MANSFIELD TOWN

A COMPLETE RECORD 1910-1990

Best Wishes

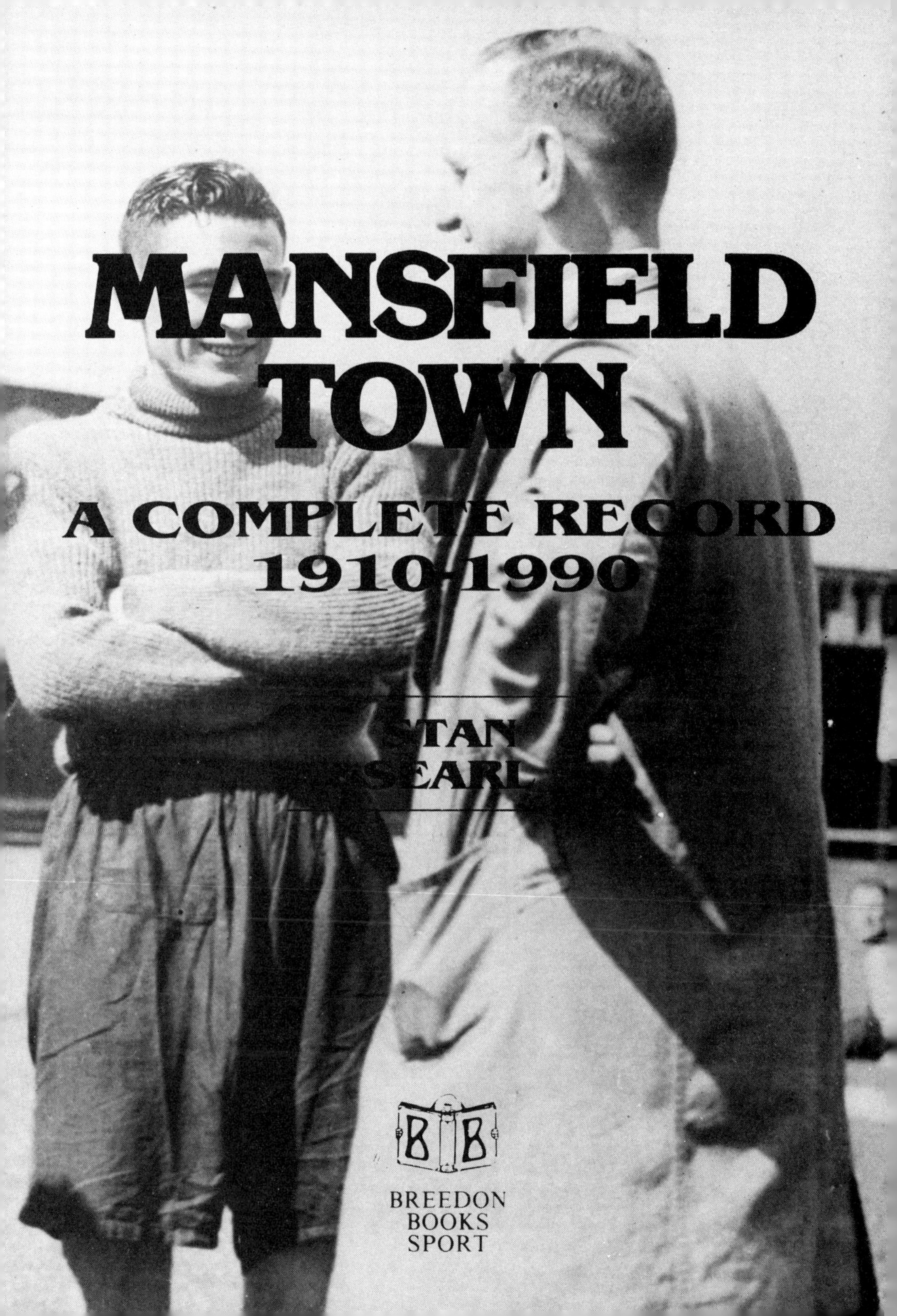

MANSFIELD TOWN

A COMPLETE RECORD 1910-1990

STAN SEARL

BREEDON
BOOKS
SPORT

First published in Great Britain by
The Breedon Books Publishing Company Limited
44 Friar Gate, Derby DE1 1DA
1990

ISBN 0 907969 70 4

Printed by Butler and Tanner Limited, Frome, Somerset.
Jacket printed by Arkle Print Ltd, Northampton.

Contents

Introduction

IDEALLY, the appropriate introduction to the official history of Mansfield Town would be for the author to state that he had followed the club 'man and boy' since the year dot.

But, as I lived in the neighbouring town of Sutton-in-Ashfield, three miles from Field Mill, and since I was ten years old only about 50 yards from the home of Sutton Town, supporting Mansfield would have been akin to treachery in that neck of the woods.

The fact that Notts County were my team was acceptable, although the doings of the Snipes (as Sutton Town were nicknamed, because the bird figured on the coat of arms of the town) were paramount in the local pubs and clubs.

Even when Mansfield became a Football League club in 1931, there was little interest in Sutton and district in the Field Mill 'goings on'.

As a schoolboy I recall trips to Meadow Lane to see the legendary Dixie Dean and Hughie Gallacher in action with the Magpies.

But I also recall those trips by special train (child's fare sixpence return), with my father, to those outlying soccer hotbeds of Ilkeston, Heanor, Belper and Matlock to follow Sutton's fortunes.

After the war, and with a son growing up, it was back to Meadow Lane for our weekend's football, although in the mid-1950s the local amateur soccer scene began to occupy a great deal of my time.

Indeed, it was involvement in local football that eventually led to the opportunity to launch a new career and when I was 46, I became a full-time journalist with the *Mansfield Chronicle Advertiser*, more popularly known as the 'CHAD'.

That was when my involvement with Mansfield Town began, although previously I had occasionally stood on the Field Mill terraces at a midweek match.

Initially my journalistic duties brought me in contact with the Stags 'A' team, then operating in the Central Alliance.

In fact I often acted as linesman, and regularly carried the kit and helped to pack the skip at the end of the match.

Then, one Friday morning in October 1969, my telephone rang and I was asked if I would consider taking over the vacant sports editor's post with the paper.

I considered — for about ten seconds — and that is when Mansfield Town turned from a passing interest into an obsession.

As my wife Dorothy was wont to say, 'He's at his second home, Field Mill.' And in some respect it was true, for hardly a day passed by without a call at the ground to 'see what was happening.'

Even when I retired in October 1985 there was hardly a let-up as my count of covering the Stags' senior matches for both the paper and *BBC Radio Nottingham* closed almost at the 1,000-mark.

'You ought to write a book on Mansfield Town,' I was often told — well, this is it. And if it has been tedious at times, and often downright frustrating, I hope you will agree that it has all been well worth the trouble.

I have made it as accurate as is possible when faced with contradicting results and names of goalscorers, and even the spelling of individual names.

The 1939-45 war years were particularly frustrating, even though the Football League kindly furnished me with the official match returns from Mansfield Town.

Unfortunately the match line-ups published in the three local Mansfield weekly papers did not always tally with the official list. However, everything possible has been done to make sure that the facts in the book are correct.

That also goes for details regarding the founding of the club which vary from what, up to now, has been accepted as official.

Stan Searl
Sutton-in-Ashfield
September 1990

Foreword

by Ian Greaves

'Why Mansfield?' was regularly fired at me by the media, and even by my closest friends, when the news broke that I had accepted the challenge in February 1983, of guiding the footballing fortunes of a Fourth Division club.

The answer was always the same: 'Because the directors wanted me to manage the club as I wanted to manage it!'.

I can say with all honesty that after the six full years at Field Mill before we amicably parted company, I never regretted my original decision — well, hardly ever anyway!

I had a marvellous relationship, first with chairman Richard Hartley, and then with Jack Pratt who succeeded him, and the board of directors, John Almond, Geoff Hall and then John Brown.

And I had a marvellous rapport with the people of Mansfield and district, who must surely be the friendliest in the country.

Although I had a fair share of managerial success before I arrived at Mansfield, those successes gave me no more delight or satisfaction than winning promotion with the Stags or that amazing day at Wembley when we returned with the Freight Rover Trophy.

Not only myself, but everyone connected with the club and the thousands and thousands of fans who lined the streets of Mansfield to welcome us home on the Monday, will ever forget that weekend.

But my inner thoughts were that if only a quarter of those fans would regularly use the turnstiles at Field Mill — then Mansfield Town could become self-sufficient, with no need to sell their best young players in order to remain in existence.

For that is a fact of life for most clubs in the same situation as Mansfield.

That is why I initiated, and put John Jarman in charge of a youth policy as soon as I arrived at Mansfield, the success of which is highlighted by the emergence of Simon Coleman and Craig McKernon, amongst others.

I hope, indeed I am sure, that the youth policy will continue, for on it depends largely the future of Mansfield Town as a senior club.

It is appropriate that this first-ever comprehensive history of the club should be compiled at this critical time in its affairs.

It will highlight and emphasize the long history of the Stags and perhaps redouble the efforts to make sure that Mansfield Town will still be adding to its annals in another 80 years from now.

Good reading!

Acknowledgements

The author wishes to thank the following for their assistance in producing this book: the *Mansfield Chronicle Advertiser*, the Football League, the Football Association, Mansfield Town FC, the *Free Press Recorder*. Thanks to individuals are due to Joe Eaton, Roger Grayson, Paul Taylor, Paul Richardson, Jack Retter and Sid Watson. I would like to give special thanks to my wife, Dorothy, whose patience must have been sorely tested in the past year, and I dedicate the book to her.

Photographic Acknowledgements

Photographs have been supplied by the *Mansfield Chronicle Advertiser, The Free Press Recorder.*

THE MANSFIELD TOWN STORY

ONE of the two main leagues with which Mansfield Town were involved from the very beginning was certainly the Midland Counties League, which began its operation on 7 September 1889 after its inaugural meeting at the Maypole Hotel in Nottingham on 17 April of that year.

A club called Mansfield Town first joined the competition for the 1892-3 season, but it should be emphasized that it had no connection with the present club. They finished third from bottom in their initial season, having played 24 games, won seven, drawn two and lost 15, goals for 26, against 70 and points 16.

The following season, 1893-4, Mansfield finished bottom with Mansfield

One of the first teams to carry the name Mansfield Town, pictured in 1894 when they amalgamated with the old Greenhalgh club. Back row (left to right): Mr W. Wilkinson, Squires, Spencer, Jarvis, Jenkinson, Jackson, W.May, Martin, J.Bramwell (trainer). Seated: Taylor, Watson, Palmer, Ray, Teddy May.

Greenhalgh, who had joined the League that season, in fifth place. Greenhalgh, who played at Field Mill, amalgamated with Mansfield Town during the close season and the new club was seventh in the 1894-5 season.

But the following season they slumped to next to bottom and at the annual meeting were not re-elected into the Midland Counties League. They were admitted to the Notts, Derby & District League for the 1886-7 season, a competition which included the reserve sides of Nottingham Forest and Notts County.

But after the 1900-01 season there was no mention in the local Press of Mansfield Town and it was Mansfield Mechanics and Mansfield Wesleyans, and then Mansfield Wesley, who became the town's two principal clubs.

So when Mansfield Wesley changed the club's name to Mansfield Town in June 1910, a fact officially confirmed by the Football Association, it is possible to trace the present club's initial competitive steps to the Notts, Derby & District League. But both Mechanics and Town were ambitious clubs and anxious to attain more senior football, and both joined the newly-launched Central Alliance for the 1911-12 campaign.

It certainly did not look to be a good move on Mansfield Town's part, for in their first season in the new league they finished next to bottom with only 12 points from 22 matches.

There was considerable improvement the following season, for the Stags finished tenth in the table with 28 points from 32 matches.

And it was noted in the *Mansfield Advertiser* in a review of the prospects for the coming 1912-13 season that Mansfield Mechanics would be staging their practice matches at their new ground at Field Mill, which had also been the home for several seasons of the Old Meeting House Football Club.

At the League's annual meeting before the start of the 1913-14 campaign, Mansfield Town were severely criticized for the poor state of their ground and warned that if there was no improvement they would not be re-elected.

Despite an outlay of much time and money, their Ratcliffe Gate headquarters showed little improvement and after the Stags had finished second from bottom they were thrown out of the League at the annual meeting on 28 April 1914.

They were immediately readmitted to the Notts, Derby & District League — poor ground and all — and finished fourth with 28 points from 26 matches.

But, by the end of that season, World War One was beginning to take its toll on the country's menfolk and sport gradually ground to a standstill. Mansfield Town were re-elected into the Central Alliance for the 1915-16 season, the last before competitive football was abandoned for the duration. So there was little joy that Mansfield finished top of the table having won all their ten matches.

It was with the Central Alliance that Mansfield Town resumed their activities for the 'victory season' of 1919-20, and at Field Mill, celebrating the return to action and their status as the town's only senior side, following the demise of Mansfield Mechanics FC, several of whose officials and players moved over to their former rivals.

The Stags finished as champions with 41 points from 30 matches and the following season they were fifth with 42 points from 34 matches, with attendances averaging over 5,000.

It was in 1920 that the Stags were involved in talks which led to the formation of the new Third Division of the Football League.

Then in 1921, the year that Mansfield Town was reconstituted, and became a limited company, the Stags were admitted to the Midland Counties League. It was reported that a crowd of over 4,000 turned up for one of the club's practice matches, to herald a season which promised a lot for the future as the club finished eighth with 42 points.

Mansfield Wesleyan Brigade FC pictured in 1902-03. Back row (left to right, players only): F.Coleman, W.Statham, F.Wilson (captain). Middle row: W.Marples, G.Smith, F.Stokes, H.Sadler. Front row: S.Benson, R.Gunthorpe, G.S.McKee, G.Abraham, J.Orton.

Mansfield Town (players only) in 1923. Back row (left to right): Coupland, Bellas, Johnson, Ryan, Brelsford, Bayliss. Front: Sheldon, Laurie, Donoven, Taylor and Death.

However, the Stags were winners of the Mansfield Charity Cup, having defeated the Midland League champions, Worksop Town, 1-0 in the Final.

There had been one disappointment before the start of the season when the Central Alliance clubs voted out Mansfield's application for their reserve side to stay in the competition. Instead, a team was entered into the Derbyshire Senior League.

The following season the Stags dropped to tenth, but in 1923-4 they topped the league with a record 68 points, 12 ahead of runners-up Grimsby Town.

The title was retained the following year, although the membership was reduced to 15 clubs after a number of Football League clubs' reserve sides had left to join the Central Combination.

In 1925-6, the membership had risen to 21 and Mansfield finished in second spot, but with another record in their possession after scoring 120 goals, nine more than champions Mexborough. They also reached the first round of the FA Cup, but lost 5-2 to Boston.

With their sights on election to the Football League, having already made several unsuccessful applications for membership, Mansfield applied for membership of the Central Combination, a competition previously exclusive to reserve teams of Football League clubs.

The Stags were admitted to the Combination at its annual meeting, but their membership was not ratified by the Football Association, although they were allowed to stay for the one season in which they finished in a mid-table position.

Readmitted to the Midland Counties League for the 1927-8 season, the Stags finished tenth with 49 points from 44 matches. And in that famous 1928-9 campaign,

The Mansfield Town line-up in the 1924-5 season which lifted the Midland League Championship for the second year running. In the subsidiary competition that season, Mansfield finished runners-up.

when Mansfield Town became a household name because of the FA Cup exploits against Wolverhampton Wanderers and Arsenal, they once more became league champions and again broke the goalscoring record with 133 for, against 72 conceded.

League performances in the next two seasons were not so memorable, with tenth position achieved in both campaigns, although the goals continued to flow with 126 in 1929-30 and 103 in 1930-31, before Football League status was achieved.

What is not generally known, however, is that it was the voting power of the full members in the First and Second Divisions which ensured Mansfield Town's elevation to the Football League. At a meeting of the Third Division North and South clubs, prior to the annual meeting, it was decided to support the re-election applications of Norwich City and Newport County to the Third Division South, a decision which was overturned by the greater voting power of the senior clubs.

'At Last' was the banner headline on the main sports page of the *Mansfield, Sutton & Kirkby Chronicle* for 5 June 1931. That day's edition announced that Mansfield Town FC had succeeded — at the seventh attempt — in their quest to become members of the Football League. At the League's annual meeting Mansfield finished second in the voting for the Third Division South which ended: Norwich City 38, Mansfield Town 25, Newport County 19, Aldershot 14 and Merthyr Town 2. Norwich had finished bottom of the table at the end of the 1930-31 season but Mansfield replaced next-to-bottom Newport County, who were also seeking re-election and who were successful in regaining their Football League status the following year.

In their previous six applications, Mansfield had asked for membership of the

This is the squad which shot the Stags to prominence in 1928-9 with their famous egg and milk training routine.

Mansfield players in a happy mood before the big match with Arsenal. Players (pictured left to right) are: Anthony, Kerry, McKenna, Chambers, Cooke, W.Marples (trainer), Allan, Freeman, Jackson, Morris and Staniforth.

Mansfield fans in a carnival mood, during Mansfield's 2-0 defeat by Arsenal.

BOROUGH OF MANSFIELD

THIRD DIVISION.

(NORTHERN SECTION.)

THE APPLICATION OF THE MANSFIELD TOWN F.C. LIMITED.

FIELD MILL GROUND,
MANSFIELD,
1925.

GENTLEMEN,

The Directors of the above Club are again making application for admittance to the 3rd DIVISION NORTHERN SECTION of the FOOTBALL LEAGUE, for the second successive year, and sincerely trust that on this occasion we shall be successful, and are confident of this success if you will be good enough to give us your support.

In making this application we claim that our past records are of no mean character. During the past Four Seasons in the MIDLAND COUNTIES LEAGUE our records are as follows:—

FIRST SEASON — FINISHED 8TH.
SECOND SEASON — FINISHED 12TH.
THIRD SEASON — WINNING THE CHAMPIONSHIP.
FOURTH SEASON — do. do. do.

RECORDS AS FOLLOWS:—

1923–1924.—Played 42, Won 31, Lost 5, Drawn 6.
Goals For 96, Against 31, Points 68.

Thus beating previous record of 64 points obtained by Sheffield United Reserve in Season 1906–7 by 4 points.

1924 1925.

PLAYED	WON	LOST	DRAWN
28	20	4	4

GOALS FOR	AGAINST	POINTS.
83	29	44

We consider the above very satisfactory from this standpoint alone.

Ever since the club was formed, no disturbance has taken place on the ground, and further we have never had a player sent off the field.

Our Ground is up-to-date, having down one side a complete Stand with seating accommodation for 2,000 persons. On the Popular side covered accommodation for 1,000 persons, this stand being terraced and will be extended if we are admitted to membership. The whole of the Ground accommodating 20,000 persons. The playing piece is entirely enclosed with a new wood fencing.

…oms are on the ground and are up-to-date for Home … Players and Referee's Lavatories.

… complete with Hot and Cold Showers.

…esmen's Room is separate, and fitted with Bath and …ot and Cold Water.

…ce separate, and Officials Room all in one complete … Ground. Our Ground at entrances is fitted with …rged exits. (Extra Turnstiles will be installed if we …

…gates last two seasons were 6,000, and we anticipate …otball an average gate of 10,000. We have on several … at Midland League Matches, and nearly £600 in an …

… the leading town in the North Midland Coal Fields with …0, and it is estimated will be doubled within the next …drawing capacity of 200,000 people served by an excellent …e.

… Club plays within 15 miles radius of Mansfield.

…o well served by Two Railway Companies, viz., L. M. & S. Rly. … Both stations being close to ground.

… is also very central for the majority of Clubs in the Third …

…perations are in progress of five new coal mines within a …iles of the town.

…cial position is sound; with assets to the value of £3,000 … a substantial balance in hand at Bank. We intend seeking … personal interview at an early date, and shall be pleased to …y count on your support and rely on your vote.

…usion we feel assured that Mansfield Town F.C. would be … Division Football.

…g you in anticipation for your support,

We are,

Yours faithfully,

Sec. Manager.

Above: The Stags' first programme in the League.
Opposite: An application to join the Football League in 1925.

Third Division North, but in 1931 switched their attentions to the Southern Section. It was a move which, in the opinion of the local sports paper, attracted the support of several Northern Section clubs who appreciated Mansfield's action in not opposing Rochdale and Nelson, who were also seeking to join the Third Division North.

Much of the credit for Mansfield's elevation to Football League status must go to their secretary-manager at that time, Jack Hickling. He, in turn, paid tribute to assistance afforded by neighbours Nottingham Forest, Notts County, Leicester City, Chesterfield, Derby County, Sheffield Wednesday and Sheffield United, who not only voted for Mansfield, but also actively canvassed other clubs on their behalf.

A member of the club's playing staff, full-back Claude White, accompanied Hickling on his campaigning visits to clubs in the north of England and the Birmingham area. And the Rev J.Lowndes, president of the North Notts Football League and vicar of Blidworth, one of the numerous mining villages surrounding Mansfield, used his persuasive powers on Lancashire and Yorkshire clubs, it was reported.

So Mansfield Town became a Football League club as they came of age after emerging from the local Mansfield Wesley team in 1910, after the Mansfield Wesleyan Chapel trustees had requested that the club change its name as 'it no longer has any connection with either the chapel or school'.

The newspaper reported that the Mayor of Mansfield, H.Garratt, had personally written to the mayor of every town possessing a Football League club.

On the weekend of the Football League's annual meeting, the local newspaper told its readers that no less than 15 people had been in London working for the club's aim. These included T.Stevens, W.W.Fenton, H.Jackson, F.S.Smith, the

An historic picture as the Stags line up for their first League match, when Swindon visited Field Mill.

secretary-manager of the Mansfield & Sutton Co-operative Society, and a well-known local baritone, Eric Edwards.

The newspaper observed: 'On Saturday evening at the Palace Hotel, Mr Edwards sang. And again on Sunday afternoon, on the River Thames.' Then at the secretary-manager's banquet at Frascati's on Sunday evening, Mr Edwards 'received an ovation for his rendering of several songs.'

So, the initial season was launched with great optimism, both at the club and in the town and surrounding districts. The first home match, on the opening day of the season, saw Swindon Town provide the opposition and, as the local newspaper reported: 'Field Mill seemed to be the goal of every sportsman in the town and for miles around.

'Special trains brought large contingents of spectators from Kirkby and Shirebrook, and buses arriving from Warsop, Pleasley, Sutton, Blidworth and Clipstone were crowded from one o'clock onwards.'

The official attendance was 12,232, breaking the previous record of 10,600 on the occasion of an FA Cup tie against Walsall several seasons earlier. The local Press, however, maintained that there were closer to 13,000 in the ground as the official figures did not include season-ticket holders.

Mansfield's 3-2 win over Swindon added to the optimism of the management and supporters but before the season was many weeks old, the enormity of the club's task in establishing itself in the League became increasingly apparent.

And with the season in its final weeks there was every prospect that Mansfield would have to go cap in hand to the annual meeting seeking re-election. However, a finish to their programme of three wins, a draw and three defeats, was enough to lift the Stags into third-from-bottom place.

Harry Johnson was top scorer with 32 goals from 40 appearances, with George Bowater on ten goals the only other forward to reach double figures.

Mansfield at Hornsea following an early-morning work-out. Unfortunately it did not do them much good – they went down 4-1 to Hull in the Cup. Pictured (left to right) are J.G.Hickling, Sam Robinson, Harry Wake, Joe Readman, Mac England, Jim Wilson, George Clifford, Harry Broome, Cyril Gilhespy, Billy Death, Arthur Weightman and trainer Wilf Marples.

One cause for concern in the first season in the Football League was that Mansfield failed to win any of their 21 away games. And although the transfer from the Southern Section to the Northern Section was greeted with some relief, life did not become all that much easier for the fledgeling League club.

But at least a slightly higher final placing was achieved. The Stags finished 16th with 35 points — three more than in the previous season — from 42 matches.

However, their away form continued to be a stumbling block with only one success away from home and that not coming until 18 March 1933 when Darlington were beaten 3-1 at Feethams. Three away draws were managed, at Wrexham, Stockport and Doncaster, and there were several disastrous scorelines on Mansfield's travels — 1-8 at Walsall, 0-6 at Accrington, 0-7 at Crewe and 2-6 at Barnsley.

There were a few consolation results at home with Rotherham defeated 9-2 (still the Stags' record win), 7-1 against Hartlepools United and 5-0 against New Brighton.

Mansfield did not enjoy the luck of the draw in the FA Cup. They had gone down 4-1 at Hull City in the first round the previous season and now, drawn at Walsall in the opening round of 1932-3, they lost by an identical scoreline at Fellows Park.

Johnson and Bowater were again the leading goalscorers and the only forwards to reach double figures, Johnson with 30 goals from 38 matches and Bowater with 18 from 38.

The following campaign of 1933-4 was a difficult season for the Stags, both on and off the field. The club was plagued by financial as well as playing difficulties and in December they parted company with their secretary-manager, Jack Hickling, who had played a leading role in Mansfield's successful bid for Football League status.

Hickling's letter of dismissal was dated 11 December 1933 and the club's trainer, Harry Martin, was put in charge and officially appointed trainer-manager on 11 January 1934.

There was another struggle to avoid the need to seek re-election but the Stags eventually finished sixth from bottom with 34 points from 11 wins and 12 draws, one place worse off than in the previous season.

However, some consolation was gleaned from the fact that the goal-average showed some improvement with 81 goals for and 88 against, compared to 84 for and 100 against in 1932-3. Away form was again a big disappointment with wins only at Darlington and Rotherham, although five away games were drawn.

Harry Johnson was again the top scorer with 18 and Kilcar, the only other forward into double figures, netted 12.

There were a few bright patches in a disappointing season, including a new attendance record at Field Mill for the match against neighbours Chesterfield.

Mansfield also reached the semi-finals of the Northern Section Cup after wins in the early rounds at Walsall and at home to Chesterfield. In the last four, Mansfield went down 4-0 to Stockport County.

There was also disappointment in the FA Cup, for after holding New Brighton to a goalless draw away from home in the first round, the Stags were trounced 4-0 in the replay.

A great deal of internal reorganization had been implemented at Field Mill and evidence of the sweeping changes came in the fact that only six of the season's playing staff were retained. Only two, Ernest England and Harry Johnson, remained of those who helped to launch Mansfield in the Football League in 1931.

Although Mansfield Town's troubles were by no means over, the 1934-5 season saw the club reach eighth position in the Third Division North, their best final placing since entering the League. They had a run of 11 weeks without defeat, which took them into fourth place at the end of December, and two months later the Stags again reached that position.

Away form continued to be a problem, though, for despite their improved final position, only three games were won and five drawn away from Field Mill.

The Stags made encouraging progress in the FA Cup, beating Accrington Stanley 6-1 in the first round and Tranmere Rovers 4-2 in the second before bowing out to Burnley, 4-2 in round three.

Chesterfield put Mansfield out of the Northern Section Cup, but there was some consolation in the fact that they were the winners of the largest trophy of the lot, the Bass Charity Vase.

Harry Johnson headed the scoring list for yet another season, with 17 goals which took him to over 100 for the club and 300 in his career. This time he was closely challenged by S.Hunt whose 14 goals included three penalties.

There was also a significant improvement in the financial position at Field Mill, but mainly because of the £1,300 transfer fee received from Manchester City for Ron Dellow, who was described as 'the find of the season'. Dellow, incidentally, made only ten League appearances for City (scoring four goals) before returning to the Third Division North with Tranmere Rovers in March 1936.

Mansfield Town pictured in 1934-5. Back row (left to right): Edmonds, Ashley, Kilcar, Bytheway, Fawcett, Dransfield. Front row: Slade, Hawley, Johnson, Law, Atkinson.

It is worthy of note that Mansfield Town Reserves finished third in the Central Combination in the 1934-5 season.

In 1935-6, the Stags were flirting, yet again, with the possibility of requiring to seek re-election before managing to finish 19th in the table.

But there was a significant entry in the minutes of the club's management committee meeting on 25 October 1935 which read: 'Confirmed the signing of player E. Harston from Bristol City for a fee of £250'.

Ted Harston made only 29 first-team appearances for Mansfield Town that season, but scored 26 goals including two penalties and three hat-tricks. And, of course, there was much more to come.

Mansfield had won only three games before Harston made his debut, at Southport on 19 October when he scored all the Stags' goals in a 3-3 draw.

But the Stags still hovered around the re-election zone for the next few months, until a 5-0 home victory over York City on 21 March launched a storming finish to the season. In their final nine matches, Mansfield gained five wins and three draws and were beaten only once to lift themselves clear of the danger zone.

There was disappointment yet again in the FA Cup as Mansfield bowed out in the first round, beaten 3-2 at Hartlepool. And in the Northern Section Cup, after holding Chesterfield 2-2 at Saltergate in the opening round, they lost the replay 4-0 at Field Mill.

Harston finished with 27 League and Cup goals, with team captain E. Dransfield an ever-present, making 42 League and three Cup appearances.

There were also managerial problems during 1935. In March, Harry Martin was

Some familiar faces from 1936-7. Left to right: Hart, Bungay, Vaux, Perfect, Roy, Littledyke, Rattray, Speed.

told he would not be re-engaged for the following season and resigned as requested by the board. Trainer Charlie Bell was installed as manager the following month, but in December he reported to the board that he had lost control of the players and staff and offered to resign if paid £450, to which the directors agreed.

In January 1936, a local man, Harry Wightman, was appointed but gave up the position in May, although offered an increase of £75 per year to stay on.

Season 1936-7 saw the Stags again finish over half-way up the table in ninth place with 44 points from 42 matches, level on points with Carlisle United, Wrexham and Port Vale.

Now in charge at Field Mill was Harry Parkes, who had previously managed Lincoln City. However, it was the exploits of Ted Harston which brought the club the sort of publicity and limelight they had not enjoyed since their Cup exploits of 1928.

Ted Harston's contribution was immense. Mansfield Town scored 91 League goals in the season, 55 of which were put away by Harston. His total included one seven-goal feat (against Hartlepools on 23 January 1937) two fives, one four and four hat-tricks. He also added three goals in the FA Cup.

Harston was transferred to Liverpool during the 1937 close season, for a £3,000 fee, but after playing only four matches for the Anfield club he broke a leg and was lost to the Football League scene.

Another pleasing feature of the season was that 17 points were gained away from home, from five wins and seven draws, Mansfield's best performance on opposition territory since joining the League.

Hopes of a good FA Cup run were raised when Barrow were defeated 4-0 in the first round but in the next round, Bournemouth won 3-0 at Field Mill. There was no joy, either, in the Northern Section Cup as Port Vale ended the Stags' hopes in the first round by winning 2-0 at Field Mill.

The Nottinghamshire County Cup competition was launched in this season and Mansfield crashed 5-1 at home to Notts County in the opening round.

The promotion and relegation situation at the end of the previous season saw Mansfield back in the Southern Section of Division Three for 1937-8, a situation hardly welcomed at Field Mill.

However, whilst the Stags hardly set the division alight, they did finish in 14th position, comfortably clear of the danger zone. It was particularly pleasing as Mansfield had to field a completely new forward line, not one of the previous season's attack being retained.

Naturally, the departure of Harston was a blow but his replacement, H.Crawshaw, scored 25 of the Stags' 62 League goals that season.

There was another managerial change in January 1938, when Harry Parkes' request to leave to take up the trainer's post at Notts County was granted 'with regret'.

The Stags' trainer, Jack Poole, was put in temporary charge, although it was not until May that he was officially appointed trainer-manager, a position he was to hold through most of the difficult war years.

One of the bright spots of the 1937-8 season was on the financial side, brought about by a third-round FA Cup meeting with Leicester City. An attendance of 15,890 watched the match at Field Mill, paying record receipts of £1,220. Leicester ran out winners by a narrow 2-1 margin.

Press reports on the match rated Mansfield unlucky to lose, declaring they deserved at least a draw against the First Division club, who scored the winner only three minutes from time.

In round one the Stags won 2-1 at non-League Wellington Town but enjoyed good fortune in the second round, for Lincoln City were leading 2-1 when the game was abandoned after 62 minutes. When the match was replayed, Mansfield won by the same margin to earn that meeting with Leicester City.

In the Southern Section Cup, the Stags failed to progress further than the opening round after losing 1-0 at Crystal Palace. They fared better in the County Cup, beating Nottingham Forest 2-1 in the Final after a 3-1 semi-final victory over Newark Town.

Mansfield dropped two places in the Southern Section in 1938-9, finishing 16th with 39 points from 42 matches. Once again it was their results away from home which disappointed and kept them at the wrong end of the table for much of the season.

Only two victories were achieved in away games, although the Stags did manage seven draws. At Field Mill, ten of the 21 games were won and only three lost, with eight draws which perhaps saved the day in the final reckoning. Added to the share of away spoils, they prevented a drop into the re-election battle.

It was significant that T.Dutton headed the goalscoring charts with only 12 goals, with his nearest rival having only seven.

However, it was in the FA Cup that Mansfield Town again hit the national headlines. The Stags required a replay before progressing at the expense of Workington in the first round. Then four matches were needed before Halifax Town emerged triumphant in round two. A 1-1 draw at The Shay, in front of 14,208 fans, was followed by a 3-3 draw at Mansfield, where 6,083 watched the game. Only 2,500 saw the second replay at Doncaster Rovers' Belle Vue ground and a meagre 1,219 were at Old Trafford where the Yorkshiremen finally went through 2-1.

This Mansfield team might have gone on to greater things – had it not been for World War Two. Back row (left to right): E.Bell, A.Statham, G.Stimpson, J.Hughes, O.Collier, F.Speed, Jack Poole (manager). Front row: J.Turner, C.Gardner, S.Carter, R.Bungay, T.Dutton, L.Barke.

In the Southern Section Cup, Notts County were defeated 3-0 in the first round at Field Mill before Port Vale proved to be an unsurmountable obstacle in round two with Mansfield going down 3-1 away from home.

Notts County were defeated 3-2 after extra-time in the semi-final of the County Cup before the Stags drew 2-2 with Forest in the Final.

After only three games of the 1939-40 season, the Football League programme was suspended upon the outbreak of war. Mansfield had begun the season with a 5-4 defeat at the hands of Crystal Palace at Field Mill. A 2-1 midweek victory at Watford was followed by a 2-2 draw at Torquay United, but on that last Saturday of peace the atmosphere was unreal and football was the last thing on people's minds.

The following day, Prime Minister Neville Chamberlain made his famous broadcast to the nation and Britain was at war with Germany. Many footballers were soon in the Army, others engaged in important war work. Whatever, when the Government agreed that some form of regionalized soccer could resume, Mansfield Town, like every other club, had to rely on guest players to complete their ranks.

Mansfield's season resumed in the East Midlands Section with a 2-1 defeat at Grimsby on 21 October 1939. Their final game of the season was a 2-2 draw with Sheffield United at Field Mill on 6 June 1940. The game was officially United's home match but Bramall Lane was required for cricket. The Stags finished fifth in the East Midlands Section and one of the highlights of the season was a 6-4 win over Notts County, although the Magpies later beat Mansfield 5-3 in a preliminary round match of the War Cup. Other big scores in this strange season were a 6-2 defeat at Nottingham Forest and a 5-4 win at Lincoln City.

In 1940-41, Mansfield finished 17th in the South Regional League. Again there were some peculiar events. The game against Nottingham Forest on 14 December was abandoned after 60 minutes with the Stags leading 2-1 and the result was ordered to stand, such were the difficulties in rearranging matches. In the Midlands Cup, Mansfield were unable to fulfil the home leg of their second-round game against Lincoln City and went out after the Imps had won their home leg 4-2. One man who did enjoy the season was centre-forward Tex Rickards, who scored 38 goals for the Stags.

In 1941-2, Mansfield finished 33rd out of 38 clubs in the Northern Division, although it should be said that, of course, they did not play every club twice. In fact, the Stags played only 29 games this season, including War Cup games. Because of postponements, Mansfield were unable to complete their qualifying games in the latter competition.

The 1942-3 season saw them finish bottom of the Cup qualifying table and bottom of both League competitions. By now there was a 'first championship' which was played until Christmas and a 'second championship' which went on until the end of the season and also included the Cup games, the results of some games counting towards both competitions. The Stags took some hammerings, losing 10-0 to Derby County with former Rams' reserve wing-half George Hannah in Mansfield's ranks, and taking drubbings from Sheffield Wednesday (9-1 and 10-2 in consecutive weeks) and Lincoln City (7-1 and 8-1).

In the first championship of 1943-4, which ended on 27 December, Mansfield finished 18th out of 50 clubs in the Northern competition. The Stags earned 20 points from their 18 matches, level with Derby County, but well ahead of Chesterfield, Nottingham Forest and Notts County.

But in the second championship, played up to 6 May 1944, Mansfield had dropped to 47th out of 50 with 13 points from 14 matches. The Stags had played the least number of matches than any other club in the competition, the majority managing 20 or 21 games.

In both competitions the matches were mainly local derbies, home and away, against Derby County, Nottingham Forest, Notts County, Lincoln City, Chesterfield, Leicester City, Sheffield Wednesday, Sheffield United and Rotherham United.

Particularly in the second competition, results went the way of the home side. One match, against Notts County at Field Mill, was abandoned after only ten minutes because of fog, with a Tex Rickards goal giving Mansfield the early advantage. A replay was impossible and the Stags picked up the two points as a result when the game was called off.

Over 50 players were called upon during the season with some well-known names amongst them. Sam Weaver, the former Hull City, Chelsea, Newcastle United and England wing-half, known universally as 'the king of the long throw', and who was later to become associated with Mansfield Town for over 25 years, had a single outing against Nottingham Forest on 5 February. Cliff Hubbard (ex-West Ham) and Luton Town's Fred Hogg, who later joined the Stags permanently, were also in the side on a dozen occasions.

In August 1944, Mansfield lost manager Jack Poole, who moved to Notts County as trainer. Lloyd Barke, the team captain, who had been a permanent member of the team throughout the war, was appointed acting manager.

It took seven games before Mansfield managed a win and the club did not do too well in the competition covering the first half of the season, which concluded on 23 December 1944, as they completed 18 matches for 15 points and were 39th out of 54 clubs.

Again in the second part of the season, Mansfield fell behind with their matches, completing only 12 games for 11 points to finish 49th.

In the League North Cup qualifying competition, staged between 25 December 1944 and 17 March 1945, Mansfield failed to get through to the closing rounds, missing the cut-off point by nine places.

Arsenal's Les Jones was one of the top players who made a dozen appearances for the Stags during the season, but there was still a great reliance on the old stalwarts like Cyril Poole, George Marlow of Lincoln City, Lloyd Barke, Ernest Bramley, who was formerly with Rotherham and Notts County, and Jim Harkin.

And if the competition staged as the Third Division North (South Region) saw Mansfield firmly entrenched at the bottom with only 11 points from 20 matches, the qualifying matches for the Third Division South Cup were much more encouraging.

The Stags finished third with 20 points from 16 games, only one point away from qualifying for the final stages of the competition.

From a spectators' point of view, it was almost a return to normality with opposition at Field Mill not seen since before the war. Queen's Park Rangers, Ipswich Town, Norwich City, Watford, Clapton Orient, even Southend United, were making the trip north.

And if the results did not quite match the expectations, at least it was a pleasure to see new faces. Although 'guesting' players were still allowed, several who had been away in the Armed Forces were beginning to return. Goalkeeper Vic Cromack, who had spent much of the war in a prisoner-of-war camp, was back on a regular basis.

Centre-forward Sid Carter, who had signed in 1938-9, was back; and later was to become Mansfield trainer and one of their longest-serving members. Sammy Chessell, who had spent much of the war years as a forward, had begun to establish himself as a regular full-back, and Fred Hogg had become a permanent member of the Stags' staff.

The FA Cup was back for 1945-6, run on a two-legged basis from first to sixth rounds. Mansfield beat Midland League club Gainsborough Trinity 5-4 on aggregate in the first round and Grimsby Town 4-2 over two legs in the second before going out to Sheffield Wednesday. The Stags managed a goalless draw at Field Mill but went down 5-0 at Hillsborough.

It was back to normal for the Football League in 1946 but with many young men still in uniform, settled sides were at a premium. In some respects Mansfield Town were fortunate in that several of the players available had assisted the club almost throughout the war years.

Lloyd Barke, the caretaker manager since August 1944, when Jack Poole left to become trainer at Notts County, was superceded by former England and Huddersfield Town full-back Roy Goodall exactly 12 months later. Barke remained with the club for much of the 1946-7 season, but lost his place for the final nine matches and was not retained.

The season began on a confident note with only one defeat in the opening eight games, half of which were away from home, picking up 10 points in the process. Then things began to go wrong and by the advent of 1947, the Stags had managed to add only 11 points to the total they had achieved by the end of September.

The second half of the season proved to be even more disastrous with only seven more points earned for a final tally of 28 and bottom place in Division Three South, Mansfield's worst-ever performance in the League, even to this day. Happily, although the Stags had to apply for re-election for the first and only time, it was virtually a cut-and-dried affair with the member clubs automatically readmitting the applicants from Third South and North in this first post-war season.

However, there was one bright spot during the season and that was the arrival of left winger Harry Oscroft, who was to play a prominent part in one of Mansfield

Mansfield Town pictured in 1946-7. Back row (left to right): Copestake, Bryant, Cromack, Chessell, Bramley, Hogg. Front: Harper, Harkin, Barke, Smith, Calverley.

Mansfield Town playing staff and directors line up for the camera in 1948.

Town's purple patches a few seasons later. Oscroft, of course, was discovered playing for the local Mansfield Colliery side, one of the many young players from the district to make the grade with their home-town club.

It was back to the Third Division North for the 1947-8 campaign and, whereas in comparison with the previous season, the early results did not give rise to a great deal of confidence, the final outcome of eighth in the table equalled the Stags' previous highest placing in 1934-5.

The most significant early happening at Field Mill was the arrival of centre-half Johnny Grogan from Leicester City. His experience played a significant part in the Stags' revival.

Promotion was very much on the cards by the beginning of April but the final seven results were even worse than the opening seven, for only one win and two draws were achieved in the final period.

In the first round of the FA Cup, Mansfield met a non-League club who were to become real headline-makers after they were elected to the Football League some years later. Wimbledon made the Stags fight all the way at Plough Lane before Mansfield won by the only goal of the game, scored by Roy Cooling. It was Cooling who put away the only goal in the second round as hosts Oldham Athletic bowed out of the competition.

That gave Mansfield a third-round home tie with First Division Stoke City. A disappointing crowd of only 10,500 watched the game with many fans staying away believing that the match was an all-ticket affair and a sell-out. There might have been even fewer spectators but for frantic appeals on the local Rediffusion system, notifying the fans that there was plenty of room at the ground. It was all in vain, however, for the Stags went down 4-2 with an Oscroft goal and a Len Butt penalty providing their scores.

Another non-League outfit, Gloucester City, were Mansfield's opponents in the first round of the FA Cup in 1948-9 and the outcome was another solid win for the Stags, this time by 4-0 with a hat-trick by Stan Mercer and a goal from Oscroft.

Northampton Town were the hurdle which Mansfield had to clear to go into the third round for the second season in succession. The Stags won 2-1 after extra-time — goals again from Oscroft and Mercer — in those early post-war days when midweek replays were avoided if at all possible. That set up a meeting with a Second Division club on their way to promotion. Preston North End just managed a win by the odd goal in three in front of 33,000 fans at Deepdale.

In the meantime Mansfield were regularly pulling in five-figure attendances at Field Mill, although League results did not quite match up to 1946-7, but a late run took them from 15th in mid-April to tenth at the end of the season.

Harry Oscroft was top marksman with 14 goals, with George Banks and Roy Cooling in joint second spot with seven each. Also on the list was a player who,

Mansfield Town pictured in 1947-8. Back row (left to right): Allcock, Oscroft, Croft, Wright, Devey, Chessell, Jack Clough. Front: Brown, Smith, Hogg, W.Fox, Shell.

four years later, was to become Mansfield's manager. Stan Mercer was that man, with six goals to his credit.

An important signing during the 1949 close season was the former England and Stoke City forward, Freddie Steele, who took over as player-manager at Field Mill. It was Steele's 18 goals which lifted the Stags into another eighth placing in the Third Division North. Oscroft was also amongst the goals with 12 in the season.

The highlight of the 1949-50 campaign came on 29 October, when Hartlepools United were the visitors and were hammered 7-1 with Steele and Oscroft both collecting hat-tricks.

On 13 January, Oscroft was on his way to Stoke City for a £30,000 fee — yet another departure which did not go down well with the home fans. They were even less pleased with some later results, for the Stags crashed 7-1 at Rochdale on 4 March and 6-3 at Chester on the final day of the season.

There was not much joy in the FA Cup either, despite a 4-1 first-round home win over Walsall in front of 16,300 spectators. There were 23,545 fans at Belle Vue to see Doncaster Rovers beat Mansfield by a single goal.

It took Mansfield 46 years to reach the heady heights of Division Two instead of the three seasons the Mansfield board had predicted when Football League status was achieved in 1931, but the Stags were desperately unlucky in 1950-51. They finished second in Division Three North with 64 points, but were foiled by Rotherham United whose 71 points, the second-highest ever, took them into the Second Division when only one club from each Third Division section was promoted.

The Stags' meeting with the Millers turned out to be decisive, United winning 3-0 at Millmoor and picking up a point in a 1-1 draw at Field Mill. But the question

The Mansfield team which lost 4-2 at home to Stoke in the third round of the FA Cup in 1948. Back row (left to right): Croft, Gregson, Devey, Searson, Jones, W.Fox. Front row: Edwards, Cooling, Banks, Butt, Oscroft.

was whether Mansfield's run to the fifth round of the FA Cup diverted attention from their progress in the League.

Walthamstow Avenue gave Mansfield a real battle in the first round at Field Mill before losing 1-0 to a Freddie Steele goal. Another non-League side, Chelmsford City, bit the dust in the second round, beaten 4-0 at home with Bill Donaldson (two), Eddie Barks and Billy Coole getting the goals.

Then there were two matches to remember in the fourth-round tie with First Division Sheffield United, who were held to a goalless draw at Bramall Lane in front of 48,696 fans. A crowd of 20,314 paid £4,013 to watch the Stags win the replay 2-1 with goals from Steele and Sid Ottewell. That earned them a fifth-round tie with First Division Blackpool at Bloomfield Road. The Seasiders were then a real force with the legendary Stanley Matthews their dangerman.

Mansfield went down 2-0 and took a real pasting in the local newspapers. Headlines declared: 'The Last Act Fell Flat' and 'Stags Cup Exit Was Not Impressive'.

The report in the *Mansfield, Sutton & Kirkby Chronicle* read: 'No one could say that the vanquished left the field in a blaze of glory with no sign of the do-or-die storming finish we had hoped for.

'It was in the end, stale, flat and unprofitable and all because it seemed that the Stags, haunted by the 'Matthews complex' adopted negative tactics not very effectively, instead of playing the sort of game that proved its worth against Sheffield United.

A Mansfield line-up from the early 1950s, possibly a Reserve side. Pictured are back row (left to right): Stan Mercer, N.Field, J.McLean, S.Brierley, G.Sharpe, L.Mayfield, S.Watson. Front row: W.Wheatley, E.Beech, K.Reeve, B.Bishop, L.Simmonds.

Mansfield Town supporters pose for a send-off photograph before setting off to Blackpool for the fourth round FA Cup meeting with the Seasiders (and Stanley Matthews) on 10 February 1951.

Freddie Steele (far right) pictured at an informal get-together with the players in July 1951.

The Stags let off steam before the big match with Blackpool. Sadly they went down 2-0 at Bloomfield Road.

'It was a bitter disappointment for the many thousands of Mansfield fans among the 33,060 at the game who made the trip to Blackpool.'

There was great optimism in the town that 1951-2 was to be 'The Season', particularly with Steele still at the helm and the majority of the previous season's players still available. And the fact that only two games were lost in the first 18 League outings confirmed that optimism. The Stags stormed to the top of the table after a 4-1 home win over Scunthorpe United on 3 November 1951 and retained top spot for the next two weeks, after a 1-1 draw at Tranmere and a 4-0 victory over Southport at home.

But then their fortunes took a complete turnaround as Steele made his farewell appearance at Stockton in the FA Cup on 24 November, before he moved back to his native Potteries to manage Port Vale. It was by no means a memorable farewell, for the Stags were held to a 1-1 draw by the non-Leaguers, who defeated a 'Steeleless' Mansfield 2-0 at Field Mill in the replay.

That launched a disastrous spell which brought only three League wins in the next 13 matches, seven of which were defeats, and saw the Stags slump from first to ninth at one stage. But then experienced manager George Jobey was called in to stop the rot and by the end of the season a creditable sixth position was achieved.

The 1952-3 season was an important period in the club's history, although not for anything the Stags achieved in the League. The programme got away to a poor start with a 4-1 defeat at Chesterfield before the following three matches brought a maximum six points to leave Mansfield third in the table by the beginning of September.

Then they hovered around the top six and had a great start to an FA Cup campaign which was to figure large in the annals of the club. Non-League Scarborough were hammered 8-0 in the first round, with Oscar Fox netting a hat-trick for the Stags. In the second round Accrington Stanley were beaten 2-0 at Peel Park to set up a story-book third-round meeting with Second Division Nottingham Forest.

On 10 January 1953, a crowd of 24,467 packed into Field Mill to set a new attendance record which has not been challenged since then and certainly will not be in the future. What a game they witnessed. There was some splendid football from both sides, despite the difference in their status, before Forest scraped through 1-0. Unfortunately, Mansfield's fortunes in the League took a turn for the worse

Another shot hits the back of the net and Scarborough are on their way to an 8-0 defeat in the FA Cup in 1952-3.

A section of the 24,467 crowd when the Field Mill attendance record was broken at the FA Cup round three meeting with neighbours Nottingham Forest on 10 January 1953.

and they finished 18th and were also beset by financial problems. Indeed, Forest made a return visit to Field Mill on 30 April to take part in an 'Aid the Stags' game.

A new man was in charge at Field Mill in time for the start of the 1953-4 campaign, after the dismissal of George Jobey. Stan Mercer was the new manager. He had joined the club as a player in 1948, when Roy Goodall was manager, but was forced to end his playing days through injury after scoring ten goals in only 15 League and Cup games. To Mercer fell the task of lifting Mansfield Town out of the doldrums.

After his playing days were prematurely ended, Mercer stayed on as a member of the backroom staff, serving under both Steele and Jobey, and he was popular with officials and players alike.

The club held a comfortable mid-table position by the turn of the year, although yet again there had been disappointment in the FA Cup. After holding Hartlepools to a 1-1 draw at the Victoria Ground in the first round, the Stags crashed 3-0 in the replay.

But by way of compensation there was a geat improvement in the League and after the acquisition of George Darwin and 'Digger' Daley towards the end of 1953, Mansfield gradually climbed up the table to finish a creditable seventh.

Results continued to please the fans at the start of the 1954-5 season and home attendances were regularly into five figures as the Stags maintained a position just outside the top six until after their 3-1 defeat at Bradford City in the first round of the FA Cup.

Then the Stags began to suffer and at one stage, in early April, they had slipped to 19th before a run of four games without defeat, including three wins in a row, stopped the rot. But that was followed by only one point from the final three games to leave Mansfield 13th at the end of the season.

There was little to enthuse over as 1955 was seen out with only 19 points earned

Mansfield Town pictured in 1953-4. Back row (left to right): Stan Mercer (manager), D.Bradley, K. Murray, T.Wilkinson, C.Adam, N.Plummer, E.Barks, A.Daley, D.Wright, S.Carter (trainer). Front: S.Watson, G.Darwin, E.Ryan, A.Gaskill, J.Eaton, W.Hudson, B.MacGregor.

from 26 League games, as well as an end to the Stags' FA Cup hopes when they were beaten 2-1 at York in the second round after winning 2-0 at home to Stockport County in round one.

And 1956 was only a couple of weeks old before Mercer had left the club, not, it should be added, because of the poor results but because of a matter of principle. Mercer was asked to also assume the duties of club secretary in addition to his commitments on the managerial side. That he was willing to do, but when he was told that he could not expect a consequent rise in salary, he resigned.

That made way for the appointment of the flamboyant Charlie Mitten as Mansfield's player-manager. Mitten made his debut on 4 February 1956, in a home meeting with Wrexham in which the Welshmen were beaten 6-1. The goals really began to flow in the second half of the season with Tranmere Rovers and Rochdale both hammered 6-0 at Field Mill and Bradford trounced 5-0.

Nevertheless, the Stags had to settle for a lowly 18th final placing in Division Three North, mainly because of their poor away record which saw only one win and five draws in 23 outings. One added bonus had been the relegation of Derby County. Mansfield opened the season in front of 24,159 fans at the Baseball Ground and there were over 9,000 at Field Mill to see the return game in December.

There was only a slight improvement in the Stags' fortunes in 1956-7 as they

Charlie Mitten, pictured with the side he led in 1956-7. Back row (left to right): Dixon, Jayes, Murray, Wright, Bradley, Watson. Front row: Anderson, Chapman, Jepson, Darwin, Mitten.

finished two places higher. Unfortunately, a total of 91 goals scored was minimized because no fewer than 90 were conceded. George Darwin headed the scoring list with 19 goals from 35 games, and it was that kind of form which made him a target for Derby manager, Harry Storer, who signed Darwin for £4,000, plus Rams full-back Keith Savin, in May 1957.

Mitten weighed in with 11 goals, four from the penalty-spot, and newcomer Jim Glazzard, who joined Mansfield from Everton and made his debut on Christmas Day, scored ten in 20 outings.

There was still no joy in the FA Cup, for after being held to a 1-1 draw at home by Workington in front of 11,383 fans, Mansfield lost the replay 2-1.

Support, though, was good at home, despite the Stags' erratic form, with 10,932 turning up for the penultimate home game of the season, against Hartlepools, which saw Mansfield win handsomely, 4-1.

However, at Crewe, in the final away game, ten goals were scored with Alexandra winning 6-4. Then to end a disappointing season, Southport won 2-1 at Field Mill. There were another two large attendances against Derby County, who went on to win the Third Division North title that year. At Field Mill in October, over 16,000 fans saw the Stags go down 2-1. At the Baseball Ground in March a crowd of almost 23,000 witnessed a 4-0 Derby win.

In 1957-8, Mansfield reached the third round of the FA Cup in what was to be Charlie Mitten's last season with the Stags before he moved on to manage Newcastle United. The highlight came in the second round, after Mansfield made progress with a 2-0 home win over Halifax Town. That paired the Stags with non-League Wigan Athletic in a second-round tie which brought 12,900 into Springfield Park to witness a thrilling 1-1 draw. By contrast, only 5,576 turned up for the replay at Field Mill which saw the Stags win 3-1. Incidentally, those scores were to be repeated when the teams again met in the FA Cup almost 20 years later.

It is perhaps best to draw a veil over the third-round meeting with Bristol Rovers at Eastville because Mansfield crashed 5-0 before a crowd of over 20,000. Eastville was not one of the Stags' favourite venues, for they never managed a win there in either League or Cup.

The League programme got away to a terrible start when 10,447 fans trudged up Quarry Lane to see visitors Rochdale win 4-2. But Mansfield made amends by winning 4-1 at Carlisle United in their next match and, indeed, lost only five games in 27 League and Cup outings up to the turn of the year, to end 1957 with 31 points in the bag and a place in the third round of the FA Cup.

That Cup defeat by Bristol Rovers hit the team hard, for they lost their next four League games before getting back on song at Bradford's Park Avenue ground with a 2-0 win on 15 February. Indeed, for a time Mansfield looked possible promotion candidates before poor away form cost them dearly, with six defeats in their final seven games on opponents' grounds leaving them sixth in the table at the end of a season in which promotion could have been a real possibility.

It was as well that the Stags finished high up the table in the final season of Division Three North's existence, for below half-way would have seen them as members of the newly-launched Fourth Division.

However, there was not the best of starts for Mansfield's new manager, Sam Weaver, who had replaced Charlie Mitten in June 1958. For at the end of his first season, the Stags managed to escape the drop into the new bottom division by only one place as they finished 20th in the new Third Division.

However, Weaver had brought a new face to Field Mill, a face which intrigued the home fans for his first signing was Lindy Delapenha, one of the few coloured players in the English game at that time. Delapenha, who was born in the West

Indies, began his career with Portsmouth but moved to Middlesbrough after one season and made almost 300 League and Cup appearances whilst with 'Boro.

Perhaps the opening game of the 1958-9 season gave an indication of the disappointments to follow as Mansfield crashed 6-1 at home to Southampton, Derek Reeves scoring four goals for the visitors.

Indeed, it was not until the fourth game of the new campaign that Mansfield managed a win. That was against Bradford City at Field Mill and they also won their next match, against Halifax Town. But then it was another four matches before Mansfield again picked up two points.

It is interesting to note that in only six matches were the Stags able to keep a clean sheet. Apart from the six goals conceded in the opening match, Mansfield were on the end of some heavy defeats. Twice they gave away five goals, on six occasions four goals and on one occasion, against Plymouth Argyle, they conceded eight goals at Home Park. The final weeks of the season provided a traumatic period for the club as only three points were earned from the last seven games.

If anything, Mansfield's start to their second season in Division Three was even worse than their first in the newly-created section. Only four points were gained from the first six matches of 1959-60 and by the end of the year a further 12 points were all that had been added. Yet the first half of the season was not without highlights, which included a 6-2 romp at home to Wrexham, a 4-3 home success over Queen's Park Rangers and a 4-4 draw with Reading.

The third round of the FA Cup was also reached, after Mansfield disposed of Accrington Stanley and Chester to earn another Cup meeting with Blackpool. Before the trip to Bloomfield Road on 9 January, the Stags had lost consecutive matches at Norwich City and Halifax Town — not the best of preparations.

The Seasiders won 3-0 and Mansfield's disappointment was clear as they lost their next match, at home to Bury, 5-1. With only 27 points in the bag at the end of March, the Fourth Division clearly beckoned and, despite a win and a draw at Newport County and Brentford respectively, and a 2-0 home victory over York City in mid-April, the Stags finished third from bottom, and were relegated, although they finished with a flourish by winning 6-3 at Field Mill over Port Vale in their penultimate match.

Four of Mansfield's last five fixtures were at Field Mill and maximum points from all four were required if Division Three status was to be preserved. It was a tall order in the circumstances, especially considering how the Stags' season had gone, and it seemed as though Mansfield's first taste of Fourth Division football was inevitable well before the final run-in of home matches.

Season 1960-61, Mansfield Town's first in the Fourth Division, was one to forget as quickly as possible, at least as far as results went. Yet, for an entirely different reason, it turned out to be one of the most important campaigns in the club's history all because of one man, that mercurial inside-forward of the game's glorious early post-war era, Raich Carter.

On 12 February 1960, Carter replaced Sam Weaver as manager of Mansfield Town. Although, in the remaining four months of that season, he could not stem the Stags' slide towards Divison Four, and still found good results hard to come by in 1960-61 as Mansfield finished 20th, Carter laid the foundations for one of the most memorable periods in Mansfield Town's history.

Always willing to give youth a chance, he threw three local youngsters in at the deep end only weeks after their 17th birthdays, and never had cause to regret his decision. All three survived the test and went on to attain the highest standards in their profession.

Goal machine Ken Wagstaff and winger Mike Stringfellow were the first to make their debuts, both on 30 August 1960 in a 2-1 win at Rochdale in which Wagstaff

Raich Carter welcomes new players Ken Wagstaff, Brian Phillips and Brian Tarrant to the club in 1960.

Raich Carter with his full playing staff in the 1960-61 season. Back row (left to right): Stringfellow, Townsend, Coates, Wragg, Jones. Middle: Sid Carter (trainer), Toon, Clarke, Tarrant, Wyllie, Bradley, Phillips, Watson, Joe Eaton (secretary). Front: Spedding, Fitzsimmons, Morris, Raich Carter (manager), Wagstaff, Delapenha, Ward, Williams.

scored twice. The youngest of the trio, Peter Morris, was introduced on 24 February 1961, in a 3-1 win at Workington.

Meanwhile, as in the League, the Stags' Cup fortunes continued to be on a downward trend. Leicester City handed out a 4-0 beating at Filbert Street in the first round of the League Cup and after a 3-1 home win over non-Leaguers Blyth Spartans in the first round of the FA Cup, a 3-0 defeat at Accrington Stanley in the next round brought an early exit from that competition.

Carter's three youngsters, all of whom had made excellent progress the previous season, established themselves in the senior side in 1961-2, but Carter made an important signing in the first week of the season when he obtained the transfer of experienced forward Roy Chapman from Lincoln City. Chapman struck up an immediate rapport with the youngsters, Wagstaff and Stringfellow, and it showed when comparing the League scoring records from the previous season.

In 1960-61, Mansfield scored 71 goals but conceded 78. In 1961-2, they netted 98 and conceded 63. The highlight of the season, however, from the fans' point of view at least, was the switching-on of Mansfield's new floodlights by former England captain Billy Wright, on the evening of 5 October. That was when the Stags entertained Second Division Cardiff City in the second round of the League Cup, having seen off Exeter City by 5-2 in the opening round. The Cardiff match ended 1-1 in front of 17,380 fans, with Cardiff winning the replay at Ninian Park, 2-1.

But the supporters were beginning to sit up and take notice, for five-figure attendances were becoming the norm and over 10,000 saw Mansfield beat Grimsby Town 3-2 at Field Mill in the first round of the FA Cup. Again, however, expectations of a good Cup run came to nothing in the next round when Mansfield went down 4-2 at Southport.

Still, there were encouraging signs as Mansfield hoisted their final League placing to 14th to give rise to hopes that Division Three was not too far away. Carter had made another important capture in early December 1961, when he persuaded Irishman Sammy Chapman to move from Portsmouth for his second spell at Field Mill.

Chapman played an important role as those promotion hopes were realized in the 1962-3 season as the Stags finished fourth to regain the Third Division status they had surrendered four seasons earlier. Between them, Wagstaff and Chapman scored a total of 78 League and Cup goals — 41 by Wagstaff and 37 by Chapman — with Mansfield's overall goal-tally in the League being 108.

There was also plenty to keep the Stags busy in Cup competitions. Halifax Town were beaten 3-2 at The Shay in the opening round of the League Cup and Chester were held to a 2-2 draw at Sealand Road in round two before they dumped Mansfield out in the replay, winning by a single goal at Field Mill.

Non-League Hounslow Town almost gave the Stags the KO in the first round of the FA Cup, Mansfield managing a 3-3 draw at Hounslow with two goals in the final minutes. The Stags made no mistake in the replay, however, as they romped to a 9-2 win, Ivan Hollett and Roy Chapman both collecting hat-tricks in the process.

There was even more sensation in the next round when Crystal Palace were held to a 2-2 draw at Selhurst Park. Indeed, Mansfield were winning 2-1 until Palace were awarded a penalty in the dying seconds. The entire Mansfield side, with the exception of goalkeeper Colin Treharne, were booked for 'applauding' the referee off the pitch at the final whistle. Fortunately there was no spin-off in the replay on the Monday evening at Mansfield, where 17,118 fans saw Palace crushed 7-2.

That gave the Stags a third-round meeting with Ipswich Town which was delayed until 9 January because of snow, but still attracted a 17,032 attendance as the First Division side were pushed to the limit before winning 3-2. That was a blow, but it paled into insignificance three days later, when Raich Carter left the Stags to become manager of Middlesbrough.

The question was who could step into Carter's shoes and it was not long before the answer was provided as the distinguished Burnley defender, Tommy Cummings, took over, initially as player-manager, to keep the Stags on course for a place in Division Three.

Cummings made his debut on 18 March, in a 2-2 home draw with Aldershot. He was injured in that match and was on the sidelines until 11 May, when he returned for the final five League outings as Mansfield recovered from a shaky period to ensure promotion.

Cummings played in the first four League matches and one League Cup game at the start of 1963-4 before finally hanging up his boots. Nevertheless, he proved to be a highly successful manager and was then the longest-serving boss at Mansfield — where he stayed for almost four and a half years — since the club had been elected to the League.

In Mansfield's first season back in the Third Division they finished seventh with Wagstaff and Chapman still very much on song. Wagstaff scored 29 League goals and Chapman 19 in League, the latter despite missing ten matches through injury in September and October.

Once again Mansfield gained little joy from the two Cup competitions, losing 5-1 at Elland Road to Leeds United in the second round of the League Cup after beating Watford 2-1 in the previous round. In the FA Cup they failed to surmount the first hurdle, going down 3-2 at Oldham in front of another 17,000-plus attendance.

That great Field Mill favourite, Ken Wagstaff (arm raised), in action against Coventry City in 1964.

There was a sour note, not only for Mansfield, but also for English football in general, when details of soccer bribery were revealed in a Sunday newspaper. The scandal involved several First Division players and England internationals and the Stags were sucked into the controversy. A number of these players, including Mansfield's Brian Phillips, were suspended *sine die*.

The centre-half's ban was lifted in the 1980s and he gained distinction by leading local club, Rainworth Miners' Welfare, to the FA Vase Final at Wembley in 1984.

The 1964-5 season turned a little sour for Mansfield. There could have been celebrations but they finished third in the table with 59 points, level with Bristol City, and a single point behind the champions, Carlisle United. Unfortunately, only two clubs were promoted and Bristol City went up by virtue of a better goal-average, the second time the Stags had fought their way to the brink of a place in Division Two, only to be disappointed.

They did, however, achieve a famous League Cup second-round victory over Second Division Manchester City at Maine Road, winning 5-3. Alas, the Stags went down 3-2 at Coventry City in the next round.

But for many Mansfield fans the biggest tragedy of the season came on 12 November 1964 when their idol, Ken Wagstaff, was transferred to Hull City for £40,000. Certainly, the Tigers never had any cause to regret their decision to sign Wagstaff, for he gave them marvellous service for many seasons.

However, there are many Mansfield supporters who have never forgiven the club,

Mansfield Town pictured in 1964-5. Back row (left to right): Ivan Hollett, Colin Toon, Wilf Humble, Alan Humphreys, John Gill, Colin Treharne, Albert Scanlon, Roy Chapman. Front row: Brian McCready, Peter Morris, Ken Wagstaff, Mick Jones, Alan Tyrer.

even to this day, for parting with this home-grown talent who was possibly the most popular man ever to play at Field Mill.

It must be said, though, that manager Cummings moved swiftly to plug the gap left by Wagstaff's departure. And an effective replacement he certainly found. Former England Under-23 centre-forward Bill Curry joined Mansfield from Derby County and made his debut on 6 February 1965 at Grimsby. Curry's impact at Field Mill was explosive, for in the 16 matches to the end of the season he scored 15 goals, including four goals in one match and two hat-tricks.

Only once in his four full seasons at Field Mill did Tommy Cummings see his side out of the top ten and that was in 1965-6, when they slumped to 19th. Wagstaff had gone, Roy Chapman rejoined Lincoln City, centre-half John Gill had moved to Hartlepools and it was rebuilding time.

Centre-half Bill Williams was signed from West Bromwich Albion and inside-forward Tommy Mitchinson from Sunderland, both making their debuts on 8 January 1966 at Southend United.

But the rebuilding process was traumatic at times with some devastating defeats — a crushing 6-0 trouncing at Bristol Rovers, a 6-2 hammering at Swindon and a 6-4 reverse at Brighton. Even worse were a 7-1 hammering by Peterborough United and a 5-1 defeat by Swindon, both at Field Mill. But by mid-April there were signs that the Stags were getting back on the rails.

England Under-23 goalkeeper Alan Humphreys took over towards the end of the season and he continued into 1966-7. Bill Curry, who had scored only a modest

A goal for hot-shot Harry Middleton as he beats the diving Watford 'keeper in 1965.

A typical action shot of Bill Curry, climbing above the Brighton defence during the opening match of the 1965-6 season on 21 August. The Stags won 3-1, Curry scoring twice.

Mansfield Town pictured in 1965-6. Back row (left to right): Bill Poynton, Peter Morris, Colin Nelson, Colin Treharne, John Gill, Wilf Humble. Front row: John Gregson, Brian McCready, Bill Curry, Harry Middleton, Albert Scanlon.

14 goals in the last campaign, had a new partner up front in Stewart Brace, signed from Watford. And full-back Bill McKinney had been recruited from Bournemouth to tighten up the defence.

The Stags scored 90 League goals that season and raised themselves to ninth place by the close of the campaign. Brace and Curry each netted 26 League and Cup goals and Mitchinson weighed in with 12. For a change there was even a little light relief in the Cup competitions, with a satisfying first-round success over Notts County in the League Cup — 1-1 at Meadow Lane and 3-1 in the replay at Field Mill.

That brought a confrontation with Second Division Wolves at Molineux. Wolves were on their way into Division One and won 2-1 against a Stags side given plenty of credit for their performance.

Mansfield reached the fourth round of the FA Cup before bowing out at Hillsborough, beaten 4-0 by Sheffield Wednesday in front of a 49,049 crowd who paid £14,400. There had been 17,332 at Field Mill in the previous round when Middlesbrough were defeated 2-0. Scunthorpe United and Bangor City, both at Mansfield, were the stepping stones in the first two rounds.

Another local player had been recruited towards the end of the season, Kirkby-in-Ashfield born Dick Edwards, who had made his name with Notts County, the club he joined as a youngster. He was to have two spells with the Stags before the end of his playing career.

A young player by the name of Stuart Boam, who had shown promise in the 'A' team, was given a run-out with the seniors in the final match of the season at Leyton Orient. He looked distinctly promising at centre-half, despite a 4-2 defeat.

It is a fact of life for clubs in the lower regions of the Football League that

Mansfield Town pictured in 1966-7: Back row (left to right): Taylor, Richardson, Morris, Humphreys, Wilson, Derco, Elliott. Middle row: Carter, Mallinson, Coleman, Brace, Ferns, Gregson, Curry, McKinney, Weaver. Front row: McGeorge, Mitchinson, Williams, Cummings, Overton, Burns, Aldread.

having given someone their first taste of management, senior clubs sit up and take notice when the newcomer does well. No doubt Tommy Cummings, because of his distinguished career as a player with Burnley, had been closely watched and his record with Mansfield could stand up to the closest of scrutinies.

On 5 July 1967, Cummings' appointment as manager of Second Division Aston Villa was announced. Villa acknowledged the co-operation of the Mansfield Town directors, who had released their manager from his five-year contract.

One month later, from a sizeable list of applicants which included a number of well-known names, Tom Eggleston emerged as the new boss at Field Mill. It was Eggleston's first managerial post but he was no stranger to the machinations of football's backroom, for he had been the right-hand man of successful manager Harry Catterick, both at Sheffield Wednesday and Everton, after a playing career which had taken in Derby County, Leicester City and Watford.

Eggleston took over at a time when Mansfield's finances were stretched to the limit and it was of immediate importance to sell players rather than delve into the transfer market on their own behalf. Cummings did his former club a favour by obtaining the transfers, first of Tommy Mitchinson and then Dick Edwards. After Edwards' move to Villa in early March — Mitchinson's move in late August had given slight release from financial headaches at Field Mill — there was a little cash available for possible strengthening of Mansfield's playing staff.

This was when Eggleston's extensive experience and involvement in soccer's market-place under his former boss Harry Catterick was put to good use. He had already thrown 20-year-old Stuart Boam back in at the deep end, three matches into the season and his gamble had been justified. In October he had obtained the signature of Alexander Montgomery Pate — 'Sandy' to his friends — at a give-away price from Watford and no one needs reminding what a bargain that turned out to be.

In early March, Eggleston signed four players in a hectic 48 hours, all for modest fees. They were Jim Goodfellow and Nick Sharkey from Leicester City, Phil Waller from Derby County and Dudley Roberts from Coventry City.

But the newcomers needed time to settle and that was a commodity which was quickly running out. In the end, however, the Stags avoided relegation on goal-average, Grimsby Town going down instead by 0.008 of a goal.

Indeed, the Stags would still have been relegated, but for the fact that Peterborough United had been sent down to Division Four as punishment for illegal payments to players. That stroke of good fortune for Mansfield was justified the following season and helped by another master-stroke in the transfer market, when Eggleston persuaded the experienced John Quigley to move to Mansfield from Bristol City.

Glaswegian Quigley had made his name with Nottingham Forest and was in their FA Cup-winning side in 1959 and also had a couple of seasons at Huddersfield Town. He had been recruited to replace long-serving Peter Morris, who joined Ipswich Town in February 1968 for what must surely have been a bargain £10,000 fee.

Soon after his arrival at Field Mill, Eggleston had appointed Walter (Jock) Basford as his right-hand man and a highly-effective partnership it turned out to be. The 1968-9 season brought Mansfield Town considerable success in the FA Cup as they reached the sixth round for the first time in the club's history, with some memorable victories on the way.

In Eggleston's initial season at Mansfield, their FA Cup hopes had foundered ignominiously at the first hurdle in the North-East, at non-League Tow Law Town, where the original game had been postponed at half-time because of a blizzard. The home side won the second meeting 5-1.

Ironically, it was Tow Law Town who launched Mansfield on their record-breaking run in 1968-9. At Field Mill, the Stags won 4-1, although the non-Leaguers scored first. After a 2-2 draw at Millmoor against Rotherham United in the second round,

Bob Ledger, supported by Dudley Roberts, pressures the Tow Law Town defence in the first match of the famous 1968-9 Cup run.

Mansfield won the replay 1-0 with a Bob Ledger goal. The tie was watched by an aggregate attendance of 23,255.

Second Division Sheffield United went down 2-1 at Mansfield in the third round in front of a 17,430 crowd but it must be admitted that Fourth Division Southend United were a little unfortunate to go out 2-1 at Field Mill in the fourth round, this time with over 16,000 packing the ground.

That set up a meeting with one of the League's glamour clubs, West Ham United, who boasted three World Cup stars in their line-up — England captain Bobby Moore, Martin Peters and centre-forward Geoff Hurst, the man who scored a hat-trick in the 1966 World Cup Final.

Whether the fact that the match was postponed on no fewer than three occasions because of snow had any effect on the Hammers, when they eventually suffered a 3-0 defeat, is hard to assess. But the fact remains that 21,117 spectators watched a rip-roaring Cup tie in which United were made to pay dearly for missed chances early in the game. It was reported that Mansfield fans sang and danced in the streets until the small hours of the morning as they celebrated the Stags' success.

Leicester City provided the opposition in the sixth round, again at Field Mill, with a young Peter Shilton in their goal. Mansfield again gave a good account of themselves but a late goal by Rodney Fern sent City through. They eventually reached the FA Cup Final where they lost 1-0 to Manchester City.

The Stags' Cup commitments perhaps hindered their progress in the League but they finished a comfortable 15th with hopes of better things to come.

There was certainly some improvement in the final League placing the following season of 1969-70, when the Stags lifted themselves to sixth. But the highlight was again to come in the FA Cup as Mansfield reached the fifth round before bowing out at Elland Road, beaten 2-0 by the mighty Leeds United, who were on their way to that memorable Cup Final against Chelsea which went to an Old Trafford replay and was won after extra-time by the Pensioners.

The Stags lost 1-0 to Bury at Gigg Lane in a League meeting in September but drew 2-2 at the same venue in the first round of the Cup, and won the replay 2-0. Shrewsbury Town lost 2-1 in front of their own fans in the second round and Barnsley were beaten 3-2 in round three at Field Mill, in front of 14,387 fans.

And so it was to Bloomfield Road, yet again, to meet Blackpool in the FA Cup. The Seasiders had seen off Arsenal in a third-round replay to earn this home tie, the third time that Mansfield had to travel to Blackpool in that competition. But Blackpool, on their way out of Division One that season, failed to make it a hat-trick of Cup wins over the Stags.

Dai Jones scored both Mansfield goals in their 2-0 win, watched by a 23,715 crowd. His first came two minutes after the start and the second two minutes from the end. But the real hero of the 90 minutes was undoubtedly goalkeeper Graham Brown, who pulled off a string of incredible saves. It was estimated that Mansfield Town supporters made up half of the 48,903 attendance for the fourth round tie at Elland Road on 7 February 1970, and to a man they maintained that, had a 13th-minute strike by the Stags been allowed to stand, then the final 2-0 scoreline to Leeds may well have been the other way round.

Not for the first time a referee, on this occasion W.Castle of Sedgeley, refused to believe that Dudley Roberts could leap so high to head the ball without 'climbing'

The Stags squad that enjoyed such a memorable Cup run. Back row (left to right): Clive Walker, Ray Keeley, Malcolm Partridge, Dave Hollins, Graham Brown, Stuart Boam, Phil Waller, Mick Hopkinson. Front row: Dudley Roberts, Sandy Pate, Jim Goodfellow, John Stenson, Johnny Quigley, Dai Jones, Nick Sharkey, Brian Bates.

on his marker, Paul Reaney this time, to set up the chance for Jim Goodfellow to crash home.

Unfortunately, Mansfield's Cup exploits had left them with a great deal of leeway to make up as the season ran its course. And having to play 14 games in March and April perhaps cost them a chance of bidding for promotion, although it should be added that six of the matches were won.

In the author's opinion, had Tom Eggleston stayed at Field Mill, then the Stags would have tasted Second Division football several years earlier than 1977-8, when they finally achieved that status. But an offer of a two-year contract, at £10,000 a year, to manage Greek club Ethnikos was one which Eggleston could hardly have turned down and he took up his new post on 1 August 1970, with the blessing of the Mansfield board.

So, for the third time in a few years, Mansfield Town had become the stepping-stone for an ambitious football manager to reach big-time soccer, as Eggleston followed in the path trodden by Raich Carter and Tommy Cummings. It was no surprise that the Stags were inundated with applications for the vacant post but in the end, Eggleston's assistant, trainer-coach Jock Basford, became the Stags' new boss, obviously with the hope that the appointment would ensure a continuation of the successful policy of the previous two years.

A 6-2 win over Chesterfield in the first round of the League Cup kept those hopes alive, as did Mansfield's showing against the mighty Liverpool in the next round with a goalless draw at Field Mill and a moral victory in the replay at Anfield, where the Stags led 2-1 with only eight minutes left. Liverpool were then awarded a controversial penalty to equalize and went on to win 3-2 in extra-time in front of a 31,087 crowd.

Dai Jones (right) scores against Bradford City on 30 January 1971 – but could not prevent the Stags from slipping to a 5-3 home defeat.

In the League there was an early 1-0 win at Villa Park, watched by 30,856 fans, although on three occasions the Stags conceded five goals in a match, at Shrewsbury and at home to Plymouth Argyle and Bradford City. Nevertheless, a final position of seventh was achieved, a satisfactory state of affairs considering the upheavals during the close season.

But the FA Cup was again a disappointment, for after a 2-0 home win over Wrexham in the first round, Mansfield crashed out at Scunthorpe in round two, beaten 3-0.

There was activity in the transfer market, too, with talented youngster Malcolm Partridge joining Leicester City for £50,000 on 14 September to ease Mansfield's growing financial problems, which over the years never seemed far away.

Quigley was appointed player-coach in November 1970 and teenage goalkeeper, Rod Arnold, on loan from Wolves, made his debut at Fulham on 6 February and went on to make 16 League appearances through to the end of the season.

Incidentally, Mansfield used five goalkeepers in this season, with Graham Brown, the regular 'keeper, picking up injuries which required loan replacements by Birmingham's Jim Herriott and Notts County's Mike Rose, as well as Arnold and Des Finch.

The season ended on a high note with the Stags lifting the County Cup after a 1-0 win over Nottingham Forest in the Final. They had beaten Notts County in the semi-final by a similar margin.

The 1970-71 season had hardly ended when the news broke that the popular

Mansfield Town pictured in 1970-71. Back row (left to right): John Stenson, Sandy Pate, Jimmy Goodfellow, Clive Walker, Dudley Roberts, Phil Waller, Barry Foster. Third row: John Quigley, Stuart Boam, John Saunders, Des Finch, Graham Brown, Malcolm Partridge, Jimmy Sutton, Dai Jones. Second row: Frank Milford, Tommy Eggleston, John Almond, Arthur Patrick, George Bunting, Joe Eaton, Jock Basford, Sam Weaver. Front row: Colin Foster, Ian Wright.

local boy, centre-half Stuart Boam, had signed for Middlesbrough for £45,000. Whether his departure could be pin-pointed as the reason it is hard to say, but the season turned out to be a disaster.

Not a goal was scored at home in any senior competition until 22 November, when Fourth Division Chester were beaten 4-3 in a first-round FA Cup replay after a 1-1 draw at Sealand Road. Of course, it was also the Stags' first home win of the season.

By then, Basford and player-coach Quigley had been dismissed, although the departure of Quigley was something of a surprise, for he was at least expected to act as caretaker manager, if not actually succeed Basford. It is worthy of note that 16 League matches had been completed before Basford was dismissed on 8 November, from which only eight points had been earned. The Stags had also been dismissed from the League Cup by Chesterfield, who were held to a goalless draw at Saltergate, but who then crushed Mansfield 5-0 at Field Mill.

There had been encouraging performances away from home with another 1-0 win at Villa Park and draws at Tranmere, Halifax and Blackburn Rovers. Basford's fate was sealed, however, by a 5-0 drubbing at home by Bournemouth, followed by a 2-0 defeat at Notts County which could so easily have been much more decisive.

The Stags' chairman, Arthur Patrick, had a busy day on Thursday 11 November, during the week after the manager had gone. In the morning he signed the experienced forward Frank Wignall from Derby County, for a remarkably low fee of £8,000. And in the afternoon he appointed Danny Williams as the new manager.

The Mansfield Town playing staff pictured for the 1971-2 season. Back row (left to right): C.Foster, J.Bingham, C.Harrington, R.Harford, G.Brown, G.Crawford, J.Saunders, P.Waller, C.Walker, R.Clarke. Middle row: D.Jones, J.Stenson, B.Roberts, A.Jarvis, S.Pate, B.Foster, D.Roberts, D.Thompson. Front row: M.Donovan, B.Hill, B.Grozier, D.Colin.

Take that! Frank Wignall in goalscoring action against Gillingham in 1972.

Mansfield Town pictured in 1972-3. Back row (left to right): C.Foster, D.Roberts, J.Saunders, C.Walker. Middle row: A.Green, K.Bird, M.Laverick, G.Brown, D.Longhorn, S.Ellis, D.Thompson. Front row: J.McCaffrey, J.Fairbrother, F.Wignall, B.Foster, A.Jarvis.

Williams, who lived in Bournemouth, was contacted on the Wednesday afternoon and travelled up to meet the Mansfield board the following day. One of his first duties was to agree to the transfer of Ray Harford to Port Vale. Harford had been signed by Jock Basford as a replacement for Stuart Boam and was probably on the receiving end of the Mansfield fans' resentment at the transfer of their idol. The player was never given a real chance to settle.

Then Williams turned to his former club, Sheffield Wednesday, to sign centre-half Sam Ellis, who was best-remembered as the teenager thrown into the 1966 FA Cup Final against Everton because the regular pivot was injured. Williams also recruited a youngster from Bournemouth, Dennis Longhorn, who was later to play a significant role in the Field Mill proceedings.

However, by the time Ellis and Longhorn arrived, the Stags were out of the FA Cup, beaten 4-2 in the second round by Tranmere Rovers in a replay at Prenton Park after a 2-2 draw at Mansfield.

Centre-forward John Fairbrother, who had been signed by Basford in late September, began his Mansfield career on a quiet note but gradually found his scoring touch to finish with 18 goals as hopes rose of avoiding the relegation which had threatened for all of the first half of the season.

Indeed, Mansfield had to collect two points from their final home game, against Wrexham, to retain their Third Division status and, after taking a 1-0 lead, they seemed well on course. But a fluke goal scored from all of 35 yards caught goalkeeper Graham Brown off his line and curled into the net for an equalizer which sent the Stags down to Division Four by 0.003 of a goal.

There was a grandstand finale to 1972-3, for when the Stags met Cambridge United at the Abbey Stadium on 28 April, in front of 10,542 fans — including a massive following from Mansfield — whoever won the match would earn promotion to Division Three. Twice Mansfield were ahead and twice they gifted equalizers to United within minutes. Then Cambridge snatched the winner in the 61st minute. It was hugely disappointing, for the Stags had looked the main promotion candidates from early in the season and headed the table for several weeks just before the turn of the year.

The start of the season was marred by an unusual occurrence during Mansfield's first match, against Northampton Town. Whilst living in Bournemouth, Danny Williams had noted the performance of a young forward, 20-year-old Alan Green, and had signed him for Mansfield during the close season. The newcomer had shown up well in pre-season games and had earned his place against the Cobblers. Almost on half-time, Green was seen to stagger and hold his chest. It was thought that he had taken a knock and he did not reappear after the break. It was subsequently revealed, however, that he had a heart attack whilst on the field and was advised not to play again.

There was a good start to the League Cup competition with a 3-1 home win over Lincoln City, but Charlton Athletic ended the Stags' run in the next round, winning 4-3 at The Valley. And Mansfield's interest in the FA Cup lasted only one round with a 2-1 defeat at York City.

Another of Mansfield's home-grown products, centre-half John Saunders, was on the move in October when he joined Huddersfield Town for £30,000. That transfer had been made possible by the tremendous form shown by newcomer Kevin Bird, who had moved to Mansfield on a three-month trial from his home-town club, Doncaster Rovers, on the recommendation of Williams' assistant, Frank Marshall. The move was made permanent when Saunders left for pastures new.

Mansfield finished sixth in the table in their first season back in Division Four and many believe that, had Duncan McKenzie been allowed to stay longer on loan from Nottingham Forest, the Stags may well have made a quick return to the Third Division.

McKenzie had a loan spell at Field Mill towards the end of the 1969-70 season, when he made seven appearances (plus three as substitute), scoring three goals. But in this second period with Mansfield, he made six full appearances scoring seven goals, the sort of form which earned his recall by struggling Forest.

Williams also introduced several other players who were to make an important impact on the outstanding events which were to follow in the mid-70s. Jim McCaffrey joined the Stags from Nottingham Forest, Paul Matthews signed from Leicester City and emerging from the youth ranks were Colin and Barry Foster. And back at the club for another loan spell was Rod Arnold, whose move was to be made permanent in time for the next season.

Frank Wignall and John Fairbrother had departed during the close season, Wignall to be player-manager of non-League King's Lynn and Fairbrother to Torquay United. But a new arrival on the Field Mill scene was striker Terry Eccles, signed for a sizeable fee from Blackburn Rovers. And back with the club was centre-half Dick Edwards, who was originally signed by manager Tom Cummings and followed him to Aston Villa. Edwards had left football to take up a singing career after Torquay United had given him a free transfer.

Without a doubt, promotion is always achieved by a team with a good away record to supplement its home form and the previous season the Stags had lost only once at Field Mill, winning 15 and drawing seven. But 17 points from their 23 away games still had not given them a place in Division Three.

In 1973-4 their home form was still good, with 13 wins, eight draws and only two defeats, but not a single away League game was won and with only nine drawn games their final League placing suffered accordingly as Mansfield struggled to reach 17th.

Duncan McKenzie (far left) puts Mansfield four-up after 86 minutes against Workington in March 1973.

Chesterfield had again knocked Mansfield out of the League Cup, this time after a first-round replay following Mansfield's 1-1 draw at Saltergate. A single goal gave the Spireites victory at Field Mill. There were also replays in both the first and second rounds of the FA Cup, at York and Scunthorpe, before hopes of a money-spinning Cup run disappeared with 1-0 defeat at the Old Showground.

During this season the Football League allowed matches to be played on Sundays for the first time, to relieve a backlog of fixtures caused by the weather and to take account of power restrictions caused by an industrial dispute. Mansfield were one of the first clubs to apply to play on the sabbath and were the first to obtain permission, their home meeting with Peterborough being played on Sunday, 20 January 1974.

During the first week in March, Danny Williams was persuaded to return to the scene of his major managerial triumphs at Swindon Town, but not before he had sold Dennis Longhorn to Sunderland in exchange for John Lathan plus a sizeable cash adjustment. He had also transferred long-serving Dudley Roberts to Lincoln City.

Williams just missed one of the season's highlights, when Sandy Pate made his 300th consecutive appearance in Mansfield's colours at Colchester on 22 March 1974.

That event preceded the appointment of a new manager by just over a week, for on 4 April, Dave Smith took over at Field Mill. The former Burnley player, who later had spells with Brighton and Bristol City and whose career was halted after breaking his leg for the fifth time, had spent 11 years in a coaching capacity with Newcastle United, Sheffield Wednesday and Arsenal. All new managers, by necessity, are optimists but Smith could hardly have envisaged what was to transpire in his first full season in charge.

Mansfield made two important signings before the start of the 1974-5 season, their most momentous since becoming a Football League club. Gordon Hodgson,

Mansfield Town during the 1973-4 season, just before manager Williams returned to Swindon Town on 7 March 1974. Back row (left to right): T.Eccles, D.Longhorn, S.Pate, R.Arnold, F.Marshall, G.Brown, D.Roberts, C.Foster, D.Edwards. Middle: D.Hailwood, A.Shore, M.Donovan, Danny Williams, M.Laverick, P.Jones, P.Christopher, K.Bird. Front: P.Matthews, C.Walker, J. McCaffrey, B.Foster, D.Thompson.

a left-sided midfield player joined the Stags from Newcastle United. And on the recommendation of Danny Williams, centre-forward Ray Clarke signed for Mansfield for a modest £8,000 fee.

Smith also signed a former Barnsley youngster, Doug O'Connor, who showed up well in early matches but then faded into the background as the side took on a familiar look from mid-October. O'Connor and Colin Foster were the scorers as the season opened with a 2-1 home win over Southport but the second outing, at Doncaster in the League Cup, saw Kevin Bird break an ankle against his former club as the Stags went down 2-1.

Undeterred, Mansfield won 1-0 at Scunthorpe in the following match to end a sequence of 38 League and Cup away games without a win. And when they defeated Exeter City at St James' Park on 7 September, the Stags held the proud record of being the last club in the Football League with a 100 per cent record.

Indeed, by the turn of the year, Mansfield had lost only twice in the League, at Stockport and Hartlepool, and had picked up an incredible 41 points from 25 matches. In addition, they were through to the third round of the FA Cup after a first-round win over Wrexham and another of those Cup meetings with non-League Wigan Athletic which had required a Field Mill replay win to ensure further progress.

The third-round visit of Cambridge United saw 10,486 fans go through the turnstiles to see a 1-0 win for the Stags. Then a 16,623 attendance saw Third Division Bury beaten 2-1 at Gigg Lane in the fourth round.

The fifth round brought First Division Carlisle United to Field Mill, where 18,293 fans saw Mansfield play the better football but United grab the winning goal they scarcely deserved in a match that was televised.

Whether it was the disappointment of being eliminated from the FA Cup or

Mansfield Town in 1974-5. Back row (left to right): Dave Smith (manager), C.Walker, D.Hailwood, T.Cook, R.Arnold, A.Shore, C.Foster, B.Foster, J.Haselden (trainer-coach). Front: P.Matthews, J.McCaffrey, T.Eccles, K.Bird, S.Pate, G.Hodgson, M.Laverick, D.O'Connor, J.Lathan.

not, the Stags lost for the third time in the League in their following match, at Doncaster, and in the middle of March failed to pick up a point in consecutive matches at Rotherham and Newport.

But promotion was almost achieved and on 5 April, a 2-0 home win over Hartlepool made it a certainty. Four matches later, Mansfield Town collected the Fourth Division championship in real style with a 7-0 win against Scunthorpe United in front of 11,020 celebrating fans at Field Mill. It was also a fitting occasion for Sandy Pate to record his 400th first-team appearance.

This was Mansfield's first-ever Football League title and a marvellous achievement in which twin strikers Ray Clarke and Terry Eccles had played a major role by scoring 45 goals between them, 28 being credited to Clarke.

Gordon Hodgson, who had been a revelation in midfield, contributed ten goals and in all, 12 players put their name on the Stags' score-sheet. In central midfield Paul Matthews had been one of the unsung heroes.

The championship had been won with 68 points, the next to the highest in the Fourth Division up to then, Notts County having achieved the title with 69 points in 1970-71. Mansfield had not lost a League match at home and their record showed 28 wins, 12 draws and six defeats, with 90 goals scored and 40 conceded.

Pre-season results before the start of the 1975-6 campaign were encouraging, with Anglo-Scottish Cup successes over Leicester City and Hull City at Field Mill and a 1-1 draw with West Bromwich Albion at The Hawthorns. And if the first game back in Division Three brought a 2-1 home defeat by Shrewsbury Town, a League

Chairman Arthur Patrick (left) joins in the dressing-room celebrations after promotion was clinched in a 2-0 win over Hartlepool on 5 April 1975, with five matches still to go.

Cup 6-0 win on aggregate over two legs against Scunthorpe United and a 2-0 League win at Colchester redressed the balance.

The Stags' next five League outings failed to produce a win until 27 September, when Walsall went down 4-1 at Mansfield. There was, though, further progress in the League Cup with a 2-1 success at Wrexham and a 3-0 victory on aggregate in the quarter-final of the Anglo-Scottish Cup. All this perhaps delayed the sounding of the alarm bells at Quarry Lane.

League results continued to point the Stags firmly on to a path back to Division Four but the fans were fed League Cup victories over Coventry City and Wolverhampton Wanderers to keep them happy.

By the end of 1975, however, only 11 points had been won in the League and Mansfield found themselves adrift at the bottom of the table. Even two marvellous performances, against First Division Middlesbrough in the Anglo-Scottish Cup, albeit the overall result being a 4-0 aggregate defeat in the semi-final, could not hide the anxiety. Nor could an even better showing when Mansfield made their first appearance in the fifth round of the League Cup, where Manchester City won 4-2 at Maine Road, a defeat that was mainly self-inflicted.

All this Cup activity, which must surely have detracted from the Stags' main aim of consolidating their Third Division status, was further compounded by the first-round action in the FA Cup, which was protracted to three matches before Mansfield beat Wrexham 2-1 at Villa Park in a match watched by a meagre crowd of 1,470. Both sides must have wondered why the decision was made to play the match in Birmingham, when the toss of a coin would have meant that the sides shared reasonable gate receipts.

At least the second round was a quick and painless affair with Lincoln City winning 2-1 at Field Mill against a Mansfield team who surely had much more important matters on their minds by mid-December. There had been some criticism

The Stags, with Peter Morris at the helm, in 1976-7. Back row (left to right): I. Wood, M. Saxby, K. Randall, I. Mackenzie, P. Evans, R. Arnold, G. Hodgson, T. Eccles, K. Bird, C. Foster. Front row: Gerry Clarke, I. McDonald, P. Matthews, S. Pate, Peter Morris, J. McCaffrey, M. Laverick, B. Foster, Jock Basford.

that manager Smith had not previously played his major trump card of the season since the return to Division Three — the striking partnership of Clarke, Eccles and Jimmy McCaffrey.

The trio had been together in the side on only three occasions prior to 7 February 1976, when there was the first evidence of a resurgence in Mansfield's fortunes with a 2-2 home draw against Hereford United. Four days later, Hereford won the return match by a single goal, very much against the run of play, and there was a feeling in the Mansfield camp that things were on the mend.

The following Saturday, a debut victory goal in injury time at Halifax Town by young Mick Saxby started a run of 19 matches without defeat, which lifted Mansfield to a final 11th position, a situation unthinkable a couple of months earlier. But by then there had been controversy at the club when in mid-April, Dave Smith was sacked in a move which shocked and angered the fans.

The real reason for the board's action has never been revealed and until all parties concerned have finally left football, I doubt if it will. Perhaps it is sufficient to say that both Terry Eccles and Mick Laverick, who had been placed on the transfer list at their own request, both immediately withdrew their requests upon Smith's departure. For my own part, all I have to say is that a situation arose which meant that either the board, the players or the manager had to go.

Dave Smith's assistant, Mick Buxton, was acting manager for the remainder of the season and there were calls for his promotion to the permanent post. But Mansfield turned to a former crowd favourite at Field Mill, Peter Morris, to guide his former

Terry Eccles (right) goes for goal against Tranmere on 18 September 1976, but he failed to get on the score-sheet in a 1-1 draw.

club as player-manager. Morris had assisted both Ipswich Town, whom he joined from Mansfield, and then their neighbours, Norwich City, into the First Division. And there is no doubt in my mind that his midfield skills played a major part in the successes achieved in his first season in charge at Field Mill.

Morris suffered a set-back, however, before he had even accepted the post, when striker Ray Clarke was sold to Sparta Rotterdam for £90,000. I believe, with hindsight, that he made an initial mistake when he failed to confirm that Mick Buxton would remain assistant manager, instead being allowed to follow Dave Smith, who had been appointed manager of Southend United.

It is a rare occasion when it is possible to pin-point exactly, an incident or a match which is the key to promotion or relegation. But Mansfield Town's second-round FA Cup defeat, 5-2 by neighbouring non-League side Matlock Town on 15 December 1976, undoubtedly forced the Stags into the transfer market and brought striker Ernie Moss to Field Mill.

The previous season Smith had signed former Chesterfield forward Kevin Randall from Notts County. Randall and Moss had enjoyed a fruitful partnership at Chesterfield and this proved to be just as effective at Mansfield. Indeed, it was the key to the Stags' elevation to the Second Division at the end of the season with their second championship in three seasons.

Morris also signed another player with Chesterfield connections in Billy McEwan, whose midfield industry augmented the Moss-Randall threat up front. His first signing, however, was winger Johnny Miller from Ipswich Town. That — and the eventual arrival of Moss — meant that the popular Jimmy McCaffrey and Terry Eccles were soon on their way to Huddersfield Town, whom Mansfield had defeated after a replay in the first round of the FA Cup.

The Stags were never far away from the top half-a-dozen clubs. Indeed, as they went into the Easter holiday sequence of three matches they were third in the table, a point behind front-runners Brighton and Rotherham United. But results had not

Kevin Randall hammers in his hat-trick goal against Reading on 8 November 1976. He scored all four that day – including two from the penalty-spot.

been too promising in the run-up to the holiday with a 2-0 defeat at Bury, a 1-1 home draw with Chester and a 3-1 defeat at leaders Brighton in the three previous outings.

However, a maximum six points from three most difficult fixtures over the holiday, at Port Vale and against Chesterfield and Shrewsbury Town at home, confirmed the Stags as potential promotion favourites. Seven matches remained, four away from home, and only one was lost, 2-1 at Reading, and one drawn, 2-2 at Gillingham.

And on 2 May the Second Division dream became a reality as promotion was made certain with a 2-0 win over Portsmouth at Field Mill, although celebrations were tempered by an injury during the game to Barry Foster, who was carried off with a double fracture of his right leg.

With two games left, the Stags' aim was to provide the championship as icing on the cake. A 3-0 win against Northampton Town ended their home programme on a high note. Now all that was left was a trip to Wrexham, possibly the best side in the division over the season, but with their player-manager Arfon Griffiths sidelined the Welshmen had slipped somewhat in the run-in period.

They lost twice in a week to promotion rivals Crystal Palace, when one point would have been sufficient to ensure them a place in Division Two. Yet two points from their last match of the season, when they entertained Mansfield, would still have earned promotion. There were 20,764 spectators packed into the Recreation Ground, including several hundred Palace supporters, who had made the trip from London. Palace manager Terry Venables, who was attending a reserve match, kept an open telephone line to the ground throughout the game.

Big Ernie Moss strikes after only five minutes of the 1-1 draw with Chester in 1977.

Gordon Hodgson proudly displays the Division Three trophy, after the presentation prior to Mansfield's celebration friendly with Norwich City on Wednesday 18 May 1977.

It was an emotional 90 minutes, full of Welsh passion and endeavour, but Mansfield kept their cool and as Wrexham wasted their chances, the Stags relaxed their tight defensive grip in the closing stages to move forward and clinch the title with a goal in the very last seconds of the match — almost inevitably set up by Kevin Randall and put away by Ernie Moss.

At the start of 1977-8, Mansfield Town's first-ever match in Division Two was marred by what in more recent years was to become a festering sore on the face of football — crowd disorder.

Hordes of Stoke City's so-called supporters rampaged through Mansfield's town centre before the match and it required firm control by the local police to prevent problems caused by the visiting fans both before and during the match. But at least the Stags had a winning start to life at a higher level, with a 2-1 win from a Pat Sharkey penalty and a goal from close-season signing, striker Dave Syrett, who had cost £25,000 from Swindon Town. Sharkey, a Northern Ireland international, and 18-year-old defender Ian Phillips were also close-season recruits from Ipswich Town.

There were fruitless journeys to Crystal Palace and Southampton for the next two games but in September and early October, the Stags appeared to be finding their feet at the higher level with a run of four games without defeat. It was also noticeable that Syrett and Ernie Moss were beginning to establish a good understanding up front. Indeed, the pair had scored a total of 13 goals between them up to November.

It was obvious, though, that Moss was having problems with a pelvic injury

The Stags' first goal in Division Two as Dave Syrett slips the ball past Stoke City goalkeeper Peter Shilton.

and after the home game against Luton Town on 12 November, he was sidelined for the rest of the season after an operation to cure the problem.

It was the Stags' failure to secure a replacement for Moss which led to a downturn in the club's fortunes and it perhaps indicated that the decisions to transfer Kevin Randall and Ian McDonald to York City, Billy McEwan to Peterborough United and Paul Matthews to Rotherham United were a little hasty.

I am aware that the idea was to build up cash to delve into the transfer market for a quality player. Unfortunately, Mansfield's need arose at a period when there were comparatively rich pickings in the North American Soccer League, not only for star players but also for those of more moderate ability who had experience in the top two divisions in England.

Typical was the case of Newcastle United's midfielder Graham Oates, who agreed to join the Stags on a month's loan with the prospect of a permanent move, but the next day cried off because he had received an offer from America in the meantime. One of the mysteries of the season was the fact that Kevin Randall, who had experienced Second Division football with Notts County and had headed the scoring list with 19 goals in the Third Division championship season, was not allowed to start a single game before he moved, very reluctantly, to York City.

Peter Morris was feeling the strain of combining the task of playing and managing the club and had only ten outings before he left Field Mill under a cloud in February to become assistant manager at Newcastle United.

Former Everton boss, Billy Bingham, took over but his expertise failed to prevent the slide back into Division Three at the end of the season. Analysing the season's statistics, one sees that the first 27 games produced 18 points. Thirteen from the last 15 when Bingham was in charge tells its own story.

However, of more significance was the fact that five penalties were missed in the season and every one cost a point at least. It may well be that even if every one had been made to count, it still would not have saved the Stags from relegation — but who knows?

Certainly it was tight at the foot of the table. Hull City were at the bottom with 28 points. Mansfield Town had 31 and Blackpool, also relegated, had 37. Then there were no fewer than seven clubs who had sweated it out with 38 points, the majority no doubt happy that safety had not depended on goal-average.

Manager Billy Bingham signed a three-year contract in time for the start of the 1978-9 season and had also been busy in the transfer market. For some time the Stags had been keeping a watchful eye on non-League Bangor City's 6ft 2in defender, John McClelland, and on 23 May 1978 he became a Mansfield player for what eventually turned out to be a bargain fee of £10,000.

Bingham also paid £20,000 to sign Tranmere Rovers winger Russ Allen, the son of former England star and then West Bromwich Albion manager, Ronnie Allen. He also picked up a £10,000 fee from Colchester United for the signature of Pat Sharkey.

One familiar name was missing from Mansfield playing staff, that of Sandy Pate who was given a free transfer at the end of a distinguished career with the Stags which had stretched to 11 years. Another popular player, Gordon Hodgson, was on his way in late September, transferred to Oxford United for a fee reported to be more than £30,000.

Making his mark right from the start of the season was another local youngster making good, centre-half Mick Saxby, who had begun to realize his potential the previous season. He linked up well with McClelland and played a prominent part in the Anglo-Scottish Cup successes of that season which saw Mansfield reach the semi-final before going out to Second Division Burnley on penalties. On the way there were memorable encounters with Scottish club, Partick Thistle, in the quarter-final.

On 19 September, Ernie Moss returned to senior action in the County Cup Final with Nottingham Forest, which the Reds won 4-0. But Moss was on his way back to Chesterfield to complete a full circle in his career, the Spireites paying out £30,000 for the privilege of signing a player whom they had launched on a soccer career.

I might add that this was another hasty decision which I have no doubt was the cause for later regret at Field Mill.

There was an important transfer deal on 16 March, when Dave Syrett moved to Walsall for £75,000 which involved the transfer the other way of striker Terry Austin for a modest £30,000. Austin made an immediate impact as he scored in his first two outings in a 1-1 draw at Chester and at Hillsborough as Sheffield Wednesday were beaten 2-1.

Mansfield finished 18th in the Third Division, too close to the relegation area for comfort, but performances had justified some optimism that better things were on the way.

Yet during the 1979 close season there was more turmoil to rock the Field Mill boat. Manager Billy Bingham had been away on holiday in Australia and during his absence, Second Division Luton Town had made an offer in excess of £200,000 for talented central defender Mick Saxby, a record for any Mansfield player. A proviso was that the Stags would take striker Steve Taylor, rated at £65,000, which would also be a record pay-out for the club. Mansfield were willing to accept the deal but waited until Bingham returned, having been kept informed of events.

As I understand it, the Mansfield manager interviewed Taylor on Friday, 6 July and agreed personal terms. Luton were informed of this and also met Saxby over the weekend to settle the player's terms. The signings were due to take place on the Monday but Bingham had a change of heart and declared he was not interested in Taylor. But chairman Arthur Patrick had given his word to his Luton counterpart that the deal would go through, as both players had agreed terms, and when Bingham refused to accept the transfer, he was dismissed and the player-cash swop was completed.

John Lathan having a splashing time during the match with Bury on 13 October 1979.

Three weeks later there was a new man in charge at Field Mill as Mick Jones gained the vote of the board from a long list of applicants. Jones, a former Notts County player, had spent 20 successful months in charge of non-League Kettering Town, whom he had lifted from near extinction to a Wembley Final in the FA Trophy. He brought with him Jeff Lee, his assistant at Kettering.

Unfortunately, at the end of Jones' first season in charge, Mansfield returned to Division Four, although there had been some progress in competitions to brighten up an otherwise poor season. York City were beaten on the away-goals rule in the two-legged first round of the League Cup and in a thrilling second round, the Stags lost 4-3 at Reading but clinched a place in the third round with a 4-2 victory at Field Mill. Then they crashed out 3-0 at home to Queen's Park Rangers.

Blyth Spartans and Doncaster Rovers provided a passage into the third round of the FA Cup, where First Division Brighton proved to be too tough a hurdle to surmount.

Only 20 points had been won by the end of 1979 and the second half of the season was to prove to be even less profitable, for by the end of the campaign only 16 more had been added. In fact between January and May, only four matches produced maximum points for Mansfield Town.

The 1980-81 season was the first when, under the new Football League regulations, clubs could agree to play matches on Sundays and it was left to Darlington and Mansfield — pioneers of Sunday soccer in the special circumstances of the early 1970s — to be the first to take advantage.

They met on Sunday, 15 February in front of an unusually large crowd, for Feethams,

Kevin Bird (left) scores in the FA Cup third round game against Carlisle United on 3 January 1981. The Stags drew 2-2 at Field Mill but went down 2-1 in the replay at Brunton Park.

of 5,932 together with a flotilla of national journalists, photographers and television cameras who watched a 2-2 draw.

This was also the season in which central defender Adrian Burrows broke a leg at Bury. Burrows is, of course, the youngest son of the late Horace Burrows of Sheffield Wednesday and England fame, who played for Mansfield the season before the Stags' election to the Football League and who had been transferred to Wednesday before it was known that Mansfield were to join the Third Division South.

And this was also the season that John McClelland received his World Cup call from Northern Ireland and former Mansfield boss, Billy Bingham. Striker Terry Austin was on the move at his own request, realizing a £100,000 fee from Huddersfield Town when the transfer went through on 19 November.

Jim Lumby arrived as his replacement, costing £35,000 from Tranmere Rovers, and after five games was sent off at Hereford United and earned a five-match suspension. Rod Arnold also picked up another injury, which kept him out of the side for the final eight League games and both County Cup matches. A lad called Steve Sutton was loaned by Nottingham Forest to help out their neighbours, and give Sutton an extended taste of League football, an experience which stood him in good stead in later years.

A respectable seventh final placing was achieved by the Stags but it was perhaps a disappointing state of affairs, considering that Mansfield had been hot promotion candidates in February, but had picked up only eight points from their last 13 matches.

There were also reasonable Cup runs with a place in round three of the FA Cup being achieved before Carlisle United won after a replay. Doncaster Rovers were beaten in the two-legged first round of the League Cup, but Barnsley saw off the Stags at Oakwell after extra-time in round two, following a goalless draw at Field Mill.

There was sensation before Mansfield left for their Friday night meeting with Stockport County on 1 May, when it was announced that the chairman, Arthur Patrick, had not only given up the post but had also left the board altogether. He was replaced by vice-chairman John Almond. Four days later there were other departures from Field Mill when Mick Jones and his assistant Jeff Lee were sacked after 20 months in charge.

The 1981-2 campaign was Mansfield Town's Golden Jubilee season in the Football League and they pinned their hopes on something extra special to celebrate upon the appointment of another local player made good, Stuart Boam. He took over as player-manager on 6 July, after a distinguished career with Middlesbrough, whom he captained into the First Division, and latterly with Newcastle United.

But before Boam took over at Field Mill, Mansfield's World Cup star John McClelland, whose contract had expired, joined Glasgow Rangers for £90,000, a real bargain-buy for Rangers in the light of McClelland's future achievements. Boam went back to his two former clubs, signing midfielder Charlie Bell from Middlesbrough and appointing Geoff Allen from Newcastle as his assistant.

But fortune did not favour the local boy on this occasion, for after only a handful of appearances he was sidelined by a back injury which eventually required surgery. Nor did Boam appear to have any luck on the managerial side, for after Mansfield reached the second round of the League Cup with a victory over Scunthorpe United, Bradford City knocked the Stags out on aggregate. There was no joy, either, in the FA Cup as Doncaster Rovers cut short Mansfield's hopes in the first round, winning by a single goal at Field Mill.

It was touch and go in the final weeks of the season as the Stags just scraped clear of the need to seek re-election by one point in 20th position. The final outcome could have been a little more comfortable but for a deduction of two points for the playing of a unregistered player at Crewe on 13 March. This involved Colin Calderwood, one of Mansfield's up-and-coming young central defenders, whose registration had been sent to the Football Association and the Football League on the same day and registered in Mansfield's post book.

The FA had received the forms, but the Football League had not and although Mansfield appealed against the decision to deduct two points, their plea was turned down, although fortunately Mansfield's League status was not put in jeopardy by the loss of the points.

The poor results had seen the financial problems at Field Mill reach almost crisis proportions and manager Boam's retained list reflected the situation. Only eight players were kept on, with nine first-team regulars allowed to go, three of whom had refused new terms. Amongst the free-transfer men were Adrian Burrows, Arthur Mann, 'Player of the Year' Nöel Parkinson, Les McJannet, Barry Foster, Ian Wood, Jim Lumby and Brian Thomson.

But before the start of the season, the whole financial aspect surrounding the club had changed for the better. At a press conference on 19 July, it was announced that a Nottingham businessman, Richard Hartley, who had been commercial director with Notts County, had taken over as chairman of Mansfield Town.

Player-manager Stuart Boam (right), leading by example against Bournemouth in 1981.

The new chairman made an immediate impact when it was also announced that four new and experienced players were joining the club, two of whom had been involved in transfer deals of over £100,000. The new men were striker John Dungworth, from Shrewsbury Town, defender Keith Kennedy, a former Bury captain, John Matthews, a midfielder who had cost Sheffield United a six-figure fee when he signed from Arsenal, and Joe Laidlaw, who had given Mansfield the run-around at Hereford the previous season.

However, early results were far from encouraging with defeats in all three pre-season Football League Trophy matches. And after an initial 2-1 home League win over Blackpool on 28 August, the Stags had to wait until 18 September and a win at Hereford before they picked up another two points.

Morale was low at the club with attendances regularly dipping below 3,000. Indeed, on Friday, 17 December the lowest-ever attendance in the League at Field Mill — 1,293 — watched the game against Torquay United.

Even with three points for a win, Mansfield had collected only 34 points after a 3-2 home win over Hull City on 3 January. And when the next three matches were lost — two of them at home — Boam and his assistant were inevitably dismissed. That was on 26 January, after only 1,655 fans had seen Hereford United win 1-0 at Field Mill four days earlier.

The announcement of Boam's successor surprised, even shocked, the football world. It seemed hardly believable that a manager of the stature of the experienced Ian Greaves, who it was well-known had turned down offers from far bigger clubs, should opt to take charge of a struggling Fourth Division side.

But after watching the Stags in action from the Port Vale terraces — they lost 4-1 — Greaves accepted the position. His first task was to appoint an assistant and from a pile of applications he nominated John Jarman. Then Greaves signed a couple of young players who had caught his eye on his travels — Mark Kearney from Everton and Tony Lowery from West Bromwich Albion.

However, there was no significant change in Mansfield's League placing as they were tenth when Boam left and tenth at the end of the season. There were some significant incidents during the season, though. Rod Arnold set a new appearance record, passing the previous best held by Sandy Pate. It is also perhaps worthy of mention that a youngster by the name of Simon Coleman of Worksop, signed for the club on schoolboy forms in late April. And on 26 February 1983, the Stags played their 2,000th League game and celebrated in style with a 2-1 win over Chester.

When Greaves released his retained list at the end of the season, he was clearly making way for some new blood. Joe Laidlaw, Keith Kennedy and Paul Cannell had already gone, but the decision to release Kevin Bird, Charlie Bell and John Matthews raised a few eyebrows, although Matthews had requested a move with a year of his contract to run.

When Mansfield Town's players reported for 1983-4 pre-season training, there was evidence of an impressive recruiting programme, possibly without precedent at Field Mill. Former England, Leicester City and Sunderland full-back Steve Whitworth, Stewart Barrowclough, who was in his second spell with Barnsley, and whose transfers over the years had pulled in hundreds of thousands of pounds for his clubs, and England Under-21 midfielder Gerard Keegan, previously with Manchester City and Oldham Athletic, all made their bow in Mansfield's colours.

There was even England and Liverpool's Emlyn Hughes, willing to help out if Greaves thought it necessary. But just as the season began, the manager made the first of his two most important signings, both of whom were to make vital contributions to the club. The second was still a couple of seasons away, but initially the acquisition of central defender George Foster from Derby County was one of inestimable value.

The Fourth Division, though, is a hard taskmaster, as a 4-0 hammering at Bristol

City in the opening League match clearly indicated, particularly for players more accustomed to the subtleties of the higher divisions.

Greaves had little luck in his home-town meetings with former clubs, both of whom he had taken in the top section while in charge. Huddersfield Town did their former boss no favours when they toppled Mansfield out of the League Cup by a 7-2 aggregate. Then Bolton Wanderers were equally unaccommodating as they dismissed the Stags from the FA Cup in the second round, winning 2-0 after Mansfield's 3-0 win over Doncaster Rovers had paved the way for Greaves' return to Burnden Park.

There was little joy for Mansfield, either, in the League, for the club was hard pressed to stay just clear of the re-election zone in 19th place at the end of the season, with six wins in nine games easing the Stags' fears.

Notable departures during the season were Bobby Hutchinson, who cost the Stags £15,000 when he signed from Tranmere in 1982, and John Dungworth, who moved to Rotherham United for a modest £5,000 in February. The lowest point of the season was a 7-1 drubbing by Aldershot at the Recreation Ground; the highlight, a 7-1 win over Halifax at Field Mill during one of Mansfield's brighter spells.

It was also a season which saw the departure of one of the club's favourite goalkeepers and the advent of another who was to be equally as favoured by the fans. Injury finally put paid to the Field Mill career of Rod Arnold, just short of his 500th appearance, with his replacement, on loan initially, of young Kevin Hitchcock from Nottingham Forest. The season also saw the continued blossoming of another home-grown central defender, Colin Calderwood, and a well-earned Player of the Year award for George Foster.

'We can look forward to a good future,' was Ian Greaves' prediction at the end of the previous season. And his team-building continued with the introduction of four new players for the start of the 1984-5 campaign. Noël Luke, from West Brom, Gary Pollard, formerly with Port Vale, and goalkeepers Kevin Hitchcock and Andy Beasley, who were no strangers to Field Mill, both having spent on-loan periods at the club during the previous campaign.

A couple of good League wins, at Port Vale and a 5-1 home victory against Rochdale, plus a couple of new faces, got the season off to a fine start. Mick Vinter, the former Notts County and Wrexham striker, cost £10,000 from Oxford United and was at Mansfield for the start of the campaign. And Paul Garner, a long-serving Sheffield United defender or midfield player, moved to the Stags on 13 September.

But defeat by Scunthorpe United in the first round of the League Cup, plus two home defeats in succession and a series of drawn games, which really should have brought three points, put the season into perspective. There there was also disappointment in the FA Cup, with a second-round defeat at Bradford City after an excellent 2-1 home win over Rotherham United in the previous round.

Yet there was plenty to stir the emotions later in the season in a new competition called the Freight/Rover Trophy, which had replaced the Associate Members Cup of the previous season as an exclusive Third and Fourth Division affair. In the first round Mansfield scored an aggregate 4-3 victory over Hull City, who were on their way into the Second Division. They then took revenge over Bradford City at Valley Parade to set up the Stags for a third-round meeting with Burnley which ended 1-1 before Mansfield won 5-3 on penalties.

There was great satisfaction for Ian Greaves as the Stags toppled Bolton 2-1 at Burnden Park in the area semi-final. And there was great optimism that Mansfield could clinch a place in the Wembley Final when they were paired at home with Wigan Athletic in the Northern area final. George Foster gave Wigan the lead with an own-goal, then 40 seconds from the end of the 90 minutes he equalized with a rare personal goal to earn extra-time, which also failed to break the deadlock. Alas, Wigan were more deadly from the penalty-spot and won 3-1 to take them to Wembley where they lifted the trophy.

It was a disappointing end to Mansfield's season, although there had been some improvement in the final League position as the Stags lifted themselves to 14th. And another piece of team-building slipped into place towards the end of 1984 when one of Greaves' former Bolton stars, striker Neil Whatmore, joined the Stags on loan from Burnley in late November. He was sent back to Turf Moor at the end of February after completing a three-month loan period, only to return a week later as a permanent member of the Field Mill staff.

But on his way was Dave Caldwell, who had joined the Stags as a youngster and really should have made more of an impact on the game than he eventually did. There was a tremendous shock for the club on 1 November, when chairman Richard Hartley resigned because of business reasons, with the club fortunate to have John Pratt to step into his shoes.

All season, Field Mill had been the home for another sport as the newly-formed Mansfield Marksman Rugby League Football Club took up residence in September.

The 1985-6 season was the one for which Ian Greaves had been planning — and the one that the Mansfield fans had been hoping for as the Stags finally returned to Division Three. It was also the one when Greaves made that second vital signing.

Keith Cassells had been high on Greaves' shopping list ever since he took over at Field Mill, after having the player under his wing while manager at Oxford United. Cassells had seen further service with Southampton, who had paid £100,000 for his signature, and Brentford, where he was a member of the Bees' unsuccessful Freight/Rover Trophy Final line-up against Wigan.

It had taken Greaves two years to persuade Cassells to leave his home base of London, but his arrival at Mansfield could not have been more emphatic. In his debut appearance in the opening game of the 1985-6 season, he collected a hat-trick in a 4-0 win over Hereford United, linking up well with another newcomer, former Port Vale winger Neville Chamberlain. Also making his debut at Mansfield

Mansfield Town's 1985-6 line-up. Back row (left to right): Mike Galloway, Mark Kearney, Kevin Hitchcock, Mike Graham, Andy Beasley, Gary Pollard, Keith Cassells, David Logan. Middle: Nöel Luke, Tony Lowery, Mick Vinter, George Foster, Neil Whatmore, Les Robinson, John Cunningham, Paul Garner. Front: John Jarman (assistant manager), Bill Dearden (trainer-coach), Neville Chamberlain, Simon Coleman, Nigel Foster, Nicky Andersen, Craig McKernon, Ian Stringfellow, Kevin Kent, Ian Greaves (manager).

was Kevin Kent, a name to earn a permanent place in the club's history books in the near future.

But the pre-season period had also seen Greaves in an angry and bitter mood as young Colin Calderwood, at the end of his contract, agreed to re-sign for the Stags but 24 hours later announced that he had joined Lou Macari at Swindon Town. A League tribunal set the transfer fee at £27,500 and 50 per cent of any

Neil Whatmore (right) on target for the Stags during the 1-1 draw with Wrexham in 1985.

Neville Chamberlain gets in a shot on the Swindon goal in 1986. He scored in the 1-1 draw.

Neil Whatmore (right) congratulates Keith Cassells on scoring his debut hat-trick against Hereford in 1986.

future transfer fee, a figure made a mockery by Calderwood's contribution to Swindon's success, with the sort of form which Greaves had predicted.

In the subsequent illegal payments scandal which shocked soccer in mid-1990, Mansfield were awarded a further £2,500 for the transfer of Calderwood, which according to the Football League 'there were facts which have emerged, which were not available to the tribunal which set the original fee.'

Mansfield's Milk Cup successes, in which they defeated Middlesbrough 2-0 at home in the opening round and then drew 4-4 in an Ayresome Park thriller in the second leg, could very well have seen the departure of Ian Greaves. When the Stags held First Division Chelsea to a 2-2 draw in the next round at Mansfield, and put up a great show at Stamford Bridge in the second leg, despite going down 2-0, West Bromwich Albion left no one in doubt that they wanted Greaves as their new manager.

There were demonstrations at Mansfield's matches with supporters pleading with Greaves to stay and overtures from the club's directors with the same aim in mind. Happily, he decided to turn down the West Brom bid, much to everyone's relief, for it was doubtful if the subsequent successes achieved by Mansfield would have come their way without his guidance.

The Freight/Rover Trophy, under its new formula of a preliminary round group play-off, saw Mansfield have to repeat their initial meetings with Notts County and Doncaster Rovers as they finished all level on points, before making progress.

That saw them paired with Darlington at Feethams in the area quarter-final. But the Stags were finding it difficult to field a side because of a heavy injury list and sought a brief postponement. The request was turned down and with several 16-year-olds in their line-up, Mansfield went down 3-0.

Of more importance, though, Greaves was able to maintain the Stags' League

The Stags in a party mood after their victory over Bristol City in the Freight/Rover Trophy Final at Wembley in May 1987.

placing in the top four, despite a difficult final three months, finally clinching promotion in third place with a 4-0 home win over Hartlepool United on 22 April.

There was a satisfying start to the 1986-7 season, when the Stags lifted the County Cup, beating Notts County in the semi-final and Nottingham Forest in the Final at the City Ground after another penalty competition, a system of deciding sudden-death matches at which Mansfield appeared to becoming adept.

Their familiarity with the system was to pay huge dividends when the Stags and their fans enjoyed the ultimate experience for any club, an appearance in a Wembley Cup Final. That came on 24 May, when the Stags met Bristol City, the holders, in the Freight/Rover Trophy Final. In a match which was a great credit to both teams and to the Third Division, Mansfield lifted the trophy after the first-ever penalty competition at Wembley in an event of high drama.

Kevin Kent gave Mansfield the lead early in the second half and 18-year-old substitute Ian Stringfellow, who had scored a vital goal in the first leg of the Northern area final against Chester, hit the bar within minutes of getting into the action.

City grabbed an equalizer with only three minutes of normal time left and extra-time failed to provide a clear-cut decision. When Keith Cassells, who had covered practically every blade of the Wembley grass, missed his spot-kick in the penalty competition, it appeared that Bristol City would be returning the trophy to Ashton Gate.

But goalkeeper Kevin Hitchcock, who had a superb game, saved two further penalties, albeit with his legs, to provide Tony Kenworthy with the daunting task of taking the decisive spot-kick. He sent his former Sheffield United teammate Keith Waugh the wrong way, and the 25,000 Stags fans at Wembley went into deliriums of delight which were continued when the team returned to Mansfield the following day for a civic reception. It was estimated that over 15,000 people lined the streets as the team toured the town in an open-topped bus as the greatest day in the club's history was appropriately celebrated.

For the record, the others successful from the spot were Kevin Kent, Gary Pollard, Mark Kearney and young Ian Stringfellow.

League affairs had perhaps been forgotten in the euphoria, but the Stags claimed a creditable tenth final placing on their return to Division Three. During the season the Stags had drawn 17 games, a factor which gave cause for some concern.

One young player who will perhaps always relish his move to Field Mill was 19-year-old Jason Danskin, who was taken on loan from Everton and made his debut against York City on 28 March. After only a couple of outings he was signed permanently by the club and was in the Wembley line-up. Unfortunately he was unable to claim a first-team spot the following season and was released from his contract.

Keith Cassells had been named Player of the Year in May 1987 and also the most consistent player in the Third Division by *Match Magazine*, so it came as a great shock when it was announced that the popular striker had turned down the offer of a new contract, expressing a wish to move nearer to his native London.

"If we could move Mansfield a hundred miles down the M1 there would be no problem," declared Greaves. However, after much debate Cassells had a change of mind and agreed to stay for another season.

The manager also announced the signing of midfield player Steve Charles for £15,000 from Wrexham. Charles, a former Sheffield United player, could have become a Mansfield player three years earlier but decided to join the Welsh club, whom he captained for a couple of seasons.

The Stags began the new season with a game against Bristol City who, like the previous season, still could not win a match against Mansfield, this time losing

Kevin Kent does a lap of honour after scoring for Mansfield in the Freight/ Rover Trophy Final at Wembley.

2-0 at Field Mill. And the Littlewoods Cup provided a real boost to the Stags' morale as Second Division Birmingham City were beaten 3-2 on aggregate.

That lined Mansfield up for an away first-leg against First Division Oxford United, one of Greaves' former clubs, who were in the doldrums when he had taken over the managerial reins but promotion challengers when he left after the Maxwell takeover.

Before the game, Mansfield suffered a blow when Mark Kearney, converted from a full-back to a ball-winning midfielder by Greaves, broke a leg in the home game against Fulham on Friday, 4 September. Nevertheless, the Stags put up a tremendous performance at the Manor Ground against an Oxford side who were hoping for a repeat of their previous season's 6-0 win over Gillingham from the Third Division.

But on this occasion United were more than thankful to settle for a 1-1 draw with substitute Dean Saunders scoring an equalizer three minutes from time to cancel out Kevin Kent's breakthrough goal in the 50th minute. Oxford had learned the lessons of the first meeting and won the second leg 2-0 at Field Mill, but only after a Steve Charles own-goal almost at the start of the second half had turned a game dominated until then by Mansfield. Saunders scored Oxford's second with Ray Houghton involved in the build-up, one of the player's last outings before joining Liverpool.

Despite another fearsome injury list, Mansfield still had plenty to shout about in both the Freight/Rover Trophy — now renamed the Sherpa Van Trophy — and in the FA Cup. The Stags looked well on their way to another Wembley visit

Mansfield Town's 1988-9 playing staff. Back row (left to right): Mark Place, Nicky Andersen, Simon Coleman, Jason Milner, Andy Beasley, Brian Cox, Mark Kearney, Tony Kenworthy, David Hodges. Third row: Steve Williams, Paul Garner, Steve Chambers, Dennis Pettitt (physiotherapist), Billy Dearden (trainer-coach), Ian Greaves (manager), John Jarman (assistant manager), Steve Charles, Keith Cassells, Paul Brogan. Second row: Gareth Price, Mick Graham, Tony Lowery, George Foster, Kevin Kent, Gordon Owen, Ian Stringfellow, John Ryan, Craig McKernon. Front row: Gary Bircumshaw, Tony Clarke, Justin Elkinston, Kevin Gray, Sean Hood, Ricky Ellerton. Shane Reddish, Jason Milner, David Parker.

with wins over Doncaster Rovers and Hartlepool in the preliminary round of the Trophy and Scunthorpe United in the first round.

The signs were still promising when they led Preston North End by a single goal at Deepdale in the area quarter-final but Gary Brazil, who had been sent back to Preston after a pre-season trial at Mansfield, scored two late goals in a five-minute spell, the equalizer stemming from a mistake by goalkeeper Hitchcock, to end the Wembley dream.

The Trophy match was the fourth of five occasions on which the Stags were destined to meet Preston. Ironically, they had been paired in the League at Field Mill the Saturday before meeting at Deepdale in the first round of the FA Cup. A 1-1 draw in Lancashire and a great 4-2 win for Mansfield in the replay led to a local derby in the second round with Lincoln City, who had dropped into the Vauxhall Conference at the end of the previous season. A right royal battle it turned out to be, with seven goals, a sending off, an above average crowd and a Kevin Kent winner two minutes from time.

Another non-League outfit, Bath City, came out of the hat as Mansfield's third-round opponents and the Stags won 4-0 for a place in the fourth round for the first time in ten years and a meeting with the eventual Cup winners, Wimbledon.

The Plough Lane club could well have missed their successful trip to Wembley, had Steve Charles put away a 71st-minute penalty and the First Division side not been gifted a couple of simple goals. Neither of them, though, by the Dons' feared striker, John Fashanu, who came off second-best in a real battle with George Foster.

"I really enjoyed it today," said Fashanu after the match. "We both got stuck in and there was not the moaning and groaning I usually get every week in the First Division."

But Ian Greaves was not so complimentary. "We have three culprits today who will be crying for a week. This was a typical Third Division game and we blew it."

With all the glamour games out of the way, attention could be focussed on the League programme, which was giving cause for concern. Only eight points were earned from the last 12 games and there were anxious moments after a 1-1 draw at Vale Park in the final match before it was announced that Rotherham United had lost and Mansfield had avoided the relegation play-offs.

On the transfer front the Stags signed England Under-21 international John Ryan from Oldham Athletic for £15,000 in October, after he spent a month on loan at Mansfield. And on 11 January, Greaves paid £35,000 for much-travelled Gordon Owen from Bristol City. Owen was one of the two City players who failed from the penalty-spot at Wembley the previous May in the Freight/Rover Trophy Final.

Outgoing Wembley hero, goalkeeper Kevin Hitchcock, had been snapped up by Chelsea for a record £250,000 just before the transfer deadline in March to give some immediate assistance to the Stags' growing financial difficulties.

The overriding incident during the 1988-9 season was the departure of Ian Greaves, which was announced on 6 February, two days after he had mysteriously been absent from the match against Notts County at Meadow Lane. I have no hesitation in declaring that no one at Field Mill — and I include the chairman and directors — wished to see the very popular manager leave. He had occupied the post for six years, almost to the day — longer than any other manager since the club was elected to the Football League.

When Greaves took over at Field Mill, he made the comment that whenever he departed, he hoped that he left the club better prepared to face the future than when he took over. The future is unpredictable in the current soccer climate but Greaves could be well satisfied with his achievements whilst with the Stags.

Mansfield's youth policy, which he initiated within days of taking over, had been successful almost since its inception and had been a lifesaver in the several periods in which injuries had made team selection something of a headache.

Once again, results had not come up to expectation, with Notts County handing out a 5-0 hammering in the first leg of the Littlewoods Cup at Meadow Lane before the Stags regained a little pride with a 1-0 win at home in the second leg.

County were held to a 1-1 draw in the preliminary round of the Sherpa Van Trophy but with a great chance of progress when they met Chesterfield at Saltergate, the Stags threw it away.

Chesterfield had gone down 3-1 to Mansfield at the same venue a week earlier and when Simon Coleman gave Mansfield the lead after 13 minutes, another Stags' win seemed on the cards.

But Steve Charles missed from the penalty-spot just before half-time, after Bob Bloomer had equalized in the 36th minute. And seconds before the half-time whistle, Dave Waller gave Chesterfield the lead. Early in the second half, young Nicky Andersen was sent off for collecting two yellow cards in the space of a minute and the Stags never recovered.

Greaves was perhaps a little disillusioned when, after an excellent showing by his side in the FA Cup first round, when they held Sheffield United to a 1-1 draw, they deserved better than a 2-1 defeat in the replay. Then there was a 6-2 trouncing at Molineux by Wolves which did the morale no good at all.

Central defender George Foster was immediately appointed the club's player-manager with coach Billy Dearden as his second in command. Both men faced a tremendous task to follow in Greaves' footsteps. Happily, though, Foster was able to keep the club in a comfortable mid-table position, although the final game of the season was a sad occasion.

Keith Cassells had made it clear that he would be leaving Mansfield at the end of the campaign and his last appearance in a Mansfield shirt was at Aldershot, when he came on as substitute for the final 15 minutes.

Keith Cassells leaves the pitch after making his last home appearance – as an emergency goalkeeper – for Mansfield.

Nevertheless, the season did have its plusses with the emergence of Craig McKernon as a quality full-back after the transfer of Mick Graham to Carlisle United right at the start of the season. Just before the transfer deadline in March, the new manager was able to complete a transfer which had frustrated his former boss, when he signed experienced striker Trevor Christie from Walsall for £30,000.

The growing authority of central defender Simon Coleman was beginning to attract the attention of senior clubs and Gordon Owen had been placed on the transfer list at his own request, declaring he did not like the method of play used by the Stags.

However, several youngsters were beginning to catch the eye, particularly Ian Hathaway, a 20-year-old signed from non-League Bedworth United and already being talked about as another Jimmy McCaffrey. There was also Graham Leishman, a 19-year-old striker signed from Irlam Town. Then there was David Hodges, still only 18, who had come up through the junior ranks to make the first team.

This was Mansfield's second season in the Second Division of the Central League, the leading competition for Football League clubs' reserve sides. Certainly, the higher grade of football was proving a useful vehicle for the development of the undoubted talent among the youngsters at the club.

The Stags had a new defender to start the 1989-90 season as Steve Prindiville and cash was taken in return for the transfer of John Ryan to neighbours Chesterfield. And the experienced former Notts County and Aston Villa midfield player, David Hunt, was another newcomer.

But one of Mansfield's biggest disappointments over the past two or three seasons had been to see the career of local boy Ian Stringfellow interrupted by injury and illness, for this nephew of former Mansfield star Mike Stringfellow, had the sort of quality and scoring ability about his play to attract the praise of the harshest of critics.

It was discovered that he had been suffering from glandular fever but he was able to resume at the start of the 1989-90 season and half-a-dozen goals in the first couple of months augured well both for the player and club. Unfortunately, a recurrence of the illness and then the need for a hernia operation again interrupted what is hoped will eventually be a rewarding career.

But the big news of the early season was a £500,000 bid by Middlesbrough for the services of Simon Coleman, which considering the financial problems and, more so, the player's own future, could hardly be turned down.

Almost before that news had been digested, Arsenal came in with a £200,000 offer for defender Craig McKernon. Unfortunately, the experienced defender Tony Kenworthy, who would have been invaluable in plugging the gap left by the departure of Coleman, was an absentee for most of the season because of an Achilles problem which eventually required an operation.

The loan of Don O'Riordan from Notts County looked to have solved the back-four problem but County's asking fee at the end of his month's loan did not match Foster's assessment and so he returned to Meadow Lane. From the beginning of December, Mark Smalley, who began his career with Nottingham Forest and spent a couple of months on loan with the Stags from Leyton Orient, eventually joined the staff permanently.

And the Stags paid out £30,000 to Hull City for defender Malcolm Murray to bring their spending since the departure of the two youngsters up to £125,000, some £80,000 of which had gone on Leicester City's 20-year-old striker Steve Wilkinson.

Then at the beginning of March, another £80,000 was paid out for the transfer from Notts County of young midfield player Wayne Fairclough. Later in the month, Martin Clark was taken on loan to the end of the season from Nottingham Forest,

No wonder he's happy! Steve Wilkinson celebrates a five-star show after scoring all five goals against Birmingham in April 1990.

Mansfield Town pictured prior to 1990-91 season. Back row (left to right): Graham Leishman, Steve Chambers, Mark Smalley, Andy Beasley, Jason Pearcey, Mark Kearney, Paul Brogan (now with Cheltenham), Dave Hodges. Third row: Kevin Randall (youth development officer), David Hunt, Steve Charles, Kevin Gray, Tony Lowery, Ian Stringfellow, Malcolm Murray, Wayne Davidson, Wayne Fairclough, John Newman (chief scout), Dennis Pettitt. Second row: Jason Milner, Steve Mills, Steve Prindiville, Steve Wilkinson, Bill Dearden, George Foster (player-manager), Ian Hathaway, Kevin Kent, Trevor Christie, Damien O'Brien. Front row: Jonathon Jordan, Chris Perkins, Graham Mowbray, Kevin Wilson, Geoff Hall, Paul Shaw, Peter Morgan, Adam Jones, Chris Parkins, Mark Tucker.

who had paid £125,000 for the young Scot. He later joined the Stags for a fee reported to be in the region of £50,000.

Drastic measures had been required, for the Stags found themselves anchored at the bottom of the table in mid-December. But the signings, and the fact that the poor home record early in the season greatly improved, gradually lifted the club clear of the danger zone and into 15th position, exactly as at the end of the previous season.

Ironically, Mansfield had won almost as many matches at home as the leaders but their away record was the third worst in the division.

A feature of the season was the strong support which followed the teams to away matches and there were many disgruntled fans in a strong following at Wigan for the first round of the FA Cup. The Stags went down 2-0 and it could so easily have been more.

There was also some disappointment early in the season after a good aggregate win over Northampton in the opening round of the Littlewoods Cup. Mansfield gave a splendid performance against First Division Luton Town at Mansfield, despite

a 4-3 defeat, but they crashed 7-2 in the second leg. However, with a side decimated by injury and playing on Luton's hated plastic pitch, at least there was some sympathy for the Stags.

The newly named Leyland/DAF Trophy competition also turned a little sour, for after finishing all-square with Leyton Orient in the preliminary round — Brentford went out — the Stags won through to the first round by beating Orient in the play-off. They had to travel to newly-elected Maidstone United where they were beaten 2-1.

Sadly, the Stags also had to surrender a piece of silverware that had graced the Field Mill trophy case for three seasons. The Nottinghamshire FA County Cup found its way to the City Ground after Forest won 4-0 in the Final.

George Foster has had a tough baptism in his first taste of football management, a period made doubly difficult because he is also involved in playing and is a key figure in the side with little opportunity for a respite. He began the 1990-91 season knowing that this would be the campaign in which he had to prove himself. Mansfield Town supporters earnestly hoped that he would succeed.

The Field Mill Story

IN THE past few years there has been the prospect of a new home for Mansfield Town as the financial pressures which have always been present, even from the club's earliest days, seemingly required Field Mill to be handed over to developers in an effort to ensure the club's existence.

Yet Mansfield Town without Field Mill — or Field Mill without the Stags for that matter — seems barely imaginable, although after the club had spent their first season as tenants of the ground in 1919-20, it appeared that a new home had to be found — and found quickly.

In the end, however, Mansfield Town owed much to their patron, the Duke of

The view of Field Mill for visiting clubs – the original main stand was eventually replaced by the more modern West Stand.

Portland, who declared: "Field Mill should be tenanted by the leading club in the town."

That was after a dispute involving two local branches of ex-servicemen's organizations had left the Stags the innocent 'pig in the middle' regarding the use of the ground. At the end of World War One, the Duke generously gifted the use of the piece of land on Quarry Lane, which had been the venue for football, cricket and numerous other sporting activities since the mid 1800s, to the Mansfield branch of the Discharged and Disabled Soldiers and Sailors Federation, at a peppercorn rent of one shilling per year, and also handed over a donation of £5 to the branch funds.

In the agreement drawn up by the Duke's agent, Major Warner Turner, there was also a proviso that the ground should only be used for sporting purposes and that it would also be available to members of the Old Comrades of the Great War, the other local ex-servicemen's organization, who would have equal rights on the ground.

Unfortunately, the secretary of the DDSSF, one Mr Holmes, omitted to inform the Old Comrades of their rights. And on 21 May 1919, following a meeting on 19 April between three Federation branch officials and three officials of Mansfield Town FC, the club was granted tenancy of Field Mill on alternate Saturdays during the football season, initially for one season.

To clarify the situation, perhaps it should be explained that from 1912 to 1916, the ground was the headquarters of Mansfield Mechanics FC, who were undoubtedly the leading club in the town at that period. To supercede the Mechanics as tenants, Mansfield Town had to agree to enclose the ground, make it fit for use by July 1919 and also provide dressing-room accommodation. The club had to bear all the expense.

The negotiations were carried on very much behind closed doors, for a move was afoot for Mansfield to have just one senior team instead of the Town and Mechanics, as before the war. With this in mind, there had been exploratory meetings between officials of the two clubs and other interested parties in the town. A well-attended public meeting was also held and a further one planned when the possibility of a town stadium capable of housing not only a top-class soccer side, but also athletics and other activities, was to be discussed.

When the Stags made the shock announcement that they had obtained tenancy of Field Mill and would be launching the re-emergence of senior football in Mansfield as members of the Central Alliance, these plans were abandoned. Mechanics also fell by the wayside and it was observed in the *Mansfield Advertiser* of 29 August 1919: 'The Mechanics, sadly, are with us no more and it will be strange times without them, for they have been an essential part of the winter sport for many years past. Amalgamation with Mansfield Town is very much in the offing.' That indeed turned out to be a sound prediction.

A few days before the DDSSF signed the agreement relative to Field Mill, the Mansfield Shoe Company, who before the war had rented the ground during the summer for use by their cricket club, approached Major Warner Turner enquiring if the Duke would be willing to sell the ground to them for use as a sports field for their employees, as the cricket club was 'now defunct and unlikely to be resurrected'. However, they failed in their bid and were informed of the arrangements involving the ex-servicemen's organizations.

As was perhaps inevitable, the Old Comrades eventually discovered their rights and with Major Muschamps, whose family owned the New Hucknall Colliery at Huthwaite, as their spokesman, their arguments with the DDSSF grew in intensity, as indeed did Mansfield Town's anxiety as to their future use of the ground, with both ex-servicemen's organizations claiming use of the venue on alternate weekends.

Major Warner Turner suggested that they should amalgamate for sporting purposes but they failed to agree and Mansfield Town were informed in early August 1920 by the DDSSF that the ground would not be available for them in the 1920-21 season.

Before then, the Stags, represented by their secretary Mr H.Willett and two committee members, had secretly had meetings with Major Turner in an effort to purchase the ground and had indicated that, if successful in their bid, they would agree to allow the ex-servicemen its use free of charge.

They explained that they had gone to great expense enclosing the ground, putting up a stand and building dressing-room accommodation. Incidentally, much of the material used in these projects had come from the army camp which had been erected at nearby Clipstone during the war.

An aerial view of Field Mill and surrounding area taken in 1930. The track for greyhound racing is clearly visible, but greyhound racing was discontinued after Mansfield were elected to the Football League in 1931.

The Mansfield Borough Brass Band accompany the home supporters on their way along Quarry Lane to one of Mansfield Town's early games in the Football League in 1931.

Fans make their way to the ground via Quarry Lane

At the gates of Field Mill. In the background, right, are the players' dressing-rooms.

By this time the DDSSF and Old Comrades had placed the whole matter in the hands of their respective solicitors, which brought a rebuke from the Duke, who expressed his disappointment that the matter was being dealt with in a legal way.

Again Major Turner intervened on behalf of the Duke, saying that, as the club was an innocent party in the wrangle, it would be a pity if they were thrown off the ground. This had the desired effect and on 20 August 1920, the Stags were told that their tenancy was to be renewed for another year.

By then, however, another party, the Mansfield Chamber of Commerce, had entered the arena. On 3 June 1920, John L. Birks, an ironmonger who traded in Leeming Street, Mansfield, and who was also on the Mansfield Town committee, informed the Duke's agent that the traders of Mansfield were anxious to buy Field Mill to provide a sports stadium in the town and would form a company with that project in mind.

It was a move which brought a response from Major Muschamps, who declared that the Old Comrades were anxious to bring good football to Field Mill and intended to join the Midland League.

The Duke, in the meantime, had grown impatient with the wrangling and on 30 August 1920, through Major Turner, informed Mr Birks that he was prepared to sell for £500, reserving the mineral rights and providing that the area should always be used for sporting activities. In addition he included a clause which prevented the sale of beer, wines and spirits at the ground.

By 23 November 1920, the agent was officially informed that the Mansfield Athletic Ground Company was to be launched with 10,000 ten-shilling shares. The DDSSF attempted to intervene but their efforts were turned down and before the end of the year they were informed that their tenancy would end on 30 April 1921.

On 30 December 1920, the draft company agreement was submitted to and approved by the Duke, with a revision of the sale of beers, wines and spirits clause and a proviso that the ex-servicemen should be allowed use of the ground when required — 'if practical'.

The agreement was signed on 16 February 1921, with John Birks, C.W.Chadburn, Ernest Champion (of the Carpenters Arms), John Dixon, J.G.Hickling, Frank Oliver (of the Dial Head Hotel), S.Richardson, C.J.Vallance, H.Walkerdine and H.Willett named as company officials with Marchant & Co as the new company's solicitors.

The new company lost no time in obtaining further plots of land surrounding Field Mill and owned by the Duke, in order to provide better access to the ground and make room for more spectators.

On 21 May 1921, a month after Town officially took over the ground, the first of six plots were purchased, with two more added before the end of the year. Further sections were added in 1927 and 1928, with the sixth acquired on 31 January 1947, but by then the club had purchased the ground from the Mansfield Athletic Ground Company, as announced at the club's 23rd annual meeting on 6 March 1946, by director Col Mein. But not before another threat had arisen to challenge their tenancy of the ground.

In 1928, the Mansfield Greyhound Company, with their general manager Bernard Meggitt of Mansfield, racing manager F.Parker of Hasland, and directors J.W.Hough of Rainworth and R.S.Warboys of Pleasley Hill, were granted joint tenancy of Field Mill, and a track was laid surrounding the playing area.

The inaugural meeting was on Saturday, 26 May 1928 and it was noted in the local Press that the track was the first in England to have a public-address system. Eventually, the greyhound company were anxious to get the football club off the land and attempted to buy up as many shares in the Athletic Ground Company as possible.

Fortunately, they were not successful and when Football League status was achieved, greyhound racing was banned from the ground and subsequently the activities were transferred to Sutton Town's Avenue Ground, just off Mansfield Road in the town, where it carried on for several years after the end of World War Two. Eventually the land was sold for housing development.

In the meantime the football club gradually bought up more and more parcels of land surrounding Field Mill, until it was possible to lay out a full-size grass practice pitch as well as two five-a-side courts and a sizeable car-park, all of them floodlit.

There was also, for a time, a social club aptly called The Antlers Club, now used as a boys' club and a gymnasium for the playing staff and which also houses the Stags' commercial department and club shop.

It may well be that eventually this will fall into the hands of the developers. Indeed, only a few short years ago plans were announced for the construction of a new purpose-built stadium near to the King's Mill Hospital complex, with Field Mill becoming a retail development area.

The plans never came to fruition because of strong objections to the proposed site for the new stadium. However, it appears inevitable that eventually there must be a comparable scheme if the club is to survive in a time when the financial implications of running a Football League club are becoming more and more complex. When that happens it will mean the end of over a century of sporting activities in the Quarry Lane area.

IN THE BEGINNING

WHEN Mansfield Town's new Popular Stand, which in 1966 was replaced by the current West Stand (the former grandstand on the Hurst Park racecourse), was officially opened in 1927, reference was made to the fact that Field Mill had been a sporting venue for over 70 years.

When the area was purchased by the Mansfield Athletic Ground Company in 1921, there was also a mention that Mansfield Greenhalgh had played on the ground 70 years earlier. Without a doubt the venue often referred to as the Mill Ground in the earliest local newpaper, the *Mansfield Reporter*, was used in the middle of the 19th century, or thereabouts, as a recreational area for the workers at the nearby Field Mill.

This, along with Matlock Mill, was rented from the Duke of Portland by the Greenhalgh family for their cotton-doubling business. Indeed, in the 1870s the area was referred to as the Greenhalgh Ground and on 28 May 1875, local newspapers contained a report of the Greenhalgh & Sons Works' sports meeting on the ground 'adjoining the Field Mill works', which also included a football match.

At that time, the Greenhalgh family contained four sons, all of whom played football, it was said, for Notts County. And one, Harwood Greenhalgh was a member of the first England team to meet Scotland in an international match.

But one of the town's main sporting venues was Parr's Ground on Newgate Lane, where many local cricket and football matches were held. Mansfield & District Football Club, which was founded in 1870, used this ground and were reported to open their 1871 season at the venue against the Field Mill Football Club — presumably this was a team from the mill workers.

On 20 August 1875, a report stated that the Greenhalgh cricket team were to meet a team from the *Nottingham Guardian* on the Greenhalgh Ground. And in 1880, surprisingly on 16 January, the *Mansfield Advertiser* reported that the Greenhalgh FC opened the season with a match 'on their ground on Quarry Lane

The home team's bath and dressing-room which were in use up to 1966 when the new West Stand was opened.

The very spartan away team facilities in the old Mansfield dressing-rooms.

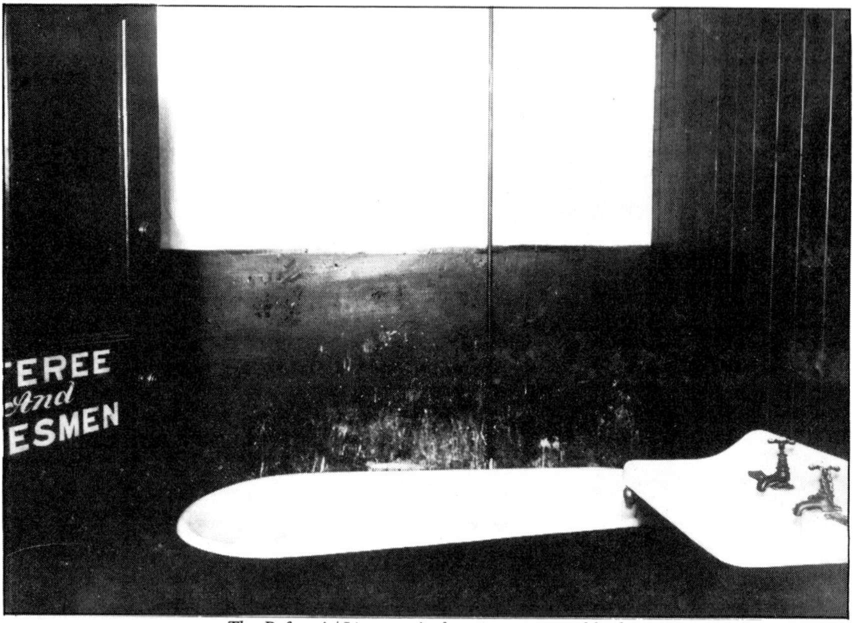

The Referee's/Linesmen's changing-room and bath.

The boardroom which was situated under the original Popular Stand before moving to the West Stand in 1966.

The secretary-manager's office.

To the back is the area allocated for the visiting directors and in front is the Press area with personal telephones.

with a Worksop XI'. Apparently the home team started the match with only seven players, but eventually made up the team and won 3-2.

Incidentally, Greenhalgh FC were nicknamed 'The Brown Paper Parcellers' because, apparently, their playing kit was always carried around in brown paper parcels, instead of a wicker basket or case.

By the 1890s the ground was in regular use for both cricket and football, although athletic meetings and cycle-racing were often on the programme. Indeed, when the then Mansfield Town (no connection with the current Mansfield Town) amalgamated with Mansfield Greenhalgh in 1894 to become Mansfield FC, it was decided that the Field Mill ground would be used for football and the Stanhope Street venue for cricket.

After Mansfield Town had become permanent tenants of the ground in 1921, their supporters' club erected a stand on the ground in 1924, again mainly using materials from the former Clipstone army camp. This stand was badly damaged in a gale in 1938 and was eventually replaced by the current Bishop Street stand.

There was also a fire in the Popular Stand on 23 August 1947, which destroyed the centre part of the building. Fortunately, the chairman of the club at the time, Mr W.Hornby, and the groundsman, Mr Stevens, were making a check after the opening match of the season in Division Three North against York City, spotted the fire and were able to alert the fire brigade in time to save the majority of the stand.

Floodlit football is an accepted part of the sport these days, even at the lowest level, but it is not generally realized that Mansfield Town and Field Mill were pioneers of football under lights in this country. On Saturday, 22 February 1930, the North Notts League Senior Cup Final between Welbeck Athletic and Ollerton Forest was staged at Field Mill, and as the programme stated 'by aid of artificial light'.

While the Mansfield squad were being put through pre-season training, workmen in the background were preparing the North End terracing in August 1949.

The idea came from the Mansfield Town secretary-manager Jack Hickling, who was the former secretary of the North Notts League. Four wooden towers were set up on the corners of the field, with banks of 16, 1,000-watt lamps on each tower. These had been flown over specially from Holland and provided by the electrical firm of Phillips. A special service was laid on from the Corporation Electricity Department with the cable running through Titchfield Park up to the ground to carry the load.

Several footballs were painted white to be used in the game, with buckets of whitewash available to repaint them at 15-minute intervals if necessary. This was found to be a precaution which was not required, so successful was the experiment. Over 6,000 spectators turned up for the match and there were representatives from some of the country's top football clubs, including Arsenal and Tottenham Hotspur, and also officials from the comparatively new Wembley Stadium.

The match was won by Ollerton Forest, who received the cup from Mr A.G.Hines, vice-president of the Football Association. In his programme notes, Mr Hickling predicted that in the near future not only football, but also rugby, hockey, tennis, boxing, and even cricket, would be played at night by artificial light. The only question is, why did it take something like 30 years for that prediction to be realized?

It should be said, however, that Mansfield Town had played under floodlights as early as the 1931-2 season, when they had a free weekend and went to meet a Dutch XI at The Hague.

In 1956, the North Stand was erected and ten years later the old Popular Stand

The new West Stand under construction behind the main Popular Stand. The structure was originally on the Hurst Park racecourse, which was closed down.

Rolling and laying of the new pitch to level the previous seven-foot slope towards Quarry Lane.

Development of the training ground after the purchase of allotments in 1946.

Former Wolverhampton and England captain Billy Wright addresses the 17,380 fans at the League Cup meeting with Second Division Cardiff City on 5 October 1961, before switching on Mansfield Town's original floodlights.

The new West Stand rises above the old stand during the 1965-6 season.

was replaced by the West Stand, but not before a great deal of controversy. During the 1960s, Mansfield Town Supporters' Club possessed one of the most successful lottery competitions in the country, with an estimated 90,000 entries each week. When the Hurst Park racecourse was closed, it was the Supporters' Club which arranged to purchase the stand and agreed to provide some of the finance. Unfortunately, the income from the lottery was gradually reduced and the club's directors were forced to find the cash required to pay for the stand, which lay for a couple of years in sections behind the Popular Stand because sufficient funds were not available to pay for its erection.

However, the stand was eventually completed and was first in use on 15 December 1966, although cash was still short and a full complement of seating could not be afforded for some time.

In the meantime, the floodlighting system was installed and opened by former England captain, Billy Wright, on 5 October 1961, on the occasion of the League Cup meeting with Second Division Cardiff City.

What the future holds for this long-established stadium is difficult to foresee. Having spent over 20 years covering the affairs of the club and travelling with the team wherever their fixtures took them, I, and many others, have always rated Field Mill as one of the better grounds in the lower divisions, and comparable with some in Division Two. It seems inconceivable that its capacity has now been reduced to less than half of that which watched the FA Cup meeting with Nottingham Forest in complete safety in the 1952-3 season, particularly when it compared with many in other parts of the country where ground safety requirements appear to be far less demanding.

With these requirements increasing season by season, it seems that the only solution is to desert Field Mill and start again from scratch at another venue. But then there is the question — where does the money come from to fund such a venture and where should the new stadium be located?

STAGS

Managers

Jack Hickling

January 1928-December 1933

JACK Hickling took over as secretary-manager of Mansfield Town on 5 January 1928, after J.E.(Teddy) Davison had resigned to join Nottingham Forest in a similar role. Hickling was already well-known in sporting circles, as the report of his appointment in the *Mansfield Chronicle* indicated. 'Mr Hickling is known on every football field in the country', it read, perhaps a little grandiosely.

Nevertheless, Hickling had served in almost every facet of the game. He had played in local league soccer until his career was cut short by cartilage problems, he had refereed at junior and senior level, and he had worked as a club and league secretary and served as a Notts FA councillor and as a director of Notts County FC.

As a referee, Hickling was appointed to the Football League list and officiated in matches all over Great Britain and in France, Belgium and North Africa. Indeed, the list of offices held by him at one time or another, in addition to those already mentioned, includes secretary of Mansfield Mechanics FC, general secretary of the North Notts Football League, chairman of the Mansfield Charity Cup competition and director of the Mansfield Ground & Athletic Co, which controlled Field Mill after World War One. As secretary of the North Notts League he took a party of local footballers to Libya, where they won all six games.

He was, of course, secretary-manager of the Stags during the period when they embarked on the famous FA Cup run in season 1928-9, when they beat Second Division Wolves before losing to Arsenal at Highbury in the fourth round. During the Cup run it was Hickling who instigated the 'egg and milk' training schedule, which earned the club national headlines.

And there can be no doubt that it was Jack Hickling who inspired the Stags' successful bid to join the Football League in 1931, after six previous applications.

Nevertheless, a minute of a special meeting of the Mansfield board of directors on 8 December 1933, reads: 'It was unanimously resolved that as Mr Hickling had failed to carry out his duties as secretary-manager to the satisfaction of the board, his services be dispensed with'.

The truth behind that stark note was that Hickling had maintained many other interests during his spell at Field Mill, including the promoting of boxing and wrestling matches at the ground, which possibly interfered with his duties for the club.

But it should also be added that one month earlier, the board had asked the secretary-manager to take a reduction in salary in view of the club's difficult financial situation. He refused.

In 1934, he was still allowed use of the ground for wrestling matches but the board refused him permission to stage a match between women, and also denied him the strange spectacle of a man wrestling a bullock.

Harry Martin
December 1933-March 1935

A NATIVE of Selston, Harry Martin was appointed the club's trainer-coach on 16 November 1933 and moved up to acting manager on 11 December that year. He was officially appointed manager on 11 January 1934.

Martin had a distinguished playing career as an outside-left with Nottingham Forest and Sunderland, earning an England cap against Scotland whilst at Roker Park. He also played for England against Ireland and appeared in two Victory internationals against Scotland in 1919. He then worked as an official with Rochdale and York City before joining Mansfield.

Whilst with Mansfield Town, Martin was responsible for the signing of Ron Dellow, who was subsequently sold to Manchester City in January 1935 for a 'substantial' fee.

After a board meeting on 7 March 1935, Martin was told he would not be re-engaged for the following season and asked to resign. Although he requested an explanation, considering the position of the club when he took over, none was forthcoming and he left the club.

The Stags had finished 19th in 1933-4 when he took over in mid-season, but ninth in the following campaign, after his first full season in charge. In that same season, Mansfield won through to the third round of the FA Cup, beating Accrington Stanley and Tranmere Rovers on the way before losing 4-2 to Burnley in front of 20,790 spectators at Turf Moor.

Although things had not gone so well in his final season at Field Mill, it was perhaps significant that on the Saturday following his resignation, Mansfield surrendered a seven-month unbeaten home record when they lost 3-2 to Southport.

One of the directors of the club, Mr W.F.Lager, resigned in protest at Martin's dismissal.

Charles Bell
March-December 1935

AFTER dismissing Harry Martin, Mansfield Town had what they considered a 'ready-made' replacement in Charles Bell, who was already at the club.

Bell had been appointed trainer on 25 July 1934. He was a centre-forward with Glasgow Rangers before being transferred to Arsenal before the war. He made only one League appearance for the Gunners, but what a memorable one it was. Turning out at Filbert Street in a Second Division game against Leicester Fosse in December 1914, Bell scored both Arsenal's goals in their 2-1 win.

Surprisingly, he did not play again and during World War One, served with the Footballers' Battalion of the Middlesex Regiment, in which he attained the rank of captain.

He was demobbed in 1920 and resumed his playing career with Barrow, top-scoring for them in 1920-21 when they won the Lancashire Combination title. Bell also had a spell with Queen's Park Rangers and was trainer-coach at Reading.

During a spell as manager of Notts County, he led them into Division One in 1922-3 and he was also manager of Wigan Borough.

In a wide and varied career, he spent periods coaching in Italy, Portugal, Brazil and in France, where he was with Marseille for three years. Not surprisingly, he became a fluent linguist.

But Bell failed to come up to expectations as manager at Field Mill and towards the end of December 1935 it was announced that he had been released at his own request. The facts were that at a board meeting on 19 December, the chairman reported that the manager had informed him that he was losing control of the players and staff and would resign if paid £450, to which the directors agreed.

Bell, however, had already done Mansfield a great service by signing Ted Harston, from Bristol City for a £250 fee in October 1935. Harston, of course, was to find a niche in the record books of the Football League.

Harold Wightman
January-May 1936

FOLLOWING the departure of Charlie Bell, Mansfield Town received 45 applications for the post of manager and on 15 January 1936, Harry Wightman, a native of Sutton-in-Ashfield, was appointed.

Wightman had played for his local club, Sutton Town, when only 14 and then Mansfield Mechanics and Eastwood Rangers. He signed for Chesterfield when he was 17 and after two years moved to Nottingham Forest, where he stayed for four seasons of wartime football. In May 1919, Wightman, a centre-half or full-back, was transferred to Derby County, where he stayed for ten years, making 180 League appearances. In addition to playing he was assistant to the Rams' manager, George Jobey. He had a second spell with Chesterfield, from May 1929 to May 1930, before being appointed manager-coach of Notts County.

Wightman then joined Luton Town as manager in June 1931 and stayed there for four and a half years, during which time the Hatters won the Third Division South title. He left in October 1935 to become Derby County's chief scout, before Field Mill beckoned.

Wightman notified the directors that he wished to leave at the end of the season and, despite being offered an extra £75 per year and a three-year contract to remain, he declined and was released on 4 May, as it transpired, to join Nottingham Forest as their first manager, a post he held until March 1939.

On reflection, perhaps Wightman could well have decided that his decision to leave Mansfield was a little premature, for the following season Ted Harston hit the headlines and his scoring prowess helped lift the Stags to ninth place in the table. Harold Wightman died in Nottingham in April 1945, aged 50.

Harry Parkes
May 1936-January 1938

THERE were a number of applications for the vacant managerial position at Field Mill and Hayden Green of Birmingham and a Mr Lowes of Barrow were short-listed. In the meantime, however, news had filtered through that Harry Parkes, who had been manager at Lincoln City for eight years, was anxious for a change.

Mansfield director Mr W.M.Hornby was asked to ascertain if this was correct and, if so, to ask Parkes to attend a meeting on 11 May. The two other candidates also attended this meeting for interview and afterwards it was reported in the minutes that Mr Parkes was indeed interested in moving to Mansfield.

He was offered £10 per week, plus the same bonuses as at Lincoln, and a three-year contract. At a meeting of the club's finance committee on 21 May, it was announced that Harry Parkes was Mansfield Town's new manager.

Parkes had begun his career with West Bromwich Albion and made his debut against Notts County in an FA Cup tie in 1906. Before managing Lincoln, he had been in charge at Chesterfield for five years and was with Newport County for three years. He asked for his release from Mansfield in January 1938, in order to take up a similar position with Notts County.

That was granted to take effect after the third-round FA Cup game against Leicester

City, on 8 January at Field Mill when the First Division side won 2-1, in front of 15,890 fans.

Parkes, of course, had negotiated the transfer of Ted Harston to Liverpool in June 1937, for an undisclosed fee, although at a board meeting on 31 March 1937, when Liverpool's interest was reported by the manager, a £3,000 fee was placed on the player.

Jack Poole
May 1938-August 1944

AFTER the departure of Harry Parkes, the appointment of a new manager was, to quote the minutes of a board meeting on 11 January 1938, 'put off indefinitely', and trainer Jack Poole was given overall control of the players 'in the meantime'. It was not until 24 May 1938 that Poole's appointment as trainer-manager was confirmed.

It was to be a traumatic period for the new manager. After only one full season of League football, the competition was suspended upon the outbreak of war and Poole had the burden of finding players to fill the side during the difficult years ahead. He did as well as anybody could until resigning to take up the position of trainer with Notts County in August 1944. Poole later worked in a similar capacity at Derby County and in August 1956 became trainer-coach to Central Alliance side, Sutton Town.

Poole was a native of Kirkby-in-Ashfield and his first club was Sutton Junction. During World War One he played for Nottingham Forest and Sheffield United and after joining the Army he was stationed in Sunderland and regularly played senior football in the area. He signed for Sunderland after demobilization and stayed for five years at Roker Park, making 152 League and Cup appearances for the Wearsiders, including 39 when they were First Division runners-up in 1922-3.

In May 1923 he signed for Bradford City and made 90 successive League appearances over the next three seasons. In 1927 he was appointed reserve-team player-coach at Valley Parade and in 1930 became first-team trainer. He joined Mansfield in August 1935. Jack Poole died in March 1967, aged 74.

Lloyd Barke
August 1944-May 1945

DEFENDER Lloyd Barke had been with Mansfield Town since 25 June 1937, when he joined the club along with Welsh international goalkeeper Jack Hughes, and at the same time as the departure of Ted Harston to Liverpool. His spell as player-manager linked the reigns of Jack Poole and Roy Goodall towards the end of wartime football.

Until he left the Stags in 1947, there were very few occasions when Lloyd was not in the line-up and he captained the side for most of the ten years he was at Field Mill. He played regularly for Mansfield throughout the war and guested for Notts County when the Stags were without a game. Lloyd's final appearance in Mansfield's colours was on 7 April 1947, in a 2-1 defeat at Ipswich.

Lloyd then spent three seasons with Denaby United before moving to Sutton Town as player-manager, then in turn to Heanor Town, when former Derby and England winger Sammy Crooks was with the club, Ilkeston Town and Belper Town.

Lloyd was born at Nuncargate and attended the same school as future England cricketers Harold Larwood, Bill Voce and Joe Hardstaff. He played football for his school and for Nottinghamshire Boys. After spells with East Kirkby Welfare and Bleak Hall United, he was spotted by Scunthorpe United and played for them in the Midland League before moving to Sheffield United, where he quickly claimed a regular first-team spot.

Barke spent five years at Bramall Lane and was unlucky to miss the 1936 FA Cup Final at Wembley, when an ulcerated leg kept him out of the side which was beaten by Arsenal. In later years he turned his attention to scouting for clubs and whilst serving Derby County he discovered Phil Boyer, who went on to represent England, although he left the Rams without playing in the first-team.

Roy Goodall
May 1945-August 1949

FORMER England full-back Roy Goodall was serving in the Army as a company quartermaster-sergeant instructor at the Epperstone Manor Auxiliary Hospital when he applied for the post of manager at Mansfield. Goodall, who had been trainer at Nottingham Forest since May 1937, took up his duties in May 1945 and faced the daunting prospect of preparing the club for a return to peacetime football.

It was an arduous task as players returned in dribs and drabs from the Armed Forces and, after a difficult first half of 1945-6, his initial season in charge, the Stags finished bottom of the Third Division South (North Region) with only 11 points from 29 matches.

There was, however, a great improvement in the second half of the campaign and Mansfield just failed to qualify for the final rounds of the Division Three South Cup, finishing third in the qualifying matches behind Queen's Park Rangers and Walsall.

At the end of 1946-7, with normal League football resumed, the Stags had to seek re-election to the Third Division South for the first time. They were readmitted but switched to the Northern Section, finishing eighth the following season and tenth in 1948-9, after which Goodall left Field Mill.

Goodall enjoyed a marvellous playing career after joining Huddersfield Town as an 18-year-old from his native Dronfield Woodhouse FC in 1921 and remained with the club until 1937, when his playing career was ended by a knee injury. Between 1926 and 1934 he won 25 England caps and skippered his country on several occasions. Surprisingly, it was never an honour he achieved with his club.

He was a member of the Huddersfield team which won the Football League Championship in three consecutive seasons from 1923 and finished runners-up in the following two seasons. He also gained two FA Cup runners-up medals. After leaving Leeds Road he was appointed trainer at Forest. From Mansfield, Goodall returned to Huddersfield as trainer until October 1964, when he became assistant trainer until his retirement in July 1965. He died in January 1982, aged 80.

Freddie Steele
August 1949-December 1951

FORMER Stoke City and England centre-forward Freddie Steele guided Mansfield during one of their best periods since they became a Football League club. Steele took over at Field Mill in time for the start of the 1949-50 season and, although in the twilight of his playing career, still managed to score 19 goals from only 20 League and two FA Cup games in his first full season, as the Stags finished tenth in the table.

The following season he took the club to the brink of Division Two when they finished runners-up to Rotherham United, in the days when only one club from the Northern section and one from the Southern were promoted. It is perhaps arguable that the Stags' FA Cup exploits that season proved a diversion that cost them promotion. They reached the fifth round before going out to First Division Blackpool and Steele scored some important goals, none more so than one against Second Division Sheffield United in a fourth-round replay.

Steele joined Mansfield from Stoke City for £750 in August 1949. He was released in December 1951, reluctantly it must be admitted, after he was in the side held to a goalless draw at non-League Stockton in the first round of the FA Cup. Perhaps it was significant that Stockton won the replay at Field Mill against a Stags side minus Steele.

He returned to his native Potteries to manage Port Vale and guided them to an FA Cup semi-final in 1954 as one of the few Third Division clubs to progress that far. He retired from playing in May 1953 remaining as manager until January 1957. He managed Vale again from October 1962 to February 1965.

Freddie Steele began his career with Stoke as a 15-year-old groundstaff lad in 1931, the year that Mansfield Town became a Football League club. He spent 18 years at the Victoria Ground, during which time he won three England caps and played for the Football League. He died in April 1976, aged 60.

George Jobey
January 1952-May 1953

MANSFIELD turned to the vastly experienced George Jobey, former manager of Derby County, to succeed Freddie Steele. In many ways, though, it was perhaps a strange appointment. Jobey had been out of football since 1941, after being suspended from the game 'permanently' following a joint FA-League inquiry into Derby's affairs between 1925 and 1938, when it appeared that the Rams had attracted and kept some of the best players in the country by making illegal bonus payments. Five Derby directors were suspended *sine die* and, although, Jobey's ban was lifted in 1945, he spent his time running a hotel until Mansfield tempted him back.

At least one person currently connected with Mansfield Town has cause to recall the arrival of the new manager at Field Mill, for it was Jobey who provided the Stags' long-serving secretary, Joe Eaton, with his first taste of League football, against Crewe Alexandra in November 1952.

And it was whilst Jobey was manager that the current Field Mill attendance record was established, at the third-round FA Cup tie against Nottingham Forest on 10 January 1953, when 24,467 passed through the turnstiles to see the Reds win 1-0.

But in that season, Mansfield finished perilously close to the re-election places, only just scraping clear in 18th place — and this after they had finished sixth the previous season. Jobey was dismissed after the board claimed that he had 'lost interest'.

George Jobey was born at Heddon on Tyneside and played for Newcastle United, Arsenal (he scored the Gunners' first-ever goal at Highbury), Bradford City and Leicester City. He was in Newcastle's 1909 League Championship side and played in the 1911 FA Cup Final for the Magpies. During World War One, Jobey appeared for Hamilton Academical and in 1920 became player-manager of Northampton Town. He was manager of Wolves when they won the Third Division North title in 1923-4, but had left the game to run a hotel when Derby tempted him back as their manager in August 1925.

From then until the outbreak of war he took some excellent players to the Baseball Ground and although he was not afraid to back his judgement with cash, three of his greatest signings — Jack Barker, Jack Bowers and Sammy Crooks — cost nothing. He was in charge throughout the Rams' most consistent period in Division One, notwithstanding their title wins under Brian Clough. George Jobey died at his Derby home in May 1962, aged 76.

Stan Mercer
August 1953-January 1956

STAN Mercer was one of football's unluckiest players, for after losing much of his career to World War Two, his playing days were eventually cut short by injury.

He was born in Birkenhead in September 1919 and played for Blackpool as an amateur, in addition to winning several medals in junior football. He served in the RAF as a PT instructor and in 1946 joined Leicester City, whom he had assisted during the war. Mercer's stay at Filbert Street lasted only a few months before he was transferred to Accrington Stanley in January 1947. In two seasons at Peel Park, he made 68 League appearances and netted 36 goals. He was Stanley's top scorer in 1947-8 and it was that form which attracted Mansfield boss Roy Goodall, who signed Mercer in October 1948.

He made his debut that month and in 15 consecutive League and Cup outings for the Stags he scored ten goals, including two hat-tricks, before a knee injury put him out of the game.

Mercer took over the managerial reins at Mansfield in August 1953, after serving the club as trainer following his premature retirement as a player. High scoring was one of the features of that season as Mansfield hit seven against York City, six against Darlington and Crewe, and five against both Tranmere and Grimsby. The Stags conceded five at York City and Accrington.

But there was disappointment in the FA Cup in his first season, for after holding Hartlepools United to a 1-1 draw at the Victoria Ground, Mansfield were beaten 3-0 in the replay at home, which attracted a crowd of only 6,273.

In January 1956, Mercer resigned 'on principle' after rejecting a call from the directors to undertake secretarial duties in addition to his work with the players — and without an increase in salary.

He left behind several good players, including George Darwin and 'Digger' Daley, both crowd-pleasers. Mercer went to live at Lytham St Anne's and became an administrator at the Premium Bonds office, from where he retired in 1989.

Charlie Mitten
February 1956-June 1958

WHEN Stan Mercer left the club, Mansfield looked for another player-manager in the hope that he could lead the Stags to the kind of success achieved in the

Steele era. And they certainly could not have chosen a more flamboyant personality than Charlie Mitten, who had shocked the soccer world by becoming one of several top-class British players to go to Colombia in search of a football fortune in the early 1950s.

Mitten's football pedigree was unquestionable. He was born in Rangoon, where his father was serving in the Army, in 1921 and later lived in Scotland before signing for Manchester United as a junior in 1936. During the war Mitten guested for several clubs, helping Chelsea to two Wembley Cup Finals, and between 1946 and 1949 he made over 150 League and Cup appearances at outside-left, scoring an average of a goal every three games and winning an FA Cup-winners' medal in 1948. He had the distinction of scoring a hat-trick of penalties in a First Division match against Aston Villa.

After his South American adventure — he was suspended by the FA for 18 months — Mitten joined Fulham in January 1952 and in five years at Craven Cottage, scored 33 goals in 160 League and Cup games. From there he moved to Mansfield.

Mitten certainly proved to be a shot in the arm for Mansfield Town and after the Stags finished 18th in the season he took over, brighter days beckoned. Several new faces appeared on the playing staff and one, almost as influential as the manager himself, was Sammy Chapman, who was persuaded to join Mansfield from Shamrock Rovers for the first of his two spells at Field Mill. Chapman marked his debut on 6 October 1956 with a goal against Halifax Town and followed up with another in his second match and a hat-trick in his fifth.

Mitten also contributed greatly in his first full season by scoring a dozen goals and missing only a couple of games throughout a campaign in which his close control continued to delight spectators.

The Stags finished 16th in that season and climbed to sixth by the end of 1957-8, when they enjoyed a run into the third round of the FA Cup before going down 5-0 at Bristol Rovers.

But prospects looked distinctly promising, with Fred Morris knocking in 17 goals, Sam Chapman hitting the same number up to February when he was transferred to Portsmouth, and Mitten weighing in with another dozen.

However, as has happened so often at Mansfield when the club has blooded newcomers into the managerial stakes, a more senior club beckoned and one could hardly blame Mitten for accepting a move to manage Newcastle United. He spent three years at St James' Park and later managed Manchester's White City greyhound stadium. His son, John, was a professional with Newcastle.

Sam Weaver
June 1958-January 1960

MENTION the name of Sam Weaver and most older fans will recall the 'King of the Long Throw,' for it was this aspect of his game that put Weaver in the football history books. His ability to throw a football from the touch-line to the far side of the penalty area laid on many goals for his colleagues.

Weaver arrived at Field Mill as trainer-coach in 1956, when Charlie Mitten was in charge, to launch a relationship with the club which was to last over 25 years. When Mitten left in June, Weaver was invited to take over and, although he relinquished the post after 18 months, it was not the only time he was in charge at Field Mill. Over the next 20 years he held the fort on numerous occasions during the many managerial changes at the club.

The Stags had slumped to 20th place in Weaver's first season and after he handed over to Raich Carter in January 1960, they dropped into Division Four, two years after the disappearance of the North and South Third Divisions. After Carter took over at Mansfield, Weaver remained at Field Mill as assistant trainer until 1967 and then became chief scout before retiring. He was born at Pilsley, Derbyshire, in 1909 and played for Hull City, Newcastle United and Chelsea, winning three England caps whilst with Newcastle. He guested for Leeds United during World War Two and played one game for the Stags in 1945-6. After the war he signed for Stockport County and after retiring as a player in 1947, worked as a coach at Leeds and as Millwall trainer before joining Mansfield. Weaver played two first-class cricket games for Somerset in 1939 and from 1956 was masseur to Derbyshire CCC for a while. He died in April 1985 and his ashes were scattered on the Field Mill pitch.

Raich Carter
February 1960-January 1963

THERE have been some distinguished occupants of the managerial chair at Field Mill since Mansfield Town were elevated to Football League status, men whose prowess in their playing days was legendary. And Raich Carter, probably the finest inside-forward to ever wear an England shirt, is undoubtedly the most famous of them all.

Even today, the exploits of the club whilst under his control, are still the topic of conversation when older Mansfield Town supporters gather to discuss their favourite team.

Yet his initial season in charge saw the Stags finish 20th in Division Four, although there were encouraging signs as Carter carried out his promise to give youth a chance. It was during the 1960-61 campaign that the new manager threw three local youngsters in at the deep end, all of them shortly after their 17th birthdays.

Ken Wagstaff and Mike Stringfellow were the first to receive the Carter 'sink or swim' treatment, in the opening month of the season, followed by Peter Morris in February. The fact that all three went on to make names for themselves at the highest level is testimony to Carter's ability, not only to discover but also to develop young players and make sure they achieved what their early potential had indicated.

It could be said that whilst he was in charge at Mansfield, Raich Carter had the town living, eating and sleeping football as never before. And never more so than in his final season before he went to manage Middlesbrough.

The Stags finished fourth in the table in the 1962-3 season, thus regaining their Third Division status, and they also enjoyed a run to the third round of the FA Cup, beating Crystal Palace after a controversial tie before losing to Ipswich Town.

Carter, who was born at Hendon, Sunderland, in 1913, made his name with the Wearsiders before the war, winning League Championship and FA Cup medals with them before joining Derby County as a guest player. He signed permanently for the Rams in 1945 and, alongside Peter Doherty, helped Derby win the FA Cup in 1946.

Two years later, Carter moved to Hull City and as player-manager took the Tigers to the Third Division North title. He played for Cork Athletic in the League of Ireland, helping them to an FAI Cup Final victory, and was manager of Leeds United from May 1953 to June 1958. Another player whose career was savaged by war, Carter's 13 England caps were scant reward for his talent. He played three first-class cricket games for Derbyshire in 1946. Carter now lives in retirement at Willerby, near Hull.

Tommy Cummings
January 1963-July 1967

YET another player who had made a name for himself in the First Division, England 'B' international Tommy Cummings was named as Carter's successor for his baptism into the world of football management.

Cummings held the post for just over four years and it is significant that he was the Stags' longest-serving manager in modern times until Ian Greaves' six-year stay at Field Mill.

Cummings, who made 434 League appearances as centre-half for Burnley, first came as player-manager. He made his debut in the Stags' line-up at home to Aldershot on 18 March 1963, but was injured. This kept him out of the side until May, when he appeared in the final four matches of the season.

He also turned out for the first five games — four in the League and one League Cup tie — the following season before hanging up his boots.

In his first full season, Mansfield finished seventh in the table and were unbeaten at home, winning 15 and drawing eight of their games at Field Mill. Had their away form been only half as good, then promotion to Division Two would have been a certainty. As it was, only five matches were won and three drawn on their travels.

The following season promotion again eluded Mansfield as they finished third, with their home form — only two defeats — again the springboard. Their away form improved with seven wins and seven draws but it was particularly disappointing, for Mansfield finished level on 59 points with Bristol City — one point behind the champions, Carlisle United — but lost out on goal-average.

Cummings had to surmount a formidable obstacle in November 1964, when he presided over the transfer of Ken Wagstaff to Hull City, a move which still rankles Stags supporters, even today.

But the former Burnley star had the answer when he signed Bill Curry, a former England Under-23 striker, from Derby County in the February. Curry immediately obliged by scoring 16 goals in the remaining 17 matches, including two hat-tricks and one four.

There were some problems the following season and the Stags dropped to 19th in the table, but in Cummings' last season with the club they were back on song, climbing to ninth with another of the manager's shrewd signings, Tommy Mitchinson, playing a leading role.

In July 1967, Aston Villa persuaded Cummings to take over at Villa Park. He was sacked after only 16 months at Villa and, after a spell out of football, coached abroad and scouted for a number of clubs, including Burnley and Sunderland.

Tommy Eggleston
July 1967-July 1970

DEFENDER Tommy Eggleston was born in Mitcham, Surrey, on 21 February 1920 and joined Derby County as an amateur in December 1936, turning professional in February 1937. A wing-half, he played only once in the Rams' first team before war interrupted his career. After serving as a Petty Officer in the Royal Navy, Eggleston was transferred to Leicester City in July 1946 and made 34 appearances in his one season at Filbert Street before joining Watford, where he stayed for five years and made over 177 League appearances.

Eggleston was appointed to the coaching staff at Vicarage Road in February 1948, became coach at Brentford in 1953 and then went back to Watford before taking coaching jobs at Sheffield Wednesday and Everton, each time working under

Harry Catterick. In the close season of 1967 he became manager of Mansfield Town and appointed the experienced Jock Basford as his assistant, but little went right in their first season in charge.

Relegation was avoided only by 0.008 of a goal and even that would not have saved the Stags, but for the fact that Peterborough United, who had finished well up the table, were demoted after being found guilty of making illegal payments to some of their players.

But after centre-half Dick Edwards had followed manager Tommy Cummings to Aston Villa, Eggleston used the incoming transfer money wisely to recruit several experienced players to his staff.

His key capture, inside-forward John Quigley, arrived in time for the start of the 1968-9 season, a campaign which was to make an indelible mark on the pages of Mansfield's history.

The Stags made it to the sixth round of the FA Cup for the first time and, like their non-League predecessors of 1928, hit the headlines by seeing off some experienced opposition. None was more formidable than First Division West Ham United, with an array of World Cup talent in their line-up, who were beaten 3-0 in the fifth round.

Another First Division outfit, Leicester City, finally ended the Stags' aspirations by a single goal in the sixth round. It is worth recalling that a certain Peter Shilton was in City's goal on that occasion.

There was almost a repeat performance in 1969-70, when Leeds United were the stumbling block in the fifth round. The euphoria was increasing the confidence of the side and lifted the Stags to sixth in the table from 15th the previous season.

But as Mansfield prepared for what was expected to be a positive bid to reach Division Two in 1970-71, Eggleston was lured away by the opportunity to manage the top Greek club, Ethnikos.

He later coached another leading Greek side, Panahaiki, before returning to England and resuming his partnership with Harry Catterick at Everton. Ill health forced Catterick out of the game and Eggleston, a qualified physiotherapist, first joined Plymouth Argyle in that capacity and then Ipswich Town. He has a private practice in Ipswich these days and still helps out when required at Portman Road.

Jock Basford
July 1970-November 1971

AFTER much speculation, and a sizeable list of applicants for the vacant post at Field Mill, the Mansfield board decided that Jock Basford should continue the task he had shared with Eggleston for three years.

And for his first season in full control, Basford certainly justified the directors' confidence in him by guiding the side to an impressive goalless draw against mighty

Liverpool in the opening round of the League Cup at Field Mill, in front of 12,532 fans. In the replay at Anfield, the Stags were leading 2-1, watched by 31,807 fans, until a debatable penalty eight minutes from time earned Liverpool extra-time and an eventual 3-2 win.

The Stags kept up the momentum in the League to finish in seventh place and as a bonus they defeated Notts County in the Notts FA Cup semi-final, then overcame Nottingham Forest in the Final.

Basford had picked up one Manager of the Month award that season, but the first half of the following season was a disaster. So disastrous, in fact, that Mansfield did not score a goal in front of their home fans until the FA Cup replay against Chester on 22 November. In the League they had to wait until 18 December, against Plymouth Argyle.

By then Basford and his assistant, John Quigley, had gone. They were dismissed on Monday, 10 November and after Sam Weaver had taken temporary charge for three days, Danny Williams took over.

On reflection, the close-season transfer of central defender Stuart Boam to Middlesbrough and talented young forward Malcolm Partridge to Leicester City may well have brought in much-needed finance, but the loss of the two players certainly had a big impact on Mansfield's potential.

However, Basford's talents were not lost to Mansfield Town for good. Within a year he was back as youth coach under Williams, a position he held, despite managerial changes, until his sudden death in March 1982, only hours after the author had been in his company at Field Mill.

Danny Williams
November 1971-March 1974

'THE best uncapped wing-half in England' was the accolade given by the sports writers of the day to former Yorkshire miner Danny Williams during 15 seasons with Rotherham United, for whom he made some 620 senior appearances in the early post-war era.

After his playing days were over, Williams went on to manage Rotherham before quitting in February 1965 to run a sports outfitters' shop in the town. Within two months, however, he was appointed manager of Swindon Town, whom he took to national fame with a League Cup Final victory over Arsenal and promotion from Division Three.

Williams, then, seemed just the man to improve the fortunes of Sheffield Wednesday, who appointed him their manager in the summer of 1969. Alas, his time at Hillsborough was something of a disaster as the Owls crashed out of Division One and struggled at the wrong end of Division Two before he was axed in January 1971.

Ten months later, Williams was back in football as manager of Mansfield Town. He just failed to prevent Mansfield being relegated at the end of the 1971-2 season, after they squandered the opportunity to collect two points from their final home game of the season, against Wrexham, by drawing 1-1 when a win would have preserved their Third Division status.

It was perhaps little consolation, but the Stags did end the season in style by retaining the Notts County Cup with a 3-1 win over Notts County.

In their first season back in Division Four, the Stags looked to be heading straight back to the Third Division until a run of only two wins in their final ten League games pushed them back into sixth place.

But 1973-4 was another of those seasons when the Stags did well at home, with 13 wins, eight draws and only three defeats, but failed miserably away from Field Mill. They went through the entire season without an away victory, although managing nine draws which saw them finish 17th in the table.

However, in March, Williams had returned Swindon Town with the blessing of the Mansfield directors, who did not stand in his way when approached by the club who were anxious to return to their former glories and turned to the man who had achieved so much for them in the late 1960s.

As it turned out, Williams was to make an early return of the favour by transferring to Mansfield a Swindon centre-forward who made quite an impact on the next highly-successful and historic season for the Stags. After leaving Swindon a second time, Williams retired to South Yorkshire.

Dave Smith
April 1974-April 1976

SCOTSMAN Dave Smith was a full-back with Burnley, Brighton and Bristol City before he turned to coaching with Sheffield Wednesday, Newcastle United and Arsenal. It was at Mansfield however, where he had his first taste of being in sole charge when he took over as manager on 4 April 1974.

With only two major close-season signings — striker Ray Clarke, who came from Swindon Town on Danny Williams' recommendation, and midfielder Gordon Hodgson from Newcastle United, on the advice of Sam Weaver — Mansfield gave every indication in the opening weeks of the season that they were going to be a major force, with both players key figures.

The Stags were the last team in the Football League with a 100 per cent record, a situation which lasted until 20 September when they lost 3-2 at Stockport County. By the turn of the year they had lost only one other match, 2-1 at Hartlepool, and had 41 points from 25 matches. In addition, they were through to the third round of the FA Cup after wins over Wrexham and non-League Wigan Athletic after a replay.

Cambridge United were their third-round victims and after two further successes in the League, Third Division Bury were beaten 2-1 at Gigg Lane in the fourth round of the Cup in front of 16,623 fans. The Cup run ended on 15 February 1975, when Carlisle United scraped a 1-0 win at Field Mill in front of another bumper attendance of 19,293, plus the television cameras.

A week later, the Stags lost their third League match of the season in a cracker at Doncaster. And in March, Mansfield lost two matches inside 48 hours at Rotherham and Newport County to bring fears that the team might be running out of steam.

But they were soon back in the groove and on 5 April, against Hartlepool, they picked up the two points they needed to ensure promotion. Four matches later it was luckless Scunthorpe United who were on the receiving end of seven-goal thrashing as Mansfield Town achieved their first-ever championship in the League, achieved with 68 points, a total exceeded previously in the division only by Notts County. Town's League record makes interesting reading, for they had lost on only six occasions in the League throughout the season and had not been defeated at Field Mill.

There was high drama the following season, with see-sawing fortunes and, in the final month, a controversy which still rages. Hopes were high that the Third Division would be taken by storm but by 11 February, when Mansfield lost 1-0 at Hereford United in midweek, they had only 16 points from 27 matches and were three points adrift at the bottom of the table.

It was ironic that, in the meantime, Mansfield had reached the semi-final of the Anglo-Scottish Cup and the fifth round of the League Cup, a competition in which they defeated First Division Coventry City and Wolves before bowing out to Manchester City at Maine Road.

Better times were to follow as teenager Mick Saxby headed an injury-time debut goal at Halifax to spark off a 19-match unbeaten run which finally lifted the Stags to 11th in the table. But with four matches remaining, Dave Smith was dismissed by the board of directors, a controversial decision which is still a topic of conversation today. Smith was out of a job for only a couple of weeks, as Southend United stepped in to appoint him their new boss.

And although it took him a litle longer, he took United into the Third Division in his second season in charge. But a boardroom battle resulted in his dismissal, and Smith left football to work in insurance before accepting an offer to manage Plymouth Argyle. He was a popular figure in Plymouth, for within 18 months he had achieved what so many others had failed to do by bringing Second Division football back to Home Park.

Plymothians were unhappy when, in the summer of 1988, Smith accepted an attractive offer to manage Dundee United, but he had an unhappy spell in Scotland and returned to the Football League as manager of Torquay United.

Peter Morris
July 1976-February 1978

WIDESPREAD speculation on the identity of Dave Smith's successor was resolved in July when Mansfield Town turned to one of their local boys made good, Peter Morris, to lead the club as player-manager.

Morris began his career at Field Mill and made his League debut in the 1960-61 season, when just past his 17th birthday. By the time he was 19 he was captain of the side and it was surprising that it took so long before he was whisked away into a higher grade of football.

Morris joined Ipswich Town in February 1968 and helped them to win promotion to Division One in his first season. In 1974, after 213 League appearances for Ipswich, he moved to Norwich City and was in their League Cup Final line-up in his first season, when they lost to Aston Villa, and when they also achieved promotion to Division One.

Morris had always been a quality player and quickly fitted in as player-boss at Mansfield as though he had never been away. Despite an early exit from the League Cup, after the opening round had gone to three meetings with Scunthorpe, Mansfield's League results were reasonably satisfactory. But then there was a second-round FA Cup disaster which later turned out to have a profound bearing on the Stags' second League title in three seasons.

Local non-League club Matlock Town went to Field Mill and hammered Mansfield 5-2. Within days Morris went to Peterborough United to sign striker Ernie Moss and thus renewed a formidable striking partnership with Moss' former Chesterfield friend and colleague, Kevin Randall, who had joined Mansfield the previous season from Notts County.

Billy McEwan was also recruited from Chesterfield, to give more bite to the Mansfield midfield, and as Moss scored seven goals in his first eight outings, with Randall also hitting the target with some regularity, promotion again became the talking point.

By the end of January, the Stags had climbed into second spot, and when maximum points came from the Easter holiday programme, from tough games at Port Vale and at home to Chesterfield and fellow promotion hopefuls Shrewsbury Town, Division Two looked possible.

Promotion was finally achieved against Portsmouth on 2 April, a match marred by an injury to Barry Foster, who broke a leg. On the last day of the season, a single-goal win at Wrexham in front of a 20,764 crowd saw the Stags move into Division Two for the first time in their history — and as champions, too. But the euphoria did not last long. Half-way through the following season a quick return to Division Three seemed on the cards. Morris departed well before relegation arrived, to become assistant manager at Newcastle United under the man who had signed him for Norwich City, Bill McGarry — not a move which was popular with the Mansfield fans. Morris later had a spell as manager of Crewe Alexandra and Peterborough United, and now manages non-League Kettering Town.

Billy Bingham
March 1978-July 1979

MANSFIELD Town chairman Arthur Patrick moved quickly in an effort to preserve the Stags' newly-won Second Division status by calling in experienced manager and former Sunderland and Northern Ireland international star, Billy Bingham.

Bingham's hopes of keeping Mansfield in Division Two almost vanished in his

Billy Bingham pictured with (left to right): Steve Johnson, Les McJannet, Aidey Burrows and Glen Chambers.

first few weeks at Field Mill when a 1-0 home win over Hull City was followed by a run of five consecutive defeats. Indeed, after Morris's departure, Mansfield won only four and drew three of their remaining 15 League matches.

But in the final reckoning, after their Second Division status was surrendered on the final day of the season, at Millwall, it was the Stags' failings from the penalty-spot which really brought about relegation. On no fewer than five occasions penalty awards were wasted and, without exception, every one cost a point. Indeed, Mansfield drew twice with Tottenham Hotspur — and in both matches a missed penalty cost them victory.

The following season Mansfield again enjoyed some success in the Anglo-Scottish Cup, once more reaching the semi-final where they were beaten by Burnley after a penalty competition.

But relegation for the second year running appeared well on the cards until a run-in of six consecutive home games — in a rearranged programme brought about by matches having been postponed during the second half of the season — produced eight points out of 12 and a safe 18th place in the table.

During the close season, Mansfield were involved in the £200,000 transfer of another of their local home-grown central defenders, Mick Saxby to Luton Town. Preliminary negotiations were conducted in the absence of Bingham, who was on holiday in Australia. The whole transaction involved the transfer of striker Steve Taylor to Mansfield for £75,000 and on his return, Bingham finalized the deal and agreed personal terms with Taylor. But over the weekend before the final signings, Bingham changed his mind about the player, to the consternation of both clubs. The Mansfield board insisted that, as a matter of honour, the deal should go through and as the manager again refused to sanction the deal, he was dismissed.

Bingham was born in Belfast in 1931 and began his career with Glentoran moving on to Sunderland, for whom he made 206 League appearances, in 1950. Transferred to Luton Town he played for the Hatters against Nottingham Forest in the 1959 FA Cup Final and joined Everton a year later. A superb dribbler and crosser of the ball, Bingham loved to take on his full-back and was a great favourite at Goodison Park. After scoring 26 goals in 98 senior appearances for the Merseysiders and appearing in the 1962-3 League Championship team, he moved to Port Vale in 1963. His playing days were ended by a broken leg two years later.

Bingham went into management with Southport, then the Greek national side before taking over as Everton boss in May 1973. In 1974-5 it seemed as though he might take them to the First Division title before they slipped away to finish fourth. In January 1977, as Everton slumped to 13th place, Bingham was sacked. He went to manage PAOK Salonika of Greece before taking the Mansfield job.

Bingham, who was capped 56 times for Northern Ireland and was in the side which reached the 1958 World Cup quarter-final, later managed the national side to the 1982 and 1986 World Cup finals.

Mick Jones
July 1979-May 1981

MICK Jones, a former Notts County and Peterborough United defender whose career was ended prematurely because of a knee injury, had been hitting the headlines in the 1978-9 season as manager of non-League Kettering Town.

Jones had taken over the club which was close to closure and revived their flagging fortunes in a very short time. So much so, in fact, that he led the team out at Wembley that season for the FA Trophy Final and guided the Poppies to the runners-up spot in the Southern League Premier Division with a goalscoring record which was one of the best in the country, with 109 scored and 43 conceded in 42 matches.

Jones, who was born in Sunderland in 1947, began his career as a Derby County junior under Tim Ward but did not figure in the Rams' first team before Brian Clough transferred him to Notts County in July 1969. He earned championship medals with both Notts County and Peterborough, whom he joined in August 1973, and was assistant manager to Ronnie Fenton at Notts County, resigning in protest when Fenton was dismissed.

Jones was given the task of attempting a 'Kettering' at Field Mill, where Mansfield's fortunes had been flagging to say the least. He was joined by his assistant at Kettering, Jeff Lee, and there were some hopeful signs early on when the Stags reached the third round of both the League and FA Cups. But in the League, the signs were ominous, with only eight points earned from the first 12 matches.

There was a marginal improvement in the middle of the campaign but results fell away again and it was back to Division Four for Mansfield at the end of the season.

One of the few successes of a disappointing campaign was the form of centre-forward Terry Austin, who scored 23 goals. He was sold to Huddersfield Town in late November the following season, for £100,000, and in January his replacement, Jim Lumby, joined Mansfield from Tranmere Rovers for £35,000.

The Stags still felt that they had a real opportunity of achieving a quick return to Division Three but this rapidly disappeared in the run-in to the end of the season when only eight points were taken from the final 13 matches.

Within days of the season's end there was a shock for Mansfield fans as Arthur Patrick, chairman for 14 years, gave up his directorship.

Five days later, Mick Jones was sacked by the new chairman, former vice-chairman John Almond. Jones later had a spell as assistant manager to Roy McFarland at Bradford City and with McFarland was involved in an unseemly row in November 1982, when Derby County allegedly 'poached' the pair. Derby had to pay a large fine and compensation to the Valley Parade club but, although McFarland survived the appointment of Arthur Cox at the Baseball Ground, Jones did not and later had a spell as manager of Peterborough United.

In 1989-90 Jones spent a period as coach at Blackpool before taking up a similar position back at Notts County. In July 1990 he was appointed assistant manager to Neil Warnock.

Stuart Boam
July 1981-January 1983

ONCE again Mansfield Town turned to a former player who had gone on to make a name for himself, in the hope that he might revive the club's fortunes as manager.

Stuart Boam, who was born in Kirkby-in-Ashfield in 1948, served the Stags superbly as a central defender after being converted from a midfield player in the Stags 'A' team by chance. The recognized centre-half failed to turn up for a Central Alliance game, Boam was pressed into action in the position and the rest is history.

He had played for the senior team in the final League game of the season and after missing the first three matches of the 1967-8 campaign, took over the position and rarely missed a match before he was transferred to Middlesbrough for £45,000 in the 1971 close season.

At Ayresome Park, Boam made 378 League and Cup appearances after making his 'Boro debut on the same day as former England World Cup hero, Nobby Stiles. When Jack Charlton became manager he appointed Boam club captain and he skippered Middlesbrough to promotion to Division One before being transferred to Newcastle United in August 1979, for £100,000. He made 69 League appearances for the Magpies before returning to Mansfield.

Boam never had the good fortune he might have expected on his return to Field Mill. He was plagued by a back injury which required hospital treatment and kept him sidelined for almost all of the two seasons he was at the club. Thus, he was not able to lead from the front as expected.

He managed to play in only the first six games of the season and by the end of the campaign Mansfield had just scraped clear of the need to seek re-election by finishing in 20th position, in what was a disappointing Golden Jubilee Year marking their election to the Football League.

There was a boardroom shake-up during the 1982 close-season, with Nottingham businessman Richard Hartley, a former Notts County director, taking over as chairman and John Almond resuming his position as vice-chairman.

With three points for a win introduced the previous season, Mansfield's haul by the start of 1983 was only 31 from 21 games and Friday, 17 December had seen the lowest-ever Football League attendance at Field Mill when only 1,293 fans watched a game against Torquay United.

Only one win in the first four outings of the New Year finally saw Boam and his assistant, Geoff Allen, dismissed. Boam signed for Hartlepool United on a non-contract basis in 1982 and then moved to Guisborough as player-manager.

Ian Greaves
February 1983-February 1989

'WHY a Fourth Division club in general and a minnow like Mansfield Town in particular?' That was a question repeatedly aimed at Ian Greaves when his appointment as the Stags' new manager was announced.

It was a justifiable question in the circumstances, for Greaves had, in turn, revitalized Huddersfield Town and Bolton Wanderers, steering them both into Division One as well as rescuing Oxford United from the doldrums before the Maxwell take-over ended his association with the club.

There were also signs that Greaves would be able to repeat the feat at his next club, Wolverhampton Wanderers, before yet another boardroom battle saw him once again available.

"Why Mansfield?" he asked. "Because they want me to run them the way I would want to run it." And that is just what he did for all the six years he was at Field Mill, a period which makes Ian Greaves the longest-serving manager in the history of Mansfield Town.

Perhaps one of his regrets, however, was that chairman Richard Hartley, whose enthusiasm persuaded Greaves to take on the Mansfield challenge, gave up the position in October 1984, although the manager was equally at home with his new chairman, John Pratt.

Greaves' first two years, at least from the point of view of results, were disappointing as the Stags finished 19th in 1983-4 and 14th the following season.

He admitted that he had a great deal to learn in dealing with Fourth Division football, particularly after recruiting several players who had made their names in the higher divisions — and even at international level — but who had been unable to adjust.

But from the outset the new manager had insisted on the formation of a positive youth policy at Mansfield and he appointed John Jarman as his assistant with this in mind. That policy quickly paid dividends with the advent of outstanding teenagers in Colin Calderwood, now captain of Swindon Town, Mike Galloway, now one of Scotland's top players, and Les Robinson, who recently joined Oxford United. Others were Simon Coleman and Craig McKernon, who recently brought in over £700,000 in transfer fees to Mansfield.

More important, Greaves achieved promotion for the Stags in 1985-6 and also took the club to Wembley and success in the Freight/Rover Trophy in May 1987 with a penalty-competition win over Bristol City after extra-time.

Two years earlier, Mansfield could well have made a trip to Wembley in the same competition but were beaten on penalties by Wigan Athletic in the Northern Area Final at Mansfield, Wigan going on to win the trophy.

There was a public outcry and demonstrations on the Field Mill pitch before and after matches when West Bromwich Albion sought to persuade Greaves to move to The Hawthorns — and intense relief when he turned down the offer.

During his spell at Mansfield, Greaves made some judicious signings, none more so than that of central defender George Foster, who picked up three Player of the Year awards after arriving in the 1983 close season.

Mark Kearney, the current captain, Kevin Kent, Tony Lowery and Paul Garner were all Greaves-inspired signings who have served the club loyally. None was more popular, however, than Keith Cassells, who moved north from Brentford in August 1985. Cassells marked his debut with a hat-trick in the opening game of the season and in his four seasons at Field Mill never failed to reach double-figures on the score-sheet at the end of a season. Like that of Greaves, his departure was greeted with great regret, for there can be no doubt in anyone's mind that Ian Greaves had no need to give up his post at Field Mill.

Born in Oldham in 1932, he began his career with Buxton as a full-back before joining Manchester United's Busby Babes in 1954, going on to make 67 League appearances and appearing in the 1958 FA Cup Final defeat by Bolton Wanderers before moving to Lincoln and then Oldham Athletic. He managed Huddersfield Town into Division One in 1970 and in August 1974 became assistant manager to Jimmy Armfield at Bolton, taking over as manager when Armfield moved to Leeds United two months later.

In 1977-8 he was named Second Division Manager of the Season, when he took Bolton to the title. A year earlier he had steered the Trotters to a League Cup semi-final. In 1980, though, he was sacked with Bolton rooted at the foot of Division One. He returned to football as assistant manager of Hereford United before joining Oxford. Greaves is now coaching two days a week at Bury and scouting part-time for Manchester United.

George Foster
February 1989-

WHEN chairman John Pratt announced on Monday, 6 February that Ian Greaves had parted company with the Stags, it was perhaps no surprise when he also revealed that the club captain, George Foster, had been offered the position of player-manager.

Foster had made no secret of the fact that management was his eventual aim and, with that in mind he had worked closely with Ian Greaves, learning the requirements of the job.

Foster had over 500 League appearances under his belt in a career which had spanned Plymouth Argyle, Torquay United, Exeter City, Derby County and

Mansfield Town, quite an achievement considering that when was a teenager, Foster was advised to give up the game because of an injury. He joined Derby in June 1982, Rams' manager John Newman paying a £40,000 fee for his transfer from Plymouth after his loan spells at Torquay and Exeter. Foster proved a real battler in Derby's defence and helped in the Rams' successful fight against relegation from the Second Division in 1982-3, after Peter Taylor took over as manager.

Foster joined Mansfield in August 1983 and was in the Stags' team that was promoted from Division Four in 1986 and won the Freight/Rover Trophy 12 months later.

His career as Mansfield's manager began well enough with an unbeaten five-match run, but thereafter there were problems, although a final position of 15th in Division Three was achieved after some fighting performances, particularly in wins against promotion-chasing Sheffield United and Wolverhampton Wanderers.

Foster's first full season in charge gave him an early indication of the headaches of management as Mansfield found themselves bottom of the table around the half-way stage of the campaign. An inability to perform in front of the home fans was their main stumbling block and it did not help when two of the Stags' rising stars, Simon Coleman and Craig McKernon, were whisked away by bigger clubs.

But the signing of striker Steve Wilkinson, who finished the club's top scorer in the League and defender Malcolm Murray stabilized the team and, despite some heart-stopping moments during the run-in at the end of the season, Mansfield again finished 15th.

Foster also enjoyed good service from a player whom he signed soon after taking over as player-manager — striker Trevor Christie, who was for so long a target of Ian Greaves. Christie weighed in with 17 goals and this, combined with a revival in fortunes at home, eased the long-standing relegation worries.

A-Z of Stags Stars

Mansfield in 1953-4. Back row (left to right): S.Carter, D.Bradley, E.Barks, D.Wright, W.McGregor, N.Plummer, S.Watson. Front: C.Adam, O.Fox, K.Murray, G.Darwin, A.Daley.

Like many players in that era who eventually signed for Mansfield Town, Charlie Adam began his career with Leicester City before moving to Field Mill when George Jobey was in charge of the Stags. Adam had joined City in 1946 and in five seasons at Filbert Street, the Glasgow-born outside-left, who had begun his career with Strathclyde, had chalked up 158 League appearances and scored 22 goals. He was still the epitomy of consistency whilst at Mansfield, making 93 League appearances and scoring six League goals. In his first season with the Stags, Adam scored twice for the side which dismissed non-League Scarborough 8-0 on their own ground in the first round of the FA Cup. After Mansfield had defeated Accrington Stanley 2-0 away in the next round, he was in the line-up which met neighbours Nottingham Forest in the third round, in front of an attendance of 24,467, the biggest crowd ever seen at Field Mill. The Stags lost by a single goal.

	LEAGUE		*FA CUP*		*TOTAL*	
	App	*Gls*	*App*	*Gls*	*App*	*Gls*
1952-53	40	4	3	3	43	7
1953-54	36	2	2	0	38	2
1954-55	17	0	0	0	17	0
	93	6	5	3	98	9

CHARLIE ADAM

Goalkeeper Rod Arnold made his Mansfield Town debut against Fulham at Craven Cottage on Saturday, 6 February 1971, when he was only 18 and on loan from his home-town club, Wolverhampton Wanderers. Arnold went on to make 17 appearances as he played out the season at Field Mill. An offer of £10,000 to Wolves to make Arnold's move permanent received no response from Molineux but the youngster was back on loan with Mansfield towards the end of the 1972-3 season, to make a further 13 appearances. Before the start of the next campaign, the Stags finally got their man and Arnold joined Mansfield's permanent staff. It was worth the wait because this time, Town got him on a free transfer. Neither Arnold or Mansfield had cause to regret the move, for his first-team place was never challenged in his 13 seasons at the Mill. Indeed, his only absences from the side were through injuries, which included a broken arm and a cartilage problem which required an operation. He chalked up his 400th League appearance on 3 November 1983 in a 4-0 win at Hartlepool and had raised that total to 440 before he was injured in the 4-0 defeat at Reading on Wednesday 19 October 1984. The injury suffered at Elm Park finally ended his career. Arnold also made one Watney Cup appearance, 16 in the Anglo/Scottish Cup and three in the Football League Trophy.

	LEAGUE		*FA CUP*		*FL CUP*		*OTHERS*		*TOTAL*	
	App	*Gls*	*App*	*Gls*	*App*	*Gls*	*App*	*Gls*	*App*	*Gls*
1970-71	17	0	0	0	0	0	0	0	17	0
1972-73	13	0	0	0	0	0	0	0	13	0
1973-74	29	0	1	0	0	0	1	0	31	0
1974-75	46	0	6	0	1	0	0	0	53	0
1975-76	39	0	0	0	4	0	6	0	49	0
1976-77	46	0	3	0	3	0	0	0	52	0
1977-78	42	0	2	0	2	0	0	0	46	0
1978-79	28	0	1	0	2	0	7	0	38	0
1979-80	43	0	3	0	5	0	3	0	54	0
1980-81	38	0	4	0	4	0	0	0	46	0
1981-82	45	0	1	0	4	0	0	0	50	0
1982-83	43	0	3	0	2	0	3	0	51	0
1983-84	11	0	2	0	2	0	0	0	15	0
	440	0	26	0	29	0	20	0	515	0

ROD ARNOLD

TERRY AUSTIN

Terry Austin joined the Stags as part of a bargain deal which took striker Dave Syrett to Walsall in exchange for the player and a reported £45,000 fee. Austin made his debut at Chester on Saturday, 31 March 1979 and scored in the 1-1 draw. He was also on target in his next game, a 2-1 victory at Sheffield Wednesday, and finished the season with five goals from 16 outings to share second-highest scorer spot for the club. Austin netted 19 League goals the following season, after manager Billy Bingham had been dismissed during the close season and Mick Jones had taken over as manager. But his efforts failed to prevent Mansfield being relegated to the Fourth Division. After only four months in the bottom division, Austin was on the move again, this time for a £100,000 fee to Huddersfield Town, managed at that time by Ian Greaves, who in 1986 was to take the Stags back into the Third Division. Austin scored ten goals in 39 appearances for the Terriers before spells with Doncaster Rovers and Northampton Town. The player must have liked the Mansfield air, for he never left the town and is currently a highly-successful insurance company executive.

	LEAGUE		*FA CUP*		*FL CUP*		*TOTAL*	
	App	*Gls*	*App*	*Gls*	*App*	*Gls*	*App*	*Gls*
1978-79	16	5	0	0	0	0	16	5
1979-80	46	19	3	1	5	2	54	22
1980-81	22	7	0	0	4	1	26	8
	84	31	3	1	9	3	96	35

Defender Lloyd Barke joined Mansfield Town in 1937 from Yorkshire neighbours, Sheffield United, and was a Stags regular through the war years, as well as serving the club as acting manager from 14 August 1944, after trainer-manager Jack Poole left Mansfield to become trainer at Notts County. Barke also guested occasionally for Notts County during the war years. He was born in the Nottinghamshire village of Nuncargate, which produced England cricketers Harold Larwood, Bill Voce and Joe Hardstaff, and began his soccer career with Midland League side Scunthorpe United. He was with that club for less than a season before moving on to Bramall Lane, where he stayed for five years. His last appearance for the Stags was on 7 April 1947 in a 2-1 defeat at Ipswich Town. After leaving Field Mill, Barke, nicknamed 'The Iron Man', spent three years with Denaby United before joining Sutton Town as player-manager. He played until he was 41, with Heanor Town (when the famous Derby County winger, Sammy Crooks was with the club), Ilkeston Town and Belper Town. Barke was also an accomplished cricketer and played for Annesley Colliery in the Notts & Derby Alliance and Blidworth Colliery in the Bassetlaw League.
(See also *Stags Managers*)

	LEAGUE		*FA CUP*		*D3S CUP*		*TOTAL*	
	App	*Gls*	*App*	*Gls*	*App*	*Gls*	*App*	*Gls*
1937-38	42	0	3	0	1	0	46	0
1938-39	40	0	6	0	2	0	48	0
1945-46	-	-	6	0	-	-	6	0
1946-47	32	0	1	0	0	0	33	0
	114	0	16	0	3	0	133	0

LLOYD BARKE

EDDIE BARKS

Edwin Barks — Eddie to his friends — was one of the real characters of the game. He was one of those players who hated the boredom of training, but whose perpetual-motion displays at half-back on match days belied the fact. His trademark was a broad grin that never seemed to disappear, no matter the situation. Even, we are told, when he was designated to man-mark the elusive Stanley Matthews in the FA Cup meeting with Blackpool at Bloomfield Road, when Freddie Steele was manager. Ilkeston-born Barks began his career with non-League Heanor Town, but was soon 'discovered' by Nottingham Forest, playing 66 League games for the Reds from 1946 to 1948 before moving down the road to Field Mill. He topped the 200 mark for the Stags in his seven seasons with the club, during which time he served under four managers.

	LEAGUE		*FA CUP*		*TOTAL*	
	App	*Gls*	*App*	*Gls*	*App*	*Gls*
1948-49	16	2	0	0	16	2
1949-50	32	0	2	0	34	0
1950-51	36	3	5	1	41	4
1951-52	45	1	2	0	47	1
1952-53	28	0	1	0	29	0
1953-54	33	0	1	0	34	0
1954-55	23	0	1	0	24	0
	213	6	12	1	225	7

KEVIN BIRD

The 20-year-old defender's world appeared to be in ruins when, after only one season as a professional with his home-town club, Doncaster Rovers, he was given a free transfer. But his potential had been recognized by former Rovers coach, Frank Marshall, who had joined Danny Williams, the new manager at Mansfield Town. Bird was offered a three-month trial period at Field Mill at the start of the 1972-3 season and it soon became apparent that Doncaster's loss would be Mansfield's gain. On 21 October, only days after signing a full contract, Bird made his debut in a 4-1 home win over Chester City, on his way to making over 400 appearances for the club, and becoming one of the most feared central defenders in the lower divisions. He was no mean scorer of goals, either, particularly in set-piece situations, grabbing over 60 whilst in Mansfield's colours. Bird's final appearance for the Stags was on 7 May 1983, at Peterborough, and, typically, he was one of the scorers, although Mansfield went down 3-2. He moved to Huddersfield Town, then did the round of local non-League clubs.

	LEAGUE		*FA CUP*		*FL CUP*		*OTHERS*		*TOTAL*	
	App	*Gls*	*App*	*Gls*	*App*	*Gls*	*App*	*Gls*	*App*	*Gls*
1972-73	26	2	1	0	0	0	0	0	27	2
1973-74	44	8	3	0	2	0	1	0	50	8
1974-75	28	7	6	0	1	0	0	0	35	7
1975-76	26/2	6	4	0	6	3	6	1	42/2	10
1976-77	37/1	8	0	0	3	0	0	0	40/1	8
1977-78	34	4	0	0	2	0	0	0	36	4
1978-79	44	4	1	0	2	1	5	0	52	5
1979-80	38	7	3	0	5	1	3	0	49	8
1980-81	42	5	4	1	4	0	0	0	50	6
1981-82	25/1	2	0	0	4	1	0	0	29/1	3
1982-83	28/1	2	2	0	2	0	3	0	35/1	2
	372/5	55	24	1	31	6	18	1	445/5	63

Mansfield Town has spawned a number of local players who have gone on to make their name in football. But Kirkby-in-Ashfield-born Stuart Boam was one who very nearly got away. He had an unsuccessful spell with Nottingham Forest after being spotted in local youth football and then turned to Mansfield, mainly as a wing-half or inside-forward. He had not really impressed until fate took a hand. The author was covering a Central Alliance match involving the Stags 'A' team, when the scheduled centre-half failed to arrive. The manager of the team at that time was Jack Jepson and he moved the young Boam into the centre of the defence for that game. Boam played a blinder and the rest is history. The youngster was given one outing with the senior side, at Leyton Orient on the final Saturday of the season. And on 22 September 1969, Boam was back in the first-team to launch in earnest a career at Field Mill which saw him an almost ever-present until he was snapped up for £40,000 by Middlesbrough in the close season of 1972. Boam captained the Boro' side which saw the club promoted to the First Division. Then, after a spell with Newcastle United, for whom he signed in 1977, he returned to Mansfield in 1981, to become player-manager of the club in its Golden Jubilee year in the Football League. Alas, he was plagued by injury and things did not go well. Eventually, he was dismissed in 1983. After a short spell with Hartlepool United, he left the game for a career in industry in his home town.

(See also *Stags Managers*)

STUART BOAM

	LEAGUE		*FA CUP*		*FL CUP*		*TOTAL*	
	App	*Gls*	*App*	*Gls*	*App*	*Gls*	*App*	*Gls*
1966-67	1	0	0	0	0	0	1	0
1967-68	44	0	1	0	0	0	45	0
1968-69	46	1	7	0	1	0	54	1
1969-70	46	1	6	0	3	0	55	1
1970-71	38	1	2	0	1	0	41	1
1981-82	4/4	1	0	0	2	0	6/4	1
1982-83	7	0	0	0	0	0	7	0
	186/4	4	16	0	7	0	209/4	4

Full-back Don Bradley was born in 1924, three miles from Field Mill in the local colliery village of Clipstone. His football career began with West Bromwich Albion in 1942 but, despite being at The Hawthorns for seven years, he did not play in a League game for the Throstles. Bradley signed for Mansfield in August 1949 and was soon to be handsomely rewarded for his patient wait for a League baptism. It came at Southport on 28 August 1949, in a 1-1 draw, and his professional career ended on 23 October 1961, with a 2-1 League Cup replay defeat at Ninian Park. The original tie at Mansfield, which ended in a 2-2 draw, was an important milestone in the club's history as the Field Mill floodlights were switched on by Billy Wright. In all

	LEAGUE		*FA CUP*		*FL CUP*		*TOTAL*	
	App	*Gls*	*App*	*Gls*	*App*	*Gls*	*App*	*Gls*
1949-50	36	0	2	0	-	-	38	0
1950-51	42	1	6	0	-	-	48	1
1951-52	46	0	2	0	-	-	48	0
1952-53	32	0	3	0	-	-	35	0
1953-54	32	3	2	0	-	-	34	3
1954-55	43	1	1	0	-	-	44	1
1955-56	29	1	1	0	-	-	30	1
1956-57	23	0	2	0	-	-	25	0
1957-58	5	0	0	0	-	-	5	0
1958-59	23	0	1	0	-	-	24	0
1959-60	35	0	3	0	-	-	38	0
1960-61	29	0	2	0	1	0	32	0
1961-62	9	0	0	0	3	0	12	0
	*384	6	25	0	4	0	413	6

* One appearance v Accrington Stanley not included after their record was expunged.

Bradley made 413 appearances, including 384 in the League, a club record which stood for ten years until beaten by another full-back, Sandy Pate. Bradley's record could have been even more impressive, but for a number of serious injuries which kept him sidelined for long periods. Pate and Clive Walker formed a full-back partnership which Mansfield fans of the late 1960s and early 1970s will long remember. But Bradley's partnership with Sam Chessell in the previous decade was just as famous.

DON BRADLEY

One thing has to be said, above all others, about goalkeeper Graham Brown — he was a tryer. Indeed, he would otherwise never have made his mark in professional soccer. Brown was born of Salvation Army officer parents in Matlock but football was always his ambition. He played for non-League Crawley Town as a 20-year-old but was convinced that he had the ability to perform at Football League level. Brown had unproductive trials with Millwall, Brighton and Watford and even when he widened his bid for a football career by moving his attentions further north, to Mansfield Town, and impressed manager Tom Eggleston, he was told that the Stags could not afford to sign him and that he should come back next season. Back he came and this time his persistence paid off,

GRAHAM BROWN

although the competition was tough, to say the least, for Brown vied with Welsh Under-23 international goalkeeper, Dave Hollins, for a place in the Stags' League side. It was Brown, though, who got the early vote and he made 33 senior appearances that season. Hollins played in the first three rounds of the FA Cup, but then Brown took over for the fourth and fifth-round ties against Blackpool and Leeds United. He became Mansfield's recognized first-team 'keeper for two seasons but in February 1971 he was injured and a Wolves youngster called Rod Arnold took over on loan for the rest of the season. However, Brown was still first-choice for the following two seasons until Arnold again had an on-loan period with the Stags, starting in March 1973 and once more running to the end of the season. This later loan period became permanent and at the end of 1972-3, Brown moved to Doncaster Rovers. He later played for Portland Timbers in America, Swansea City, Southport, York City and Rotherham United before rejoining Mansfield on a non-contract basis in 1981, for a short period before retiring. He now keeps in touch as a part-time League scout alongside his regular job as a sales representative.

	LEAGUE		*FA CUP*		*FL CUP*		*TOTAL*	
	App	*Gls*	*App*	*Gls*	*App*	*Gls*	*App*	*Gls*
1969-70	33	0	2	0	2	0	37	0
1970-71	19	0	1	0	2	0	22	0
1971-72	40	0	4	0	2	0	46	0
1972-73	33	0	0	0	2	0	35	0
1973-74	17	0	3	0	2	0	22	0
1981-82	1	0	0	0	0	0	1	0
	143	0	10	0	10	0	163	0

COLIN CALDERWOOD

Glaswegian Colin Calderwood is another of Mansfield Town's youngsters who came up through the apprentice and junior ranks and quickly began to show his potential. So much so, that he made his senior debut in a 2-0 win at Crewe on 13 March 1982, when he was only 17 years and 52 days old. That was his only first-team outing that season but by November the following season he had claimed a regular senior place. Calderwood's move to Swindon Town just before the start of the 1985-6 season was a bitter blow for Mansfield, who received a paltry £27,500 fee for the player, set by an independent transfer tribunal. Mansfield's disappointment was even more understandable, for Calderwood continued to prove the original estimates of his ability absolutely right. He was appointed Swindon Town's team captain and played a prominent role in helping the Wiltshire club climb into the Second Division. Calderwood was involved in the recent 'illegal payments' scandal at Swindon. He was one of several people initially questioned after police investigations, but was released. The Football League ordered Swindon to pay extra fees to clubs from whom they had recruited players. Mansfield received an extra £2,500 for Calderwood, but still believe the original tribunal-fixed fee was underestimated.

	LEAGUE		*FA CUP*		*FL CUP*		*AM CUP*		*TOTAL*	
	App	*Gls*	*App*	*Gls*	*App*	*Gls*	*App*	*Gls*	*App*	*Gls*
1981-82	1	0	0	0	0	0	0	0	1	0
1982-83	28	0	3	0	0	0	0	0	31	0
1983-84	27/3	1	1	1	2	0	1	1	31/3	3
1984-85	41	0	2	0	2	0	*6	0	51	0
	97/3	1	6	1	4	0	*7	1	114/3	3

*Six in Freight/Rover Trophy

David Caldwell signed for Mansfield when he was 18, in June 1979 from Highland League club, Inverness Caledonian. Some believed that the Stags had discovered another Ken Wagstaff, for Caldwell had the pace and control to get past defenders and an ability to score goals. What was not realized in those early days, was that he also had a short temper on the field. He made his senior debut in 1979-80 and served Mansfield well before joining newly-promoted Chesterfield in the 1985 close season, for £12,000. On the debit side he amassed 36 bookings, eight periods of suspension and one sending off. Unsettled, he had already been on loan to Carlisle United in late 1984 but did not impress there, nor at Swindon Town where he spent a month before returning to Mansfield in March 1985. He had a couple of seasons at Saltergate but then picked up two suspensions in quick succession and was sold to Torquay United, for £4,000. Dismissed on three further occasions, he was suspended for eight weeks. Caldwell later played in Belgium and South Africa and returned to Torquay on loan.

	LEAGUE		*FA CUP*		*FL CUP*		*OTHERS*		*TOTAL*	
	App	*Gls*	*App*	*Gls*	*App*	*Gls*	*App*	*Gls*	*App*	*Gls*
1979-80	1/2	0	0	0	0	0	0	0	1/2	0
1980-81	23/5	8	4	2	4	1	0	0	31/5	11
1981-82	31/2	9	1	0	4	0	0	0	36/2	9
1982-83	34/1	10	3	0	1	0	2/1	0	40/2	10
1983-84	37/1	21	2	1	2	1	0/1	0	41/2	23
1984-85	19/1	9	2	1	2	0	2	1	25/1	11
	145/12	57	12	4	13	2	4/2	1	174/14	64

DAVE CALDWELL

One of the most popular strikers to wear a Mansfield Town shirt, Keith Cassells had four excellent seasons with the Stags and it could well have been more, but for the player's avowed intention to retire from the game. He turned down the offer of a further lucrative contract at Field Mill at the close of the 1988-9 season and joined the Hertfordshire police force, despite attempts by several other clubs to obtain his signature. Cassells joined Mansfield from Brentford for the start of the 1985-6 season and scored a hat-trick on his debut on the opening day of the campaign, as Hereford United were defeated 4-0. He never failed to reach double figures in his goal tally in every season with the club. Cassells began his career with Watford, who signed the London postman from non-League Wembley in November 1977. A short spell with Peterborough United followed before the player moved to Oxford United, then under the guidance of Ian Greaves. Under Greaves, Cassells began to attract the attention of more senior clubs and in March 1982 he moved to Southampton for a £100,000 fee. Things did not work out as well as expected at The Dell and Cassells returned to his native London and Brentford FC in February 1983. He was in the Bees' losing line-up in the Freight/Rover Trophy Final in May 1985. There was ample consolation for Cassells, however, when he returned to Wembley in the same competition two years later and helped Mansfield lift the trophy. He was also a key performer when the Stags won promotion from the Fourth Division at the end of the 1985-6 season.

KEITH CASSELLS

	LEAGUE		*FA CUP*		*FL CUP*		*F/Rov*		*TOTAL*	
	App	*Gls*	*App*	*Gls*	*App*	*Gls*	*App*	*Gls*	*App*	*Gls*
1985-86	40	13	2	0	3	1	2	1	47	15
1986-87	46	15	1	0	2	1	8	1	57	17
1987-88	40	10	4	3	4	1	4	1	52	15
1988-89	36/1	14	0	0	2	0	0	0	38/1	14
	162/1	52	7	3	11	3	14	3	194/1	61

Roy Chapman had been on the football scene for several years before he arrived at Mansfield Town in August 1961 to form a vital part of perhaps the most lethal scoring partnership in the Stags' history. Manager Raich Carter had plunged three local youngsters in at the deep end the previous season, and Ken Wagstaff, Peter Morris and Mike Stringfellow had begun to mature into class players. The influence which the experienced Chapman had on Wagstaff's career is inestimable, and the pair became the scourge of defences in the Third and Fourth Divisions, putting away a total of 175 League goals between them in the four seasons they were partners. Chapman scored over 200 goals in 400 League appearances, spread over 20 seasons, and played in every division of the Football League. He began his career with Aston Villa, but did not hit the headlines until he moved to Lincoln City, where he made 105 appearances and scored 45 goals between 1957 and 1961. At Field Mill, he added 136 League appearances and 78 goals to his growing tally before returning to Lincoln for another 69 appearances and 31 goals. In two years with Port Vale, he kept up his scoring prowess, hitting 38 goals in 77 games before concluding his career with Chester and a modest nine games and three goals. Unhappily, Roy had a heart attack while playing five-a-side football and died in 1983, but his son, Lee Chapman, still keeps the family name firmly in the soccer headlines.

ROY CHAPMAN

	LEAGUE		*FA CUP*		*FL CUP*		*TOTAL*	
	App	*Gls*	*App*	*Gls*	*App*	*Gls*	*App*	*Gls*
1961-62	37	20	0	0	1	0	38	20
1962-63	44	30	5	5	3	2	52	37
1963-64	36	19	1	1	1	0	38	20
1964-65	19	9	2	0	1	2	22	11
	136	78	8	6	6	4	150	88

Belfast-born Sammy Chapman's first English club was Mansfield Town, with whom he had two spells. Signed by the Stags from Shamrock Rovers in October 1956, he made 63 appearances and scored 26 goals for the club — not a bad return for a wing-half — before moving to Portsmouth in February 1958. Almost three years later, and 48 appearances and ten goals further on, Chapman was back at Field Mill, this time for 105 appearances and another 15 goals. He played a significant role in one of Mansfield's most successful periods, when Raich Carter was in charge. He is still active in English football, coaching youngsters taking their first steps in the profession with Football League clubs.

	LEAGUE		*FA CUP*		*FL CUP*		*TOTAL*	
	App	*Gls*	*App*	*Gls*	*App*	*Gls*	*App*	*Gls*
1956-57	21	10	2	0	-	-	23	10
1957-58	29	15	4	2	-	-	33	17
1961-62	20	8	0	0	0	0	20	8
1962-63	40	5	4	0	1	0	45	5
1963-64	45	2	1	0	2	0	48	2
	155	40	11	2	3	0	169	42

SAMMY CHAPMAN

SAM CHESSELL

Defender Sammy Chessell followed in his father's footsteps, who was a professional with Brighton and Hove Albion. A native of that hotbed of soccer talent five miles from Field Mill, Shirebrook, Sam's potential was realized when playing for local side, Welbeck Colliery. He made his official debut for his only League club, Mansfield Town, in 1945 at Gainsborough Town in the FA Cup and was already a first-team regular before he teamed up with Don Bradley and goalkeeper Dennis Wright to become the first three names on a Stags' senior team-sheet for something like seven seasons. Altogether, Chessell made 256 League appearances in his nine years at the club and enjoyed a reputation throughout the League as a hard, but scrupulously fair footballer. One lasting memory of his career came at Carlisle United on New Year's Day 1948 when he broke his leg — almost at the same time as his wife was presenting him with twin daughters! Chessell appeared in the Stags' colours during the war years when he was a teenager, operating mainly as a forward, and gave every indication that Mansfield perhaps missed out when they converted him into a full back, for he was no mean scorer of goals.

	LEAGUE		*FA CUP*		*TOTAL*	
	App	*Gls*	*App*	*Gls*	*App*	*Gls*
1946-47	35	1	0	0	35	1
1947-48	22	1	2	0	24	1
1948-49	36	2	3	0	39	2
1949-50	32	0	2	0	34	0
1950-51	46	0	6	0	52	0
1951-52	24	0	2	0	26	0
1952-53	45	3	3	0	48	3
1953-54	16	0	1	0	17	0
	256	7	19	0	275	7

Cockney striker Ray Clarke spent only a couple of seasons with Mansfield, but when he was sold to Sparta Rotterdam for £90,000 during the 1975 close season, Stags' supporters were almost as livid as when all-time favourite Ken Wagstaff was transferred to Hull City during the 1964-5 campaign. Clarke had been a prolific scorer in the reserve sides of Tottenham and Swindon Town, but did not reproduce that form in occasional senior outings with both of those clubs. He was recommended to Mansfield by manager Danny Williams, who had been allowed to return to his former club, Swindon, by the Stags Board, although under contract at Field Mill. Clarke's impact at Mansfield soon proved what a favour Williams had afforded his previous club. Clarke immediately hit up the sort of striking partnership with Terry Eccles, who had been top scorer for Mansfield the previous season, that managers dream about. And with new Mansfield boss Dave Smith at the helm, the Stags simply steamrollered their way through the Fourth Division to the club's first-ever championship since being elected to the Football League in 1931. It was the Clarke-Eccles partnership that enabled Mansfield to consolidate their newly-won position. After languishing six points adrift at the bottom of the table, they finished 11th after a run of 19 games without a defeat. Clarke spent three years on the Continent, first with Sparta Rotterdam and then Bruges. He returned to England and had spells with Brighton & Hove Albion and Newcastle United before injury brought his career to an early close.

RAY CLARKE

	LEAGUE		*FA CUP*		*FL CUP*		*TOTAL*	
	App	*Gls*	*App*	*Gls*	*App*	*Gls*	*App*	*Gls*
1974-75	46	28	6	2	1	0	53	30
1975-76	45	24	4	0	6	3	55	27
	91	52	10	2	7	3	108	57

DAVID COATES

Geordie David Coates launched his career in football as a 17-year-old with Hull City and appeared in 61 senior League games for the Tigers, scoring 13 goals whilst at Boothferry Park. In March 1960, the inside-forward moved to Mansfield, following his former boss, Raich Carter, who had taken over the Field Mill hot seat a month earlier as Mansfield dropped into the Fourth Division. Before he joined neighbours Notts County in July 1964, Coates had chalked up 159 League appearances for the Stags and scored 17 goals and played a leading role as promotion back to the Third Division came at the end of the 1962-3 season. Coates spent two seasons at Meadow Lane, making 66 League appearances for the Magpies before continuing his career as a coach with several top clubs.

	LEAGUE		*FA CUP*		*FL CUP*		*TOTAL*	
	App	*Gls*	*App*	*Gls*	*App*	*Gls*	*App*	*Gls*
1959-60	5	0	0	0	-	-	5	0
1960-61	38	5	2	1	1	0	41	6
1961-62	40	3	2	0	3	1	45	4
1962-63	40	5	1	0	2	0	43	5
1963-64	36	4	1	0	2	0	39	4
	*159	17	6	1	8	1	173	19

* One appearance v Accrington Stanley not included after their record was expunged.

When Geordie Bill Curry made the short move from Derby County to Mansfield Town in February 1965, he knew that in Ken Wagstaff he had a hard act to follow at Field Mill. But the explosive start to Curry's Mansfield career — 15 goals, including two hat-tricks and one four-goal strike in a match, in the last 16 League games of the season — did a great deal to placate the local fans, angry at the transfer of the popular Wagstaff. Curry had begun his career at Newcastle United and scored 34 goals in 80 appearances spread over four seasons. He was signed by Brighton for a £12,000 fee in July 1959 and scored 26 goals in his one full season at the Goldstone Ground before joining Derby County for £10,000 in October 1960. His scoring prowess continued with the Rams and he collected 63 goals in 148 outings before joining the Stags. After one season with Chesterfield, his League career ended. Curry, who won one England Under-23 cap whilst with Newcastle, later played for Boston United, served Worksop Town as trainer and managed Boston FC and Sutton Town. He died of cancer on 20 August 1990, aged 55.

	LEAGUE		*FA CUP*		*FL CUP*		*TOTAL*	
	App	*Gls*	*App*	*Gls*	*App*	*Gls*	*App*	*Gls*
1964-65	16	15	0	0	0	0	16	15
1965-66	36	14	1	0	1	0	38	14
1966-67	45	22	4	3	3	1	52	26
1967-68	5	2	1	0	1	0	7	2
	102	53	6	3	5	1	113	57

BILL CURRY

Sadly, 'Digger' Daley, as he was popularly known by the Mansfield supporters, died in 1975, at the comparatively early age of 48, but his memory lives on for those who saw him at his best. Daley was one of that breed of flamboyant, aggressive wingers so beloved by fans everywhere. Mansfield-born, he had two spells at Field Mill, first joining the club in September 1946 from local youth team, Pleasley Boys' Club. The following year he moved to Hull City, after failing to break into the Stags' senior side, and in his two years at Boothferry Park he managed only seven first-team League outings. A couple of seasons with Doncaster Rovers followed, but it was not until he joined Scunthorpe United that his form really began to blossom. In only one season at The Old Showground, Daley made 35 appearances and scored nine goals, the sort of form which again attracted his hometown club, whom he rejoined in November 1953. However, in the meantime he had sharpened up his game with non-League sides Worksop Town, Boston United and Corby Town. And it showed at Mansfield where, in just over two seasons, he added 24 goals to his tally in 98 appearances. 'Digger' then continued to delight the crowds at Stockport County (73 appearances, 17 goals) and Crewe Alexandra (14 appearances, one goal) where he stayed for only four months of the 1958-9 season before moving to Coventry City, where he ended his senior career with 55 appearances and a further ten goals.

ALAN (DIGGER) DALEY

	LEAGUE		*FA CUP*		*TOTAL*	
	App	*Gls*	*App*	*Gls*	*App*	*Gls*
1953-54	29	12	0	0	29	12
1954-55	41	12	1	0	42	12
1955-56	27	1	2	0	29	1
	97	25	3	0	100	25

A modest fee paid to Huddersfield Town proved to be money well spent for pacey George Darwin, who had begun his professional career at Leeds Road as an 18-year-old after being snapped up from local Chester-le-Street side, Kimblesworth Juniors, by the Yorkshire club. Darwin had failed to make the Huddersfield senior team, but he quickly established himself at Field Mill after being signed in November 1953, soon after he reached the age of 21, by manager Stan Mercer. In May 1957 he made the short trip to join Derby County, but not before he had chalked up 126 League appearances for the Stags and averaged a goal every two games for a total of 63. His scoring prowess continued for the Rams and Darwin netted 32 League goals in 94 appearances before leaving the Baseball Ground for a short spell with Rotherham United. After only nine months at Millmoor he ended his career with Barrow, knocking in a further 28 goals in 92 appearances in his two years at Holker Street.

GEORGE DARWIN

	LEAGUE		*FA CUP*		*TOTAL*	
	App	*Gls*	*App*	*Gls*	*App*	*Gls*
1953-54	26	17	2	0	28	17
1954-55	28	8	1	0	29	8
1955-56	37	19	2	1	39	20
1956-57	35	19	1	0	36	19
	126	63	6	1	132	64

LLOYD (LINDY) DELAPENHA

Lindy Delapenha was another winger who is remembered with affection by Mansfield Town supporters. In his era, he was a rarity in that he was coloured and at that time, few coloured players were in evidence in Football League sides. Delapenha was born in the West Indies in 1927 but emigrated to England as a youngster. He began his soccer career with Portsmouth in April 1948 and it says much for his talent that in 12 years in the game he had only three clubs, totalling 383 League games and 117 goals. He made only eight appearances in his two years with Pompey but after being transferred to Middlesbrough in April 1950, he added 260 appearances and 90 goals to his tally. Signed by Mansfield's new manager Sam Weaver in June 1958, after Charlie Mitten had left to take over the Newcastle United hot seat, he made 115 appearances for the Stags and scored 27 goals before bowing out of the Football League scene. Lindy is now residing back in his native West Indies where he holds a senior position in the sports department of the Jamaican Broadcasting Corporation.

	LEAGUE		*FA CUP*		*TOTAL*	
	App	*Gls*	*App*	*Gls*	*App*	*Gls*
1958-59	39	9	1	0	40	9
1959-60	41	10	3	0	44	10
1960-61	35	8	1	0	36	8
	115	27	5	0	120	27

RAY DEVEY

Ray Devey was one of those unfortunate players whose careers were interrupted just at the wrong time by World War Two. Born in Birmingham in 1917, Devey joined Birmingham as a teenager and looked certain to make a name for himself as a quality wing-half. He returned to St Andrew's after the war but managed only a single first-team outing in the 1946-7 season. Transferred to Field Mill in August 1947, he quickly claimed a senior spot with his consistent displays, making his debut at York City on 23 August 1947. In two years with the Stags, Devey made a total of 76 appearances, scoring six goals, but then dropped out of the Football League scene as a player. However, until a couple of years ago he was in charge of the youth team at the club which launched his professional career — Birmingham City.

	LEAGUE		*FA CUP*		*TOTAL*	
	App	*Gls*	*App*	*Gls*	*App*	*Gls*
1947-48	41	1	3	0	44	1
1948-49	34	3	3	0	37	3
1949-50	1	0	0	0	1	0
	76	4	6	0	82	4

Had striker Terry Eccles been born only a few years later, he would surely have been a target for the bigger clubs. Big and brave, Eccles undoubtedly played a major role in one of the most successful periods enjoyed by Mansfield Town in their 69 years in the Football League. Born in Leeds in 1953, he joined Blackburn Rovers straight from school and made his first-team debut when only 17, completing 33 senior appearances and 13 as substitute in his three years with the Ewood club and scoring six goals. He was persuaded by fellow Yorkshireman Danny Williams, then manager of Mansfield Town, to move to Field Mill in July 1973 and in the 1973-4 season he topped the scoring list with 22 goals from 50 League and Cup games. And it was his link-up with Ray Clarke the following season which spearheaded Mansfield to their first-ever League championship with a total of 45 goals between them. He also played his part the following season as the Stags turned almost certain relegation, after being adrift at the bottom of the table at the turn of the year, to a comfortable 11th position by the end of the season with a run of 19 games without defeat. In January 1977 he was transferred to Huddersfield Town and made 41 appearances and scored six goals for the Terriers before he tried his luck with Greek side, Ethnikos, where he mainly operated as a central defender. Back in England he signed for York City in September 1979 and added a further 64 appearances and 16 goals to his career total before retiring from the game to become a publican in a village near York.

	LEAGUE		*FA CUP*		*FL CUP*		*TOTAL*	
	App	*Gls*	*App*	*Gls*	*App*	*Gls*	*App*	*Gls*
1973-74	44	20	4	2	2	0	50	22
1974-75	32	17	5	3	1	0	38	20
1975-76	29/3	3	2	2	3/1	1	34/4	6
1976-77	10	7	2	1	3	1	15	9
	115/3	47	13	8	9/1	2	137/4	57

TERRY ECCLES

Kirkby-in-Ashfield-born Dick Edwards first came to the notice of senior clubs when playing for the local East Kirkby Welfare Juniors. And it was to Notts County that he turned to take his initial steps in a football career. A quality central defender, Edwards made 219 League appearances for the Magpies and scored 18 goals between 1959 and 1966, before he moved to Field Mill when Tommy Cummings was the manager at Mansfield. Forty-five appearances and one goal later he followed Cummings to Aston Villa, where the former Burnley star had taken over as manager. In his 27 months at Villa Park, Edwards made 68 senior appearances before joining Torquay United in June 1970 to add a further 99 senior games to his credit. Then it was back to Field Mill, three years further on, to add another 31 appearances to the list. Once again Torquay beckoned and he picked up several Player of the Year awards before ending his career on the non-League scene. In the meantime, Dick had added another string to his bow — that of night-club entertainer, a career which sees him a popular Country and Western turn at local Torquay night-spots every summer.

	LEAGUE		*FA CUP*		*FL CUP*		*TOTAL*	
	App	*Gls*	*App*	*Gls*	*App*	*Gls*	*App*	*Gls*
1966-67	13	0	0	0	0	0	13	0
1967-68	32	1	1	0	1	0	34	1
1973-74	31/2	1	0	0	1	0	32	1
	76/2	2	1	0	2	0	79/2	2

DICK EDWARDS

ERNEST ENGLAND

Full-back Ernest England was born at Shirebrook, the colliery village only a few miles from Field Mill, and after a distinguished career with some of the country's top soccer clubs, he returned to captain his local club in their early seasons in the Football League. England joined Sunderland at the age of 18 and made his debut against Manchester City on 27 December 1919. He went on to make 334 appearances for the Wearsiders before, in October 1930, moving to West Ham United for a £500 fee. At Upton Park, England made only five League appearances and it was from the Hammers that he joined Mansfield in August 1931, in time for the Stags' opening match in Division Three South. After making a total of 136 League and Cup appearances for Mansfield in four seasons, he left to become trainer to Notts County. In August 1936 he returned to Field Lane as assistant trainer for two seasons. Ernest England died at his Radcliffe-on-Trent home in February 1982, at the age of 81.

	LEAGUE		*FA CUP*		*D3N CUP*		*TOTAL*	
	App	*Gls*	*App*	*Gls*	*App*	*Gls*	*App*	*Gls*
1931-32	42	2	1	0	0	0	43	2
1932-33	29	0	1	0	0	0	30	0
1933-34	36	1	2	0	1	1	39	2
1934-35	23	0	2	0	0	0	25	0
	130	3	6	0	1	1	137	4

This much-travelled striker maintained at Mansfield what he managed at all of his other clubs — his ability to score goals. Born in February 1941 in Cricklewood, Fairbrother's early football was played with Bennett's End, from where he was recruited by Watford in 1959 when he was 18. After a couple of seasons, in which he made 40 appearances and scored 19 goals at Vicarage Road, he moved to non-League Worcester City but was back in the Football League in 1965 with Peterborough United, with whom he averaged almost a goal every two games with 37 in 69 outings. He was transferred to Northampton Town in February 1968 and maintained his scoring ability with 56 goals in 156 first-team games. Fairbrother made his Mansfield Town debut on 18 September 1971, in a match at Chesterfield, after being signed by manager Jock Basford only three months before Basford was dismissed. He justified his signing by scoring 22 League and Cup goals in his first season, despite Mansfield being relegated to Division Four by .003 of a goal. In the following season he again topped the 20-goal mark and in the next close season was transferred to Torquay United. As with his previous clubs, Fairbrother was able to keep up his strike rate with Mansfield, having made 90/2 League and Cup appearances for the Stags and scoring 43 goals.

	LEAGUE		*FA CUP*		*FL CUP*		*TOTAL*	
	App	*Gls*	*App*	*Gls*	*App*	*Gls*	*App*	*Gls*
1971-72	41	18	4	4	0	0	45	22
1972-73	42/2	20	1	1	2	0	45/2	21
	83/2	38	5	5	2	0	90/2	43

JOHN FAIRBROTHER

ARTHUR FITZSIMMONS

Dublin-born Arthur Fitzsimmons collected 26 full caps for the Republic of Ireland in a distinguished career and also represented the League of Ireland whilst a member of his first club Shelbourne. Fitzsimmons, who was born on 6 December 1929, was transferred to Middlesbrough in May 1949 for £18,000 along with Peter Desmond. Both men hit the headlines in September that year when they made their international debuts before playing a Football League game. In nine years at Ayresome Park, inside-forward Fitzsimmons made 223 League appearances and scored 54 goals. In March 1958, he moved to Lincoln City and made seven appearances, winning his last cap, before Mansfield Town paid out a £6,000 fee to take him to Field Mill a few months later. He was a first-team regular for most of his two seasons with the Stags, adding a further 68 League and Cup outings and 25 goals to his tally.

	LEAGUE		*FA CUP*		*FL CUP*		*TOTAL*	
	App	*Gls*	*App*	*Gls*	*App*	*Gls*	*App*	*Gls*
1959-60	38	15	3	1	-	-	41	16
1960-61	24	8	2	1	1	0	27	9
	62	23	5	2	1	0	68	25

Barry and Colin Foster both made their senior debuts in the 1971-2 season, having come up through Mansfield Town's junior sides. They were not related in any way, Barry being discovered whilst playing in schools football in the Worksop area and Colin in the Nottingham district. But both were defenders, Barry a left-back and Colin mainly operating in the centre of the defence. In fact, they made their senior debuts together, on 4 September 1971 at Plymouth Argyle, although Colin had been on the substitute's bench on one occasion the previous season. The son of a miner, Barry delayed turning full-time professional until he had completed his course as a mining electrician at his local colliery. It was some three seasons after his debut that Barry eventually arrived permanently on the senior scene. That was in the 1974-5 season, when he finally took over from the previous incumbent of the left-back position, Clive Walker. It was said of Barry that he rarely had a spectacular game but always maintained consistent good form throughout his 328 senior appearances. But his one real regret after finally hanging up his boots was that he never scored a senior goal in his career. Barry's high came with his England Youth Cap, and his low came on the evening promotion to Division Two was achieved for the first time in Mansfield's history, when the celebrations were marred by him breaking a leg during the 2-0 win over Portsmouth on 2 April 1977. He never drifted into non-League soccer like many of his contemporaries, but played a bigger part in the family market-trading business which still operates in the North Nottinghamshire and South Yorkshire areas.

BARRY FOSTER

	LEAGUE		*FA CUP*		*FL CUP*		*ASC*		*TOTAL*	
	App	*Gls*	*App*	*Gls*	*App*	*Gls*	*App*	*Gls*	*App*	*Gls*
1971-72	9	0	0	0	0	0	0	0	9	0
1972-73	11/2	0	0	0	0	0	0	0	11/2	0
1973-74	19/3	0	4	0	0/1	0	0	0	23/4	0
1974-75	40	0	6	0	1	0	0	0	47	0
1975-76	44	0	4	0	6	0	7	0	61	0
1976-77	39	0	1	0	3	0	0	0	43	0
1977-78	25	0	2	0	0	0	0	0	27	0
1978-79	39	0	1	0	2	0	7	0	49	0
1979-80	15	0	1	0	4	0	3	0	23	0
1980-81	13	0	2	0	0	0	0	0	15	0
1981-82	28	0	1	0	1	0	0	0	30	0
	282/5	0	22	0	17/1	0	17	0	338/6	0

Nottingham-born Colin Foster had earmarked himself for a successful soccer career even during his apprentice days, when he captained the championship-winning youth team in the Midland Intermediate League. He was discovered by Mansfield, playing for Nottingham Schools and the County schools representative sides. Colin had a taste of the senior scene at Field Mill before his namesake Barry, when he was named as substitute midway through the previous season, and finally made his first-team debut along with Barry on 4 September 1971 at Plymouth. Apart from that, their two careers ran almost parallel, except that Colin ended his association with Mansfield Town at the end of the 1978-9 season, when he was transferred to Peterborough United for a modest £13,000. Known in the trade as a 'hard man', Colin was also no mean scorer of vital goals from set-pieces. And there is no doubt that he could have claimed a place in many teams as a goalkeeper, a position he took over with some relish on several occasions when the regular custodian was injured during a game. After a couple of seasons at London Road, Colin graduated into non-League soccer management with Corby Town and then with King's Lynn, also playing for both clubs.

	LEAGUE		*FA CUP*		*FL CUP*		*AM CUP*		*TOTAL*	
	App	*Gls*	*App*	*Gls*	*App*	*Gls*	*App*	*Gls*	*App*	*Gls*
1971-72	1	0	0	0	0	0	0	0	1	0
1972-73	6	0	0/1	0	0	0	0	0	6/1	0
1973-74	24/3	1	4	1	1	0	0	0	29/3	2
1974-75	42/1	3	6	0	1	0	0	0	49/1	3
1975-76	34/2	1	0/1	0	3/1	0	4	0	41/4	1
1976-77	44	9	3	1	0	0	0	0	47	10
1977-78	35	3	2	0	2	0	0	0	39	3
1978-79	9/4	0	0	0	2	0	3	0	14/4	0
	195/10	17	15/2	2	9/1	0	7	0	226/13	19

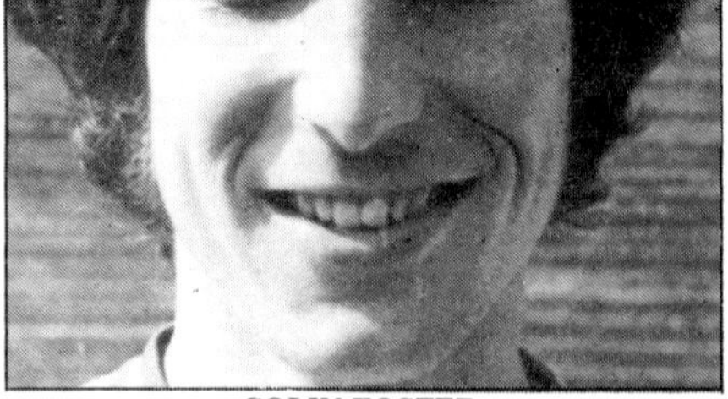

COLIN FOSTER

Oscar Fox was born just over the border in neighbouring Derbyshire in the mining village of Clowne, only a few miles from Field Mill where he was to spend most of his career. But he learned his trade at Hillsborough with Sheffield Wednesday when they were a Second Division outfit before the war. As with many of his contemporaries, Fox's career was interrupted by the outbreak of hostilities but at the end of the war he rejoined Wednesday and between 1946 and 1949 he appeared in the inside-forward position for the Owls on 44 occasions. The move to Field Mill came in June 1950, when England international centre-forward Freddie Steele was manager. One of Fox's biggest disappointments whilst he was with Mansfield was missing, because of injury, all the 1950-51 FA Cup run in which the Stags reached the fifth round before being knocked-out by Stanley Matthews' Blackpool. He hung up his boots at the conclusion of the 1956-7 season after his final appearance for Mansfield on 23 April 1957 in the 4-1 home win over Hartlepool, and thus completed 258 League and Cup appearances and 34 goals. Sadly Oscar Fox, who worked in engineering after finishing in football and who regularly turned up at Field Mill every year for a chat about old times, died in January 1990, only a fortnight after his 69th birthday and after a short illness.

	LEAGUE		*FA CUP*		*TOTAL*	
	App	*Gls*	*App*	*Gls*	*App*	*Gls*
1950-51	34	5	0	0	34	5
1951-52	43	10	2	0	45	10
1952-53	38	5	3	4	41	9
1953-54	38	2	2	0	40	2
1954-55	41	4	1	0	42	4
1955-56	37	2	2	0	39	2
1956-57	17	2	0	0	17	2
	248	30	10	4	258	34

OSCAR FOX

PAUL GARNER

Yorkshireman Paul Garner did not move far from his native county in his 18-year professional career, apart from a five-match loan spell with Gillingham in 1983. Equally at home in midfield or at left-back, Garner earned England Youth honours while with his first club, Huddersfield Town, whom he joined when only 17. After 96 League outings while at Leeds Road, he was transferred to Sheffield United in November 1975 and in nine distinguished seasons at Bramall Lane, he put together 248 appearances before he was persuaded by manager Ian Greaves to sign for Mansfield on 13 September 1984. Garner spent five more seasons at Field Mill and made 102 appearances, although dogged by injuries during his Mansfield campaigns. He finally hung up his boots in 1989, to take up a career in the insurance business after the knee injury which plagued him at Mansfield finally ended his attempt to continue his career in non-League football.

	LEAGUE		*FA CUP*		*FL CUP*		*OTHERS*		*TOTAL*	
	App	*Gls*	*App*	*Gls*	*App*	*Gls*	*App*	*Gls*	*App*	*Gls*
1984-85	38/1	2	1	0	0	0	6	0	45/1	2
1985-86	28	4	0	0	1	0	5	0	34	4
1986-87	21/1	2	1	0	1	0	7/1	0	30/2	2
1987-88	14/5	0	2	0	0	0	2	0	18/5	0
1988-89	1/1	0	0	0	0	0	0	0	1/1	0
	102/8	8	4	0	2	0	20/1	0	128/9	8

JOHN GILL

John Gill was born at Wednesbury, Staffordshire, in February 1941 and discovered by Nottingham Forest playing in schoolboy football. He joined the City Ground staff on leaving school but he never made the senior side and, soon after his 20th birthday, he moved 15 miles down the road to Field Mill and made his senior debut in the heart of the Stags' defence on the opening day of the 1961-2 season in a game at Carlisle United. In his five seasons with Mansfield, John Gill made over 150 League and Cup appearances before moving on to Hartlepools United on 2 February 1966. Before he finally disappeared from the League scene, he had added a further 202 first-team appearances to his record. And whilst at the Victoria Ground, he achieved something he had failed to do at Field Mill — he scored a League goal.

	LEAGUE		*FA CUP*		*FL CUP*		*TOTAL*	
	App	*Gls*	*App*	*Gls*	*App*	*Gls*	*App*	*Gls*
1961-62	19	0	2	0	0	0	21	0
1962-63	14	0	0	0	3	0	17	0
1963-64	41	0	1	0	1	0	43	0
1964-65	46	0	2	0	2	0	50	0
1965-66	18/1	0	1	0	2	0	21/1	0
	138/1	0	6	0	8	0	152/1	0

This likeable Scot was born in Edinburgh in July 1938 and had only three clubs in a successful career which, not surprisingly began north of the border, with Third Lanark. However, he really took off when he attracted the attentions of Leicester City and joined the Filbert Street staff in May 1963. After four seasons at Leicester, Goodfellow moved on Mansfield, as a number of City players had in the past, making his debut along with three other new signings, Nick Sharkey, also from Leicester City, Phil Waller from Derby County, and Dudley Roberts from Coventry City, on 16 March at Brighton. All four were destined to play their part in one of Mansfield's most successful FA Cup periods when the Stags became a household name throughout the country. Goodfellow was in the side which went unchanged throughout the competition in the 1968-9 season and reached the sixth round before bowing out to his former club, Leicester City. After missing the first round the following season, he put away a vital penalty in the third round against Barnsley. And after Mansfield were paired with mighty Leeds United at Elland Road in the fifth round, the Stags' fans are still convinced that if Goodfellow's strike — which was disallowed before a goal had been scored — had stood, then Mansfield could well have made it to the quarter-final for the second year running. Instead they went down 2-0. Goodfellow left Mansfield in 1971 and entered the catering and hotel trade on the south coast, at the same time spending a couple of seasons in non-League football.

	LEAGUE		*FA CUP*		*FL CUP*		*TOTAL*	
	App	*Gls*	*App*	*Gls*	*App*	*Gls*	*App*	*Gls*
1967-68	12	0	0	0	0	0	12	0
1968-69	39	6	7	0	1	0	47	6
1969-70	30	6	4	1	2	1	36	8
1970-71	15/4	2	2	0	1	0	18/4	2
	96/4	14	13	1	4	1	113/4	16

JIMMY GOODFELLOW

Winger John Gregson did not move far from his home town of Skelmersdale to launch his Football League career, for Blackpool discovered his talents whilst he was playing for his local club, Skelmersdale Town, and he moved to Bloomfield Road only days after his 18th birthday. First-team opportunities for the youngster were few and far between in his five seasons with the Seasiders and in May 1962, again only days after his birthday, he moved on to Chester. After only eight months and 32 appearances, he collected his kit again to join Shrewsbury Town, with whom he added a further 56 League appearances to his record. However, once more his stay was only a brief one, for 18 months later the former Burnley player, Tommy Cummings, who had replaced Raich Carter as the Mansfield Town boss, negotiated the transfer of the talented winger. Even then Gregson's wanderings were not over, for after three seasons, and 81 League and Cup appearances for the Stags, he joined Lincoln City, before leaving the Football League scene for the final spell of his career with Cambridge United, who were then in the Southern League.

	LEAGUE		*FA CUP*		*FL CUP*		*TOTAL*	
	App	*Gls*	*App*	*Gls*	*App*	*Gls*	*App*	*Gls*
1964-65	24	2	1	0	0	0	25	2
1965-66	30	3	0	0	2	0	32	3
1966-67	21/1	0	0	0	3	0	24/1	0
	75/1	5	1	0	5	0	81/1	5

JOHN GREGSON

JOHN GROGAN

Mansfield Town have been well-served by central defenders, almost since their foundation and Johnnie Grogan is a name which always crops up when the older supporters reminisce over previous occupiers of this vital position. Like many other of the Stags' players over the years, his original club was Leicester City, who discovered the young Scot prior to the war playing for Shawfield Juniors. He returned to Filbert Street in 1946, but after only one season and 17 senior appearances, he made the short move to Field Mill, joining the club in September 1947. He served them well for the next five seasons and was an ever-present in two seasons, 1948-9 and 1950-51, but had the disappointment of never scoring a goal for the Stags over his five seasons with them. Grogan was born in Paisley in October 1915.

	LEAGUE		*FA CUP*		*TOTAL*	
	App	*Gls*	*App*	*Gls*	*App*	*Gls*
1947-48	34	0	3	0	37	0
1948-49	42	0	3	0	45	0
1949-50	37	0	2	0	39	0
1950-51	46	0	6	0	52	0
1951-52	42	0	2	0	44	0
	201	0	16	0	217	0

Winger Brian Hall first came to Mansfield Town's notice whilst playing for the Derbyshire non-League side, Belper Town, and moved to Field Mill in April 1959, making his debut against Bournemouth at Field Mill on 25 April in the penultimate match of the 1958-9 season. Brian, no relation to Ian Hall, made 72 appearances and scored 19 League goals for the Stags in just over six seasons before moving to Colchester United in March 1965 to become a firm favourite with the Layer Road fans. His career with the Essex club saw him make 324 League appearances and score 29 goals before dropping out of League football in 1972. He was born at Burbage in March 1939.

	LEAGUE		*FA CUP*		*FL CUP*		*TOTAL*	
	App	*Gls*	*App*	*Gls*	*App*	*Gls*	*App*	*Gls*
1958-59	2	1	0	0	-	-	2	1
1959-60	15	3	1	0	-	-	16	3
1960-61	4	0	0	0	0	0	4	0
1961-62	14	3	2	2	0	0	16	5
1962-63	16	4	1	1	3	2	20	7
1963-64	11	6	0	0	0	0	11	6
1964-65	10	2	0	0	2	0	12	2
	72	19	4	3	5	2	81	24

BRIAN HALL

IAN HALL

An all-round sportsman, Ian Hall had a distinguished career as a batsman with his native Derbyshire, as well as making his mark in football with Derby County and Mansfield Town. But the Sutton Scarsdale-born inside-forward began his soccer career as an amateur with Wolverhampton Wanderers after earning England Schoolboy honours. After his move to the Baseball Ground he added England Youth caps to his collection. After two seasons, 44 appearances and 13 goals for the Rams, Hall moved to Mansfield in September 1962, not doubt persuaded by the fact that former Derby star, Raich Carter, was in charge of the Stags. He made 159 League and Cup appearances during his six-season stay with the club, continuing his cricketing career with Derbyshire for a time after hanging up his football boots. Indeed, Hall, an opening bat and good close fielder, scored 11,666 runs (nine centuries) altogether for his county. He then spent four years at Birmingham University, gaining an honours degree in Physical Education and Social Administration. Twelve months at Loughborough College followed to earn his teaching certificate and then as his varied career continued, Hall lectured at Leicester Polytechnic for a year before assuming the duties of secretary of Scarborough CC for two years. He became a house-master at Ashbourne's Queen Elizabeth Grammar School and now teaches history at Hasland Hall School, Dronfield. Ian Hall continues his contact with cricket as a radio commentator both on Derbyshire and, occasionally, Nottinghamshire matches. And to complete a full circle he has more recently taken up commentating on soccer phone-in lines.

	LEAGUE		*FA CUP*		*FL CUP*		*TOTAL*	
	App	*Gls*	*App*	*Gls*	*App*	*Gls*	*App*	*Gls*
1962-63	16	1	2	1	1	0	19	2
1963-64	7	1	1	1	0	0	8	2
1964-65	34	4	2	1	1	0	37	5
1965-66	41	1	1	0	1	0	43	1
1966-67	34	3	4	0	1	0	39	3
1967-68	13	0	0	0	0	0	13	0
	145	10	10	3	4	0	159	13

Bristol City were paid what was then considered a 'substantial' transfer fee of £250 for the services of Teddy Harston in October 1935, and certainly Mansfield had no cause to regret their outlay over the next two seasons. Harston had previous spells with Sheffield Wednesday, Barnsley and Reading before joining City, but had not achieved the success he subsequently enjoyed at Field Mill. He made his debut at Southport on 19 October 1935 and scored a hat-trick to mark his arrival on the Mansfield scene in a 3-3 draw which gave the Stags their first away point of the season. His initial season could be described as highly satisfactory, as he scored 26 goals in 29 appearances, but this paled into insignificance compared with his exploits in 1936-7. Harston missed only one match in the campaign and scored 55 League goals, as well as three in the FA Cup, to share the top goalscorer honours with Joe Payne of Luton. During the season he netted seven hat-tricks, scored seven goals in one game against Hartlepool United, and five goals in each of two other matches. According to the minutes of a board meeting on 31 March 1937, manager Harry Parkes reported that Liverpool FC had made an enquiry about the transfer of Harston to Anfield. A price of £3,000 was placed on the player's head, but when the move was completed in the close season there was no mention of the fee which changed hands, only the usual description 'substantial'. As it turned out Harston broke a leg after playing only five games for the Reds, and did not appear again in the League. Two years later, a local newspaper reported that Harston had moved into non-League football and was playing for Ramsgate Town.

TED HARSTON

	LEAGUE		*FA CUP*		*D3N CUP*		*TOTAL*	
	App	*Gls*	*App*	*Gls*	*App*	*Gls*	*App*	*Gls*
1935-36	29	26	1	1	1	0	31	27
1936-37	41	55	2	3	1	0	44	58
	70	81	3	4	2	0	75	85

Cockney-born, at Custom House in the East End of London, goalkeeper Kevin Hitchcock was spotted by Nottingham Forest playing in youth football with a Barking club. He was taken on the City Ground staff, signed professional forms in August 1983 and was loaned out to Mansfield Town, making his debut at Colchester on 10 March 1984. Hitchcock made 14 appearances that season, plus one in the County Cup against his parent club, Forest. The youngster impressed so much in those matches and had become so popular with the supporters that his move was made permanent during the close season, for a modest fee but with a proviso that any future transfer fees were to be shared equally with Forest, a requirement which Mansfield were later to regret. Hitchcock kept 21 clean sheets in his first full season with Mansfield and helped the club to reach with Northern Area Final of the Freight/Rover Trophy, in which Wigan won through to Wembley after a penalty shoot-out at Field Mill. He repeated the feat the following year as Mansfield gained promotion to Division Three, but it was in the 1986-7 season that Hitchcock reached the peak of his popularity when he saved two spot-kicks in the penalty shoot-out at Wembley against Bristol City to bring the Freight/Rover Trophy to Mansfield. He was transferred to Chelsea, for £250,000 in March 1988, half of which was claimed by Forest. However, a series of injuries has marred his progress, and he has seen little first-team football since leaving Mansfield.

KEVIN HITCHCOCK

	LEAGUE		*FA CUP*		*FL CUP*		*OTHERS*		*TOTAL*	
	App	*Gls*	*App*	*Gls*	*App*	*Gls*	*App*	*Gls*	*App*	*Gls*
1983-84	14	0	0	0	0	0	0	0	14	0
1984-85	43	0	2	0	2	0	6	0	53	0
1985-86	46	0	2	0	4	0	3	0	55	0
1986-87	46	0	1	0	2	0	8	0	57	0
1987-88	33	0	5	0	4	0	3	0	45	0
	182	0	10	0	12	0	20	0	224	0

Geordie Gordon Hodgson was a member of Newcastle United junior teams whilst at school but did not join the Magpies' full-time staff until he had completed his grammar school education at the age of 18. Nevertheless, he earned England Youth International honours and, although first-team outings were infrequent, he was a member of United's FA Cup squad for the unsuccessful trip to Wembley in 1974. The stylish midfield player with a cultured left foot had attracted the attention of Mansfield's chief scout, the legendary Sam Weaver, who persuaded the Stags' new boss, Dave Smith, that his signing was a 'must'. And Weaver was proved correct as Hodgson played a major role in Mansfield's first-ever League championship in the 1974-5 season and again when the club lifted the Third Division title two seasons later, to ensure Mansfield's one and only stay, so far, in Division Two. Hodgson moved to Oxford United in September 1978 and two years later joined Peterborough United, where he ended his League career to join the local police force.

	LEAGUE		*FA CUP*		*FL CUP*		*TOTAL*	
	App	*Gls*	*App*	*Gls*	*App*	*Gls*	*App*	*Gls*
1974-75	44	10	6	1	1	0	51	11
1975-76	46	7	4	0	6	0	56	7
1976-77	46	4	3	0	3	0	52	4
1977-78	42	2	2	0	2	0	46	2
1978-79	6	0	0	0	2	0	8	0
	184	23	15	1	14	0	213	24

GORDON HODGSON

Pinxton-born Ivan Hollett's first club was Derby County, where he played as an amateur, but he first came to the notice of senior clubs whilst playing for local senior non-League team, Sutton Town. He joined the Field Mill staff shortly after his 18th birthday in August 1958, signed by Sam Weaver, who had played for Sutton Town in his younger days. Hollett also served under Raich Carter and Tommy Cummings before a tragedy for neighbouring Chesterfield saw Hollett move to the Derbyshire club. In December 1964, in an horrific motor accident, the Spireites lost four of their senior players. Centre-forward Roger Hunt died in the crash and Doug Wragg, Ron Powell and Peter Stringfellow suffered injuries which caused a premature end to their careers. As a neighbourly gesture, Hollett was allowed to move to Saltergate as several clubs rallied round to help out the club. He made over 150 appearances for Chesterfield over the next four seasons and scored 65 goals before joining Crewe Alexandra. Whilst at Gresty Road, Hollett was the subject of a transfer bid by First Division Stoke City which was accepted. But he suffered a serious injury in the match prior to completing the move and the opportunity to play in the top division was lost. He subsequently had spells with Cambridge United and Hereford United before returning to the Mansfield area and joining the mining engineering industry. In recent years he has been in charge of coaching the young players on schoolboy forms with Mansfield Town.

IVAN HOLLETT

	LEAGUE		*FA CUP*		*FL CUP*		*TOTAL*	
	App	*Gls*	*App*	*Gls*	*App*	*Gls*	*App*	*Gls*
1958-59	2	0	0	0	-	-	2	0
1959-60	21	15	0	0	-	-	21	15
1960-61	26	10	0	0	0	0	26	10
1961-62	15	3	0	0	3	1	18	4
1962-63	19	9	3	5	3	1	25	15
1963-64	10	1	0	0	0	0	10	1
1964-65	5	2	0	0	0	0	5	2
	98	40	3	5	6	2	107	47

DAVE HOLLINS

Dave Hollins was born in Bangor, North Wales, and his brother, John, in Guildford, Essex. So, although they both followed football as a career with some success, Dave was a Welsh international, whilst John played for England. And, of course, whilst John was a midfield dynamo, Dave earned his honours as a goalkeeper. It was with Brighton & Hove Albion that Dave began his career, joining the Goldstone staff in November 1955. He made 66 appearances for Brighton before his transfer to Newcastle United in March 1960. In February 1967, Hollins moved south to join Mansfield, then under the guidance of Tommy Cummings, and just six months before Tom Eggleston took over the reins at Field Mill. He was in the successful FA Cup line-up in season 1968-9 when the Stags reached the sixth round, the furthest they had ever gone in the competition. And he played in the first three rounds the following season but lost his place to Graham Brown for the next two rounds as the Stags went as far as the fifth round. Dave had a short spell on loan with Nottingham Forest towards the end of that season and in the 1970 close season, he joined Aldershot to round off his career.

	LEAGUE		*FA CUP*		*FL CUP*		*TOTAL*	
	App	*Gls*	*App*	*Gls*	*App*	*Gls*	*App*	*Gls*
1966-67	13	0	0	0	0	0	13	0
1967-68	41	0	1	0	1	0	43	0
1968-69	44	0	7	0	1	0	52	0
1969-70	13	0	4	0	1	0	18	0
	111	0	12	0	3	0	126	0

Although Wilf Humble was born in that hotbed of soccer talent, Ashington, which produced the Charltons and Milburns etc, the only senior club in his career was Mansfield Town. He was 23 when he moved into the Football League after playing with his home-town club, and after seven seasons at Field Mill, he left the game to become a pillar of Mansfield industry, forming his own highly-successful company manufacturing industrial clothing. But until his untimely death in 1988, he continued to enjoy his football, raising considerable amounts of money for local charities with his All-Star XI. Before his Mansfield career concluded in 1966, the consistent full-back had made over 200 appearances, with perhaps his best memory coming in the 1961-2 season, when he scored his only League goal, against Colchester United on 15 January 1962, upon his return after missing the previous 27 matches through injury. Wilf Humble scored one further goal — in the FA Cup first-round match at Accrington Stanley on 14 November 1959, when the Stags won 2-1 and went on to reach the third round.

	LEAGUE		*FA CUP*		*FL CUP*		*TOTAL*	
	App	*Gls*	*App*	*Gls*	*App*	*Gls*	*App*	*Gls*
1959-60	37	0	3	1	-	-	40	1
1960-61	14	0	0	0	0	0	14	0
1961-62	21	1	0	0	0	0	21	1
1962-63	41	0	5	0	1	0	47	0
1963-64	46	0	1	0	2	0	49	0
1964-65	17	0	0	0	0	0	17	0
1965-66	22	0	1	0	2	0	25	0
	198	1	10	1	5	0	213	2

WILF HUMBLE

Alan Jarvis was one of several internationals to play for Mansfield Town but unfortunately his career at Field Mill was cut short by an injury which, ironically, he did not receive pursuing his football career. Whilst playing squash to maintain his fitness during the 1973 close season, he lost the sight in one eye after being struck by the ball and was forced to give up the professional game. The classy midfielder was born in Wrexham in August 1943 and began his career at Goodison Park in 1961, when he was 18, after joining the club as a junior. But he failed to make the Everton senior side and in June 1965 he was transferred to Hull City, where he made over 150 appearances and gained his three Welsh caps. He was transferred to Mansfield in March 1971 and was popular with the fans before sustaining the injury which ended his career when he was only 29.

	LEAGUE		*FA CUP*		*FL CUP*		*TOTAL*	
	App	*Gls*	*App*	*Gls*	*App*	*Gls*	*App*	*Gls*
1970-71	12	0	0	0	0	0	12	0
1971-72	40/2	0	4	0	2	0	46/2	0
1972-73	24/4	0	1	0	1	0	26/4	0
	76/6	0	5	0	3	0	84/6	0

ALAN JARVIS

BRIAN JAYES

This talented half-back joined his home-town club, Leicester City, as a 20-year-old but managed only three senior appearances in his one season at Filbert Street. He then joined the almost customary exodus of City players in the decade after the war, to Field Mill. Jayes had an excellent start to his career with Mansfield, making his debut in a 5-1 home win over Carlisle United on 25 August 1956. He had two long spells on the sidelines because of injury during his period at Mansfield, but still managed to make 125 League and Cup appearances before leaving the club and the senior game in 1960. But like many half-backs in his day, his goals were few and far between. Indeed, his only score for the Stags came on 8 April 1958, in a 2-1 home win against Halifax Town.

	LEAGUE		*FA CUP*		*TOTAL*	
	App	*Gls*	*App*	*Gls*	*App*	*Gls*
1956-57	42	0	2	0	44	0
1957-58	34	1	4	0	38	1
1958-59	19	0	1	0	20	0
1959-60	20	0	3	0	23	0
	115	1	10	0	125	1

HARRY JOHNSON

Harry Johnson held the unique distinction of being one of that rare breed of senior soccer players, who have scored over 300 goals in a career. And he was unique by virtue of the fact that he was the only one of that select band who was a part-time player, for his full-time daytime occupation when he was not 'steeling' goals, was as a metalurgist in a Sheffield steelworks. Between 1919 and 1930, he scored 225 League and Cup goals for Sheffield United, a club to which his family gave tremendous service over the years. His father won three FA Cup medals with the Blades, was in their Championship-winning side in 1897-8 and also gained international honours. His younger brother, Tom, played in United's FA Cup-winning team in 1936. Whilst with Mansfield, Harry added another 114 goals to his tally, scored in only 172 League and Cup outings. Although a mere 'midget' by centre-forward standards — he was only 5ft 8in tall and never weighed more than 10st — he was rarely injured. But to illustrate his resilience, in March 1934 he broke his wrist in a game at Barrow. The X-ray revealed that he had broken the wrist in six other places over the years without him realizing. Harry Johnson died in May 1981 at the age of 82.

	LEAGUE		*FA CUP*		*FL CUP*		*TOTAL*	
	App	*Gls*	*App*	*Gls*	*App*	*Gls*	*App*	*Gls*
1931-32	40	32	1	0	0	0	41	32
1932-33	38	30	1	1	0	0	39	31
1933-34	32	18	2	2	1	2	35	22
1934-35	39	17	3	5	0	0	42	22
1935-36	14	7	0	0	1	0	15	7
	163	104	7	8	2	2	172	114

David Jones was yet another Leicester City player who moved on to Mansfield to complete his career in football. And he was yet another Welsh international to figure on the Stags' playing staff. This dependable full-back was also another player whose career was restricted by World War Two, a career which began at Ebbw Vale and extended to Orient and Millwall and seven Welsh international caps before the start of hostilities. He resumed his career with Leicester in 1946 and after one season and 33 appearances was recruited by Mansfield. After making his debut on 4 October 1947, in a home meeting with Rotherham United, Jones missed only one match during his stay at Field Mill.

	LEAGUE		*FA CUP*		*TOTAL*	
	App	*Gls*	*App*	*Gls*	*App*	*Gls*
1947-48	33	0	3	0	36	0
1948-49	41	0	3	0	44	0
	74	0	6	0	80	0

DAVID JONES

Neath-born David Jones, more popularly known as Dai by the Field Mill faithful, made the transition from his local club Ton Pentre to Millwall to launch his professional football career in 1964. But after only a single season at The Den, he was back in his native Wales with Newport County, where the 'poaching' qualities of this exuberant forward earned him 25 League goals in 82 outings, an asset which attracted the attention and made him one of the earliest signings of the new Mansfield manager, Tom Eggleston. Dai Jones made his debut on 23 December 1967 and forged an immediate understanding with another striker, Bob Ledger, who had joined the Stags at the same time. Jones' impact was immediate, for he scored six goals in his first five games, Ledger putting away three in the same period. Jones was out of action injured during the successful 1968-9 FA Cup run which saw Mansfield reach the sixth round, but he played a prominent role the following season when the Stags made it to the fifth round. He was particularly effective in the fourth-round meeting with First Division Blackpool, scoring both goals in the Stags' 2-0 win, the first after two minutes and the second two minutes from time. The Welshman spent just over another year at Field Mill before returning, at his own request, to Newport County in November 1971 for a nominal £500 fee.

	LEAGUE		*FA CUP*		*FL CUP*		*TOTAL*	
	App	*Gls*	*App*	*Gls*	*App*	*Gls*	*App*	*Gls*
1967-68	22	8	0	0	0	0	22	8
1968-69	19/4	4	0/1	0	0	0	19/5	4
1969-70	31/3	10	4/1	2	0	0	35/4	12
1970-71	39/2	9	0/1	0	3	0	42/3	9
1971-72	5/5	1	0	0	0	0	5/5	1
	116/14	32	4/3	2	3	0	123/17	34

DAVID (DAI) JONES

Mark 'Scouse' Kearney was obviously a native of Liverpool, whose first taste of professional football was with Everton, who had discovered the youngster playing for local non-League outfit, Marine. He joined the Toffeemen as a 19-year-old but, as so often happens, saw little hope of a regular first-team spot at Goodison Park. However, the experienced manager, Ian Greaves, who had just surprised the soccer world by taking over the reins at Fourth Division Mansfield in February 1983, had noted the youngster on his travels and made him his first signing for the Stags. Kearney moved to Field Mill primarily as a left-back, but it was not long before his 'no compromise' attitude saw Greaves decide to use the youngster as his hard-man midfielder. He became the king-pin of Greaves' team selections and it was a bitter blow for the Stags when he broke a leg in an innocuous-looking tackle early in the home game with Fulham in the fourth League match of 1987-8 season, when Mansfield were hoping to build on their Freight/Rover Trophy success of the previous season. Kearney was out for the remainder of the season and was badly missed. And he took time to settle when he resumed in the following campaign. When skipper George Foster was appointed player-manager following the shock departure of Ian Greaves in February 1989, almost six years to the day he took over, Kearney was appointed team captain.

MARK KEARNEY

	LEAGUE		*FA CUP*		*FL CUP*		*FR Trophy*		*TOTAL*	
	App	*Gls*	*App*	*Gls*	*App*	*Gls*	*App*	*Gls*	*App*	*Gls*
1982-83	11	1	0	0	0	0	0	0	11	1
1983-84	17	2	0/1	0	2	0	0	0	19/1	2
1984-85	37/1	4	2	0	2	0	6	1	47/1	5
1985-86	30	7	2	0	3	1	1	0	36	8
1986-87	43	10	1	0	1	0	7	1	52	11
1987-88	4	0	0	0	2	0	0	0	6	0
1988-89	44/1	2	0/2	1	2	0	2	0	48/3	3
1989-90	42	3	1	0	4	1	4	1	51	5
	228/2	29	6/3	1	16	2	20	3	270/5	35

RAY KEELEY

Ray Keeley's soccer career began as an apprentice at The Valley with Charlton Athletic, when Jock Basford was in charge of coaching the youngsters at the club. But he managed only a single first-team outing in his first season as a professional in 1964. A spell with Exeter City followed and after 45 appearances and ten goals in two seasons at St James' Park, he dropped out of the League and had a couple of seasons with Crawley Town. However, Basford, now Tom Eggleston's assistant, had not forgotten the youngster's potential and he persuaded Eggleston to sign the Londoner just prior to the 1968-9 season. He held down a regular first-team place, apart from when injured, during that campaign and played in every round of the successful FA Cup run which took the Stags to the sixth round. He scored three vital goals in that run, his most memorable being the one against First Division West Ham, who went down 3-0 at Field Mill in round five, the shock result of the competition that season. Keeley had a series of injuries the following season which kept him sidelined for weeks and he was able to make only 15 League and Cup appearances throughout the campaign. Subsequently, he was given a free transfer and dropped out of the League.

	LEAGUE		*FA CUP*		*FL CUP*		*TOTAL*	
	App	*Gls*	*App*	*Gls*	*App*	*Gls*	*App*	*Gls*
1968-69	37/3	4	7	3	1	1	45/3	8
1969-70	11/1	1	3/1	2	1	0	15/2	3
	48/4	5	10/1	5	2	1	60/5	11

Kevin Kent achieved many memorable occasions throughout his football career, even as a schoolboy when he played for his home-town schools team Stoke Boys. He also made the Staffordshire County team and had an England trial. But his outstanding moment will never be forgotten by the thousands of Mansfield Town supporters who made the trip to the 1987 Freight/Rover Trophy Final, when he achieved the supreme moment for any professional player — he scored at Wembley. To cap his afternoon, he was one of the successful penalty-takers in the only penalty competition to take place beneath the twin towers so far, as Mansfield snatched a dramatic victory. Surprisingly, his professional career was launched, not at Stoke as might have been expected, but at West Bromwich Albion as an apprentice. However, after only one senior appearance he moved to Newport County for one season before being recruited by manager Ian Greaves at the start of the 1985-6 season. He spent the first month with his new club almost as a permanent substitute, but had every cause to recall with pleasure his first full senior outing with Mansfield. That was against Chelsea in the second round of the Milk Cup, after Mansfield had disposed of another Second Division club, Middlesbrough, in the previous round. The Blues were held to a 2-2 draw in the first leg at Mansfield, but the Stags bowed out of the competition at Stamford Bridge, losing 2-0. Promotion to Division Three, however, was the icing on the cake for Mansfield at the end of that season in which Kent played his part, and also in the following season when the club's new-found status was consolidated. Indeed, the Staffordshire lad has been a key figure in Mansfield plans right from the day he signed, during which time his skill, flair and enthusiasm have never diminished.

KEVIN KENT

	LEAGUE		*FA CUP*		*FL CUP*		*FR Trophy*		*TOTAL*	
	App	*Gls*	*App*	*Gls*	*App*	*Gls*	*App*	*Gls*	*App*	*Gls*
1985-86	31/2	8	2	0	2	0	1/1	0	36/3	8
1986-87	46	7	1	0	2	1	8	3	57	11
1987-88	45	10	5	3	4	1	4	2	58	16
1988-89	36/3	5	2	1	0	0	2	0	40/3	6
1989-90	38	2	1	0	0	0	3/1	0	42/1	2
	196/5	32	11	4	8	2	18/2	5	233/7	43

One of defender Tony Kenworthy's biggest disappointments in a career which has spanned nearly 15 years was the fact that a string of niggling injuries sidelined him virtually for the entire campaign in 1989-90, the first full season in which his central defender partner, George Foster, was in charge. An ankle problem was followed by an equally long-term knee injury and then by a damaged Achilles tendon which required an operation. His experience was badly missed by Mansfield in a difficult season, experience which had blossomed during his 10 years with Sheffield United. Leeds-born Kenworthy joined the Bramall Lane staff as an apprentice and turned full-time professional during the 1975-6 season. He made over 250 League appearances for the Blades and also earned England Youth honours. He moved to Mansfield on loan just before the transfer deadline in March 1986, to boost the Stags' successful bid for promotion. The move was made permanent in time for the following season and Mansfield fans will always remember the Yorkshireman as the player who remained calm and collected to score that winning penalty at Wembley in May 1987. He also played a major role in the Northern Area Final at Chester which earned the Stags a Wembley place. Another former Blade, Paul Garner, was injured in the opening minutes and Kenworthy took over at left-back to help restrict Chester to a single goal as they sought to close a 2-0 gap from the first leg. Kenworthy's soccer future is in the balance after his Achilles operation, but it will be a tragedy if his sound defensive qualities are lost to the game.

	LEAGUE		*FA CUP*		*FL CUP*		*FR Trophy*		*TOTAL*	
	App	*Gls*	*App*	*Gls*	*App*	*Gls*	*App*	*Gls*	*App*	*Gls*
1985-86	13	0	0	0	0	0	3	0	16	0
1986-87	36	0	1	0	2	0	6/1	0	45/1	0
1987-88	29/1	0	3	0	1	0	1	0	34/1	0
1988-89	19/1	0	2	0	2	0	2	0	25/1	0
1989-90	1	0	0	0	0	0	0	0	1	0
	98/2	0	6	0	5	0	12/1	0	121/3	0

TONY KENWORTHY

TOM KNOX

Glaswegian Tom Knox was a rare breed of footballer in his day — an 'out-and-out' outside-left. It was a quality which saw Chelsea sign the 22-year-old from his first club, East Stirling, and which also persuaded Newcastle United to take the winger back north just after the great Jackie Milburn had ended his magnificent ten-year career with the Magpies. Knox made only 20 senior appearances in his two seasons at Stamford Bridge, and first-team appearances were almost as rare in a similar period at St James' Park, for he pulled on the famous black and white stripes on only 24 occasions. He fared somewhat better after moving to Field Mill in March 1967, appearing 34 times in the Stags' senior side before moving on again to Northampton in November of the same year. With the Cobblers he had 28 senior games before disappearing from the League scene.

	LEAGUE		*FA CUP*		*FL CUP*		*TOTAL*	
	App	*Gls*	*App*	*Gls*	*App*	*Gls*	*App*	*Gls*
1966-67	13	2	0	0	0	0	13	2
1967-68	21	3	1	0	1	1	23	4
	34	5	1	0	1	1	36	6

JOHN LATHAN

It was a reluctant John Lathan who agreed in the end to move to Mansfield Town from his home-town club, Sunderland, in the player plus cash deal which saw Dennis Longhorn move to Roker Park from the Stags. But the busy midfielder, who had joined Sunderland as an apprentice and had over 50 senior outings with the club after signing professional in April 1969, had no call to regret the move. Indeed, he was very much a part of the Mansfield line-up which earned the club's first-ever League championship in 1974-5, the season after he had made the move in February 1974. But the following season his appearances were restricted by injury and, just before the end of January 1976, he moved to Carlisle United for a reported £11,000 fee. After two seasons at Brunton Park, which included a short spell on loan with Barnsley, he spent a period abroad but returned to join Portsmouth in March 1978. In August 1979 he joined Mansfield for the second time, but was not retained after one season and another short spell abroad followed. He was training to deal with sports injuries whilst in his final spell with Mansfield and recently was back in England, looking for a position in that field.

	LEAGUE		*FA CUP*		*FL CUP*		*TOTAL*	
	App	*Gls*	*App*	*Gls*	*App*	*Gls*	*App*	*Gls*
1973-74	17	5	0	0	0	0	17	5
1974-75	45	9	6	0	0	0	51	9
1975-76	10/2	0	0	0	2	1	12/2	1
1979-80	29	1	2	0	3	0	34	1
	101/2	15	8	0	5	1	114/2	16

Mick Laverick was another of those local youngsters, discovered by Mansfield Town, who went on to make his mark in the football profession. He joined the Stags as an apprentice and came up through the ranks along with several other local notables, including Colin and Barry Foster and John Saunders, to make his debut on 12 August 1972, in a 1-0 home win over Northampton Town. The young midfield player never really commanded a regular first-team place, but could always be relied upon for a consistent performance whenever called up for senior duty. When manager Dave Smith was dismissed near the end of the 1975-6 season and moved almost immediately to Southend United, his first excursion into the transfer market was to sign Laverick, who had just completed five seasons at Field Mill. In three seasons at Roots Hall, Laverick made well over 100 appearances before he became a target of Huddersfield Town, moving to Leeds Road in June 1979. After two seasons at Huddersfield, he joined York City, but had a short loan spell with the Huddersfield club before moving into non-League football with clubs in the vicinity of his home village of Ollerton in Nottinghamshire, where his father had moved when he was a youngster from his native North East to work in the local colliery. More recently, Mick Laverick became a prison officer but still finds time to coach players in his home village, competing in local amateur football.

	LEAGUE		*FA CUP*		*FL CUP*		*TOTAL*	
	App	*Gls*	*App*	*Gls*	*App*	*Gls*	*App*	*Gls*
1972-73	12/5	2	1	0	1	1	14/5	3
1973-74	30/6	5	1/1	0	2	1	33/7	6
1974-75	9/2	3	0/1	0	1	0	10/3	3
1975-76	22/3	3	1	1	3	2	26/3	6
1976-77	0	0	0	0	2	0	2	0
	73/16	13	3/2	1	9	4	85/18	18

MICK LAVERICK

Bob Ledger began his soccer career as a winger with Huddersfield Town, a club he joined as a junior, and made over 70 League and Cup appearances for the Terriers in his six seasons at Leeds Road. But it was with Carlisle United that his career really took off, not as a winger but as the target man in the attack. He chalked up over 250 senior League and Cup outings for United in five seasons, including 222 in the League, before moving to Field Mill in November 1967 as one of manager Tom Eggleston's first signings after taking over in the previous August. Ledger played a vital role in Mansfield's remarkable FA Cup run in the 1968-9 season, which took them to the sixth round before bowing out to Leicester City, after they had knocked out West Ham United, England World Cup stars and all. But the following season, before the Stags had embarked upon another FA Cup run which took them to the fifth round, Ledger had returned to his favourite North-West to join Barrow, where he ended his outstanding career. However, Bob Ledger is by no means a forgotten man at Field Mill, where the supporters always admired his skill and commitment in one of the club's most outstanding periods.

	LEAGUE		*FA CUP*		*FL CUP*		*TOTAL*	
	App	*Gls*	*App*	*Gls*	*App*	*Gls*	*App*	*Gls*
1967-68	15/2	4	0	0	0	0	15/2	4
1968-69	34/1	9	7	3	0	0	41/1	12
1969-70	2/3	1	0	0	1	1	3/3	2
	51/6	14	7	3	1	1	59/6	18

BOB LEDGER

Birmingham-born Jack Lewis, who was christened John, was already a talented 16-year-old junior on West Bromwich Albion's books when World War Two broke out. Like many of his contemporaries, the hostilities restricted his career but he still had many years before him when war ended, although it was 1948 before he really made his mark. Given a free transfer by Albion, he joined Mansfield Town on a month's trial in August 1948 and became part of the permanent staff well before the end of the four weeks. He made his senior debut on 30 August 1948, in a home game against Bradford City, and celebrated with a 1-0 victory. But all-told he pulled on a first-team shirt on only four occasions that season. However, by the 1949-50 campaign he had established himself as a regular member of the senior side in that purple patch in the Stags affairs, affectionately known as the 'Freddie Steele' era. The powerful half-back was a member of the team which battled their way into the fifth round of the FA Cup in 1950-51 and the meeting with Stanley Matthews and Blackpool. But, on the other side of the coin, he was in the line-up which drew 1-1 away with non-League Stockton in the first round the following season (he scored the equalizer from the penalty-spot) but then lost the replay 2-0 at Field Mill. After his initial season, Lewis rarely missed a game in the following three, achieving maximum appearances in 1950-51 and 1951-52. But gradually he gave way to younger players in his fifth and final season at Field Mill, and his last in the Football League. He was a very proficient golfer and won the Professional Footballers' Association tournament. Indeed, he could have taken up golf in the professional ranks and been assured of an excellent living. When he reached the end of his football career, he became a representative for a golf equipment company, participating in tournaments all over Great Britain, as part of his duties.

JACK LEWIS

	LEAGUE		*FA CUP*		*TOTAL*	
	App	*Gls*	*App*	*Gls*	*App*	*Gls*
1948-49	4	0	0	0	4	0
1949-50	39	1	2	0	41	1
1950-51	46	5	6	0	52	5
1951-52	46	4	2	1	48	5
1952-53	28	1	3	0	31	1
	163	11	13	1	176	12

DENNIS LONGHORN

Whilst in between clubs after being dismissed by Sheffield Wednesday, Danny Williams lived in Bournemouth and kept in touch with football in general and AFC Bournemouth in particular. And he was impressed by the form shown by a young midfield player, Southampton-born Dennis Longhorn, who had joined the club as an apprentice. Longhorn turned professional when he was 18, although he had made his League debut whilst still in the junior ranks. In his four seasons at Dean Court, he made only 30 first-team appearances but did enough to bring him to Williams' attention. Within a month of taking over the Mansfield hot seat in the first week of November 1971, Williams had made the young midfield player his first transfer target, bringing him to Field Mill in time to make his debut on 18 December against Plymouth. The Stags lost that one 3-2, but had something to celebrate as these were the first League goals scored at home in that season. The skilful midfield player spent three seasons at Field Mill before joining Sunderland in February 1974, in a deal which took John Lathan to Mansfield, plus a £20,000 fee. Longhorn spent three seasons at Roker Park before moving to Sheffield United, then Aldershot and Colchester United, where he completed his career.

	LEAGUE		*FA CUP*		*FL CUP*		*TOTAL*	
	App	*Gls*	*App*	*Gls*	*App*	*Gls*	*App*	*Gls*
1971-72	26/1	1	0	0	0	0	26/1	1
1972-73	39/1	2	1	0	2	1	42/1	3
1973-74	28/1	2	4	0	1	0	33/1	2
	93/3	5	5	0	3	1	101/3	6

Tony Lowery was a player from the North-East who slipped through the scouting nets of the major clubs in the area, despite being a member of the same county schoolboy team as England and Liverpool star Peter Beardsley. Born in Wallsend, he was a member of the Ashington FC side which has provided more than its fair share of soccer greats over the years. The midfielder started his Football League career with West Bromwich Albion when he was 19, but found first-team opportunities at a premium at The Hawthorns. A loan spell with Walsall whetted his appetite for a senior place and when his talents were recalled by John Jarman, Ian Greaves' assistant in the new management team at Field Mill, Lowery had no hesitation in making the move. He has been a key figure in the Stags' plans for most of the eight seasons he has been with the club. Indeed, he missed only a few senior matches until the most recent two campaigns, when injury sidelined him for much of the time. Hoping for a change of fortune, Lowery asked for a transfer in February 1990, confident that he still has a great deal to offer for several seasons yet. Mansfield agreed but he will be badly missed. Mansfield supporters reckon that 'if Tony plays well, then the team plays well'.

	LEAGUE		*FA CUP*		*FL CUP*		*FR Trohpy*		*TOTAL*	
	App	*Gls*	*App*	*Gls*	*App*	*Gls*	*App*	*Gls*	*App*	*Gls*
1982-83	1	0	0	0	0	0	0	0	1	0
1983-84	44	6	2	0	2	0	1	0	49	6
1984-85	45	3	2	1	1	0	6	2	54	6
1985-86	40	5	2	0	4	0	3/1	1	49/1	6
1986-87	44	5	1	0	2	0	8	1	55	6
1987-88	44	0	5	1	4	0	4	1	57	2
1988-89	11/1	0	2	0	2	0	2	0	17/1	0
1989-90	14	0	1	0	4	0	1	0	20	0
	243/1	19	15	2	19	0	25/1	5	302/2	26

TONY LOWERY

Goal poacher Jim Lumby spent just over one season at Field Mill, but what the Stags would give for a player with his scoring touch these days. He was born in Grimsby and followed in his father's footsteps by becoming a Grimsby Town player soon after his 19th birthday. (Lumby senior was on the Blundell Park staff in pre-war days.) Jim junior knocked in 12 League goals in 28 outings before moving into non-League with Brigg Town for a couple of seasons before Scunthorpe United took notice of his goal-grabbing ability, signing him in March 1977. In just over a season at the Old Showground, Lumby netted 28 League goals in 55 outings, the sort of form which attracted the attentions of Carlisle United. He found goals a little harder to come by at Brunton Park, but after joining Tranmere Rovers he regained his scoring touch to add a further 21 League goals to his record in 43 games. In January 1981 he moved on to Mansfield, his final League club, and scored an average of more than one goal every three games. Even after his playing days ended, Jim Lumby has kept close to football — as the licensee of a pub near to the Grimsby Town ground in Cleethorpes.

	LEAGUE		*FA CUP*		*FL CUP*		*TOTAL*	
	App	*Gls*	*App*	*Gls*	*App*	*Gls*	*App*	*Gls*
1980-81	11/1	4	0	0	0	0	11/1	4
1981-82	38/1	14	0	0	4	3	42/1	17
	49/2	18	0	0	4	3	53/2	21

JIM LUMBY

JIM McCAFFREY

	LEAGUE		*FA CUP*		*FL CUP*		*TOTAL*	
	App	*Gls*	*App*	*Gls*	*App*	*Gls*	*App*	*Gls*
1972-73	45	7	0	0	2	1	47	8
1973-74	37/3	3	4	1	1	0	42/3	4
1974-75	37/2	6	6	2	0/1	0	43/3	8
1975-76	35/1	2	2	0	4	0	41/1	2
1976-77	16/2	3	3	0	3	2	22/2	5
	170/8	21	15	3	10/1	3	195/9	27

Ask any keen Mansfield Town fan to name his favourite player from the past two decades and the name of the 'wizard of the wing', Jim McCaffrey, will be high on the list. Luton-born McCaffrey was a member of the nearby St Albans Boys team when he was spotted by a Leeds United scout and offered a trial at Elland Road. He was turned down by United but Nottingham Forest had begun to take notice and he joined the City Ground staff. Soon, McCaffrey was in the England Youth side, playing alongside Steve Perryman, Steve Whitworth, Len Cantello and Tony Towers in the 'Little World Cup' qualifying rounds. He played in three of the four qualifying matches — in the one he missed, England defeated Ireland 10-1 — but they still failed to qualify. McCaffrey began to challenge for a first-team place with Forest and was a substitute 15 times before making his full debut at Hillsborough. But his chances were limited and in July 1972 he was snapped up on a free transfer by Mansfield manager, Danny Williams. Crosswords are one of his favourite pastimes and during his stay at Field Mill he was certainly a puzzle to many opposing defenders. He was an integral member of Dave Smith's Division Four championship side and the following season played a leading role as Division Three status was consolidated. At the start of the Peter Morris managerial era, and with the arrival of winger Johnnie Miller, McCaffrey gradually fell from favour. With 170 League appearances and 21 goals to his credit he moved to Huddersfield for a season and had similar spells with Portsmouth and Northampton Town. Then, with an eye on the future, he took over a newsagent's business in the Lake District and more recently moved to a similar venture in Leicestershire. He still plays Sunday soccer.

Central defender John McClelland is the only player to receive an international call-up whilst on the books of Mansfield Town. He was drafted into the Northern Ireland squad shortly after Billy Bingham had been appointed national team manager. Bingham, of course, was fully aware of the defender's ability from his days as the Stags' boss. McClelland went on gain 52 caps for his country. He skippered the side and figured in the 1982 and 1986 World Cups in Spain and Mexico. The Belfast-born player could well have made his name as a striker, for in 1974, whilst with Portadown, he joined Cardiff City as a forward. However, after making only a single appearance he was released and joined Bangor City, where he was spotted by Mansfield Town. He joined the Stags in May 1978, the first of Bingham's close-season signings, and quickly established himself in the first team with performances very akin to those of Liverpool's Alan Hansen. In the summer break of 1981 the popular McClelland was transferred to the top Scottish club, Rangers, for a £90,000 fee, and captained the side. He was on the move again in 1984, for £250,000 this time, to Watford where he was again appointed captain. From there he was transferred to Leeds United in the summer of 1989 but was kept out of the side for a time by injury. He had a spell back with Watford for a loan period half-way through the season, before returning to Elland Road and the first team for the vital run-in to the Second Division championship.

JOHN McCLELLAND

	LEAGUE		*FA CUP*		*FL CUP*		*TOTAL*	
	App	*Gls*	*App*	*Gls*	*App*	*Gls*	*App*	*Gls*
1978-79	33/3	1	1	0	2	0	36/3	1
1979-80	43	1	3	1	2/1	1	48/1	3
1980-81	46	6	4	0	4	1	54	7
	122/3	8	8	1	8/1	2	138/4	11

Midfield man Ian McDonald was the sort of player to make Bill Shankly reach for Liverpool's cheque book when the Barrow-born youngster was earning rave reviews with Workington. He began his career in the apprentice ranks of his home-town club and turned professional in May 1971, but Barrow's days as a Football League club were numbered and they were voted out of the League at the end of 1971-2. McDonald was the only professional on the club's books when a dispute saw him move on to Workington in February 1973 and 11 months later he appeared to have the world at his feet after a move to Liverpool. Three days after signing he played for Liverpool Reserves and impressed by scoring a goal. But he also broke his foot and on the Monday morning was back home with it in plaster. Trying to get back too early cost him almost a whole season and when he did return, places in the side were even harder to attain. He scored twice against Nottingham Forest Reserves in November but did not get another outing until January. A loan spell with Colchester followed but they could not afford the asking price for the player. Then a proposed move to Blackburn failed to materialize, so when Dave Smith, on the crest of a wave after achieving promotion the previous season, came in with a £10,000 bid, McDonald welcomed the move. Yet again, things did not quite work out as planned and York City was his next club where, from November 1977 to November 1981, he made over 200 League and Cup appearances and scored 29 goals. He joined Aldershot in November 1981 and has made over 300 League appearances for them, captaining the side and more recently coaching the young players at the Recreation Ground.

IAN McDONALD

	LEAGUE		*FA CUP*		*FL CUP*		*TOTAL*	
	App	*Gls*	*App*	*Gls*	*App*	*Gls*	*App*	*Gls*
1975-76	32/2	4	4	1	5	3	41/2	8
1976-77	15/7	0	2	0	0	0	17/7	0
1977-78	0	0	0	0	0/1	0	0/1	0
	47/9	4	6	1	5/1	3	58/10	8

In a period after World War Two, it seemed a natural progression of a Leicester City player's career to move to Mansfield Town and full-back Bill McGregor was another of the Filbert Street staff to make the trip. Born in Paisley, he first came to the notice of Leicester whilst a member of the local Mossdale YMCA team. He moved to Filbert Street in April 1947 but in his four seasons with the club, he found first-team appearances at a premium and figured in the side on only nine occasions. However, his move to Mansfield in time for the 1953-4 season saw him realize his true potential, as 118 League and five FA Cup outings in his three seasons at Field Mill clearly indicate.

BILL McGREGOR

	LEAGUE		*FA CUP*		*TOTAL*	
	App	*Gls*	*App*	*Gls*	*App*	*Gls*
1953-54	42	0	2	0	44	0
1954-55	39	0	1	0	40	0
1955-56	38	0	2	0	40	0
	119	0	5	0	124	0

CRAIG McKERNON

Craig McKernon is another of Mansfield Town's long list of home-grown players to show the potential to reach the big-time. In McKernon's case this is partly due to a positional change worked out by manager Ian Greaves. McKernon, a midfielder who hails from the Gloucester area, had a couple of first-team outings in the 1984-5 season, when he was barely 17, and made 11 full League and Cup appearances the following season. In 1986-7 he played in 14 League and Cup games, although not really threatening to claim a regular first-team spot. It was early in the 1988-9 season, however, that his career really took off. Right-back Mike Graham was transferred to Carlisle United, virtually in the opening week of the season, and Greaves, with injuries causing a lack of cover in defence, had noted Craig's occasional performance at full-back in the Reserves. He gambled on the youngster giving him time to rectify the gap in his back-four but McKernon did rather more and made the position his own. His electrifying pace was a match for any winger and his previous experience in midfield and up front, helped him become a threat to opposing defences and gave an added dimension to the Mansfield attack. A move to Wolves looked on the cards in December 1989, but Arsenal beat them to it with a £200,000 bid. Unfortunately, McKernon suffered a knee injury in his first game for the Gunners' reserve side and required a cartilage operation, but the Highbury staff have high hopes of him.

	LEAGUE		*FA CUP*		*FL CUP*		*F/Rov*		*TOTAL*	
	App	*Gls*	*App*	*Gls*	*App*	*Gls*	*App*	*Gls*	*App*	*Gls*
1984-85	1/1	0	0	0	0	0	0	0	1/1	0
1985-86	7/4	0	0	0	0	0	3	0	10/4	0
1986-87	13/5	0	0/1	0	1	0	0/1	0	14/7	0
1987-88	9/5	0	2	0	0/3	0	2	0	13/8	0
1988-89	42	0	2	0	1	0	1	0	46	0
1989-90	7	0	0	0	3	0	1	0	11	0
	79/15	0	4/1	0	5/3	0	7/1	0	95/20	0

ARTHUR MANN

Scotsman Arthur Mann, a classy midfield player, started his long career with Scottish League club, Hearts, but it was not long before he moved over the border to join Manchester City, a couple of months before his 21st birthday. Two seasons at Old Trafford and a short loan spell with Blackpool followed before he became a Notts County player in July 1972. It was at Meadow Lane that his career really took off, for in six seasons with the Magpies, Mann made well over 250 League and Cup appearances. Mansfield Town showed an interest in the player during the early weeks of the 1979 close season, but he decided to accept an offer from Shrewsbury Town, signing in June of that year. However, he never settled at Gay Meadow and with the season only a couple of months old, he switched to Field Mill. In three seasons with the Stags he made 114 League and 15 Cup appearances, picking up a Player of the Year trophy in the process. Mann then tried his hand on the management side of the game and in 1989-90 was assistant manager to Alan Buckley at Grimsby Town.

	LEAGUE		*FA CUP*		*FL CUP*		*TOTAL*	
	App	*Gls*	*App*	*Gls*	*App*	*Gls*	*App*	*Gls*
1979-80	35	0	3	0	0	0	38	0
1980-81	44	2	4	0	4	0	52	2
1981-82	35/2	1	1	0	3/1	0	39/3	1
	114/2	3	8	0	7/1	0	129/3	3

Although Jarrow-born Chris Marron had his first taste of senior soccer with local club South Shields, his first Football League club was Chesterfield and he joined the Saltergate staff in 1947. In his four seasons with the Spireites, centre-forward Marron made 108 League appearances and scored 44 goals. It was that sort of form which attracted the attention of Chesterfield's neighbours, Mansfield Town. He made the short trip to Field Mill in June 1952 and before he moved on to complete his career with Bradford, he had made 53 League appearances for the Stags and added 25 goals to his growing tally. For the Park Avenue club, Marron made two appearances, scoring one goal, before leaving the League scene. He managed local club Heanor Town in the early 1960s. Marron still lives in Mansfield and is a respected member of the local business community.

	LEAGUE		*FA CUP*		*TOTAL*	
	App	*Gls*	*App*	*Gls*	*App*	*Gls*
1952-53	39	16	3	2	42	18
1953-54	14	9	0	0	14	9
	53	25	3	2	56	27

CHRIS MARRON

Paul Matthews joined his home-town club, Leicester City, straight from school as an apprentice. He turned professional in 1964, when he was 18, which was remarkable when one considers that he did not play football until he was 15. Matthews was educated at a grammar school where they played rugby and he represented Leicestershire at fly-half. Soccer, though, was to be his sport and he joined a men's team when only 15. In six seasons at Filbert Street he made 56 League appearances and scored five goals. Then, after a short spell on loan to Southend United, he was signed by Danny Williams for Mansfield Town. Although the player had been used mainly as a winger at Leicester, he was converted into a central midfielder at Field Mill and under Williams, and later Dave Smith, Matthews enjoyed perhaps the most successful years of his career. He was an influential member of Smith's Fourth Division championship side and also played an important role the following season when the Stags turned what appeared certain relegation at Christmas into a final placing of 11th, following a 19-match unbeaten run. Peter Morris took over as player-manager for the following season and Matthews could only find a first-team place when the new boss was injured. In October 1977 he moved to Rotherham United and then completed his career with Northampton Town. Paul Matthews still lives in Leicester and imparts some of his soccer experience to non-League clubs in the area.

	LEAGUE		*FA CUP*		*FL CUP*		*TOTAL*	
	App	*Gls*	*App*	*Gls*	*App*	*Gls*	*App*	*Gls*
1972-73	16	1	0	0	0	0	16	1
1973-74	12/1	0	0	0	0	0	12/1	0
1974-75	44	2	6	0	0	0	50	2
1975-76	28/1	1	4	0	3	0	35/1	1
1976-77	17/1	2	1	1	0	0	18/1	3
1977-78	4	0	0	0	2	0	6	0
	121/3	6	11	1	5	0	137/3	7

PAUL MATTHEWS

Centre-forward Harry Middleton won England Youth international honours whilst with his first Football League club, Wolverhampton Wanderers, the first of six in his 13-year professional career. He was born in Birmingham in March 1937 and joined Wolves as a junior, but had only one senior outing after turning professional in August 1954. Middleton was transferred to Scunthorpe United in September 1959 and in his one season at the Old Showground scored 11 goals in 29 League appearances. Portsmouth was his next port of call in June 1961 and, again, his stay was for one season, in which he made 17 League appearances and scored five goals. Then it was on to Gay Meadow and just over two seasons with Shrewsbury Town, making 85 appearances and scoring 37 goals. He arrived at Field Mill in November 1964, being signed by the former Burnley star, Tom Cummings, in a double transfer which also brought John Gregson to the club. Middleton spent 16 months with the Stags before he resumed his travels after adding a further 24 goals in 45 games to his record. Fellows Park, Walsall, was his final destination, where in the concluding two seasons of his professional career he took his goals total over the century-mark with 26 in 56 outings.

HARRY MIDDLETON

	LEAGUE		*FA CUP*		*FL CUP*		*TOTAL*	
	App	*Gls*	*App*	*Gls*	*App*	*Gls*	*App*	*Gls*
1964-65	24	16	1	0	0	0	25	16
1965-66	21/1	8	1	0	2	1	24/1	9
	45/1	24	2	0	2	1	49/1	25

JOHN MILLER

The talented Johnnie Miller joined his home-town club, Ipswich Town, as a junior, after school and county honours as a centre-forward. He signed professional forms in June 1968, when he was 18, by which time he was playing on the wing. In his five seasons at Portman Road, Miller managed only 37 senior outings and scored two goals. He was on the verge of asking for a transfer when neighbours Norwich City came in with a £47,000 bid and he was transferred to the Carrow Road staff in October 1974. It was there that Miller met up with Peter Morris, who made Miller his first signing in July 1976, after taking over as player-manager at Mansfield. Miller signed as a non-contract player for Port Vale in September 1980 but eventually dropped out of League soccer and settled in Mansfield, where he assisted several of the local non-League clubs. He is now an employee of the Ashfield District Council and is on the staff of one of their leisure centres.

	LEAGUE		*FA CUP*		*FL CUP*		*TOTAL*	
	App	*Gls*	*App*	*Gls*	*App*	*Gls*	*App*	*Gls*
1976-77	40	5	3	0	3	0	46	5
1977-78	32	5	2	1	2	0	36	6
1978-79	28/3	4	1	0	2	1	31/3	5
1979-80	9/1	0	0	0	0	0	9/1	0
	109/4	14	6	1	7	1	122/4	16

Manager Tom Cummings was also responsible for taking classy midfielder Tommy Mitchinson to Mansfield Town from his home-town club, Sunderland, where his career had begun as a junior. So impressive was Mitchinson during his two seasons with the Stags that he was Cummings' first signing after taking over as manager of Aston Villa during the 1967 close season. Mitchinson had also impressed the Roker Park management team as a junior and was on contract before his 18th birthday. Regular senior places, though, were at a premium in those halcyon Sunderland days and the young player managed only 16 in his three seasons in the first-team squad. He made the move south in January 1966 and immediately became a big hit with the Mansfield fans, who were far from happy when the player was lured away by their former manager. Mitchinson spent just under two years at Villa Park, making 49 League appearances before he joined Torquay United in May 1969. He found the seaside air much to his liking and in three seasons at Plainmoor made 108 League appearances. His final club was Bournemouth, where he ended his senior career in 1972 after 32 League appearances for the Dean Court club.

	LEAGUE		*FA CUP*		*FL CUP*		*TOTAL*	
	App	*Gls*	*App*	*Gls*	*App*	*Gls*	*App*	*Gls*
1965-66	28	5	0	0	0	0	28	5
1966-67	46	10	4	2	3	0	53	12
1967-68	2	0	0	0	1	1	3	1
	76	15	4	2	4	1	84	18

TOMMY MITCHINSON

Winger Fred Morris was discovered as a teenager playing for his local club, Oswestry Town, and signed for Walsall in May 1950, for £500. In almost six seasons with the Saddlers he made 210 League appearances, scoring 43 goals, before signing for Mansfield Town, for £1,500, in March 1957. At Field Mill, Morris figured in 60 League and Cup games, scoring 19 goals, and was described by one reporter as having a 'tearaway style' and a player 'who pleased the crowd with his dashing work'. In February 1958, Morris signed for Liverpool, who were then still trying to get out of Division Two. They paid £7,000 for him and he made his debut the following September. In two seasons at Anfield he made 47 League appearances and scored 14 goals before further moves took him to Crewe, Gillingham and Chester in that order before he joined non-League Altrincham in the close season of 1962. Morris finally settled in Chester and launched his own successful building contractor's business.

	LEAGUE		*FA CUP*		*TOTAL*	
	App	*Gls*	*App*	*Gls*	*App*	*Gls*
1956-57	10	2	0	0	10	2
1957-58	46	15	4	2	50	17
	56	17	4	2	60	19

FRED MORRIS

PETER MORRIS

At the age of 12, Peter Morris attracted the Stags' attention, when he was playing for a church team in his home village of New Houghton. And after making the local schoolboys' representative team, he joined Ladybrook Colts, which was virtually Mansfield Town's nursery side. Morris signed for Town immediately on leaving school, teaming up with two other local boys, Ken Wagstaff and Mike Stringfellow, and made his Mansfield debut at Workington on 24 February 1961, when he was only 17. Before he was 19, he was appointed skipper, such was the quality of his play and leadership. Seven years, almost to the day, after making his League debut, he was transferred to Ipswich and in six seasons at Portman Road made over 250 League and Cup appearances and played in the UEFA Cup. He won promotion with both Ipswich and Norwich and played for the Canaries in the 1975 League Cup Final. Although their manager, John Bond, was prepared to offer him another two-year contract, when the possibility arose of a return to Mansfield as player-manager, he was allowed to leave. (See also *Stags Managers*.)

	LEAGUE		*FA CUP*		*FL CUP*		*TOTAL*	
	App	*Gls*	*App*	*Gls*	*App*	*Gls*	*App*	*Gls*
1960-61	13	0	0	0	0	0	13	0
1961-62	40	10	2	0	2	0	44	10
1962-63	33	6	5	0	3	0	41	6
1963-64	45	3	1	0	2	0	48	3
1964-65	46	7	2	0	2	0	50	7
1965-66	39/1	4	1	0	2	0	42/1	4
1966-67	41	13	3	0	3	0	47	13
1967-68	29	7	1	0	1	0	31	7
1976-77	32	3	3	0	3	0	38	3
1977-78	9	0	1	0	0	0	10	0
	327/1	53	19	0	18	0	364/1	53

Ernest Moss, 'Big Ern' to his countless friends and admirers on the terraces, has played for seven clubs in his professional career and was still playing, at the age of 41, for non-League Kettering Town. And he was still a threat to defenders and, as always, a great favourite with the fans. He left school with five GCE 'O' levels and started work in local government at Matlock in Derbyshire. Football, though, was very much a part of his life and he was noted by his home-town club, Chesterfield, when a member of the local works side, Chesterfield Tube. He joined the Spireites a few days before his 19th birthday in October 1968

ERNIE MOSS

and in his first full season scored 20 goals in 44 games and collected a Fourth Division championship medal. He gave marvellous service to Chesterfield, scoring 94 goals in 271 League outings overall before his transfer to Peterborough United in January 1976, for a £16,000 fee. Moss stayed for less than a year at London Road before joining Mansfield Town in December. At Field Mill he teamed up with the Stags' new player-manager, Peter Morris, and his former partner at Chesterfield, Kevin Randall. It was this proven Derbyshire duo who inspired Mansfield to their second championship success in three seasons and a place in Division Two for the first time in their history. The Stags lasted only one season in the higher division but most Mansfield fans are adamant that had not Ernie Moss, who had scored six goals in 15 matches, been sidelined by a pelvic injury for much of the season, Mansfield would almost certainly have enjoyed a longer stay in the Second Division. It cost Chesterfield £35,000 to regain the player's signature in January 1979 and he added another 105 appearances and 33 goals to his tally before moving to Port Vale, Lincoln City and Doncaster Rovers, where he scored 15 goals in 43 matches to earn another championship medal. Moss has played for non-League Kettering for the past two seasons and, although his 41st birthday is now behind him, it is quite possible that he has more seasons in front of him. He is also a partner in a successful sports outfitting business with outlets in Chesterfield and Matlock.

	LEAGUE		*FA CUP*		*FL CUP*		*TOTAL*	
	App	*Gls*	*App*	*Gls*	*App*	*Gls*	*App*	*Gls*
1976-77	29	13	0	0	0	0	29	13
1977-78	15	6	0	0	2	0	17	6
1978-79	12/1	2	0	0	0	0	12/1	2
	56/1	21	0	0	2	0	58/1	21

Ernie Moss scores the opening goal in the 2-0 win over Portsmouth in May 1977 – a result which assured the Stags of promotion to Division Two.

KEN MURRAY

Darlington-born forward Ken Murray cut his soccer teeth playing for the famous amateur club, Bishop Auckland. Then, just after his 21st birthday, he realized an ambition when his home-town club finally took him on their staff. Murray spent two seasons at Feethams and attracted attention from other clubs by scoring 19 goals in 70 League outings. Mansfield manager Stan Mercer was particularly impressed and took Murray to Field Mill in July 1953. In almost four seasons at Mansfield he made nearly 150 League and Cup appearances and scored 61 goals before being transferred to Oldham Athletic in March 1957, for £1,500. Murray spent just under a year at Boundary Park, skippering the Latics for a spell, and scored 14 goals in 35 League games before being transferred to Wrexham in February 1958. He then had a spell with Southern League Yeovil Town before ending his League career with Gateshead. When he retired in the 1960 close season, after Gateshead had been voted out of the League, he had career figures of 112 goals in 293 League games.

	LEAGUE		*FA CUP*		*TOTAL*	
	App	*Gls*	*App*	*Gls*	*App*	*Gls*
1953-54	40	21	2	0	42	21
1954-55	37	13	0	0	37	13
1955-56	38	17	1	0	39	17
1956-57	25	9	2	1	27	10
	140	60	5	1	145	61

Harry Oscroft joined his local club, Mansfield Town, as an inside-forward after he was discovered virtually on the Field Mill doorstep, playing for Mansfield Colliery. He was born in March 1926 and was one of the many local miners who joined the Stags soon after World War Two when the distinguished Huddersfield and England defender, Ray Goodall, was team manager at Mansfield. It was as a goalscoring outside-left that Oscroft came into his own, however, after Freddie Steele became player-manager of Mansfield, although Oscroft was already a firm favourite with the local fans, regularly reaching double figures each season. He had joined the Stags in March 1947 and in the closing weeks of that season scored three goals in 12 outings. Before he left for Stoke City in January 1950, he had netted 40 goals in 113 appearances and greatly improved on that record at the Victoria Ground, chalking up 326 League outings and reaching a century of goals. His final move in League football was to neighbouring Port Vale, where he took his total career League and Cup outings close to the 500 mark and his goals tally to over 150.

	LEAGUE		*FA CUP*		*TOTAL*	
	App	*Gls*	*App*	*Gls*	*App*	*Gls*
1946-47	12	3	0	0	12	3
1947-48	40	11	3	1	43	12
1948-49	38	14	3	2	41	16
1949-50	23	12	2	0	25	12
	113	40	8	3	121	43

HARRY OSCROFT

Much-travelled Sidney Ottewell arrived at Field Mill as Harry Oscroft departed and he helped to ease the fans' resentment at the popular Oscroft's move to the Potteries. Indeed, Ottewell launched his spell with Mansfield very much as the local winger had done, with three goals in 13 matches to the end of the season. In the following two seasons he continued to earn the respect of local supporters, as well as that of Mansfield's opponents. An aggressive player with an explosive shot, Ottewell scored 21 League goals in 67 outings before joining his final League club, Scunthorpe United in March 1952. Ottewell was born at Horsley, Derbyshire, in October 1919 and began his professional career with neighbouring Chesterfield, who plucked him from the ranks of mining club, Holbrook MW. From Saltergate, he went to Birmingham City but his stay at St Andrew's was short. After only six months and five appearances, he was transferred to Luton Town but again he did not linger long. After seven months his travels continued with a move to Nottingham Forest. In 18 months at the City Ground, he made 31 first-team appearances before switching to Mansfield Town. After ending his playing days in the League, Ottewell moved back to the Midlands and kept in touch with football as a non-League manager.

	LEAGUE		*FA CUP*		*TOTAL*	
	App	*Gls*	*App*	*Gls*	*App*	*Gls*
1949-50	13	3	0	0	13	3
1950-51	38	15	6	1	44	16
1951-52	16	3	1	0	17	3
	67	21	7	1	74	22

SID OTTEWELL

NOËL PARKINSON

Noël Parkinson was a busy-bee of a midfield player and it was not a popular decision when he was allowed to leave Field Mill on a free transfer at the end of the 1981-2 season, only a week after receiving the club's Player of the Year award. He was one of eight players to go when, along with Adrian Burrows and Arthur Mann, he refused terms as times were hard and getting harder at Mansfield. Hull-born Parkinson began his career as an Ipswich Town apprentice but failed to break into the first-team. After short loan spells with Bristol Rovers and Brentford, he was snapped up by Mansfield Town manager Mick Jones during the 1980 close-season. He quickly became one of the crowd's favourites at Field Mill, where he made 66 League appearances in his couple of seasons with the club. Scunthorpe United was his next port of call and again he pleased the local fans before an injury brought his career to a premature end. But Parkinson is still very popular in the Scunthorpe area as a match commentator on local radio, in a brash and breezy style which was so typical of his approach as a player.

	LEAGUE		*FA CUP*		*FL CUP*		*TOTAL*	
	App	*Gls*	*App*	*Gls*	*App*	*Gls*	*App*	*Gls*
1980-81	35	4	2	3	4	1	41	8
1981-82	31/4	9	1	0	1/1	0	33/5	9
	66/4	13	3	3	5/1	1	74/5	17

No Mansfield Town records would be complete without reference to Alexander Montgomery Pate — Sandy to his friends. Sandy Pate wrested the Stags' long-standing appearances record from another full-back, Don Bradley, although goalkeeper Rod Arnold eventually took over the mantle a few seasons later. But in achieving the record, Pate set one of his own with 366 consecutive appearances stretching from 21 September 1968 and a home game against Rotherham United, to a pre-season Anglo-Scottish Cup meeting with Hull City on 9 August 1975. The young Scot had been spotted by Watford whilst playing for Renfrew Juniors, a favourite venue for English clubs hoping to tempt young Scottish talent over the border. Pate was barely 20 at the time but managed 14 first-team outings in just over 18 months at Vicarage Road. His potential had been noted in what manager Tom Eggleston always referred to as 'my little black book' and he signed for Mansfield in time to make his debut at Stockport on 13 October 1967, as one of the new manager's first captures. Pate gave outstanding service to the Stags, captaining the side for many seasons and leading them to the club's first-ever League championship in 1975, when the Fourth Division title was earned. He was also a member of the team which reached the sixth round of the FA Cup in 1968-9 with wins over West Ham and Sheffield United. Pate also played his part the following season, when the Stags had a goal controversially disallowed with the score at 0-0 against Leeds United at Elland Road in the fifth round. Mansfield were on top until then but Leeds went on to win 2-0. He also skippered the side in 1975-6, when the Stags reached the fourth round of the League Cup, the furthest the club has been in that competition. Mention has to be made of the three goals scored by Sandy Pate in his Mansfield career. He broke his duck on 16 August 1972 with a goal in the 3-1 League Cup win over Lincoln City. The other two were in the League two years apart, against Sheffield Wednesday in a 3-0 home win on 18 April 1976, and in a 1-1 draw with Orient at home on 29 March 1978. Pate is now very much an adopted son of Mansfield and is a successful and highly-respected licensee and businessman with his hotel the 'Mecca' of the local sporting public.

SANDY PATE

	LEAGUE		*FA CUP*		*FL CUP*		*TOTAL*	
	App	*Gls*	*App*	*Gls*	*App*	*Gls*	*App*	*Gls*
1967-68	34	0	1	0	0	0	35	0
1968-69	39	0	7	0	1	0	47	0
1969-70	46	0	6	0	3	0	55	0
1970-71	46	0	2	0	3	0	51	0
1971-72	46	0	4	0	2	0	52	0
1972-73	46	0	1	0	2	1	49	1
1973-74	46	0	4	0	2	0	52	0
1974-75	46	0	6	0	1	0	53	0
1975-76	40/1	1	4	0	4/1	0	48/2	1
1976-77	14	0	0	0	3	0	17	0
1977-78	9	1	1	0	0	0	10	1
	412/1	2	36	0	21/1	1	469/2	3

A proud moment for Sandy Pate, with the Fourth Division trophy in 1975.

MALCOLM PARTRIDGE

Malcolm Partridge was another youngster to come up through Mansfield's apprentice ranks and who made his mark in League football. A native of Clowne, near Chesterfield, the young midfielder served notice of his potential as a schoolboy, playing both at local and county level. After his spell in the Stags' junior ranks he became a full-time professional in September 1968, a month after his 18th birthday, although he had already made his Football League debut the previous season. In all, he made 62 first-team appearances before attracting the attention of Leicester City, for whom he signed in September 1970 for a £50,000 fee, only a few days after Mansfield had held mighty Liverpool to a goalless draw in the League Cup at Field Mill. Partridge was not quite as successful as had been hoped for at Filbert Street and after a short loan spell with Charlton Athletic he joined Grimsby Town in March 1975, for what was the most successful period of his career. In his three and a half years with the Mariners, he made 134 first-team appearances and scored 24 goals before his next and final move took him to Scunthorpe United, where he added 91 appearances and 21 goals to his record before ending his Football League career as a central defender.

	LEAGUE		*FA CUP*		*FL CUP*		*TOTAL*	
	App	*Gls*	*App*	*Gls*	*App*	*Gls*	*App*	*Gls*
1967-68	5	1	0	0	0	0	5	1
1968-69	16/2	3	0	0	1	0	17/2	3
1969-70	39	13	5/1	2	3	0	47/1	15
1970-71	5	3	0	0	2	3	7	6
	65/2	20	5/1	2	6	3	76/3	25

Norman Plummer was another of the Leicester City players to take what at one time was a familiar path from Filbert Street to Mansfield Town. He made the move in July 1952 after 66 League appearances (one goal) and was one of the earlier signings of the Stags' new boss, veteran manager George Jobey, who took over at Field Mill after the popular Freddie Steele departed. Plummer, who began with Leicester ATC, was given the task of leading Mansfield and he missed only two League matches in his first two seasons with the Stags. All told he had 166 League outings for Mansfield, and scored five goals, all of these in his appearances as an emergency centre-forward in the 1953-4 campaign. Mostly, however, Plummer was a solid 'stopper' centre-half.

	LEAGUE		*FA CUP*		*TOTAL*	
	App	*Gls*	*App*	*Gls*	*App*	*Gls*
1952-53	45	0	3	0	48	0
1953-54	45	5	2	0	47	5
1954-55	38	0	1	0	39	0
1955-56	38	0	2	0	40	0
	166	5	8	0	174	5

NORMAN PLUMMER

Of all the inside-forwards, or midfield players as they are now known, who have worn Mansfield Town's colours with distinction, John Quigley was arguably one of the most popular and certainly one of the most effective skippers ever appointed by the club. He captained the side in their two outstanding FA Cup runs, in 1968-9 to the sixth round, and the following season to the fifth round. He was eventually appointed asssitant to manager Jock Basford, but left Field Mill when both were dismissed in November 1971. Whilst with Mansfield, Quigley made well over 100 appearances and after leaving League football he spent several years coaching in the Middle East. Quigley made his name with Nottingham Forest and was a member of their FA Cup-winning side in 1959. The Glasgow-born Scot joined the Reds from Ashfield Juniors in July 1957 and before he moved to Huddersfield Town in February 1965, made 236 League appearances and scored 51 goals. He admitted, though, that his happiest days as a player were with Bristol City between October 1966 and July 1968, before he moved to Mansfield for £3,000. He made 66 League appearances whilst at Ashton Gate.

	LEAGUE		*FA CUP*		*FL CUP*		*TOTAL*	
	App	*Gls*	*App*	*Gls*	*App*	*Gls*	*App*	*Gls*
1968-69	46	2	7	0	1	0	54	2
1969-70	43	0	6	0	0	0	49	0
1970-71	16	0	0	0	3	0	19	0
	105	2	13	0	4	0	122	2

JOHN QUIGLEY

Kevin Randall could well have realized an ambition to join his home-town club, Manchester United. After attracting attention whilst playing schools football with the Droylsden and Ashton-under-Lyne teams, he trained at Old Trafford and played for United's 'B' and junior teams. But his first taste of senior competitive football was in the Lancashire Combination with Droylsden and it was from there that he was recruited by Bury, when he was 20. Randall stayed only eight months at Gigg Lane before he joined Chesterfield on a free transfer in July 1966. It was in the middle of his five-year stay at Saltergate that he forged, with Ernie Moss, one of the most effective striking partnerships in the lower divisions. Randall was transferred to Notts County for £20,000 in August 1972, after he had made almost 300 League and Cup outings and scored well in excess of a century of goals for Chesterfield. In his three years at Meadow Lane, he did not lose his scoring touch, putting away another 40-odd goals in 125 senior matches. He signed for Mansfield in November 1975 and a year later renewed his scoring partnership with Moss, who arrived at Field Mill from Peterborough United. The old lethal rapport was still there and they spearheaded the Stags' march into the Second Division, for the first time in the club's history, at the end of the 1976-7 season, with Randall top scorer with 17 goals. Randall was on the move again in October 1977, after spending Mansfield's early days in the Second Division on the substitute's bench. He joined York City for £7,000 and in his three years at Bootham Crescent, first as a player and then player-coach, he served City well. A spell as manager at York followed and then for a time he was player-manager of Goole Town before returning to Chesterfield as manager. In 1989, after being dismissed by Chesterfield, he returned to Mansfield Town as the club's youth development officer.

	LEAGUE		*FA CUP*		*FL CUP*		*TOTAL*	
	App	*Gls*	*App*	*Gls*	*App*	*Gls*	*App*	*Gls*
1975-76	18	3	1	0	0	0	19	3
1976-77	44	17	3	1	1	0	48	18
1977-78	0/4	0	0	0	0	0	0/4	0
	62/4	20	4	1	1	0	67/4	21

KEVIN RANDALL

JOE READMAN

Forward Joe Readman has a unique place in Mansfield Town's history as the first player to score a Football League goal for the club. That was in the opening Third Division South match of the 1931-2 season, when Swindon Town lost 3-2 at Field Mill in front of what was given as a record 11,000 attendance, but which the local newspapers declared was nearer 13,000. Readman joined the Stags from Millwall and gave Bolton Wanderers as a former club, although he never appeared in the Trotters' first team. He stayed at Field Mill for two seasons, during which time he also operated occasionally as a wing-half.

	LEAGUE		*FA CUP*		*TOTAL*	
	App	*Gls*	*App*	*Gls*	*App*	*Gls*
1931-32	39	5	1	0	40	5
1932-33	34	7	1	0	35	7
	73	12	2	0	75	12

Centre-forward Ken Reeve was on Grimsby Town's books before the start of World War Two, when he was a teenager. And at the end of hostilities he rejoined his home-town club, who had discovered the local youngster playing for Humber United. In his one season as a senior at Blundell Park, he made 22 first-team appearances and scored four goals. Then he was on the move to Doncaster Rovers in July 1948 and was top scorer at Belle Vue in the following season before Freddie Steele persuaded him to join the Stags. For a couple of seasons at Field Mill, Reeve was virtually his boss's understudy, but still managed 51 appearances and 20 goals. With Steele's departure to manage Port Vale, Reeve really came into his own and before completing his five seasons with Mansfield, he had headed the scoring list in 1951-2, with 21 League goals, to become the club's top scorer in post-war football. He was described as 'fast and tricky, with a powerful shot' and that was well illustrated by his 62 goals in 139 senior outings for the Stags.

	LEAGUE		*FA CUP*		*TOTAL*	
	App	*Gls*	*App*	*Gls*	*App*	*Gls*
1949-50	27	8	0	0	27	8
1950-51	24	12	4	0	28	12
1951-52	37	21	2	0	39	21
1952-53	32	10	0	0	32	10
1953-54	19	11	0	0	19	11
	139	62	6	0	145	62

KEN REEVE

Dudley Roberts was one of a quartet of players recruited by manager Tom Eggleston in March 1968, after central defender Dick Edwards had been sold to Aston Villa. Derby-born Roberts was signed from Coventry City, where his father was a long-serving forward and a great favourite with the fans. Roberts and fellow defender Phil Waller, and forwards Nick Sharkey and Jim Goodfellow, all made their debuts in the same match at Brighton on 16 March. But Eggleston's decision to utilize the former Sky Blue, who had been taught his trade by that peer of centre-halves, George Curtis, as a target man, had a vital bearing on what was to become one of Mansfield's most successful periods since their election to the Football League. Roberts' power in the air became almost legendary and, as well as setting up goals for his colleagues, he scored 66 in the League in almost 200 appearances with Mansfield, mostly it should be added, with his head. He figured prominently in the two record-setting FA Cup runs in 1968-9 to the sixth round and the following season to the fifth round. And one of the most memorable moments came in the 22nd minute of the fifth-round tie with West Ham United on 26 February, when he opened the scoring as Mansfield went on to defeat the First Division side —World Cup stars and all — 3-0. Rumours of a move to top clubs were rampant in most of his early seasons with Mansfield, but they were resisted, perhaps to the player's detriment. Finally, after seven seasons at Field Mill, he moved to Doncaster Rovers and then Scunthorpe United where he scored 17 goals in 56 League appearances. In 1975 there were several offers from continental clubs but Roberts, who in his later career had been troubled by a knee injury, decided to call it a day. He and his family never left Mansfield and he joined the East Midlands Electricity Board as a storekeeper, a position he still holds.

DUDLEY ROBERTS

	LEAGUE		*FA CUP*		*FL CUP*		*TOTAL*	
	App	*Gls*	*App*	*Gls*	*App*	*Gls*	*App*	*Gls*
1967-68	6/2	0	0	0	0	0	6/2	0
1968-69	42	10	7	4	0/1	0	49/1	14
1969-70	43	18	6	1	2	0	51	19
1970-71	45	22	2	1	3	1	50	24
1971-72	15/1	1	1	0	2	0	18/1	1
1972-73	16/2	8	0	0	0	0	16/2	8
1973-74	27/1	7	3	0	2	0	32/1	7
	194/6	66	19	6	9/1	1	222/7	73

Over the years, Leicester City has been the destination of many young Scotsmen hoping to make their way in English football. Many successfully made the trip and Edinburgh-born Bobby Roberts, who attracted City's attention while in Motherwell's ranks, followed this trend. Roberts spent six years at Filbert Street and made 224 League appearances and scored 26 goals from midfield. Among the highlights of his playing career are a Scottish Under-21 cap and a Scottish Football League representative appearance. In September 1970, Roberts joined Mansfield, shortly after the departure of Malcolm Partridge to Filbert Street, and his signing owed much to the persistence of manager Jock Basford, who had pursued the player for some considerable time. But his stay lasted only a couple of seasons before he joined the coaching staff of Coventry City. A further move took him to Colchester, first as a player, then as manager. Roberts did an excellent job for United on a shoestring budget but eventually followed the way of all managers when he was dismissed. Then he had a spell as Wrexham boss in even more difficult financial circumstances, before again having to make way. More recently, Roberts has been back at his first English club, Leicester City, on the coaching staff.

	LEAGUE		*FA CUP*		*FL CUP*		*TOTAL*	
	App	*Gls*	*App*	*Gls*	*App*	*Gls*	*App*	*Gls*
1970-71	39	2	2	0	0	0	41	2
1971-72	37/4	2	3	1	2	0	42/4	3
	76/4	4	5	1	2	0	83/4	5

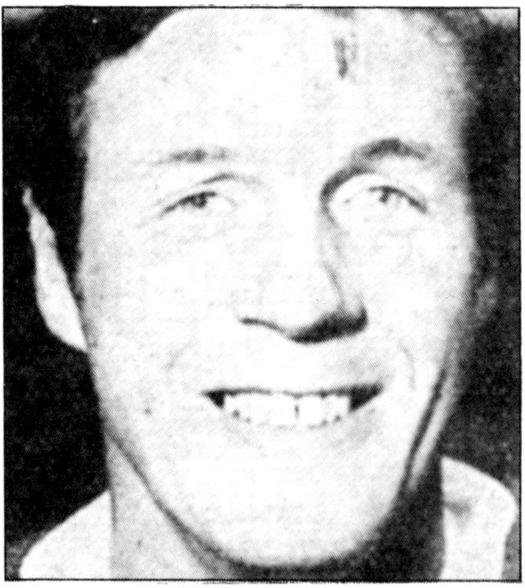

BOBBY ROBERTS

Worksop-born John Saunders was another product of Mansfield's seemingly unending conveyor belt of local central defenders, who came through the ranks to claim a regular first-team place before moving on to more senior clubs. And again, he had his first taste of senior action some months before his 19th birthday, at Queen's Park Rangers in a second-round League Cup replay. He played in a couple of League games just over a month later and then a foot injury kept him out of action for much of the remainder of the season. It was not until midway through the 1970-71 season that he was to command a regular first-team spot. In October 1972, Ian Greaves paid £20,000 to take the player to Huddersfield Town, where in three seasons Saunders had 121 League outings before he moved to Barnsley. At Oakwell he added another 149 League games to his career record before shorter spells with Lincoln City and Doncaster Rovers took him to the end of his Football League career. Then it was back to Worksop and the local senior outfit, Worksop Town, where after spells as player, captain and then manager he eventually progressed to become the chairman of the club.

	LEAGUE		*FA CUP*		*FL CUP*		*TOTAL*	
	App	*Gls*	*App*	*Gls*	*App*	*Gls*	*App*	*Gls*
1969-70	2	0	0	0	1	0	3	0
1970-71	29	0	0	0	2	0	31	0
1971-72	44	2	4	0	0	0	48	2
1972-73	14	0	0	0	2	0	16	0
	89	2	4	0	5	0	98	2

JOHN SAUNDERS

MICK SAXBY

Mick Saxby was another of Mansfield's 'home grown' products, who went on to pull in what was at the time a club record fee when he was transferred to Luton Town for £200,000 in July 1979. Saxby, a central defender, came up through the apprentice ranks at Field Mill and had a dream Football League debut at Halifax Town on 14 February 1976, when still six months away from his 19th birthday. He had been called up to replace the regular centre-half, Kevin Bird, who had picked up a knee injury in the previous match in midweek at Hereford United and required a cartilage operation. Saxby headed the winner deep in injury time to give Mansfield only their second victory of 1976 and launch a dramatic unbeaten run of 19 games without defeat which took the Stags from points adrift at the bottom of the Third Division table to a respectable final 11th position. His move to Kenilworth Road in July 1979 was part of a deal which brought Steven Taylor to Mansfield for a then club record pay-out of £75,000. For a time it seemed that Saxby was going to hit the heights with some splendid performances for his new club. But a serious knee injury curtailed his progress and, despite loan periods with Grimsby Town and Lincoln City in an effort to revive his career, he was eventually compelled to give up the professional game. He made a further attempt with non-League outfits in the Mansfield area but eventually called it a day and became a local publican.

	LEAGUE		*FA CUP*		*FL CUP*		*TOTAL*	
	App	*Gls*	*App*	*Gls*	*App*	*Gls*	*App*	*Gls*
1975-76	1/1	1	0	0	0	0	1/1	1
1976-77	10	0	0	0	0	0	10	0
1977-78	19/2	0	0/1	0	0	0	19/3	0
1978-79	46	4	1	0	2	0	49	4
	76/3	5	1/1	0	2	0	79/4	5

ALBERT SCANLON

Albert Scanlon was a nephew of Charlie Mitten but it was not during his uncle's spell as manager of Mansfield Town between 1956 and 1958 that Scanlon moved to Field Mill. Indeed, it was some four years further on before manager Raich Carter took the former Manchester United winger to Mansfield. Scanlon came up through the junior ranks at Old Trafford after joining his local club straight from school and he was one of the survivors of the Munich air crash in February 1958. He made 115 League appearances for United and scored 34 goals, winning England Under-23 caps and representing the Football League on five occasions. In November 1960 he moved to Newcastle United, but after just over 12 months he was on the move again, this time to Lincoln City, before joining Mansfield in April 1963, just before Carter left the club to manage Middlesbrough. Scanlon served Mansfield well in his four seasons at Field Mill, during which time he had 108 senior outings and scored 21 goals.

	LEAGUE		*FA CUP*		*FL CUP*		*TOTAL*	
	App	*Gls*	*App*	*Gls*	*App*	*Gls*	*App*	*Gls*
1962-63	15	3	0	0	0	0	15	3
1963-64	36	5	1	0	2	1	39	6
1964-65	37	7	2	0	1	1	40	8
1965-66	20	6	0	0	2	1	22	7
	108	21	3	0	5	3	116	24

A future in football was confidently predicted for Nick Sharkey at an early age, for he won two Scottish Schoolboy caps. Further honours followed after he joined Sunderland at the age of 17, when he figured in the Scottish Under-23 side. In his six years at Roker Park, Sharkey averaged more than a goal every two games, scoring 51 in 99 senior appearances. He joined Leicester City in October 1966, but found it difficult to claim a first-team place despite five goals in only six League appearances. Mansfield paid a £10,000 fee for the player in March 1968 and he joined the Stags along with Dudley Roberts, Phil Waller and Jim Goodfellow. He was a regular in the first-team in his initial full season, and was a member of the team in the great FA Cup run which took Mansfield to the sixth round after defeating First Division West Ham United 3-0, with Sharkey netting the third 'killer' goal. He kept his place until half-way through the following campaign, but figured mainly on the substitute's bench for the remainder of the season and was then given a free transfer. Sharkey then had a couple of seasons back in the North-East with Hartlepool, where he made 55 League appearances and scored 12 goals.

	LEAGUE		*FA CUP*		*FL CUP*		*TOTAL*	
	App	*Gls*	*App*	*Gls*	*App*	*Gls*	*App*	*Gls*
1967-68	13	2	0	0	0	0	13	2
1968-69	40/1	13	7	4	1	0	48/1	17
1969-70	14/1	2	0	0	3	0	17/1	2
	67/2	17	7	4	4	0	78/2	21

DOMINIC (NICK) SHARKEY

Wilf Slack was a local boy made good. He was born at Skegby, only a few miles from Field Mill, and first came to the notice of Football League clubs whilst playing for Sutton Junction. Before joining Mansfield during their second season in the Football League, he had vast experience and included Blackpool, Portsmouth and Merthyr among his previous clubs and also assisted local club, Shirebrook, one of the leading sides in the area at the time. Originally an outside-left, his position when joining the Stags, he dropped back to left-half and quickly settled down in the position to become one of Mansfield's most consistent and reliable players.

	LEAGUE		*FA CUP*		*D3N CUP*		*TOTAL*	
	App	*Gls*	*App*	*Gls*	*App*	*Gls*	*App*	*Gls*
1932-33	25	0	0	0	0	0	25	0
1933-34	42	0	2	0	3	0	47	0
1934-35	31	0	3	0	0	0	34	0
1935-36	22	0	1	0	2	0	25	0
	120	0	6	0	5	0	131	0

WILF SLACK

FRED SPEED

Fred Speed was the type of player which most football club managers dream about — a play-anywhere type who always did a good job. He joined Mansfield from York City in time for the 1936-7 season and had spells at left-half, inside-left, left-back and right-back before eventually moving to centre-half and making the position his own. Speed had a reputation as a solid two-footed player, quick to the tackle and with the ability to make good use of the ball. Originally he was from Newark Town, from where he joined Hull City and helped them to gain promotion to Division Two in 1933. During his three seasons with the Stags, Speed topped a century of appearances and that figure could well have been exceeded, but for the start of World War Two.

	LEAGUE		*FA CUP*		*D3N CUP*		*TOTAL*	
	App	*Gls*	*App*	*Gls*	*App*	*Gls*	*App*	*Gls*
1936-37	34	0	1	0	1	0	36	0
1937-38	39	5	3	0	1	0	43	5
1938-39	27	0	6	0	2	0	35	0
	100	5	10	0	4	0	114	5

CHRIS STANIFORTH

If there is any positive memory for the much older fan reminiscing on the earliest days of Mansfield Town, then surely it must be the shining bald dome of forward Chris Staniforth. He served the Stags with distinction in their non-League days and was player-coach in the initial season in the Football League. Born in Carrington, Nottingham, Staniforth was a star in local schoolboy football and a career in the sport was a natural progression. He played for Creswell Colliery, from where he joined Chesterfield in 1919, then had the first of his four spells with Mansfield Town in 1921. He joined Oldham Athletic in May 1922 and made his debut on 14 October that year, but Athletic were relegated to the Second Division at the end of the season. In May 1924 he was back at Field Mill, but in December the following year, a fee of £800 took him to Notts County. Given a free transfer at the end of that season, he returned to Field Mill in May 1926, only for another £800 to change hands as he returned to County a year later. However, it was another brief visit, for he was back with the Stags in time to lead the side in that important 1928-9 season, in which their FA Cup exploits brought the club national recognition, and no doubt played a great part in them eventually gaining admission to the League. Of course, he will always be remembered as the player who failed from the penalty-spot in the epic Cup meeting with Arsenal. In 1932, Staniforth moved to local club, Sutton Town, and then to Worksop Town a year later, eventually returning to be player-manager of Creswell Colliery.

	LEAGUE		*FA CUP*		*TOTAL*	
	App	*Gls*	*App*	*Gls*	*App*	*Gls*
1931-32	8	2	0	0	8	2
	8	2	0	0	8	2

Coach Jock Basford remembered young forward John Stenson from during the time he was at The Valley in a similar coaching capacity for Charlton Athletic. So it was hardly surprising that when the 19-year-old player became available, Jock persuaded his boss, Tom Eggleston, that the youngster who had played for England Schoolboys and then for England Youth whilst with Charlton, would be a useful addition to the Field Mill staff and a fee of around £5,000 was paid out. Catford-born Stenson was involved in three campaigns with the Stags, the final one in 1971-2 ending in relegation to the Fourth Division. During his final season at Field Mill, he had a short spell on loan at Peterborough United and at the end of the campaign was given a free transfer by Mansfield's new manager, Danny Williams. Stenson joined Aldershot but stayed for only one season scoring four goals in 34 appearances before dropping out of the Football League.

	LEAGUE		*FA CUP*		*FL CUP*		*TOTAL*	
	App	*Gls*	*App*	*Gls*	*App*	*Gls*	*App*	*Gls*
1969-70	39/1	7	5	1	3	0	47/1	7
1970-71	45	12	2	1	3	3	50	16
1971-72	19/3	2	2/1	0	1	0	22/4	2
	103/4	21	9/1	2	7	3	119/5	25

JOHN STENSON

Full-back George Stimpson was born in Giltbrook near Nottingham and began his footballing career with Kimberly Amateurs. He then had four years with Notts County and served them well, both at right and left-back, before joining Exeter City where he spent two years. City were anxious to keep the reliable defender but his wish to get back to his native county saw him accept Mansfield Town's offer. Stimpson joined the Stags in time for the 1937-8 season and made his debut against Northampton Town at Field Mill on 28 August 1937. He captained the side for a time and continued playing for Mansfield throughout the first season of the war. After finishing his soccer career he entered the engineering industry.

	LEAGUE		*FA CUP*		*D3S CUP*		*TOTAL*	
	App	*Gls*	*App*	*Gls*	*App*	*Gls*	*App*	*Gls*
1937-38	40	0	3	0	1	0	44	0
1938-39	42	0	6	0	2	0	50	0
	82	0	9	0	3	0	94	0

GEORGE STIMPSON

IAN STRINGFELLOW

It seems appropriate that a nephew of Mike Stringfellow should follow in his uncle's footsteps and become a Mansfield Town player. That is what Ian Stringfellow did as soon as he left school and the predictions are that he could achieve even more in the game than his relative, for the youngster has received rave notices from the time he made his debut just before his 17th birthday. Unfortunately, his career so far has been plagued by injury and illness, more recently glandular fever and the need for a hernia operation. Mansfield certainly missed his skills in setting up scoring chances for his colleagues and his own ability to find the back of the net. Stringfellow had an early taste of the Wembley atmosphere when he came on as substitute in the Freight/Rover Trophy Final against Bristol City in 1987, and hit the bar with a fine header only seconds after he had joined the action. The Stags are hopeful that 1990-91 will see the youngster over his fitness problems and regularly back in the side. He was born at Kirkby-in-Ashfield and before he moved with his family to Retford, he attended the Vernon Road Infants School in the town. His soccer skills came to prominence, however, when playing for the Queen Elizabeth Grammar School in Retford and for Bassetlaw Schools. He joined Mansfield Town as an apprentice on leaving school and the club is certain that he will have a distinguished future in the game.

	LEAGUE		*FA CUP*		*FL CUP*		*L/DAF*		*TOTAL*	
	App	*Gls*	*App*	*Gls*	*App*	*Gls*	*App*	*Gls*	*App*	*Gls*
1985-86	0/3	0	0	0	0	0	0	0	0/3	0
1986-87	12/9	4	1	0	1	0	2/2	1	16/11	5
1987-88	22/8	8	3/1	1	4	2	0/1	0	29/10	11
1988-89	0/8	1	0/1	0	2	0	2	0	4/9	1
1989-90	16/2	3	0/1	0	4	3	0/1	0	20/4	6
	50/30	16	4/3	1	11	5	4/4	1	69/38	23

MIKE STRINGFELLOW

Winger Mike Stringfellow was one of a trio of young teenagers thrown in at the deep end by manager Raich Carter soon after their 17th birthday. The Nuncargate-born youngster was spotted playing for Mansfield Schools and the Notts Youth team and joined the Mansfield groundstaff on leaving school. He entered the professional ranks in February 1960 and quickly attracted the attention of senior clubs by his skilful play on the left wing. In January 1962, almost on his 19th birthday, he joined Leicester City for a £20,000 fee, and was the first of the local trio to leave. He served City well for more than 12 years, during which time he topped over 250 appearances and scored close on a century of goals. More recently, Mike Stringfellow has gone into the newsagent's business, first in Sutton-in-Ashfield and then in Alfreton.

	LEAGUE		*FA CUP*		*FL CUP*		*TOTAL*	
	App	*Gls*	*App*	*Gls*	*App*	*Gls*	*App*	*Gls*
1960-61	33	6	2	0	1	0	36	6
1961-62	24	4	2	1	3	1	29	6
	*57	10	4	1	4	1	65	12

* One appearance v Accrington Stanley not included after their record was expunged.

England Youth international Dave Syrett went to Mansfield Town from the club where he began his career as an apprentice, Swindon Town. He was one of player-manager Peter Morris' major signings as the Stags prepared for a first taste of Second Division soccer in the 1977-8 season. A native of Salisbury, Syrett earned schoolboy honours with the South-West of England representative side. He first came to Swindon's notice playing in a youth team managed by one of the club's directors. The young player saw four managers in quick succession in charge at Swindon, whilst progressing through the youth ranks. Fred Ford invited him for trials at the County Ground, Dave Mackay signed him on and guided him in the early months of his career, Les Allen saw him blossom into a striker of note and when Danny Williams returned to manage Swindon from Mansfield, Syrett became a first-team regular. He made over 120 first-team appearances for the club and scored 37 goals, top-scoring with 15 in 1975-6. In fact it was Syrett who kept Ray Clarke out of the Swindon line-up and led to his move to Mansfield in 1974. In the season prior to joining Mansfield, Syrett had a two-month period on loan with Wolves and might have become a regular member of the Molineux staff but for the fact that he was recalled by Swindon because they were hit by a crop of injuries. He struck up an immediate understanding with Ernie Moss at Field Mill, but when Moss was sidelined by a pelvic injury there was little support for him up front and the Stags were back in the Third Division at the end of the season. Whilst with the Stags, Syrett had 65 first-team League outings and scored 20 goals before he moved to Walsall as part of the deal which brought Terry Austin to Field Mill in March 1979. His stay at Fellows Park was only a short one, for in August of the same year he moved to Peterborough United and scored 24 goals in 75 outings before concluding his Football League stint with a season at Northampton Town, where he made 42 appearances and scored 13 goals.

DAVE SYRETT

	LEAGUE		*FA CUP*		*FL CUP*		*TOTAL*	
	App	*Gls*	*App*	*Gls*	*App*	*Gls*	*App*	*Gls*
1977-78	42	16	2	0	2	0	46	16
1978-79	23	4	1	0	2	0	26	4
	65	20	3	0	4	0	72	20

Barrie Thomas was the sort of player worth his weight in gold, no matter which era you take into consideration, for he was a natural goalscorer. His original club, Leicester City, did not quite take this into consideration when they allowed the youngster, who had come up through the junior ranks, to join Mansfield Town on a free transfer after only seven senior outings in which he scored three goals, even though Thomas had gained England Youth honours whilst at Filbert Street. In fact the Stags took him on more or less as a stand-by, but his potential was soon realized and by the end of his first season at Field Mill he had scored 23 League goals — a post-war club record. After two years at Mansfield, in which he made 72 League appearances and scored 48 goals, he moved on to Scunthorpe United, then a Second Division outfit. If anything his goal-scoring qualities were even greater with United, bringing him 67 goals in 88 appearances, a record which tempted Newcastle United to step in with a successful £40,000 bid in January 1962. Unfortunately, injuries restricted his first-team outings at St James' Park, although before he returned to Scunthorpe in November 1964 he had added a further 26 goals to his record in 52 appearances. Thomas' final club was Barnsley, with whom he lifted his goals-tally to over 200 with 18 in 43 games.

	LEAGUE		*FA CUP*		*TOTAL*	
	App	*Gls*	*App*	*Gls*	*App*	*Gls*
1957-58	32	23	0	0	32	23
1958-59	34	21	1	1	35	22
1959-60	6	4	0	0	6	4
	72	48	1	1	73	49

BARRIE THOMAS

DAVE THOMPSON

David Thompson was an out-and-out winger who began his career as a youngster with Wolverhampton Wanderers, but after four years at Molineux, in which he managed only eight senior outings, he was transferred to Southampton. However, in four years at The Dell he pulled on a first-team shirt on only 21 occasions. Then it was off to Mansfield Town in October 1970 and he was a first-team regular for most of his four years at Field Mill. In December 1973, Thompson joined Chesterfield for a four-figure fee but he left the club in a controversial manner after scoring five goals in 14 appearances. Thompson's family were Yorkshire farmers and he joined the family business.

	LEAGUE		*FA CUP*		*FL CUP*		*TOTAL*	
	App	*Gls*	*App*	*Gls*	*App*	*Gls*	*App*	*Gls*
1970-71	34	8	2	0	0	0	36	8
1971-72	40	4	4	2	2	0	46	6
1972-73	38/2	8	1	0	2	0	41/2	8
1973-74	17	1	3	1	2	0	22	2
	129/2	21	10	3	6	0	145/2	24

COLIN TOON

Full-back Colin Toon was discovered playing for local side, New Houghton, and signed as a professional in July 1957, soon after his 17th birthday. Originally he was a right winger but developed into a solid and consistent right-back. In all he made well over 200 League appearances, despite breaking a leg early in the 1963-4 season. He served Mansfield well for nine years and the Stags were his only club. After leaving the Football League he joined a supermarket chain and became a foreman storeman. Toon can still be seen in action on the football field as a member of a local ex-professionals XI which earns a great deal of much-needed finance for local charities. It would be remiss to fail to mention the only goal Colin Toon ever scored at senior level for Mansfield. That was at Workington on 14 March 1963 — but the Stags lost 3-2, with Brian Hall the other scorer.

	LEAGUE		*FA CUP*		*FL CUP*		*TOTAL*	
	App	*Gls*	*App*	*Gls*	*App*	*Gls*	*App*	*Gls*
1957-58	7	0	0	0	-	-	7	0
1958-59	17	0	0	0	-	-	17	0
1959-60	19	0	1	0	-	-	20	0
1960-61	42	0	2	0	1	0	45	0
1961-62	44	0	2	0	3	0	49	0
1962-63	42	1	5	0	0	0	47	1
1963-64	16	0	0	0	2	0	18	0
1964-65	17	0	2	0	0	0	19	0
1965-66	9	0	0	0	0	0	9	0
	*213	1	12	0	6	0	231	1

*One appearance v Accrington Stanley not included after their record was expunged.

Colin Treharne is rated by the more mature Mansfield Town supporters as one of the best goalkeepers the club has ever had other than Ron Arnold. And that, considering that the Stags have had more than their fair share of quality 'keepers, is praise indeed. He played 32 games in his first full season, then was an ever present in the following two campaigns. In July 1966, he moved to Lincoln City but stayed only one season. On leaving professional football, Treharne went into the frozen food business in which he is still engaged, living in the Lincolnshire town of North Hykeham. For a time he also kept up his interest in football as manager of local Scunthorpe side, Ashby United. He also had a spell with Ilkeston Town.

	LEAGUE		*FA CUP*		*FL CUP*		*TOTAL*	
	App	*Gls*	*App*	*Gls*	*App*	*Gls*	*App*	*Gls*
1961-62	32	0	2	0	1	0	35	0
1962-63	46	0	5	0	3	0	54	0
1963-64	46	0	1	0	2	0	49	0
1964-65	38	0	2	0	2	0	42	0
1965-66	29	0	1	0	2	0	32	0
	191	0	11	0	10	0	212	0

COLIN TREHARNE

Alan Tyrer joined his home-town club, Everton, as a junior and signed professional forms when he was 17. He found a first-team place hard to come by at Goodison and after five years with the club was transferred to Mansfield in June 1963. Whilst with Everton, Tyrer had only nine first-team League outings and at Field Mill he switched between inside and outside-left before gaining a regular place at outside-right towards the last quarter of the season. In August 1965 he was transferred to Arsenal but in two years at Highbury he did not figure in the Gunners' senior side. Two years later he was on the move again, this time to Bury, but again could not command a regular senior spot. That move came in August 1967 and 11 months later he was again transferred, this time to Workington. In seven years with the club he made 228 League appearances and scored 18 goals before bowing out of the Football League scene.

	LEAGUE		*FA CUP*		*FL CUP*		*TOTAL*	
	App	*Gls*	*App*	*Gls*	*App*	*Gls*	*App*	*Gls*
1963-64	23	4	0	0	1	0	24	4
1964-65	18	1	1	0	2	1	21	2
	41	5	1	0	3	1	45	6

ALAN TYRER

DENNIS UPHILL

Inside-forward Dennis Uphill was already a much-travelled player before he arrived at Field Mill in March 1957. But apart from Tottenham Hotspur, where the Bath-born player began his career as a junior, he served all five of his subsequent clubs well. His main claim to fame during his 30 months with Mansfield was that he scored his 100th League goal in the Stags' final game of the 1957-8 season. Uphill signed professional forms for Spurs in September 1948, just a month after his 18th birthday, but in two seasons at White Hart Lane, he managed only half a dozen League outings and scored two goals. In February 1952 he joined Reading and in three seasons at Elm Park made 92 League appearances and netted a very creditable tally of 43 goals. Uphill's next club was Coventry City, where he moved in October 1955, and again his record — 17 goals in 49 matches — was a very acceptable contribution. Charlie Mitten took the player to Mansfield in March 1957 and it is worthy of note that in the final 13 fixtures of the 1956-7 season, the newcomer scored six goals. Uphill left Mansfield in June 1959, during the reign of Sam Weaver, and was recruited by Watford, where in 51 senior outings in the League he showed his scoring potential had not diminished by netting 30 goals. Crystal Palace was his final club, the move being made in October 1960, and once more the goals continued to flow, with 17 in 63 League games before he bowed out of the League scene to join Rugby Town.

	LEAGUE		*FA CUP*		*TOTAL*	
	App	*Gls*	*App*	*Gls*	*App*	*Gls*
1956-57	13	6	0	0	13	6
1957-58	26	13	0	0	26	13
1958-59	44	19	1	2	45	21
	83	38	1	2	84	40

Striker Mick Vinter could well have annexed his home county's signature tune *The Lincolnshire Poacher* as his own personal property, for the Boston-born player had a flair for poaching goals for every club with which he was associated during his career. Indeed, during the 1989-90 season, when he assisted Matlock Town, he showed that his goal-grabbing instincts were still very much an asset. Notts County realized the youngster's potential when he was with Boston United as a teenager and took him on to the Meadow Lane staff in March 1972, just before his 18th birthday. In a seven-year stint with the Magpies, Vinter saw first team action in over 150 games and scored 53 goals when County were a Second Division outfit. A £150,000 fee saw Vinter transferred to Wrexham in June 1979, soon after the Welsh club had been promoted into the Second Division. At the Racecourse he added a further 90 appearances and 25 goals to his record before another £25,000 changed hands and he moved to Oxford United. In two seasons with United, Vinter saw action with the first team on 67 occasions in the League and scored 21 goals before he finally arrived at Field Mill, with a £10,000 fee the key to the move back nearer home.

MICK VINTER

	LEAGUE		*FA CUP*		*FL CUP*		*FR Trophy*		*TOTAL*	
	App	*Gls*	*App*	*Gls*	*App*	*Gls*	*App*	*Gls*	*App*	*Gls*
1984-85	31/2	3	0	0	2	1	4	0	37/2	4
1985-86	21	4	1/1	0	4	2	5	0	31/1	6
	52/2	7	1/1	0	6	3	9	0	68/3	10

No history of Mansfield Town would be complete without reference to Ken Wagstaff, the man who was undoubtedly the most popular player ever to wear a Stags' shirt. And considering the number of local youngsters who have cut their soccer teeth at Field Mill and gone on to make their mark at a high level in the sport, it is appropriate that he was another home-grown player plucked from a local team. Langwith Woodland Imps was the club and it was whilst with this Mansfield Youth League team that Wagstaff had a trial with Rotherham United and was turned down. But Raich Carter had no such qualms and threw Wagstaff into first-team action on 30 August 1960, well before his 18th birthday on 24 November, along with another talented local youngster, Mike Stringfellow. Wagstaff scored both the goals in a 2-1 win at Rochdale and went on to score nine goals in 27 League games in his first season. In 1961-2 he scored 12 in 42 League outings plus three in the Cup, then reached his peak in 1962-3 as his striking partnership with Roy Chapman blossomed. Wagstaff scored 34 League goals in 44 matches and added seven more in five FA Cup outings. The goals continued to flow in 1963-4, with 29 in 46 League games, but time was running out for Mansfield Town and the almost inevitable move to a more senior club came on 12 November 1964, when he joined Hull City for a then sizeable £40,000 fee. Wagstaff had made almost 200 League and Cup appearances for the Stags and scored 105 goals and before he left the Football League scene after 11 years at Boothferry Park, that total had soared to over 300 in the League and Cup, with 173 in 347 League matches for the Tigers. He spent some time playing and coaching in Australia before returning to become a local publican near Hull, where he is still revered, even more so, if that were possible, than at Mansfield.

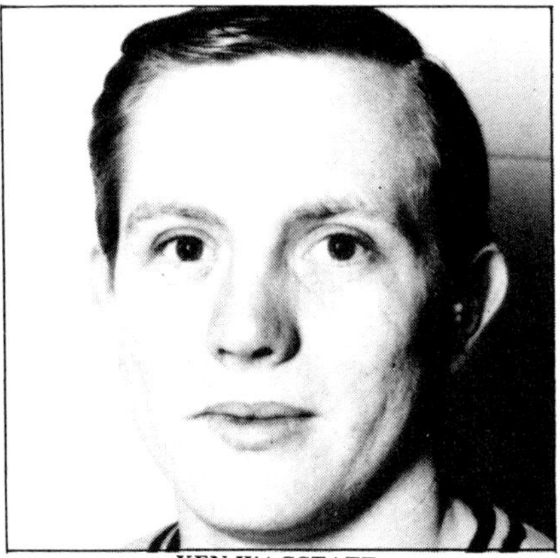

KEN WAGSTAFF

	LEAGUE		*FA CUP*		*FL CUP*		*TOTAL*	
	App	*Gls*	*App*	*Gls*	*App*	*Gls*	*App*	*Gls*
1960-61	27	9	0	0	0	0	27	9
1961-62	42	12	2	0	3	3	47	15
1962-63	44	34	5	7	0	0	49	41
1963-64	46	29	1	0	2	0	49	29
1964-65	22	9	0	0	2	2	24	11
	*181	93	8	7	7	5	196	105

*One match v Accrington Stanley not included after their record was expunged.

Manager Tom Eggleston used to say that defender Clive Walker was a product of his 'little black book'. That was where he kept references of players he had noted on his travels, players who might prove useful at a later date. Walker turned out to be 'more than useful,' for he spent six glorious years with Mansfield in which the Stags enjoyed outstanding success, particularly in the FA Cup. This pacey left-back, whose additional asset was his ability to support his forwards with dangerous breaks down the flanks, was born in Leicester and joined City as an apprentice when he was 16, after earning English Schools international honours. After three years at Filbert Street, during which time he made 17 first-team appearances, Walker was transferred to Northampton Town. That was in October 1966 and in the following two seasons he was a regular in the Cobblers' line-up, and it was a little surprising when he was given a free transfer at the end of that second season. But out came that 'little black book' and although Walker and his family were away on holiday, a note from manager Eggleston lay on the door-mat when they returned. Within 24 hours he was a Mansfield Town player, starting a full-back partnership with Sandy Pate which is rated among one of the best ever enjoyed by the Stags. For the next five seasons, Walker only rarely, and always because of injury, was out of the Mansfield line-up. But youth will out and waiting in the wings was a youngster who was to become a Mansfield Town stalwart — Barry Foster. Walker picked up an injury at Cambridge United on 24 September 1974 and gave way to Foster in the following game. The youngster took full advantage of the opportunity to make the left-back spot his own property. Given a free transfer at the end of the 1974-5 season, Walker's next club was non-League Chelmsford City, but it was not long before he was back with Northampton Town, first as coach, and then for a spell as manager before reverting to coach, a position he held at the end of the 1989-90 season.

CLIVE WALKER

	LEAGUE		*FA CUP*		*FL CUP*		*TOTAL*	
	App	*Gls*	*App*	*Gls*	*App*	*Gls*	*App*	*Gls*
1969-70	45	1	6	0	3	0	54	1
1970-71	46	2	2	0	3	0	51	2
1971-72	41	0	4	0	2	0	47	0
1972-73	40	3	1	0	2	1	43	4
1973-74	42	2	4	1	2	0	48	3
1974-75	9/6	0	0	0	1	0	10/6	0
	223/6	8	17	1	13	1	253/6	10

A Yorkshireman, born in Leeds, wing-half Phil Waller was allowed to slip over the border into Derbyshire and join Derby County as a junior. He turned professional in May 1961 and remained at the Baseball Ground until 1968, topping the century-mark in appearances and playing in the 1967-8 League Cup semi-final against Leeds United before moving to Mansfield Town for £6,000 as soon as the Cup run was over in March. Waller became a vital member of new boss Tom Eggleston's successful FA Cup team in 1968-9 and again the following season. And even when Eggleston moved on, Waller was still very much part of new manager Jock Basford's plans. Waller spent five seasons at Field Mill and had planned well for his future, for when he finally left the game, he was a partner in a highly-successful motor business in Mickleover on the outskirts of Derby. Waller played in two Northern Premier League championship-winning teams with Boston United and also saw service with Ilkeston Town, where he was player-manager, Matlock Town, Burton Albion, Belper and Kimberley Town.

	LEAGUE		*FA CUP*		*FL CUP*		*TOTAL*	
	App	*Gls*	*App*	*Gls*	*App*	*Gls*	*App*	*Gls*
1967-68	13	0	0	0	0	0	13	0
1968-69	45	1	7	0	1	0	53	1
1969-70	40	0	6	1	3	1	49	2
1970-71	34/3	0	2	0	3	0	39/3	0
1971-72	21/3	0	4	0	2	0	27/3	0
	153/6	1	19	1	9	1	181/6	3

PHIL WALLER

Sid Watson was another of the band of local players recruited by Mansfield Town and who gave the club loyal service which extended well into double figures of years. During the war years he served as a Bevan Boy at Pleasley Colliery and then joined a local beer, soft drinks and mineral water merchants after the end of hostilities. He continued working for the firm in the afternoons after signing for the Stags as a part-time player from Palterton Welfare in January 1949. Watson signed full-time professional forms a year later and made his senior debut on 22 December 1951, at home to Workington. His final senior game, ten years later, was on 3 May 1961 in a goalless draw at Gillingham. When he left League soccer, Watson returned to his original job and stayed until 1970, when he joined the staff of the Coalite company at Bolsover. In 1983 he became a member of the transport staff at the local King's Mill Hospital, where he is still employed. After Mansfield Town he played for four years with Ilkeston Town and was playing in local football for Coalite FC when he was 51. Watson still found time to help out at Field Mill, coaching the youngsters in the 'A' and 'B' teams. He was also a good cricketer and was piling on the runs for local Bassetlaw League side, Pleasley Colliery, when he was 55. Unlike many former Mansfield players, Sid Watson regularly attends most of their home matches.

	LEAGUE		*FA CUP*		*FL CUP*		*TOTAL*	
	App	*Gls*	*App*	*Gls*	*App*	*Gls*	*App*	*Gls*
1951-52	21	1	0	0	-	-	21	1
1952-53	30	1	3	1	-	-	33	2
1953-54	39	0	2	1	-	-	41	1
1954-55	39	1	1	0	-	-	40	1
1955-56	42	1	2	0	-	-	44	1
1956-57	41	1	2	0	-	-	43	1
1957-58	25	4	2	0	-	-	27	4
1958-59	24	0	1	0	-	-	25	0
1959-60	22	0	0	0	-	-	22	0
1960-61	9	0	1	0	1	0	11	0
	292	9	14	2	1	0	307	11

SIDNEY WATSON

Defender Steve Whitworth had a great football pedigree — playing for England at Schools, Youth, Under-23 and winning seven full caps. So Mansfield Town were fortunate that Whitworth completed an outstanding career at Field Mill at the invitation of manager Ian Greaves as the new manager prepared for his first full season after taking over in February 1983. Whitworth was born at Coalville, Leicestershire, and it was hardly surprising that his talent was recognized by Leicester City at a very early age. He signed for them in November 1969, after progressing through the Filbert Street youth teams, and went on to complete 352 League outings and collect a Second Division championship medal before moving to Sunderland for £125,000 in October 1981. Whitworth was a key player as Sunderland gained promotion to Division One as runners-up in 1979-80. In 1981 he moved to Bolton Wanderers soon after the Trotters, with Greaves in charge, had made it to the First Division. The experienced defender found it hard to adjust to Fourth Division football after arriving at Field Mill, although he was almost an ever-present in his two seasons there. However, there was one moment to treasure for Whitworth in his final season in the Football League — and one equally big disappointment. In the 41st minute of a 1-1 draw with Hereford United on 23 March 1985 he scored his first-ever senior goal in over 650 appearances, albeit from the penalty-spot. He repeated the feat twice more in the closing weeks of the season, one in the Freight/Rover meeting with Burnley. The disappointment came on 20 May 1985, when Mansfield lost to Wigan Athletic in a penalty competition in the Freight/Rover Trophy Northern Area Final at Field Mill, when a win would have taken Whitworth to Wembley for his final appearance. He was granted a transfer at the end of the season as he wished to take up a business appointment in the south of England.

STEVE WHITWORTH

	LEAGUE		*FA CUP*		*FL CUP*		*FR Trophy*		*TOTAL*	
	App	*Gls*	*App*	*Gls*	*App*	*Gls*	*App*	*Gls*	*App*	*Gls*
1983-84	41	0	2	0	2	0	1	0	46	0
1984-85	39	2	2	0	2	0	5	0	48	2
	80	2	4	0	4	0	6	0	94	2

FRANK WIGNALL

International forward Frank Wignall arrived at Field Mill during an eventful week at Mansfield Town. It began on Monday, 8 November 1971 when manager Jock Basford and his assistant John Quigley were sacked. Chairman Arthur Patrick dashed over to the Baseball Ground on the Thursday to sign Wignall, for what was a modest £8,000 fee considering he had scored six First Division goals for Derby that season. The same afternoon the chairman announced the appointment of Danny Williams as the new Mansfield manager. By then the Stags had already adopted the look of a side on its way to relegation and, if the undoubted quality and experience of the former England forward was expected to resolve the dire situation, then the final outcome was a disappointment. Mansfield went down but only just, by 0.003 of a goal as Wignall failed to make the expected impact. He stayed only two seasons with the club before being given a free transfer and moved into non-League soccer as manager of King's Lynn. He joined Burton Albion in 1974, was national coach in Qatar and then managed Shepshed Charterhouse from July 1981 to March 1983. His career had begun with Everton in 1958, after being discovered playing with Lancashire club, Horwich RMI. After five years at Goodison Park, Wignall moved to Nottingham Forest, where in four years he made 155 League appearances and scored 47 goals. His next club was Wolves and then Derby County as Brian Clough took the Rams into Division One and then to the League Championship. Wignall gained two England caps and represented the Football League.

	LEAGUE		*FA CUP*		*FL CUP*		*TOTAL*	
	App	*Gls*	*App*	*Gls*	*App*	*Gls*	*App*	*Gls*
1971-72	23/2	8	2	0	0	0	25/2	8
1972-73	27/4	7	1	0	2	1	30/4	8
	50/6	15	3	0	2	1	55/6	16

Apart from a short spell with non-League club Wisbech Town, George Williams had spent his League career in Yorkshire before moving to Mansfield Town in July 1957, in Charlie Mitten's first season as the Stags' boss. Mainly operating as a wing-half, Williams, nevertheless, was not averse to a run-out in the forward line if required. He had his first taste of senior football with Rotherham United, after coming up through the club's junior ranks, but moved to Sheffield United in May 1954. However, it was whilst he was with Wisbech that he received the call from Bradford City to sign for them in June 1956, although his stay at Valley Parade lasted only 13 months. It was then that Williams arrived at Field Mill, for what was probably the best spell of his career. He spent five seasons with the Stags after making his debut at Darlington on 1 February 1958, the start of a career with Mansfield in which he made well over 150 appearances.

	LEAGUE		*FA CUP*		*FL CUP*		*TOTAL*	
	App	*Gls*	*App*	*Gls*	*App*	*Gls*	*App*	*Gls*
1957-58	12	0	0	0	-	-	12	0
1958-59	29	1	0	0	-	-	29	1
1959-60	32	2	3	0	-	-	35	2
1960-61	45	2	1	0	0	0	46	2
1961-62	36	0	2	0	3	0	41	0
	*154	5	6	0	3	0	163	5

* One match v Accrington Stanley not included after their record was expunged.

GEORGE WILLIAMS

Ian Wood, who was born in Kirkby-in-Ashfield, was another in the long list of local lads who turned to Mansfield Town in the hope of launching a career in professional football. The surprising fact is that Wood had all the makings of turning into a top-class defender but then in the end retired early to join the family butchers' business. He came up through the apprentice ranks at Field Mill, turning full-time professional in June 1976 when he had reached his 18th birthday. By then he had already made his Football League debut, on 11 October 1975 against Peterborough United, only four months and 17 days after his 17th birthday. He was not quite the youngest player at that time to wear a Stags senior shirt, for he was pipped by Peter Morris some 15 years earlier. He went on to complete 135 League games before being given a free transfer at the end of the 1981-2 campaign. Undoubtedly Wood endured the highs and lows of a soccer career while with the Stags. He was with the club in the heady days of promotion as champions of the Fourth Division, and in the first-team squad when the feat was repeated in the Third Division two seasons later. He made 40 senior League and Cup appearances in the Second Division, but then saw the other side of the coin as the Stags slipped all too quickly back into the Fourth Division. Ian Wood had a short spell with Aldershot but, after making only 14 appearances in 1982-3, he decided to hang up his boots.

	LEAGUE		*FA CUP*		*FL CUP*		*TOTAL*	
	App	*Gls*	*App*	*Gls*	*App*	*Gls*	*App*	*Gls*
1975-76	2	0	0	0	0	0	2	0
1976-77	13/1	0	2	0	0	0	15/1	0
1977-78	36	1	2	0	2	0	40	1
1978-79	6/11	0	1	0	0	0	7/11	0
1979-80	21	0	2	0	4	1	27	1
1980-81	21/2	4	2	0	0	0	23/2	4
1981-82	36	4	1	0	3/1	1	40/1	5
	135/14	9	10	0	9/1	2	154/15	11

IAN WOOD

Ian Wood (left) pictured in action against Hartlepool on 16 March 1981 when the Stags lost the Division Four match 1-0.

There is one anecdote that long-serving goalkeeper Dennis Wright enjoys relating over his pint in Palterton Welfare. He first became associated with Mansfield Town as a youngster just before World War Two, when he was on their books as a reserve goalkeeper. Leicester City arrived for a wartime fixture with only nine players, not an unusual occurrence for clubs in those days, and Wright, who was on leave, was one of the two players loaned to the visitors. He played at centre-forward and, although City lost 3-2, he scored both their goals. So, perhaps the Stags missed out by using him in goal, although he was an exceptionally fine 'keeper and a wonderful servant to the club. In over 15 years as a player at Field Mill he made 400 appearances and then spent a number of years as a groundsman. He decided very early on that he was going to be a goalkeeper, for he was a star in that position for his local schoolboy team, Chesterfield Boys. He joined local club, Clay Lane Rangers, and before hostilities commenced he had been discovered by Mansfield and signed as an understudy to Welsh international, Jack Hughes. After the outbreak of war, Wright joined the Army and was stationed in Northern Ireland where he guested for Glentoran, winning a Unity Cup-winners' medal. He also played for the Army in Scotland and on the Continent and recalls playing for the British Army XI against a team of internationals and restricting the defeat to a very slender one. In 1945 he was permanently back with Mansfield and on first-team duty. He lost his place for a time to Harold 'Polly' Searson, but when Searson was transferred to Leeds United, Wright regained his place. Wright's first senior match as the Football League got back to normal action in 1946 was at home to Watford on 9 October 1946 in a 2-0 win. His final League outing was on 22 September 1956 at home to Oldham Athletic in a 4-2 defeat, although he did play in a friendly match two days later against a Managers XI at Field Mill in front of 6,658 fans, when Mansfield won 6-5. It is perhaps indicative of Wright's popularity that over 14,000 fans packed into Field Mill for his testimonial game on 5 May 1951, when a Mansfield Town XI v Stoke City XI match ended 1-1. Neil Franklin, Tim Ward and Jack Stamps boosted the Mansfield side, whilst Harry Oscroft led the Stoke team. After giving up the post of groundsman at Field Mill, Dennis Wright took over the stewardship of a local miners' welfare club, a position he held until he retired.

	LEAGUE		*FA CUP*		*TOTAL*	
	App	*Gls*	*App*	*Gls*	*App*	*Gls*
1946-47	32	0	1	0	33	0
1947-48	15	0	0	0	15	0
1948-49	27	0	3	0	30	0
1949-50	41	0	2	0	43	0
1950-51	45	0	6	0	51	0
1951-52	46	0	2	0	48	0
1952-53	29	0	1	0	30	0
1953-54	46	0	2	0	48	0
1954-55	43	0	1	0	44	0
1955-56	46	0	2	0	48	0
1956-57	9	0	0	0	9	0
	379	0	20	0	399	0

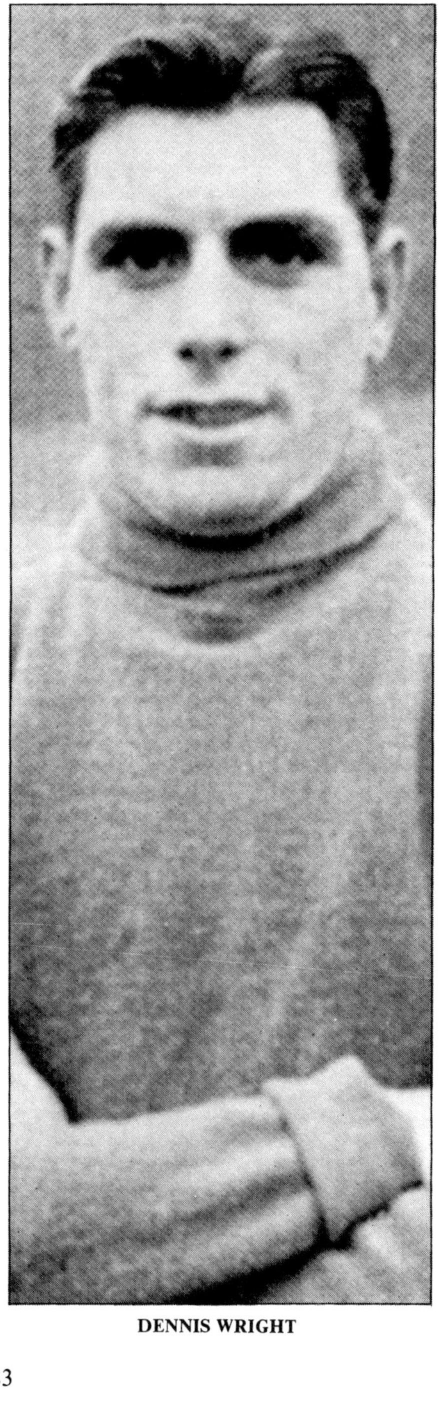

DENNIS WRIGHT

ROBINSON WYLLIE

When Mansfield Town were searching for an experienced goalkeeper towards the end of the 1950s, they turned to Robinson Wyllie, who was with the third club in his career, Plymouth Argyle. Wyllie, who was born in Dundee, had begun his career with his local team, Dundee United, before he signed for Blackpool in May 1953. After two seasons and 13 senior outings he joined West Ham United in May 1956, but again could make only 13 senior League appearances before he was on the move once more, this time to Plymouth. Within just over a year, Wyllie was on his way to Field Mill, another signing by manager Sam Weaver. It was with Mansfield that Wyllie enjoyed the most successful period of his career. He made his Mansfield debut on 3 October 1960, at Shrewsbury, although it was perhaps not an occasion to recall with any pleasure for Mansfield lost 6-3. However, Wyllie missed only one match throughout the remainder of the campaign and was an ever-present the following season. In 1961-2 he was a regular up to 14 October, after which he was replaced by Colin Treharne. Indeed, only three matches before his final outing with the Stags, the 'keeper was in the line-up for the League Cup second round meeting with Cardiff City on 5 October, when the Field Mill floodlights were switched on by Billy Wright.

	LEAGUE		*FA CUP*		*FL CUP*		*TOTAL*	
	App	*Gls*	*App*	*Gls*	*App*	*Gls*	*App*	*Gls*
1959-60	34	0	3	0	-	-	37	0
1960-61	46	0	2	0	1	0	49	0
1961-62	12	0	0	0	2	0	14	0
	*92	0	5	0	3	0	100	0

* One appearance v Accrington Stanley not included after their record was expunged.

Mansfield Town 1960-61. Back row (left to right): W.Humble, B.Williams, D.Bradley, R.Wyllie, G.Jones, L.Delapenha, S.Carter (trainer). Front: D.Wragg, A.Fitzsimmons, I.Hollett, T.Emery, S.Watson.

New signing Martin Clark is welcomed to Field Mill by Bill Dearden.

Match to Remember 1 — 12 January 1929

Wolverhampton Wanderers 0 Mansfield Town 1

McLachlan

MANSFIELD Town had become a force in non-League football after taking over the tenancy of Field Mill immediately following the end of World War One. But it still took seven separate applications before they eventually were admitted to the Football League in 1931 and there is little doubt that their exploits in the FA Cup in the 1928-9 season, and the accompanying publicity surrounding their supposed 'egg and milk' training methods, played no mean part in obtaining senior status.

They dismissed Ardsley, winning the replay 2-0 on 14 November 1928 after a 2-2 draw away four days earlier. Then, on 24 November they saw off Shirebrook 4-2 to earn a meeting with Barrow on 8 December. The Stags won at Holker Street with a Harold Morris goal to set up a trip to Molineux to meet Wolves, FA Cup winners on three occasions.

The match report in the *Mansfield Advertiser* said that Mansfield were a capable and well-balanced side with no lack of confidence and they never allowed the Wolves to settle down to their normal game.

They kept the ball swinging about with long passes to either wing and Cooke and McLachlan replied with accurate centres. The vital goal came after 26 minutes, when Cooke put over a high centre to find Morris, who was closely marked. Nevertheless he tapped the ball to McLachlan, who lifted it over Lewis's head into the net. Morris had the ball in the net a second time before the interval but his effort was disallowed for offside.

Mansfield did not make the mistake of trying to sit on their advantage in the second half and, although the Wolves rallied to threaten the Stags' goal, the Mansfield defenders and goalkeeper Staples never faltered.

Wolverhampton Wanderers: Lewis; Williams, Shaw, Brown, Hollingsworth, J.Kay, Richards, Green, Weaver, Marshall, Baxter.
Mansfield Town: Staples; Anthoney, Jackson, Kay, Chambers, McKenna, McLachlan, Staniforth, Morris, Kerry, Cooke.

Referee: J.Tilston (Chester) — *Attendance: 21,000 (£1,354)*

The Mansfield team that made history in 1929. Back row (left to right, players only): Freeman, Chambers, Jackson, Staples, Anthoney, McKenna. Front row: McLachlan, Staniforth, Morris, Kerry, Cooke. The trainer with the towel is Wilf Marples.

Arsenal 2 Mansfield Town 0

Peel, Jack

'WITH their colours still flying, and after they had more than merely held their own for nine-tenths of the game, Mansfield Town went down gallantly to the formidable Arsenal at Highbury on Saturday'. That was how the *Mansfield Advertiser* prefixed their report on this match.

The newspaper added: 'It was a splendid game to watch, packed full of thrills and incident, and but for the tragedy of a missed penalty the Stags might still have enhanced further their reputation. To Arsenal the victory, but to Mansfield the honour.'

Over 2,000 Mansfield supporters made the trip to North London for the match and the outstanding incident for them was the penalty miss by the Stags' captain, Chris Staniforth, who took on the task himself when all his other colleagues declined.

That incident came in the 33rd minute, when Morris was brought down by Butler. Staniforth fired in a powerful, low shot but too near to goalkeeper Lewis, who beat the ball down with his fists, caught it on the rebound and cleared.

Goalkeeper Staples to the rescue, punching the ball clear during an Arsenal attack.

Despite the disappointment, Mansfield continued to hold their own and it was not until nine minutes from time that the Gunners finally broke through against the run of play.

The local paper described the goal thus: 'Anthoney conceded a corner in tackling Brain. Hulme placed the flag-kick splendidly and from a crowd of players, Peel succeeded in heading past Staples, who had come off his line in an endeavour to punch away.'

Two minutes later it was all over as David Jack 'evaded the Mansfield defence in tricky style' and finished off with a left-foot drive which Staples had no chance of saving, although he did manage to touch the ball as it went just inside the post.

Arsenal: Lewis; Parker, Hapgood, Baker, Butler, Blythe, Hulme, Jack, Brain, Peel, Jones.
Mansfield Town: Staples; Anthoney, Jackson, Kay, Chambers, McKenna, McLachlan, Staniforth, Morris, Kerry, Cooke.

Referee: F.W.Reeve (Devonport) *Attendance: 44,493 (£2,982 13s 4d)*

Match to Remember 3 — 29 August 1931

Mansfield Town 3 Swindon Town 2

Readman, Broome 2 *Morris, Lawley*

ALL previous attendance records at Field Mill were broken as Mansfield Town made their Football League debut in the Third Division South.

Reports of the match indicated that some spectators grew impatient with the formalities as the Mayor of Mansfield was introduced to each player and there were loud cries of: 'Get on with it!'

When the two teams finally 'got on with it' there was plenty to keep the spectators happy, particularly in the first half. But the home fans had a shock when Morris gave the visitors the lead with the game only four minutes old, when he headed in a fine cross from Nicholls.

Swindon quickly settled down but the Stags gradually began to get the measure of their opponents. It was Gilhespy who inspired Mansfield's first goal in the Football League and sparked off a spell of scoring in the final 15 minutes of the first half.

Joe Readman had the honour of scoring the Stags' initial goal as he headed in Gilhespy's centre. Swindon replied immediately and regained the lead within two minutes. But Gilhespy was again Mansfield's inspiration as he took the ball to the corner and sent over a centre which Broome trapped and turned into the net.

And it was Broome who dashed in to intercept a Stansfield back-pass attempt to give Mansfield the lead just before the interval and, as it turned out, the Stags' first-ever maximum points in the League.

The second period did not live up to the opening half as both sets of players began to feel the effects of a very hot afternoon. The match report said: 'The afternoon was more in keeping with cricket and ice cream than the exertions of soccer'.

There were no further goals, although Wilson in the Mansfield goal was called upon to make two superb saves to preserve the home advantage. At the final whistle the home fans invaded the pitch to cheer the Mansfield players into the dressing-rooms.

Mansfield Town: Wilson; Clifford, England, Wake, Davis, Blackburn, Gilhespy, Readman, Johnson, Broome, Baxter.
Swindon Town: Cope; Stansfield, Girvan, Godfrey, Greenwell, Braithwaite, Nicholls, Starsmore, Morris, Laycock, Lawley.

Referee: A.J.Jewell (London) *Attendance: 12,232*

Match to Remember 4 — 23 January 1937

Mansfield Town 8 Hartlepools United 2

Harston 7, Rattray — *Proctor (pen), Wigham*

TED Harston was obviously the man of this match, but his efforts were the outcome of some remarkable teamwork, all the more impressive in view of the ground conditions with the pitch a veritable quagmire in places.

The centre-forward's personal triumph was due, in no small measure, to the scant attention he received from Hartlepools' centre-half Dick Hardy.

The result was that he had ample opportunities and found the weak spots in the defence time and time again, although missing one or two sitters.

Nevertheless, the visitors were by no means submissive and fought hard up to the last 15 minutes when they lost goalkeeper Billy Moore through injury. Thereafter the Stags did pretty well as they liked.

Harston's two opening goals were against the run of play, for Hartlepools showed plenty of forward skill in the early stages of the game.

The first goal came after 13 minutes and was one of the 'prettiest' seen at the ground, according to a local reporter. Harston received a clever cross pass from Horne and raced up the field and across goal, beating Proctor on the way, and placed the ball past Moore.

Rattray then dribbled down the wing, beating two defenders before crossing for Harston to shoot into goal.

Then a save by Moore led to Mansfield's third goal after 30 minutes. The ball went out to Roy, who returned it for Rattray to tap in. Proctor then reduced the arrears from the penalty-spot to conclude the first-half scoring.

Harston scored twice in as many minutes soon after the restart, the first from Roy's centre and the second following a Vaux free-kick.

On the hour, Harston scored his fifth goal, from Roy's centre, and five minutes later added his sixth, after which Johnny Wigham scored Pools' second.

Harston's club and personal record-breaking seventh goal came from a Rattray centre. He miskicked a first-time effort but recovered to make sure at a second attempt.

Hartlepools were down to ten men for the final 15 minutes when goalkeeper Moore went off injured and centre-half Hardy took over between the sticks.

Mansfield Town: Black; Vaux, Bungay, Brown, Hart, Wood, Rattray, Atkinson, Harston, Roy, Horne.
Hartlepools United: Moore; Proctor, Allison, Hill, Hardy, Graham, Scott, Wigham, McCambridge, Robertson, Self.

Referee: C.Fletcher (Cambridge) — *Attendance: 2,696*

Match to Remember 5 — 31 January 1951

Mansfield Town 2 Sheffield United 1

(after extra-time)

Steele, Ottewell — *Thompson*

SEVERAL local factories closed down for the afternoon and many others staggered their lunch hours to enable anyone who wished to attend this Wednesday afternoon fourth-round FA Cup replay at Field Mill. The morning shifts at a number of collieries also began early to allow the miners to attend the match.

The previous Saturday, Mansfield had held their Second Division neighbours to a goalless draw at Bramall Lane in front of 48,696 fans. Now well over 20,000 fans packed into Field Mill for the replay, thus breaking the ground attendance record. They saw the Stags qualify to meet Blackpool in the fifth-round, the furthest Mansfield had progressed in the competition at that time.

It was a pulsating game, wrote a local reporter, with Mansfield beginning in a workmanlike manner and Sheffield showing signs of nervousness under pressure, with miskicks frequent.

The first big thrill came after only five minutes when Coole flighted in a centre. Ottewell was unable to collect it but Steele ran in and tried a first-time shot which Ted Burgin had to go full length to save.

There were innumerable free-kicks in a typical Cup-tie in which over-robust methods repeatedly held up play.

United took the lead against the run of play. No sooner had Thompson wasted a possible chance than he again received the ball from the great Jimmy Hagan and made amends by finding the net.

It was some 17 minutes after the restart before Sheffield's goalkeeper, Burgin, handled the ball again, but five minutes later the crowd went wild as Steele equalized. The former England international hooked the ball over his shoulder past the helpless Burgin, following a centre by Ottewell.

Then in the 23rd minute of extra-time, Ottewell netted the winner. Burgin saved from Coole at the expense of a corner and when his accurate flag-kick came over, it was headed neatly into the net.

Mansfield Town: Wright; Chessell, Bradley, Antonio, Grogan, Lewis, Coole, Reeve, Steele, Barks, Ottewell.
Sheffield United: Burgin; Furniss, Cox, Hitchin, Latham, Fountain, Thompson, Brook, Bottom, Hagan, Jones.
Referee: F.H.Gerrard (Preston) *Attendance: 20,314*

Match to Remember 6 10 February 1951

Blackpool 2 Mansfield Town 0

Mudie, Brown

'MANSFIELD's exit from the Wembley stakes at the fifth-round hurdle surprised no one. But the way they went out did!

'It was a bitter disappointment to the many thousands of local supporters who travelled to Blackpool on Saturday, that the end turned out to be such an anti-climax'.

The *Mansfield Chronicle* no doubt voiced the opinion of Mansfield's supporters of the period, who had hoped to see a repeat of the 'do-or-die' attitude of the Sheffield games.

'Mansfield's approach was stale, flat and unprofitable', declared the reporter. 'All because it seemed that the Stags were haunted by the 'Matthews complex' and adopted negative tactics (not very effectively) instead of playing the kind of game that proved its worth against Sheffield United'.

When Mansfield announced their team just before the start, with Eddie Barks at outside-left, it was realized that his sole job would be to mark Matthews.

'This he did for all of the 90 minutes', said the match report. 'And it was to the detriment of the balance of the team!'

With their right wing under heavy supervision, it left the Blackpool left flank with an unusual amount of freedom, which was exploited to the full by the fast-moving Bill Perry, the report added.

And it was from this wing that the first goal came as Stan Mortensen veered to the left and, although he fell injured, Jackie Mudie collected the ball and scored.

Just before half-time Matthews won a corner and when it came over, Wright beat out a Mortensen header, but only as far as Allan Brown, who scored from the rebound.

Although they were two goals down, Mansfield carried on in the second half with the same plan of campaign and the system which had paid them no dividends in the first half.

'It would have been difficult to beat the Blackpool defence on a normal showing', declared the report, 'but with Mansfield's depleted attack it was hopeless. Shimwell had a holiday, and goalkeeper Farm was bored with the whole proceedings!'

The reporter remarked that when Chessell went off with an injured leg after 19 minutes of the half and returned limping on the left wing, this gave the forward line the best appearance of the afternoon, and almost produced a goal when Ottewell intercepted a careless clearance and sent a pass through the middle, only to see Shimwell just beat the chasing Coole and Chessell to the ball.

Blackpool: Farm; Shimwell, Garrett, Johnston, Hayward, Kelly, Matthews, Mudie, Mortensen, Brown, Perry.

Mansfield Town: Wright; Chessell, Bradley, Antonio, Grogan, Lewis, Coole, Reeve, Steele, Ottewell, Barks.

Referee: W.J.Edwards (Somerset) *Attendance: 33,060*

Mansfield Town during the Freddie Steele era. Back row (left to right): Lewis, Field, McLean, Wright, Bramley, Barks, Steele, Bradley, Carter (trainer). Middle row: Simmons, Grogan, Simpson, Ketley, Evans, Mayfield, Chessell. Front row: Ottewell, Ryan, Fox, Watson, Reeve.

Match to Remember 7 — 10 January 1953

Mansfield Town 0 Nottingham Forest 1

Ardron

THE general opinion of the first-ever FA Cup meeting between two of Nottinghamshire's three Football League clubs was that it did not produce the expected rip-roaring, thrill-a-minute affair.

But it did produce something infinitely more satisfying — a 90-minute feast of good football.

Ironically, however, both sides appeared to be affected by the same malady — an inability to turn good approach work into goals.

That was evident early on when Forest's Wally Ardron failed to get a foot to the ball close in, when it seemed the simplest of tasks.

And after having a goal disallowed for offside, Mansfield's Ken Reeve failed completely to connect when picked out by a perfect centre from Charlie Adam.

Forest's new right-wing combination of Tommy Martin and Alan Moore caused the majority of problems for the Mansfield defence and it was from good work by these two that Ardron turned in the winner in the 13th minute, to leave the Stags' long-serving goalkeeper, Dennis Wright, helpless.

This was Wright's first senior outing for over four months, having missed the previous 19 matches after breaking a wrist at Barrow on 20 September. And he played brilliantly.

Forest were kept on the defensive for long periods in the second half and did well to prevent an equalizer.

This was Field Mill's biggest-ever attendance and one which will now never be exceeded. It brought in gate receipts of £2,838 15s.

Earliest arrivals at Field Mill for the game were three Forest supporters, who turned up at the ground at 9.15am and were joined half an hour later by a couple of Mansfield fans.

Mansfield Town: Wright; Chessell, Bradley, Barks, Plummer, Lewis, Coole, Fox, Marron, Reeve, Adam.
Nottingham Forest: Walker; Whare, Hutchinson, French, Gager, Burkitt, Moore, Martin, Ardron, Scott, Collindridge.

Referee: W.Ling (Cambridgeshire) *Attendance: 24,467 (£2,838 15s)*

Match to Remember 8 — 26 November 1962

Mansfield Town 7 Crystal Palace 2

Wagstaff 3, Chapman 2, Hall, Askey — *Phillips (og), Summersby*

PALACE had earned an FA Cup second-round replay at Selhurst Park on the Saturday, thanks to a last-minute penalty awarded to the home side by Middlesbrough referee Kevin Howley.

And after the final whistle, as the players left the field, the entire Mansfield team, with the exception of goalkeeper Colin Treharne, 'applauded' the referee as he made his way to the dressing-room.

For this, ten Mansfield players were booked, although Mr Howley failed to notify all ten and they did not realize the fact until reading about it in the Sunday newspapers.

It was an injudicious action by the referee, which brought a great deal of unwelcome publicity for Mansfield and could have made the replay an explosive affair.

There could have been some ugly scenes if the Stags had not smoothed things over by turning in another of their goal-happy performances.

Mansfield's 'golden boy', Ken Wagstaff, simply tore Palace apart and scored a hat-trick as well as missing three other good chances. Roy Chapman weighed in with a brace and Ian Hall and Colin Askey tidied it up with a goal apiece.

From a financial point of view it turned out well for both sides. A crowd of 13,414 watched the affair at Selhurst Park, over 17,000 were at the replay.

Mansfield Town: Treharne; Toon, Humble, S.Chapman, Phillips, Morris, Askey, I.Hall, Wagstaff, R.Chapman, Weir.
Crystal Palace: Glazier; Howe, Little, Long, Evans, Werge, Uphill, Summersby, Burridge, Smillie, Allen.

Referee: K.Howley (Middlesbrough) *Attendance: 17,118*

Match to Remember 9 — 26 February 1969

Mansfield Town 3 West Ham United 0

Roberts, Keeley, Sharkey

IT took a long time for this fifth-round FA Cup tie to be concluded, for it was postponed no fewer than five times because of heavy snowfalls.

But it was well worth the wait as Mansfield hammered the Hammers, their three World Cup stars, Bobby Moore, Martin Peters and Geoff Hurst and all.

It was the first occasion that the Stags had ever defeated a First Division side

Dudley Roberts (number 10) gives the Stags a shock 22nd-minute lead against mighty West Ham.

and part of a rare season in which the club defeated teams from five other divisions on their way to the sixth round of the FA Cup.

That was made up of Northern League amateurs Tow Law Town, Third Division Rotherham United, Second Division Sheffield United, Fourth Division Southend United and First Division West Ham.

And whatever else, because of the postponements, Mansfield appeared for the first and only time so far in the draw for the FA Cup semi-finals.

It was all over after only 49 minutes, by which time Mansfield were 3-0 in front. West Ham had their chances early on, but once Dudley Roberts had given the Stags the lead after 22 minutes, the writing was on the wall for the Hammers.

Ray Keeley made it 2-0 in the 37th minute and Nick Sharkey killed off the opposition four minutes into the second half.

Mansfield fans thronged the streets, celebrating until the early hours of the morning, chanting and even singing Christmas carols.

Mansfield Town: Hollins; Pate, Hopkinson, Quigley, Boam, Waller, Keeley, Sharkey, Ledger, Roberts, Goodfellow.
West Ham United: Ferguson; Bonds, Howe, Peters, Stephenson, Moore, Redknapp, Lindsay(Boyce 14 mins), Brooking, Hurst, Sissons.

Referee: E.T.Jennings (Stourbridge) *Attendance: 21,117*

Match to Remember 10 — 8 March 1969

Mansfield Town 0 Leicester City 1

Fern

MANSFIELD'S dream of appearing in the FA Cup semi-final was shattered in the 58th minute of the sixth-round tie when Rodney Fern met Len Glover's cross to beat goalkeeper Dave Hollins with a neat header.

But Leicester's real strength was in defence where David Nish, Bobby Roberts, John Sjoberg, Peter Rodrigues and Graham Cross gave nothing away. And in goal there was the up-and-coming Peter Shilton, who pulled off a couple of fine saves to frustrate the Stags, who found goal chances few and far between.

Indeed, Dudley Roberts, Bob Ledger and Nick Sharkey were never as effective as they had been in the earlier rounds and were never really able to shake of the shackles imposed by the City back line.

Leicester may well have had a more decisive passage into the semi-final, but for two excellent saves by Hollins and the intervention of the woodwork.

Indeed, until the breakthrough, Mansfield had looked as safe in defence as the visitors. But with the need to attempt to force an equalizer, more gaps were created, and Hollins was the stumbling block which prevented further goals.

Mansfield Town: Hollins; Pate, Hopkinson, Quigley, Boam, Waller, Keeley, Sharkey, Ledger, Roberts, Goodfellow.
Leicester City: Shilton; Rodrigues, Nish, Roberts, Sjoberg, Cross, Fern, Gibson, Lochhead, Clarke, Glover.

Referee: K.Howley (Middlesbrough) *Attendance: 23,500*

Dudley Roberts (number 10) and Phil Waller (6) challenge John Sjoberg and Peter Shilton watched by Leicester players Graham Cross (left) and Allan Clarke.

Match to Remember 11 — 7 February 1970

Leeds United 2 Mansfield Town 0

Giles, Clarke

ASK any one of the 10,000 Mansfield fans who made the trip to Elland Road for this fifth-round FA Cup tie and they still remain convinced that Jimmy Goodfellow's 13th-minute effort, which got the 'thumbs down' from the referee, should have counted.

Had Mr Castle had the opportunity to see Dudley Roberts in action previously, he would have required no convincing of Roberts' ability to climb unaided above defenders to almost unbelievable heights to win the ball in the air.

That was what the ex-Coventry player had done to claim the ball at the expense of the challenging Paul Reaney, to set up the opening for Goodfellow's strike.

The referee remained unconvinced of Roberts' ability in that direction and ruled that he had 'climbed' over the defender, so the goal was disallowed.

Had it counted, then who knows what would have happened. But what did happen was that, like the highly professional First Division team they were, Leeds took

A tense moment at Field Mill as the draw for the fourth round of the FA Cup is made. Players gather round the radio with Jock Basford, chairman Arthur Patrick and manager Tommy Eggleston.

Allan Clarke (number 8), one of the scorers in Leeds' 2-0 win, goes for goal again.

full heed of the warning and the threat from this Third Division outfit. And, in a razor-sharp burst, two goals in seven minutes killed off the Stags.

An Eddie Gray corner in the 27th minute was only partially cleared and headed back into the box for Johnny Giles to pivot and flash the ball into the net.

Then Mick Jones darted after a ball which appeared destined to go out of play and managed to screw it back for the lethal left foot of Allan Clarke to do the rest.

But there were never any signs after that of 'how many' as Mansfield buckled down to the task in hand. In fact, with a little more steadiness in front of goal, they might have made it a much tighter finish. And they certainly deserved the standing ovation afforded them by both sets of fans at the final whistle.

Leeds United: Sprake; Reaney, Cooper, Bremner, Charlton, Hunter, Lorimer, Clarke, Jones, Giles, Gray.
Mansfield Town: Brown; Pate, Walker, Quigley, Boam, Waller, Partridge, Stenson, Jones, Roberts, Goodfellow.

Referee: W.Castle (Sedgeley) *Attendance: 48,093*

Match to Remember 12 8 September 1970

Mansfield Town 0 Liverpool 0

'IT was almost Leeds United all over again', summed up a local newspaper as it reported on the Stags' second-round League Cup meeting with the mighty Liverpool at Field Mill.

At Elland Road, Mansfield had what, on the face of it, appeared to be a perfect goal disallowed. And so it was against Liverpool. Manager Jock Basford was adamant after the game that there had been no infringement before Dudley Roberts nodded in what could have been the winner in the 75th minute. Alas, referee Corbett of Wolverhampton was equally certain that Dudley had done 'a bit of pushing' before he got up to the ball.

But a fighting display by the Stags earned them a replay at Anfield, although Liverpool fans would argue that Mansfield were fortunate to be in with a chance, even as early as the half-way stage.

Certainly, the Mansfield woodwork had rarely been rattled on so many occasions as in the first 45 minutes of this game. However, it was significant that most of the visitors' efforts were from long range and only rarely did they make an opening inside the box.

Five times in the first half, the woodwork prevented the Stags from falling behind. Twice Emlyn Hughes set the crossbar quivering and Peter Thompson showed obvious frustration when a couple of explosive efforts suffered a similar fate. Then an upright prevented Bobby Graham from providing the breakthrough.

Mansfield goalkeeper Graham Brown was also at his superb best when he pulled off fine saves from the same three players.

But the tide began to turn and Ray Clemence needed two attempts before claiming a fierce shot from Malcolm Partridge. Then a Roberts header was turned away for a corner when it appeared a certain winner, before Hughes managed to block another tremendous drive by Partridge.

It was all Mansfield in the final 15 minutes and Liverpool were mighty relieved to hear the final whistle.

Mansfield Town: Brown; Pate, Walker, Quigley, Saunders, Waller, Partridge, Stenson, D.Roberts, Sutton, Jones.
Liverpool: Clemence; Lawler, R.Evans, Smith, Lloyd, Hughes, Callaghan, A.Evans, Graham, Hall, Thompson.

Referee: D.A.Corbett (Wolverhampton) *Attendance: 12,532*

Match to Remember 13 22 September 1970

Liverpool 3 Mansfield Town 2
(after extra-time)

Hughes, Smith (pen), Evans *Sutton, Stenson*

CONTROVERSY also surrounded the League Cup replay at Anfield when Liverpool, who were trailing 2-1 with only nine minutes left, were awarded a debatable penalty. It was put away by Tommy Smith to earn the Reds extra-time.

And three minutes from the end of the first period, Alun Evans applied the finishing

The Stags, pictured in 1970. Back row (left to right): Walker, Roberts, Finch, Brown, Boam, Waller. Middle: B.Foster, Goodfellow, Saunders, Partridge, I.Wright, C.Foster. Front: Stenson, Pate, Quigley, Jones, Sutton.

touch to a Steve Heighway cross from the byline to put Liverpool in front for the first time in the match.

With the replay only 90 seconds old, Mansfield had handed out a real shock when a 30-yard effort by Jimmy Sutton rebounded off the underside of the crossbar and bounced down over the line.

It was 15 minutes before the home side were able to draw level with a superb effort by Emlyn Hughes, who picked up the ball on the edge of the Mansfield penalty area and went past three defenders across the face of the goal before firing a shot into the opposite corner of the net, giving Graham Brown no chance.

The Stags regained the lead 20 minutes into the second half after a move involving John Quigley, Dudley Roberts and John Stenson was rounded off by a Stenson header.

Clive Walker was the player alleged to have handled when the penalty was awarded, despite strong protests by Mansfield and a discussion between referee and linesman.

From then on the Stags had their backs to the wall, although looking dangerous on the break. But mainly they had Graham Brown to thank for keeping Liverpool at bay with a performance that fully deserved the standing ovation afforded him by the home fans at the end of the match.

Liverpool: Clemence; Lawler, Lindsay, Smith, Lloyd, Hughes, Hall, A.Evans, Graham, McLaughlin, Heighway.
Mansfield Town: Brown; Pate, Walker, Quigley, Saunders, Waller, Goodfellow, Stenson, D.Roberts, Sutton, Jones.
Referee: D.A.Corbett (Wolverhampton) *Attendance: 31,087*

Match to Remember 14 28 April 1973

Cambridge United 3 Mansfield Town 2

Walton 2, Ross (pen) *McCaffrey, Roberts*

PROMOTION to Division Three or another term in the Fourth — they were the stark alternatives for Mansfield in this final League game of the 1972-3 season at the Abbey Stadium.

Success for the Stags would have meant a quick return to the Third Division after being relegated the previous season. In the final reckoning, if it was a gift goal which gave Wrexham a point in the final game of the previous campaign and sent Mansfield down, then it was an identical situation which kept them anchored in Division Four when they had every opportunity to achieve promotion.

Twice Mansfield hushed the packed home fans by grabbing the lead. But twice they gifted equalizing goals and then allowed Ron Walton to skip past two defenders to fire in a 61st-minute winner with his second goal of the game.

The Stags' epitaph in the local Press was undeniable: 'It is not always the most skilful or most deserving side football-wise that takes the honours in the Football League. But often the one that possesses character to shrug off disasters and fight back with sheer guts and determination to succeed.'

Early on Jim McCaffrey rattled the home upright with a fine effort and Mansfield more than deserved the lead provided by McCaffrey from the rebound after goalkeeper Peter Vasper had only been able to block a fierce drive by Paul Matthews.

Within four minutes the Stags had wasted all their previous effort by conceding an unnecessary free-kick just outside of the penalty area, from which Walton equalized.

Dudley Roberts regained the advantage two minutes from half-time and again it was McCaffrey who was involved in the build-up. Again, however, the Stags let it slip in first-half injury time.

Goalkeeper Rod Arnold certainly appeared to have been impeded when he attempted to punch away a right-wing cross. The ball went straight to Ross, who chipped it towards the top corner of the net and Sandy Pate had little option but to punch the shot over the bar, Ross sending Arnold the wrong way from the resultant penalty.

Cambridge had got over their early jitters in the second half and Greenhalgh had the ball in the net soon after the restart. It was the same player who was the architect of the move which resulted in the Walton goal which ensured Cambridge achieved promotion.

Cambridge United: Vasper; Thompson, Akers, Guild, Rathbone, Watson, Eades, Greenhalgh, Lill, Ross, Walton.
Mansfield Town: Arnold; Pate, Walker, Jarvis(Fairbrother), Ellis, Bird, Thompson, Roberts, Wignall, Matthews, McCaffrey.
Referee: J.K.Taylor (Wolverhampton) *Attendance: 10,542*

Match to Remember 15 — 9 November 1974

Brentford 2 Mansfield Town 3

Cross, Simmons — *Clarke, McCaffrey, Bird*

THE author has covered well over 1,000 matches during his 20 years involvement with the affairs of Mansfield Town. And he rates this Stags performance as the best-ever by the club on opposition territory.

Brentford were eighth from bottom, whilst Mansfield headed the Fourth Division. But as the Stags discovered throughout this championship season, no matter what the opposition's placing, they always managed to pull out their best when up against the leaders.

Ray Clarke gave Mansfield a 28th-minute lead in a match played throughout in pouring rain, before Roger Cross, who had scored a hat-trick in the corresponding match the season before, equalized in the 55th minute.

But these were mere incidentals in a match which was already full of blood-tingling stuff. And to fuel it even further, Dave Simmons gave Brentford the lead in the 73rd minute.

It seemed then that the Stags were in for a yet another shock defeat at one of their least favourite venues over the years. That was until five minutes later when Jim McCaffrey was involved in a sweet move down the right which scattered the Brentford defence to enable him to volley in an equalizer.

Six minutes from time, with the home fans urging on their side in the hopes of achieving victory, Kevin Bird silenced the terraces by looping a header over the 'keeper after a corner had not been cleared, to give Mansfield the points.

Brentford: Sherwood; Bence, Scales, Smith, Lawrence, Riddick, Graham, Metchick, Simmons, Cross, Salvage.
Mansfield Town: Arnold; Pate, B.Foster, Matthews, C.Foster, Bird, Lathan, Eccles, Clarke, Hodgson, McCaffrey.
Referee: L.Shapter (Torquay) *Attendance: 5,560*

Jimmy McCaffrey keeps cool to score against Brentford in one of the Stags' best-ever away performances.

Match to Remember 16 — 21 April 1975

Mansfield Town 7   Scunthorpe United 0

Clarke 2, Hodgson, Eccles, Lathan 2, Bird

MANAGER Dave Smith inherited the Field Mill hot seat on Wednesday, 3 April 1974 — and one year, two weeks and six days later he had guided the Stags to their first championship since they were elected to the Football League 44 years earlier.

And what a way to make sure of moving up into Division Three as champions, having lost only six League games all season and scored 90 goals against 40 conceded.

Even at half-time of this game there was little sign of the goal-avalanche to come, for United had packed their penalty area well to restrict Mansfield to a 2-0 advantage by the interval, with Ray Clarke and Gordon Hodgson the scorers in a seven-minute spell midway through the opening session.

Terry Eccles got the second half away to a flyer four minutes after the restart. And it was something of a surprise that it took the Stags all of a further 24 minutes before man of the match Lathan scored a well-deserved goal to launch a late goal blitz, the ball helped into the net by Eccles.

Ray Clarke beats the despairing dive of goalkeeper Norris during the Stags' 7-0 win over Scunthorpe which clinched the Division Four championship.

Clarke joined in after 77 minutes, and Lathan put away his second nine minutes from time to leave Kevin Bird to round off the historic occasion in the 86th minute.

The success could hardly have been described as 'surprising', for the Stags had reached the top of the division in the second week of September and, apart from a period when they were involved in the FA Cup and had fallen behind with their League programme, they had never relinquished the proud placing.

In addition to their League achievements, Mansfield had also found time to reach the fifth round of the FA Cup, where they were dismissed by First Division Carlisle United, who, although outplayed on the day, managed to scrape a 1-0 victory.

Mansfield Town: Arnold; Pate, B.Foster, Matthews, Madden, Bird, Lathan, Eccles, Clarke, Hodgson, McCaffrey.
Scunthorpe United: Norris; Lynch, Peacock, Simpkin, Atkin, Money, Collier, Oates, Charnley, Roberts, Pilling.

Referee: C.L.Newsome (Shropshire) *Attendance: 11,020*

Match to Remember 17 3 December 1975

Manchester City 4 Mansfield Town 2

Royle, Oakes, Tueart, Hartford *Clarke, Bird*

THINGS may not have gone right for Dave Smith and his team immediately after Mansfield's return to Division Three. And success in the League Cup was little

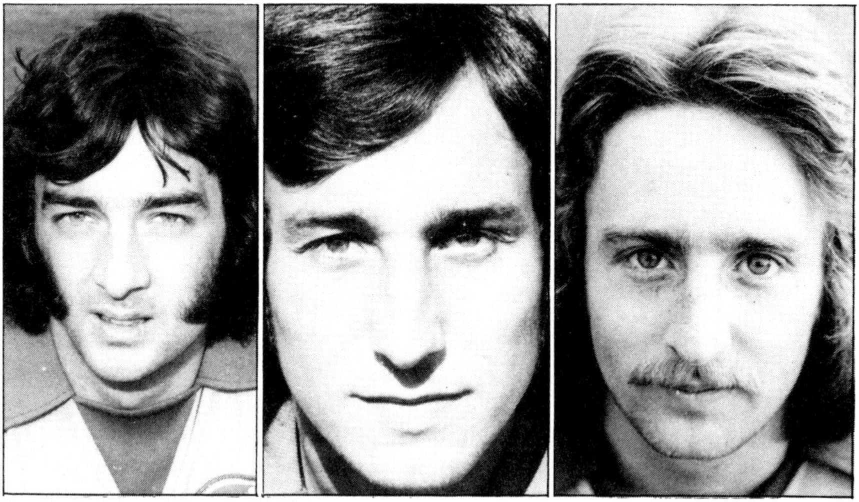

Ray Clarke (left) and Kevin Bird (right) were on target against Manchester City, while Colin Foster (centre) did his best to keep out the highly-rated City attack.

consolation when the Stags languished at the foot of the table with a quick return to Division Four a possibility, even with the season not yet at the half-way stage.

But Mansfield had reached the fifth round for the first time in their history with victories over senior clubs Coventry City and Wolverhampton Wanderers on their way to Maine Road. And so their game against Manchester City ranks as one of the high spots in the Stags' story.

City ended Mansfield's run, but most agreed that the Stags defeat was mainly self-inflicted. An injudicious Sandy Pate back-pass gifted City with their third goal. Then Terry Eccles inexplicably miskicked with the goal at his mercy when an equalizer looked a certainty with the Stags 3-2 down.

Joe Royle provided City's ninth-minute breakthrough, only for Ray Clarke to cancel it out eight minutes later as Joe Corrigan failed to clear one of a series of corners won by Jim McCaffrey, who caused the home defence some early nightmares.

Asa Hartford set up City's second goal in the 36th minute, although it was a miskick by Tommy Booth as the centre came across which deceived the Mansfield defence and left Alan Oakes with a simple tap-in chance.

It was Dennis Tueart who made Mansfield pay for the Pate back-pass in the 56th minute, to give his side the cushion of a 3-1 lead. But that was narrowed by Kevin Bird in the 61st minute.

However, it was all over with four minutes remaining after Roy Brown had blocked Hartford's first effort but could do little as the rebound fell kindly for the same player.

There was a standing ovation from the home fans for the Stags, who left still feeling that they should have been in the semi-finals and not the First Division outfit.

Manchester City: Corrigan; Clements, Donachie, Doyle, Watson, Oakes, Barnes, Booth, Royle, Hartford, Tueart.

Mansfield Town: R.Brown; Pate, B.Foster, McDonald, Madden, Bird, Matthews (Mackenzie), Eccles, Clarke, Hodgson, McCaffrey.

Referee: K.Burns (Stourbridge) *Attendance: 30,022*

Match to Remember 18 — 9 April 1977

Port Vale 1 Mansfield Town 4

Harris — *Randall, Bird 2, C.Foster*

MANSFIELD had been hovering around the top three in the Third Division for much of the 1976-7 season. But it was this match at Vale Park on Easter Saturday, at the start of a tough three-match holiday programme, which heralded the start of the Stags' successful final push towards promotion to Division Two, and the club's second championship in three seasons.

Player-manager Peter Morris had stated that four points were a minimum requirement from the Easter matches and six a passport to Division Two.

A maximum six was the eventual reward against formidable opposition which also included fellow promotion-chasers Shrewsbury Town and neighbours Chesterfield. But until Kevin Bird put away the first of his two goals in the 52nd minute at Vale Park, there had been little sign of the Stags' true form.

Kevin Randall had given the visitors the lead against the run of play with a breakaway goal in the 23rd minute to keep up his record of having scored every time he had played against the Potteries side, whether for Chesterfield, Notts County or Mansfield.

That lead had lasted only four minutes, however, as Dave Harris provided Vale's deserved equalizer following a corner. But a reshuffled formation in the second half, as player-manager Morris failed to reappear because of a calf injury, turned the game on its head.

Bird's goal followed a fine cross from Barry Foster, helped on by Randall. And his second in the 79th minute was a real stunner, with Randall once again involved. Then Colin Foster killed off the opposition with a great header from a Johnny Miller corner four minutes from time.

Port Vale: Connaughton; McLaren, Griffiths, Dulson, Harris, Lamb, Bailey, Brownbill, Cullerton, Beamish, Beech.
Mansfield Town: Arnold; Bird, B.Foster, McEwan, C.Foster, Wood, Morris(McDonald), Moss, Randall, Hodgson, Miller.

Referee: M.R.Garner (Liverpool) — *Attendance: 4,389*

Match to Remember 19 — 14 May 1977

Wrexham 0 Mansfield Town 1

Moss

MANSFIELD were already assured of a place in Division Two the following season when they arrived at the Recreation Ground, Wrexham. But for the club and the 3,500 of their fans who made the trip into North Wales, the championship as the icing on the cake was the aim.

Two points were absolutely crucial for Wrexham, for after leading the way for most of the season, they had lost at home the previous Wednesday to Terry Venables' Crystal Palace, who had scored twice in the last 90 seconds to deny the Welshmen the point they required to ensure promotion, and virtually booked their own place in Division Two.

Wrexham had to defeat the Stags to redress the balance and keep Palace in Division Three — but the emotion and pressure of the day took its toll on the home side.

They certainly had the opportunity to collect both points, which in the end would not have denied Mansfield the championship, anyway.

But whilst the Stags kept their cool, the Welshmen were caught up by the fervour of their 17,000 or so fans in the 20,000 crowd. Their frantic response often produced long periods of prolonged pressure but this was coupled with the squandering of chances which, on another day, might have brought the vital goals.

Billy Ashcroft, who had scored 27 goals in the season, twice had the goal at his mercy with time and space in which to pick his spot, but failed miserably each time.

Then there was Mansfield's Player of the Year, goalkeeper Rod Arnold, who added to the home side's frustrations with superlative saves to deny Graham Whittle and Ashcroft.

And to cap it all, with the Wrexham fans already streaming from the ground convinced that all was lost, the old firm of Moss and Randall made doubly sure only 90 seconds from time with a classic goal right out of their repertoire.

Randall slipped past his marker and crossed from the byline for Moss to collect his 20th goal of the season.

One Mansfield player needed convincing that it was all over and the Stags had won and were the champions. Rod Arnold was knocked out right on the half-time whistle and had to be led to the dressing-room. Although he resumed, he could recall little of what had gone on in the 90 minutes.

Wrexham: Lloyd; Evans, Dwyer, Davies, Roberts, Thomas, Shinton, Sutton, Ashcroft, Whittle, Lyons. Substitute: Cegielski.
Mansfield Town: Arnold; Bird, Wood, McEwan, Mackenzie, C.Foster, Morris, Moss, Randall, Hodgson, McDonald. Substitute: Matthews.

Referee: H.Hackney (Barnsley) *Attendance: 20,706*

Ian Mackenzie gets a lift from Kevin Bird, and Billy McEwan also joins in the celebrations, following the 1-0 victory over Wrexham at the Racecourse Ground which made sure of the Second Division title.

Three of the players involved in the tense penalty defeat by Burnley – Johnny Miller (left), scorer Dave Syrett (centre) and Gary Saxby.

Match to Remember 20 — 7 November 1978

Burnley 0 Mansfield Town 1
(after extra-time – Burnley won 8-7 on penalties)

Syrett

PENALTY competitions to decide drawn matches, not a common occurrence in the late 1970s, were nevertheless, becoming near to a little habit-forming for Mansfield Town in the 1978-9 Anglo-Scottish Cup competition.

The Stags had seen off top Scottish club Partick Thistle in the second leg of their quarter-final tie at Field Mill in similar fashion, winning 3-1 on penalties after an aggregate score over the two legs of 3-3.

Reserve goalkeeper Martin New was the hero on that occasion after replacing the injured Rod Arnold in the 65th minute of a bruising encounter. He pulled off two magnificent saves in extra-time and then capped a fine performance by saving Thistle's first two penalty attempts.

But at Turf Moor, Arnold, now recovered, did not match New's penalty peformance against the Second Division side, although he kept the Stags in the game with a couple of superb stops in the second half of normal time.

Burnley had won 2-1, somewhat fortunately, in the first leg at Field Mill. But the Stags cancelled out the advantage in the 31st minute with a fine goal from Dave Syrett.

From then on it was something of a rearguard action for Mansfield, but Burnley could not find a way through either in the 90 minutes or in the extra period.

It was 6-6 in the penalty situation with Kevin Bird, Bob Curtis, Mark Goodwin, Barry Foster, Dave Syrett and Mick Saxby duly finding the back of the net for Town.

There was controversy when Gary Saxby, who had replaced Mick Coffey during the game, was turned away from the penalty-spot. But John McClelland gave Mansfield a 7-6 lead. Then there was jubilation in the Mansfield camp when Burnley's full-back, Derek Scott, hit the post with his side's seventh effort.

The celebrations were short-lived, however, when he was ordered to retake the kick because Arnold had been standing just off his line, and he succeeded with this second attempt. Dennis Martin saw Alan Stevenson save Mansfield's eighth spot-kick and when Billy Rodaway hammered in Burnley's eighth, unlucky Stags were out of the competition.

Burnley: Stevenson; Scott, Brennan, Noble, Thompson, Rodaway, Hall, Ingham, Fletcher, Kindon, James.
Mansfield Town: Arnold; Curtis, B.Foster, Coffey(G.Saxby), M.Saxby, McClelland, Miller, Bird, Syrett, Goodwin, Martin.

Referee: J.Butcher (Kendal) *Attendance: 6,871*

Match to Remember 21 15 December 1982

Bradford City 3 Mansfield Town 2

Campbell, Lester, McNiven *Dungworth, Bell*

'BRADFORD trip was so unnecessary,' read the headline fronting the report of the second-round FA Cup tie at Field Mill — and no one would disagree with that sentiment.

The tie ended in a 1-1 draw, despite City being reduced to ten men after only 20 minutes when Northern Ireland international striker Bobby Campbell was sent off for a 'professional foul' after fisting out a Dave Caldwell header to prevent a certain goal.

Incidentally, it was the second time in the same season that Campbell had been dismissed at Field Mill, for he had suffered the same fate in the Milk Cup meeting between the clubs in September.

Campbell made his mark in the replay by putting away the equalizer on the half-hour, after John Dungworth had given Mansfield the lead in the 21st minute.

But by then referee Neil Midgley of Salford had mystified everyone by disallowing a Dave Caldwell effort as early as the third minute, after the intervention of a linesman, the first of two inexplicable decisions.

Mark Lester blasted Bradford ahead five minutes from half-time, only for Charlie Bell to level matters five minutes into the second half. There was a touch of farce about David McNiven's eventual 68th-minute winner. Campbell failed to make contact with a low cross from Ian Mellor and as the ball ran kindly for Mark Ellis, his centre produced a miskick by Terry Gray. That set up the chance which McNiven could hardly have missed.

Again, however, referee Midgley and his linesmen were at fault, for it was inconceivable that they alone should fail to spot Peter Jackson's handling offence inside the box in the 76th minute.

The player made no secret of the fact after the game, although his confirmation was not required, for the fans at the other end of the ground had a clear sight of the incident.

So City were all set for a third-round confrontation with their Yorkshire neighbours Barnsley, a meeting which would have suited the Stags in view of its financial implications.

Bradford City: McManus; Podd, Chapman, Lester, Cooke, Jackson, Ellis, Gray, Campbell, McNiven, Mellor.
Mansfield Town: Arnold; Bird, Kennedy, Bell, Ayre, Calderwood, Matthews, Hutchinson, Dungworth, Caldwell, Nicholson.

Referee: N.Midgley (Salford) *Attendance: 3,081*

Mansfield Town 1 Wigan Athletic 1
(after extra-time - Wigan won 3-1 on penalties)

G.Foster *G.Foster (og)*

IT WAS only two years later that Mansfield Town made the long hoped-for trip to Wembley to return with the Freight/Rover Trophy.

But they were certainly hot favourites to have made the trip in May 1985, when the luck of the draw coupled them with Wigan Athletic in the Northern area final of the competition, and at Field Mill too.

Thus, Mansfield were only 90 minutes away from a trip to the twin towers, for the area final was sudden-death, unlike the two-legged affair of more recent times.

The start was delayed for 15 minutes to enable the long queues at the turnstiles to get into the ground, but it was well worth the wait.

There was a set-back for the Stags with the game only 15 minutes old when Tony Kelly's innocuous-looking shot from 15 yards looked to be going wide until it was deflected into the net by skipper George Foster.

It was Wigan's first effort at goal and for the rest of the half the visitors had to defend in depth to protect their slender advantage.

Wigan looked livelier in the second period and it required two excellent saves by Kevin Hitchcock to prevent the Lancastrians from extending their lead. Colin Methven also had a goal ruled out.

Neil Whatmore fires in a shot during the Freight/Rover Trophy Northern Area Final which ended in a 1-1 draw with Wigan, who went on to win the penalty shoot-out.

Even so, it appeared that Mansfield's Wembley dream had already turned into a nightmare as the game moved into the final minute.

Then, with only 40 seconds left, Neil Whatmore gained possession and beat two defenders to square the ball to George Foster, who blasted in the equalizer from 25 yards for his first goal of the season.

In the extra period, Mansfield created the better chances, without accepting a single one, and then it was Wigan's goalkeeper, Roy Tunks, who became his side's hero and the villain of the piece as far as Mansfield were concerned.

He saved the first three of Mansfield's penalty attempts from Steve Whitworth, Mick Vinter and Neil Whatmore. And although Gary Pollard did get one past Tunks and Hitchcock pulled off one save, it was unfancied Wigan whose Wembley dream came true.

Mansfield Town: Hitchcock; Whitworth, Logan, Garner, Foster, Calderwood, Lowery, Whatmore, Caldwell, Vinter, Kearney.
Wigan Athletic: Tunks; Cribley, Butler, Kelly, Walsh, Methven, Lowe, Barrow, Bennett, Newell, Langley.

Referee: A.Saunders (Newcastle) *Attendance: 9,214*

Match to Remember 23 22 April 1986

Mansfield Town 4 Hartlepool United 0

Cassells 2, Kelly (og), Chamberlain

THE broad grin on manager Ian Greaves' face said it all as Mansfield celebrated their return to Division Three in style. The Stags had achieved their manager's aim, first avowed when he took charge just over three years earlier.

Keith Cassells (second right) opens the scoring for the Stags with an 18th-minute header in the 4-0 win over Hartlepool.

But perhaps the grin was just as much about relief as pleasure, for the Stags had just gone through a period of 'promotion nerves' which had seen them without a win in their four previous matches.

There were no signs of nerves, however, right from the start of the 90 minutes as Mansfield warmed to the task of clinching a place in Division Three backed by some 5,500 fans, and at the same time ending the diminishing hopes of United.

Keith Cassells unlocked the door to promotion with a goal after only 18 minutes. He won a free-kick and picked himself up to glance in Paul Garner's perfectly-flighted cross.

But it was an unfortunate own-goal 11 minutes later which really turned the game Mansfield's way. Garner was again involved as he produced another decisive cross which Neville Chamberlain flicked on to Cassells, who turned and aimed a pass at the unmarked Kevin Kent, only to see the ball deflected by full-back Tom Kelly into his own net.

United rallied towards the close of the first half and in the opening period of the second, but Hitchcock pulled of a fine save to deny Paul Dobson. And when George Foster got back to clear a goal-bound lob from Tony Smith off the line, it was obvious it was going to be the Stags' night.

Cassells scored his second goal in the 68th minute and Chamberlain wrapped up their Third Division return nine minutes from time with his 20th goal of the season to launch the celebrations on the terraces.

Mansfield Town: Hitchcock; Graham, Garner(Collins), Lowery, Foster, Pollard, Kent, Kenworthy, McKernon, Cassells, Chamberlain.
Hartlepool United: Blackburn; Carney, Kelly, Hogan, Smith, Linighan, Honour, Dobson, Borthwick, Walker, Proudlock(Knobbs).

Referee: R. Guy (Kirkby) *Attendance: 5,523*

Match to Remember 24 15 April 1987

Chester City 1 Mansfield Town 0
(Mansfield won 2-1 on aggregate)
Woodthorpe

WELL over 3,000 Mansfield fans made the midweek trip to Sealand Road for the second-leg confrontation of the Freight/Rover Trophy Northern area final against Chester.

And it is doubtful if any side's 1-0 defeat away from home has ever been as rapturously received and wildly celebrated as this was by the jubilant Stags supporters at the final whistle.

The pressures on Mansfield became even harder to bear when, after only eight minutes, full-back Paul Garner was led from the field with a fractured cheekbone after a wild challenge by Milton Graham.

Three minutes later Wembley looked a million miles away when Colin Woodthorpe drove home a 30-yard free kick to reduce Mansfield's 2-0 first-leg advantage provided by Ian Stringfellow and Keith Cassells a week earlier. Town now led by a single goal and there were 79 minutes of the encounter still to come.

But Mansfield's defence was superb as Chester poured men forward. They restricted the home side to three clear chances in what remained of the first half. Top scorer Gary Bennett fluffed the first, but it required two dramatic goal-line clearances to keep the Stags on course for Wembley. Tony Lowery just managed to block Bennett's neat flick, but it was Tony Kenworthy, who had come on as substitute to fill the left-back spot vacated by the injured Garner, who turned the game Mansfield's way with a headed clearance right on half-time when it seemed the ball was on its way into the net.

Chester rarely threatened after that, although Gary Pollard was called upon to make two timely interceptions when it appeared that the home fans might have something to shout about. By then, though, it was only the Stags fans who could be heard.

Chester City: Stewart; Greenhough, Woodthorpe, Fazackerley(Croft), Abel, Butler, Kelly, Barrow, Bennett, Rimmer, Milton Graham.
Mansfield Town: Hitchcock; Mike Graham, Garner(Kenworthy), Lowery, Foster, Pollard, Kent, Danskin, Stringfellow(Chamberlain), Cassells, Kearney.

Referee: G. Courtney (Spennymoor) *Attendance: 8,787*

Skipper George Foster celebrates with the fans following the Stags' Freight/Rover Trophy success against Chester.

Match to Remember 25 — 24 May 1987

Bristol City 1 Mansfield Town 1

(after extra-time – Mansfield won 5-4 on penalties)

Riley *Kent*

MANSFIELD was almost a ghost town on this Sunday morning as over 25,000 Stags fans made their way to Wembley unaware of the dramatic happenings they were to witness later in the day.

It is doubtful if a professional script writer could have created a more exciting finale than the one which unfolded in the brilliant sunshine of West London.

Mansfield's heroes were the two Kevins — Kent and Hitchcock — whilst Bristol City, holders of the Freight/Rover Trophy, looked to Glynn Riley to play his part in the nerve-tingling afternoon.

Kent achieved the ambition of every professional footballer by scoring at Wembley, to give Mansfield the lead in the 57th minute.

And it could have been 2-0 within minutes, for substitute Ian Stringfellow, who had taken over from Neil Whatmore, headed against the bar soon after getting into the action.

Keith Cassells twice went close and Mark Kearney had a goal-bound effort deflected for a corner.

There was no lack of incident at the other end, either, with the highlight of the

It's a goal! Kevin Kent (right) gives Mansfield the lead in the 57th minute.

afternoon the confrontation between Mansfield's skipper George Foster and experienced Scottish international Joe Jordan.

Hitchcock pulled off the save of the match as he somehow palmed a David Moyes header away for a corner for just a foretaste of his later contribution.

There seemed only one winner as the minutes ticked away, but with only three minutes remaining, Riley found an equalizer after two previous shots had been blocked.

Extra-time produced no clear-cut decision and so, for the first time at Wembley, it was left to penalties to settle the issue.

Cassells, who must have covered every blade of grass in the 120 minutes, failed with his penalty and suddenly City were one penalty away from repeating their win of the previous year.

But they had reckoned without Hitchcock, who saved Gordon Owen's spot-kick with his legs to allow Kent to level the score at 4-4 after the first five each.

Then he repeated the effort to leave Kenworthy with the unenviable task of clinching the win with Mansfield's sixth penalty, against a former Sheffield United colleague in Keith Waugh.

Kenworthy called upon all of his vast experience to send Waugh the wrong way and the massed ranks of Mansfield fans went wild with delight.

The celebrations continued the next day when the successful team paraded through the town in an open-top bus to be greeted by thousands of ecstatic supporters.

Bristol City: Waugh; Newman, Williams, Moyes, McPhail, Llewellyn, Owen, Marshall(Fitzpatrick), Riley, Walsh(Curle), Jordan.
Mansfield Town: Hitchcock; Graham, Garner, Lowery, Foster, Kenworthy, Kent, Danskin(Pollard), Whatmore(Stringfellow), Cassells, Kearney.

Referee: A.Gunn (Burgess Hill) *Attendance: 58,586 (£324,592)*

Joe Eaton (back left) pictured with the Mansfield Board – J.B.Almond, B.Chambers. Seated: G.Bunting (vice chairman), A.F.Patrick (chairman), R.J.Windsor in 1968.

JOE EATON – TRULY 'MR MANSFIELD TOWN'

NO history of Mansfield Town Football Club would be complete without a section devoted to their club secretary, Joe Eaton, who has been connected with the club longer than anyone else, past or present.

That association began 43 years ago, in August 1947 when the young Joseph David Eaton was signed for the club on amateur forms by former England international full-back, Roy Goodall. Joe had been discovered whilst playing for Langwith Boys' Club in the North Notts Youth League, a club which has produced several notable players in its time, including England international defender Ray Wilson, the popular Ken Wagstaff and Peter Morris, among others.

Joe was brought up on the Duke of Portland's estate at Welbeck, where his father was chauffeur and his uncle the Duke's head gamekeeper. His grandfather, too, had been in the Duke's service. On leaving school, Joe joined the staff of the Mansfield Brewery as a clerk, a job he returned to after completing his National

Service. By then, however, Freddie Steele was the manager at Field Mill and he signed the young Eaton as a part-time professional.

In February 1952 he made his debut in Mansfield's reserve side and a memorable one it was too, for he scored a couple of goals. His consistent scoring qualities at that level earned him a senior outing against Crewe Alexandra at Field Mill on 1 November 1952, when the Stags won 3-0. He had another game on 20 December against Chesterfield, again at home, but this time Mansfield lost 4-1.

In all, Joe made four first-team appearances, the other two coming the following season in a 2-0 win at Chester on 24 March 1954 and his final outing on 3 April at home against Hartlepool. The Stags won 1-0 and Joe Eaton scored the goal. He said: "I thought I was a certainty for the next match at Vale Park on 5 April and I travelled with the side. But after Stan Mercer, who was manager then, had looked at the pitch, he took me on one side and said he was leaving me out because of the very heavy conditions. That didn't go down well, although I have to admit I was only a bit of a stripling in those days."

By then, of course, Joe had been appointed assistant secretary in 1953 under Bert Mee. Mee retired because of ill health and a few weeks later, in July 1956, Joe took over the running of the club. He is the longest-serving and one of the most respected club secretaries in the Football League and certainly one of the most knowledgeable in soccer affairs. There are several who have laid claim to being 'Mr Mansfield Town,' but surely none who could have a more worthy claim for the title than Joe Eaton.

Mind you, it could have all been so different, for he had the unenviable task of writing out the notification to other clubs that he had been given a free transfer. Indeed, Bradford Park Avenue came in with an offer to sign the young player, but fortunately as it turned out for Mansfield Town, he turned it down.

'Mr Mansfield' Joe Eaton, accompanied by Mrs Maureen Eaton, left, join in the Fourth Division championship celebration. Also pictured are directors John Almond and John Brown with their wives, Mrs Ray Clarke (right) and Rod Arnold.

Stags' Pre-Football League Days

Below are listed Mansfield Town's results from the first season after Mansfield Wesley had changed their name. Except where stated, the games are in the league competition applicable to the respective season.

1910-11 (Notts & Derby District League)
Sep 3 v Sutton Junction (a) 2-2
Carter 2
Sep 10 v Long Eaton St Helen's (h) 3-1
W. Wheatley, J. Wheatley 2
FA Cup Preliminary Round
Sep 17 v Market Harborough (a) 5-0
Middleton 2, J. Wheatley 2, Hall
Sep 21 v Alfreton Town (h) 1-4
Bowles (pen)
Notts Senior Cup
Sep 24 v Players Athletic (h) 2-1
J. Wheatley 2
FA Cup 1st Qualifying Round
Oct 1 v Loughborough Corinthians (h) 3-0
Ball 2, J. Wheatley
Oct 8 v Ilkeston United (a) 1-5
Middleton
FA Cup 2nd Qualifying Round
Oct 15 v Basford United (h) 2-2
Ball, J. Wheatley (pen)
Played at Basford. Mansfield's ground not available.
Replay
Oct 20 v Basford United (a) 3-1
J. Wheatley 2, Hardy
Oct 22 v Clay Cross 6-1
James 2, J. Wheatley 2 (1 pen), Ball, Middleton
Notts Senior Cup 2nd Round
Oct 29 v Stanton Hill Victoria (h) 1-1
James
FA Cup 3rd Qualifying Round
Nov 5 v Hinckley United (a) 2-1
J. Wheatley, Ball
Nov 12 v Belper Town (a) 3-4
J. Wheatley 2, Temple
FA Cup 4th Qualifying Round
Nov 19 v Blackwell Colliery (h) 0-1
Nov 26 v Blackwell Colliery (a) 3-0
J. Wheatley 2, Ball
Dec 3 v Tibshelf 2-1 (h)
J. Wheatley (pen), Walker og
Notts Senior Cup 2nd Round Replay
Dec 10 v Stanton Hill Victoria (a) 2-2
Middleton, J. Wheatley
2nd Replay
Dec 17 v Stanton Hill Victoria (n) 4-2
J. Wheatley 4
(at Sutton Town's ground)
Dec 26 v Long Eaton St Helen's (a) 2-0
J. Wheatley, W. Wheatley
Dec 27 v Ripley 3-0 (h)
J. Wheatley 3
Dec 28 v Sutton Town (a) 1-2
J. Wheatley
Dec 31 v Heanor United (h) 3-1
Middleton, W. Wheatley, J. Wheatley
Jan 7 v Stanton Hill Victoria (a) 1-3
J. Wheatley (pen)
Jan 14 v Mansfield Mechanics (h) 1-3
Middleton
Att: 3,000
Jan 21 v Tibshelf (a) 0-2
Notts Senior Cup
Jan 28 v Notts County Reserves (h) 1-1
Ball
Replay
Feb 1 v Notts County Reserves (a) 0-4
Feb 4 v Sutton Town (h) 1-1
J. Wheatley
Feb 11 v Clay Cross (a) 1-3
J. Wheatley
Feb 18 v Blackwell Colliery (h) 2-2
J. Wheatley 2, (1 pen)
Feb 25 v Mansfield Mechanics (a) 3-1
Smedley, W. Wheatley, J. Wheatley
Mar 4 v Ilkeston United (h) 2-1
James, Ball
Mar 8 v South Normanton (h) 1-0
Middleton
Mar 11 v Derby County Reserves (h) 5-3
James 2, J. Wheatley 2, Middleton
Mansfield Charity Cup Semi-final
Mar 18 v Mansfield Mechanics (h) 2-4
James, Middleton
Mar 25 v South Normanton (a) 2-0
James, Belton
Mar 29 v Derby County Reserves (a) 0-2
Apr 1 v Pinxton (h) 2-3
Wheeliker (og), W. Wheatley (pen)
Apr 5 v Sutton Junction (h) 1-1
Gelsthorpe
Apr 8 v Eastwood Rangers (a) 2-2
W. Wheatley, Middleton
Apr 15 v Eastwood Rangers (h) 2-1
J. Wheatley, Smith
Morning
Apr 17 v Pinxton (a) 2-1
J. Wheatley, Smith
Afternoon
Apr 17 v Stanton Hill Victoria (h) 1-1
Middleton
Apr 22 v Heanor (a) 1-2
J. Wheatley
Apr 24 v Alfreton (a) 0-4
Apr 26 v Belper (h) 2-1
Horsman, W. Wheatley
Apr 29 v Ripley (h) 3-1
Burgin 2, Middleton
Final placing: 9th: 34-15-6-13-66-58-36.

1911-12 (Central Alliance)
Sep 2 v Sutton Town (a) 2-3
Smedley, Middleton (pen)
Sep 9 v Peterborough GN Loco (a) 3-1
J. Wheatley 2, Ball
Sep 16 v Walsall Reserves (h) 0-3
FA Cup 1st Qualifying Round
Sep 30 v Hinckley United (a) 0-1
Oct 7 v Mansfield Mechanics (a) 1-4
Middleton (pen)
Oct 14 v Derby County Reserves (h) 1-3
W. Wheatley
Notts Senior Cup 1st Round
Oct 28 v Retford (h) 1-0
Ball
Dec 2 v Ilkeston United (h) 1-4
W. Wheatley
Notts Senior Cup 2nd Round
Dec 9 v Arnold St Mary's (h) 2-2
Wheatley (pen), Middleton
Replay
Dec 16 v Arnold St Mary's (a) 3-2
Staley, Ball, W. Wheatley
Dec 23 v Grantham Town (h) 2-1
Middleton 2
Dec 25 v Grantham Avenue (a) 1-4
Middleton
Dec 30 v Sutton Junction (a) 1-5
W. Wheatley
Jan 13 v Ilkeston United (a) 0-5
Notts Senior Cup 3rd Round
Jan 27 v Sutton Junction (a) 1-1
Evans
Replay
Feb 3 v Sutton Junction (h) 2-1
Bagnall, Middleton
Feb 10 v Derby County Reserves (a) 1-3
Ball
Notts Senior Cup Semi-final
Feb 17 v Notts County Reserves 1-3
Middleton
Feb 24 v Sutton Town (h) 1-2
J. Wheatley
Mar 6 v Peterborough GN Loco (h) 1-2
Bagnall
Mar 9 v Grantham Town (a) 2-4
Jones, Middleton
Mar 16 v Nottingham Forest (h) 1-0
Jones (pen)
Mar 30 v Sutton Junction (h) 2-4
Middleton, Ball
Apr 5 v Nottingham Forest (a) 2-4
Bagnall, Walker
Apr 6 v Long Eaton Corinthians (a) 3-2
Middleton 2, Ball
Apr 8 v Grantham Avenue (h) 5-0
J. Wheatley 2, Smedley, Jones, Middleton
Apr 9 v Long Eaton Corinthians (h) 2-1
Jones, Middleton
Apr 20 v Mansfield Mechanics (h) 1-3
Ball
Position 11th: 22-6-0-16-35-62-12.

1912-13 (Central Alliance)
Sep 3 v Sutton Town (h) 0-1
Sep 8 v Sutton Town (a) 1-2
Jones
Sep 12 v Derby County Reserves (a) 0-4
FA Cup Preliminary Round
Sep 14 v Market Harborough (h) 2-1
Bentell 2
Sep 21 v Walsall Reserves (a) 1-0
Barnett
Notts Senior Cup 1st Round
Sep 28 v Notts Rangers (h) 5-0
Blacknell 2, Statham, Whitehead, Ball
Oct 5 v Kettering (h) 4-1
Barnett 3, Whitehead
FA Cup 1st Qualifying Round
Oct 12 v Netherfield (a) 3-2
Statham, Whitehead, Blackwell
Oct 19 v Stanton Hill Victoria (a) 3-2
Blackwell 3
Oct 26 v Grantham Town (a) 1-0
Barnett
Match abandoned bad light.
FA Cup 2nd Qualifying Round
Nov 2 v Long Eaton Corinthians (h) 5-2
Blackwell 2, Radford 2, Barnett
Nov 9 v Mansfield Mechanics (h) 0-1
FA Cup 3rd Qualifying Round
Nov 16 v Sutton Town (a) 1-3
Thompson (pen)
Nov 23 v Kettering (a) 5-0
Blackwell 4, Ball
Dec 7 v Ilkeston United (h) 0-2
Dec 14 v Sutton Junction (h) 1-2
Blackwell
Dec 21 v Peterborough GN Loco (a) 0-4
Dec 26 v Mansfield Mechanics (a) 0-3
Dec 26 v Grantham Avenue (h) 1-0
Blackwell
Dec 28 v Leicester Fosse Reserves (a) 0-4
Jan 4 v Stanton Hill Victoria (h) 2-1
Barnett, Blackwell
Jan 18 v Sutton Junction (a) 1-4
Barnett
Notts Senior Cup 1st Round
Jan 25 v Kirkby Town (a) 7-1
Barnett 2, Blackwell 2, Statham, Hardy, Whitehouse
Feb 1 v Long Eaton St Helen's (h) 0-1
Feb 8 v Shirebrook (a) 3-1
Blackwell 3
Notts Senior Cup Semi-final
Feb 15 v Sutton Junction (a) 0-3
Feb 22 v Peterborough GN Loco (h) 3-0
Barnett 2, Blackwell
Mar 1 v Ilkeston United (a) 1-2
Mee
Mar 8 v Shirebrook (h) 3-1
Blackwell 2, Barnett
Mar 15 v Long Eaton St Helen's (a) 2-4
Mee 2
Mar 22 v Ripley (h) 5-1
Blackwell 3, Mee, Thompson
Mar 24 v Grantham Avenue (a) 3-1
Blackwell 2, Barnett
Mar 25 v Ripley (a) 0-1
Mar 29 v Leicester Fosse Reserves (h) 0-2
Apr 2 v Derby County Reserves (a) 1-3
Statham
Apr 5 v Eastwood Rangers (a) 2-0
Barnett, King (pen)
Apr 9 v Grantham Town (h) 2-1
Blackwell, King (pen)

Apr 12 v Gresley Rovers (h) 2-0
Blackwell, Stringfellow
Mansfield Charity Cup Semi-final
Apr 14 v Mansfield Mechanics (a) 1-1
Blackwell
Apr 19 v Gresley Rovers (a) 1-1
Hardy
Apr 23 v Walsall Reserves (h) 5-1
Blackwell 5
Apr 26 v Eastwood Rangers (h) 0-1
Position 10th: 32-13-2-17-50-54-28.

1913-14 (Central Alliance)
Sep 6 v Shirebrook (h) 3-3
Spriggs 2, Middleton (pen)
Mansfield Charity Cup Final
Sep 8 v Sutton Town (a) 0-3
Sep 13 v Ilkeston United (a) 0-3
Sep 29 v Kettering (a) 1-1
Middleton
FA Cup Preliminary Round
Sep 27 v Mapperley (h) 3-1
Riley 2, Middleton
FA Cup 1st Qualifying Round
Oct 11 v Netherfield (h) 2-2
Barnett, Dexter
Replay
Oct 16 v Netherfield (a) 4-0
Middleton 3, Bailey
Oct 18 v Holwell Works (h) 1-2
Dexter
Oct 25 v Ilkeston United (h) 1-2
Green
FA Cup 2nd Qualifying Round
Nov 1 v Hinckley United (h) 1-3
Woollett
Nov 8 v Gresley Rovers (h) 2-2
Middleton 2
Nov 15 v Mansfield Mechanics (a) 1-1
Middleton
Nov 22 v Sutton Town (a) 0-4
Nov 29 v Leicester Fosse Reserves (h) 5-0
Flanders 2, Middleton, Woollett, Parnell
Dec 6 v Long Eaton (a) 2-2
Foster, Parnell
Dec 13 v Gresley Rovers (a) 0-2
Dec 20 v Kettering (h) 1-0
Middleton
Dec 25 v Mansfield Mechanics (h) 0-4
Dec 26 v Holwell Works (a) 3-0
Ward 2, Foster
Dec 27 v Shirebrook (a) 1-6
Middleton
Jan 3 v Derby County Reserves (h) 1-2
Flanders
Jan 10 v Sutton Junction (a) 1-3
Parnell
Jan 17 v Sutton Junction (h) 3-2
Foster, Middleton, Ward
Notts Senior Cup 1st Round
Jan 24 v Sutton Junction (h) 1-2
Middleton
Jan 31 v Grantham Town (h) 1-1
Smith
Feb 14 v Long Eaton (h) 1-2
Flanders
Mar 1 v Grantham Avenue (h) 1-1
A.Smith
Mar 7 v Grantham Town (a) 0-3
Mar 14 v Leicester Fosse Reserves (a) 0-2
Mar 22 v Notts County Reserves (h) 2-1
Woollett, Hankin
Apr 4 v Notts County Reserves (a) 1-4
Marshall
Apr 9 v Leicester Imperial (a) 0-1
Apr 10 v Sutton Town (h) 2-1
Middleton (pen), Timmins
Apr 12 v Grantham Avenue (a) 1-1
Smith
Apr 22 v Derby County Reserves (a) 0-3
Position: 15th: 30-6-7-17-38-62-19
Not re-elected to Alliance because ground not up to standard.

1914-15 (Notts & Derby League)
Sep 2 v Bolsover (h) 1-4
Holden
Sep 5 v Chesterfield Municipal Reserves (a) 1-3
Blackwell
Sep 12 v Chesterfield Municipal Reserves (h) 1-5
Congrove
FA Cup Preliminary Round
Sep 26 v Sutton Town (a) 0-5
Oct 3 v New Hucknall (a) 0-3
Byron Cup
Oct 17 v Newhall Swifts (a) 0-11
Oct 31 v New Whittington (a) 3-3
Holden, Bingham, Middleton
Nov 14 v Staveley (h) 1-1
Holden
Nov 28 v Pinxton (h) 1-1
Bingham
Dec 12 v Staveley (h) 3-5
Smith 2 (1 pen), Woollett
Dec 19 v South Normanton (a) 2-5
Bingham 2 (1 pen)
Dec 25 v Alfreton (a) 0-1
Dec 26 v Alfreton (h) 4-2
Collins 2, Smith, Middleton
Jan 2 v Matlock (h) 2-1
Smith 2
Jan 9 v Hardwick Collieries (h) 3-2
Woollett, Bingham, Holden
Jan 16 v Pinxton Collieries (a) 0-2
Jan 23 v New Whittington (h) 2-1
Collins 2
Jan 30 v Matlock (a) 1-2
Collins
Feb 6 v South Normanton (h) 5-1
Collins 3, Holden, Cooper
Feb 13 v Bolsover (a) 0-4
Mar 6 v Tibshelf (h) 3-2
Morton 2, Middleton
Mar 13 v Newhall Swifts (a) 3-1
Collins 2, Middleton
Mar 20 v Tibshelf (a) 3-2
Collins, Morton, Middleton
Mar 27 v Hardwick Collieries (a) 3-2
Collins, Foster, Middleton
Apr 3 v Ripley (a) 2-2
Collins, Morton
Apr 5 v New Hucknall (h) 3-1
Morton 2, Collins
Apr 10 v Ripley (h) 2-0
Collins, Housley

Apr 24 v Newhall Swifts (h) 3-0
Housley, Middleton, Collins
Position: 4th: 26-12-4-10-52-56-28.

1915-16 (Central Alliance)
Sep 4 v Ilkeston United (a) 3-4
Housley 2, Bryan
Sep 11 v New Hucknall (a) 3-2
Brown 2, Smith
Sep 18 v Shirebrook (h) 1-2
Smith (pen)
Sep 25 v Sutton Town (h) 4-2
Smith, Brown, Housley, Foster
Oct 2 v Sutton Town (a) 1-2
Housley
Oct 16 v Shirebrook (a) 1-3
Bryan
Oct 23 v Loughborough Corinthians (h) 0-2
Oct 30 v Ilkeston United (h) 0-6
Nov 6 v Long Eaton Corinthians (a) 5-2
Harrison, Ward, Middleton, Foster 2
Nov 13 v Sutton Junction (a) 2-3
Brown, G.Smith
Nov 27 v New Hucknall (h) 0-1
Dec 4 v Mansfield Mechanics (a) 2-1
Foster, Brown
Dec 11 v Sutton Junction (h) 6-0
Foster 3, Housley, Middleton, Ward
Dec 18 v Long Eaton Corinthians (h) 3-0
Dexter, Housley, Middleton
Dec 25 v Mansfield Mechanics (h) 2-0
Housley, Olton
Dec 27 v Loughborough Corinthians (a) 0-1
Position: 6th: 16.7.0.9.34.31.14
Comforts Fund Match
Dec 31 v Mansfield Mechanics (a) 0-4
Housley 2, Middleton, Cockle (og)
Abandoned 70 mins
Subsidiary competition
Jan 8 v Sutton Town (h) 3-1
Brown, Congrieve, Middleton
Jan 15 v New Hucknall (a) 2-1
Brown, G.Smith
Jan 22 v Sutton Junction (a) 6-0
Middleton 3, Brown, Congrieve, Unknown
Jan 29 v Shirebrook (h) 2-1
Middleton, Dexter (pen)
Feb 5 v Mansfield Mechanics (h) 6-0
Middleton 3, Congrieve 2, G.Smith
Feb 12 v Sutton Town (a) 4-2
Housley 2, Foster 2
Feb 19 v New Hucknall (h) 2-1
Housley 2
Mar 4 v Shirebrook (a) 1-0
Congrieve
Mar 11 v Mansfield Mechanics (a) 6-0
Congrieve 2, Middleton, T.Smith, Housley, Bryan
Mar 18 v Sutton Junction (h) 10-1
Congrieve 3, Middleton 3, Housley 2, T.Smith 2
Position: 2nd: 10-10-0-0-42-7-20

1919-20 (Central Alliance)
Aug 30 v Hucknall Byron (h) 3-2
Middleton 2, J.Tremmelling
Sep 6 v Shirebrook (a) 1-1
Housley
Sep 13 v Sutton Junction (h) 4-6
Housley 2, Middleton 2
Notts Senior Cup 2nd Round
Sep 20 v Woodhouse Exchange (h) 3-1
Housley, Middleton, Ward
FA Cup Preliminary Round
Sep 27 v Shirebrook (a) 1-3
J.Tremmelling
Oct 4 v Sutton Junction (a) 4-1
Middleton, J.Tremmelling 3
Oct 18 v New Hucknall (h) 6-1
Housley 2, Shuttleworth, J.Tremmelling, Richardson 2 (1 pen)
Nov 1 v Long Eaton (a) 2-2
J.Tremmelling, Scrimshaw
Nov 22 v Welbeck Colliery (h) 2-0
Housley, Middleton
Notts Senior Cup 1st Round
Nov 29 v Mansfield Colliery (a) 3-1
Shuttleworth 2, Housley
Dec 6 v Leicester Reserves (h) 2-1
Middleton, Shuttleworth
Notts Senior Cup 2nd Round
Dec 13 v Kirkby Colliery (h) 2-2
Richardson 2 (1 pen)
Replay
Dec 20 v Kirkby Colliery (a) 2-1
Middleton, Shuttleworth
Dec 25 v Chesterfield Reserves (h) 8-2
J.Tremmelling 3, Housley 2, Shuttleworth 2, Middleton
Dec 26 v Shirebrook (h) 2-0
Middleton, Housley
Dec 27 v Sutton Town (h) 2-1
Middleton, J.Tremmelling
Jan 3 v Grantham Town (a) 1-1
Housley
Jan 10 v Gresley Rovers (h) 5-1
Middleton 3, Housley, Shuttleworth
Jan 17 v Ilkeston United (a) 2-0
Housley, Middleton
Notts Senior Cup 3rd Round
Jan 24 v Notts County Reserves (h) 1-0
Housley
Jan 31 v Welbeck Colliery (a) 0-1
Feb 8 v Ilkeston United (h) 2-1
Scrimshaw, Middleton
Feb 14 v Kettering (a) 0-1
Feb 21 v Kettering (h) 3-0
Middleton, Housley, S.Tremmelling
Feb 28 v Derby County Reserves (a) 1-0
Shuttleworth
Mar 7 v Loughborough Corinthians (h) 2-1
Housley, Congrieve
Notts Senior Cup Semi-final
Mar 11 v New Hucknall (a) 0-1
Mar 14 v Sutton Town (a) 6-1
J.Tremmelling 3, Scrimshaw, Congrieve 2
Mar 21 v New Hucknall (a) 4-2
Middleton 2, Shuttleworth, J.Tremmelling
Mar 28 v Gresley Rovers (a) 0-2
Apr 2 v Hucknall Byron (a) 1-0
J.Tremmelling
Apr 5 v Leicester Reserves (a) 1-2
Housley
Apr 6 v Long Eaton (h) 5-2
Housley 3, Middleton, Shuttleworth
Apr 10 v Grantham Town (h) 8-0
J.Tremmelling 3, Middleton 3, Shuttleworth, Congrieve
Apr 12 v Chesterfield Reserves (a) 3-4
Housley, Middleton, J.Tremmelling

Apr 17 v The Rest (h) 1-0
Housley
Apr 24 v Derby County Reserves (h) 1-3
Congrieve
Mansfield Charity Cup
Apr 28 v Shirebrook 0-1
May 1 v Loughborough Corinthians (a) 0-4
Position: 1st: 30-19-3-8-81-41-41

1920-21 (Central Alliance)
Aug 28 v Long Eaton (h) 7-0
Foster 3 (1 pen), J.Smith, Middleton, Housley 2
Sep 4 v Grantham Town (h) 4-1
Foster 3 (1 pen), Middleton
Sep 11 v Sutton Town (a) 4-3
Foster 2, Housley, Middleton
Sep 18 v Grantham Town (a) 0-4
FA Cup Preliminary Round
Sep 25 v Sutton Junction (h) 8-1
Foster 6, Middleton, Housley
Oct 2 v Loughborough Corinthians (h) 1-1
Middleton
Oct 6 v Shirebrook (h) 5-0
Foster 2, Richardson 2 (2 pens), Scrimshaw
FA Cup 1st Qualifying Round
Oct 9 v Hucknall Byron (h) 2-1
Middleton, Foster
Abandoned Fog
Oct 11 v Hucknall Byron (h) 5-0
Foster 3, Housley 2
Oct 16 v Shirebrook (a) 2-1
Foster, Scrimshaw
FA Cup 2nd Qualifying Round
23 Oct v Grantham Town (a) 3-1
Middleton, Scrimshaw, Housley
Oct 30 v Welbeck Colliery (a) 3-2
S.Tremmelling, Richardson, Middleton
Notts Senior Cup 2nd Round
Nov 3 v Mansfield Colliery (h) 1-0
Scrimshaw
FA Cup 3rd Qualifying Round
Nov 6 v Boots Athletic (h) 3-0
Housley 3
Nov 13 v New Hucknall (a) 3-0
Scrimshaw, J.Smith, Cottam
FA Cup 4th Qualifying Round
Nov 20 v Scunthorpe United (a) 1-0
Housley
Nov 27 v Sutton Junction (h) 2-1
Housley 2
FA Cup 5th Qualifying Round
Dec 4 v Worksop Town (a) 2-2
Scrimshaw, J.Smith
Replay
Dec 8 v Worksop Town (h) 1-4
Middleton
Abandoned Fog
Notts Senior Cup 3rd Round
Dec 11 v Newark Athletic (a) 5-2
Housley 2, J.Smith, Scrimshaw 2
FA Cup 5th Qualifying Round Replay
Dec 13 v Worksop Town (h) 0-8
Dec 18 v Retford Town (h) 4-1
Middleton 2, Housley 2
Dec 25 v Chesterfield Reserves (h) 2-2
Housley 2
Dec 27 v Welbeck Colliery (h) 6-2
Housley 4, Holt, Middleton
Dec 28 v Ilkeston United (a) 2-3
Price, Middleton
Jan 1 v Sutton Junction (a) 4-2
Housley 2, Scrimshaw, Holt
Jan 8 v Chesterfield Reserves (a) 2-0
Dowson, Middleton
Jan 15 v Hucknall Byron (h) 1-0
Housley
Notts Senior Cup 4th Round
Jan 22 v Sutton Town (a) 0-0
Replay
Jan 26 v Sutton Town (h) 2-0
J.Smith, Scrimshaw
Jan 29 v Leicester Fosse Reserves (a) 0-5
Feb 5 v Gresley Rovers (a) 0-3
Feb 12 v Ilkeston United (h) 1-1
Dowson
Feb 19 v New Hucknall (h) 1-1
Scrimshaw
Feb 26 v Loughborough Corinthians (a) 1-6
Hibbard
Notts Senior Cup Semi-final
Mar 5 v New Hucknall (h) 3-0
Cottam, Middleton, Housley
Mar 12 v Retford Town (a) 1-3
J.Tremmelling
Mar 19 v Derby County Reserves (h) 1-0
Scrimshaw
Notts Senior Cup Final
Mar 25 v Nottingham Forest (h) 2-2
Middleton 2 (1 pen)
Mar 26 v Sutton Town (h) 1-1
Housley
Mar 27 v Hucknall Byron (a) 0-1
Apr 2 v Gresley Rovers (h) 3-0
Leafe, Housley, Staniforth
Apr 6 v Kettering (h) 3-0
Staniforth 2, Middleton
Apr 9 v Leicester Reserves (h) 2-0
Staniforth 2
Apr 12 v RAF Cranwell (a) 3-3
Staniforth 2, Housley
Mansfield Charity Cup Semi-final
Apr 16 v Woodhouse Exchange (h) 0-1
Notts Senior Cup Final Replay
Apr 20 v Nottingham Forest (a) 1-2
Holt
Apr 23 v Kettering (a) 0-5
Apr 27 v Long Eaton (a) 1-0
Housley
Apr 30 v Derby County Reserves (a) 1-3
Housley
May 7 v RAF Cranwell (h) 5-1
Richardson 2, Housley, Middleton, Staniforth
Position: 5th: 34-18-6-10-76-56-42

1921-22 (Midland League)
Aug 27 v Worksop (h) 2-0
Middleton 2
Aug 31 v Gainsborough Trinity (h) 1-1
J.Smith
Sep 3 v Castleton (a) 1-2
Staniforth (pen)
Sep 10 v Wakefield City (a) 2-1
Sharpe, Staniforth
Sep 17 v Wombwell (a) 2-1
Staniforth, Sharpe

FA Cup Preliminary Round
Sep 24 v Mansfield Colliery (h) 8-0
Staniforth 5, Sharpe 2, Housley
Oct 1 v Rotherham United (h) 0-0
FA Cup 1st Qualifying Round
Oct 8 v Stanton Hill DDSS (h) 6-0
Staniforth 2 (1 pen), Mayfield 2, Sheldon, J.Smith
Oct 12 v Denaby United (h) 2-0
Staniforth, J.Smith
Oct 15 v Wath Athletic (h) 4-1
Staniforth 2, J.Smith, Housley
FA Cup 2nd Qualifying Round
Oct 22 v Grantham Town (h) 2-0
Frith, Clarke
Oct 27 v Scunthorpe United (a) 1-3
Housley
Oct 29 v Boston (h) 2-1
Staniforth 2
FA Cup 3rd Qualifying Round
Nov 5 v Welbeck Colliery (a) 2-1
J.Smith 2
Nov 12 v Wakefield City (h) 1-2
Clarke
FA Cup 4th Qualifing Round
Nov 19 v Gainsborough Trinity (a) 2-1
Foster 2
Nov 26 v Hull City Reserves (a) 2-3
T.Smith, Foster
FA Cup 5th Qualifying Round
Dec 3 v Darlaston (h) 2-0
Frith, Foster
Dec 10 v Barnsley Reserves (h) 2-1
Foster 2
Dec 14 v Mexborough (h) 1-1
Foster
FA Cup 6th Qualifying Round
Dec 17 v Walsall (h) 1-1
Staniforth
Replay
Dec 22 v Walsall (a) 0-4
Dec 24 v Hull City Reserves (h) 2-0
Tomlinson, Staniforth
Dec 26 v Wath Athletic (a) 1-0
Sheldon
Dec 31 v Grimsby Town Reserves (a) 1-3
Mite
Jan 7 v Castleford (h) 2-0
Staniforth 2
Jan 14 v Wombwell (h) 4-2
Staniforth 3, Foster
Notts Senior Cup 1st Round
Jan 21 v Nottingham Forest (a) 1-1
Foster
Jan 28 v Denaby United (a) 0-3
Notts Senior Cup Replay
Feb 4 v Nottingham Forest (h) 0-1
Feb 8 v Lincoln City Reserves (h) 6-2
Clarke 3, Mite, Frith, Staniforth
Feb 11 v Doncaster Rovers Reserves (a) 2-3
Jones, Clarke
Feb 15 v Notts County Reserves (h) 1-1
Mite
Feb 18 v Mexborough (a) 0-1
Feb 25 v Grimsby Town Reserves (h) 1-0
Foster
Mar 4 v Barnsley Reserves (a) 0-2
Mar 8 v Harrogate (a) 3-2
Staniforth, Gibson 2 (1 pen)
Mar 11 v Rotherham United (a) 0-3
Mar 15 v Harrogate (h) 3-0
Wynn, Gibson (pen), Staniforth
Mar 18 v Sheffield Wednesday Reserves (a) 1-1
Staniforth
Mar 22 v Scunthorpe United (h) 3-1
Clarke 2, Mite
Mar 25 v Rotherham United (h) 2-0
Staniforth 2
Apr 1 v Lincoln City (a) 2-2
Staniforth, Gibson
Apr 8 v Sheffield Wednesday Reserves (h) 0-1
Apr 10 v Notts County Reserves (a) 2-1
Gibson, Staniforth
Apr 15 v Nottingham Forest Reserves (h) 1-2
Mite
Apr 22 v Doncaster Rovers (h) 3-1
Staniforth 2, Housley
Apr 26 v Gainsborough Trinity (a) 3-1
Staniforth 2, Clarke
Apr 29 v Rotherham United (a) 0-1
May 1 v Nottingham Forest Reserves (a) 0-3
Position 6th: 42-20-7-15-68-57-47

1922-23 (Midland League)
Aug 26 v Worksop Town (h) 0-0
Aug 30 v Rotherham United (h) 1-2
Greatorex
Sep 2 v Nottingham Forest Reserves (h) 5-0
Greatorex 3, Clarke, Donoven
Sep 9 v Chesterfield (a) 2-3
Reed 2
Sep 16 v Gainsborough Trinity (a) 0-1
Sep 20 v York City (a) 1-4
Greatorex
FA Cup Preliminary Round
Sep 23 v Langwith Athletic (h) 2-1
Donoven 2
Sep 28 v Nottingham Forest Reserves (a) 2-1
Greatorex 2 (1 pen)
Sep 30 v Boston (h) 2-2
Reid, Greatorex
Oct 6 v Notts County Reserves (a) 0-0
FA Cup 1st Qualifying Round
Oct 7 v Shirebrook (h) 3-1
Greatorex 3
Oct 14 v Wombwell (a) 0-0
FA Cup 2nd Qualifying Round
Oct 21 v Sutton Junction (h) 3-0
Donoven 2, Sheldon
Oct 25 v Barnsley Reserves (h) 5-1
Donoven 2, Sheldon, Greatorex, Clarke
Oct 28 v Denaby United (h) 0-2
Associaton Cup 3rd Qualifying Round
Nov 4 v Sutton Town (h) 4-1
Clarke 2, Reed, Donoven
Nov 11 v Wath Athletic (h) 2-0
Greatorex 2
Nov 25 v Wombwell (h) 3-0
Rowell, Greatorex 2
FA Cup 4th Qualifying Round
Nov 28 v Coalville Swifts (a) 2-0
Greatorex 2
FA Cup 5th Qualifying Round
Dec 2 v Wath Athletic (h) 1-0
Villiers
Dec 9 v Chesterfield (h) 0-1

FA Cup 6th Qualifying Round
Dec 16 v Halifax Town (h) 0-2
Notts Senior Cup 1st Round
Dec 23 v Langwith Athletic (h) 6-0
Donoven 2, Reed 2, Howell, Woodland
Dec 25 v Lincoln City (h) 5-0
Reed 3, Donoven, Clarke
Dec 26 v Doncaster Rovers (h) 1-0
Howell
Jan 1 v Hull City Reserves (a) 1-1
Howell
Jan 6 v Scunthorpe United (a) 1-2
Howell
Jan 13 v Grimsby Town (h) 2-5
Greatorex, Sheldon
Friendly
Jan 20 v Aston Villa (h) 2-2
Greatorex, Reed
Jan 24 v Castleford (a) 1-2
Bryan
Notts Senior Cup 2nd Round
Jan 27 v Sutton Town (a) 0-0
Feb 3 v Sheffield Wednesday (h) 2-3
Howell 2
Feb 8 v Rotherham United (a) 2-1
Greatorex, Reed
Notts Senior Cup Replay
Feb 10 v Sutton Town (h) 3-1
Howell 2, Greatorex
Feb 17 v Sheffield Wednesday Reserves (a) 4-5
Howell, Bryan (pen), Reed, Donoven
Feb 24 v Scunthorpe United (h) 1-1
Howell
Mar 3 v Wath Athletic (a) 1-2
Donoven
Mar 7 v Notts County Reserves (h) 2-3
Howell, Greatorex
Notts Senior Semi-final
Mar 10 v Player Athletic (h) 2-2
Donoven 2
Mar 15 v Barnsley (h) 3-2
Greatorex 2, Howell
Mar 17 v Rotherham United (a) 2-0
Howell, Donoven
Notts Senior Cup Replay
Mar 19 v Player Athletic (h) 3-0
Donoven, Howell, Bayliss
Mar 21 v Mexborough (h) 2-0
Howell, Sheldon
Mar 24 v Lincoln City (a) 0-3
Notts Senior Cup Final
Mar 30 v Newark Athletic (h) 2-1
Howell, Greatorex
Mar 31 v Worksop Town (a) 1-4
Howell
Apr 2 v Hull City Reserves (h) 5-1
Sheldon, Frith 2, Reed, Clarke
Apr 3 v Gainsborough Trinity (h) 8-3
Donoven 2, Frith 2, Bayliss, Sheldon, Reed, Clarke
Apr 7 v Rotherham United (h) 1-0
Donoven
Apr 12 v Mexborough (a) 1-2
Greatorex
Apr 14 v Boston (a) 0-1
Apr 21 v Grimsby Town (h) 4-0
Donoven 4
Apr 25 v Castleford (h) 3-1
Greatorex, Donoven, Bayliss, (pen)
Apr 28 v Doncaster Rovers (a) 0-2
May 1 v Denaby United (a) 1-2
Greatorex
May 5 v York City (h) 3-0
Lowde, Sydney, Clarke
Position 12th: 42-17-6-19-79-64-40

1923-24 (Midland League)
Aug 25 v Worksop Town (h) 0-1
Aug 27 v Worksop Town (a) 0-0
Sep 1 v Castleford (h) 4-0
Sheldon, Dean, Bryan, Donoven
Sep 8 v Boston (a) 2-0
Donoven, Death
Sep 12 v Chesterfield Reserves (h) 2-0
Death, Bellas
Sep 15 v Boston (h) 2-1
Death, Donoven
Sep 22 v Sutton Town (a) 0-0
Sep 29 v Barnsley (h) 3-0
Donoven, Lawrie, Bayliss (pen)
FA Cup 1st Qualifying Round
Oct 6 v Shirebrook (h) 1-1
Death
Replay
Oct 10 v Shirebrook (a) 2-4
Donoven 2
Oct 13 v Gainsborough (a) 0-0
Oct 20 v Hull City Reserves (h) 3-1
Donoven 2, Lawrie 1
Oct 27 v Rotherham United (h) 5-3
Donoven 2, Lawrie, Taylor, Bryan
Nov 3 v Hull City Reserves (a) 1-2
Lawrie
Nov 10 v Rotherham United (a) 0-0
Nov 17 v Gainsborough Trinity (h) 3-0
Taylor 2, Donoven
Nov 24 v Doncaster Rovers (a) 3-1
Taylor, Death, Donoven
Dec 1 v Mexborough (a) 2-2
Taylor, Donoven
Dec 8 v York City (h) 5-2
Taylor 3, Coupland, Sheldon
Dec 15 v Lincoln City (a) 2-0
Donoven 2
Notts Senior Cup 1st Round
Dec 22 v Lenton (h) 7-0
Gillatt 2, Donoven 2, Death, Bryan, Hardstaff (pen)
Dec 25 v Sutton Town (h) 4-1
Gillatt 2, Donoven, Death
Dec 26 v Notts County Reserves (a) 2-1
Death 2 (1 pen)
Dec 29 v Grimsby Town (h) 2-0
Death, Sheldon
Jan 1 v Wath Athletic (a) 0-2
Jan 5 v Grimsby Town (a) 1-0
Donoven
Jan 12 v Doncaster Rovers (h) 3-0
Donoven, Taylor, Death
Jan 19 v Lincoln City (h) 9-3
Donoven 5, Death 2, Taylor 2
Notts Senior Cup 2nd Round
Jan 26 v Notts County Reserves (a) 3-1
Donoven 2, Taylor
Jan 31 v Nottingham Forest Reserves (a) 0-1
Feb 9 v Wombwell (h) 4-1
Taylor 2, Donoven, Coupland

Feb 16 v Wombwell (a) 2-1
Gillatt, Death
Feb 23 v Nottingham Forest (h) 3-1
Bryan, Lawrie, Donoven
Feb 27 v York City (a) 1-1
Flint
Mar 1 v Rotherham United (h) 5-2
Donoven 2, Taylor 2, Death
Mar 8 v Rotherham United (a) 2-1
Taylor, Gillatt
Notts Senior Cup Semi-final
Mar 15 v Newark Town (h) 1-1
Gillatt
Mar 22 v Mexborough (h) 2-0
Taylor 2
Notts Senior Cup Replay
Mar 26 v Newark Town (h) 0-0
Mar 31 v Denaby United (h) 1-0
Donoven
Apr 5 v Chesterfield (a) 3-0
Flint, Donoven, Taylor
Notts Senior Cup Replay
Apr 7 v Newark Town (a) 2-4
Donoven (pen), Lawrie
Mansfield Charity Cup
Apr 9 v Sutton Town (a) 0-4
Apr 12 v Barnsley (a) 0-1
Apr 19 v Scunthorpe United (a) 2-0
Donoven, Holden
Apr 21 v Wath Athletic (h) 2-1
Lawrie, Holden
Apr 22 v Scunthorpe United (h) 6-0
Flint 3, Donoven 2, Lawrie
Apr 26 v Denaby United (h) 3-2
Donoven 2, Flint
Apr 30 v The Rest (h) 4-1
Bayliss, Bellas, Donoven 2
May 1 v Castleford (a) 3-1
Donoven 2, Flint
May 3 v Notts County Reserves (h) 1-0
Donoven
Position 1st: 42-31-6-5-98-31-68

1924-25 (Midland League)
Aug 30 v Frickley Colliery (h) 5-0
Staniforth 3, Donoven 2
Sep 6 v Rotherham United (h) 2-1
Staniforth 2
Sep 13 v Boston (a) 1-2
Sheldon
FA Cup Preliminary Round
Sep 20 v Sneinton (h) 6-1
Staniforth 2, Donoven 2, Sheldon, Gillatt
Sep 27 v Gainsborough Trinity (h) 1-1
Bryan
FA Cup 1st Qualifying Round
Oct 4 v Whitwell (h) 7-0
Staniforth 4, Bayliss, Sheldon, Gillatt
Oct 11 v Rotherham United (a) 1-1
Donoven
FA Cup 2nd Qualifying Round
Oct 18 v Sutton Junction (h) 3-0
Donoven 2, Robson
Oct 25 v Denaby United (h) 4-0
Robson 2, Donoven, Brelsford
FA Cup 3rd Qualifying Round
Nov 1 v Grantham Town (h) 1-0
Kennie
Nov 8 v Lincoln City (h) 3-0
Staniforth, Robson, Sheldon
FA Cup 4th Qualifying Round
Nov 15 v Doncaster Rovers (a) 2-3
Donoven 2
Nov 22 v Wombwell (h) 7-1
Donoven 3, Staniforth 2, Bryan, Gillatt
Nov 29 v Scunthorpe United (h) 3-0
Donoven 3
Dec 6 v Scunthorpe United (a) 3-2
Donoven 2, Gillatt
Dec 13 v Castleford (h) 9-0
Donoven 3, Coupland 3, Staniforth 2, Gillatt
Notts Senior Cup 1st Round
Dec 20 v Notts County Reserves (h) 0-1
Dec 25 v Sutton Town (h) 6-1
Staniforth 3, Donoven, Coupland, Gillatt
Dec 26 v Sutton Town (a) 2-0
Donoven, Gillatt
Dec 27 v Wath Athletic (h) 7-1
Staniforth 3, Kennie 2, Gillatt, Moore
Jan 1 v Wath Athletic (a) 3-2
Hemstock 2, Jones
Jan 3 v Boston (h) 3-2
Hemstock 2, Jones
Jan 10 v Frickley Colliery (a) 1-1
Hemstock
Jan 17 v Mexborough (h) 1-1
Chambers
Jan 24 v Gainsborough Trinity (a) 3-0
Donoven 2, Chambers
Jan 28 v Castleford (a) 0-1
Jan 31 v Worksop Town (h) 0-0
(Abandoned waterlogged)
Feb 7 v Mexborough (a) 2-1
Sheldon, Coupland
Feb 9 v Denaby United (a) 2-1
Donoven, Coupland
Feb 14 v York City (h) 2-0
Donoven, Jones
Feb 18 v York City (a) 3-0
Sheldon, Donoven, Dring (pen)
Feb 21 v Lincoln City (a) 1-4
Bryan
Feb 25 v Worksop Town (h) 2-0
Donoven, Sheldon
Feb 28 v Worksop (a) 1-3
Taylor
Subsidiary Competition
Mar 7 v Lincoln City (h) 2-1
Dring 2
Mar 12 v Worksop Town (a) 1-0
Donoven
Mar 21 v Gainsborough Trinity (h) 2-0
Donoven 2
Mar 28 v Gainsborough Trinity (a) 2-1
Donoven, Dring
Apr 1 v Worksop Town (h) 3-0
Dring, Donoven, Hunt (og)
Apr 11 v Sutton Town (a) 1-2
Donoven
Apr 13 v Sutton Town (h) 4-0
Donoven 2, Dring 2
Apr 18 v Boston (a) 0-3
Apr 22 v The Rest (h) 4-1
Donoven 3, Jones
Apr 23 v Scunthorpe United (a) 1-0
Donoven

Apr 25 v Boston (h) 3-0
Dring 2, Donoven
Chesterfield Charity Cup
Apr 25 v Chesterfield (a) 0-5
May 2 v Scunthorpe United (h) 4-3
Donoven 2, Dring 2
Position 1st: 28-20-4-4-83-27-44
Subsidiary Competition
Position 2nd: 12-9-0-3-23-15-18
Lincoln C. champions on goal-average

1925-26 (Midland League)
Aug 29 v Grantham Town (h) 1-1
Taylor
Sep 1 v Ilkeston United (a) 2-2
Taylor, Bell
Sep 5 v Wombwell (h) 4-3
Taylor 2, Cell, Heathcote
Sep 12 v Worksop Town (a) 2-0
Heathcote, Breedon
Sep 19 v Lincoln City (h) 0-1
Sep 22 v Ilkeston United (h) 4-0
Heathcote 3, Wilson
Sep 26 v Scunthorpe United (a) 0-3
Sep 30 v Long Eaton (h) 6-0
Hart 3, Bell, Heathcote 2
Oct 3 v Boston (a) 0-2
Friendly
Oct 5 v Manchester City (h) 3-4
Dyson, Taylor, Heathcote
Oct 10 v Scunthorpe United (h) 3-1
Bell, Taylor, Dyson
Oct 17 v Boston (h) 2-3
Bell, Hart
Oct 24 v Grantham Town (a) 5-2
Hart 3, Dyson 2
Oct 31 v Worksop (h) 5-0
Hart 3, Taylor, Dyson
FA Cup 4th Qualifying Round
Nov 14 v Gainsborough Trinity (a) 2-0
Heathcote, Hart
Nov 21 v Gainsborough Trinity (h) 6-1
Hart 2 (1 pen), Sheldon 2, Taylor, Heathcote
FA Cup 1st Round Prop
Nov 28 v Boston (a) 2-5
Hart, Heathcote
Dec 5 v Alfreton (h) 1-1
Hart
Dec 12 v Alfreton (a) 5-3
Hart 3, Dyson 2
Notts Senior Cup 1st Round
Dec 19 v Sutton Town (h) 7-1
Heathcote 5 (1 pen), Bryan, Bell
Dec 25 v Shirebrook (h) 4-0
Hart 2, Bell 2
Dec 26 v Shirebrook (a) 7-1
Heathcote 3, Dyson 2, Sheldon, Bell
Jan 1 v Mexborough (a) 1-5
Heathcote
Jan 2 v Mexborough (h) 2-3
Hart, Garner (pen)
Jan 9 v Lincoln City (a) 1-1
Bell
Jan 16 v Castleford (h) 10-1
Hart 5 (2 pens), Dyson 2, Heathcote, Bell 2
Notts Senior Cup
Jan 23 v Nottingham Forest (h) 0-0
Jan 30 v Gainsborough Trinity (a) 1-3
Dyson
Notts Senior Cup Replay
Feb 1 v Nottingham Forest (a) 2-1
Heathcote 2
Feb 6 v Frickley Colliery (h) 3-2
Heathcote 2, Sheldon
Notts Senior Cup Semi-final
Feb 13 v Notts County (h) 1-0
Bell
Feb 20 v Newark Town (a) 5-0
Taylor 3, Heathcote, Bell
Feb 27 v Wath Athletic (a) 1-0
Sharpe
Mar 6 v York City (a) 2-2
Taylor, Sharpe
Mar 13 v Newark Town (a) 6-1
Taylor 3, Bradley 2, Heathcote
Mar 20 v York City (h) 5-1
Taylor 3, Bradley, Sharpe
Mar 27 v Denaby United (a) 1-1
Bradley
Notts Senior Cup Final
Apr 2 v Players Athletic (h) 6-0
Taylor 3, Davis 2, Sharpe
Apr 3 v Wath Athletic (h) 4-0
Sharpe, Davis, Jones, Taylor
Apr 5 v Sutton Town (h) 2-0
Bryan, Taylor
Apr 6 v Sutton Town (a) 0-1
Apr 10 v Denaby United (h) 1-0
Taylor
Apr 17 v Frickley Colliery (a) 0-4
Apr 18 v Castleford (a) 7-0
Moore 3, Taylor 4
Apr 24 v Loughborough (a) 1-1
Sheldon
Apr 26 v Long Eaton (a) 1-3
Taylor
May 1 v Loughborough Corinthians (h) 6-1
Taylor 3, Sheldon 2, Jones
Position 2nd: 40-23-7-10-120-54-53

1926-27 (Midland Combination)
Town were invited to join the Midland Combination which was sanctioned by the FA for Football League reserves sides only. Mansfield were expelled but the FA later relented.
Aug 28 v Rotherham United (h) 1-1
Laycock
Sep 4 v Hull City (a) 0-2
Sep 11 v Halifax Town (h) 2-0
Laycock, Beresford
Sep 18 v Bradford Park Avenue (a) 3-0
Sharp, Dickinson, Laycock
Sep 25 v Rochdale (h) 4-3
Baxter 2, Beresford 2
Oct 2 v Barnsley (a) 2-1
Staniforth 2
Oct 16 v Doncaster Rovers (h) 4-1
Staniforth 3, Baxter
Combination Cup
Oct 23 v Nottingham Forest (a) 0-0
Combination Cup
Oct 28 v Notts County (a) 4-1
Staniforth 4
Oct 30 v Rochdale (a) 1-0
Staniforth

Nov 6 v Notts County (h) 4-1
Staniforth 2, Sharp, Laycock
FA Cup 4th Qualifying Round
Nov 13 v Burton Town (h) 2-2
Staniforth, Beresford
Nov 20 v Grimsby Town (a) 1-1
Staniforth
FA Cup 1st Round
Nov 27 v Wellington Town (a) 2-1
Staniforth, Laycock
Dec 4 v Stockport County (h) 4-1
Staniforth 2, Laycock, Sheldon
FA Cup 2nd Round
Dec 11 v Walsall (a) 0-2
Notts Senior Cup 1st Round
Dec 18 v Newark Town (h) 1-1
Laycock
Dec 25 v Chesterfield (h) 7-1
Beresford 2, Staniforth, Laycock, Sharp, Bryan, Sheldon
Dec 27 v Chesterfield (a) 1-1
Laycock
Dec 28 v Nottingham Forest (h) 3-0
Laycock 2, Beresford
Notts Senior Cup Replay
Jan 1 v Newark Town (a) 2-2 a.e.t.
Baxter 2
Jan 8 v Halifax Town (a) 0-0
Notts Senior Cup 2nd Replay
Jan 12 v Newark Town (h) 4-0
Beresford 2, Staniforth, Laycock
Jan 15 v Bradford Park Avenue (h) 5-1
Beresford 2, Laycock, Staniforth, Baxter
Notts Senior Cup 2nd Round
Jan 22 v Sutton Junction (h) 15-1
Staniforth 5, Laycock 4, Sheldon 2, Baxter 2, Buckley, Baxter
Combination Cup
Jan 26 v Notts County (h) 2-2
Staniforth 2
Jan 29 v Nottingham Forest (a) 2-3
Dyson, Beresford
Feb 5 v Barnsley (h) 3-1
Dyson 2, Beresford
Feb 12 v Doncaster Rovers (a) 2-2
Combination Cup
Feb 19 v Rotherham United (h) 2-2
Baxter (2 pens)
Feb 26 v Notts County (a) 2-5
Laycock, Baxter
Mar 5 v Hull City (h) 2-2
Baxter, Staniforth
Mar 12 v Nottingham Forest (h) 3-0
Staniforth 2, Beresford
Combination Cup
Mar 19 v Grimsby Town (a) 1-2
Beresford
Mar 26 v Grimsby Town (h) 4-1
Dyson 2, Beresford, Staniforth
Apr 2 v Chesterfield (a) 1-0
Staniforth
Apr 9 v Nottingham Forest (h) 5-0
Taylor 3, Dyson 2
Notts Senior Cup Final
Apr 15 v Notts County (a) 5-1
Staniforth 4, Sharpe
Apr 18 v Rotherham (a) 3-0
Dyson, Staniforth, Beresford
Combination Cup
Apr 19 v Grimsby (h) 3-3
Sharp, Baxter 2
Combination Cup
Apr 23 v Doncaster Rovers (h) 5-0
Staniforth 2, Buckley, Beresford, Baxter
Mansfield Charity Cup
Apr 27 v Shirebrook (h) 5-3
Staniforth 3, Beresford, Dyson
Combination Cup
Apr 30 v Doncaster Rovers (a) 1-0
Baxter
Combination Cup
May 2 v Rotherham United (a) 2-3
Dyson, Beresford, Staniforth
May 4 v Stockport County (a) 2-0
Staniforth, Laycock
Combination Cup
May 7 v Chesterfield (h) 8-1
Staniforth 3, Laycock 2, Beresford 2, Sharp
Position 2nd: 24-15-6-3-62-28-36
Supplementary Cup: Position 1st: 12-7-4-1-35-13-18

1927-28 (Midland League)
Aug 27 v Scarborough (a) 2-3
Milner, Keetley
Aug 29 v Wath Athletic (a) 2-2
Fisher, Keetley
Sep 3 v Scarborough (h) 1-1
Bryan
Sep 5 v Gainsborough Trinity (a) 2-5
Milner, Vincent (og)
Sep 10 v Boston (a) 0-2
Sep 14 v Worksop Town (h) 1-1
Bradley
Sep 17 v Grimsby Town (a) 2-1
Bradley, Keetley
Sep 21 v Heanor (h) 8-2
Bradley 3, Sheldon, Hamby, Meads, Jackson, Keetley
Sep 24 v Mexborough (h) 3-3
Hamby, Bradley, Sheldon
Oct 1 v Notts County (h) 4-1
Fisher 2, Sheldon, Jackson
Oct 8 v Wombwell (a) 1-1
Fisher
Oct 15 v Wath Athletic (h) 4-1
Jackson 2, Hardy, Bratley (og)
Oct 22 v Boston (h) 7-2
Morfitt 2, Keetley 3, Fisher, Roe
Oct 24 v Mexborough (h) 3-3
Morfitt, Keetley, Fisher
Oct 29 v Notts County Reserves (a) 0-2
Nov 5 v Scunthorpe United (h) 5-1
Keetley 2, Fisher, McKenna, Jackson
FA Cup 4th Qualifying Round
Nov 12 v Gainsborough Trinity (a) 0-5
Nov 19 v Frickley Colliery (h) 1-1
Sheldon
Nov 26 v Heanor (a) 3-0
Moore 2, Morfitt
Dec 3 v Grimsby Town (h) 2-2
Milner, Keetley
Dec 10 v Staveley (a) 2-1
Keetley, Morfitt
Notts Senior Cup 1st Round
Dec 17 v Nottinghamshire (h) 8-2
Moore 3, Bradley 3, Keetley, Sheldon
Dec 24 v Nottingham Forest (h) 1-7
Morfitt

Dec 26 v Shirebrook (a) 2-3
Dyson, Moore
Dec 27 v Shirebrook (h) 3-5
Moore 2, Morfitt
Dec 31 v Denaby United (h) 3-1
Jackson, Bradley 2
Jan 2 v Denaby United (a) 2-4
Bradley, Morfitt
Jan 7 v Newark Town (a) 2-3
Dyson, Morfitt
Jan 14 v York City (h) 5-1
Bradley 4, Morfitt
Notts Senior Cup 2nd Round
Jan 21 v Nottingham Forest (h) 1-1
Milner
Friendly
Jan 28 v Bolton Wanderers (h) 6-1
Moore 5, Housley
Feb 2 v Frickley Colliery (a) 3-0
Morfitt, Dyson, Bradley
Notts Senior Cup Replay
Feb 4 v Nottingham Forest (a) 0-4
Feb 11 v Staveley (h) 2-2
Morfitt, Dyson
Feb 15 v York City (a) 5-2
Morfitt 2, Webb, Dyson, Goddard
Feb 18 v Worksop Town (a) 0-3
Feb 25 v Grantham Town (a) 1-1
Dyson
Mar 3 v Gainsborough Trinity (h) 2-4
Morfitt, Goddard
Mar 10 v Loughborough Corinthians (a) 4-3
Moore 2, Fisher, Morfitt
Mar 17 v Wombwell (h) 10-1
Moore 3, Dyson 3, Fisher, Morfitt 2, Bryan
Mar 24 v Mexborough (a) 2-2
Moore 2
Mansfield Charity Cup Semi-final
Mar 31 v Sutton Town (h) 3-0
Moore 2, Morfitt
Apr 7 v Newark Town (h) 3-0
Jackson, Dyson 2
Apr 9 v Ilkeston United (a) 3-2
Morfitt 2, Fisher
Apr 10 v Ilkeston United (h) 4-1
Moore, Jackson, Dyson, Morfitt
Apr 14 v Lincoln City (h) 5-2
Moore 2, Morfitt, Dyson 2
Apr 19 v Scunthorpe United (a) 1-5
Moore
Apr 21 v Lincoln City (a) 2-1
Fisher, Cooke
Friendly
Apr 25 v Wolverhampton Wanderers (h) 1-2
Morfitt
Apr 28 v Loughborough Corinthians (h) 4-0
Moore, Linley, Goddard, Morfitt
Apr 30 v Nottingham Forest (a) 0-6
Mansfield Charity Cup Final
May 1 v Shirebrook (h) 2-1
Morfitt, Fisher
May 5 v Grantham Town (h) 1-0
Anthoney
Position 10th: 44-19-11-14-117-97-49

1928-29 (Midland League)
Aug 25 v Grantham Town (h) 4-3
Morris 2, Staniforth 2
Aug 29 v Grimsby Town (h) 6-0
Morris 3, Staniforth 2, Kay
Sep 1 v Newark Town (a) 4-1
Morris 2, Paterson, Staniforth
Sep 3 v Worksop (a) 0-3
Sep 8 v Staveley (h) 5-0
Morris 2, Staniforth, Cooke, Chambers
Sep 12 v Scarborough (h) 5-1
Staniforth 2, Morris 2, Greatorex
Sep 15 v Grantham Town (a) 0-1
Sep 22 v Nottingham Forest (h) 3-1
Morris 2, Kay
Sep 29 v Gainsborough Trinity (a) 1-1
Staniforth
Oct 3 v Boston (h) 2-2
McLachlan, Morris
Oct 6 v Frickley Colliery (a) 0-0
Oct 13 v Notts County Reserves (h) 4-1
Morris 3, Cooke
Oct 17 v York City (a) 1-0
Staniforth
Oct 20 v Gainsborough Trinity (h) 5-2
McLachlan 2, Morris, Kerry, Keating
Friendly
Oct 24 v Sheffield Wednesday (h) 1-5
Garnham
Oct 27 v Notts County Reserves (a) 3-2
Morris 2, Cooke
Oct 29 v Rotherham United (a) 2-11
Kerry, Morris
Nov 3 v Worksop Town (h) 2-0
Staniforth 2
FA Cup 4th Qualifying Round
Nov 10 v Ardsley (a) 2-2
McLachlan, Staniforth
Replay
Nov 14 v Ardsley (h) 2-0
McLachlan, Kerry
Nov 17 v Newark Town (h) 2-3
McLachlan, Kerry
FA Cup 1st Round
Nov 21 v Shirebrook (a) 4-2
Morris 2, McKenna, Kerry
Dec 1 v York City (h) 2-1
Morris, Cooke
FA Cup 2nd Round
Dec 8 v Barrow (a) 2-1
Morris 2
Dec 15 v Hull City (h) 2-1
Kerry, Kay
Notts Senior Cup 1st Round
Dec 22 v Woodthorpe (h) 6-0
Atkins 2, Rice, Freeman, Garnham, Price (og)
Dec 25 v Shirebrook (h) 2-0
Morris, McLachlan
Dec 26 v Shirebrook (a) 3-1
Cooke 2, Kerry
Dec 29 v Nottingham Forest (a) 1-7
Morris
Jan 1 v Denaby United (a) 0-3
Jan 5 v Scunthorpe United (h) 5-0
McLachlan 2, Morris 2, McKenna
FA Cup 3rd Round
Jan 12 v Wolverhampton Wanderers (a) 1-0
McLachlan
Jan 19 v Lincoln City (a) 1-2
McKenna

FA Cup 4th Round
Jan 26 v Arsenal (a) 0-2
Feb 2 v Denaby United (h) 8-0
Morris 2, Anthoney 2, Staniforth, Kerry, Cooke, McLachlan
Notts Senior Cup 2nd Round
Feb 2 v Nottinghamshire (h) 4-1
Garnham 2, Hickling, Burton
NB: Reserves played in Cup.
Feb 9 v Scunthorpe United (a) 3-0
Staniforth 2, Morris
Feb 16 v Wombwell (h) 4-1
Cooke 2, Kerry, Morris
Feb 23 v Wombwell (a) 5-3
Kerry, Cooke, Kay, McLachlan, Staniforth
Mar 2 v Wath Athletic (h) 3-3
Kerry, Staniforth, McLachlan
Mar 9 v Lincoln City (h) 6-0
Staniforth 3, Kerry, Morris, Jackson (pen)
Mar 13 v Loughborough Corinthians (h) 4-1
Morris 2, Staniforth, Kerry
Mar 16 v Mexborough (a) 1-1
Cooke
Mar 20 v Scarborough (a) 1-2
Cooke
Notts Senior Cup Semi-final
Mar 20 v Nottingham Forest (a) 0-2
NB. The Reserves played in the Cup.
Mar 23 v Mexborough (h) 3-2
Grice, Cooke, Staniforth
Mar 29 v Hull City (a) 3-1
McLachlan, Grice, Kerry
Mar 30 v Barnsley (h) 4-2
Grice 2, Cooke, McLachlan
Apr 1 v Rotherham United (h) 3-0
Grice 2, Staniforth
Apr 6 v Grimsby Town (a) 3-2
McLachlan, Cooke, Jackson (pen)
Apr 11 v Wath Athletic (a) 1-1
Grice
Apr 13 v Frickley Colliery (h) 2-2
Grice 2
Apr 15 v Chesterfield (a) 0-0
Apr 17 v Doncaster (h) 4-1
Morris 2, Kay, Chambers
Apr 20 v Staveley (a) 0-0
Apr 24 v Loughborough Corinthians (a) 3-0
Staniforth, McLachlan, Kerry
Apr 27 v Chesterfield (h) 3-0
Morris 2, Kerry
Apr 29 v Doncaster Rovers (a) 3-0
McLachlan, Kerry, Morris
Mansfield Charity Cup Final
May 1 v Grantham Town (h) 2-2
Morris, McLachlan
NB. Mansfield allowed Grantham to keep trophy for the full 12 months.
May 2 v Boston (a) 0-4
May 4 v The Rest (h) 1-0
Swaby (og)
Reserve side completed Midland League fixtures for seniors at Barnsley.
Pos: 1st. 50-31-10-9-132-71-72

1929-30 (Midland League)
Aug 31 v Grantham Town (h) 4-0
Gibson, McLachlan, Staniforth, Chambers
Sep 2 v Worksop Town (a) 8-3
McLachlan 2, Daykin 2, Roseboom 2, Stimpson, Cook (og)
Sep 7 v Denaby United (a) 3-2
Staniforth, Roseboom, Gibson
Sep 9 v Hull City (a) 3-1
Gibson 2, McLachlan
Sep 14 v Mexborough (h) 4-0
Grice, McLachlan 2, Gibson
Sep 18 v Denaby United (h) 4-2
Kay 2, Staniforth 2
Sep 21 v Grantham Town (a) 1-0
Kay
Sep 25 v Loughborough Corinthians (h) 1-2
Gibson
Sep 28 v Staveley (h) 2-2
Gibson 2
Oct 2 v Scarborough (h) 1-2
Gibson
Oct 5 v Chesterfield (a) 2-3
Gibson 2
Oct 9 v Frickley Colliery (a) 0-2
Oct 12 v Worksop Town (h) 4-2
Whylde, Roseboom 2, Gibson 2
Oct 19 v Notts County (h) 4-7
McLachlan 2, Gray, Roseboom
Oct 23 v Wombwell (h) 2-0
Gibson 2
Oct 26 v Mexborough (a) 3-0
Murphy, Gray, Gibson
Nov 2 v Chesterfield (h) 2-1
Gray, Gibson
Nov 9 v Newark Town (a) 1-0
Gibson
Nov 16 v Nottingham Forest (h) 6-1
McLachlan 4, Murphy, Gibson
Nov 23 v Notts County (a) 0-5
FA Cup 1st round
Nov 30 v Manchester Central (h) 0-2
Dec 7 v Newark Town (h) 9-0
Wannacott 2, Gray 2, McLachlan 4, Gray
Dec 14 v Loughborough Corinthians (a) 0-2
Dec 21 v Bradford (h) 4-3
Gray, McLachlan, Gibson, Kay (pen)
Dec 25 v Shirebrook (a) 4-3
Kay 2, McLachlan 2
Dec 26 v Shirebrook (h) 3-1
McLachlan 2, Gibson
Dec 28 v Wath Athletic (a) 2-1
Gibson, Murphy
Jan 1 v Hull City (a) 3-4
Kay (2 pens), Murphy
Jan 4 v Doncaster Rovers (h) 5-2
Wonnacott 2, Whylde, Gray, Kay (pen)
Jan 11 v Wath Athletic (h) 7-0
Gibson 3, Gray 2, Murphy, Wannacott
Jan 18 v Gainsborough (a) 1-3
Murphy
Jan 25 v Frickley Colliery (h) 3-0
Gibson, Murphy, Gray
Notts Senior Cup 1st round
Feb 1 v Sutton Town (h) 4-0
Murphy 2, McLachlan, Gibson
Feb 8 v Boston (h) 1-2
Gibson
Feb 15 v Nottingham Forest (a) 2-3
Murphy, McLachlan
Feb 22 v Lincoln City (a) 0-1
Mar 1 v Rotherham United (h) 7-0
Murphy 3, Gibson 2, Gray 2

Mar 4 v Scarborough (a) 1-3
Kay
Mar 8 v Doncaster Rovers (a) 2-1
A.Smith 2
Mar 15 v Bradford (a) 2-3
McLachlan, Kay (pen)
Mar 19 v Wombwell (a) 0-3
Mar 22 v Scunthorpe United (h) 1-3
Shaw
Mansfield Charity Cup
Mar 26 v Nottingham University (h) 3-1
Smith, Wonnacott, Jackson
Notts Senior Cup Semi-final
Mar 29 v Nottingham Forest (a) 3-6
McLachlan, Gray, Smith
Apr 5 v Gainsborough Trinity (h) 1-1
Gray
Apr 12 v Scunthorpe United (a) 1-2
Smith
Apr 18 v Barnsley (a) 1-1
Murphy
Apr 19 v Rotherham United (a) 2-1
Shaw 2
Apr 21 v Barnsley (h) 2-3
Murphy, Whylde
Apr 22 v Grimsby Town (h) 1-1
Roseboom
Apr 23 v Staveley (a) 1-3
Frith
Apr 26 v Lincoln City (h) 3-1
Gray 2, Whylde
Apr 30 v Grimsby Town (a) 1-8
Shaw
May 3 v Boston (a) 0-5
Pos: 10th. 50-25-4-21-126-98-54

1930-31 (Midland League)
Aug 30 v Grantham Town (h) 2-2
Hill, Jackson
Sep 3 v Hull City (h) 5-1
Devlin 2, Chappell, Hill, Murphy
Sep 6 v Scarborough (h) 4-0
Devlin, Hill, Jackson (pen), Belton (og)
Sep 10 v Loughborough Corinthians (a) 6-6
Hill 2, Devlin 2, Goddard, Jackson (pen)
Sep 13 v Scarborough (a) 6-3
Murphy 2, Hargreaves, Frith, Hill, Higginbottom (og)
Sep 17 v Wombwell (h) 4-2
Devlin 2, Hill, Goddard
Sep 20 v Grantham Town (a) 0-0
Sep 24 v Loughborough Corinthians (h) 1-1
Murphy
Sep 27 v Boston (h) 3-0
Hargreaves, Murphy 2
Oct 1 v Notts County (h) 4-1
Devlin 3, Goddard
Oct 4 v Grimsby Town (h) 0-2
Oct 18 v Bradford PA (h) 2-0
Murphy, Frith
Oct 25 v Newark Town (a) 0-0
Nov 1 v Gainsborough Trinity (a) 2-0
Nov 3 v Rotherham United (a) 2-2
Murphy, Hill
Nov 8 v Nottingham Forest (h) 1-3
Devlin
FA Cup 4th Qualifying Round
Nov 15 v Highgate (h) 10-1
Devlin 5, Hill 4, Hargreaves
Nov 22 v Gainsborough Trinity (h) 4-2
Devlin 2, Hill, Frith
FA Cup 1st Round
Nov 29 v Halifax Town (a) 2-2
Devlin, Chambers
Replay
Dec 3 v Halifax Town (h) 1-2
Murphy
Dec 6 v Newark Town (h) 2-2
Hargreaves, Hill (pen)
Dec 13 v Lincoln City (h) 1-3
Chappell
Dec 20 v Doncaster Rovers (h) 4-1
Devlin 2, Hill 2
Dec 25 v Shirebrook (h) 2-1
Goddard, Devlin
Dec 26 v Shirebrook (a) 1-1
Hargreaves
Dec 27 v Barnsley (h) 2-1
Goddard, Hargreaves
Jan 3 v Barnsley (a) 3-3
Hill 2, Ogle (og)
Jan 10 v Chesterfield (h) 6-2
Frith 2, Goddard 2, Hill, Trotman
Jan 17 v Boston (a) 1-1
Goddard
Jan 24 v Frickley Colliery (h) 4-0
Goddard 2, Trotman, Hargreaves
Notts Senior Cup 1st Round
Jan 31 v Welbeck Athletic (a) 3-1
Hill 2, Chambers
Feb 7 v Denaby United (h) 3-2
Goddard, Hill, Hargreaves (pen)
Feb 14 v Lincoln City (a) 0-2
Feb 21 v Frickley Colliery (a) 1-7
Hill
Mar 7 v Bradford City (a) 2-4
Hill, Trotman
Notts Senior Cup Semi-final
Mar 14 v Newark Town (h) 4-0
Frith 2, Hill 2
Mar 21 v Grimsby Town (a) 0-5
Mar 28 v Mexborough (h) 5-0
Grice 4, Trotman
Apr 1 v Bradford City (h) 1-2
Trotman
Notts Senior Cup Final
Apr 3 v Notts County (h) 7-0
Hill 3, Trotman, Hargreaves, Frith, Murphy
Apr 4 v Chesterfield (a) 0-2
Apr 6 v Scunthorpe United (h) 3-4
Goddard 2, Hill
Apr 7 v Mexborough (a) 1-1
Goddard
Apr 11 v Denaby United (a) 1-2
Hill
Apr 18 v Nottingham Forest (a) 2-5
Trotman, Murphy
Apr 20 v Bradford City (a) 1-5
Frith
Apr 25 v Rotherham United (h) 3-2
Hill 3
Apr 30 v Wombwell (a) 2-1
Frith 2
May 2 v Scunthorpe United (a) 2-0
Frith, Hill
Pos: 10th. 46-19-11-16-103-95-49

League Facts & Figures

MANSFIELD Town have completed 52 seasons as members of the Football League (not including wartime football) — 2,338 matches up to the end of the 1989-90 campaign.

In that period they gained 2,458 points, remembering that from season 1981-2, three points were on offer for a win.

In 13 seasons, 42 matches were played (12 in the lower divisions plus one in Division Two), and in 38 seasons 46 matches were played.

In 1961-2, 44 were played because Accrington Stanley resigned from the League. One match had been completed against Accrington, but this was deleted from the records.

Also, in 1981-2, the Stags had two points deducted for playing an ineligible player — Colin Calderwood at Crewe on 13 March. That was the youngster's debut although still an apprentice, and he had signed his Football League and Football Association registration forms, which had both been posted on the same day and recorded in the club's post book. It was confirmed that the Association forms had arrived at Lancaster Gate, but there was no trace of the League forms being received at Lytham St Annes.

Fortunately the loss of the points did not result in the Stags having to apply for re-election, although it was close as they finished 20th in Division Four.

In Mansfield's career in the Football League, 625 home matches were won: 300 drawn and 244 lost with 2,260 goals scored and 1,348 conceded.

On opposition territory 238 matches were won: 297 drawn and 634 lost with 1,271 goals scored and 2,157 conceded.

The Stags went through four seasons without losing at match at Field Mill, in 1950-51, 1963-4, 1974-5 and 1976-7 — the last two when the club's only championships were achieved.

Twice they went through a season without an away win, in 1931-2 and 1973-4. Indeed, in the first two seasons in the League the Stags won only once on opposition territory and that was 3-1 at Darlington on 18 March 1933.

The late 1950s were particularly devastating from a 'goals conceded' aspect. For five consecutive seasons the 'goals against' column made horrific reading as it rose from 81 in 1955-6 to 90, 92, 98 and finally 110 in season 1959-60.

Although it should be added that in those five seasons the Stags themselves scored 89, 91, 100, 73 and 81 goals respectively . . .how about that for entertaining football!

The highest number of goals scored away from home was 47 in the 1962-3 promotion season, when in Mansfield's 46 matches a grand total of 177 goals were scored, 61 of which were at Field Mill, plus the 20 conceded.

But the highest number ever put in the opposition net at home was in 1957-8 when the League table read 'home goals for 68, against 42!' Those certainly were the days.

Appended is a complete record of Mansfield's achievements in the Football League.

Mansfield in the Football League 1931-32 to 1989-90

		HOME					*AWAY*						
	P	W	D	L	F	A	W	D	L	F	A	Pts	Pos
					DIVISION THREE SOUTH								
1931-32	42	11	5	5	54	45	0	5	16	21	63	32	20th
					DIVISION THREE NORTH								
1932-33	42	13	4	4	57	22	1	3	17	27	78	35	16th
1933-34	42	9	7	5	49	29	2	5	14	32	59	34	17th
1934-35	42	16	3	2	55	25	3	6	12	20	37	47	8th
1935-36	42	13	5	3	55	25	1	4	16	25	66	37	19th
1936-37	42	13	1	7	64	35	5	7	9	27	41	44	9th
					DIVISION THREE SOUTH								
1937-38	42	12	5	4	46	26	3	4	14	16	41	39	14th
1938-39	42	10	8	3	33	19	2	7	12	11	43	39	16th
1946-47	42	8	5	8	31	38	1	5	15	17	58	28	22nd
					DIVISION THREE NORTH								
1947-48	42	11	4	6	37	24	6	7	8	20	27	45	8th
1948-49	42	13	6	2	39	15	1	8	12	13	33	42	10th
1949-50	42	12	4	5	37	20	6	8	7	29	34	48	8th
1950-51	46	17	6	0	54	19	9	6	8	24	29	64	2nd
1951-52	46	17	3	3	50	23	5	5	13	23	37	52	6th
1952-53	46	11	9	3	34	25	5	5	13	21	37	46	18th
1953-54	46	15	5	3	59	22	5	6	12	29	45	51	7th
1954-55	46	14	4	5	40	28	4	5	14	25	43	45	13th
1955-56	46	13	6	4	59	21	1	5	17	25	60	39	18th
1956-57	46	13	3	7	58	38	4	7	12	33	52	44	16th
1957-58	46	16	3	4	68	42	6	5	12	32	50	52	6th
					DIVISION THREE								
1958-59	46	11	5	7	38	42	3	8	12	35	56	41	20th
1959-60	46	11	4	8	55	48	4	2	17	26	64	36	22nd
					DIVISION FOUR								
1960-61	46	10	3	10	39	34	6	3	14	32	44	38	20th
1961-62	44	14	3	5	51	19	5	3	14	26	47	44	14th
1962-63	46	16	4	3	61	20	8	5	10	47	49	57	4th

			HOME						*AWAY*				
	P	W	D	L	F	A	W	D	L	F	A	Pts	Pos
				DIVISION THREE									
1963-64	46	15	8	0	51	20	5	3	15	25	42	51	7th
1964-65	46	17	4	2	61	23	7	7	9	34	38	59	3rd
1965-66	46	10	5	8	31	36	5	3	15	28	53	38	19th
1966-67	46	12	4	7	48	37	8	5	10	36	42	49	9th
1967-68	46	8	7	8	32	31	4	6	13	19	36	37	21st
1968-69	46	14	5	4	37	18	2	6	15	21	44	43	15th
1969-70	46	14	4	5	46	22	7	7	9	24	27	53	6th
1970-71	46	13	7	3	44	28	5	8	10	20	34	51	7th
1971-72	46	5	12	6	19	26	3	8	12	22	37	36	21st
				DIVISION FOUR									
1972-73	46	15	7	1	52	17	5	7	11	26	34	54	6th
1973-74	46	13	8	2	47	24	0	9	14	15	45	43	17th
1974-75	46	17	6	0	55	15	11	6	6	35	25	68	1st
				DIVISION THREE									
1975-76	46	8	11	4	31	22	8	4	11	27	30	47	11th
1976-77	46	17	6	0	52	13	11	2	10	26	29	64	1st
				DIVISION TWO									
1977-78	42	6	6	9	30	34	4	5	12	19	35	31	21st
				DIVISION THREE									
1978-79	46	7	11	5	30	24	5	8	10	21	28	43	18th
1979-80	46	9	9	5	31	24	1	7	15	16	34	36	23rd
				DIVISION FOUR									
1980-81	46	13	5	5	36	15	7	4	12	22	29	*49	7th
1981-82	46	8	6	9	39	39	5	4	14	24	42	47	20th
1982-83	46	11	6	6	32	26	5	7	11	29	44	61	10th
1983-84	46	9	7	7	44	27	4	6	13	22	43	52	19th
1984-85	46	10	8	5	25	15	3	10	10	16	23	57	14th
1985-86	46	13	8	2	43	17	10	4	9	31	30	81	3rd
				DIVISION THREE									
1986-87	46	9	9	5	30	23	6	7	10	22	32	61	10th
1987-88	46	10	6	7	25	21	4	6	13	23	38	54	19th
1988-89	46	10	8	5	32	22	4	9	10	16	30	59	15th
1989-90	46	13	2	8	34	25	3	5	15	16	40	55	15th

*Two points deducted

Stags Against Other League Clubs

Mansfield Town have played 87 clubs in the Football League since 1931-32. Below is the Stags' record against each club. Some clubs changed their names (eg Clapton Orient became Leyton Orient then Orient and then Leyton Orient again) and some clubs modified their titles (eg Swansea Town became Swansea City). In all cases the current name used by each club covers all games under previous names.

		HOME					*AWAY*				
	P	W	D	L	F	A	W	D	L	F	A
Accrington Stanley	38	12	4	3	40	19	4	6	9	25	38
AFC Bournemouth	34	7	6	4	23	23	2	5	10	20	38
Aldershot	32	11	2	3	31	14	4	3	9	15	31
Aston Villa	4	1	1	0	3	1	2	0	0	2	0
Barnsley	30	6	4	5	22	25	2	6	7	17	29
Barrow	44	13	2	7	50	37	4	6	12	24	44
Birmingham City	2	1	0	0	5	2	0	0	1	1	4
Blackburn Rovers	6	1	1	1	3	3	0	2	1	2	4
Blackpool	22	1	7	3	10	15	3	2	6	11	18
Bolton Wanderers	10	1	2	2	4	5	1	2	2	2	5
Bradford	18	6	2	1	18	9	4	2	3	12	6
Bradford City	46	12	7	4	36	22	6	7	10	34	44
Brentford	30	7	5	3	22	14	3	3	9	16	27
Brighton & Hove Albion	30	7	4	4	23	23	2	0	13	11	41
Bristol City	22	6	2	3	22	14	2	3	6	11	23
Bristol Rovers	36	12	3	3	33	11	0	6	12	16	44
Burnley	4	1	1	0	4	1	0	0	2	1	4
Bury	42	8	7	6	32	39	3	6	12	16	32
Cambridge United	6	3	0	0	7	2	0	1	2	6	9
Cardiff City	16	2	3	3	13	15	0	3	5	2	14
Carlisle United	44	15	2	5	50	23	4	4	14	22	51
Charlton Athletic	2	0	0	1	0	3	0	1	0	2	2
Chester City	68	23	8	3	66	25	12	11	11	38	53
Chesterfield	50	12	6	7	38	29	7	7	11	30	39
Colchester United	34	5	7	5	21	19	5	3	9	13	21
Coventry City	6	1	1	1	8	9	1	0	2	4	7
Crewe Alexandra	62	19	8	4	75	35	7	7	17	38	53
Crystal Palace	18	3	4	2	11	9	0	1	8	8	29
Darlington	58	22	5	2	85	35	8	5	16	38	49
Derby County	4	0	1	1	2	3	0	0	2	0	8
Doncaster Rovers	38	10	5	4	39	22	8	3	8	28	26
Exeter City	32	9	4	3	32	21	5	4	7	19	23
Fulham	16	3	1	4	10	11	2	5	1	9	5
Gateshead	32	7	4	5	27	21	4	3	9	24	36
Gillingham	42	13	7	1	37	15	1	10	10	17	36
Grimsby Town	28	8	5	1	28	12	5	3	6	17	22
Halifax Town	56	21	5	2	72	32	9	8	11	30	38
Hartlepool United	58	25	1	3	84	20	6	7	16	34	59
Hereford United	16	3	4	1	15	7	1	1	6	7	16
Huddersfield Town	4	1	0	1	2	2	0	0	2	0	3
Hull City	30	7	5	3	26	20	2	4	9	14	37
Ipswich Town	4	1	0	1	4	4	0	0	2	2	7

		HOME					AWAY				
	P	W	D	L	F	A	W	D	L	F	A
Leyton Orient	22	5	4	2	17	12	2	2	7	9	21
Lincoln City	28	9	3	2	29	17	4	5	5	16	20
Luton Town	12	4	2	0	12	4	1	3	2	9	11
Middlesbrough	4	0	1	1	5	6	0	0	2	0	2
Millwall	16	3	5	0	13	5	1	1	6	3	14
New Brighton	18	7	1	1	29	8	2	2	5	7	13
Newport County	18	6	2	1	14	7	3	2	4	7	7
Northampton Town	40	16	2	2	45	16	6	3	11	16	28
Norwich City	8	2	2	0	13	9	0	1	3	3	10
Notts County	22	4	3	4	17	13	1	3	7	10	22
Oldham Athletic	46	12	4	7	45	35	2	9	12	22	40
Oxford United	14	4	2	1	11	8	1	0	6	8	17
Peterborough United	34	5	8	4	20	21	5	0	12	27	34
Plymouth Argyle	14	2	1	4	11	14	1	2	4	8	14
Portsmouth	2	1	0	0	2	0	0	1	0	2	2
Port Vale	40	10	3	7	40	24	3	8	9	20	36
Preston North End	14	2	2	3	10	11	3	0	4	7	10
Queen's Park Rangers	20	5	2	3	26	25	1	4	5	6	16
Reading	44	8	11	3	39	32	0	5	17	20	47
Rochdale	60	20	5	5	71	33	5	10	15	31	48
Rotherham United	44	11	5	6	49	22	1	4	17	18	48
Scunthorpe United	38	10	6	3	40	24	6	6	7	25	31
Sheffield United	8	0	2	2	5	7	1	0	3	3	8
Sheffield Wednesday	8	2	2	0	6	2	2	2	0	4	1
Shrewsbury Town	32	8	3	5	24	17	4	5	7	20	28
Southampton	6	1	0	2	6	8	0	0	3	3	11
Southend United	34	10	4	3	39	19	4	5	8	22	30
Southport	48	14	6	4	67	29	4	9	11	34	46
Stockport County	64	18	9	5	59	32	4	9	19	41	71
Stoke City	2	1	0	0	2	1	0	1	0	1	1
Sunderland	4	0	0	2	1	6	0	0	2	1	5
Swansea City	18	5	2	2	17	7	4	1	4	13	14
Swindon Town	38	5	10	4	23	23	2	4	13	19	45
Thames	2	1	0	0	4	0	0	0	1	3	6
Torquay United	40	13	4	3	38	18	8	6	6	23	25
Tottenham Hotspur	2	0	1	0	3	3	0	1	0	1	1
Tranmere Rovers	68	15	11	8	60	34	6	8	20	37	66
Walsall	44	10	7	5	39	27	4	5	13	17	42
Watford	20	5	2	3	15	10	3	1	6	9	19
Wigan Athletic	12	2	0	4	6	10	0	1	5	2	14
Wimbledon	6	1	2	0	4	3	0	1	2	4	6
Wolverh'ton Wanderers	2	1	0	0	3	1	0	0	1	2	6
Workington	32	8	4	4	57	28	6	5	5	27	25
Wrexham	56	16	7	5	57	28	5	7	15	27	56
York City	58	17	5	7	62	30	4	5	20	38	68

1931-32

Secretary/Manager: J.G.Hickling

1	Aug	29	(h)	Swindon T	W 3-2	Broome 2, Readman	12,232
2		31	(a)	Norwich C	D 1-1	Davis	13,913
3	Sep	5	(a)	Clapton O	L 0-4		8,138
4		7	(h)	Watford	W 3-2	Gilhespy, Readman, Broome	8,662
5		12	(h)	Torquay U	L 2-4	Johnson 2	8,499
6		16	(a)	Watford	L 1-4	Johnson	7,309
7		19	(a)	Bristol R	D 1-1	England (pen)	10,770
8		26	(h)	Queen's Park R	D 2-2	Johnson 2	4,107
9	Oct	3	(a)	Bournemouth	L 2-3	Johnson, Baxter	7,674
10		10	(h)	Crystal P	D 1-1	Gilhespy	10,849
11		17	(a)	Cardiff C	L 0-2		7,688
12		24	(h)	Northampton T	W 2-0	Johnson 2	7,015
13		31	(a)	Reading	L 1-4	Gilhespy	8,083
14	Nov	7	(h)	Southend U	D 4-4	Johnson 2, Readman, Broome	8,833
15		14	(a)	Fulham	L 1-2	Johnson	16,977
16		21	(h)	Thames	W 4-0	England (pen), Johnson, Staniforth, Death	7,644
17	Dec	5	(h)	Exeter C	W 3-1	Johnson 2, Featherby	6,602
18		12	(a)	Coventry C	L 1-5	Readman	11,046
19		19	(h)	Gillingham	W 3-1	Bowater 2, Johnson	5,400
20		25	(h)	Brighton & HA	D 3-3	Bowater, Readman, Featherby	10,848
21		26	(a)	Brighton & HA	L 0-4		16,516
22	Jan	2	(a)	Swindon T	L 2-5	Johnson 2	4,481
23		9	(a)	Crystal P	L 1-2	Featherby	10,817
24		13	(a)	Brentford	D 1-1	Johnson	4,902
25		16	(h)	Clapton O	W 4-3	Johnson 2, Weightman, Bowater	6,719
26		23	(a)	Torquay U	D 2-2	Broome, Death	3,370
27		30	(h)	Bristol R	L 0-3		7,118
28	Feb	6	(a)	Queen's Park R	D 1-1	Bowater	12,079
29		13	(h)	Bournemouth	W 2-1	Bowater, Broome	5,479
30		27	(h)	Cardiff C	L 1-2	Johnson	8,316
31	Mar	5	(a)	Northampton T	L 0-3		5,777
32		12	(h)	Reading	L 1-7	Johnson	6,228
33		19	(a)	Southend U	L 2-5	Fisher, Johnson	6,710
34		25	(a)	Luton T	L 1-3	Johnson	7,621
35		26	(h)	Fulham	L 1-2	Storer	5,910
36		28	(h)	Luton T	W 5-2	Johnson 3, Bowater 2	5,588
37	Apr	2	(a)	Thames	L 3-6	Johnson, Featherby 2	1,070
38		9	(h)	Brentford	W 2-0	Broome 2	4,932
39		16	(a)	Exeter C	L 0-3		5,478
40		23	(h)	Coventry C	D 3-3	Johnson 2, Staniforth	4,492
41		30	(a)	Gillingham	L 0-2		2,936
42	May	7	(h)	Norwich C	W 5-2	Johnson 2, Bowater 2, Gilhespy	4,107

FINAL LEAGUE POSITION: 20th in Division Three South

Appearances
Goals

FA Cup

1	Nov	28	(a)	Hull C	L 1-4	Death	10,000

Appearances
Goals

Baxter TW	Blackburn GF	Bowater G	Broome WH	Chambers B	Clifford G	Davis CF	Death WH	England E	Featherby LW	Fisher F	Gilhespy C	Jepson J	Johnson H	Lloyd C	Phoenix AF	Readman JA	Robinson A	Robinson SH	Small T	Staniforth C	Staples A	Storer JA	Wake HW	Weightman A	White C	Wilson J	
11	6		10		2	5		3			7		9			8							4			1	1
11	6		10		2	5		3			7		9			8							4			1	2
11	6		10		2	5		3			7		9			8							4			1	3
11	6		10		2	5		3			7		9			8							4			1	4
11	6		10	5	2			3			7		9			8							4			1	5
11			10	5	2			3			7		9			8							4	6		1	6
11			10	5	2			3			7	9				8							4	6		1	7
11			10	5	2			3			7		9			8							4	6		1	8
11			10	5	2			3			7		9			8							4	6		1	9
11			10		2			3			7		9			8		5					4	6		1	10
11			10		2			3			7		9			8		5					4	6		1	11
11			10		2			3			7		9			8		5					4	6		1	12
11			10		2			3			7		9			8		5					4	6		1	13
			10		2		11	3			7		9			8		5					4	6		1	14
							11	3			7		9			8		5		10			4	6	2	1	15
							11	3			7		9	2		8		5		10			4	6		1	16
					2		11	3	10				9			8		5	7				4	6		1	17
					2		11	3	10				9			8		5	7				4	6		1	18
		7			2		11	3	10				9		4	8		5						6		1	19
		7			2		11	3	10				9		4	8		5						6		1	20
		7			2		11	3	10				9		4	8		5						6		1	21
			8		2		11	3	10		7		9			4		5						6		1	22
		7	8		2		11	3	10				9			4		5			1			6			23
		7	8		2		11	3	10				9			4		5			1			6			24
		7	8		2		11	3	10				9			4		5			1			6			25
		7	8		2		11	3	10				9			4		5			1			6			26
		7	8		2		11	3	10				9			4		5			1			6			27
		11	8	5	2			3	10				9			4					1	7		6			28
		11	8	5	2			3	10				9			4					1	7		6			29
		11	8		2			3	10				9			4		5			1	7		6			30
		11	8	5	2			3	10				9			4						7		6		1	31
		11	8	5	2			3	10				9			4						7		6		1	32
	6	11			2	5		3	10	8			9			4					1	7					33
	6	11	8		2			3	10				9			4		5			1	7					34
11	6		8		2			3								9		5		10	1	7	4				35
	6	11	8		2			3					9			4		5		10	1	7					36
		11	8		2			3	10				9			4		5				7		6		1	37
	6	11	8		2			3	4				9					5		10		7				1	38
	6	11	8		2			3	4				9					5		10	1	7					39
	6	11	8		2			3	4				9					5		10		7				1	40
	6	11	10		2			3			7		9			8		5					4			1	41
	6	11	8					3			7		9			4	2	5		10						1	42
14	14	22	34	9	39	5	14	42	22	1	19	1	40	1	3	39	1	28	2	8	13	13	20	28	1	29	
1		10	8			1	2	2	5	1	4		32			5				2		1		1			

Baxter TW	Blackburn GF	Bowater G	Broome WH	Chambers B	Clifford G	Davis CF	Death WH	England E	Featherby LW	Fisher F	Gilhespy C	Jepson J	Johnson H	Lloyd C	Phoenix AF	Readman JA	Robinson A	Robinson SH	Small T	Staniforth C	Staples A	Storer JA	Wake HW	Weightman A	White C	Wilson J	
			10		2		11	3			7		9			8		5					4	6		1	1
			1		1		1	1			1		1			1		1					1	1		1	
							1																				

1932-33

Secretary/Manager: J.G.Hickling

1	Aug	27	(h)	Chester	W	1-0	Hoyland	8,009
2		31	(a)	New Brighton	L	0-1		3,331
3	Sep	3	(a)	Barrow	L	0-1		4,657
4		5	(h)	New Brighton	W	5-0	Johnson 4, Hoyland	4,636
5		10	(h)	Carlisle U	W	3-1	Johnson 2, Bowater	7,573
6		17	(a)	York C	L	3-4	Raynor, Johnson, Bowater	4,313
7		24	(h)	Crewe A	W	4-0	S.Robinson, Johnson 2, Hoyland	7,856
8	Oct	1	(a)	Rochdale	L	1-2	Johnson	5,945
9		8	(h)	Southport	W	4-0	Johnson, Hoyland, Bowater 2	5,827
10		15	(a)	Barnsley	L	2-6	Johnson 2	5,145
11		22	(h)	Hull C	W	2-1	Fisher, Johnson	8,436
12		29	(a)	Doncaster R	D	2-2	Anthoney, Johnson	5,767
13	Nov	5	(h)	Darlington	D	3-3	Johnson 3	7,346
14		12	(a)	Stockport	D	2-2	Bowater 2	5,498
15		19	(h)	Gateshead	L	1-2	Cropper	6,823
16	Dec	3	(h)	Wrexham	D	0-0		5,557
17		10	(h)	Rochdale	W	4-1	Readman, Prior 2, Bowater	4,441
18		17	(h)	Halifax T	D	2-2	Broome, Johnson	4,668
19		24	(a)	Hartlepools U	L	3-6	Prior, Johnson, Bowater	3,872
20		26	(a)	Rotherham U	L	0-3		5,580
21		27	(h)	Rotherham U	W	9-2	Readman 3, Hoyland 3, Bowater 3	7,192
22		31	(a)	Chester	L	2-5	Anthoney, Hoyland	6,618
23	Jan	2	(a)	Accrington S	L	0-6		2,477
24		7	(h)	Barrow	W	2-1	Readman, Bowater	4,633
25		19	(a)	Walsall	L	1-8	Bowater	3,068
26		21	(a)	Carlisle U	L	1-3	Johnson	4,328
27		28	(h)	York C	W	2-0	Johnson, Hoyland	4,127
28	Feb	4	(a)	Crewe A	L	0-7		3,771
29		18	(a)	Southport	L	2-5	Johnson 2	2,307
30	Mar	4	(a)	Hull C	L	1-4	Prior	8,630
31		11	(h)	Doncaster R	D	2-2	Readman, Bowater	4,651
32		18	(a)	Darlington	W	3-1	Johnson 2, Prior	2,678
33		25	(h)	Stockport	L	1-2	Prior	5,070
34	Apr	1	(a)	Gateshead	L	2-3	Johnson, Bowater	2,413
35		8	(h)	Walsall	W	2-0	Fisher, Bowater	4,023
36		10	(a)	Tranmere R	L	0-3		1,737
37		14	(h)	Barnsley	L	0-1		5,994
38		15	(a)	Wrexham	D	1-1	Readman	7,775
39		17	(h)	Accrington S	L	1-3	Prior	3,869
40		22	(h)	Tranmere R	W	2-0	Fisher 2	2,859
41		29	(a)	Halifax T	L	1-5	Johnson	2,305
42	May	6	(h)	Hartlepools U	W	7-1	Fisher, Johnson 2, Wannacott 2, Bowater 2	2,381

FINAL LEAGUE POSITION: 16th in Division Three North — Appearances

Goals

FA Cup

1	Nov	26	(a)	Walsall	L	1-4	Johnson	9,838

Appearances

Goals

Anthony G	Bowater G	Broome WH	Butler EL	Chambers B	Clough J	Cropper R	Cupit W	Davies R	England E	Fisher F	Foster WH	Herring C	Hoyland W	Johnson H	Lloyd CF	Parsons J	Prior J	Raynor GS	Readman JA	Robinson A	Robinson SH	Siviter E	Slack W	Wannacott CB	Weightman AW	Wilson J	
2					1		7	4	3				10	9					8		5		11		6		1
2					1		7	4	3				10	9					8		5		11		6		2
2	11	10			1			4	3					9				7	8		5				6		3
2	11				1			4	3				10	9				7	8		5				6		4
2	11				1			4	3				10	9				7	8		5				6		5
2	11				1			4	3				10	9				7	8		5				6		6
2	11				1			4	3				10	9				7	8		5				6		7
2	11				1			4	3				10	9				7	8		5				6		8
2	11				1	8		4	3				10	9			7				5				6		9
2	11				1	8		4	3				10	9			7				5				6		10
2	11		5		1			4	3	8			10	9			7								6		11
2	11		5		1			4	3				10	9		8	7								6		12
2	11		5		1				3				10	9		8	7		4						6		13
2	11				1	8			3				10	9			7		4		5				6		14
2	11					8			3				10	9				7	4		5				6	1	15
2	11					8			3				10	9				7	4		5				6	1	16
2	11	8							3			6		9			7		4		5			10		1	17
2	11	8							3			6		9			7		4		5			10		1	18
2	11	8							3					9			7		4		5			10	6	1	19
2	11	8							3					9			7		4		5		6	10		1	20
2	11	8						4	3				10				7		9		5		6			1	21
2	11	8						4	3				10				7		9		5		6			1	22
	11	8		5				4	3				2				7		9				6	10		1	23
2	11	8				9			3				10				7		4		5		6			1	24
2	11	8							3					9			7		4		5		6	10		1	25
	11								3				10	9	2		7	8	4		5		6			1	26
2	11	8			1				3				10	9			7		4		5		6				27
4	11		5		1				3				10	9			7			2	8		6				28
2	11				1			4	3				10	9			7		8		5		6				29
2	11	10			1			4						9	3		7		8		5		6				30
2	11	10			1			4						9	3		7		8		5		6				31
3	11		5		1									9			7		4	2	8		6	10			32
3	11		5		1									9			7		4	2	8		6	10			33
3	11		5		1									9			7		4	2	8		6	10			34
3	11		5		1					8				9			7		4	2			6	10			35
3	11		5		1					8				9			7		4	2			6	10			36
3	11		5		1					8				9			7		4	2			6	10			37
3	11		5		1					8				9			7		4	2			6	10			38
3	11	10	5		1					8				9	2		7		4				6				39
3			5		1					8	11		10	9			7			2	4		6				40
			5		1					8	11		3	9			7			2	4		6	10			41
3	11				1					8				9			7			2	5	4	6	10			42
39	38	14	14	1	30	6	2	18	29	9	2	2	25	38	4	2	32	9	34	11	33	1	25	15	17	12	
2	18	1				1				5			9	30			7	1	7		1			2			

2	11					8			3				10	9				7	4		5				6	1	1
1	1					1			1				1	1				1	1		1				1	1	
														1													

1933-34

Manager: J.G.Hickling to December 1933, then H.Martin from January 1934.

1	Aug	26	(h)	Hartlepools U	D 1-1	Munnings	7,101
2		28	(h)	Tranmere R	D 0-0		5,121
3	Sep	2	(a)	Wrexham	L 0-5		6,320
4		4	(a)	Tranmere R	L 2-3	Raynor, Johnson	6,877
5		9	(h)	Southport	D 2-2	Butler 2	5,101
6		16	(a)	Darlington	W 4-1	Munnings 2, Raynor, Johnson	4,158
7		23	(h)	Gateshead	D 1-1	Raynor	5,057
8		30	(a)	Accrington S	D 1-1	Hill	4,271
9	Oct	7	(h)	Chesterfield	L 0-3		14,184
10		14	(a)	Rochdale	D 2-2	Butler, Methven	5,334
11		21	(a)	York C	L 0-1		5,261
12		28	(h)	Chester	W 2-1	Johnson 2	4,007
13	Nov	4	(a)	Doncaster R	L 0-1		5,786
14		11	(h)	Barrow	L 0-5		4,824
15		18	(a)	Carlisle U	L 2-3	Foster, Opp own-goal	3,335
16	Dec	2	(a)	Halifax T	L 2-4	Raynor, Johnson	5,781
17		9	(h)	Crewe A	W 4-1	Butler, Raynor, Johnson, Foster	2,465
18		16	(a)	New Brighton	L 1-5	Munnings	2,101
19		23	(h)	Rotherham U	W 3-0	Johnson, Kilcar 2	3,818
20		25	(h)	Walsall	L 1-2	Prentice	7,675
21		26	(a)	Walsall	D 0-0		10,251
22		30	(a)	Hartlepools U	L 1-3	Johnson	2,759
23	Jan	6	(h)	Wrexham	D 1-1	Johnson	3,523
24		13	(h)	Stockport C	D 1-1	Kilcar	5,191
25		20	(a)	Southport	D 3-3	Livingstone, Johnson, Kilcar	2,316
26		27	(h)	Darlington	W 4-0	Slack, Kirk, Raynor, Bytheway	4,439
27	Feb	3	(a)	Gateshead	L 3-5	England (pen), Butler, Raynor	2,482
28		10	(h)	Accrington S	W 5-0	Munnings, Johnson 2, Kilcar, Bytheway	4,441
29		17	(a)	Chesterfield	L 2-3	Clayton, Johnson	12,298
30		24	(h)	Rochdale	W 5-0	Johnson 2, Bytheway 2, Munnings	4,502
31	Mar	3	(h)	York C	L 0-2		4,843
32		10	(a)	Chester	D 1-1	Johnson	3,728
33		17	(h)	Doncaster R	D 1-1	Bytheway	4,524
34		24	(a)	Barrow	L 3-6	Johnson 2, Kilcar	3,453
35		30	(h)	Barnsley	L 1-5	Methven	8,422
36		31	(h)	Carlisle U	W 6-0	Methven 3, Munnings, Hill, Kilcar	3,301
37	Apr	2	(a)	Barnsley	L 1-6	Methven	10,814
38		7	(a)	Stockport C	L 1-3	Kilcar	8,789
39		14	(h)	Halifax T	W 6-1	Hill 2, Methven 2, Kilcar 2	3,262
40		21	(a)	Crewe A	L 1-2	Kilcar	2,467
41		28	(h)	New Brighton	W 5-2	Goodacre, Raynor, Kilcar, Bytheway 2	2,472
42	May	5	(a)	Rotherham U	W 2-1	Hill, Methven	1,324

FINAL LEAGUE POSITION: 17th in Division Three North

Appearances
Goals

FA Cup

1	Nov	25	(a)	New Brighton	D 0-0		4,000
R		29	(h)	New Brighton	L 3-4	Raynor, Johnson 2	6,300

Appearances
Goals

Division Three North Cup

1	Jan	29	(a)	Walsall	W 2-1	Prentice, Foster
3	Mar	21	(h)	Chesterfield	W 4-1	England (pen), Prentice, Johnson 2
SF	Apr	16	(a)	Stockport C	L 0-4	

Mansfield received a bye in round two

Appearances
Goals

Ashley JA	Butler EL	Bytheway G	Clayton J	Edwards JA	England E	Foster WH	Goodacre R	Hill H	Johnson H	Keeling H	Kilcar SP	Kirk WH	Livingstone A	Maddison	Mee GW	Methven H	Munnings CE	Prentice D	Raynor F	Robinson SH	Siviter E	Slack W	Williams C	Wood WH	
	5				3		2		9				10		11		7	8			4	6	1		1
	5		4		3		2	8	9	10					11		7					6	1		2
	5		4		3		2	8	9	10					11		7					6	1		3
	5		4		3		2	10	9						11		7		8			6	1		4
	5		4		3		2	10	9				6				7		8			11	1		5
	5				3	11	2	10	9				4				7		8			6	1		6
	5				3		2	10	9				4		11		7		8			6	1		7
	5				3		2	10	9				4		11		7		8			6	1		8
	5		4		3		2	10	9						11		7		8			6	1		9
	5				3		2	10					4		11	9	7		8			6	1		10
	5				3		2	10	8				4		11	9	7					6	1		11
	5				3		2	10	9				4		11		7	8				6	1		12
3	5'						2	10	9				4		11		7	8				6	1		13
3	5					11	2	10	9				4				7	8				6	1		14
3	5					11	2	10	9				4				7	8				6	1		15
2	5			1	3	11			9	10			4				7	8				6			16
2	5			1	3	11			9	10			4				7	8				6			17
2	5			1	3	11		8	9	10			4				7					6			18
2	5	11		1	3				9		10	7	4					8				6			19
2	5	11		1	3				9		10	7	4					8				6			20
2	5	11		1	3				9	10		7	4					8				6			21
2	5	11		1	3				9	10		7	4					8				6			22
2	5	11		1	3				9	10		7	4					8				6			23
2	5	11		1	3						10		4				7	8	9			6			24
2	5	11		1	3				9		10		4				7		8			6			25
2	5	11		1	3				9		10	7	4						8			6			26
2	5	11		1	3				9		10	7	4						8			6			27
2	5	11		1	3				9		10						7	8				6		4	28
2	5	11	4	1	3				9		10						7	8				6			29
2	5	11	4	1	3				9		10						7	8				6			30
2	5	11	4		3				9		10						7	8				6	1		31
2	5	7			3	11			9		10							8				6	1	4	32
2		7			3	11			9		10		5					8				6	1	4	33
2		11			3				9		10		5				7	8				6	1	4	34
2		11			3						10		5			9	7	8				6	1	4	35
2		11	4		3			8			10		5			9	7					6	1		36
2		11	4		3			8			10		5			9	7					6	1		37
2		11	4	1	3			8			10		5			9	7					6			38
2		11	4	1	3			8			10		5			9			7			6			39
3		11	4	1			2	8			10		5			9			7			6			40
3		11	4	1			2	8			10		5			9			7			6			41
3		11	4	1			2	8			10		5			9			7			6			42
30	32	24	15	20	36	8	18	22	32	8	21	7	33		11	10	29	21	15		1	42	22	5	
	5	7	1		1	2	1	5	18		12	1	1			9	7	1	8			1			

1 own-goal

2			4		3	11		10	9					5			7		8			6	1		1
2			4		3	11		10	9								7		8	5		6	1		R
2			2		2	2		2	2					1			2		2	1		2	2		
									2										1						

3			4	1		11	2				10	7		5		9		8				6		4	1
2		11			3				9		10		5				7	8				6	1		3
3	5	11	4	1			2	8			9					10			7			6	1		SF
3	1	2	2	2	1	1	2	1	1		3	1	1	1		2	1	2	1			3		1	
					1	1			2									2							

1934-35

Manager: H.Martin to 21 March 1935, then C.Bell from 5 April 1935.

1	Aug	25	(a)	Halifax T	L	1-2	Hawley	9,386
2		29	(h)	Lincoln C	L	3-4	Atkinson, Johnson, Bytheway	8,669
3	Sep	1	(h)	Rotherham U	W	2-1	Johnson 2	6,588
4		3	(a)	Lincoln C	L	0-4		8,376
5		8	(a)	Walsall	D	2-2	Dellow, Johnson	7,011
6		15	(h)	Chesterfield	W	1-0	Dellow	8,424
7		19	(a)	Accrington S	L	0-2		1,604
8		22	(a)	Stockport C	W	2-0	Atkinson, Kilcar	5,932
9		29	(a)	Barrow	L	0-3		3,927
10	Oct	6	(h)	Carlisle U	W	3-0	Dellow 2, Atkinson	5,069
11		13	(a)	Rochdale	L	0-1		3,684
12		20	(h)	Crewe A	W	4-1	Hunt, Kilcar, Parker, Dransfield	5,753
13		27	(a)	Hartlepools U	D	1-1	Johnson	2,206
14	Nov	3	(h)	Doncaster R	W	2-0	Atkinson, Johnson	5,638
15		10	(a)	Southport	W	2-1	Dellow, Atkinson	2,827
16		17	(a)	Chester	D	1-1	Hunt	5,026
17	Dec	1	(h)	York C	W	5-1	Atkinson, Johnson, Hunt, Dellow 2	5,227
18		15	(h)	Accrington S	W	2-1	Edmonds, Atkinson	4,327
19		22	(a)	Gateshead	D	2-2	Dellow, Hunt	2,028
20		25	(h)	Wrexham	W	4-0	Dellow, Atkinson, Johnson, Hunt	9,554
21		26	(a)	Wrexham	W	3-1	Dellow, Johnson, Bytheway	9,115
22		29	(h)	Halifax T	W	4-0	Johnson 2, Hunt 2	8,144
23	Jan	5	(a)	Rotherham U	L	0-3		5,740
24		16	(a)	New Brighton	L	1-2	Edmonds	2,075
25		19	(h)	Walsall	W	4-2	Johnson 2, Hunt, Bytheway	5,251
26		26	(a)	Chesterfield	D	0-0		5,026
27	Feb	2	(h)	Stockport C	W	3-2	Atkinson, Hunt (pen), Bytheway	5,295
28		9	(h)	Barrow	W	3-2	Hunt (pen), Bytheway 2	5,204
29		23	(h)	Rochdale	W	1-0	Edmonds	4,788
30	Mar	2	(a)	Crewe A	D	1-1	Johnson	3,720
31		9	(h)	Hartlepools U	W	2-1	Johnson, Bytheway	4,006
32		16	(a)	Doncaster R	L	1-2	Hunt	15,764
33		23	(h)	Southport	L	2-3	J.Hunter, Hunt	3,023
34		30	(a)	Chester	L	2-3	Atkinson, Bytheway	5,160
35	Apr	6	(h)	New Brighton	W	2-1	Johnson, Hunt (pen)	3,152
36		13	(a)	York C	L	1-2	Johnson	3,504
37		19	(h)	Tranmere R	W	4-2	Edmonds, Atkinson, Bytheway, Hunt	6,876
38		20	(h)	Darlington	D	2-2	Atkinson, Bytheway	3,962
39		22	(a)	Tranmere R	L	0-3		3,916
40		25	(a)	Carlisle U	D	1-1	Bytheway	2,622
41	May	1	(a)	Darlington	L	0-1		2,479
42		4	(h)	Gateshead	D	1-1	Bytheway	2,541

FINAL LEAGUE POSITION: 8th in Division Three North

Appearances

Goals

FA Cup

1	Nov	24	(h)	Accrington S	W	6-1	Johnson 2, Dellow, Atkinson, Hunt 2	7,750
2	Dec	8	(h)	Tranmere R	W	4-2	Johnson 2, Dellow, Hunt	12,553
3	Jan	12	(a)	Burnley	L	2-4	Johnson, Hunt (pen)	20,790

Appearances

Goals

Division Three North Cup

1	Jan	30	(a)	Chesterfield	L	1-8	Carr (pen)	

Appearances

Goals

Ashall T	Ashley JA	Atkinson G	Barks W	Barlow GA	Bytheway G	Carr A	Cooke TV	Dellow RW	Dransfield E	Edmonds AJ	England E	Fawcett DH	Hawley S	Hufton C	Hunt SW	Hunter JB	Jepson A	Johnson H	Kilcar SP	Livingstone A	Page S	Parker ESH	Slack W	Wright E	
	3	7			11	5			2	4		1	8					9	10					6	1
	3	7			11	5			2	4		1	8					9	10				6		2
	3		8		11	5		7	2			1						9	10	4			6		3
	2		8		11	5		7			3	1						9	10	4			6		4
	2	8			11			7		4	3	1			10			9		5			6		5
	2	8						7		4	3	1						9	10	5		11	6		6
	2	8						7		4	3	1						9	10	5		11	6		7
	2	8			11			7		4	3	1						9	10	5			6		8
	2	8			11			7		4	3	1						9	10	5			6		9
		8	10		11			7	2	4	3	1						9		5			6		10
		8	10		11			7	2	4	3	1						9		5			6		11
		8						7	2	4	3	1			9				10	5		11	6		12
		8				5		7	2	4	3	1						9	10			11	6		13
	5	8						7	2	4	3	1			10			9				11	6		14
	5	8		2				7		4	3	1			10			9				11	6		15
	5	8		2				7		4	3	1			10			9				11	6		16
	5	8						7	2	4	3	1			10			9				11	6		17
	5	8			11			7	2	4	3	1			10			9					6		18
	5	8				3		7	2	4		1			10			9				11	6		19
	5	8				3		7	2	4		1			10			9				11	6		20
	5	8			11	3		7	2	4		1			10			9					6		21
	5	8			11	3		7	2	4					10		1	9					6		22
	5	8			11	3		7	2	4		1			10			9					6		23
	5	8			11	3		7	2	4					10		1	9						6	24
	5	8			11	3		7	2	4		1			10			9						6	25
	5	8			11			7	2	4	3	1			10			9						6	26
	5	8			11				2	4	3	1	9		10	7								6	27
	5	8			11				2	4	3	1	9		10	7								6	28
	5	8			11				2	4	3	1			10	7		9					6		29
10	5	8			11				2		3	1		4		7		9						6	30
10	5	8			11				2		3	1		4		7		9						6	31
	5	8							2		3	1			10	7		9				11	6	4	32
	5	8			11				2		3	1			10	7		9					6	4	33
	5	8		3	11				2	4		1			10	7		9					6		34
	5	8		3	11				2	4		1			10	7		9					6		35
	3	8			11		5		2	4		1			10	7		9					6		36
	3	8			11		5		2	4		1			10	7		9					6		37
	3	8			11		5		2	4		1			10	7		9						6	38
	3	8			11		5		2			1		4	10	7		9						6	39
	3	8			11		5		2			1			10	7		9					6	4	40
	3	8			11		5		2	4		1			10	7		9						6	41
	3	8			11		5		2			1			10	7		9					6	4	42
2	38	40	4	4	31	12	7	24	34	33	23	40	4	3	29	16	2	39	10	10		11	31	15	
		12			12			10	1	4			1		14	1		17	2			1			

Ashall T	Ashley JA	Atkinson G	Barks W	Barlow GA	Bytheway G	Carr A	Cooke TV	Dellow RW	Dransfield E	Edmonds AJ	England E	Fawcett DH	Hawley S	Hufton C	Hunt SW	Hunter JB	Jepson A	Johnson H	Kilcar SP	Livingstone A	Page S	Parker ESH	Slack W	Wright E	
	5	8						7	2	4	3	1			10			9				7	6		1
	5	8			11			7	2	4	3	1			10			9					6		2
	5	8			11	3		7	2	4					10		1	9					6		3
	3	3			2	1		3	3	3	2	2			3		1	3				1	3		
		1						2							4			5							

Ashall T	Ashley JA	Atkinson G	Barks W	Barlow GA	Bytheway G	Carr A	Cooke TV	Dellow RW	Dransfield E	Edmonds AJ	England E	Fawcett DH	Hawley S	Hufton C	Hunt SW	Hunter JB	Jepson A	Johnson H	Kilcar SP	Livingstone A	Page S	Parker ESH	Slack W	Wright E	
	5	8	10		7	3			2	4		1	9								11			6	1
	1	1	1		1	1			1	1		1	1								1			1	
						1																			

1935-36

Manager: C.Bell to 19 December 1935, then H.Wightman from 14 January to 4 May 1936.

1	Aug	31	(h)	Oldham A	W	1-0	Allen	11,102
2	Sep	4	(a)	Wrexham	L	1-5	Whittam	7,593
3		7	(a)	Halifax T	L	0-1		11,090
4		11	(h)	Wrexham	W	3-2	Hunter 2, Whittam	6,342
5		14	(h)	Darlington	W	4-2	Allen 3, Johnson	6,130
6		16	(a)	Rotherham U	L	1-2	Hunter	6,299
7		21	(a)	Gateshead	L	1-3	Johnson	3,220
8		28	(h)	Tranmere R	L	2-3	Johnson, Allen (pen)	6,674
9	Oct	5	(a)	Walsall	L	0-7		7,636
10		12	(h)	Carlisle U	D	1-1	Atkinson	4,228
11		19	(a)	Southport	D	3-3	Harston 3	1,534
12		26	(h)	Chester	D	0-0		5,561
13	Nov	2	(a)	Lincoln C	W	2-1	Hunter, Harston	6,623
14		9	(h)	Rochdale	W	3-0	Lockie, Harston, Clenshaw	4,762
15		16	(a)	York C	L	5-7	Johnson 2, Clenshaw 2, Bytheway	3,643
16		23	(h)	Barrow	L	1-3	Whittam	4,034
17	Dec	7	(h)	Chesterfield	L	0-1		6,230
18		14	(a)	Stockport C	L	1-6	Clenshaw	5,268
19		21	(h)	Crewe A	D	1-1	Harston	2,645
20		25	(a)	Hartlepools U	L	1-4	Harston	5,679
21		26	(h)	Hartlepools U	W	4-0	Atkinson 2, Johnson, Harston	2,595
22		28	(a)	Oldham A	L	1-4	Atkinson	5,473
23	Jan	4	(h)	Halifax T	W	3-2	Atkinson 2, Johnson	3,756
24		11	(a)	New Brighton	L	0-1		2,208
25		18	(a)	Darlington	L	1-2	Clenshaw	2,927
26	Feb	1	(a)	Tranmere R	L	2-4	Anderson, Harston	8,717
27		8	(h)	Walsall	D	2-2	Harston, Whittam	4,681
28		15	(a)	Carlisle U	L	0-3		4,918
29		22	(h)	Southport	W	5-1	Harston 3, Anderson, Clenshaw	3,662
30		29	(a)	Rochdale	L	1-3	Harston (pen)	2,227
31	Mar	7	(h)	Lincoln C	D	2-2	Harston, Anderson	5,007
32		14	(a)	Chester	L	0-4		5,533
33		21	(h)	York C	W	5-0	Atkinson 2, Anderson 2, Opp own-goal	4,367
34		28	(a)	Barrow	D	2-2	Harston 2	2,829
35	Apr	4	(h)	New Brighton	W	2-0	Harston 2 (1 pen)	3,220
36		10	(h)	Accrington S	W	3-1	Harston, Anderson 2	6,165
37		11	(a)	Chesterfield	L	1-2	Parker	10,523
38		13	(a)	Accrington S	D	1-1	Atkinson	2,771
39		14	(h)	Gateshead	W	3-1	Harston 3	3,599
40		18	(h)	Stockport C	W	2-1	Harston, Wood	4,508
41		25	(a)	Crewe A	D	1-1	Bytheway	1,827
42	May	2	(h)	Rotherham U	W	8-2	Bytheway 2, Harston 2, Parker 2, Atkinson, Anderson	3,264

FINAL LEAGUE POSITION: 19th in Division Three North

Appearances

Goals

FA Cup

1	Nov	30	(h)	Hartlepools U	L	2-3	Atkinson, Harston	6,000

Appearances

Goals

Division Three North Cup

1	Oct	30	(a)	Chesterfield	D	2-2	Hunter, Whittam
R	Nov	12	(h)	Chesterfield	L	0-4	

Appearances

Goals

Allen J	Anderson GR	Atkinson GA	Ashley JA	Barlow G	Bartley PJ	Bisby CC	Black D	Brown A	Bytheway G	Clenshaw LJ	Cooke TV	Darville GM	Dransfield E	Fawcett DH	Field E	Gabbitas H	Gilmore HP	Grundy W	Harston E	Hufton C	Hunter JB	Johnson H	Lockie T	Moran J	Parker ESH	Pritchard T	Slack W	Whittam EA	Wood L	Wright E	
10		7	3		9				11				2	1			4						5				6	8			1
10		7		3	9				11				2	1			4						5				6	8			2
10		7		3					11				2	1								9	5				6	8		4	3
10				3					11				2	1							7	9	5				6	8		4	4
10									11		5		2	1							7	9	5				6	8		4	5
10		8		3					11				2	1							7	9	5				6			4	6
10		8		3					11		5		2	1							7	9					6			4	7
10		8		3					11		5		2	1							7	9					6			4	8
		8		3						11			2	1							7	9				5	6	10		4	9
		8								11		3	2	1	9						7		5				6	10		4	10
		8								11		3	2	1			4		9		7		5				6	10			11
		8								11		3	2	1			4		9		7		5				6	10			12
		8								11		3	2	1			4		9		7		5				6	10			13
		8							7	11		3	2	1			4		9				5				6	10			14
		8							7	11		3	2	1			4					9	5				6	10			15
		8							7	11		3	2	1						4		9	5				6	10			16
		8							7	11		3	2	1			4		9				5				6	10			17
		8							7	11	5	3	2	1			4					9						10	6		18
		8							7	11	5	3	2	1			4		9										6	10	19
		8							7	11	5	3	2	1			4		9										6	10	20
		8							7	11		3	2	1			4		10			9							6	5	21
		8							7	11		3	2	1			4		10			9							6	5	22
		8				3			7	11			2	1			4		10			9							6	5	23
		8				3			7	11			2	1			4		9									10	6	5	24
		8				3			7	11			2	1			4		9									10	6	5	25
	8	7				3							2	1			4		10			9						11	6	5	26
	8	7				3				11			2	1			4		9									10	6	5	27
	8	7				3				11			2	1			4		9									10	6	5	28
	10	8				3		4	7	11			2	1					9								6			5	29
	10	8				3		4	7	11			2	1					9								6			5	30
	10	8						4	7	11			2	1					9					3			6			5	31
	10	8						4	7	11			2	1				6	9					3						5	32
	10	8					1	4	7	11			2					6	9					3						5	33
	10	8					1	4	7	11			2					6	9					3						5	34
	10	8					1	4	7	11			2					6	9					3						5	35
	10	8					1	4	7	11			2					6	9					3						5	36
	8	7					1	4					2			9	6		10					3	11					5	37
	8	7					1	4					2		10				9					3	11				6	5	38
	10	8					1	4	7				2						9					3			11		6	5	39
	10	8					1	4	7				2						9					3			11		6	5	40
	10	8					1	4	7				2						9					3	11				6	5	41
	10	8				3	1	4	7				2						9						11				6	5	42
8	17	40	1	7	2	9	10	14	32	27	6	13	42	32	2	1	20	5	29	1	10	14	14	11	4	1	22	20	16	32	
5	8	10							4	6									26		4	7	1		3			4	1		

1 own-goal

		8							7	11		3	2	1			4		9				5				6	10			1
		1							1	1		1	1	1			1		1				1				1	1			
		1																	1												

		8								11		3	2	1			4				7	9	5				6	10			1
		8							7	11		3	2	1			4		9				5				6	10			R
		2							1	2		2	2	2			2		1		1	1	2				2	2			
																					1							1			

1936-37

Manager: W.H.Parkes

1	Aug	29	(h)	Barrow	W 2-1	Atkinson, Harston	7,657
2	Sep	1	(a)	Rochdale	W 3-1	Harston 3	5,297
3		5	(a)	York C	D 1-1	Atkinson	7,504
4		9	(h)	Rochdale	W 6-2	Harston 5, Atkinson	7,404
5		12	(h)	Carlisle U	L 1-4	Atkinson	6,665
6		19	(a)	Hartlepools U	L 0-3		7,178
7		26	(h)	Southport	W 3-0	Speed, Atkinson, Harston	6,556
8	Oct	3	(a)	Tranmere R	W 2-0	Harston 2 (1 pen)	6,791
9		10	(h)	Halifax T	W 3-0	Harston 3	7,731
10		17	(h)	Hull C	W 5-2	Harston 4, Anderson	9,776
11		24	(a)	New Brighton	D 0-0		4,722
12		31	(h)	Lincoln C	D 2-2	Roy, Harston	13,228
13	Nov	7	(a)	Accrington S	W 3-0	Harston 2, Bungay	3,334
14		14	(h)	Oldham A	L 1-2	Rattray	9,650
15		21	(a)	Port Vale	L 1-5	Atkinson	8,983
16	Dec	5	(a)	Stockport C	L 1-3	Anderson	5,913
17		19	(a)	Darlington	D 0-0		3,936
18		25	(h)	Crewe A	L 1-4	Roy	7,663
19		26	(a)	Barrow	D 2-2	Harston 2	3,921
20		28	(a)	Crewe A	L 1-2	Littledyke	2,534
21	Jan	1	(a)	Gateshead	D 3-3	Harston 2, Rattray	4,753
22		2	(h)	York C	L 1-2	Harston	4,008
23		9	(a)	Carlisle U	W 2-1	Wood, Atkinson	6,162
24		16	(h)	Rotherham U	W 4-1	Horne 2, Atkinson, Harston	4,137
25		23	(h)	Hartlepools U	W 8-2	Harston 7, Rattray	2,696
26		30	(a)	Southport	L 2-3	Harston, Rattray	3,558
27	Feb	6	(h)	Tranmere R	L 2-3	Pressgrave, Cartwright	6,348
28		13	(a)	Halifax T	D 0-0		4,970
29		20	(a)	Hull C	L 0-3		4,249
30		27	(h)	New Brighton	L 2-3	Harston, Anderson	3,229
31	Mar	6	(a)	Lincoln C	L 0-2		7,877
32		13	(h)	Accrington S	W 2-1	Harston, Anderson	3,385
33		20	(a)	Oldham A	D 1-1	Atkinson	6.479
34		26	(h)	Chester	W 5-0	Harston 2, Anderson 2, Atkinson	6,920
35		27	(h)	Port Vale	W 7-1	Harston 5, Wood, Anderson	6,348
36		29	(a)	Chester	L 1-5	Harston	9,448
37		30	(h)	Wrexham	W 3-0	Harston 3 (1 pen)	4,579
38	Apr	3	(a)	Rotherham U	L 1-4	Anderson	4,890
39		10	(h)	Stockport C	L 0-2		6,359
40		17	(a)	Wrexham	W 3-2	Rattray, Harston 2	2,170
41		24	(h)	Darlington	W 3-1	Harston 2, R.Cooke	4,072
42	May	1	(h)	Gateshead	W 3-2	Harston 2, Horne	3,123

FINAL LEAGUE POSITION: 9th in Division Three North

Appearances
Goals

FA Cup

1	Nov	30	(a)	Barrow	W 4-0	Harston 3, Anderson	7,231
2	Dec	12	(h)	Bournemouth	L 0-3		11,200

Appearances
Goals

Division Three North Cup

1	Nov	11	(h)	Port Vale	L 0-2		1,008

Appearances
Goals

Anderson GR	Atkinson GA	Black D	Briggs R	Brown A	Bungay RH	Cartwright H	Cooke TV	Dransfield E	Harston E	Hart EA	Hill A	Horne A	Jones OH	Littledyke R	Moran J	Perfect FT	Poole C	Pressgrave G	Rattray CR	Roy JR	Speed F	Vaux E	Wainwright W	Wood L	Wright E	
	8	1		4				2	9	5					3				7	11	10			6		1
	8	1		4	10				9	5					3	2			7	11	6					2
	8	1		4	10				9	5					3	2			7	11	6					3
	8	1		4	10				9	5					3	2			7	11	6					4
	8	1		4	10				9	5					3	2			7	11	6					5
	8			4					9	5			1	10	3	2			7	11	6					6
10	8			4					9	5			1		3	2			7	11	6					7
10	8			4					9	5			1		3	2			7	11	6					8
10	8			4					9	5			1		3	2			7	11	6					9
10	8			4					9	5			1		3	2			7	11	6					10
10	8			4					9	5			1		3	2			7	11				6		11
10	8	1		4					9	5					3	2			7	11	6					12
	8	1		4	10				9	5					3	2			7	11	6					13
	8	1		4	10				9	5					3	2			7	11	6					14
	8			4	10			2	9	5			1		3				7	11				6		15
10	8			4					9	5			1		3				7	11		2		6		16
10				4		8			9	5			1		3			7		11	6	2				17
	8			4					9	5			1	10	3			7		11	6	2				18
	8			4					9	5			1	10				7		11	3	2		6		19
	8			4					9	5			1	10				7		11	3	2		6		20
				4					9	5		10	1	8	3				7	11	6	2				21
	11				3				9	5		10	1	8					7		6	2		4		22
	8	1		4	3				9	5		10							7	11		2		6		23
	8	1		4	3				9	5		10							7	11		2		6		24
	8	1		4	3				9	5		10							7	11		2		6		25
	8	1		4	3				9	5		10							7	11		2		6		26
		1			3	8			9	5		10						7	11		6	2		4		27
	8	1		4	3				9		11	10							7		5	2		6		28
	8	1	11	4	3				9			10							7		5	2		6		29
10	7	1		4	3				9	5		8					11				6	2				30
10	11	1		4	3				9			8							7		5	2		6		31
10	11	1			3	8			9			4							7		5	2		6		32
10	11	1			3	8						4		9					7		5	2		6		33
10	11	1		4	3				9			8							7		5	2		6		34
10	11	1		4	3				9			8							7		5	2		6		35
10	11	1			3				9			4		8					7		5	2		6		36
10	11	1			3				9			4		8					7		2		5	6		37
10	11	1			3	8			9			4							7			2	5	6		38
10	11	1		4	3				9			8							7		5	2		6		39
10	11	1			3		8		9			4							7		5	2		6		40
10	11	1			3		8		9			4							7		5	2		6		41
	8	1	11		3				9		4	7									10	2	5	6		42
20	39	28	2	32	28	5	2	2	41	28	2	22	14	9	19	13	1	5	36	25	34	26	3	26		
8	10				1	1	1		55			3		1				1	5	2	1			2		

Anderson GR	Atkinson GA	Black D	Briggs R	Brown A	Bungay RH	Cartwright H	Cooke TV	Dransfield E	Harston E	Hart EA	Hill A	Horne A	Jones OH	Littledyke R	Moran J	Perfect FT	Poole C	Pressgrave G	Rattray CR	Roy JR	Speed F	Vaux E	Wainwright W	Wood L	Wright E	
10	8			4					9	5			1		3	2			7	11				6		1
10	8			4					9	5			1		3	2			7	11	6					2
2	2			2					2	2			2		2	2			2	2	1			1		
1									3																	

Anderson GR	Atkinson GA	Black D	Briggs R	Brown A	Bungay RH	Cartwright H	Cooke TV	Dransfield E	Harston E	Hart EA	Hill A	Horne A	Jones OH	Littledyke R	Moran J	Perfect FT	Poole C	Pressgrave G	Rattray CR	Roy JR	Speed F	Vaux E	Wainwright W	Wood L	Wright E	
	10	1		4		8			9							2			7	11	6	3			5	1
	1	1		1		1			1							1			1	1	1	1			1	

1937-38

Manager: W.H.Parkes to 4 January 1938, then J.Poole from 4 May 1938.

1	Aug	28	(h)	Northampton T	W	4-1	Crawshaw 3, Holmes	9,619
2	Sep	4	(a)	Bristol R	D	0-0		7,996
3		8	(h)	Walsall	W	3-1	Horne 2, Crawshaw	7,979
4		11	(h)	Gillingham	W	3-1	Crawshaw 2, Speed	7,921
5		15	(a)	Brighton & HA	L	0-2		6,294
6		18	(h)	Torquay U	D	1-1	Speed	7,393
7		25	(a)	Clapton O	W	2-1	Crawshaw 2	8,590
8	Oct	2	(h)	Southend U	D	2-2	Crawshaw 2	8,330
9		7	(a)	Notts C	L	0-2		13,632
10		9	(a)	Queen's Park R	D	1-1	Crawshaw	14,142
11		16	(a)	Exeter C	L	0-4		4,894
12		23	(h)	Swindon T	W	2-0	Crawshaw, Sams	5,264
13		30	(a)	Aldershot	L	0-1		5,680
14	Nov	6	(h)	Millwall	D	1-1	Horne	8,400
15		13	(a)	Reading	L	2-3	Horne, Sams	7,910
16		20	(h)	Crystal P	W	2-0	Bungay, Crawshaw	8,207
17	Dec	4	(h)	Newport C	D	1-1	Holmes	2,946
18		18	(h)	Watford	L	0-1		5,274
19		25	(h)	Cardiff C	W	3-0	Crawshaw, Holmes 2	12,114
20		27	(a)	Cardiff C	L	1-4	Johnston	37,726
21	Jan	1	(a)	Northampton T	L	0-3		6,401
22		15	(h)	Bristol R	W	1-0	Read	3,222
23		22	(a)	Gillingham	D	0-0		5,590
24		29	(a)	Torquay U	W	1-0	Read	2,467
25	Feb	5	(h)	Clapton O	W	3-1	Crawshaw 2, Read	5,394
26		12	(a)	Southend U	W	1-0	Speed (pen)	5,375
27		19	(h)	Queen's Park R	W	3-2	Speed, Turner, Crawshaw	9,072
28		26	(h)	Exeter C	L	2-3	Turner, Horne	7,187
29	Mar	5	(a)	Swindon T	D	3-3	Turner, Read, Johnston	7,728
30		12	(h)	Aldershot	W	2-0	Horne, Crawshaw	7,173
31		19	(a)	Millwall	L	0-1		29,253
32		26	(h)	Reading	W	5-1	Crawshaw 4, Turner	6,521
33	Apr	2	(a)	Crystal P	L	0-4		13,105
34		9	(h)	Notts C	L	1-2	Crawshaw	11,190
35		15	(a)	Bournemouth	L	4-5	Speed, Turner, Crawshaw, Read	8,616
36		16	(a)	Newport C	L	0-1		8,087
37		18	(h)	Bournemouth	W	3-2	Crawshaw, Read, Johnston	7,198
38		23	(h)	Bristol C	L	3-5	Read 2, Johnston	7,233
39		27	(a)	Bristol C	L	1-2	Read (pen)	15,231
40		30	(a)	Watford	L	0-2		9,222
41	May	2	(a)	Walsall	L	0-2		2,022
42		7	(h)	Brighton & HA	D	1-1	Shaw	4,417

FINAL LEAGUE POSITION: 14th in Division Three South

Appearances
Goals

FA Cup

1	Nov	27	(a)	Wellington T	W	2-1	O'Connor, Bungay	6,000
2	Dec	15	(h)	Lincoln C *	W	2-1	Crawshaw, Holmes	8,000
3	Jan	8	(h)	Leicester C	L	1-2	Johnston	15,890

* Replayed after match was abandoned after 62 minutes, score 2-1

Appearances
Goals

Division Three South Cup

1	Sep	27	(h)	Crystal P	L	0-1	

Appearances
Goals

Barke JL	Black D	Bungay RH	Crawshaw H	Fielding H	Holmes HH	Horne A	Hughes JI	Johnston C	Morris A	O'Connor FR	Paterson W	Read CW	Rudkin GW	Sams A	Shaw F	Speed F	Stamps JD	Stimpson G	Turner JK	Vaux E	Wood L	
4		3	9		10	7	1	11			5				8	6		2				1
4		3	9		10	7	1	11			5				8	6		2				2
4		3	9		10	7	1	11			5				8	6		2				3
4		3	9		8	7	1	11			5			10		6		2				4
4		3	9			7	1	11			5			10	8	6		2				5
4			9			7	1	11			5			10	8	6		2		3		6
6			9			7	1	11		4	5			10	8	3		2				7
6			9		11	7	1			4	5		10		8	3		2				8
6		3	9	7		8	1	11		4	5					10		2				9
6		3	9	7	11	8	1			4	5					10		2				10
6		3	9	7	11	8	1			4	5					10		2				11
6	1		9	7	11	8				4	5			10		3		2				12
6	1		9		11	8				4	5			10	7	3		2				13
6			9		8	7	1	11		4	5			10		3		2				14
6			9			7	1	11		4	5			10		3	8	2				15
6		8	9		11		1	7		4	5			10		3		2				16
6		8	9		11		1	7		4	5			10		3		2				17
6		10	9		8	7	1	11		4	5					3		2				18
6			9		10		1	11		4	5	8				3		2	7			19
6			9		10		1	11		4	5	8				3		2	7			20
6			9		11		1			4	5	8		10				2	7	3		21
4		3	9				1	11			5	8				6		2	7	10		22
4		3	9		10		1	11			5	8				6		2	7			23
4		3	9				1	11			5	8			10	6		2	7			24
4		3	9				1	11			5	8			10	6		2	7			25
4		3	9				1	11			5	8			10	6		2	7			26
4		3	9				1	11			5	8			10	6		2	7			27
4		3				8	1	11			5	9			10	6		2	7			28
6		3	9			8	1	11		4	5	10						2	7			29
4		3	9			8	1	11			5	10				6		2	7			30
4		3	9			8	1	11			5	10				6		2	7			31
4		3	9			8	1	11			5	10				6		2	7			32
2		3	9			8	1	11		4	5	10				6			7			33
2		3	9				1	11			5	10			8	6			7		4	34
4		3	9				1	11			5	10			8	6		2	7			35
4		3	9				1	11			5				8	6		2	7		10	36
4		3	9				1	11			5	10			8	6		2	7			37
4	1	3	9					11			5	10			8	6		2	7			38
5		3	9				1	11		4	6	10			8			2	7			39
5		3	9				1	11				10			8	6		2	7		4	40
5		3	9				1	11	4						8	6		2	7		10	41
4		3	9				1	11			6	10			8	6		2	7			42
42	3	32	41	4	17	22	39	36	1	18	40	22	1	11	22	39	1	40	24	3	4	
		1	25		4	6		4				9		2	1	5			5			

4		10	9			11	1	7		6	5			8		2		3				1
6		10	8		9	7	1	11		4	5					3		2				2
4		3	9		10	8	1	11			5					6		2	7			3
3		3	3		2	3	3	3		2	3			1		3		3	1			
			1		1			1		1												

6	1		9			7		11		4	5			10	8	3		2				1
1	1		1			1		1		1	1			1	1	1		1				

1938-39

Manager: J.Poole

1	Aug	27	(a)	Bristol R	L 0-3		11,050
2		31	(h)	Cardiff C	D 2-2	Dutton 2	6,959
3	Sep	3	(h)	Brighton & HA	W 4-2	Bungay 2, Carter, Dutton	5,830
4		7	(a)	Exeter C	L 0-2		6,297
5		10	(a)	Bournemouth	D 1-1	Dutton	9,414
6		17	(h)	Walsall	D 0-0		5,918
7		24	(a)	Port Vale	L 0-3		8,100
8	Oct	1	(a)	Queen's Park R	L 0-3		12,519
9		8	(h)	Southend U	W 3-1	Gardiner, Dutton, Wilson	5,472
10		15	(h)	Watford	D 0-0		6,491
11		22	(a)	Swindon T	W 2-1	Somerfield, Wilson	11,853
12		29	(h)	Bristol C	W 3-2	Turner, Somerfield, Dutton (pen)	7,398
13	Nov	5	(a)	Aldershot	L 0-3		6,848
14		12	(h)	Notts C	W 2-0	Turner, Dutton	9,852
15		19	(a)	Northampton T	W 4-3	Somerfield 3, Dutton	8,774
16	Dec	3	(a)	Clapton O	D 0-0		8,204
17		17	(a)	Crystal P	L 2-6	Bell, Carter	10,224
18		24	(h)	Bristol R	L 1-3	Gardiner	3,343
19		26	(a)	Ipswich T	L 1-5	Dutton	3,774
20		27	(h)	Ipswich T	L 0-1		6,486
21		31	(a)	Brighton & HA	L 0-3		7,084
22	Jan	11	(h)	Newport C	L 0-2		1,419
23		14	(h)	Bournemouth	W 2-0	Turner, Somerfield	3,098
24		28	(h)	Port Vale	W 2-0	Carter, Bungay (pen)	3,742
25	Feb	2	(a)	Walsall	D 0-0		2,980
26		4	(h)	Queen's Park R	D 2-2	Dutton, Mee	5,523
27		11	(a)	Southend U	L 0-2		6,195
28		18	(a)	Watford	L 0-2		7,254
29		25	(h)	Swindon T	D 1-1	Turner	4,111
30	Mar	4	(a)	Bristol C	L 0-2		8,270
31		8	(h)	Torquay U	W 4-0	Gardiner 2, Carter 2	800
32		11	(h)	Aldershot	W 1-0	Carter	3,218
33		18	(a)	Notts C	D 1-1	Harkin	11,629
34		25	(h)	Northampton T	D 1-1	Carter	4,039
35	Apr	1	(a)	Newport C	D 0-0		10,600
36		7	(h)	Reading	D 0-0		6,635
37		8	(h)	Clapton O	W 1-0	Flowers	4,188
38		10	(a)	Reading	D 0-0		9,225
39		15	(a)	Torquay U	L 0-3		3,209
40		22	(h)	Crystal P	D 0-0		3,016
41		29	(a)	Cardiff C	D 0-0		5,886
42	May	6	(h)	Exeter C	W 4-2	Harkin (pen), Flowers, Dutton 2	2,632

FINAL LEAGUE POSITION: 16th in Division Three South

Appearances
Goals

FA Cup

1	Nov	26	(a)	Workington	D 1-1	Somerfield	3,132
R		30	(h)	Workington	W 2-1	Somerfield, Dutton	5,111
2	Dec	10	(a)	Halifax T	D 1-1	Somerfield	14,208
R		14	(h)	Halifax T	D 3-3	Bell, Dutton, Wilson	6,083
2R		19	(n*)	Halifax T	D 0-0		2,500
3R		21	(n†)	Halifax T	L 1-2	Somerfield	1,219

*Played at the Belle Vue Ground, Doncaster. †Played at Old Trafford, Manchester.

Appearances
Goals

Division Three South Cup

1	Oct	12	(h)	Notts C	W 3-0	Bell, Gardiner, Wilson
2	Feb	13	(a)	Port Vale	L 1-3	Bell

Appearances
Goals

Match	Barke JL	Bell E	Black D	Bramley E	Bungay RH	Carter S	Collier A	Dutton T	Flowers TJ	Gardiner A	Harkin J	Hodgetts J	Hughes JI	Mee B	Paterson W	Somerfield A	Speed F	Statham A	Stimpson G	Turner JK	Wilson A
1	4	8				9	3	10					1		5		6		2	7	11
2	4	8			3	9		10		7			1		5		6		2		11
3		8			3	9	4	10		7			1		5		6		2		11
4	6	8			3	9	4	10		7			1		5				2		11
5	6	8			3	9	4	10		7			1		5				2		11
6	6	8			3	9	4	10					1		5				2	7	11
7	6	8			11	9	4	10					1		5		3		2		7
8	6	8			3		4	10		9			1				5		2	7	11
9	5	8			3		4	10		9			1				6		2	7	11
10	5	8			3		4	10		9			1				6		2	7	11
11	5	8			3		4	10					1			9	6		2	7	11
12	5	8			3		4	10					1			9	6		2	7	11
13	5	8			3		4	10					1			9	6		2	7	11
14	5	8			3		4	10					1			9	6		2	7	11
15	5	8	1		3		4	10								9	6		2	7	11
16	5	8	1		3		4	10								9	6		2	7	11
17	5	8	1		3	9	4			10								6	2	7	11
18	5	8	1		3			6		10					4	9			2	7	11
19	5	8	1		3	9		11		10					4		6		2		7
20	5	8			3	9		10		4		11	1			7	6		2		
21	5	8			3			10		4			1			9	6		2	7	11
22	5	8			6		4	11		10			1			9	3		2	7	
23	5				6	10	4	11		8			1			9	3		2	7	
24	5				6	10	4	11		8			1			9	3		2	7	
25	5				6	10	4	11		8			1			9	3		2	7	
26	5					9	3	10		8			1	11			6	4	2	7	
27	5	8			3	9		10			4		1	11			6		2	7	
28	5	8			3			10			4		1	11		9	6		2	7	
29	5	8			3			10			4		1	11		9	6		2	7	
30	5			2		9		10		8	4		1	11			6		3	7	
31				2		9		10		8	4		1	11	5		6		3	7	
32	6			2		9		10		8	4		1	11	5				3	7	
33	6			2		9		10		8	4		1	11	5				3	7	
34	6			2		9			10	8	4		1	11	5				3	7	
35	6			2		9			10	8	4		1	11	5				3	7	
36	6			2		9		10		8	4		1	11	5				3	7	
37	6			2		9		11	8		4		1	7	5		10		3		
38	6	8		2		9		11	10		4		1		5				3	7	
39	6	8		2		9		11	10		4		1		5				3	7	
40	6			2		9		11	10	8	4		1		5				3	7	
41	6			2		9		10		8	4		1	11	5				3	7	
42	6	8		2				11	10	9	4		1		5				3	7	
	40	28	5	13	27	27	21	39	7	27	16	1	37	13	21	15	27	2	42	34	20
		1			3	7		12	2	4	2			1		6				4	2

Round	Barke JL	Bell E	Black D	Bramley E	Bungay RH	Carter S	Collier A	Dutton T	Flowers TJ	Gardiner A	Harkin J	Hodgetts J	Hughes JI	Mee B	Paterson W	Somerfield A	Speed F	Statham A	Stimpson G	Turner JK	Wilson A
1	5	8	1		3		4	10								9	6		2	7	11
R	5	8	1		3		4	10								9	6		2	7	11
2	5	8	1		3		4	10								9	6		2	7	11
R	5	8	1		3		4	10								9	6		2	7	11
2R	5	7	1		3			10		8					4	9	6		2		11
3R	5	8	1		3			10		7					4	9	6		2		11
	6	6	6		6		4	6		2					2	6	6		6	4	6
		1						2								4					1

Match	Barke JL	Bell E	Black D	Bramley E	Bungay RH	Carter S	Collier A	Dutton T	Flowers TJ	Gardiner A	Harkin J	Hodgetts J	Hughes JI	Mee B	Paterson W	Somerfield A	Speed F	Statham A	Stimpson G	Turner JK	Wilson A
1	5	8			3		4	10		9			1				6		2	7	11
2	5	8			3	9		10			4		1	11			6		2	7	
	2	2			2	1	1	2		1	1		2	1			2		2	2	1
		2								1											1

1939-40

Manager: J Poole

1	Aug	26	(h)	Crystal P	L	4-5	Ward 2, Flowers, Glassey	7,658
2		30	(a)	Watford	W	2-1	Akers 2	
3	Sep	2	(a)	Torquay U	D	2-2	Akers, Ward	

Competition abandoned upon outbreak of war | Appearances
Goals

East Midland Section

1	Oct	21	(a)	Grimsby T	L	1-2	Robertson	22,357
2		28	(h)	Sheffield U	W	4-2	Hubbard 2, Robertson, Smith	3,000
3	Nov	4	(a)	Barnsley	L	1-2	Smith	2,500
4		11	(a)	Nottingham F	L	2-6	Hillard 2	3,000
5		18	(h)	Doncaster R	W	2-1	Rickards, Robinson	2,500
6		25	(h)	Sheffield W	W	5-3	Smith 2, Hubbard, Robertson, Rickards (pen)	1,600
7	Dec	2	(a)	Lincoln C	L	2-3	Rickards, Hubbard	2,000
8		9	(h)	Rotherham U	D	1-1	Hubbard	2,000
9		23	(a)	Sheffield W	L	0-2		2,000
10	Jan	13	(h)	Notts C	W	6-4	Lucas 3, Hubbard 3	2,200
11		20	(a)	Chesterfield	L	0-4		1,500
12	Mar	9	(h)	Nottingham F	W	3-0	Matthews 3	3,000
13		16	(a)	Doncaster R	L	1-4	Burrows, Beaumont	2,500
14		22	(a)	Notts C	D	2-2	Robertson, Hubbard (pen)	4,000
15		30	(h)	Lincoln C	L	4-5	Rickards, Harkin, Hubbard, Robertson	1,400
16	Apr	6	(a)	Rotherham U	W	2-1	Robertson 2	1,200
17	May	4	(h)	Grimsby T	W	4-1	Hunter, Lucas, Hubbard, Opp own-goal	1,000
18		18	(h)	Chesterfield	W	3-1	Lucas 2, Beaumont	2,000
19		25	(h)	Barnsley	W	3-2	Hubbard 3	2,000
20	Jun	8	(a*)	Sheffield U	D	2-2	Hubbard, Lucas	2,500

FINAL LEAGUE POSITION: 5th in East Midland Section | Appearances
Goals

Match 17 was a War Cup Preliminary Round
*Match 21 played at Field Mill because Bramall Lane required for cricket.

Akers W	Bailey E	Barke L	Barsby G	Beaumont L	Bedford G	Biddlestone	Bramley J	Borrows J	Carr	Clarke J	Corkhill W	Downham J	Egan H	Fillingham J	Flowers I	Glassey R	Gregg W	Harkin J	Hillard J	Hubbard C	Hunt K	Hunter J	Lucas W	Matthews E	McDonagh C	Moody J	Moore W	Nelson W	Patterson	Poole C	Rickards T	Robertson J	Robinson J	Simms TJ	Smith E	Speed F	Stephenson E	Stimpson G	Sullivan M	Turner J	Wainwright T	Ward TEG	
7		5				1		2							10	11		4									6												3	8			9	1
7		6				1	11									10		4										2	5									3	8			9	2
7		6				1	11									10		4										2	5									3	8			9	3
3		3				3	2	1							1	3		3									1	2	2									3	3			3	
3															1																											3	

Akers W	Bailey E	Barke L	Barsby G	Beaumont L	Bedford G	Biddlestone	Bramley J	Borrows J	Carr	Clarke J	Corkhill W	Downham J	Egan H	Fillingham J	Flowers I	Glassey R	Gregg W	Harkin J	Hillard J	Hubbard C	Hunt K	Hunter J	Lucas W	Matthews E	McDonagh C	Moody J	Moore W	Nelson W	Patterson	Poole C	Rickards T	Robertson J	Robinson J	Simms TJ	Smith E	Speed F	Stephenson E	Stimpson G	Sullivan M	Turner J	Wainwright T	Ward TEG	
		5						2										4		8						1						7			10	6		3		11		9	1
		3									4			5				6	11	9						1					7	10			8			2					2
	5	3									4							6	11	9						1						10			8			2		7			3
		3									4			5				6	11	9						1						10			8			2		7			4
	5										4						3	8		9						1					7	10	11						2			6		5
		5									4						3	6		8						1					11	9	10		7			2					6
		5									4						3	6		8						1					11	9	10		7			2					7
		5									4						3	6		8						1					11	9	10		7			2					8
											4						3	6		9						1					7	10	11		8			2			5		9
	5	3		11							4							6		9			10			1					7	8							2					10
		6		10	5				3									4		9						1				11	7	8							2					11
				11	5					6							3	4					10	9		1					7	8							2					12
		3		11	5		9											6		4			10			1					7	8							2					13
		6		11	5												3	4		10				9		1					7	8							2					14
		3	6	11	5													8		9						1					7	10		4				2					15
		3		11	5													4		9			10			1					7	8		6				2					16
		6		11	5													4		9			10		3	1					7	8							2					17
		3		11	5								8					4		9	1	7	10											6				2					18
		5		11									9					2		4	1	7	8											6			10	3					19
		5		11									8					2		9	1	7	10									4		6				3					20
		5		11								1	8					2		9		7	10									4		6				3					21
	3	18	1	12	8		1	1	1	1	9	1	4	2			7	21	3	20	3	4	9	2	1	17				1	14	19	5	6	8	1	1	21		3	2	1	
				2			1											1	2	17		1	7	3							5	7	1		4								

1 own-goal

1940-41

Manager: J.Poole

1	Aug	31	(h)	Norwich C	W 4-0	Hubbard 2, Flowers, Beaumont	1,000
2	Sep	7	(a)	Northampton T	L 1-6	Hubbard	1,500
3		14	(h)	Stoke C	L 2-3	Egan 2	
4		21	(a)	Stoke C	L 0-5		2,000
5		28	(h)	Northampton T	W 3-1	Hubbard, Rickards, Harkin	2,000
6	Oct	12	(h)	Birmingham	W 4-1	Robertson 2, Rickards, Egan	2,000
7		19	(a)	Birmingham	L 1-4	Simms	1,000
8		26	(h)	Walsall	D 6-6	Rickards 4, Egan, Robertson	1,500
9	Nov	2	(a)	Walsall	W 3-1	Rickards, Beaumont, Egan	500
10		9	(a)	Leicester C	L 2-3	Robertson, Barke	1,500
11		16	(h)	Leicester C	W 3-2	Rickards, Egan, Robertson	2,000
12		23	(a)	West Brom A	L 2-4	Rickards 2 (1 pen)	300
13		30	(h)	West Brom A	D 3-3	Rickards, Harkin, Hubbard	2,000
14	Dec	14	(h)	Nottingham F	W 2-1*	Rickards, Akers	500
15		21	(a)	Nottingham F	W 4-1	Rickard 2, Hunter, Egan	500
16		25	(h)	Stoke C	W 7-2	Rickards 2, Egan 2, Harkin, Robertson, Hubbard	
17	Jan	4	(h)	Northampton T	W 3-1	Rickards 2, Beaumont	1,000
18		11	(a)	Northampton T	D 3-3	Rickards 3	1,500
19		25	(a)	Lincoln C	L 2-4	Egan, Robertson	
20	Feb	15	(h)	Stoke C	W 6-1	Rickards 3, Robertson, Beaumont, Egan	2,000
21		22	(a)	Stoke C	L 0-2		1,200
22	Mar	1	(a)	West Brom A	W 3-2	Egan 2, Lucas	1,500
23		8	(h)	West Brom A	W 6-2	Rickards 3 (1 pen), Harkin 2, Egan	3,000
24		15	(a)	Leicester C	D 2-2	Beaumont, Robertson	6,000
25		22	(h)	Leicester C	L 1-2	Hubbard	5,000
26		29	(a)	Lincoln C	L 1-3	Rickards	
27	Apr	15	(h)	Lincoln C	D 1-1	Beaumont	
28		12	(h)	Rotherham U	L 0-1		
29		14	(h)	Bradford	W 5-1	Rickards 2, Hubbard 2, Beaumont	
30		19	(a)	Walsall	D 1-1	Hubbard (pen)	1,500
31		26	(h)	Walsall	D 2-2	Harkin, Rickards	500
32	May	3	(a)	Doncaster R	L 1-2	Rickards	1,241
33		10	(h)	Grimsby T	W 3-1	Rickards 3	600
34		17	(h)	Doncaster R	W 6-1	Beaumont 3, Rickards 2, Lucas	500
35	Jun	7	(h)	Chesterfield	L 1-4	Rickards	600

FINAL LEAGUE POSITION: 17th in South Regional Competition

Appearances

Goals

Matches 17, 18 and 19 Midlands Cup.
Mansfield were unable to play their round two home leg with Lincoln — round decided on second leg at Sincil Bank, 25 January 1941.
*Match 14 abandoned after 60 minutes, but result to stand.
Matches 20, 21, 22, 23, 24 and 25 War Cup.

Akers W	Allen J	Ashton P	Barke L	Barsby G	Beaumont L	Briggs R	Corkhill W	Downham J	Egan H	Flowers I	Gilmour T	Hall G	Hardwick H	Harkin J	Hays C	Hesford RS	Hillard J	Hubbard C	Hunt K	Hunter J	Jackson	Johnstone R	Lucas W	Marshall E	Mayfield G	McCall R	McDonald G	Mills	Poyser G	Richards	Rickards T	Rigby W	Robertson J	Simms TJ	Stimpson G	
			3		11			1	8	10				4				9								5							7	6	2	1
			3		10	11		1	8					4				9								5							7	6	2	2
			3		11			1	8	10				4			7	9								5								6	2	3
			5		11		4		9	10				7				1								3		6						8	2	4
			5		11		4		10					6				9	1							2				3	7		8			5
			5		11		4		10					6					1							2				3	9		8	7		6
			5		11		4		10					6					1			3				2					9		8	7		7
			5		11		4		10					6					1			3				2					9		8	7		8
			5		11		4		10					6					1			3				2					9		8	7		9
			5		11		4		10					6		1						3				2					9		8	7		10
			5		11		4		10					6		1				7		3				2					9		8			11
			5		11		4		10				1	6				8				3				2					9		7			12
		1	5		11		4		10					6				8		7		3				2					9					13
8			5		11				10					6		1		4		7		3				2					9					14
			5		11				10					6		1		4		7		3				2					9		8			15
			5						11					6				10		7		2				4			3		9	1	8			16
		1	5		11		2		10					3				4		7				6							9		8			17
		1	5		11		4		10					2				8		7		3		6							9					18
		1	5		11				10					3				4		7				6		2					9		8			19
		1	5		11				10					4				7				3		6		2					9		8			20
		1	5		11				10					4				7				3		6		2					9		8			21
		1	5		11				10					4				7				3	8	6		2					9					22
		1	5		11				10					4				7				3	8	6		2					9					23
			5		11				10					4				1				3	8	6		2					9		7			24
		1	5		11				8					4				7				3	10	6		2					9					25
		1	5		11									4				7				3	10	6		2					9		8			26
	5	1			11						7			4				6				3	10			2					8		9			27
		1	5		11				10		6			4						7		3				2					9		8			28
		1	5		11				10		6			3				4		7						2					9		8			29
		1	5		11				10		6			4						7		3				2					9		8			30
	3	1	5		11				10		6			8				4								2					9		7			31
	3	1	5		11				10		6			8				4								2					9		7			32
		1	5	7	11				10		6			3				4								2					9		8			33
	4		5	7	11							2		3				1			6		10								9		8			34
	4	1	5	7	11										6			2							3		10				9		8			35
1	5	18	34	3	34	1	12	3	31	3	7	1	1	34	1	4	1	27	5	11	1	21	7	10	1	31	1	1	1	2	31	1	27	9	4	
1			1		10				14	1				6				10		1			2								38		9	1		

1941-42

Manager: J Poole

1	Aug	30	(h)	Doncaster R	W 4-1	Beaumont 2, Harkins 2	2,000
2	Sep	6	(a)	Doncaster R	L 1-4	Beaumont	2,000
3		13	(a)	Sheffield U	W 2-1	Hazard, Robertson	3,000
4		20	(h)	Sheffield U	L 2-3	Hindley, Harkin	2,500
5		27	(h)	Bradford	L 1-2	Harkin	1,500
6	Oct	4	(a)	Bradford	L 0-3		3,000
7		11	(h)	Chesterfield	L 2-4	Jeffries, Rickards	1,000
8		18	(a)	Chesterfield	W 2-1	Cairns, Jeffries	600
9		25	(a)	Barnsley	L 1-3	Barke (pen)	1,500
10	Nov	1	(h)	Barnsley	L 0-3		600
11		8	(h)	Sheffield W	W 4-0	Rickards 2, Harkin, Barke (pen)	1,200
12		15	(a)	Sheffield W	L 0-2		1,000
13		22	(a)	Rotherham U	L 0-4		1,800
14		29	(h)	Rotherham U	W 4-1	Rickards 3, Harkin	600
15	Dec	6	(h)	Grimsby T	L 1-3	Egan	500
16		13	(a)	Grimsby T	W 5-4	Rickards 2, Harkin 2, Beaumont	1,500
17		20	(h)	Lincoln C	L 0-5		1,000
18		25	(a)	Lincoln C	L 0-6		6,014
19		27	(h)	Luton T	D 3-3	Harkin, Somerfield, Barke (pen)	2,500
20	Jan	3	(a)	Luton T	L 1-2	Rickards	2,500
21		10	(a)	Lincoln C	L 2-7	Owen, Hunter	2,000
22	Feb	21	(h)	West Brom A	L 1-3	Somerfield	1,000
23	Mar	14	(h)	Nottingham F	L 1-3	Harkin (pen)	2,000
24		21	(a)	Walsall	L 0-1		874
25		26	(h)	Walsall	W 2-0	Rickards, Robertson	600
26	Apr	4	(a)	Chesterfield	L 2-5	Rickards, Hunter	2,000
27		6	(h)	Chesterfield	L 0-2		2,500
28		11	(h)	Lincoln C	L 1-8	Rickards	700
29		18	(a)	Lincoln C	D 2-2	Hunter, Rich	2,000

FINAL LEAGUE POSITION: 33rd out of 38 in North Region

Appearances
Goals

Because of postponement Mansfield were unable to complete qualifying matches in War Cup — 5 matches outstanding.
Matches 19-25 were War Cup Qualifying rounds.
Finished 3rd from 60 in qualifying table.

Ashton P	Barke L	Beaumont L	Butler J	Butler R	Cairns W	Carnham	Corkhill W	Cross B	Egan H	Galley S	Harkin J	Hazard H	Hazelby	Hindley F	Hillard	Hodgetts J	Hunter J	Ithell W	Jeffries A	Johnstone R	Jones	Keeton A	Kingswell L	Kinsell S	McCall R	Musson W	Owens W	Parr J	Platts L	Rich	Richards S	Rickards T	Robertson J	Ross L	Siviter	Somerfield	Townsend	Ward T	Webber E	Wolfe E	
1	5	11					4	7	10		6									3					2							9	8								1
1	6	11						7			4		10							3			5		2							9	8								2
1	5								11	2		10		9						3			6		4							7	8								3
	5								11	2		10		9						3	1		6		4							7	8								4
1	5							7	11		6			9						3			4		2							10	8								5
1	5	11							10		6			9					7	3					2							8	4								6
1	5	11			10				4	3	6								7						2							9	8								7
1	3	11			10				8		6								7						2							9	4						5		8
1	3	11			10				9		6							4	7						2								8						5		9
1	3	11			10						6							4	7						2							9	8						5		10
	6	11							10		8								7						2	4		3	1			9							5		11
	3	11							10		8								7				6		2				1			9	4						5		12
	6	11							10		8								7						2	4		3	1			9							5		13
	6	11							10		8								7						2	4		3	1			9							5		14
	6	11							10		8								7						2	4		3	1			9							5		15
	6	11							10		8								7						2	4		3	1			9							5		16
	5	11			10						8						7					2			6	4		3	1			9									17
	5	11				4					6						7		10						2				1				8	3						9	18
	5	11									6						7		8							4		3	1			2	10			9					19
	6	11									3						7		8							4			1		2	9	10						5		20
	6	10									4						7										11	3	1		2	9	8						5		21
	6		1						10		3						7														2	9				8	4	11	5		22
1	6								10		4				11		7		8									3			2	9							5		23
1	6			4					10		3				11		7		8												2	9							5		24
	5		1				4		11		6						7		10									3			2	9	8								25
	5		1				4		10		6					11	7							3							2	9	8								26
	5		1				4		10		6					11	7							3							2	9	8								27
	6		1	5					10		4					11	7							3								9	8						2		28
	6		1	5							4						7											3		11	2	9	8		10						29
11	29	18	6	3	5	1	4	3	21	3	27	2	1	4	2	3	13	2	17	6	1	1	5	3	18	8	1	11	11	1	9	27	20	1	1	2	1	1	15	1	
	3	4			1				1		10		1	1			3		2								1			1		12	2			2					

Match 18: Wolfe & Carnham recruited from crowd.

1942-43

Manager: J.Poole

1	Aug	29	(h)	Rotherham U	W 4-3	Rickards 2, Egan, Siviter	1,500
2	Sep	5	(a)	Rotherham U	D 0-0		1,600
3		12	(h)	Notts C	L 0-1		1,500
4		19	(a)	Notts C	L 1-3	Bicknell	2,000
5		26	(h)	Nottingham F	L 0-1		2,000
6	Oct	3	(a)	Nottingham F	L 1-3	Hunter	2,000
7		10	(a)	Lincoln C	L 1-7	Ward	2,000
8		17	(h)	Lincoln C	L 3-4	Marlow, Owen, Bicknell	2,000
9		24	(h)	Leicester C	L 1-2	Rickards	1,500
10		31	(a)	Leicester C	L 2-5	Rickards, Bicknell	3,000
11	Nov	7	(a)	Sheffield W	L 1-9	Edwards	9,569
12		14	(h)	Sheffield W	L 2-10	Bicknell 2	2,000
13		21	(a)	Chesterfield	D 1-1	Bicknell	2,000
14		28	(h)	Chesterfield	D 1-1	Edwards	1,500
15	Dec	5	(a)	Sheffield U	L 2-6	Bicknell, Marlow	2,000
16		12	(a)	Sheffield U	W 4-3	Edwards 2, Marlow 2	2,000
17		19	(h)	Derby C	D 1-1	Parr (og)	2,500
18		25	(a)	Derby C	L 0-5		8,000
19		26	(h)	Nottingham F	L 1-3	Robertson	5,000
20	Jan	2	(a)	Nottingham F	L 1-3	Hannah	1,500
21		9	(a)	Derby C	L 0-10		7,000
22		16	(h)	Derby C	D 1-1	Bicknell	2,500
23		23	(h)	Lincoln C	L 2-3	Robertson, Wilson	1,500
24		30	(a)	Lincoln C	L 1-8	Dunderdale	1,500
25	Feb	6	(h)	Notts C	L 2-4	Flowers, Opp own-goal	1,000
26		13	(a)	Notts C	L 0-2		2,000
27		20	(a)	Chesterfield	L 2–6	Barke, Bicknell	3,000
28		27	(h)	Chesterfield	W 2-1	Chessell, Opp own-goal	1,500

FINAL LEAGUE POSITION: Bottom Football League North & bottom North Second Championship. Appearances

Goals

Matches 19 to 28 War Cup — Mansfield finished third from bottom in Cup Qualifying table.

Allen J	Barke L	Bedford	Bennet R	Bicknell J	Bradshaw W	Bramley E	Chessell S	Cooke E	Dunderdale W	Egan H	Edwards	Everett H	Findley W	Flowers I	Hannah G	Harkin J	Hazard J	Hunter	Jeffries A	Jones	Lievesley	Little	Marlow G	Marsh E	Marsh W	Mills P	Oakley J	Owen W	Platts L	Poole C	Pritchard R	Richards S	Rickards T	Robertson J	Sidley	Siviter	Smith	Taylor	Ward T	Walters H	Webber E	Wilson	Winslow	Winstanley D	
	6									10						3		7				4						11	1			2	8			9					5				1
	6					3				10						4		7	11			8							1			2	9								5				2
6	5	3								10						4		8	11								1				7	2	9												3
4	6		3	9						11						2		7	10								1						8								5				4
	3			9						11		6				4		7	10							2	1						8								5				5
	4			9		3						6				8		7					11			2	1						10								5				6
	3			9												2		7		6			11				1						8				4		10		5				7
	6			9												4							10	2	3		1	11					7								5			8	8
	6			9												4							11	2	3		1						8							7	5			10	9
	6			9									10		7	4							11	2	3		1						8								5				10
	6										9			10		2							11		3		1						7		8		4				5				11
	6			9							10		8								4		11		3		1						7								5		2		12
	6			9							10		8								4		11		3		1						7								5		2		13
	5			9				3			10						6				4		11				1						7	8							2				14
	5			9				3			10						6				4		11				1						7	8							2				15
	5			9			4	2			10	6											11				1			3			7	8											16
	5			9			4	2			10	6			7								11				1			3				8											17
	5			9			4	2			10	6			7								11				1			3				8											18
	3			9			8	2			10	5			6								11				1							7							4				19
	4			9				3			10	6			7								11				1					2		8							5				20
	5			9			4	3			10	6			7								11				1					2		8											21
3	6			9	7		4	2			10																1							8				11			5				22
	6			9	7	3	4	2															11				1							8							5	10			23
	6			9			4	2	10											3			11				1							8			7				5				24
3	6			9			4	2	8					10									11				1							7							5				25
4	6			10				2												9			11				1			3				8			7				5				26
4	6			9			10	2															11				1			3				8			7				5				27
	6			9			10	2												4			11				1			3				8			7				5				28
6	28	1	1	24	2	3	11	15	2	5	12	8	3	2	6	11	2	7	4	4	4	2	22	3	6	2	26	2	2	6	1	5	16	15	1	1	6	1	1	1	23	1	2	2	
	1			9			1		1	1	4			1	1			1					4					1					4	2		1			1			1			

3 own-goals

1943-44

Manager: J.Poole until August 1944

1	Aug	28	(a)	Leicester C	L	1-4	Chessell	4,000
2	Sep	4	(h)	Leicester C	D	0-0		2,500
3		11	(a)	Rotherham U	L	1-3	Sullivan	2,500
4		18	(h)	Rotherham U	W	3-2	Marlow 2, Chessell	
5		25	(a)	Nottingham F	W	2-1	Chessell 2	5,000
6	Oct	2	(h)	Nottingham F	L	0-1		3,500
7		9	(a)	Notts C	W	2-0	Smith, Laing	3,000
8		16	(h)	Notts C	W	4-0	Marlow 2, Chessell, Smith	3,500
9		23	(h)	Lincoln C	W	1-0	Marlow (pen)	2,000
10		30	(a)	Lincoln C	L	2-7	Smith, Marlow	3,000
11	Nov	6	(h)	Sheffield W	L	0-2		6,000
12		13	(a)	Sheffield W	W	3-2	Marlow 2, Hubbard	6,000
13		20	(h)	Chesterfield	W	2-0	Hubbard, Clarke	4,000
14		27	(a)	Chesterfield	W	3-2	Marlow 2, Hubbard	2,000
15	Dec	4	(h)	Sheffield W	D	0-0		4,000
16		11	(a)	Sheffield W	L	2-4	Rickards, Chessell	8,000
17		18	(h)	Derby C	W	3-1	Smith, Marlow, Chessell	3,500
18		25	(a)	Derby C	L	3-4	Tapping 2, Barke	8,000
19		26	(h)	Lincoln C	W	2-1	Akers, Rickards	
20	Jan	1	(a)	Lincoln C	L	2-3	Rickards, Chessell	3,000
21		8	(a)	Notts C	L	0-5		4,000
22		15	(h)	Notts C *	W	1-0	Rickards	
23		22	(a)	Leicester C	L	2-5	Rickards, Opp own-goal	6,000
24		29	(h)	Leicester C	D	1-1	Marlow	5,000
25	Feb	5	(h)	Nottingham F	L	0-1		5,000
26		12	(a)	Nottingham F	W	1-0	Chessell	6,000
27		19	(a)	Derby C	W	1-0	Smith	6,000
28		26	(h)	Derby C	L	2-3	Tapping, Smith	11,000
29	Mar	18	(h)	Lincoln C	W	4-0	Owens 2, Tapping, Barke (pen)	1,000
30		25	(a)	Lincoln C	L	0-3		1,500
31	Apr	15	(h)	Notts C	W	5-0	Marlow 3, Collins, Owens	1,000
32		22	(a)	Notts C	L	2-3	Jagger, Gascoigne	1,500

FINAL LEAGUE POSITION: 18th in Football League North; 4th from bottom in Second Championship

*Abandoned after 15 minutes, result stood.

Appearances
Sub Appearances
Goals

Matches 19 to 28 War Cup Qualifying competition.
Finished 4th in League North Cup, failing to qualify.

Akers W	Allen J	Barke L	Bramley E	Calladine J	Chessell S	Clack F	Clarke J	Coleman T	Collins A	Davidson D	Dickinson N	Dawson	Egan H	Ellis S	Flowers I	Galley D	Gascoigne	Greaves	Hamilton G	Match
		5		7	9						10			1				11		1
		5			7	1													6	2
		5			7														6	3
					7	1													2	4
		5			7	1													6	5
		5			9	1									10				2	6
		5				1										2			6	7
		5			7											2			6	8
		5														2			6	9
		5				1										2			6	10
		5			10	1	7			2									6	11
		5	2			1	7												6	12
		5	2			1	7												6	13
		5	2		10	1	7												6	14
		5	2		10	1	7												6	15
		5			7											2			6	16
		5			7	1													6	17
		9						5				3					8			18
7		5	3																	19
		5	3		7	1														20
		5	2		7	1													6	21
		5	2		7	1													6	22
	6	5			7	1													4	23
		5	2		7	1													6	24
		5	2			1													4	25
		5	2		7	1													6	26
		5	2			1							9						6	27
		5	2			1							9						6	28
		5	2			1													6	29
		5	2			1													6	30
		5	2			1			8										6	31
		5	2			1													8	32
1	1	31	17	1	18	25	5	1	1	1	1	1	2	1	1	5	1	1	28	
1		2			9		1		1											

Harkin J	Hazard J	Hogg F	Holling	Hubbard C	Jaggers	Jones DO	Laing F	Marlow G	Owens M	Pilcher E	Poole C	Rickards CT	Shadwell J	Smith K	Sullivan M	Tapping F	Wood A	Woolridge J	Match
					2				4	3		6		8					1
					2				4	3	9		10	8					2
							11		4	3	9	2		8					3
		5					11		6	3	9		8	10	4				4
		2					11			3	9		8	10	4				5
							11		6	3	7		8		4				6
						8	11			3	9		7	10	4				7
						8	11			3	9		10		4				8
			7			8	11			3	9			10	4	1			9
			7				11			3	8		9	10	4				10
			9				11			3	8				4				11
			9				11			3	8		10		4				12
			9				11			3	8		10		4				13
			9				11			3	8				4				14
			9				11			3	8				4				15
			9				11			3	8		10		4				16
	8						11			3	9		10		4		2		17
6					7		11			2	10				4	1			18
	8						11			6	9		10		4	1	2		19
	8						11			6	9		10		4		2		20
	8						11			3	9		10		4				21
	8						11			3	9		10		4				22
					8		11			3	9		10				2		23
	8						11			3	9		10		4				24
	8						11			3	7		10						25
	8						11			3	9		10		4				26
	8						11			3	7		10		4				27
	8						11			3	7		10		4				28
	8						11	7		3	9		10		4				29
	8						11	7		3	9		10		4				30
	4						10	7		3	9							11	31
	4			7			10			3	9							11	32
1	14	2	8	1	4	3	30	3	5	32	31	2	23	8	25	3	4	2	
			3	1		1	15	3			5		6	1	4			1	

1 own-goal

Norton played number 1 in Match 16; J.Rutherford played number 1 in Match 8; Taylor played number 6 in Match 32; Walsh played number 9 in Match 25; Wall played number 10 in Match 3; Warburton played number 11 in Match 2; S.Weaver played number 6 in Match 25; J.Wilkinson played number 1 in Match 3.

1944-45

Acting Manager: Lloyd Barke from August 1944

1	Aug	26	(a)	Grimsby T	L	1-5	Ward	6,000
2	Sep	2	(h)	Grimsby T	D	1-1	Alsop (pen)	3,000
3		9	(h)	Rotherham U	L	1-2	Opp own-goal	4,000
4		16	(a)	Rotherham U	D	0-0		7,000
5		23	(a)	Lincoln C	L	1-3	Marlow	3,500
6		30	(h)	Lincoln C	W	1-0	Cooke	3,000
7	Oct	7	(h)	Sheffield W	W	2-0	Marlow, Cooke	4,000
8		14	(a)	Sheffield W	W	6-1	Cooke 3, Alsop 3 (1 pen)	8,000
9		21	(a)	Nottingham F	W	5-2	Marlow 2, Alsop 2, Cooke	5,000
10		28	(h)	Nottingham F	W	4-2	Wilcockson, Harkin, Marlow, Alsop (pen)	5,000
11	Nov	4	(h)	Barnsley	D	1-1	Liddle	6,000
12		11	(a)	Barnsley	L	2-3	Curry 2	7,666
13		18	(a)	Doncaster R	L	1-2	G.Poole	4,967
14		25	(h)	Doncaster R	L	0-2		3,000
15	Dec	2	(h)	Derby C	L	0-4		7,000
16		9	(a)	Derby C	L	1-7	Bramley	11,000
17		16	(a)	Sheffield U	L	0-4		4,000
18		23	(h)	Sheffield U	W	4-1	Hewitt, Akers, Tapping 2	4,000
19		26	(a)	Notts C	W	2-0	Curry, Baxter	5,000
20		30	(h)	Notts C	W	3-1	Gardner 2, Hewitt	3,000
21	Jan	6	(h)	Leicester C	D	2-2	Curry, Marlow	5,000
22		13	(a)	Leicester C	L	3-8	Rickards, Hewitt, Akers	5,000
23	Feb	3	(h)	Derby C	L	1-8	Hewitt	8,000
24		10	(a)	Derby C	L	1-7	Akers	12,000
25		17	(h)	Chesterfield	W	4-3	Curry, Hewitt, Akers, Bramley (pen)	5,000
26		24	(a)	Chesterfield	L	0-3		6,000
27	Mar	10	(a)	Nottingham F	L	1-2	Davie	10,463
28		17	(h)	Nottingham F	W	1-0	Bramley	8,000
29	Apr	2	(h)	Walsall	W	2-0	Owens, Bramley (pen)	4,000
30	May	5	(a)	Walsall	L	2-4	Curry, Wilkinson	500

FINAL LEAGUE POSITION: 39th in Football League North — Appearances

Goals

Finished 9th in North Cup, failed to qualify.
Matches 19 to 28 League Cup qualifying rounds.
Matches 29 & 30 Division Three South North Regional Cup.

Akers W	Alsop G	Armeson L	Atter A	Barke L	Baxter W	Beardall J	Bramley E	Bradley D	Brown G	Butler J	Christopher J	Cooke E	Collins A	Curry R	Davie J	Gardner J	Grout A	Harkin J	Hartley T	Hewitt J	Hogg F	Jones L	Liddle D	Long A	Marlow G	Moulson C	Owens M	Poole C	Poole G	Ranshaw J	Rickards C	Rickett W	Rossington K	Tapping F	Ward T	White F	Wilcoxson C	Williams F	
	11			6			2			1								4						7	10			3			8				9				1
7	9			5			2			1								4					6	10	11			3							8				2
7	10			5			2			1			8					4					6		11			3			9								3
	10		4	5					1				7										6		8			3		11								2	4
	9		4	5								10						8					6		7			3		11						1		2	5
8	10			5			2					9						4					6		7			3		11						1			6
	10			5			8					9						4					6		11			3		7						1		2	7
	7			5			2					9						4					10		11	6		3								1	8		8
	7			6			2					9					1	4					10		11	5		3									8		9
	7	6		5			2					9					1	4					10		11			3									8		10
	7	6		5			2					9					1	4					10		11			3									8		11
		6		5			2					9		8			1	7					10		11			3										4	12
		6		5			2							8			1	9					10		11			3	7									4	13
7		6		5			2					9					1	4					10		11			3						8					14
7				5			2							8			1	6					10		11			3					4	9					15
				5			9							8			1	6				10	7		11			3					4					2	16
10				5			2							8			1	6		9		4	7		11			3											17
7				5			2							8			1	6		10		4	11					3						9					18
7				5	4		2							8			1	6					10		11			3						9					19
9				5			2									10	1	6		8		4	7		11			3											20
				5			2							8		9		6		10		4			11			3			7								21
7				5			2									11		6		10		4						3			9			8					22
7				5			2									11	1	6		10	8	4						3						9					23
7				5			2									11	1	6			10	4						3			8			9					24
7				5			3							10			1	6		9	8	11												4				2	25
7				5			3										1	6			8	10												4				2	26
7				5			2	3						8	9		1	6			4	10										11							27
7				5			2							9			1	6	4		8	10						3				11							28
				5			2							8		11	1	6	4			10					9	3	7										29
				5		11	2	3		1	9			8					4																		10		30
16	11	5	2	30	1	1	28	2	1	4	1	9	2	13	1	6	19	28	3	7	6	13	19	2	20	2	1	26	2	4	5	2	2	9	2	4	5	8	
4	7				1		4					6		6	1	2		1		5			1		6		1		1		1			2	1		2		

1 own-goal

S.Duffield played number 7 in Match 30; S.Flewitt played number 11 in Match 26; R.Griffin played number 6 in Match 30; A.Hughes played number 9 in Match 4; A.Somerfield played number 9 in Match 26; S.Jones played number 1 in Match 22; J.Wheat played number 5 in Match 1; J.Wilkinson played number 1 in Match 21.

1945-46

Manager: Roy Goodall

1	Aug	25	(h)	Clapton O	D 2-2	Thorpe, Harkin	4,000
2	Sep	1	(a)	Clapton O	D 0-0		5,000
3		8	(a)	Watford	L 1-2	Hogg	4,648
4		12	(h)	Queen's Park R	L 2-6	Hogg, Womwell	7,000
5		15	(h)	Watford	L 1-2	Womwell	4,000
6		19	(h)	Walsall	W 6-1	Hogg 2, Womwell 2, E.Smith, Peacock	4,000
7		28	(a)	Walsall	L 0-2		3,000
8	Oct	6	(a)	Norwich C	L 1-5	Womwell	12,000
9		13	(h)	Norwich C	W 4-1	Miller, Womwell, Hogg, E.Smith	6,000
10		20	(a)	Notts C	L 0-1		20,000
11		27	(h)	Notts C	L 2-3	Harkin 2	10,000
12	Nov	3	(h)	Southend U	D 2-2	Womwell 2	3,000
13		10	(a)	Southend U	D 1-1	Womwell	5,000
14	Dec	1	(h)	Port Vale	L 1-2	Womwell	4,000
15		22	(h)	Ipswich T	L 1-2	Womwell	2,500
16		24	(a)	Port Vale	L 0-2		6,000
17		25	(h)	Northampton T	W 2-0	Carter 2	
18		26	(a)	Northampton T	L 0-4		
19		29	(a)	Queen's Park R	L 2-3	Akers, Marsh	20,000
20	Jan	12	(a)	Notts C	W 2-1	Carter, Barke (pen)	9,000
21		19	(h)	Notts C	W 2-0	Clarke, Barke	4,500
22		26	(a)	Walsall	D 2-2	Brinton, Copestake	4,000
23	Feb	2	(h)	Walsall	L 1-2	Hogg	2,500
24		9	(a)	Clapton O	W 2-0	Hewitt, Carter	9,000
25		16	(h)	Clapton O	L 1-2	Miller	4,000
26		20	(a)	Ipswich T	D 1-1	Hogg	
27		23	(h)	Queen's Park R	D 0-0		5,000
28	Mar	2	(a)	Queen's Park R	L 0-3		5,000
29		9	(a)	Ipswich T	L 1-2	Harkin	10,000
30		16	(h)	Ipswich T	W 3-0	Hogg, Copestake, Hewitt	4,500
31		23	(a)	Northampton T	D 1-1	E.Betts	10,000
32		30	(h)	Northampton T	W 3-1	Copestake, Hogg, E.Betts	4,000
33	Apr	6	(h)	Port Vale	W 2-1	Hogg, Hewitt	6,000
34		13	(a)	Port Vale	D 0-0		8,000
35		20	(a)	Watford	W 3-0	Jeffries, Everett, Hogg	6,000
36		22	(h)	Watford	W 1-0	Copestake	7,000

FINAL LEAGUE POSITION: Bottom Third Division South (North Region). First half of season Matches 20 & 25, 27-36 Division Three South (North Region) Cup — finished 3rd.

Appearances
Goals

FA Cup

1	Nov	17	(h)	Gainsborough T	W 3-0	Womwell 2, Harkins
		24	(a)	Gainsborough T	L 2-4*	C.Poole, Womwell
2	Dec	8	(a)	Grantham	W 2-1	Thorpe, Womwell
		15	(h)	Grantham	W 2-1	Hogg, Womwell
3	Jan	5	(h)	Sheffield W	D 0-0	
		10	(a)	Sheffield W	L 0-5	

*After extra-time

Appearances
Goals

Akers W	Alderston N	Allen J	Baker A	Barke L	Betts C	Betts E	Bowles J	Bramley C	Bramley E	Brinton J	Carter S	Chessell S	Copestake O	Cromack V	Everett H	Ferguson J	Fretwell L	Grant A	Harkin J	Hartley T	Hewitt J	Hogg F	Jeffries H	Mallinder D	Marsh W	Miller L	Oakley J	Peacock T	Poole G	Richmond R	Rickett W	Smith E	Smith L	Smith W	Thorpe L	Urien P	Ward T	Womwell D	
11			7	5			1	3	2		9						6		4			10													8				1
			7	5			1				9	3					6		4			10		2											8				2
			9	5								3			1	11	4					8		2							7	10	6						3
			11	5			1					3										6		2							7	10			8			9	4
	3		7	5													10		4			6		2			1			11							8	9	5
7	3			5								2							4			8					1	11				10	6					9	6
	3			5								2						1	4									11					6					9	7
7	3			5								2							4			8					1	11										9	8
7				5					2			3							4			8				11	1					10	6					9	9
7				5					2			3							4							11	1	10				8	6					9	10
7				5				2				3							6			10				11	1						4				8	9	11
7				5				2											3	6	8					11	1	10					4					9	12
				5					2			3							6		7						1						4					9	13
				5								2			6						7	8			3	11	1						4	10				9	14
				5								2			6				8						3		1			11			4	10	7			9	15
				5	7				2			3					10		6								1						4	11				9	16
		11		5							9	2							6						3								4	10	7	1		8	17
		11		5							9	2							6						3								4	10	7	1		8	18
7				5								2							10						3	11	1						4		8			9	19
8				5				2			9	3		1	6				10							11							4		7				20
				5				2			9	3	10	1	6				8							11							4		7				21
				5				2		11	9	3	10	1	6		8		7														4						22
				5				2				3	10		6				7			8				11							4			1		9	23
				5				2			9	3	10	1	6						7					11							4	8					24
				5				2			9	3	10	1	6						7	8				11							4						25
				5	11			2				3	9	1					6		7	8											4		10				26
				5	11			2				3	9	1					10		7	6											4		8				27
				5	11			2				3	9	1	6				10		7	8											4						28
				5		11		2				3	9	1	6				10		7	8											4						29
				5		11			2			3	9	1	6				10		7	8											4						30
				5		11			2			3	9	1	6				10		7	8											4						31
				5		11			2			3	9	1	6				10		7	8											4						32
				5		11			2			3	9	1	6				10		7	8											4						33
				5		11			2			3	9	1	6							8	10										4						34
				5		11			2			3	9	1	6						7	8	10										4						35
				5				2			10	3	9								8	6											4	11		1			36
9	4	2	5	36	4	7	3	14	11	1	10	33	16	15	17	1	6	1	28	1	15	23	2	4	5	11	12	5		2	2	5	31	7	11	4	2	17	
1				2		2				1	5		4		1				4		3	11	1		1	2		1				2		1	1			10	

				5					2			3			6				10		7						1	11					4		8			9	1
				5					2			3			6				10		7						1	11					4		8			9	
				5								2			6						7	10			3		1	11					4		8			9	2
				5								2			6						7	10			3		1	11					4		8			9	
8				5								2		1	6							10			3			11					4		7			9	3
8				5								2		1	6							10			3			11					4		7			9	
2				6					2			6		2	6				2		4	4			4		4	6					6		6			6	
																			1			1						1							1			5	

A.Hawkins played number 8 in Match 7; A.Kelks played number 7 in Match 36; W.Lappage played number 6 in Match 19; C.Longden played number 7 in Match 34; B.Martin played number 10 in Match 8; J.McKay played number 8 in Match 13; A.Naylor played number 7 in Match 7; C.Poole played number 11 in Match 13; V.Pulfrey played number 10 in Match 7; R.Robinson played number 4 in Match 4; W.Thorpe played number 8 in Match 16; A.Townsend played number 11 in Match 2; S.Weaver played number 6 in Match 8; A.Woodhead played number 10 in Match 13.

1946-47

Manager: Roy Goodall

1	Aug	31	(h)	Crystal P	W 3-1	Copestake, Bryant, Hogg	9,508
2	Sep	4	(a)	Watford	W 2-1	Copestake, Bryant	4,219
3		7	(a)	Torquay U	D 2-2	Bryant 2	7,258
4		9	(a)	Walsall	D 0-0		9,047
5		14	(h)	Port Vale	L 0-3		11,207
6		18	(h)	Walsall	D 1-1	Harper	7,368
7		21	(h)	Bristol R	W 3-1	Bryant 2, Calverley	9,183
8		28	(a)	Southend U	D 1-1	Harkin	10,994
9	Oct	5	(h)	Queen's Park R	L 0-3		13,459
10		9	(h)	Watford	W 2-0	Bryant 2	5,218
11		12	(a)	Leyton O	L 1-3	Bramley (pen)	9,783
12		19	(a)	Bristol C	L 2-5	Bryant 2	17,357
13		26	(h)	Swindon T	D 1-1	Hogg	7,583
14	Nov	2	(a)	Bournemouth	L 1-3	Hogg	12,562
15		9	(h)	Cardiff C	L 1-3	Hogg	9,827
16		16	(a)	Norwich C	L 1-3	Bryant	16,561
17		23	(h)	Notts C	W 1-0	Copestake	10,899
18	Dec	7	(h)	Aldershot	L 1-3	Copestake	4,429
19		14	(a)	Brighton & HA	L 0-5		7,666
20		21	(h)	Exeter C	W 1-0	Hogg	4,485
21		25	(h)	Reading	D 2-2	Copestake, Hogg	4,975
22		26	(a)	Reading	L 0-3		16,488
23		28	(a)	Crystal P	D 1-1	Harkin	15,347
24	Jan	4	(h)	Torquay U	W 1-0	Bryant	5,499
25		18	(a)	Port Vale	L 1-4	Harkin	14,390
26		23	(a)	Northampton T	L 0-3		2,713
27		25	(a)	Bristol R	L 0-1		9,401
28	Feb	1	(h)	Southend U	L 0-1		4,411
29		8	(a)	Queen's Park R	L 1-3	Bryant	7,776
30	Mar	1	(a)	Swindon T	L 1-6	Bryant	12,257
31		15	(a)	Cardiff C	L 0-5		9,384
32		22	(h)	Norwich C	D 4-4	Copestake, Carter, Betts 2	5,141
33		29	(a)	Notts C	L 1-5	Betts	12,157
34	Apr	4	(h)	Ipswich T	W 4-3	Oscroft 2, Carter, Chadbourn	5,383
35		5	(h)	Northampton T	W 3-2	Copestake, Carter, Chadbourn	5,625
36		7	(a)	Ipswich T	L 1-2	Oscroft	15,102
37		12	(a)	Aldershot	D 1-1	Betts	4,322
38		19	(h)	Brighton & HA	L 0-3		6,938
39		26	(a)	Exeter C	L 0-1		5,346
40	May	3	(h)	Bournemouth	D 1-1	Betts	5,042
41		17	(h)	Bristol C	L 1-3	Bryant	7,012
42		31	(h)	Leyton O	L 1-3	Chessell	4,412

FINAL LEAGUE POSITION: 22nd in Division Three South

Appearances
Goals

FA Cup

1	Nov	30	(a)	Northampton T	L 0-2	

Appearances
Goals

Baird JAG	Barke JL	Betts E	Binnie L	Bramley E	Brown A	Bryant E	Calverley A	Carter S	Chadbourn W	Chessell S	Copestake OF	Cromack V	Dallman W	Everett, Harold	Everett, Harry	Fox W	Harkin J	Harper D	Hewitt H	Hogg F	Jeffries W	Liddle D	Nettleship R	Oscroft H	Smith L	Thorpe L	Westland J	Wright D	
	5			2		9	11			3	8	1		6				7		10					4				1
	5			2		9	11			3	8	1		6				7		10					4				2
	5			2		9	11			3	8	1		6				7		10					4				3
	5			2		9	11			3	8	1		6				7		10					4				4
	5			2		9	11			3	8	1		6				7		10					4				5
	5			2		9	11			3		1		6				7		10		8			4				6
	5			2		9	11			3		1		6			10	7		4	8								7
	5			2		9	11			3		1		6			10	7		4	8								8
	5			2		9	11			3	8	1		6			10	7		4									9
	5			2		9	11			3	8	1		6				7		10					4				10
	5			2		9	11			3				6				7		10			8		4			1	11
	5			2		9	11			6	8			3				7		10					4			1	12
	5			2		9	11				8			3	6			7		10					4			1	13
	5			2		9	11	8		3					6			7		10					4			1	14
	5			2		8	11			3	9				6			7		10					4			1	15
	5		6	2	8	9	11			3								7		4							10	1	16
	5		6	2	8		11				9					3		7		4							10	1	17
4			6	2			11			3	9								7	8					5		10	1	18
	5		6	2		9	11			3								7		10					4		8	1	19
	5		6	2	8		11	7		3	9									10					4			1	20
	5		6	2	8		11	7		3	9									10					4			1	21
	5	11	6	2	8		7			3	9						10									4		1	22
	5	11	6	2		9	7			3	8						10									4		1	23
	5	11	6			9	7			3	8					2	10									4		1	24
	5	11	6				7			3	8					2	10									4	9	1	25
	5		6	3		9	11				7					2				8					4		10	1	26
4	5			2		9	11				7			3						10					6	8		1	27
4	5	11	6			9	7			3	8					2				10								1	28
4	5	11				9	7			3	8					2								10	6			1	29
4	5	11	6			9	7			3	8					2								10				1	30
4	5	11	8	3		9					7					2				6				10				1	31
	5	11	8	3				9			7			6		2									4		10	1	32
	5	11		3				9	8		7					2				6					4		10	1	33
		11	5					9	10	3	7					2				6				8	4			1	34
		11	5					9	10	3	7					2				6				8	4			1	35
		11	5					9	10	3	7					2				6				8	4			1	36
4		11	5					9		3	7					2				6				8			10	1	37
4		11	5					9		3	7					2				6				8			10	1	38
		11				9		8		3	7		5			2				6				10	4			1	39
		11						8		3	9		5			2		7		6				10	4			1	40
		11				9			8	3			5			2		7		6				10	4			1	41
		11				9			8	3			5			2		7		6				10	4			1	42
8	32	19	20	28	5	28	30	12	6	35	33	10	4	15	3	19	7	21	1	35	2	1	1	12	28	5	10	32	
		5		1		15	1	3	2	1	7						3	1		6				3					

Baird JAG	Barke JL	Betts E	Binnie L	Bramley E	Brown A	Bryant E	Calverley A	Carter S	Chadbourn W	Chessell S	Copestake OF	Cromack V	Dallman W	Everett, Harold	Everett, Harry	Fox W	Harkin J	Harper D	Hewitt H	Hogg F	Jeffries W	Liddle D	Nettleship R	Oscroft H	Smith L	Thorpe L	Westland J	Wright D	
	5		6	2	8		11				9					3		7		4							10	1	1
	1		1	1	1		1				1					1		1		1							1	1	

1947-48

Manager: Roy Goodall

1	Aug	23	(h)	York C	L 1-2	Croft	9,695
2		27	(a)	Crewe A	D 0-0		7,810
3		30	(a)	Oldham A	D 1-1	Hogg	14,336
4	Sep	1	(h)	Crewe A	W 3-1	Croft 2, Oscroft	10,043
5		6	(h)	Tranmere R	L 1-3	Oscroft	10,187
6		8	(h)	Carlisle U	L 2-3	Chadbourn, Hogg	8,272
7		13	(a)	Darlington	W 2-1	Chessell, Bryant	6,936
8		20	(h)	Gateshead	L 1-2	Cooling	9,879
9		27	(a)	Hartlepools U	L 0-1		7,497
10	Oct	4	(h)	Rotherham U	W 2-1	Bryant, Oscroft	13,886
11		11	(a)	Halifax T	D 1-1	Shell	6,713
12		18	(h)	Rochdale	D 1-1	Oscroft	12,268
13		25	(a)	New Brighton	D 2-2	Croft, Oscroft	5,540
14	Nov	1	(h)	Southport	W 2-0	Brown, Cooling	11,260
15		8	(a)	Lincoln C	D 0-0		15,127
16		15	(h)	Accrington S	W 1-0	Oscroft	12,527
17		22	(a)	Hull C	D 1-1	Brown	20,677
18	Dec	6	(a)	Bradford C	W 1-0	Banks	9,322
19		20	(a)	York C	W 2-1	Butt, Banks	5,863
20		26	(a)	Wrexham	L 1-2	Banks	17,683
21		27	(h)	Wrexham	W 1-0	Banks	13,128
22	Jan	1	(a)	Carlisle U	L 1-3	Edwards	9,997
23		3	(h)	Oldham A	D 1-1	Banks	12,834
24		17	(a)	Tranmere R	W 1-0	Devey	4,390
25		24	(h)	Barrow	W 1-0	Oscroft	10,701
26		31	(h)	Darlington	W 4-0	Banks 2, Edwards, Oscroft	11,605
27	Feb	7	(a)	Gateshead	L 1-2	Cooling	9,718
28		14	(h)	Hartlepools U	W 3-2	Edwards, Banks, Oscroft	12,326
29		28	(h)	Halifax T	W 3-1	Banks 3	10,664
30	Mar	6	(a)	Rochdale	W 2-1	Butt, Cooling	9,990
31		13	(h)	New Brighton	W 5-0	Butt 2, Banks, Cooling, Oscroft	10,886
32		20	(a)	Southport	D 1-1	Croft	7,032
33		26	(a)	Chester	W 2-1	Banks, Oscroft	11,209
34		27	(h)	Lincoln C	L 0-2		18,863
35		29	(h)	Chester	W 2-1	Edwards, Banks	12,770
36	Apr	3	(a)	Accrington S	L 0-1		4,622
37		5	(h)	Stockport C	L 1-2	Coole	12,760
38		10	(h)	Hull C	D 1-1	Oscroft	11,098
39		12	(a)	Rotherham U	L 1-2		20,522
40		17	(a)	Stockport C	L 0-5		11,039
41		24	(h)	Bradford C	D 1-1	Cooling	6,799
42	May	1	(a)	Barrow	L 0-1		5,341

FINAL LEAGUE POSITION: 8th in Division Three North

Appearances
Goals

FA Cup

1	Nov	29	(a)	Wimbledon	W 1-0	Cooling	
2	Dec	13	(a)	Oldham A	W 1-0	Cooling	21,067
3	Jan	10	(h)	Stoke C	L 2-4	Butt (pen), Oscroft	10,500

Appearances
Goals

Allcock K	Baird JAG	Banks G	Bramley E	Brown A	Bryant E	Butt L	Chadbourn W	Chessell S	Cochrane C	Coole W	Cooling R	Croft C	Dallman W	Devey R	Edwards W	Fox W	Grogan J	Hill WH	Hogg F	Jones DO	Kay K	Oscroft H	Searson HV	Shell FW	Smith L	Wright D	
9				7				3				11		5		2			6			8		10	4	1	1
	6			7				3				11		5		2			10			8		9	4	1	2
				7	4		6	3						5		2			10		11	8		9		1	3
				7	6			3				11		5		2			10			8		9	4	1	4
				7	6			3				11		5		2			10			8		9	4	1	5
			9	7			8	3				11	6	5		2			10						4	1	6
			9	7	6			3			10	11		5		2			8						4	1	7
			3	7	6						8	11		5		2						10		9	4	1	8
			2		9		6	3			8			4			5		10			11	1	7			9
					9			2			8	6		4			5		10	3		11	1	7			10
				7				2			8	6		4			5		10	3		11	1	9			11
				7		10		2			8	6		4			5			3		11	1	9			12
				7		10		2			8	6		4			5			3		11	1	9			13
				7		10		2			8	6		4			5			3		11	1	9			14
				7				2	10		8	6		4			5			3		11	1	9			15
		9		7				2			8	6		4			5			3		11	1	10			16
		9		7				2			8	6		4			5			3		11	1	10			17
		9				8		2			10	6		4			5			3		11	1	7			18
		9				8		2			10	6		4			5			3		11	1	7			19
		9				8		2			10	6		4			5			3		11	1	7			20
		9						2			8	6		4	7		5			3		11	1	10			21
		9						2			8	6		4	7		5			3		11	1	10			22
		9									8	6		4	7	2	5			3		11	1	10			23
		9				8						6		10	7	2	5			3		11	1		4		24
		9										6		10	7	2	5			3		11	1	8	4		25
		9				10					8	6		4	7	2	5			3		11	1				26
		9				10					8	6		4	7	2	5			3		11	1				27
		9									10	6		4	7	2	5	8		3		11	1				28
		9									10	6		4	7	2	5	8		3		11	1				29
		9				8					10	6		4	7	2	5			3		11	1				30
		9				8					10	6		4	7	2	5			3		11	1				31
		9				8					10	6		4	7	2	5			3		11	1				32
		9				8					10	6		4	7	2	5			3		11	1				33
		9				8					10	6		4	7	2	5			3		11	1				34
		9								8	10	6		4	7	2	5			3		11				1	35
		9								8	10	6		4	7	2	5			3		11				1	36
		9								8	10	6		4	7	2	5			3		11				1	37
		9				8				10		6		4	7	2	5			3		11				1	38
		9		7						10	8	6		4		2	5			3		11				1	39
		9		7						10	8	6		4		2	5			3		11				1	40
		9						2		10	8	6			7		5			3		11			4	1	41
		9								10	8	6		4	7	2	5			3		11	1				42
1	1	27	4	17	7	15	3	22	1	8	33	40	1	41	20	27	34	2	10	33	1	40	27	22	10	15	
		14		2	2	4	1	1		1	7	5		1	4				2			12		1			

		9		7				2			8	6		4			5			3		11	1	10			1
		9				10		2			8	6		4			5			3		11	1	7			2
		9				10					8	6		4	7	2	5			3		11	1				3
		3		1		2		2			3	3		3	1	1	3			3		3	3	2			
						1					2											1					

1948-49

Manager: Roy Goodall

1	Aug	21	(h)	Doncaster R	D 2-2	Oscroft 2	16,759
2		25	(a)	Bradford C	L 0-1		9,483
3		28	(a)	Hull C	L 0-4		34,000
4		30	(h)	Bradford C	W 1-0	Oscroft	13,124
5	Sep	4	(h)	Rotherham U	L 1-2	Cooling	16,208
6		6	(h)	Halifax T	W 2-1	Cooling, McCarter	11,673
7		11	(a)	Accrington S	D 1-1	Banks	7,000
8		13	(a)	Halifax T	D 2-2	Banks, Oscroft	11,000
9		18	(h)	Oldham A	W 3-2	Banks, Oscroft 2	11,997
10		25	(a)	Tranmere R	L 0-1		6,000
11	Oct	2	(h)	Chester	W 1-0	McCarter	12,508
12		9	(a)	Southport	D 1-1	Wheatley	10,000
13		16	(h)	Crewe A	W 5-1	Mercer 2, Edwards, Devey, Oscroft	12,556
14		23	(a)	York C	L 1-2	Oscroft	11,000
15		30	(h)	Stockport C	W 4-0	Mercer 3, Banks	12,000
16	Nov	6	(a)	Carlisle U	L 1-3	Cooling	12,000
17		13	(h)	Gateshead	D 1-1	Mercer	9,034
18		20	(a)	Hartlepools U	D 1-1	Wheatley	6,000
19	Dec	4	(a)	New Brighton	L 0-1		7,000
20		18	(a)	Doncaster R	D 1-1	Oscroft (pen)	15,600
21		26	(h)	Wrexham	L 1-2	Oscroft	12,400
22	Jan	1	(h)	Hull C	D 1-1	Devey	11,700
23		15	(a)	Rotherham U	L 0-1		16,647
24		22	(h)	Accrington S	W 2-0	Cooling, Oscroft	11,000
25		29	(h)	Darlington	D 2-2	Barks, Devey	14,100
26	Feb	5	(a)	Oldham A	L 0-4		15,236
27		12	(h)	New Brighton	W 2-0	Oscroft 2	9,300
28		19	(h)	Tranmere R	D 0-0		11,500
29		26	(a)	Chester	D 1-1	Banks	9,000
30	Mar	5	(h)	Southport	D 1-1	Cooling	6,296
31		12	(a)	Crewe A	L 1-3	Cooling	5,000
32		19	(h)	York C	W 3-0	Banks 2, Peters	9,000
33		26	(a)	Stockport C	L 0-2		8,000
34	Apr	2	(h)	Carlisle U	W 2-0	Wheatley, Oscroft	8,700
35		4	(a)	Rochdale	L 0-1		5,000
36		9	(a)	Gateshead	D 0-0		6,000
37		15	(a)	Barrow	L 0-1		5,000
38		16	(h)	Hartlepools U	W 1-0	Cooling	9,000
39		18	(h)	Barrow	W 2-0	McCarter 2	9,000
40		23	(a)	Darlington	W 2-1	Barks, Opp own-goal	7,400
41		30	(h)	Rochdale	W 2-0	Chessell 2	9,842
42	May	4	(a)	Wrexham	D 1-1	Peters	4,300

FINAL LEAGUE POSITION: 10th in Division Three North

Appearances
Goals

FA Cup

1	Nov	27	(h)	Gloucester C	W 4-0	Mercer 3, Oscroft	11,400
2	Dec	11	(h)	Northampton T	W 2-1*	Mercer, Oscroft	13,500
3	Jan	8	(a)	Preston NE	L 1-2	Oscroft	33,000

*After extra-time

Appearances
Goals

Banks G	Barks E	Chessell S	Coole W	Cooling R	Croft C	Devey R	Edwards W	Fox W	Grogan J	Hodgson S	Ibbotson W	Jones DO	Lennon AV	Lewis J	McCarter J	Mercer S	Oscroft H	Peters TJ	Searson HV	Wheatley W	Wright D	
9		2	8		6	4	7		5		10	3					11				1	1
9		2	8		10	4	7		5	6		3					11		1			2
9		2	10		6	8			5	4		3					11		1	7		3
9		2		8		4			5			3		6	11		10		1	7		4
9		2		8		4			5			3		6	11		10		1	7		5
9		2		8	6	4			5			3			11		10		1	7		6
9		2		8	6	4			5			3			11		10		1	7		7
9		2		8	6	4			5			3			11		10		1	7		8
9		2	8		6	4			5			3			11		10		1	7		9
9		2		8	6	4			5			3			11		10		1	7		10
8		9				4	7	2	5			3		6	11		10		1			11
8		2			6	4			5			3			11	9	10		1	7		12
8		2			6	4	7		5			3			11	9	10		1			13
8		2			6	4			5			3			11	9	10		1	7		14
8		2		10	6	4			5			3				9	11		1	7		15
8				10	6	4		2	5			3			11	9			1	7		16
8				10	6	4		2	5			3				9	11			7	1	17
8		2		10	6	4			5			3				9	11			7	1	18
8		2			6	4			5			3			11	9	10			7	1	19
8		2			6	4			5			3			11	9	10			7	1	20
8		2			6	4			5			3			11	9	10			7	1	21
8		2			6	4			5			3			11	9	10			7	1	22
8		3			6	4		2	5						11	9	10			7	1	23
9		2		8	6	4			5			3			11		10			7	1	24
10	9	2		8	6	4			5			3					11			7	1	25
8	9	2		10	6	4			5			3					11			7	1	26
	9	2		8	6	4			5			3			11		10			7	1	27
9	4	2		8	6		7		5			3			11		10				1	28
9		2		8	6	4			5			3	10				11			7	1	29
	9	2		8		4			5			3	10	6			11			7	1	30
9	4	2		8	6				5			3	10				11			7	1	31
9	4	2		8	6				5			3					11	10		7	1	32
9				8	6	4		2	5			3					11	10		7	1	33
9	4			8	6			2	5			3					11	10		7	1	34
9	4			8	6			2	5			3					11	10		7	1	35
9	4			8	6			2	5			3					11	10		7	1	36
9	4	2		8	6				5			3			11		10			7	1	37
9	4	2		8	6				5			3			11		10			7	1	38
	9	2		8	6	4			5			3			11		10			7	1	39
	9	2		8	6	4			5		10	3			11					7	1	40
	9	2	10	8	6	4			5			3			11					7	1	41
	9	2		8	6	4			5			3			11			10		7	1	42
36	16	36	5	29	38	34	5	8	42	2	2	41	3	4	26	12	38	6	15	37	27	
7	2	2		7		3	1								4	6	14	2		3		

1 own-goal

8		2			6	4			5			3			11	9	10			7	1	1
8		2			6	4			5			3			11	9	10			7	1	2
8		2			6	4			5			3			11	9	10			7	1	3
3		3			3	3			3			3			3	3	3			3	3	
															1	4	2					

1949-50

Manager: Freddie Steele

1	Aug	20	(a)	Southport	D 1-1	Reeve	11,000
2		24	(a)	Accrington S	D 2-2	Steele 2	9,000
3		27	(h)	Carlisle U	W 4-1	Steele 2, Oscroft 2 (2 pens)	15,129
4		29	(h)	Accrington S	W 2-0	Coole, Steele	15,457
5	Sep	3	(a)	Rotherham U	D 2-2	Coole, Steele	13,000
6		5	(a)	York C	D 3-3	Poole, Oscroft, McCarter	8,500
7		10	(h)	Lincoln C	W 2-1	Steele, Oscroft	16,856
8		12	(h)	York C	W 1-0	Oscroft	14,950
9		17	(a)	Barrow	W 1-0	Coole	6,000
10		24	(h)	Crewe A	W 3-0	Coole, Reeve, McCarter	17,182
11	Oct	1	(a)	Tranmere R	L 1-2	Coole	11,000
12		8	(a)	Stockport C	L 0-1		12,000
13		15	(h)	Doncaster R	L 1-2	Oscroft	19,496
14		22	(a)	Gateshead	W 1-0	Steele	12,000
15		29	(h)	Hartlepools U	W 7-1	Steele 3, Oscroft 3 (2 pens), Coole	13,112
16	Nov	5	(a)	Darlington	D 2-2	Steele, Oscroft (pen)	9,500
17		12	(h)	New Brighton	D 2-2	Steele, Oscroft	11,450
18		19	(a)	Halifax T	W 3-0	Steele 2, Oscroft	6,000
19	Dec	3	(a)	Bradford C	L 1-2	Coole	14,000
20		17	(h)	Southport	L 1-2	McCarter	7,475
21		24	(a)	Carlisle U	D 1-1	McCarter	15,000
22		26	(h)	Oldham A	W 3-1	Reeve 2, McCarter	14,859
23		27	(a)	Oldham A	L 0-1		22,252
24		31	(h)	Rotherham U	L 0-2		15,500
25	Jan	14	(a)	Lincoln C	L 0-1		14,942
26		21	(h)	Barrow	D 1-1	Godwin	11,500
27		28	(h)	Rochdale	D 1-1	Godwin	11,000
28	Feb	4	(a)	Crewe A	D 1-1	McCarter	10,000
29		11	(h)	Chester	L 0-2		9,616
30		18	(h)	Tranmere R	D 1-1	Steele	9,342
31		25	(h)	Halifax T	W 1-0	Ottewell	5,781
32	Mar	4	(a)	Rochdale	L 1-7	Antonio	10,000
33		11	(h)	Gateshead	W 1-0	Steele	8,566
34		18	(a)	Hartlepools U	W 3-1	Godwin 2, Reeve	5,000
35		25	(h)	Darlington	W 2-1	Godwin, Steele	8,577
36	Apr	1	(a)	New Brighton	W 2-1	Reeve, Godwin	8,000
37		7	(h)	Wrexham	W 1-0	Reeve	10,055
38		8	(h)	Stockport C	W 3-0	Godwin, Ottewell 2 (1 pen)	9,182
39		10	(a)	Wrexham	D 0-0		4,000
40		15	(a)	Doncaster R	W 1-0	Reeve	20,000
41		22	(h)	Bradford C	L 0-2		9,937
42		29	(a)	Chester	L 3-6	Lewis (pen), Coole, Opp own-goal	3,000

FINAL LEAGUE POSITION: 8th in Division Three North

Appearances
Goals

FA Cup

1	Nov	26	(h)	Walsall	W 4-1	Coole 2, Antonio, Steele	16,300
2	Dec	10	(a)	Doncaster R	L 0-1		23,545

Appearances
Goals

Antonio GR	Barks E	Bradley DJ	Bramley A	Chessell S	Coole W	Cooling R	Croft C	Devey R	Evans R	Fox W	Godwin V	Grogan J	Lewis J	Mayfield L	McCarter J	Oscroft H	Ottewell S	Poole CJ	Reeve K	Steele F	Wheatley W	Wright D	
	4	3		2	7							5	6		11	10			8	9		1	1
	4	3		2	7							5	6		11	10			8	9		1	2
	4	3		2	7							5	6		11	10			8	9		1	3
	4	3		2	7							5	6		11	10			8	9		1	4
	4	3		2	7							5	6		11	10			8	9		1	5
	4	3		2	7							5	6		11	10		9	8			1	6
	4	3		2	7							5	6		11	10			8	9		1	7
	4	3		2	7							5	6		11	10		9	8			1	8
	4	3		2	7							5	6		11	10			8	9		1	9
	4	3		2	7	8						5	6		11	10			9			1	10
	4	3		2	7	8	6					5			11	10			9			1	11
	4	3		2	7		6					5			11	10			8	9		1	12
	4	3			7	8						5	6		11	10		2		9		1	13
8	4	3			7							5	6		11	10		2		9		1	14
8	4	3		2	7							5	6		11	10				9		1	15
8	4	3		2	7							5	6		11	10				9		1	16
8	4	3		2	7							5	6		11	10				9		1	17
8	4	3		2	7							5	6		11	10				9		1	18
8	4	3		2	7		6						5		11	10				9		1	19
8	4	3		2	7							5	6		11	10				9		1	20
8	4	3		2	7							5	6		11	10			9			1	21
8	4	3		2	7							5	6		11	10			9			1	22
8	4	3		2	7							5	6		11	10			9			1	23
8	4	3		2	7							5	6		11				10	9		1	24
8	4	3		2	7						9	5	6		11				10			1	25
8	4	3		2	7		6				9	5			11				10			1	26
8	4	3		2	11						7	5	6				10			9		1	27
8	4			2	7						9	5	6		11		10	3				1	28
8	4			2	7						9	5	6		11		10	3				1	29
8	4	3		2	7		6				10		5		11					9		1	30
8	4	3		2	7		6						5		11		10			9		1	31
8		3		2	7		6	4			9		5		11		10					1	32
4		3			7					2	8	5	6		11				10	9		1	33
4		3			7					2	9	5	6		11		8		10			1	34
4		3			7					2	8	5	6		11				10	9		1	35
4		3			7					2	9	5	6		11		10		8			1	36
4		3			7					2	9	5	6		11		10		8			1	37
4		3			7					2	9	5	6		11		10		8			1	38
4					7					2	9	5	6		11		10	3	8			1	39
4				2	7						9	5	6		11		10	3	8			1	40
4				2							9	5	6		11		10	3	8		7	1	41
4	6		1		7				9	2	8		5	3	11		10						42
29	32	36	1	32	41	3	7	1	1	8	17	37	39	1	41	23	13	9	27	22	1	41	
1					8						7		1		6	12	3	1	8	18			

1 own-goal

Antonio GR	Barks E	Bradley DJ	Bramley A	Chessell S	Coole W	Cooling R	Croft C	Devey R	Evans R	Fox W	Godwin V	Grogan J	Lewis J	Mayfield L	McCarter J	Oscroft H	Ottewell S	Poole CJ	Reeve K	Steele F	Wheatley W	Wright D	
8	4	3		2	7							5	6		11	10				9		1	1
8	4	3		2	7							5	6		11	10				9		1	2
2	2	2		2	2							2	2		2	2				2		2	
1					2															1			

1950-51

Manager: Freddie Steele

1	Aug	19	(a)	Wrexham	D 2-2	Godwin, Ottewell	12,960
2		21	(h)	Darlington	W 2-1	Barks, Godwin	14,200
3		26	(h)	Scunthorpe U	D 1-1	Coole	11,637
4		30	(a)	Darlington	W 2-1	Steele, Ottewell	7,398
5	Sep	2	(h)	Lincoln C	D 1-1	Lewis (pen)	13,146
6		4	(h)	Bradford	W 3-2	Lewis, Steele, Ottewell	13,476
7		9	(a)	Rotherham U	L 0-3		12,904
8		13	(a)	Bradford	L 0-1		11,174
9		16	(h)	Barrow	W 4-0	Coole, Steele 2, Bradley	8,968
10		23	(a)	York C	D 1-1	Coole	9,228
11		30	(h)	Carlisle U	W 2-1	Steele 2	6,733
12	Oct	7	(a)	Crewe A	L 0-2		8,700
13		14	(h)	New Brighton	W 4-0	Coole, Steele, Ottewell, Opp own-goal	10,464
14		21	(a)	Hartlepools U	D 1-1	Ottewell	8,454
15		28	(h)	Gateshead	W 2-1	Coole, Ottewell	13,387
16	Nov	4	(a)	Stockport C	L 1-3	Ottewell	12,000
17		11	(h)	Halifax T	W 3-1	Coole, Steele 2	9,872
18		18	(a)	Bradford C	W 3-2	Coole, Steele, Donaldson	14,000
19	Dec	2	(a)	Chester	W 1-0	Coole	3,000
20		23	(a)	Scunthorpe U	D 0-0		7,000
21		25	(a)	Oldham A	L 0-2		11,000
22		26	(h)	Oldham A	W 3-1	Reeve, Lewis (pen), Opp own-goal	10,812
23		30	(a)	Lincoln C	L 0-3		
24	Jan	10	(h)	Tranmere R	W 2-1	Reeve, Steele	5,473
25		13	(h)	Rotherham U	D 1-1	Reeve	18,343
26		20	(a)	Barrow	W 3-2	Coole, Reeve 2	6,000
27	Feb	3	(h)	York C	W 3-1	Coole, Steele, Ottewell	10,152
28		17	(a)	Carlisle U	L 0-2		
29		24	(h)	Crewe A	W 4-1	Reeve, Steele, Ottewell 2 (1 pen)	9,300
30	Mar	3	(a)	New Brighton	W 1-0	Fox	3,347
31		7	(a)	Tranmere R	L 1-2	Antonio	
32		10	(h)	Hartlepools U	W 1-0	Steele	7,341
33		17	(a)	Gateshead	W 3-1	Reeve, Ottewell 2	
34		23	(h)	Accrington S	W 5-0	Coole 2, Fox, Reeve, Barks	4,563
35		24	(h)	Stockport C	W 2-1	Reeve, Ottewell	10,000
36		26	(a)	Accrington S	W 2-0	Barks, Ottewell	3,000
37		31	(a)	Halifax T	W 1-0	Coole	4,000
38	Apr	7	(h)	Bradford C	D 1-1	Ottewell	9,471
39		10	(a)	Southport	W 1-0	Coole	5,000
40		14	(a)	Rochdale	D 0-0		4,500
41		16	(h)	Rochdale	W 1-0	Reeve	11,462
42		21	(h)	Chester	W 2-1	Coole, Fox	10,288
43		23	(h)	Wrexham	D 1-1	Opp own-goal	12,090
44		28	(a)	Shrewsbury T	D 1-1	Lewis (pen)	
45		30	(h)	Shrewsbury T	W 4-0	Coole, Fox 2, Reeve	9,654
46	May	5	(h)	Southport	D 2-2	Lewis (pen), Reeve	8,431

FINAL LEAGUE POSITION: 2nd in Division Three North — Appearances

Goals

FA Cup

1	Nov	25	(h)	Walthamstow A	W 1-0	Steele	11,784
2	Dec	9	(a)	Chelmsford C	W 4-1	Donaldson 2, Coole, Barks	
3	Jan	6	(h)	Swansea C	W 2-0	Steele 2	18,000
4		27	(a)	Sheffield U	D 0-0		48,696
R		31	(h)	Sheffield U	W 2-1	Steele, Ottewell	20,314
5	Feb	10	(a)	Blackpool	L 0-2		33,060

Appearances

Goals

Antonio GR	Barks E	Bradley D	Bramley A	Chessell S	Coole W	Donaldson W	Fox O	Godwin V	Grogan J	Lewis J	Mayfield L	Ottewell S	Poole CJ	Reeve K	Steele F	Wright D	
4	8	3		2	7		10	9	5	6		11				1	1
4	8	3		2	7		10	9	5	6		11				1	2
4		3		2	7		10	8	5	6		11			9	1	3
4		3		2	11		7	8	5	6		10			9	1	4
4	8	3		2	7		10	9	5	6		11				1	5
4	8	3		2	7				5	6		10	11		9	1	6
4	8	3		2	7				5	6		10	11		9	1	7
	4	3		2	7				5	6		10	11	8	9	1	8
	4	3		2	7		8		5	6		10	11		9	1	9
	4	3		2	7		8	9	5	6		10	11			1	10
	4	3		2	7		8		5	6		10	11		9	1	11
10	4	3		2	7		8		5	6			11	9		1	12
	4	3		2	7	11	8		5	6		10			9	1	13
	4	3		2	7	11	8	9	5	6		10				1	14
	4	3		2	7	11	8		5	6		10			9	1	15
	4	3		2	7	11	8		5	6		10			9	1	16
4	8	3		2	7	11			5	6		10			9	1	17
4	8	3		2	7	11			5	6		10			9	1	18
4	8	3		2	7	11			5	6		10			9	1	19
4		3		2	7	11	8	9	5	6		10				1	20
4		3		2	7	11	8	9	5	6		10				1	21
4		3		2	7	11			5	6		10		8	9	1	22
4		3		2	7	11		9	5	6		10		8		1	23
4		3	1	2	7	11			5	6		10		8	9		24
4		3		2	7	11			5	6		10		8	9	1	25
4	8	3		2	7	11			5	6		10		9		1	26
4	8	3		2	7		10		5	6		11		9		1	27
4	8	3		2		11	7	9	5	6		10				1	28
4	10	3		2			7		5	6		11		8	9	1	29
4	10	3		2	7		8		5	6		11		9		1	30
4	10	3		2	7		8		5	6		11		9		1	31
4	10	3		2	7				5	6		11		8	9	1	32
4	10	3		2	7		8		5	6		11		9		1	33
4	10	3		2	7		8		5	6		11		9		1	34
4	10	3		2	7		8		5	6		11		9		1	35
4	10	3		2	7		8		5	6		11		9		1	36
4	10	3		2	7		8		5	6		11		9		1	37
4	10	3		2	7		8		5	6		11		9		1	38
4	10	3		2	7		8		5	6		11		9		1	39
4	10	3		2	7	11	8		5	6				9		1	40
4	10	3		2	7	11	8		5	6				9		1	41
4	10	3		2	7	11	8		5	6				9		1	42
4	10			2	7	11	8		5	6	3			9		1	43
4	10			2	7	11	8	9	5	6	3					1	44
4				2	7	11	8	9	5	6	3			10		1	45
4				2	7	11	8	9	5	6	3			10		1	46
38	36	42	1	46	44	22	34	14	46	46	4	38	7	25	18	45	
1	3	1			16	1	5	2		5		15		12	14		

3 own-goals

4	8	3		2	7	11			5	6		10			9	1	1
4	8	3		2	7	11			5	6		10			9	1	2
4		3		2	7	11			5	6		10		8	9	1	3
4	10	3		2	7				5	6		11		8	9	1	4
4	8	3		2	7				5	6		11		10	9	1	R
4	11	3		2	7				5	6		10		8	9	1	5
6	5	6		6	6	3			6	6		6		4	6	6	
	1				1	2						1			4		

1951-52

Manager: Freddie Steele to December 1951, then George Jobey from January 1952.

1	Aug	18	(h)	Stockport C	W 1-0	Donaldson	10,753
2		22	(a)	Accrington S	D 0-0		8,614
3		25	(a)	Workington	W 1-0	Geddes	6,770
4		27	(h)	Accrington S	W 3-0	Coole, Reeve, Lewis (pen)	10,520
5	Sep	1	(h)	Barrow	W 2-1	Coole, Lewis (pen)	10,609
6		4	(a)	Rochdale	L 0-1		6,046
7		8	(a)	Grimsby T	D 1-1	Steele	17,361
8		15	(h)	Wrexham	W 3-0	Ottewell 2, Reeve	8,547
9		17	(h)	Rochdale	D 1-1	Ottewell	10,413
10		22	(a)	Chesterfield	D 1-1	Steele	17,446
11		29	(h)	Bradford	W 1-0	Geddes	11,567
12	Oct	6	(h)	Bradford C	W 2-1	Fox, Steele	11,712
13		13	(a)	York C	L 0-3		7,577
14		20	(h)	Chester	W 3-1	Steele, Donaldson 2	9,550
15		27	(a)	Lincoln C	W 2-1	Coole, Steele	16,364
16	Nov	3	(h)	Scunthorpe U	W 4-1	Steele 2, Fox, Reeve	10,301
17		10	(a)	Tranmere R	D 1-1	Fox	8,215
18		17	(h)	Southport	W 4-0	Reeve 2, Fox, Donaldson	10,172
19	Dec	1	(h)	Gateshead	L 2-3	Fox, Opp own-goal	10,171
20		8	(a)	Darlington	L 1-2	Donaldson	3,024
21		15	(a)	Stockport C	L 1-2	Lewis (pen)	10,212
22		22	(h)	Workington	W 3-2	Donaldson, Fox, Evans	6,127
23		25	(a)	Hartlepools U	L 0-2		10,542
24		26	(h)	Hartlepools U	L 0-1		9,185
25		29	(a)	Barrow	D 1-1	Reeve	7,585
26	Jan	5	(h)	Grimsby T	D 2-2	Fox, Donaldson	9,471
27		12	(h)	Carlisle U	L 1-2	Lewis	8,497
28		19	(a)	Wrexham	L 1-3	Evans	7,941
29		26	(h)	Chesterfield	W 2-1	Coole, Reeve	10,411
30	Feb	2	(a)	Carlisle U	D 0-0		8,946
31		9	(a)	Bradford	W 1-0	Donaldson	10,516
32		16	(a)	Bradford C	L 1-2	Reeve	11,676
33		23	(h)	Oldham A	W 2-1	Fox, Donaldson	9,623
34	Mar	1	(h)	York C	D 1-1	Reeve	7,953
35		8	(a)	Chester	W 5-1	Evans 3, Reeve 2	5,133
36		15	(h)	Lincoln C	W 1-0	Reeve	19,043
37		22	(a)	Scunthorpe U	L 1-4	Reeve (pen)	7,552
38		29	(h)	Tranmere R	W 3-0	Fox, Evans, Reeve	3,194
39	Apr	5	(a)	Southport	W 1-0	Evans	2,630
40		12	(h)	Crewe A	W 2-1	Fox, Reeve	8,136
41		14	(a)	Halifax T	L 0-1		5,901
42		15	(h)	Halifax T	W 4-2	Reeve 3, Evans	8,214
43		19	(a)	Gateshead	L 1-4	Reeve	3,501
44		23	(a)	Crewe A	L 0-1		3,825
45		26	(h)	Darlington	W 3-2	Reeve 2 (1 pen), Coole	5,914
46	May	3	(a)	Oldham A	L 3-5	Barks, Coole, Watson	5,593

FINAL LEAGUE POSITION: 6th in Division Three North

Appearances
Goals

FA Cup

1	Nov	24	(a)	Stockton	D 1-1	Lewis (pen)	10,000
R		28	(h)	Stockton	L 0-2		5,229

Appearances
Goals

Barks E	Bradley D	Chessell S	Coole W	Donaldson W	Evans R	Field N	Fox O	Geddes A	Grogan J	Lewis J	Mayfield L	Ottewell S	Reeve K	Steele F	Watson S	Wright D	
4	3	2	7	11			8		5	6		10		9		1	1
4	3	2	7	11			8		5	6		10	9			1	2
4	3	2	7				8	10	5	6		11	9			1	3
4	3		7				8	10	5	6	2	11	9			1	4
4	3	2	7				8	10	5	6		11		9		1	5
4	3	2	7	11	9		10		5	6			8			1	6
4	3	2	7	11			8	10	5	6				9		1	7
	3	2	7	11			8	4	5	6		10	9			1	8
4	3	2	7				8	10	5	6		11	9			1	9
4	3	2	7					10	5	6		11	8	9		1	10
4	3	2	7				8	10	5	6		11		9		1	11
4	3	2	7				8	10	5	6		11		9		1	12
4	3	2	7	11			8	10	5	6				9		1	13
4	3	2	7	11			8		5	6			10	9		1	14
4	3	2	7	11			8		5	6			10	9		1	15
4	3	2	7	11			8		5	6			10	9		1	16
4	3	2	7	11			8		5	6			10	9		1	17
4	3	2	7	11			8		5	6			10	9		1	18
4	3	2		11			7	8	5	6		10	9			1	19
4	11	2		7	9		8		5	6	3	10				1	20
4	3	2		7	9		8		5	6		11	10			1	21
4	3	2		7	9		8		5	6		11			10	1	22
4	3	2		7	9		8		5	6		11			10	1	23
4	3			7	9		10		5	6	2	11	8			1	24
4	3			11	9		8		5	6	2		10		7	1	25
4	3			11	9		8		5	6	2		10		7	1	26
4	3			11	9		8		5	6	2		10		7	1	27
4	3		7	11	9		8		5	6	2		10			1	28
4	3		7	11	9		8		5	6	2		10			1	29
4	3		7	11			8		5	6	2		9		10	1	30
4	3		7	11			8		5	6	2		9		10	1	31
4	3		7	11			8		5	6	2		9		10	1	32
4	3		7	11			8		5	6	2		9		10	1	33
4	3		7	11			8		5	6	2		9		10	1	34
4	3		7	11	9				5	6	2		8		10	1	35
4	3		7	11	9				5	6	2		8		10	1	36
4	3		7		9		11		5	6	2		8		10	1	37
4	3		7		9		8		5	6	2		10		11	1	38
4	3		7		9		8		5	6	2		10		11	1	39
4	3		7		9		8		5	6	2		10		11	1	40
4	3		7	11	9		8		5	6	2		10			1	41
4	3		7		9	5	8			6	2		10		11	1	42
4	3		7		9		8		5	6	2		10		11	1	43
4	3	2	7		9	5	8			6			10		11	1	44
4	3		7		9	5	10			6	2		8		11	1	45
4	3	2	7		9	5	10			6			8		11	1	46
45	46	24	37	30	23	4	43	11	42	46	23	16	37	12	21	46	
1			6	9	8		10	2		4		3	21	7	1		

1 own-goal

4	3	2	7	11			8		5	6			10	9		1	1
4	3	2	7	11			8		5	6		10	9			1	R
2	2	2	2	2			2		2	2		1	2	1		2	
										1							

1952-53

Manager: George Jobey

1	Aug	23	(a)	Chesterfield	L 1-4	Reeve	18,116
2		25	(h)	Gateshead	W 2-0	Coole, Reeve	13,000
3		30	(h)	Tranmere R	W 1-0	Marron	12,500
4	Sep	1	(a)	Gateshead	W 2-1	Marron 2	5,400
5		6	(a)	York C	L 0-2		8,636
6		8	(h)	Workington	D 0-0		10,000
7		13	(h)	Grimsby T	D 1-1	Evans	13,000
8		17	(a)	Workington	W 1-0	Fox	6,488
9		20	(a)	Barrow	L 0-3		6,110
10		25	(a)	Scunthorpe U	W 1-0	Adam	7,252
11		27	(h)	Wrexham	L 0-2		8,000
12		29	(h)	Darlington	W 3-2	Marron, Evans, Adam	4,567
13	Oct	4	(a)	Bradford	D 1-1	Marron	9,623
14		11	(a)	Hartlepools U	L 0-2		7,000
15		18	(h)	Carlisle U	W 2-1	Fox, S.Watson	7,491
16		25	(a)	Southport	W 3-1	Marron, Reeve, Adam	5,700
17	Nov	1	(h)	Crewe A	W 3-0	Marron 2, Coole	7,602
18		8	(a)	Port Vale	D 1-1	Adam	14,176
19		15	(h)	Chester	D 2-2	Marron, Chessell (pen)	6,396
20		29	(h)	Stockport C	D 2-2	Marron 2	4,765
21	Dec	13	(h)	Rochdale	W 2-1	Scott, Marron	6,322
22		20	(h)	Chesterfield	L 1-4	Scott	6,800
23		26	(a)	Oldham A	L 0-1		25,165
24		27	(h)	Oldham A	L 0-2		11,373
25	Jan	1	(a)	Darlington	L 1-2	Fox	3,991
26		3	(a)	Tranmere R	L 0-1		8,700
27		17	(h)	York C	D 1-1	Lewis	6,964
28		24	(a)	Grimsby T	L 1-5	Chessell (pen)	13,676
29		31	(a)	Accrington S	D 2-2	Marron, Opp own-goal	2,200
30	Feb	7	(h)	Barrow	D 2-2	Marron, Reeve	5,297
31		14	(a)	Wrexham	L 0-1		6,682
32		21	(h)	Bradford	D 1-1	Evans	6,224
33		28	(h)	Hartlepools U	W 2-0	Reeve, Chessell (pen)	6,724
34	Mar	7	(a)	Carlisle U	L 0-1		8,000
35		14	(h)	Southport	D 2-2	Evans, Reeve	6,665
36		21	(a)	Crewe A	L 0-1		5,800
37		28	(h)	Port Vale	W 1-0	V.Watson	6,050
38	Apr	4	(a)	Chester	D 2-2	Reeve, V.Watson	5,282
39		6	(a)	Halifax T	W 2-1	Fox, V.Watson	4,100
40		7	(h)	Halifax T	W 2-1	V.Watson, Marron	7,953
41		11	(h)	Scunthorpe U	W 1-0	Reeve	7,314
42		13	(h)	Accrington S	D 0-0		4,574
43		18	(a)	Stockport C	D 2-2	Marron, Coole	8,000
44		20	(a)	Bradford C	L 1-2	Reeve	8,165
45		25	(h)	Bradford C	W 3-1	Fox, Reeve, V.Watson	6,230
46		29	(a)	Rochdale	L 0-1		4,000

FINAL LEAGUE POSITION: 18th in Division Three North

Appearances
Goals

FA Cup

1	Nov	22	(a)	Scarborough	W 8-0	Fox 3, Marron 2, Adam 2, S.Watson	
2	Dec	6	(a)	Accrington S	W 2-0	Fox, Adam	
3	Jan	10	(h)	Nottingham F	L 0-1		24,467

Appearances
Goals

Adam C	Barks E	Bradley D	Bramley A	Chessell S	Coole W	Eaton JD	Evans R	Field N	Fox O	Hawksford E	Lewis J	Livie G	Marron C	Mayfield L	Plummer NL	Revell GH	Reeve K	Scott K	Simpson GL	Watson S	Watson V	Wright D	Wright V	
11	4	3			7		9		8		6			2	5		10					1		1
11	4	3		2	7						6		9		5		8			10		1		2
11	4	3		2	7						6		9		5		8			10		1		3
11		3		2	7			4					9		5		8		6	10		1		4
11		3		2	7			4					9		5		8		6	10		1		5
11		3		2	7			4	8				9		5				6	10		1		6
11	4	3		2	7		9		10				8		5				6			1		7
7		3		2			9	6	8		4				5		10					1	11	8
11		3		2	7			4	8		6		9		5		10					1		9
11		3	1	2	7			4	8		6		9		5		10							10
11		3	1	2	7			4	8		6		9		5					10				11
11		3	1	2	7		9	4			6		8			5	10							12
11		3	1	2	7		9	4			6		8		5		10							13
11		3	1	2	7		9	4			6		8		5		10							14
11		3	1	2	7			4	8		6		9		5					10				15
11		3	1	2	7			4	8				9		5		10			6				16
11		3	1	2	7	10		4	8				9		5					6				17
11		3	1	2				4	8	7			9		5		10			6				18
11		3	1	2	7			4	8		6		9		5					10				19
11		3	1	2				4	8				9		5		10	7		6				20
11	4	3	1	2					8		6		9		5			7		10				21
11	4	3	1	2		10			8				9		5			7		6				22
11	4	3	1	2	7				8		6		9		5					10				23
11	4	3	1	2	7				8		6		9		5					10				24
11	4	3	1	2			9		10		6		8		5			7						25
11	4	3	1	2			9		8		6				5		10	7						26
11	4	3		2	7		9		8		6		10		5							1		27
11	4			2	7				8		6		10	3	5		9					1		28
11	4			2	7		9		8		6		10	3	5							1		29
11	4			2	7				8		6		9	3	5		10					1		30
11	4			2	7				8		6		9	3	5		10					1		31
11	4			2			9				6		10	3	5		8					1	7	32
11	4	3		2	7		9		8						5		10			6		1		33
11	4	3		2	7		9		8						5		10			6		1		34
11	4	3		2	7		9		8						5		10			6		1		35
11	4	3		2	7		9		8						5		10			6		1		36
11	4	3		2	7				8				10		5					6	9	1		37
11	4			2					7			3	10		5		8			6	9	1		38
11	4			2					7			3	10		5		8			6	9	1		39
11	4			2					7		3		10		5		8			6	9	1		40
	4			2	11				7			3	10		5		8			6	9	1		41
	4			2	11				7		3		10		5		8			6	9	1		42
	4			2	11				7			3	10		5		8			6	9	1		43
	4			2	11				7		3		10		5		8			6	9	1		44
				2	11				7		6	3	10		5		8			4	9	1		45
				2	11				7		3		10		5		8		4	6	9	1		46
40	28	32	17	45	35	2	15	16	38	1	28	5	39	6	45	1	32	5	5	30	10	29	2	
4				3	3		4		5		1		16				10	2		1	5			

1 own-goal

11		3	1	2				4	8		6		9		5			7		10				1
11		3	1	2				4	8		6		9		5			7		10				2
11	4	3		2	7				8		6		9		5					10		1		3
3	1	3	2	3	1			2	3		3		3		3			2		3		1		
3									4				2							1				

1953-54

Manager: Stan Mercer

1	Aug	19	(h)	Port Vale	L 1-2	Marron	10,410
2		22	(a)	Tranmere R	W 5-2	Reeve 2, Murray, Plummer, Adam	7,500
3		26	(a)	Bradford C	D 2-2	Plummer, Reeve	9,873
4		29	(h)	Halifax T	W 3-1	Murray, Plummer, Reeve	6,884
5		31	(h)	Bradford C	L 0-1		9,380
6	Sep	5	(a)	Carlisle U	L 0-5		9,800
7		12	(h)	Accrington S	D 1-1	Murray	7,953
8		14	(h)	Chesterfield	D 2-2	Murray 2	11,593
9		19	(a)	Grimsby T	W 2-0	Marron, Adam	12,000
10		21	(a)	Barrow	L 2-4	Murray, Reeve (pen)	3,700
11		26	(h)	Stockport C	W 3-1	Coole, Murray, Plummer	8,610
12		28	(h)	Barrow	L 2-3	Murray, Marron	6,590
13	Oct	3	(a)	Rochdale	L 0-1		9,483
14		10	(h)	Southport	W 4-2	Murray 2, Bradley 2	7,926
15		17	(a)	York C	L 1-5	Murray	6,523
16		24	(h)	Scunthorpe U	W 2-1	Marron, Bradley	8,539
17		31	(a)	Workington	D 1-1	Reeve	6,600
18	Nov	7	(h)	Gateshead	D 1-1	V.Watson	7,355
19		14	(a)	Hartlepools U	L 1-3	Daley	6,878
20		28	(a)	Barnsley	L 1-2	Daley	9,500
21	Dec	5	(h)	Bradford	D 1-1	Murray	5,439
22		12	(h)	Darlington	W 6-0	Murray 2, Darwin 2, Reeve, Daley	5,665
23		19	(h)	Tranmere R	W 2-0	Reeve, Darwin	6,102
24		25	(h)	Crewe A	W 6-0	Reeve 2, Darwin 2, Plummer, Daley	6,092
25		26	(a)	Crewe A	D 0-0		4,700
26	Jan	1	(a)	Chesterfield	D 0-0		12,359
27		2	(a)	Halifax T	L 0-2		4,750
28		9	(h)	Chester	W 2-1	Reeve, Darwin	6,532
29		16	(h)	Carlisle U	W 2-1	Daley, Darwin	6,386
30		23	(a)	Accrington S	L 1-5	Darwen	5,500
31	Feb	6	(h)	Grimsby T	W 5-1	Murray 3, Fox, Darwin	6,513
32		13	(a)	Stockport C	L 2-3	Darwin 2	6,300
33		20	(h)	Rochdale	W 2-0	Darwin, Daley	8,324
34		27	(a)	Southport	L 1-2	Darwin	3,000
35	Mar	6	(h)	York C	W 7-2	Murray, V.Watson 2, Darwin 2, Daley, Fox	6,783
36		13	(a)	Scunthorpe U	D 2-2	Murray, V.Watson	6,500
37		20	(h)	Workington	L 0-2		8,063
38		24	(a)	Chester	W 2-0	Marron, Daley	1,667
39		27	(a)	Gateshead	W 3-1	Marron 2, Murray	4,437
40	Apr	3	(h)	Hartlepools U	W 1-0	Eaton	5,948
41		5	(a)	Port Vale	D 1-1	Daley	13,218
42		10	(a)	Darlington	W 2-1	Murray, Daley	3,391
43		16	(a)	Wrexham	L 0-2		10,018
44		17	(h)	Barnsley	W 2-0	Marron 2	10,031
45		19	(h)	Wrexham	W 4-0	Darwin 2, Daley 2	8,984
46		24	(a)	Bradford	L 0-1		5,437

FINAL LEAGUE POSITION: 7th in Division Three North

Appearances
Goals

FA Cup

1	Nov	21	(a)	Hartlepools U	D 1-1	S.Watson	11,779
R		25	(h)	Hartlepools U	L 0-3		6,237

Appearances
Goals

Adam C	Allen F	Barks E	Bradley D	Chessell S	Coole W	Cuthbertson J	Daley A	Darwin GH	Eaton JD	Fox O	Goodwin E	Heather JL	Jepson B	Lill JA	Livie G	Marron C	McGregor W	Murray K	Plummer N	Reeve	Simpson GL	Sinclair D	Watson S	Watson V	Wright D	
11				2	7					4					3	10		8	5	9			6		1	1
11		5		2	7					4					3			8	9	10			6		1	2
11		5		2	7					4					3			8	9	10			6		1	3
11		5		2	7					4					3			8	9	10			6		1	4
11		5		3	7					4							2	8	9	10			6		1	5
11		5		3	7					4							2	8	9	10			6		1	6
11		6		3	7					4					5		2	8	9	10					1	7
11		6		3	7					4					5		2	8	9	10					1	8
11				3	7					4					5	9	2	8	6	10					1	9
11				3	7					4					5	9	2	8	6	10					1	10
11	6			3	7					4					5	10	2	8	9						1	11
11	3				7					4	9				5	10	2	8	6						1	12
11	6			3						4		10			5	9	2	8				7			1	13
7			11	3		10				4					5		2	8	9				6		1	14
7			11	3		10				4					5		2	8	9				6		1	15
7			11	3		10				4					3	9	2	8	5				6		1	16
7			11	9						4					3		2	8	5	10			6		1	17
7		4	3				11	10									2	8	5				6	9	1	18
7		4	3				11	10							9		2	8	5				6		1	19
7		4	3				11	10		8							2	9	5				6		1	20
		4	3				11	10		7							2	8	5	9			6		1	21
		4	3				11	10		7							2	8	5	9			6		1	22
		4	3				11	10		7							2	8	5	9			6		1	23
		4	3				11	10		7							2	8	5	9			6		1	24
		4	3				11	10		7							2	8	5	9			6		1	25
		4	3				11	10		7							2	8	5	9			6		1	26
7		4	3				11	10									2		5	9	8		6		1	27
7		4	3				11	10									2		5	9	8		6		1	28
7		4		3			9	10						11			2		5		8		6		1	29
7		4	3				9	10		8				11			2		5				6		1	30
7		4	3				11	10		8							2	9	5				6		1	31
7		4	3				11	10		8							2	9	5				6		1	32
7		4	3				11	10		8							2	9	5				6		1	33
7		4	3				11	10		8							2	9	5				6		1	34
		4	3				11	10		7							2	8	5				6	9	1	35
		4	3				11	10		7							2	8	5				6	9	1	36
7		4	3				11	10									2	8	5				6	9	1	37
		4	3				11	10	7							9	2	8	5				6		1	38
		4	3				11	10		7						9	2	8	5				6		1	39
7	6		3				11		10							9	2	8	5				4		1	40
7			3				11	10		4						9	2	8	5				6		1	41
7		4	3				11			10						9	2	8	5				6		1	42
7		4	3				11			10						9	2	8	5				6		1	43
7		4	3				11	10		8						9	2		5				6		1	44
7		4	3				11	10		8			9				2		5				6		1	45
7			3				11	10		4			9				2	8	5				6		1	46
36	4	33	32	16	12	3	29	26	2	38	1	1	2	2	16	14	42	40	45	19	3	1	39	4	46	
2			3		1		12	17	1	2						9		21	5	11				4		

Adam C	Allen F	Barks E	Bradley D	Chessell S	Coole W	Cuthbertson J	Daley A	Darwin GH	Eaton JD	Fox O	Goodwin E	Heather JL	Jepson B	Lill JA	Livie G	Marron C	McGregor W	Murray K	Plummer N	Reeve	Simpson GL	Sinclair D	Watson S	Watson V	Wright D	
11		4	3					10		7							2	8	5				6	9	1	1
11			3	4				10		7							2	8	5				6	9	1	R
2		1	2	1				2		2							2	2	2				2	2	2	
																							1			

1954-55

Manager: Stan Mercer

1	Aug	21	(h)	Barrow	L 0-5		12,494
2		25	(a)	Crewe A	L 1-2	Gaskell	6,800
3		28	(a)	Workington	D 2-2	Gaskell, Daley	8,671
4		30	(h)	Crewe A	W 4-2	Daley 2, Gaskell, Fox	10,270
5	Sep	4	(h)	Chesterfield	W 2-0	Fox, Daley	16,765
6		8	(a)	Halifax T	W 2-1	Murray, J.Adam	5,000
7		11	(h)	Accrington S	D 2-2	Murray, Daley	9,772
8		13	(h)	Halifax T	W 2-1	Murray 2	9,567
9		18	(a)	Wrexham	W 3-1	Bradley, Gaskell, J.Adam	9,121
10		22	(a)	Bradford C	L 0-1		8,621
11		25	(h)	Scunthorpe U	W 2-1	Fox, Daley	11,813
12		27	(h)	Bradford C	W 1-0	J.Adam	8,268
13	Oct	2	(a)	Barnsley	L 0-1		13,864
14		9	(a)	Carlisle U	W 2-1	Daley, Opp own-goal	6,132
15		16	(h)	Chester	W 2-1	Murray 2	9,468
16		23	(a)	Grimsby T	L 2-3	Gaskell 2	7,151
17		30	(h)	Bradford	W 2-1	Gaskell, Daley	9,221
18	Nov	6	(a)	Rochdale	L 0-2		6,557
19		13	(h)	Tranmere R	W 3-1	Gaskell, Daley, Opp own-goal	6,980
20		27	(h)	Hartlepools U	L 0-2		7,855
21	Dec	4	(a)	Gateshead	L 0-4		3,554
22		18	(a)	Barrow	D 2-2	J.Adam, Darwin	3,286
23		25	(a)	York C	L 1-3	Darwin	10,214
24		27	(h)	York C	L 1-2	Darwin	9,719
25	Jan	1	(h)	Workington	W 2-0	Murray, Opp own-goal	6,700
26		8	(a)	Oldham A	D 1-1	Hudson	9,573
27		22	(a)	Accrington S	L 2-3	Darwin, Daley	9,000
28		29	(h)	Oldham A	L 1-3	Darwin	6,838
29	Feb	5	(h)	Wrexham	W 2-1	Murray 2	5,083
30		12	(a)	Scunthorpe U	L 0-2		7,132
31		19	(h)	Barnsley	D 1-1	J.Adam	4,020
32		26	(h)	Carlisle U	D 1-1	Watson	4,070
33	Mar	5	(a)	Chester	L 0-1		4,864
34		12	(h)	Grimsby T	W 3-0	J.Adam, Jepson, Darwin	6,250
35		19	(a)	Bradford	D 0-0		5,527
36		26	(h)	Rochdale	W 3-2	J.Adam 2, Darwin	2,531
37		30	(a)	Chesterfield	L 1-4	Darwin	
38	Apr	2	(a)	Tranmere R	L 1-2	J.Adam (pen)	4,000
39		8	(a)	Southport	L 0-1		4,087
40		9	(h)	Stockport C	D 0-0		6,389
41		11	(h)	Southport	W 3-0	Murray, Gaskell, J.Adam (pen)	5,172
42		16	(a)	Hartlepools U	W 2-1	Murray, Gaskell	3,204
43		18	(h)	Darlington	W 3-1	Murray 2, Daley	4,891
44		23	(h)	Gateshead	L 0-1		4,336
45		25	(a)	Stockport C	D 2-2	Fox, Daley	4,000
46		30	(a)	Darlington	L 1-3	Gaskell	3,000

FINAL LEAGUE POSITION: 13th in Division Three North

Appearances
Goals

FA Cup

1	Nov	20	(a)	Bradford C	L 1-3	J.Adam	9,314

Appearances
Goals

Adam C	Adam J	Allen F	Barks E	Bradley D	Daley A	Darwin GH	Fox O	Gaskell A	Goodwin	Hudson WA	Jepson B	Lambert B	McDonald R	McGregor W	Murray K	Plummer N	Ryan EW	Warner R	Watson S	White W	Wilson J	Wright D	
				3	11	10	4	9		7				2	8	5			6			1	1
			4	3	11	10	7	9						2	8	5			6			1	2
			4	3	11	10	7	9						2	8	5			6			1	3
			4	3	11	10	7	9						2	8	5			6			1	4
			4	3	11	10	7	9						2	8	5			6			1	5
	10		4	3	11		7	9						2	8	5			6			1	6
			4	3	11	10	7	9						2	8	5			6			1	7
	10	3	4		11		7	9						2	8	5			6			1	8
	10		4	3	11		7	9						2	8	5			6			1	9
	10		4	3	11		7	9						2	8	5			6			1	10
	10		4	3	11		7	9						2	8	5			6			1	11
11	10			3			7	9		7				2	8	5			6			1	12
11	10		4	3		8	7	9						2		5			6			1	13
	10		4	3	11		7	9						2	8	5			6			1	14
	10		4	3	11		7	9						2	8	5			6			1	15
	10		4	3	11		7	9						2	8	5			6			1	16
	10		4	3	11		7	9						2	8	5			6			1	17
	7		4	3	11	10		9						2	8	5			6			1	18
	10		4	3	11		7	9						2	8	5			6			1	19
	10	3	4		11	8	7	9						2		5			6			1	20
7	10		4	3	11						9			2	8	5			6			1	21
	8			3	11	10			5	7	9			2	4				6			1	22
	8			3	11	10			5	7	9			2	4				6			1	23
	8		4		11	10	6		5	7	9			2					3			1	24
	8		4	3	11	10			5	7				2	9				6			1	25
	8			3	11	10	4		5	7				2	9				6			1	26
	8			3	11	10	4		5	7					9		2		6			1	27
	8			3	11	10	4	8	5						9		2		6			1	28
7	8			3	11	10	4		5					2	9				6			1	29
7	8			3	11	10	4							2	9	5			6			1	30
7	8			3	11	10	4							2	9	5			6			1	31
11	7		6	3		10	4							2	9	5			8			1	32
	7		6	3	11	10	4							2	9	5			8			1	33
11	8			3		10	4				9			2		5		6			7	1	34
11	8			3		10	4				9			2		5		6			7	1	35
7	8			3	11	10	4				9			2		5		6				1	36
7	8			3	11	10	4				9			2		5		6				1	37
7	8			3	11	10	4	9						2		5		6				1	38
7	10			3	11		4						9	2	8	5		6				1	39
7	10			3	11		8	9					2			5		6	4			1	40
7	10			3	11		4	9					2		8	5			6			1	41
7	10			3	11		4	9					2		8	5			6			1	42
7	10			3	11		4	9					2		8	5			6			1	43
	10			3	11		4	9				6	2		8	5				1	7		44
				3	11	10	4	9						2	8	5			6	1	7		45
	7			3	11	10	4	9						2	8	5			6	1			46
17	39	2	23	43	41	28	41	29	8	8	8	1	6	39	37	38	2	7	39	3	4	43	
	10			1	12	8	4	11		1	1				13				1				

3 own-goals

	10		4	3	11	8	7	9						2		5			6			1	1
	1		1	1	1	1	1	1						1		1			1			1	
	1																						

1955-56

Manager: Stan Mercer to January, then Charlie Mitten from February 1956.

1	Aug	20	(a)	Derby C	L 0-4		24,159
2		22	(h)	Scunthorpe U	W 3-2	Murray 2, Fox	9,730
3		27	(h)	Crewe A	D 1-1	Daley	6,996
4		31	(a)	Scunthorpe U	L 0-3		8,923
5	Sep	3	(a)	Hartlepools U	L 2-4	Lee, Gaskell	7,554
6		5	(h)	Oldham A	W 2-0	Gaskell 2	5,679
7		10	(h)	Stockport C	D 2-2	Murray, Gaskell	7,108
8		12	(a)	Oldham A	D 1-1	Watkin	5,417
9		17	(a)	Barrow	L 1-4	Watkin	5,919
10		19	(h)	Workington	D 0-0		6,023
11		24	(a)	Wrexham	L 0-2		7,348
12		26	(h)	Bradford C	D 0-0		5,339
13	Oct	1	(h)	Halifax T	W 3-1	Gaskell, Watkin, Opp own-goal	5,673
14		8	(h)	Darlington	D 3-3	Murray, Gaskell, Darwin	5,603
15		15	(a)	Chester	L 3-4	Watson, Wilson, Darwin	7,707
16		22	(h)	Southport	L 0-1		5,565
17		29	(a)	Tranmere R	L 0-1		3,424
18	Nov	5	(h)	Chesterfield	L 0-1		8,382
19		12	(a)	Rochdale	D 1-1	Jepson	4,660
20		26	(a)	Grimsby T	L 0-2		12,084
21	Dec	3	(h)	Carlisle U	L 0-1		6,048
22		17	(h)	Derby C	D 1-1	Watkin	9,017
23		24	(a)	Crewe A	L 1-2	Darwin	3,000
24		26	(h)	York C	W 3-1	Darwin 2, Murray	6,303
25		27	(a)	York C	D 1-1	Fox	14,265
26		31	(h)	Hartlepools U	W 5-1	Jepson 2, Darwin 3	7,297
27	Jan	14	(a)	Stockport C	L 2-7	Jepson, Darwin	4,500
28		21	(h)	Barrow	W 4-0	Darwin 2, Jepson, Daley	5,422
29		28	(a)	Gateshead	L 0-3		3,521
30	Feb	4	(h)	Wrexham	W 6-1	Darwin 3, Jepson 2, Opp own-goal	5,073
31		11	(a)	Halifax T	D 1-1	Murray	5,300
32		18	(a)	Darlington	L 1-3	Jepson	3,104
33		25	(h)	Chester	W 3-0	Jepson 2, Darwin	7,693
34	Mar	3	(a)	Southport	D 1-1	Murray	7,000
35		10	(h)	Tranmere R	W 6-0	Murray 2, Jepson 2, Darwin, Opp own-goal	8,591
36		17	(a)	Bradford	W 3-0	Murray, Darwin, Opp own-goal	5,912
37		24	(h)	Rochdale	W 6-0	Murray 3, Jepson, Darwin, Mitten	8,663
38		30	(h)	Accrington S	W 3-2	Murray, Jepson, Mitten	17,303
39		31	(a)	Chesterfield	L 1-2	Jepson	15,138
40	Apr	2	(a)	Accrington S	L 1-3	Lee	8,000
41		7	(h)	Grimsby T	L 0-2		15,562
42		9	(h)	Bradford	W 5-0	Jepson 3, Murray, Darwin	6,380
43		12	(a)	Carlisle U	L 2-5	Jepson, Mitten	5,000
44		21	(h)	Gateshead	W 3-1	Jepson 2, Murray	7,348
45		25	(a)	Bradford C	L 2-4	Murray, Jepson	3,642
46		28	(a)	Workington	L 1-2	Bradley	4,832

FINAL LEAGUE POSITION: 18h in Division Three North

Appearances
Goals

FA Cup

1	Nov	19	(h)	Stockport C	W 2-0	Watkin, Jepson	8,072
2	Dec	10	(a)	York C	L 1-2	Darwin	13,326

Appearances
Goals

Bradley D	Daley AJ	Darwin GH	Fox O	Gaskell A	Jepson BC	Lambert B	Lee H	Lill JA	Linacre W	McDonald R	McGregor W	Mitten C	Murray K	Plummer N	Ryan EW	Smith FD	Stainton JK	Warner RO	Watkin TWS	Watson S	Wilson J	Wright D	
3	11	10	4								2		8	5					9	6	7	1	1
3	11	10	4								2		8	5					9	6	7	1	2
3	11	10	4								2		8	5					9	6	7	1	3
3	7		4	9			10			2			8	5				6	11			1	4
	11		7	9			8			3	2			5				6	10	4		1	5
	11		7	9						3			8	5	2			6	10	4		1	6
		7	4	9				11		3			8	5	2				10	6		1	7
	11			9		6				3			8	5	2				10	4	7	1	8
	11			9		6				3			8	5	2				10	4	7	1	9
	11	8			9						2			5	3	7		6	10	4		1	10
	11	8			9						2			5	3	7		6	10	4		1	11
	11		8	9							2			5	3			6	10	4	7	1	12
	11		4	9							2		8	5	3				10	6	7	1	13
	11	10	4	9							2		8	5	3					6	7	1	14
	11	10		9		6					2		8	5	3					4	7	1	15
	11	10		9		6			7		2		8	5	3					4		1	16
	11	10							7		2		8	5	3			6	9	4		1	17
	11	10			9				7		2			5	3			6	8	4		1	18
	11	10	4		9				7		2			5	3				8	6		1	19
		10	4		9				7		2			5	3				8	6	11	1	20
3	11	10	4			6			7		2		9	5					8			1	21
3	11	10	4			6			7		2		9	5					8			1	22
3	11	10	4						7		2		9	5					8	6		1	23
3	11	10	4						7		2		9	5					8	6		1	24
3	11	10	4						7		2		9	5					8	6		1	25
3	11	10	4		9				7		2		8	5						6		1	26
3	11	10	4		9						2		8	5		7				6		1	27
3	11	10	4		9						2		8	5						6	7	1	28
3	11	10	4		9						2		8	5						6	7	1	29
3		10	4		9						2	11	8	5						6	7	1	30
3		10	4		9						2	11	8	5				7		6		1	31
3		10	4		9						2	11	8	5				7		6		1	32
3		10		7	9						2	11	8	5	4					6		1	33
3		10	7		9						2	11	8	5	4					6		1	34
3		10	4		9				7		2	11	8	5						6		1	35
3		10	4		9				7		2	11	8	5						6		1	36
3		10	4		9							11	8			7	2	5		6		1	37
3		10	4		9						2	11	8			7		5		6		1	38
3			4		9						2	11	8			7		5	10	6		1	39
			4	7	9		8			3		11		6			2	5	10			1	40
3		10	7		9						2	11	8	4				5		6		1	41
3		10	4		9						2	11	8					5		6	7	1	42
3		10	4		9						2	11	8					5		6	7	1	43
3		10	4		9						2	11	8			7		5		6		1	44
3		10	4		9						2	7	8					5	11	6		1	45
3		10	4		9							11	8			7	2	5		6		1	46
29	27	37	37	13	26	6	3	1	13	7	38	17	38	38	17	8	3	20	25	42	15	46	
1	2	19	2	6	22		2					3	17						4	1	1		

4 own-goals

	11	10	4		9				7		2			5	3				8	6		1	1
3	11	10	4						7		2		9	5					8	6		1	2
1	2	2	2		1				2		2		1	2	1				2	2		2	
		1			1														1				

1956-57

Manager: Charlie Mitten

1	Aug	18	(a)	Stockport C	L	1-2	Darwin	6,200
2		20	(h)	Rochdale	L	2-3	Smith, Berry	13,441
3		25	(h)	Carlisle U	W	5-1	Jepson 2, Darwin 2, Smith	7,856
4		29	(a)	Rochdale	D	0-0		7,360
5	Sep	1	(a)	Accrington S	D	3-3	Jepson, Darwin, Smith	10,000
6		3	(h)	Bradford C	W	3-1	Jepson 2, Darwin	12,104
7		8	(h)	Tranmere R	W	3-0	Jepson 2, Darwin	11,382
8		12	(a)	Bradford C	L	3-4	Jepson, Darwin, Mitten	9,022
9		15	(a)	York C	L	0-2		9,790
10		18	(a)	Southport C	D	1-1	Darwin	3,246
11		22	(h)	Oldham A	L	2-4	Mitten 2	9,794
12		29	(a)	Scunthorpe U	W	1-0	Jepson	7,774
13	Oct	6	(h)	Halifax T	W	2-0	Chapman, Murray	9,016
14		13	(a)	Workington	D	3-3	Jepson 2, Chapman	7,159
15		20	(h)	Derby C	L	1-2	Murray	16,341
16		27	(a)	Barrow	L	0-2		5,925
17	Nov	3	(h)	Darlington	W	7-3	Chapman 3, Murray 2, Darwin, Anderson	7,215
18		10	(a)	Bradford	W	4-1	Anderson, Murray, Mitten, Opp own-goal	6,456
19		24	(a)	Wrexham	D	0-0		10,482
20	Dec	1	(h)	Hull C	W	2-1	Jepson, Murray	8,895
21		8	(h)	Gateshead	L	2-4	Chapman, Murray	7,531
22		15	(h)	Stockport C	W	4-2	Watson, Jepson, Murray, Mitten	6,169
23		22	(a)	Carlisle U	L	1-6	Darwin	5,000
24		25	(a)	Chesterfield	L	0-1		12,500
25		29	(h)	Accrington S	L	1-3	Chapman	9,688
26	Jan	5	(h)	Chester	D	1-1	Glazzard	5,949
27		12	(a)	Tranmere R	L	1-3	Murray	4,671
28		19	(h)	York C	W	4-1	Chapman 2, Glazzard 2	6,916
29		26	(a)	Chester	L	2-6	Smith, Chapman (pen)	5,680
30	Feb	2	(a)	Oldham A	D	1-1	Darwin	6,929
31		9	(h)	Scunthorpe U	D	1-1	Glazzard	8,804
32		16	(a)	Halifax T	L	1-2	Mitten	5,075
33	Mar	2	(a)	Derby C	L	0-4		22,997
34		9	(h)	Barrow	L	1-3	Uphill	6,637
35		16	(a)	Darlington	W	3-1	Uphill, Glazzard, Mitten (pen)	5,566
36		23	(h)	Bradford	W	2-1	Glazzard, Darwin	7,591
37		30	(a)	Gateshead	D	1-1	Glazzard	3,333
38	Apr	6	(h)	Wrexham	W	3-1	Darwin 3	6,435
39		8	(h)	Chesterfield	W	3-0	Fox 2, Uphill	8,702
40		13	(a)	Hull C	W	2-1	Uphill, Mitten (pen)	10,550
41		15	(h)	Workington	D	2-2	Mitten 2 (1 pen)	11,346
42		19	(a)	Hartlepools U	L	1-2	Glazzard	8,804
43		20	(h)	Crewe A	W	2-1	Glazzard, Darwin	7,719
44		23	(h)	Hartlepools U	W	4-1	Uphill 2, Darwin, Mitten (pen)	10,932
45		27	(a)	Crewe A	L	4-6	Morris 2, Darwin 2	6,762
46		29	(h)	Southport	L	1-2	Glazzard	6,749

FINAL LEAGUE POSITION: 16th in Division Three North

Appearances
Goals

FA Cup

1	Nov	17	(h)	Workington	D	1-1	Murray	11,383
R		24	(a)	Workington	L	1-2	Jepson	9,070

Appearances
Goals

Anderson RJ	Berry W	Bradley D	Chamberlain DC	Chapman SEG	Crowe CA	Darwin GH	Dickson W	Elliott FFG	Flowers M	Fox O	Glazzard J	Jayes B	Jepson BC	Lambert B	Mitten C	Morris FW	Murray K	Rushby A	Ryan EW	Smith FD	Stainton JK	Statham T	Swinscoe T	Uphill DE	Warner RO	Watson S	Wright D	
		3				10	5	1		4			9		11		8		2	7						6		1
	8	3				10		1		4			9		11		2			7					5	6		2
	8	3				10						4	9		11		2			7					5	6	1	3
	8	3				10						4	9		11		2			7					5	6	1	4
	8	3				10	5					4	9		11		2			7						6	1	5
	8	3				10	5					4	9		11		2			7						6	1	6
	8	3				10						4	9		11		2			7					5	6	1	7
7	8	3				10	5					4	9		11		2									6	1	8
7	8	3				10	5					4	9		11		2									6	1	9
7		3		8		10	5					4	9		11		2									6	1	10
7	8	3				10						4	9		11		2								5	6	1	11
		3				10	5	1		2		4	9		11		8			7						6		12
		3		8		10	5	1		2		4	7		11		9									6		13
7		3		10			5	1		2		4	9		11		8									6		14
7		3		8			5	1		2		4	9		11		10									6		15
7	10	3		8			5	1		6		4			11		9				2							16
7		3		8		10	5	1				4			11		9				2					6		17
7		5	3	8		10		1				4			11		9				2					6		18
		5		8				1				4	9	3	11		10			7	2					6		19
		5		8				1				4	9	3	11		10			7	2					6		20
		3		8				1				4	9	2	11		10			7					5	6		21
		5		8				1				4	9	3	11		10			7	2					6		22
		5		8		10		1				4		3	11		2			7			9			6		23
			2			10		1	5		9	4		3	11		8			7						6		24
			2	8		10		1	5	6	9	4		3	11					7								25
			2	8		10		1	5		9	4		3	11					7						6		26
11			2	8		7		1		5	9	4		3			10									6		27
			2	8		10	5	1		3	9	4			11					7						6		28
			2	8		10	5	1		3	9	4			11					7						6		29
			2	8		10	5	1			9	4		3	11					7						6		30
11			2	8			5				9	4		3	10					7		1				6		31
			2	8	6	10	5	1			9			3	11					7						4		32
			2	8	6	10	5	1		3	9				11					7						4		33
			2		6	10	5	1				4			11					7			9	8		3		34
			2		3	10		1			9	4			11	7		5						8		6		35
			2		3	10		1			9	4			11	7		5						8		6		36
			2		3	10		1			9	4			11	7		5						8		6		37
7			2		3	10		1			9	4			11			5						8		6		38
			2		3			1		10	9	4			11	7		5						8		6		39
			2		3			1		10	9	4			11	7		5						8		6		40
11			2					1		6	9	4			10	7		5					3	8				41
			2			10		1		6	9	4			11	7		5					3	8				42
			2		6	10		1			9	4			11	7		5					3	8				43
7			2		3	9		1		10		4			11			5						8		6		44
11			2		3	9		1				4			10	7		5						8		6		45
			2		3	10		1			9	4			11	7		5						8		6		46
15	10	23	24	21	13	35	19	36	3	17	20	42	19	12	45	10	25	12	1	23	6	1	5	13	6	41	9	
2	1			10		19				2	10		13		11	2	9			4				6		1		

1 own-goal

		5		8		10		1				4	7	3	11		9				2					6		1
11		5		8				1				4	7	3	10		9				2					6		R
1		2		2		1		2				2	2	2	2		2				2					2		
													1				1											

1957-58

Manager: Charlie Mitten

1	Aug	24	(h)	Rochdale	L	2-4	Uphill, C.Mitten (pen)	10,447
2		27	(a)	Carlisle U	W	4-3	Uphill 2, Chapman 2	10,000
3		31	(a)	Crewe A	L	0-1		6,049
4	Sep	2	(h)	Carlisle U	W	2-0	Chapman, Keery	9,674
5		7	(h)	Wrexham	W	2-1	Chapman, B.Thomas	7,748
6		9	(h)	Stockport C	D	2-2	Keery, C.Mitten	8,561
7		14	(a)	Scunthorpe U	D	3-3	Keery, B.Thomas, Opp own-goal	9,533
8		16	(a)	Stockport C	D	3-3	C.Mitten 2 (1 pen), B.Thomas	8,500
9		21	(h)	Darlington	W	4-2	Chapman 2, Morris, B.Thomas	7,897
10		23	(h)	Hull C	L	1-3	Morris	6,868
11		30	(a)	Hull C	D	1-1	Keery	7,878
12	Oct	5	(h)	Bradford	W	2-1	Morris, B.Thomas	7,756
13		12	(a)	Tranmere R	W	2-1	Morris, B.Thomas	10,697
14		19	(h)	York C	W	2-1	Morris, C.Mitten	7,907
15		26	(a)	Barrow	L	1-2	Uphill	6,016
16	Nov	2	(h)	Oldham A	D	4-4	Chapman 2, Morris, Uphill	7,711
17		9	(a)	Bury	W	2-0	Chapman 2	11,895
18		23	(a)	Chester	W	2-1	B.Thomas, Chapman	7,096
19		30	(h)	Chesterfield	D	1-1	Keery	12,579
20	Dec	14	(h)	Hartlepools U	W	5-1	Keery 2, Morris 2, Chapman	8,097
21		21	(a)	Rochdale	L	0-3		4,371
22		25	(h)	Bradford C	W	5-1	Morris, Chapman, Keery, Watson, C.Mitten	7,876
23		26	(a)	Bradford C	D	1-1	Watson	17,472
24		28	(h)	Crewe A	W	2-1	Chapman, Watson	10,249
25	Jan	11	(a)	Wrexham	L	2-4	B.Thomas, Watson	6,863
26		18	(h)	Scunthorpe U	L	3-5	Keery 2, Chapman	8,336
27		25	(h)	Accrington S	L	0-2		7,153
28	Feb	1	(a)	Darlington	L	0-2		6,106
29		15	(a)	Bradford	W	2-0	B.Thomas 2	8,629
30		22	(h)	Chester	W	3-1	Griffiths 2, Morris	7,605
31	Mar	1	(a)	York C	L	1-3	Uphill	6,000
32		8	(h)	Barrow	W	4-2	B.Thomas 2, C.Mitten (pen), Morris	5,239
33		10	(h)	Workington	W	6-3	Griffiths 2, Uphill 2, C.Mitten 2	4,664
34		15	(a)	Oldham A	D	1-1	B.Thomas	6,054
35		22	(h)	Tranmere R	W	4-1	Morris 2, Keery, B.Thomas	7,255
36		29	(a)	Accrington S	L	1-4	B.Thomas	6,500
37		31	(a)	Southport	L	1-4	B.Thomas	1,405
38	Apr	5	(h)	Southport	W	3-0	Uphill 2, B.Thomas	6,658
39		7	(h)	Halifax T	W	2-1	B.Thomas, Jayes	8,325
40		8	(a)	Halifax T	L	0-4		5,882
41		12	(a)	Chesterfield	W	4-1	Morris 2, B.Thomas, Keery	12,279
42		14	(a)	Gateshead	L	1-2	Uphill	3,005
43		19	(h)	Bury	W	6-4	B.Thomas 3, Uphill, Keery, C.Mitten	10,352
44		23	(a)	Workington	L	0-4		4,700
45		26	(a)	Hartlepools U	L	0-2		4,552
46		28	(h)	Gateshead	W	3-0	Uphill, B.Thomas, C.Mitten (pen)	7,474

FINAL LEAGUE POSITION: 6th in Division Three North

Appearances
Goals

FA Cup

1	Nov	16	(h)	Halifax T	W	2-0	Chapman, C.Mitten (pen)	9,697
2	Dec	7	(a)	Wigan A	D	1-1	Chapman	12,900
R		11	(h)	Wigan A	W	3-1	Morris 2, C.Mitten	5,576
3	Jan	4	(a)	Bristol R	L	0-5		20,446

Appearances
Goals

Anderson RJ	Bradley D	Cann RG	Chamberlain DC	Chapman SEG	Crowe CA	Elliott FFG	Glazzard J	Griffiths KJ	Jayes B	Keery S	Kirkham RN	Mellor KE	Mitten C	Mitten J	Morris FW	Rushby A	Savin KA	Statham T	Swinscoe T	Thomas BEB	Thomas JC	Toon C	Uphill DE	Watson S	Williams GR	
	5			8	2	1			4	10			11		7		3						9	6		1
	5		2	8		1			4	10			11		7		3						9	6		2
	3		2	8		1			4	10			11		7	5							9	6		3
			2	8	3	1			4	10			11		7	5				9				6		4
			2	8	3	1			4	10			11		7	5				9				6		5
			2	8	3	1			4	10			11		7	5				9				6		6
11			2	8	3	1			4	10					7	5				9				6		7
			2	8	3	1			4	10			11		7	5				9				6		8
			2	8	3	1			4	10			11		7	5				9				6		9
			2	8	3	1			4	10			11		7	5				9				6		10
	3		2	8	6	1			4	10		5	11		7								9			11
			2	8	6	1			4	10		5			7		3			11			9			12
				8	6	1	9		4			5			7		3		2	11			10			13
				8	6	1			4			5	11		7		3		2	9			10			14
				8		1			4			5	11		7		3		2	9			10	6		15
				8	6	1			4	10		5	11		7		3		2				9			16
7			2	8	6	1			4	10		5	11		9		3									17
			2	8	6	1			4	10		5	11		7		3			9						18
			2	8	6	1			4	10		5	11		7		3			9						19
				8	6	1			4	9		5	11		7		3		2					10		20
				8	6	1			4	9		5	11		7		3		2					10		21
			2	8	6	1			4	9		5	11		7		3							10		22
			2	8	6	1			4	9		5	11		7		3							10		23
			2	8	6	1			4	9		5	11		7		3							10		24
			2	8	6	1			4			5	11		9		3			7				10		25
			2	9	6				4	8		5	11		7		3	1						10		26
				9		1		10	4	8		5	11		7		3					2		6		27
		5		9	6	1		10		8				11	7		3					2			4	28
				8				10		6	1	5	11		7		3			9		2			4	29
								10		6	1	5	11		7		3			9		2	8		4	30
								10		6	1	5	11		7		3			9		2	8		4	31
								10		6	1	5	11		7		3			9		2	8		4	32
								8	4	6	1	5	11		7		3			9		2	10			33
								8		6	1	5	11		7		3			9	2		10		4	34
								8		6	1	5	11		7		3			9	2		10		4	35
								8	4	6	1	5	11		7		3			9	2		10			36
								8	4	6	1	5	11		7		3			9	2		10			37
								8	4	6	1	5		11	7		3			9	2		10			38
								8	4	6	1	5	11		7		3			9	2		10			39
								8	4	6	1	5		11	7		3			9	2		10			40
										10	1	5	11		7		3			9	2		8	6	4	41
										10	1	5	11		7		3			9	2		8	6	4	42
										10	1	5	11		7		3			9	2		8	6	4	43
11										10	1	5			7		3			9	2		8	6	4	44
11										10	1	5			7		3			9	2		8	6	4	45
	5								4	10	1		11		7		3			9	2		8	6		46
4	5	1	19	29	24	27	1	14	34	42	18	34	38	3	46	8	37	1	6	32	13	7	26	25	12	
				15				4	1	13			11		15					23			13	4		

1 own-goal

7			2	8	6	1			4	10		5	11		9		3									1
			2	8	6	1	9		4	10		5	11		7		3									2
				8	6	1			4	9		5	11		7		3		2					10		R
			2	8	6	1			4	9		5	11		7		3							10		3
1			3	4	4	4	1		4	4		4	4		4		4		1					2		
				2									2		2											

1958-59

Manager: Sam Weaver

1	Aug	23	(h)	Southampton	L 1-6	Delapenha	14,038
2		27	(a)	Bradford C	D 1-1	Fraser	10,939
3		30	(a)	Accrington S	L 0-2		6,542
4	Sep	1	(h)	Bradford C	W 2-1	Kemp, B.Thomas	10,129
5		6	(h)	Halifax T	W 4-3	Uphill, B.Thomas, Keery, Delapenha	9,763
6		9	(a)	Brentford	L 0-2		13,600
7		13	(a)	Newport C	L 0-1		8,482
8		15	(h)	Brentford	D 1-1	Opp own-goal	9,166
9		20	(h)	Chesterfield	W 2-1	Anderson, Delapenha	15,943
10		22	(h)	Wrexham	W 3-1	Uphill 2, Vaughan	7,882
11		27	(a)	Notts C	W 4-3	Vaughan, Uphill, Keery (pen), Opp own-goal	16,510
12	Oct	1	(a)	Wrexham	L 1-2	Uphill	9,872
13		4	(h)	Queen's Park R	L 3-4	Keery 2, Uphill	9,622
14		11	(a)	Doncaster R	W 2-0	Uphill, Delapenha	10,200
15		18	(h)	Plymouth A	L 1-4	Downie	12,488
16		25	(a)	Tranmere R	D 2-2	Uphill, B.Thomas	11,744
17	Nov	1	(h)	Stockport C	W 2-1	B.Thomas 2	8,277
18		8	(a)	Reading	D 3-3	Uphill, Downie, B.Thomas	13,473
19		22	(a)	Southend U	L 1-5	Uphill	9,329
20	Dec	13	(h)	Bury	L 0-2		5,775
21		20	(a)	Southampton	L 2-3	Uphill (pen), B.Thomas	17,901
22		26	(a)	Hull C	L 2-5	B.Thomas 2	20,836
23		27	(h)	Hull C	D 1-1	Delapenha	7,919
24	Jan	3	(h)	Accrington S	W 3-2	B.Thomas 2, Griffiths	6,815
25		17	(a)	Halifax T	D 0-0		3,403
26		24	(a)	Bournemouth	D 3-3	B.Thomas 2, Delapenha	10,342
27		31	(h)	Newport C	W 2-1	B.Thomas 2	8,347
28	Feb	2	(h)	Colchester U	W 3-2	Uphill 2, Delapenha	5,155
29		7	(a)	Chesterfield	L 1-3	B.Thomas	10,118
30		14	(h)	Notts C	W 3-0	Delapenha, B.Thomas, Opp own-goal	13,374
31		21	(a)	Queen's Park R	D 1-1	B.Thomas	4,927
32		28	(h)	Doncaster R	W 3-1	Delapenha, Uphill (pen), B.Thomas	8,120
33	Mar	7	(a)	Plymouth A	L 3-8	Downie 2, Ripley	17,597
34		14	(h)	Tranmere R	L 0-2		5,623
35		21	(a)	Stockport C	L 1-4	Griffiths	6,300
36		27	(a)	Rochdale	D 2-2	Uphill, Griffiths	3,537
37		28	(h)	Reading	W 1-0	Williams	6,277
38		30	(h)	Rochdale	D 0-0		5,862
39	Apr	4	(a)	Colchester U	W 3-1	Uphill 2 (1 pen), B.Thomas	5,901
40		6	(h)	Norwich C	D 1-1	Nugent	7,734
41		11	(h)	Southend U	L 1-4	Uphill	7,143
42		13	(h)	Swindon T	D 0-0		5,719
43		18	(a)	Norwich C	L 0-1		21,225
44		22	(a)	Swindon T	L 1-2	Uphill	7,305
45		25	(h)	Bournemouth	L 1-3	Nugent	3,698
46		28	(a)	Bury	D 2-2	Hall, B.Thomas	5,421

FINAL LEAGUE POSITION: 20th in Division Three — Appearances

Goals

FA Cup

1	Nov	15	(h)	Bradford C	L 3-4	Uphill 2, B.Thomas	9,313

Appearances

Goals

Anderson RJ	Billington CR	Bradley D.	Delapenha LL	Downie JD	Fraser DM	Griffiths KJ	Hall BS	Hogg AR	Hollett I	Jayes B	Keery S	Kemp SP	Kirkham RN	Lambert B	McBride V	Mellor KE	Nugent WC	Ripley SK	Savin KA	Statham T	Swinscoe T	Thomas BEB	Thomas JC	Toon C	Uphill DE	Vaughan TR	Watson S	Williams GR	
	5	3	7		11	8		2		4	10				1										9			6	1
7		3			11	10				4					1	5						9	2		8		6		2
		3	10		11					4		7				5				1		9	2		8		6		3
		3	11							4	10	7				5				1		9	2		8		6		4
		3	11							4	10	7				5				1		9	2		8		6		5
		3	11			7				4	10					5				1		9	2		8		6		6
					11	8				4	10				1	5			3			7	2		9		6		7
7			11							4	10				1	5			3				2		9	8	6		8
7			11							4	10				1	5			3				2		9	8	6		9
7					11					4	10				1	5			3				2		9	8	6		10
7						10				4	11					5			3	1			2		9	8	6		11
7						10				4	11		1			5			3				2		9	8	6		12
7			11						8	4	10		1			5			3					2	9			6	13
7			11	10		8				4			1			5			3				2		9		6		14
7		3	11	10		8				4			1			5							2		9		6		15
7			11	6		10				4					1	5			3			9	2		8				16
7		3	11	6		10				4					1	5						9	2		8				17
7		3		10						4					1	5	11	6				9	2		8				18
7		3		10						4					1	5	11	6				9	2		8				19
		3	7	10												5	11	6		1		9	2		8			4	20
		3	7	10												5	11	6		1		9	2		8			4	21
		3	7	10												5	11	6		1		9	2		8			4	22
			7			10										5	11	6	3	1		9	2		8			4	23
			7			10										5	11	6	3	1		9	2		8			4	24
			7			10										5	11	6	3	1		9	2		8			4	25
			7	6		10										5	11		3	1		9	2		8			4	26
7			8	6												5	11		3	1		9	2		10			4	27
7			8	6	11											5			3	1		9	2		10			4	28
7			8	6												5	11		3	1		9	2		10			4	29
			7	6		10										5	11		3	1		9		2	8			4	30
			7	6		10										5	11		3	1		9	2		8			4	31
			7			10							1			5	11	6	3			9		2	8			4	32
			7	10													11	6	3	1	5	9		2	8			4	33
			7	10													11	6	3	1	5	9		2		8		4	34
			7			10											11		3	1	5	9		2	8		6	4	35
			8			10							1			5	11		3			7		2	9		6	4	36
		5	8			10							1				11		3			7		2	9		6	4	37
		5	8			10							1				11		3			7		2	9		6	4	38
		5	8			10							1				11		3			7		2	9		6	4	39
		5	8			10							1				11		3			7		2	9		6	4	40
		5	7			10							1				11		3			9		2	8		6	4	41
		5	7			10							1				11		3			9		2	8		6	4	42
7		5	8			10							1				11		3					2	9		6	4	43
7		5	8			10							1				11		3					2	9		6	4	44
		5	8			10	11						1	3			7							2	9		6	4	45
		5	7	10			11		8				1	3				6				9		2				4	46
18	1	23	39	18	6	28	2	1	2	19	11	3	16	2	10	32	27	12	31	20	3	34	28	17	44	6	24	29	
1			9	4	1	3	1				4	1					2	1				21			19	2		1	

3 own-goals

11		3	7			10				4					1	5						9	2		8		6		1
1		1	1			1				1					1	1						1	1		1		1		
																						1			2				

1959-60

Manager: Sam Weaver to January 1960, then Raich Carter.

1	Aug	22	(a)	Coventry C	L 0-2		19,769
2		24	(h)	Bradford C	D 0-0		11,645
3		29	(h)	Halifax T	D 1-1	Thomas	8,947
4	Sep	1	(a)	Bradford C	L 1-4	Thomas	11,309
5		5	(a)	Bury	L 1-4	Fitzsimmons	11,278
6		7	(a)	Southend U	W 2-0	Jones, Delapenha	13,500
7		12	(h)	Barnsley	L 1-4	Thomas	8,417
8		14	(h)	Southend U	D 1-1	Thomas	7,039
9		19	(a)	Southampton	L 2-5	Jones, Ripley	15,831
10		21	(a)	Colchester U	L 0-3		8,202
11		26	(h)	Reading	D 4-4	Ripley 2, Jones, Opp own-goal	5,626
12		28	(h)	Colchester U	L 1-3	Hollett	5,046
13	Oct	3	(a)	Shrewsbury T	L 3-6	Hollett 2, Ripley	8,722
14		10	(h)	Queen's Park R	W 4-3	Hollett 2, Ringstead, Jones	7,533
15		12	(a)	Port Vale	L 1-4	Jones	9,230
16		17	(a)	Grimsby T	L 1-2	Jones	11,300
17		24	(h)	Wrexham	W 6-2	Fitzsimmons 2, Ringstead, Delapenha, Jones, Nugent	5,284
18		31	(a)	York C	L 1-2	Fitzsimmons	6,868
19	Nov	7	(h)	Bournemouth	L 3-4	Fitzsimmons 3	6,797
20		21	(h)	Newport C	W 3-1	Williams, Jones, Nugent	6,996
21		28	(a)	Chesterfield	W 1-0	Fitzsimmons	9,431
22	Dec	12	(a)	Tranmere R	L 2-4	Jones, Fitzsimmons	5,204
23		26	(h)	Norwich C	W 3-2	Ringstead, Jones, Delapenha (pen)	7,657
24		28	(a)	Norwich C	L 1-5	Hall	21,250
25	Jan	2	(a)	Halifax T	L 2-4	Hall, Opp own-goal	4,397
26		16	(h)	Bury	L 1-5	Fitzsimmons	6,085
27		23	(a)	Barnsley	D 2-2	Taylor, Delapenha (pen)	4,906
28	Feb	6	(h)	Southampton	W 4-2	Anderson, Delapenha, Fitzsimmons, Hall	7,435
29		13	(a)	Reading	L 2-3	Delapenha, Taylor	5,895
30		20	(h)	Shrewsbury T	W 1-0	Fitzsimmons	6,581
31		27	(a)	Queen's Park R	L 0-2		7,734
32	Mar	5	(h)	Grimsby T	W 3-2	Hollett 2, Williams	9,111
33		12	(a)	Wrexham	L 0-3		8,460
34		19	(h)	Chesterfield	W 4-1	Jones 2, Fitzsimmons, Delapenha	11,123
35		21	(a)	Accrington S	W 1-0	Jones	3,668
36		26	(a)	Bournemouth	L 0-6		7,080
37		28	(h)	Swindon T	L 1-2	Hollett	6,409
38	Apr	2	(h)	Accrington S	W 4-1	Hollett 3, Fitzsimmons	5,284
39		4	(h)	Coventry C	L 2-4	Nugent, Delapenha (pen)	7,019
40		9	(a)	Newport C	W 1-0	Delapenha	4,473
41		15	(a)	Brentford	D 1-1	Hollett	9,575
42		16	(h)	York C	W 2-0	Nugent 2	7,234
43		18	(h)	Brentford	L 0-1		7,626
44		23	(a)	Swindon T	L 1-2	Hollett	7,963
45		25	(h)	Port Vale	W 6-3	Wragg 2, Hollett 2, Fitzsimmons, Delapenha	4,970
46		30	(h)	Tranmere R	L 0-2		5,177

FINAL LEAGUE POSITION: 22nd in Division Three

Appearances

Goals

FA Cup

1	Nov	14	(a)	Accrington S	W 2-1	Humble, Nugent	4,363
2	Dec	5	(h)	Chester	W 2-0	Jones, Fitzsimmons	11,509
3	Jan	9	(a)	Blackpool	L 0-3		18,812

Appearances

Goals

Anderson RJ	Bradley D	Coates DP	Delapenha LL	Emery AJ	Fitzsimmons AG	Hall BS	Hogg AR	Hollett I	Humble JW	Jayes B	Jones G	Kirkham RN	Lambert B	Nugent WC	Ogilvie JF	Ringstead A	Ripley SK	Statham T	Taylor J	Thomas B	Toon C	Watson S	Williams GR	Wragg D	Wyllie RG	
	5		8		10				3		9	1		11		7					2	6	4			1
	5		8		10				3	4	9	1		11		7					2	6				2
	5		8		10	11			3	4		1				7	6			9	2					3
	5		8		10	11			3	4		1				7	6			9	2					4
	5		8		10	11	2		3							7	6	1		9			4			5
	3		11	5	10				2		8					7	6	1		9			4			6
	3		8	5		11			2		10					7	6	1		9			4			7
	3		10	5		11			2		8					7	6	1		9			4			8
	3		10			11	5		2	4	8	1				7	9					6				9
	5		8				2		3	4	10	1		11		7	9					6				10
	2					11			6	3	8	1		10		4	9				5		7			11
						11	5	9	3	6	8	1		10		7					2		4			12
							5	10	3	4	8			11		7	9				2	6			1	13
	5				10		4	9	3	6	8			11		7					2				1	14
	5				10		4	9	3		8			11		7					2	6			1	15
	5		8		10		2		3	6	9			11		7							4		1	16
			8	5	10		2		3	6	9			11		7							4		1	17
	5		8		10		2		3	6	9			11		7							4		1	18
	5		8		10				3	6	9			11		7					2		4		1	19
	5		8		10				2	6	9		3	11		7							4		1	20
	5		8		10				2	6	9		3	11		7							4		1	21
	5		8		10				2	6	9		3	11		7							4		1	22
	3		8		10	11			2	6	9					7	5						4		1	23
	3		8			11		10	2	6	9					7	5						4		1	24
7	3		8		10	11			2	6	9						5						4		1	25
	5		7		9	11		10	2	6	8				3								4		1	26
			8	5	10	11			2						3	7	4		9			6			1	27
7			8	5	10	11			2						3		4		9			6			1	28
7			8	5	10	11			2						3		4		9			6			1	29
			8	5	10				2		9			11	3		4		7			6			1	30
			8	5	10				2		9			11	3		4		7			6			1	31
			8	5	7			9	2		10				3	11						6	4		1	32
			8	5	7			9	2		10				3	11						6	4		1	33
	3		11	5	8			9	2		10											6	4	7	1	34
	3		11	5	8			9	2		10											6	4	7	1	35
	3		11	5	8			9	2		10											6	4	7	1	36
	3		11	5	8			9	2		10											6	4	7	1	37
	5		11		8			9						10	3						2	6	4	7	1	38
	5		11		8			9						10	3		4				2	6		7	1	39
	5		11		8			9						10	3						2	6	4	7	1	40
	5	6	11		8			9						10	3						2		4	7	1	41
	5	6	11		8			9						10	3						2		4	7	1	42
	5	6	11		8			9						10	3						2		4	7	1	43
	5	6	11		8			9						10	3						2		4	7	1	44
	5		11		8			9						10	3						2	6	4	7	1	45
		8	11	5	10			9							3						2	6	4	7	1	46
3	35	5	41	16	38	15	10	21	37	20	31	8	3	25	17	27	19	4	5	6	19	22	32	13	34	
1			10		15	3		15			13			5		3	4		2	4			2	2		

2 own-goals

Anderson RJ	Bradley D	Coates DP	Delapenha LL	Emery AJ	Fitzsimmons AG	Hall BS	Hogg AR	Hollett I	Humble JW	Jayes B	Jones G	Kirkham RN	Lambert B	Nugent WC	Ogilvie JF	Ringstead A	Ripley SK	Statham T	Taylor J	Thomas B	Toon C	Watson S	Williams GR	Wragg D	Wyllie RG	
	5		8		10				2	6	9		3	11		7							4		1	1
	5		8		10				2	6	9		3	11		7							4		1	2
	5		8		10	11			3	6	9					7					2		4		1	3
	3		3		3	1			3	3	3		2	2		3					1		3		3	
					1				1		1			1												

1960-61

Manager: Raich Carter

1	Aug	20	(a)	Aldershot	L 0-2		6,505
2		22	(h)	Rochdale	L 0-2		8,150
3		27	(h)	Stockport C	W 2-0	Delapenha, Fitzsimmons	4,073
4		30	(a)	Rochdale	W 2-1	Wagstaff 2	5,547
5	Sep	3	(a)	Exeter C	W 2-0	Wragg 2	5,576
6		7	(a)	Wrexham	L 0-2		8,469
7		10	(h)	Peterborough U	W 1-0	Wagstaff	11,285
8		12	(h)	Wrexham	L 0-3		6,455
9		17	(a)	Southport	L 1-2	Delapenha (pen)	4,486
10		19	(h)	Carlisle U	L 1-3	Delapenha	3,110
11		24	(h)	Darlington	W 2-1	Jones 2	3,868
12		27	(a)	Carlisle U	L 1-3	Hollett	6,135
13	Oct	1	(a)	Crystal P	L 1-4	Fitzsimmons	15,018
14		8	(h)	Workington	W 2-0	Fitzsimmons, Opp own-goal	2,338
15		15	(a)	Chester	D 3-3	Wagstaff, Delapenha, Stringfellow	5,553
16		22	(h)	Crewe A	D 1-1	Coates	3,866
17		29	(a)	York C	L 2-3	Delapenha, Stringfellow	5,439
18	Nov	12	(a)	Millwall	L 0-3		8,069
19		19	(h)	Barrow	W 5-1	Hollett 3, Wragg 2	3,682
20	Dec	10	(a)	Northampton T	L 0-1		7,929
21		17	(h)	Aldershot	W 2-0	Gauld 2	3,786
22		26	(h)	Hartlepools U	W 2-1	Gauld, Fitzsimmons	6,283
23		27	(a)	Hartlepools U	L 2-3	Delapenha, Fitzsimmons	3,914
24		31	(a)	Stockport C	L 0-1		4,695
25	Jan	7	(a)	Barrow	D 1-1	Phillips	3,300
26		14	(h)	Exeter C	L 2-3	Fitzsimmons 2	4,485
27		21	(a)	Peterborough U	L 1-2	Fitzsimmons	10,628
28	Feb	4	(h)	Southport	L 1-2	Williams	3,234
29		11	(a)	Darlington	L 2-3	Wragg, Phillips	4,888
30		18	(h)	Crystal P	L 1-2	Hollett	5,878
31		24	(a)	Workington	W 3-1	Hollett 2, Wragg	2,814
32	Mar	4	(h)	Chester	W 3-1	Wragg 2, Hollettt	4,564
33		11	(a)	Crewe A	W 2-1	Coates, Hollett	6,059
34		18	(h)	York C	L 1-3	Wragg	5,062
35		22	(h)	Accrington S	D 0-0		3,095
36		25	(a)	Accrington S	W 4-1	Wagstaff 2, Wragg, Ogilvie (pen)	2,350
37		31	(a)	Oldham A	L 1-3	Hollett	13,054
38	Apr	1	(h)	Millwall	W 5-1	Stringfellow 2, Coates 2, Wragg	4,574
39		3	(h)	Oldham A	L 1-2	Williams	6,882
40		12	(h)	Bradford	L 1-2		4,699
41		15	(h)	Gillingham	W 1-0	Delapenha	4,070
42		17	(h)	Doncaster R	L 1-2	Coates	4,748
43		22	(a)	Bradford	L 1-2	Stringfellow	10,249
44		25	(a)	Doncaster R	W 3-2	Jones 2, Wagstaff	3,574
45		29	(h)	Northampton T	W 4-2	Wagstaff 2, Jones, Delapenha	4,870
46	May	3	(a)	Gillingham	D 0-0		3,164

FINAL LEAGUE POSITION: 20th in Division Four

Appearances
Goals

FA Cup

1	Nov	5	(h)	Blyth Spartans	W 3-1	Wragg, Coates, Fitzsimmons	5,727
2		30	(a)	Accrington S	L 0-3		4,467

Appearances
Goals

League Cup

1	Oct	12	(a)	Leicester C	L 0-4		7,070

Appearances
Goals

Bradley D	Clarke RJ	Coates DP	Delapenha LL	Emery AJ	Fitzsimmons AG	Gauld J	Hall BS	Hollett I	Humble JW	Jones G	Moore B	Morris PJ	Ogilvie JF	Phillips BJ	Smith TV	Stringfellow M	Tarrent BL	Toon C	Wagstaff K	Watson S	Williams GR	Wragg D	Wyllie RG	
3	6	8	11					9		10				5				2			4	7	1	1
3	6	8	10				11	9						5				2			4	7	1	2
3			8		10		11	9	2					5						6	4	7	1	3
3			10	5					2						4	11			9	6	8	7	1	4
3			10	5					2						4	11			9	6	8	7	1	5
3			11		10				2					5	4				9	6	8	7	1	6
			10		7			11	3					5	4			2	9	6	8		1	7
			10		8			11	3					5	4			2	9	6	7		1	8
		6	10		11				3	7				5	4			2	9		8		1	9
		6	7	5	10		11	9					3		4		8	2					1	10
		6	7	5	10					9	11		3				8	2			4		1	11
		6	7	5	10			8		9			3					2	11		4		1	12
				5	10		11	8		9			3		6		7	2			4		1	13
3		6	8		10					9	7			5		11		2			4		1	14
3		6	8		10					9				5		11		2	7		4		1	15
3		6	8		10			9						5		11		2	7		4		1	16
3		6	8		10					9				5		11		2			4	7	1	17
3		6	8		10					9				5		11		2			4	7	1	18
3		6	8			9		10						5		11		2			4	7	1	19
3		6	8			9		10						5		11		2			4	7	1	20
3		6	8	5	10	9										11		2			4	7	1	21
3		6	8	5	10	9										11		2			4	7	1	22
3		6	8	5	10			9								11		2			4	7	1	23
3		6	8	5	10			9			11							2			4	7	1	24
3		6	8		10						11			5				2	9		4	7	1	25
3		6	8		10									5		11		2	9		4	7	1	26
3		6	8		10									5		11		2	9		4	7	1	27
3		6	7		10			8						5		11		2	9		4		1	28
		6			10			8					3	5		11		2	9		4	7	1	29
		6			8			10					3	5		11		2	9		4	7	1	30
3		8						10				6		5		11		2	9		4	7	1	31
3		8						10				6		5		11		2	9		4	7	1	32
3		8						10				6		5		11		2	9		4	7	1	33
3		8						10				6		5		11		2	9		4	7	1	34
		8						10	3			6		5		11		2	9		4	7	1	35
		8						10				6	3	5		11		2	9		4	7	1	36
3		8						10				6		5		11		2	9		4	7	1	37
		8	10					9	3					5		11		2		6	4	7	1	38
		8	10					9	3			6		5		11		2			4	7	1	39
		8						10	3			6		5		11		2	9		4	7	1	40
		8	10						3	9		6		5		11		2			4	7	1	41
		8	10						3	9		6		5		11		2			4	7	1	42
		8	10						3			6		5		11		2	9		4	7	1	43
3			8							10		6		5		11		2	9		4	7	1	44
3		8	7							10				5		11		2	9	6	4		1	45
3		8	7							10				5		11		2	9	6	4		1	46
29	2	38	35	10	24	4	4	26	14	14	4	13	7	36	8	33	3	42	27	9	45	33	46	
		5	8		8	3		10		5			1	2		6			9		2	11		

1 own-goal

3		6	8		10					9				5		11		2			4	7	1	1
3	8	6		5	10					9	7					11		2		4			1	2
2	1	2	1	1	2					2	1			1		2		2		1	1	1	2	
		1			1																	1		

3	8	6		5	10					9	7					11		2		4			1	1
1	1	1		1	1					1	1					1		1		1			1	

1961-62

Manager: Raich Carter

1	Aug	19	(h)	Exeter C	W 3-1	Straw 2, O'Hara	7,611
2		21	(h)	Barrow	L 0-1		9,141
3		26	(a)	Wrexham	L 0-5		8,750
4		28	(a)	Barrow	D 1-1	R.Chapman	5,225
5	Sep	2	(h)	Doncaster R	W 4-0	R.Chapman 2, Straw, Stringfellow	7,879
6		4	(a)	Accrington S	D 0-0		3,500
7		9	(a)	Workington	D 1-1	Straw	4,161
8		16	(h)	York C	W 3-1	Straw 2, Hollett	8,844
9		23	(a)	Chesterfield	W 4-0	Wagstaff 2, R.Chapman 2	10,919
10		30	(h)	Gillingham	W 3-1	Wagstaff, R.Chapman, Morris (pen)	10,599
11	Oct	2	(a)	Millwall	L 0-4		9,462
12		7	(h)	Stockport C	W 2-0	Stringfellow 2	10,632
13		14	(a)	Aldershot	L 2-4	Wagstaff, R.Chapman	7,336
14		16	(h)	Millwall	D 0-0		12,431
15		21	(h)	Bradford C	L 0-1		8,983
16		28	(a)	Carlisle U	L 0-1		5,099
17	Nov	11	(a)	Chester	W 1-0	Wagstaff	4,168
18		15	(a)	Oldham A	W 3-2	Straw 2, Coates	11,204
19		18	(h)	Tranmere R	L 1-2	Morris (pen)	8,667
20	Dec	2	(h)	Hartlepools U	W 3-1	Morris, Coates, Opp own-goal	6,619
21		16	(a)	Exeter C	L 1-2	R.Chapman	3,592
22		23	(h)	Wrexham	L 1-2	R.Chapman	7,270
23		26	(h)	Rochdale	L 0-1		6,352
24	Jan	12	(a)	Doncaster R	W 1-0	Stringfellow	2,966
25		15	(h)	Colchester U	W 4-0	Humble, Wagstaff, R.Chapman, Morris (pen)	5,880
26		20	(h)	Workington	W 4-1	R.Chapman 2, S.Chapman, Hall	6,243
27	Feb	3	(a)	York C	L 1-2	R.Chapman	5,794
28		10	(h)	Chesterfield	D 2-2	Straw, Morris (pen)	8,249
29		17	(a)	Gillingham	D 2-2	S.Chapman, Straw	5,928
30		23	(a)	Stockport C	L 1-2	Straw	2,961
31	Mar	2	(h)	Aldershot	W 4-1	S.Chapman 3, Wagstaff	5,356
32		5	(a)	Southport	L 1-2	S.Chapman	4,120
33		10	(a)	Bradford C	L 1-6	R.Chapman	5,697
34		17	(h)	Carlisle U	W 5-2	R.Chapman 2, Wagstaff, Morris (2 pen)	5,558
35		19	(a)	Darlington	L 1-3	Hollett	7,578
36		23	(a)	Colchester U	L 0-2		5,730
37		26	(h)	Oldham A	W 2-0	S.Chapman, R.Chapman	5,417
38		30	(h)	Chester	W 3-0	Hall 2, S.Chapman	5,169
39	Apr	7	(a)	Tranmere R	L 0-2		4,385
40		11	(a)	Rochdale	L 2-3	Hollett, Morris (pen)	3,050
41		14	(h)	Southport	W 3-1	R.Chapman 2, Morris (pen)	4,107
42		20	(a)	Crewe A	L 2-3	Wagstaff, R.Chapman	5,343
43		21	(a)	Hartlepools U	W 1-0	Wagstaff	2,059
44		23	(h)	Crewe A	D 1-1	Coates	4,957
45		28	(h)	Darlington	W 3-0	Wagstaff 2, Morris (pen)	5,292

FINAL LEAGUE POSITION: 14th in Division Four — Appearances

NOTE: Home match v Accrington Stanley not played and Match 6 later expunged from the League records. — Goals

FA Cup

1	Nov	4	(h)	Grimsby T	W 3-2	B.Hall 2, Wagstaff	10,127
2		25	(a)	Southport	L 2-4	Straw, Stringfellow	7,311

Appearances

Goals

League Cup

1	Sep	11	(h)	Exeter C	W 5-2	Wagstaff 2, Coates, Straw, Hollett	5,994
2	Oct	5	(h)	Cardiff C	D 1-1	Stringfellow	17,380
R		23	(a)	Cardiff C	L 1-2	Wagstaff	5,800

Appearances

Goals

Bradley DJ*	Chapman RC*	Chapman SEG	Coates DP*	Gill JBA	Hall BS	Hollett I	Humble JW	McGowan J	Morris PJ*	O'Hara D	Phillips BJ*	Richards T	Straw R*	Stringfellow MD*	Toon C*	Treharne C	Wagstaff K*	Williams GR*	Wyllie RG*	
			8				3		6	10	5		9	11	2		7	4	1	1
			8				3		6	10	5		9	11	2		7	4	1	2
	10		8				3		6		5		9	11	2		7	4	1	3
3	10					8			6		5		9	11	2		7	4	1	4
3	10		8						6		5		9	11	2		7	4	1	5
3	10		8						6		5		9	11	2		7	4	1	6
3	10		8						6		5		9	11	2		7	4	1	7
3			4			10		8	6		5		9	11	2		7		1	8
3	10		8						6		5		9	11	2		7	4	1	9
	10		8	3					6		5		9	11	2		7	4	1	10
	10		8	3					6		5		9	11	2		7	4	1	11
3	10		8			9			6		5			11	2		7	4	1	12
3	10		8						6		5		9	11	2		7	4	1	13
3	10		8						6		5		9	11	2	1	7	4		14
3	10					8			6		5		9	11	2	1	7	4		15
			6	3		9				10	5		8	11	2	1	7	4		16
			10	3		9			6		5		8	11	2	1	7	4		17
			10	3	9				6		5		8	11	2	1	7	4		18
			10	3	9				6		5		8	11	2	1	7	4		19
	10		8	3					6		5		9	11	2	1	7	4		20
	10	4	8	3					6		5		9	11	2	1	7			21
	10	8	6	3							5		9	11	2	1	7	4		22
	10	8	6	3	7						5		9	11	2	1		4		23
	9	7	4	3					6		5		8	11	2	1	10			24
	10	8	4				3		6		5		9	11	2	1	7			25
	10	8	4	5	11		3		6				9		2	1	7			26
	10	8	4	5	11		3		6				9		2	1	7			27
	10	8	4	5	11		3		6				9		2	1	7			28
	10	8	6	5			3		7				9		2	1	11	4		29
	10	8	6	5			3		7				9		2	1	11	4		30
	10	8	6				3		7		5		9		2	1	11	4		31
	10	8	6				3		7		5		9		2	1	11	4		32
	10	8	6				3		7		5		9		2	1	11	4		33
	9	8	7			10	3		6		5				2	1	11	4		34
	9		6			10	3	7			5		8		2	1	11	4		35
	9	8	10			11	3	7	6		5				2	1		4		36
	9	8	10		11		3		6		5				2	1	7	4		37
	9	8	10		11		3		6		5				2	1	7	4		38
	9	8	10		11		3		6		5				2	1	7	4		39
	11	8				10	3		6		5		9		2	1	7	4		40
	9	8			11	10	3		6		5				2	1	7	4		41
	9		8	3	11	10			6		5				2	1	7	4		42
	9		8	3	11	10			6		5				2	1	7	4		43
	9		8	3	11	10			6		5				2	1	7	4		44
	9		8		11	10	3		6		5	4			2	1	7			45
10	38	20	41	19	14	15	21	3	41	3	40	1	34	25	45	32	43	37	13	
	20	8	3		3	3	1		10	1			11	4			12			

*Denotes players whose appearance against Accrington Stanley does not appear in their totals following the record being expunged by the Football League.

1 own-goal

			10	3	7				6		5		9	11	2	1	8	4		1
			10	3	9				6		5		8	11	2	1	7	4		2
			2	2	2				2		2		2	2	2	2	2	2		
					2								1	1			1			

3			8			10			6		5		9	11	2		7	4	1	1
3	10		8			9			6		5			11	2		7	4	1	2
3			6			8				10	5		9	11	2	1	7	4		R
3	1		3			3			2	1	3		2	3	3	1	3	3	2	
			1			1							1	1			3			

1962-63

Manager: Raich Carter until 12 January, Tommy Cummings from 18 March 1963.

1	Aug	18	(h)	Rochdale	W	1-0	Wagstaff	6,121
2		22	(a)	Exeter C	W	3-0	Wagstaff 3	5,862
3		25	(a)	Brentford	W	3-1	Straw, Wagstaff, B.Hall	8,350
4		27	(h)	Exeter C	W	1-0	Wagstaff	11,173
5	Sep	1	(h)	York C	W	2-0	R.Chapman 2	10,864
6		8	(a)	Chester C	W	2-0	Morris (pen), R.Chapman	7,775
7		10	(h)	Workington	D	0-0		13,874
8		15	(h)	Crewe A	D	2-2	Wagstaff, R.Chapman	9,731
9		17	(a)	Chesterfield	D	4-4	S.Chapman, Weir, R.Chapman 2 (1 pen)	12,859
10		22	(a)	Gillingham	W	1-0	Wagstaff	11,500
11		29	(h)	Stockport C	L	0-1		9,981
12	Oct	1	(h)	Tranmere R	W	6-1	R.Chapman 3, Hollett 2, Askey	9,596
13		6	(a)	Torquay U	D	3-3	Hollett, R.Chapman, B.Hall	6,241
14		13	(h)	Lincoln C	W	2-0	R.Chapman 2 (1 pen)	12,801
15		20	(a)	Oldham A	L	2-3	R.Chapman, Weir	23,747
16		22	(h)	Chesterfield	W	3-0	Wagstaff 2, Hollett	16,673
17		27	(h)	Barrow	W	5-0	Wagstaff 2, R.Chapman 2, Opp own-goal	8,285
18	Nov	10	(h)	Darlington	W	6-0	Wagstaff 2, R.Chapman, Hollett, Weir, Morris (pen)	7,406
19		17	(a)	Southport	L	2-3	S.Chapman, Morris (pen)	2,254
20	Dec	1	(a)	Newport C	D	1-1	Opp own-goal	5,399
21		8	(h)	Oxford U	W	3-2	Askey, R.Chapman, Morris (pen)	7,729
22		15	(a)	Rochdale	L	1-3	I.Hall	2,735
23		22	(h)	Brentford	L	1-2	Hollett	9,468
24	Mar	9	(h)	Oldham A	W	4-2	Wagstaff 3, B.Hall	7,762
25		14	(a)	Workington	L	2-3	Toon, B.Hall	1,800
26		16	(a)	Barrow	L	2-3	Wagstaff 2	4,010
27		18	(h)	Aldershot	D	2-2	Wagstaff 2	10,579
28		22	(h)	Hartlepools U	W	3-1	R.Chapman 2, Hollett	7,781
29		27	(a)	Lincoln C	W	6-2	Morris, Hollett, R.Chapman, Wagstaff, Coates, Opp own-goal	5,840
30		30	(a)	Aldershot	W	3-2	Wagstaff 2, Coates	6,246
31	Apr	3	(a)	Bradford C	W	3-1	R.Chapman 2, Scanlon	2,796
32		6	(h)	Southport	W	6-1	Wagstaff 4, Coates, Scanlon	9,161
33		8	(h)	Torquay U	L	1-2	Phillips	14,262
34		13	(a)	Darlington	L	1-2	Scanlon	4,136
35		15	(a)	Doncaster R	D	1-1	Coates	8,017
36		16	(h)	Doncaster R	W	4-2	Wagstaff 2, R.Chapman 2	11,657
37		20	(h)	Newport C	W	2-1	R.Chapman 2	6,038
38		22	(a)	Tranmere R	L	1-5	R.Chapman	7,268
39		27	(a)	Oxford U	L	0-3		7,187
40		29	(h)	Bradford C	W	3-1	Wagstaff 2, S.Chapman	8,702
41	May	4	(h)	Gillingham	D	0-0		9,431
42		8	(a)	Crewe A	L	0-3		9,042
43		11	(a)	York C	L	1-2	Hollett	4,914
44		13	(a)	Hartlepools U	W	4-3	R.Chapman 2, Wagstaff, S.Chapman	2,576
45		18	(h)	Chester	W	4-0	Coates, Wagstaff, R.Chapman, Morris (pen)	7,414
46		20	(a)	Stockport C	D	1-1	S.Chapman	3,586

FINAL LEAGUE POSITION: 4th in Division Four

Appearances
Goals

FA Cup

1	Nov	3	(a)	Hounslow	D	3-3	Hollett 2, Wagstaff	6,000
R		5	(h)	Hounslow	W	9-2	Hollett 3, R.Chapman 3, Wagstaff, Askey, Weir	10,543
2		24	(a)	Crystal P	D	2-2	Wagstaff 2	13,414
R		26	(h)	Crystal P	W	7-2	Wagstaff 3, R.Chapman 2, Askey, I.Hall	17,118
3	Jan	9	(h)	Ipswich T	L	2-3	Askey, B.Hall	17,032

Appearances
Goals

League Cup

1	Sep	13	(a)	Halifax T	W	3-2	R.Chapman 2, Hollett	3,871
2		26	(a)	Chester	D	2-2	B.Hall 2	6,159
R	Oct	10	(h)	Chester	L	0-1		8,298

Appearances
Goals

Askey C	Chapman RC	Chapman SE	Coates DP	Cummings TS	Gill JBA	Hall BS	Hall IW	Hollett I	Humble JW	Jones MA	Morris PJ	Phillips AJ	Richards I	Scanlon AJ	Straw C	Toon C	Treharne C	Wagstaff K	Weir J	
7	10	8	4			11			3		6	5				2	1	9		1
7	10	6	4		5	11			3						8	2	1	9		2
7	10	6	4		5	11			3						8	2	1	9		3
7	10	6	4		5	11			3						8	2	1	9		4
7	10	6	4		5	11			3						8	2	1	9		5
7	10		4		5				3		6				8	2	1	9	11	6
7	10		6		5				3				4		8	2	1	9	11	7
7	10		4		3						6	5			8	2	1	9	11	8
7	10	6	4		5				3						8	2	1	9	11	9
7	10	6	4						3			5			8	2	1	9	11	10
7	10	6	4						3			5			8	2	1	9	11	11
7	10	6	4			11		8	3			5				2	1	9		12
7	10	6	4			11		8	3			5			9	2	1			13
7	10	6	4					8	3			5				2	1	9	11	14
7	10		4					8	3		6	5				2	1	9	11	15
7	10		4					8	3		6	5				2	1	9	11	16
7	10		4					8	3		6	5				2	1	9	11	17
7	10	4						8	3		6	5				2	1	9	11	18
7	10	4						8	3		6	5				2	1	9	11	19
7	10	4			5		8		3		6					2	1	9	11	20
7	10	4			5		8		3		6					2	1	9	11	21
7	10	4					8		3		6	5				2	1	9	11	22
7	10	4						8	3		6	5				2	1	9	11	23
7	10	4	8			11			3		6	5				2	1	9		24
	10	4	8			7			3		6	5				2	1	9	11	25
	10	4	8			7			3		6	5				2	1	9	11	26
	10	4	8	2		11	6	7	3			5					1	9		27
7	10	4	6			11	8	9	3			5				2	1			28
	8	4	10				11	7	3		6	5				2	1	9		29
	10	4	8				11	7	3		6	5				2	1	9		30
	10	4	8					7	3		6	5		11		2	1	9		31
	10	4	8			7			3		6	5		11		2	1	9		32
	10	4	8			7			3		6	5		11		2	1	9		33
	10	4	8					7	3		6	5		11		2	1	9		34
	10	4	8		5		7		3		6			11		2	1	9		35
	10	4	8		5		7		3		6			11		2	1	9		36
	10	4	8		5		7		3		6			11		2	1	9		37
	10	4	8		5		7		3		6			11		2	1	9		38
	10	4	8				7		3		6	5		11		2	1	9		39
	10	4	8			11	7		3	2	6	5					1	9		40
	10	4	8				7		3	2	6	5		11			1	9		41
		4	8	5			7	10	3	2	6			11			1	9		42
		8	4	5		7		10		2	6			11		3	1	9		43
	10	4	8	5			7			2	6			11		3	1	9		44
	10	4	8	5				7		2	6			11		3	1	9		45
	10	4	8	5				7		2	6			11		3	1	9		46
25	44	40	40	6	14	16	16	19	41	7	33	28	1	15	11	42	46	44	18	
2	30	5	5			4	1	9			6	1		3	1	1		34	3	

3 own-goals

7	10		4					8	3		6	5				2	1	9	11	1
7	10	4						8	3		6	5				2	1	9	11	R
7	10	4					8		3		6	5				2	1	9	11	2
7	10	4					8		3		6	5				2	1	9	11	R
7	10	4				11		8	3		6	5				2	1	9		3
5	5	4	1			1	2	3	5		5	5				5	5	5	4	
3	5					1	1	5										7	1	

	10		7		3	11		9		2	6	5	4		8		1			1
7	10	6			5	9		8	3	2	4						1		11	2
7	10		4		3	11	8	9		2	6	5					1			R
2	3	1	2		3	3	1	3	1	3	3	2	1		1		3		1	
	2					2		1												

1963-64

Manager: Tommy Cummings

1	Aug	24	(h)	Crewe A	W 2-1	Wagstaff 2	8,813
2		26	(a)	Port Vale	L 0-1		14,541
3		31	(a)	Crystal P	L 1-3	Morris (pen)	14,180
4	Sep	7	(h)	Walsall	W 2-1	Wagstaff, R.Chapman	8,407
5		9	(h)	Port Vale	D 1-1	Bonner	12,064
6		14	(a)	Reading	L 3-4	Wagstaff, R.Chapman 2	6,137
7		16	(h)	Notts C	W 4-0	R.Chapman 3, Scanlon	16,560
8		21	(h)	Luton T	D 1-1	Tyrer	9,565
9		28	(a)	Coventry C	W 3-0	Coates, Wagstaff, Tyrer	22,903
10	Oct	3	(a)	Notts C	L 0-1		14,014
11		5	(a)	Bournemouth	D 0-0		10,884
12		7	(h)	Shrewsbury T	W 3-1	Wagstaff 2, Tyrer	10,374
13		12	(h)	Queen's Park R	W 1-0	Wagstaff	10,869
14		16	(a)	Shrewsbury T	L 0-2		8,535
15		19	(a)	Millwall	W 1-0	R.Chapman	8,348
16		21	(h)	Brentford	D 2-2	Wagstaff 2	12,115
17		26	(h)	Colchester U	D 1-1	Wagstaff	10,278
18		29	(a)	Brentford	L 0-4		14,900
19	Nov	2	(a)	Watford	L 0-3		9,148
20		9	(h)	Southend U	W 4-1	R.Chapman 3, Wagstaff	8,125
21		23	(h)	Oldham A	D 1-1	R.Chapman	9,557
22		30	(a)	Bristol R	L 2-3	R.Chapman, Scanlon	9,104
23	Dec	14	(a)	Crewe A	L 2-3	Wagstaff 2	3,248
24		21	(h)	Crystal P	D 1-1	Scanlon	5,629
25		26	(a)	Hull C	L 1-3	I.Hall	14,132
26		28	(h)	Hull C	W 2-0	Wagstaff, Scanlon	7,790
27	Jan	4	(a)	Peterborough U	W 3-1	Morris, B.Hall 2	8,806
28		11	(a)	Walsall	L 1-3	Wagstaff	4,376
29		18	(h)	Reading	W 2-1	Morris (pen), Scanlon	5,423
30	Feb	1	(a)	Luton T	W 2-0	B.Hall, Wagstaff	6,307
31		8	(h)	Coventry C	W 3-2	R.Chapman 2, B.Hall	16,755
32		15	(h)	Bournemouth	D 1-1	Wagstaff	7,959
33		22	(a)	Queen's Park R	L 0-2		4,780
34		29	(h)	Wrexham	W 3-1	B.Hall, Wagstaff, R.Chapman	5,609
35	Mar	7	(a)	Colchester U	D 1-1	Hollett	3,666
36		9	(h)	Barnsley	W 2-1	B.Hall, Wagstaff	8,687
37		20	(a)	Wrexham	L 0-2		4,059
38		27	(a)	Bristol C	W 3-2	Wagstaff 2, Tyrer	13,914
39		28	(h)	Peterborough U	W 4-1	Wagstaff 2, R.Chapman 2	8,208
40		30	(h)	Bristol C	W 4-0	Coates 3, S.Chapman	8,714
41	Apr	4	(a)	Oldham A	L 0-1		6,460
42		6	(h)	Watford	D 1-1	Wagstaff	11,779
43		11	(h)	Bristol R	W 2-0	Wagstaff, S.Chapman	8,317
44		18	(a)	Barnsley	D 1-1	R.Chapman	5,523
45		20	(a)	Southend U	L 1-2	Wagstaff	6,562
46		25	(h)	Millwall	W 4-1	Wagstaff 2, R.Chapman, Opp own-goal	6,618

FINAL LEAGUE POSITION: 7th in Division Three

Appearances
Goals

FA Cup

1	Nov	20	(a)	Oldham A	L 2-3	I.Hall, R.Chapman	17,337

Appearances
Goals

League Cup

1	Sep	4	(h)	Watford	W 2-1	Bonner, Scanlon	7,975
2		25	(a)	Leeds U	L 1-5	Bonner	9,843

Appearances
Goals

Askey J	Bonner D	Chapman RC	Chapman SE	Coates DP	Cummings TS	Gill JBA	Govan CF	Hall BS	Hall IW	Hollett I	Humble JW	Jones MA	Morris PJ	Richards AJ	Scanlon AJ	Toon C	Treharne C	Tyrer A	Wagstaff K	
7		10	4	8	5						3		6		11	2	1		9	1
7		10	4	8	5						3		6		11	2	1		9	2
		10	4	8	5		7				3		6		11	2	1		9	3
	7	10	4	8	5						3		6		11	2	1		9	4
	7	10	4	8		5		11			3		6			2	1		9	5
	7	10	4	8		5					3		6		11	2	1		9	6
	7	10	4	8		5					3		6		11	2	1		9	7
	7		4	8		5					3		6		11	2	1	10	9	8
	7		4	8		5				10	3		6			2	1	11	9	9
	7		4	8		5				10	3		6			2	1	11	9	10
	7		4	8		5				10	3		6			2	1	11	9	11
	7		4	8		5				10	3		6			2	1	11	9	12
	7			4		5				8	3		6		11	2	1	10	9	13
	7		4	8		5					3		6		11	2	1	10	9	14
7		10	4	8		5					3		6			2	1	11	9	15
7			4	8		5				10	3		6			2	1	11	9	16
7			4	8		5				10	3	2	6				1	11	9	17
	7		4	8		5			10		3	2	6				1	11	9	18
		10	4	8		5				7	3	2	6				1	11	9	19
		10	4	8		5			7		3	2	6		11		1		9	20
		10	4	8					7		3	2	6	5	11		1		9	21
		10	4	8		5			7		3	2	6		11		1		9	22
		10	4	8		5			7		3	2	6		11		1		9	23
		10	4	8		5			7		3	2	6		11		1		9	24
		10	4	8		5			7		3	2	6		11		1		9	25
		10	4			5	8	9			3	2	6		11		1		7	26
		10	4			5	8	9			3	2	6		11		1		7	27
		10	4			5	8	9			3	2	6		11		1		7	28
		9	4			5	8	7			3	2	6		11		1		10	29
		10	4			5	8	7			3	2	6		11		1		9	30
		10	4			5	8	7			3	2	6		11		1		9	31
		10	4			5	8				3	2	6		11		1	7	9	32
		10	4			5	8	7			3	2	6		11		1		9	33
		10	4			5	8	7			3	2	6		11		1		9	34
		10	4			5		7		8	3	2	6		11		1		9	35
		10	4	6		5		7		8	3	2			11		1		9	36
		10	4	8		5					3	2	6		11		1	7	9	37
		10	4	8		5					3	2	6		11		1	7	9	38
		10	4	8		5					3	2	6		11		1	7	9	39
		10	4	8		5					3	2	6		11		1	7	9	40
		10	4	8		5					3	2	6		11		1	7	9	41
		10	4	8		5					3	2	6		11		1	7	9	42
		10	4	8		5					3	2	6		11		1	7	9	43
		10	4	8		5					3	2	6		11		1	7	9	44
		10	4	8		5					3	2	6		11		1	7	9	45
		10	4	8		5					3	2	6		11		1	7	9	46
5	12	36	45	36	4	41	10	11	7	10	46	30	45	1	36	16	46	23	46	
	1	19	2	4				6	1	1			3		5			4	29	

1 own-goal

		10	4	8		5			7		3	2	6		11		1		9	1
		1	1	1		1			1		1	1	1		1		1		1	
		1							1											

	7	8	4	10	5						3		6		11	2	1		9	1
	7		4	8		5					3		6		11	2	1	10	9	2
	2	1	2	2	1	1					2		2		2	2	2	1	2	
	2														1					

1964-65

Manager: Tommy Cummings

1	Aug	22	(a)	Bristol R	L 1-4	Morris	10,621
2		24	(h)	Brentford	W 4-1	Anderson, Wagstaff, Chapman, Scanlon	11,362
3		29	(h)	Oldham A	W 4-1	Morris (pen), Macready, Wagstaff, Hollett	9,384
4		31	(a)	Brentford	L 0-1		10,600
5	Sep	5	(a)	Exeter C	W 3-2	Cooper 2, B.Hall	8,357
6		7	(h)	Colchester U	L 0-1		11,573
7		12	(h)	Bournemouth	D 0-0		7,621
8		14	(a)	Colchester U	W 1-0	Scanlon	3,544
9		19	(a)	Peterborough U	W 5-4	Chapman 2, Scanlon, Wagstaff, Macready	10,256
10		26	(h)	Grimsby T	D 2-2	Macready, Chapman	10,620
11		28	(h)	Port Vale	D 2-2	Graham, Scanlon	10,709
12	Oct	3	(h)	Scunthorpe U	W 3-2	Chapman 2, Wagstaff	7,911
13		5	(a)	Port Vale	D 2-2	B.Hall, Cooper	4,247
14		10	(a)	Watford	L 1-3	Wagstaff	8,051
15		12	(h)	Luton T	W 2-0	Wagstaff, Opp own-goal	8,080
16		17	(h)	Workington	L 3-5	I.Hall, Cooper, Scanlon	7,227
17		21	(a)	Luton T	D 1-1	Anderson	2,874
18		24	(a)	Hull C	D 1-1	Hollett	8,482
19		26	(h)	Barnsley	W 4-3	Anderson, Wagstaff, Graham, Opp own-goal	8,245
20		31	(h)	Gillingham	W 3-1	I.Hall, Wagstaff, Graham	7,065
21	Nov	3	(a)	Shrewsbury T	D 1-1	Wagstaff	5,463
22		7	(a)	Bristol C	D 1-1	Scanlon	9,653
23		28	(h)	Reading	W 2-1	Middleton, Opp own-goal	6,480
24	Dec	12	(h)	Bristol R	W 3-0	Morris, Gregson, Chapman	4,784
25		19	(a)	Oldham A	L 1-2	Chapman	6,310
26		26	(a)	Walsall	L 1-2	Middleton	6,900
27		28	(h)	Walsall	W 2-0	Middleton, Chapman	5,209
28	Jan	2	(h)	Exeter C	W 2-1	Middleton 2	6,768
29		16	(a)	Bournemouth	L 0-2		5,562
30		30	(a)	Southend U	W 4-1	Hall 3, Middleton, Tyrer, Scanlon	5,464
31	Feb	6	(a)	Grimsby T	D 1-1	Macready	6,302
32		12	(a)	Scunthorpe U	W 1-0	Curry	5,903
33		20	(h)	Watford	W 3-0	Curry, Middleton, I.Hall	6,180
34		26	(a)	Workington	W 5-1	Curry 3, Middleton 2	4,414
35	Mar	13	(a)	Gillingham	D 0-0		11,846
36		15	(h)	Queen's Park R	W 8-1	Curry 3, Middleton 3, Gregson, Morris (pen)	9,180
37		20	(h)	Bristol C	W 3-0	Middleton 2, Curry	9,434
38		26	(a)	Queen's Park R	L 0-2		5,400
39		29	(h)	Peterborough U	D 0-0		15,354
40	Apr	3	(h)	Shrewsbury T	W 1-0	Morris	8,894
41		5	(h)	Southend U	W 6-1	Curry 4, Anderson, Morris (pen)	11,552
42		10	(a)	Reading	L 1-2	Curry	5,261
43		17	(h)	Hull C	W 2-1	Middleton 2	19,500
44		19	(h)	Carlisle U	W 2-0	Macready, Curry	13,831
45		20	(a)	Carlisle U	L 0-3		18,000
46		24	(a)	Barnsley	W 3-2	Macready 2, Morris	6,672

FINAL LEAGUE POSITION: 3rd in Division Three

Appearances
Goals

FA Cup

1	Nov	14	(a)	Oxford U	W 1-0	I.Hall	9,765
2	Dec	5	(a)	Newport C	L 0-3		5,304

Appearances
Goals

League Cup

2	Sep	23	(a)	Manchester C	W 5-3	R.Chapman 2, Wagstaff, Tyrer, Macready	8,789
3	Oct	14	(a)	Coventry C	L 2-3	Wagstaff, Scanlon	12,387

Appearances
Goals

Anderson GT	Chapman RC	Cooper JE	Curry WM	Gill JBA	Goven CP	Graham GW	Gregson J	Hall BS	Hall IW	Hollett I	Humble JW	Humphreys A	Jones MA	Middleton H	Morris PJ	Macready BL	Nelson CA	Poynton W	Scanlon AJ	Toon C	Treharne C	Tyrer A	Wagstaff K	
7	10			5		4					3		2		6	8			11		1		9	1
7	10			5		4					3	1	2		6	8			11				9	2
7				5		4				10	3	1	2		6	8			11				9	3
7				5		4				10		1	2		6	8		3	11				9	4
7		10		5		4		11				1	2		6	8		3					9	5
7		10		5		4		11				1	2		6	8		3					9	6
	10			5		4		11				1	2		6	8		3				7	9	7
	10			5		4						1	2		6	8		3	11			7	9	8
	10			5		4						1	2		6	8		3	11			7	9	9
	10			5		4							2		6	8		3	11		1	7	9	10
	10			5		4							2		6	8		3	11		1	7	9	11
	10			5		4							2		6	8		3	11		1	7	9	12
		10		5				3	4						6	8		2	11		1	7	9	13
		9		5				3	4						6	8		2	11		1	7	10	14
	10	9		5				3	4						6			2	11		1	7	8	15
		9		5	10			3	4						6			2	11		1	7	8	16
7		9		5				11	4	10			2		6					3	1		8	17
7				5		9		11	4	10			2		6					3	1		8	18
7				5		9		11	4	10			2		6					3	1		8	19
7	10			5		9			4				2		6				11	3	1		8	20
7	10			5		9			4				2		6				11	3	1		8	21
7	10			5		9			4				2		6				11	3	1		8	22
	10			5		8	7		4				2	9	6				11	3	1			23
	9			5			7		4				2	8	6				11	3	1	10		24
	9			5			7		4				2	8	6				11	3	1	10		25
	9			5			7		4				2	8	6				11	3	1	10		26
	9			5			7		4				2	8	6				11	3	1	10		27
	9			5			7		4				2	8	6				11	3	1	10		28
	9			5			7		4		3			8	6				11	2	1	10		29
				5			7		4				2	9	6	8			11	3	1	10		30
			9	5			7		4				2	10	6	8			11	3	1			31
			9	5			7		4				2	10	6	8			11	3	1			32
			9	5			7		4		3		2	10	6	8			11		1			33
			9	5			7		4		3		2	10	6	8			11		1			34
			9	5			7		4		3		2	10	6	8			11		1			35
			9	5			7		4		3		2	10	6	8			11		1			36
			9	5			7		4		3		2	10	6	8			11		1			37
			9	5			7		4		3		2	10	6	8			11		1			38
			9	5			7		4		3		2	10	6	8			11		1			39
			9	5			7		4		3		2	10	6	8					1	11		40
11			9	5			7		4		3			10	6	8	2				1			41
11			9	5			7		4		3			10	6	8	2				1			42
			9	5			7		4		3			10	6	8	2		11		1			43
			9	5			7		4		3			10	6	8	2		11		1			44
			9	5			7		4		3			10	6	8	2		11		1			45
			9	5			7		4					10	6	8	2		11	3	1			46
14	19	7	16	46	1	18	24	10	34	5	17	8	35	24	46	31	6	13	37	17	38	18	22	
4	9	4	15			3	2	2	4	2				16	7	7			7			1	9	

3 own-goals

7	10	9		5		8			4				2		6				11	3	1			1
	10			5		8	7		4				2	9	6				11	3	1			2
1	2	1		2		2	1		2				2	1	2				2	2	2			
									1															

	10			5		4		11					2		6	8		3			1	7	9	2
		9		5	10			3	4						6			2	11		1	7	8	3
	1	1		2	1	1		2	1				1		2	1		2	1		2	2	2	
	2															1			1			1	2	

1965-66

Manager: Tommy Cummings

1	Aug	21	(h)	Brighton & HA	W 3-1	Curry 2, Morris	7,647
2		25	(a)	Scunthorpe U	W 1-0	Curry	6,742
3		28	(a)	Queen's Park R	W 2-1	Anderson, Middleton	6,405
4	Sep	4	(h)	Bristol R	W 2-0	Curry 2	9,560
5		11	(h)	Hull C	L 1-2	Anderson	14,051
6		14	(a)	Watford	L 1-2	Morris	11,531
7		17	(a)	Reading	L 1-2	Middleton	7,303
8		25	(h)	Exeter C	D 0-0		7,511
9	Oct	2	(a)	Peterborough U	L 2-3	Aldread, Scanlon	8,231
10		9	(a)	Oxford U	L 1-4	Middleton	9,683
11		14	(h)	Watford	D 2-2	Scanlon 2	8,479
12		16	(h)	Swansea T	W 3-0	Middleton, Scanlon, Lee (pen)	6,767
13		23	(a)	Walsall	L 1-2	Middleton	9,334
14		30	(h)	Workington	L 0-1		5,679
15	Nov	6	(a)	Bournemouth	D 2-2	Macready, Curry	5,005
16		20	(a)	Swindon T	L 2-6	Curry 2	12,001
17	Dec	11	(h)	Brentford	W 2-0	Curry, Scanlon	3,627
18	Jan	1	(h)	Oxford U	L 1-4	Middleton	5,194
19		8	(a)	Southend U	L 0-1		7,213
20		15	(h)	Walsall	L 0-3		4,027
21		29	(a)	Brighton & HA	L 4-6	Anderson 2, Macready, Aldread	13,068
22	Feb	5	(h)	Queen's Park R	W 2-1	Anderson, Macready	4,166
23		19	(a)	Bristol R	L 0-6		7,477
24		21	(h)	Oldham A	D 1-1	Middleton	5,787
25		26	(a)	Hull C	L 0-4		28,214
26	Mar	1	(a)	Swansea T	W 2-1	Anderson, Mitchinson	8,887
27		5	(a)	Oldham A	D 1-1	Anderson	10,239
28		7	(h)	Scunthorpe U	D 2-2	Curry, Middleton	6,681
29		12	(h)	Reading	L 0-2		4,722
30		14	(h)	Gillingham	D 0-0		5,248
31		19	(a)	Exeter C	D 2-2	Morris, Hall	5,050
32		21	(h)	Shrewsbury T	L 0-3		5,753
33		26	(h)	Peterborough U	L 1-7	Mallinson	3,545
34	Apr	8	(a)	York C	L 1-2	Curry	3,253
35		9	(a)	Grimsby T	W 1-0	Macready	4,016
36		11	(h)	York C	W 4-1	Mitchinson 2, Anderson, Aldread	4,231
37		16	(h)	Swindon T	L 1-5	Gregson	3,764
38		22	(a)	Shrewsbury T	L 1-2	Mitchinson	3,585
39		25	(h)	Millwall	D 1-1	Scanlon	5,710
40		30	(h)	Grimsby T	W 2-1	Curry, Anderson	4,961
41	May	3	(a)	Gillingham	L 0-2		6,127
42		7	(a)	Brentford	W 3-0	Gregson, Curry, Mitchinson	7,970
43		9	(h)	Southend U	W 2-0	Gregson, Morris	6,545
44		16	(a)	Millwall	L 0-2		15,980
45		23	(h)	Bournemouth	W 1-0	Curry	6,285
46		27	(a)	Workington	L 0-2		2,261

FINAL LEAGUE POSITION: 19th in Division Three

Appearances
Sub Appearances
Goals

FA Cup

1	Nov	13	(h)	Oldham A	L 1-3	Macready	6,914

Appearances
Goals

League Cup

1	Sep	22	(h)	Birmingham C	W 2-1	Middleton, Scanlon	9,344
2	Oct	13	(a)	West Ham U	L 0-4		11,550

Appearances
Goals

Aldread P	Anderson GT	Burns NJ	Cheeseborough A	Curry WM	Curtin D	Gill JBA	Gregson J	Hall IW	Humble JW	Humphreys A	Jones MA	Lee R	Mallinson D	Middleton H	Mitchinson TW	Morris PJ	Macready BL	Nelson CA	Poynton W	Richardson W	Scanlon AJ	Toon C	Treharne C	Williams WT	
	7		10	9		5		4	3					8		6		2			11		1		1
	7		10	9		5		4	3					8		6		2			11		1		2
	7		10	9		5		4	3					8		6		2			11		1		3
	7		10	9		5		4	3					8		6		2			11		1		4
	7		10	9		5		4	3		2			8		6					11		1		5
	7		10	9		5		4	3		2			11		6			8				1		6
				9		5		4	3					10		6	7	2	8		11		1		7
9						5	7	4	3					8		6	10	2			11		1		8
9			10			5	7	4	3					8*		6	12	2			11		1		9
	10					5	7	4	3					9		6	8	2			11		1		10
				9		5	7	4	3			6				10	8	2			11		1		11
	7			9		5		4	3			6		8		10		2			11		1		12
	7*			9		5		4	3			12		8		6		2	10		11		1		13
	7*		10	9		5		4	3					8		6		2		12	11		1		14
	7		11	9		5		4	3							6	8	2	10				1		15
				9		5	7			1		6		8		4		2	10	3	11				16
				9		5	7	4		1	2			10		6	8			3	11				17
				9		5	7	4		1	2			10		6	8			3	11				18
				9	11		7	4			2			10	8	6				3			1	5	19
				9	11		7	4			2			10	8	6				3			1	5	20
9	7		6		11										10	4	8	2		3			1	5	21
9	7		6			12	11	4	3*	1					10		8	2						5	22
9	7		6					4		1				11	10		8	2		3				5	23
8		7	6	9							2			11	10	4						3	1	5	24
8		7	6	9							2			11	10	4						3	1	5	25
	7		6	9			11	8			2				10	4						3	1	5	26
	7		6	9			11	8			2				10	4						3	1	5	27
	7		6*	9			11	8	3		2			12	10	4							1	5	28
	7			9			11	4	3		2				10	6	8						1	5	29
	7			9				8	3		2		4		10	6					11		1	5	30
9	7						11	8	3		2		4		10	6							1	5	31
	7	9					11	8					4		10	6		2				3	1	5	32
	7	8					11	9					4		10	6		2				3	1	5	33
		10		9			11	4	3				8		7	6		2					1	5	34
				9			7	4		1	2				10	6	8	3			11			5	35
12	11			9			7	4		1	2				10	6	8*	3						5	36
9	11	12					7	4*		1	2				10	6	8	3						5	37
	11			9			7	4	3	1					10	6	8	2						5	38
			6	9			7	4		1					10		8	2			11	3		5	39
	11			9			7*	4		1	6		12		10		8	2				3		5	40
	11			9			7	4		1	6				8		10	2				3		5	41
	11*	12		9			7	4		1			6		10			2	8	3				5	42
	11			9			7	4		1			6		10	8		2		3				5	43
				9			7	4		1			6		10	8		2		3	11			5	44
			11	9			7	4		1			6		10	8		2		3				5	45
7*			6	9			11			1			4		10	12		2	8	3				5	46
10	29	5	20	36	3	18	30	41	22	17	19	3	10	21	28	39	18	32	7	12	20	9	29	28	
1		2				1						1	1	1		1	1			1					
3	9			14			3	1				1	1	8	5	4	4				6				

			11	9		5		4	3					7		6	8	2	10				1		1
			1	1		1		1	1					1		1	1	1	1				1		
																	1								

			10	9		5	7	4	3					8		6		2			11		1		1
			10			5	7	4	3					9		6	8	2			11		1		2
			2	1		2	2	2	2					2		2	1	2			2		2		
														1							1				

1966-67

Manager: Tommy Cummings

1	Aug	20	(a)	Walsall	W 2-1	Curry 2	10,287
2		27	(h)	Peterborough U	D 0-0		6,036
3	Sep	3	(a)	Torquay U	W 2-1	Brace 2	5,413
4		4	(h)	Oldham A	L 2-4	Hall 2	9,776
5		10	(h)	Brighton & HA	W 2-1	Brace, Hall	5,175
6		17	(a)	Darlington	D 1-1	Curry	7,033
7		24	(h)	Queen's Park R	L 1-7	Brace	6,262
8		27	(a)	Oldham A	D 0-0		14,687
9	Oct	1	(a)	Watford	W 1-0	Curry	5,219
10		8	(h)	Oxford U	D 1-1	Morris (pen)	5,023
11		15	(a)	Bristol R	D 4-4	Rowland 2, Mitchinson, Brace	7,599
12		17	(h)	Doncaster R	W 3-1	McKinney, Brace, Mitchinson	8,257
13		22	(h)	Colchester U	W 2-0	Mitchinson, Brace	6,028
14		29	(a)	Shrewsbury T	L 0-1		4,925
15		31	(h)	Torquay U	W 4-2	Curry, Brace, Mitchinson, Morris (pen)	6,101
16	Nov	5	(h)	Middlesbrough	L 4-5	Ferns, Curry 2, Morris (pen)	6,379
17		12	(a)	Swansea T	W 1-0	Brace	5,563
18		15	(a)	Doncaster R	W 6-4	Brace 2, Morris, McKinney, Curry 2	7,188
19		19	(h)	Bournemouth	W 1-0	Rowland	6,681
20	Dec	3	(h)	Gillingham	W 4-1	Rowland 2, Mitchinson, Brace	6,158
21		10	(a)	Workington	W 4-2	Curry 2, Brace 2	2,118
22		17	(h)	Walsall	W 4-1	Curry 2, Mitchinson, Morris (pen)	8,782
23		23	(a)	Scunthorpe U	L 1-2	Brace	6,263
24		27	(h)	Scunthorpe U	W 3-1	Rowland 2, Morris (pen)	10,292
25		31	(a)	Peterborough U	L 1-3	Curry	5,000
26	Jan	14	(a)	Brighton & HA	L 0-1		13,591
27		21	(h)	Darlington	D 2-2	Brace, Morris	7,639
28	Feb	4	(a)	Queen's Park R	D 0-0		14,728
29		11	(h)	Watford	W 2-1	Curry, Morris (pen)	11,291
30		22	(h)	Reading	W 4-2	Curry 2, Mitchinson, Morris	6,823
31		25	(a)	Oxford U	L 1-2	Morris (pen)	8,155
32	Mar	4	(h)	Bristol R	W 2-0	Morris, Mitchinson	12,813
33		11	(a)	Reading	D 2-2	Curry, Morris (pen)	5,972
34		18	(a)	Colchester U	L 0-3		4,175
35		24	(a)	Grimsby T	W 2-1	Rowland, Knox	10,145
36		25	(h)	Shrewsbury T	L 0-1		10,192
37		28	(h)	Grimsby T	W 4-0	Brace 2, Mitchinson, Opp own-goal	11,734
38	Apr	1	(a)	Middlesbrough	L 0-1		23,226
39		8	(h)	Swansea T	L 1-2	Curry	7,483
40		11	(a)	Swindon T	L 1-3	Curry	13,280
41		15	(a)	Bournemouth	W 3-1	Brace 2, Morris (pen)	5,122
42		22	(h)	Leyton O	D 1-1	Curry	8,881
43		24	(h)	Swindon T	L 1-3	Brace	7,837
44		29	(a)	Gillingham	L 2-5	Curry, Knox	4,880
45	May	6	(h)	Workington	L 0-1		3,486
46		12	(a)	Leyton O	L 2-4	Rowland, Mitchinson	4,918

FINAL LEAGUE POSITION: 9th in Division Three

Appearances
Sub Appearances
Goals

FA Cup

1	Nov	26	(h)	Bangor City	W 4-1	Curry 2, Brace, Mitchinson	6,470
2	Jan	7	(h)	Scunthorpe U	W 2-1	Brace, Mitchinson	9,446
3		28	(h)	Middlesbrough	W 2-0	Brace, Curry	17,332
4	Feb	18	(a)	Sheffield W	L 0-4		49,049

Appearances
Sub Appearances
Goals

League Cup

1	Aug	24	(a)	Notts C	D 1-1	Williams	7,002
R		29	(h)	Notts C	W 3-1	Brace 2, Burns	6,081
2	Sep	13	(a)	Wolves	L 1-2	Curry	12,098

Appearances
Sub Appearances
Goals

Aldread P	Boam SW	Brace SC	Burns NJ	Cheeseborough A	Coleman JH	Curry WM	Derco TF	Edwards RT	Ferns P	Gregson J	Hall IW	Hollins DM	Humphreys A	Knox T	McGeorge JL	Mitchinson TW	McKinney W	Morris PJ	Oldham J	Richardson W	Rowland JD	Williams WT	Wilson A	
		7		10		9			6	11			1			8	2	4		3		5		1
		7				9			6	11	10		1			8	2	4		3		5		2
		7	10			9			6	11			1			8	2	4		3		5		3
		7				9			6	11	10		1			8	2	4		3		5		4
		7				9			6	11	10		1			8	2	4		3		5		5
		7			2	9			6	11	8		1			10	5	4		3				6
		7			2	9			6	11	8		1			10	5	4		3				7
		7			2	9			6	11*	8		1		12	10	5	4		3				8
		7			2	9			6	11	8		1			10	5	4		3				9
		7			2				6	11	8		1			10	5	4		3	9			10
		7			4	9			6		8		1			10	2			3	11	5		11
		7			4	9				11	6					10	2			3	8	5	1	12
		7			4	9	6			11						10	2			3	8	5	1	13
		7			4	9			6		10					8	2			3	11	5	1	14
		7			4	9			3		8					10	2	6			11	5	1	15
		7			4	9			3	11	8				12	10	2	6				5*	1	16
		7		6	2	9			3	11	8		1			10	5	4						17
		7		6	2	9			3	11	8		1			10	5	4						18
		7		6	2	9			3		8		1		12	10*	5	4			11			19
		7			2	9			6		8		1			10	5	4		3	11			20
		7			2	9			6		8		1			10	5	4		3	11			21
		7			2	9			6		8		1			10	5	4		3	11			22
		7			2	9			6*		8		1			10	5	4		3	11	12		23
		7			2	9			6		8		1			10	5	4		3	11			24
		7			2	9			4		8		1			10	5	6		3*	11	12		25
		7				9			6	11	8		1			10	2	4		3		5		26
		7				9			6		8		1			10	2	4		3	11	5		27
		7			11	9			6		8		1			10	2	4		3		5		28
		7			2	9			6	11	8		1			10		4		3		5		29
		7			2	9			6	11	8		1			10	5	4		3				30
		7*	12		2	9			6	11	8	1				10	5	4		3				31
		7			2	9			6	11	8	1				10	5	4		3				32
		7			2	9			6		8	1		11		10	5	4		3				33
		7				9		2	6		8	1		11		10	5	4		3				34
						9		2	6		8	1		11		10	5	4		3	7			35
		12				9		2	6		8*	1		11		10	5	4		3	7			36
		7				9		2	6			1		11	8	10	5	4		3				37
		7				9		2	6			1		11	8	10	5	4		3				38
		7				9		2	6			1		11	8	10	5	4		3				39
		7				9		2	6		8		1	11	12	10	5*	4		3				40
		7			2	9		5	6			1		11	8	10		4		3				41
		7			2	9		5	6			1		11	8	10		4		3				42
8*		7	2			9		5	6	12		1		11		10		4		3				43
		7			2	8		5	6			1		11		10		4		3	9			44
		7			2	9		5	6				1	11		10		4		3	8			45
	5	11				9		4	6	7			1*			10	2		12	3	8			46
1	1	44	2	4	30	45	1	13	44	21	34	13	28	13	5	46	40	41		41	19	15	5	
		1	1							1					4				1			2		
		21				22			1		3			2		10	2	13			9			

1 own-goal

Aldread P	Boam SW	Brace SC	Burns NJ	Cheeseborough A	Coleman JH	Curry WM	Derco TF	Edwards RT	Ferns P	Gregson J	Hall IW	Hollins DM	Humphreys A	Knox T	McGeorge JL	Mitchinson TW	McKinney W	Morris PJ	Oldham J	Richardson W	Rowland JD	Williams WT	Wilson A	
		7		6	2	9			3		8		1			10	5	4			11			1
		7			4	9			6		8					10	2			3	11	5	1	2
		7			11	9			6		8		1			10	2	4		3		5		3
		7			11	9			6		8		1			10	2	4		3		5		4
		4		1	4	4			4		4		3			4	4	3		3	2	3	1	
		3				3										2								

Aldread P	Boam SW	Brace SC	Burns NJ	Cheeseborough A	Coleman JH	Curry WM	Derco TF	Edwards RT	Ferns P	Gregson J	Hall IW	Hollins DM	Humphreys A	Knox T	McGeorge JL	Mitchinson TW	McKinney W	Morris PJ	Oldham J	Richardson W	Rowland JD	Williams WT	Wilson A	
		7		10*	12	9			6	11			1			8	2	4		3		5		1
		7	10			9			6	11			1			8	2	4		3		5		R
		7			12	9			6	11	8		1			10	2	4*		3		5		2
		3	1	1		3			3	3	1		3			3	3	3		3		3		
					2																			
		2	1			1																1		

1967-68

Manager: Tom Eggleston

1	Aug	19	(h)	Southport	W 4-2	Morris 2, Brace, Rowland	5,467
2		25	(a)	Scunthorpe U	D 3-3	Curry, Knox, Opp own-goal	6,137
3	Sep	2	(h)	Oldham A	D 1-1	Knox	6,718
4		5	(a)	Northampton T	D 1-1	Brace	12,206
5		9	(a)	Bristol R	L 0-2		7,317
6		16	(h)	Barrow	L 1-2	Curry	5,550
7		23	(a)	Oxford U	L 0-2		6,515
8		25	(h)	Northampton T	W 3-2	J.Rowlands 2, Knox	5,506
9		30	(h)	Bury	D 1-1	Rowland	7,397
10	Oct	2	(a)	Peterborough U	L 0-2		9,045
11		7	(h)	Tranmere R	L 0-3		6,493
12		13	(a)	Stockport C	L 0-1		8,030
13		21	(h)	Brighton & HA	L 1-3	Morris	5,231
14		25	(h)	Peterborough U	L 2-3	Rowland, Stanton	5,123
15		28	(a)	Shrewsbury T	L 1-2	Brace	5,660
16	Nov	4	(h)	Swindon T	D 2-2	Brace, Rowland	4,619
17		11	(a)	Reading	L 1-2	Rowland	8,087
18		14	(a)	Oldham A	L 0-1		7,691
19		18	(h)	Torquay U	W 2-0	Melling, Rowland	5,295
20		25	(a)	Grimsby T	D 0-0		3,074
21	Dec	2	(h)	Gillingham	L 0-1		5,403
22		16	(a)	Southport	L 1-3	Morris (pen)	4,191
23		23	(h)	Scunthorpe U	W 3-0	Jones, Rowland, Morris (pen)	4,907
24		26	(h)	Colchester U	W 2-1	Jones, Ledger	6,679
25		30	(a)	Colchester U	W 2-1	Jones 2	4,180
26	Jan	20	(a)	Barrow	W 1-0	Jones	6,246
27	Feb	3	(h)	Oxford U	W 1-0	Morris (pen)	6,111
28		10	(a)	Bury	L 1-3	Morris	9,399
29		17	(h)	Bournemouth	D 1-1	Melling	6,093
30		23	(a)	Tranmere R	D 1-1	Ledger	6,750
31	Mar	2	(h)	Stockport C	W 1-0	Ledger	6,455
32		9	(h)	Watford	L 1-2	Edwards	6,629
33		11	(h)	Bristol R	W 3-0	Coleman, Melling, Partridge	6,377
34		16	(a)	Brighton & HA	L 0-3		7,756
35		19	(a)	Watford	W 2-1	Sharkey 2	7,325
36		23	(h)	Shrewsbury T	L 0-1		6,701
37		30	(a)	Swindon T	D 1-1	Jones	10,248
38	Apr	6	(h)	Reading	D 2-2	Melling 2	5,661
39		13	(a)	Torquay U	W 2-0	J.Rowlands, Jones	10,618
40		15	(a)	Orient	D 0-0		6,772
41		16	(h)	Orient	D 0-0		6,566
42		20	(h)	Grimsby T	D 1-1	Jones	6,277
43		23	(a)	Walsall	L 1-2	Ledger	5,598
44		27	(a)	Gillingham	L 1-2	Opp own-goal	4,008
45	May	4	(h)	Walsall	L 0-3		5,072
46		11	(a)	Bournemouth	L 0-3		4,588

FINAL LEAGUE POSITION: 21st in Division Three (escaped relegation because Peterborough United went into Division Four after the Football League found them guilty of making illegal payments).

Appearances
Sub Appearances
Goals

FA Cup

1	Dec	13	(a)	Tow Law	L 1-5	Melling	2,508

Appearances
Sub Appearances
Goals

League Cup

1	Aug	23	(h)	Lincoln C	L 2-3	Mitchinson, Knox	6,030

Appearances
Sub Appearances
Goals

Boam SW	Brace SC	Coleman JH	Curry WM	Edwards RT	Ferns P	Frude RG	Glover GJ	Goodfellow JB	Hall IW	Hollins DM	Humphreys A	Jones DAB	Knox T	Ledger RH	Melling T	McKinney W	Mitchinson TW	Morris PJ	Partridge M	Pate AM	Richardson W	Roberts DE	Rowland JD	Rowlands JH	Sharkey D	Stanton T	Waller P	Williams WT	
	7			9	6					1			11			2	10	4			3		8					5	1
	7		9	2	6					1			11			5	10	4			3		8						2
10	7		9	4	6					1			11			2					3		8					5	3
10	7	2	9	4	6					1			11					8			3							5	4
4	7			10	6					1			11			2		8			3		9					5	5
5	7		9	4	6					1			11			2		8			3		10						6
5	12	8*		6	3		10			1			11			2		4					7	9					7
5	7			6	3		10			1			11			2		4					8	9					8
5				6		8	10			1			11			2		4					7	9		3			9
5				6		9	10		8		1		11			2		4					7			3			10
5				6	3	8	10				1		11			12		4*					7	9		2			11
8				6		10	7				1		11			5		4		2				9		3			12
4'	7			10			6				1		11			5		8		2				9		3			13
5	7			6		8	12		10	1			11*					4		2			9			3			14
5	7			6		10	11		4	1								8		2	3		9						15
5	7*			6			10		4	1			11					8		2	12		9			3			16
5				6			7		10	1			11					4		2			8	9		3			17
5				6			7		10	1			11					4		2			8	9		3			18
5				6		10	7			1			11		8*			4		2			9	12		3			19
5				6		10	7			1			11		8			4		2			9			3			20
5			9	6		10				1			11		8			4		2			7			3			21
5				6			7		10	1			11		8			4			3		9			2			22
5				6					10	1		7		9	8			4		2			11			3			23
5				6					10	1		7		9	8			4		2			11			3			24
5				6					10	1		7		9	8			4		2			11			3			25
5					6				10		1	7		9	8			4		2			11			3			26
5				6					10	1		7		9	8			4		2			11			3			27
5				6					10	1		7		9	8			4		2			11			3			28
5				6		10				1		7		9	8			4		2			11			3			29
5				6			10			1		7		9	8			4		2			11			3			30
5				6	12	10	4			1		7		9	8					2			11*			3			31
5		4		6		10				1		7		9	8					2			11			3			32
5		4		10	6					1		11		9	7				8	2						3			33
5								10		1		11		9	7					2		6			8	3	4		34
5		11						10		1					7				9	2		6			8	3	4		35
5		7*						11		1				12	10				8	2		6			9	3	4		36
5		4						11		1		9			10				7	2					8	3	6		37
5		6						11		1		9		7	10					2					8	3	4		38
5		4						11		1		10			7					2				9	8	3	6		39
5		4						11		1		10			7					2				9	8	3	6		40
5		4						11		1		10			7					2		12		9*	8	3	6		41
5		4					7	11		1		10								2		12		9*	8	3	6		42
5								11		1		7		9	8					2		4			10	3	6		43
5								11		1		7		9	8					2		6			10	3	4		44
5										1		7		12	10				8	2		6	11		9*	3	4		45
5		4					7	11		1		9			10					2					8	3	6		46
44	11	13	5	32	11	12	18	12	13	41	5	22	21	15	27	11	2	29	5	34	8	6	30	12	13	37	13	4	
	1				1		1							2		1					1	2		1					
	4	1	2	1								8	3	4	5			7	1				7	3	2	1			

2 own-goals

5			9	6		10				1			11		8			4		2			7			3			1
1			1	1		1				1			1		1			1		1			1			1			
															1														

	7	2	9	6						1			11				10	4			3		8					5	1
	1	1	1	1						1			1				1	1			1		1					1	
													1				1												

1968-69

Manager: Tom Eggleston

1	Aug	10	(a)	Brighton & HA	W 2-1	Sharkey 2	9,647
2		17	(h)	Torquay U	W 2-1	Melling, Goodfellow	6,686
3		24	(a)	Orient	L 0-1		7,087
4		26	(h)	Southport	W 3-1	Ledger, Melling, Goodfellow	7,708
5		31	(h)	Tranmere R	D 1-1	Jones	7,172
6	Sep	7	(h)	Oldham A	W 4-0	Ledger 2, Goodfellow, Roberts	6,718
7		14	(a)	Barrow	L 0-3		4,742
8		18	(a)	Luton T	L 2-4	Partridge, Jones	19,315
9		21	(h)	Rotherham U	L 0-1		10,023
10		28	(a)	Gillingham	D 1-1	Sharkey	4,630
11	Oct	4	(a)	Hartlepool	D 1-1	Quigley	5,776
12		7	(a)	Southport	L 2-3	Keeley 2	3,740
13		12	(h)	Bournemouth	W 3-1	Ledger 2, Jones	5,094
14		18	(a)	Crewe A	L 1-2	Jones	4,500
15		26	(h)	Bristol R	D 0-0		5,068
16	Nov	2	(a)	Reading	L 1-2	Partridge	5,522
17		6	(a)	Plymouth A	L 0-1		6,603
18		9	(h)	Northampton T	L 0-2		4,635
19		23	(h)	Swindon T	W 2-0	Roberts, Ledger	5,471
20		30	(a)	Shrewsbury T	D 1-1	Roberts	2,594
21	Dec	14	(a)	Bournemouth	L 1-2	Ledger	6,506
22		21	(h)	Crewe A	W 2-1	Keeley, Ledger	6,337
23		26	(h)	Hartlepool	W 2-0	Ledger, Roberts	6,683
24	Jan	11	(h)	Reading	D 1-1	Sharkey	6,935
25		18	(a)	Northampton T	D 0-0		5,840
26	Feb	1	(h)	Stockport C	D 0-0		13,301
27		22	(a)	Watford	L 1-2	Roberts	13,347
28	Mar	1	(h)	Brighton & HA	W 3-2	Hopkinson, Sharkey, Opp own-goal	13,595
29		10	(a)	Stockport C	D 1-1	Sharkey	6,027
30		15	(h)	Orient	L 0-2		5,460
31		21	(a)	Tranmere R	L 1-2	Quigley	3,829
32		25	(a)	Bristol R	L 2-6	Partridge, Goodfellow	5,482
33		28	(a)	Oldham A	D 2-2	Roberts, Keeley	4,037
34	Apr	11	(a)	Walsall	L 1-3	Sharkey	5,285
35		5	(h)	Gillingham	W 2-0	Roberts, Sharkey (pen)	4,959
36		7	(h)	Luton T	W 1-0	Sharkey (pen)	8,681
37		8	(a)	Barnsley	L 0-2		8,248
38		12	(a)	Rotherham U	L 0-3		6,645
39		14	(h)	Barnsley	D 0-0		6,236
40		19	(h)	Barrow	W 4-2	Roberts 2, Sharkey, Goodfellow	5,166
41		22	(a)	Swindon T	L 0-1		21,045
42		25	(h)	Walsall	W 2-1	Waller, Sharkey	5,836
43		28	(h)	Plymouth A	W 1-0	Goodfellow	7,144
44		30	(a)	Torquay U	W 1-0	Boam	5,691
45	May	5	(h)	Watford	W 3-0	Sharkey 2, Opp own-goal	8,574
46		9	(h)	Shrewsbury T	L 1-2	Roberts	5,716

FINAL LEAGUE POSITION: 15th in Division Three

Appearances
Sub Appearances
Goals

FA Cup

1	Nov	16	(h)	Tow Law	W 4-1	Ledger 2, Keeley, Sharkey	6,361
2	Dec	7	(a)	Rotherham U	D 2-2	Keeley, Sharkey	10,379
R		9	(h)	Rotherham U	W 1-0	Ledger	12,876
3	Jan	4	(h)	Sheffield U	W 2-1	Roberts 2	17,430
4		25	(h)	Southend U	W 2-1	Roberts, Sharkey	16,160
5	Feb	26	(h)	West Ham U	W 3-0	Keeley, Sharkey, Roberts	21,117
6	Mar	8	(h)	Leicester C	L 0-1		23,500

Appearances
Sub Appearances
Goals

League Cup

1	Aug	14	(a)	Lincoln C	L 1-2	Keeley	8,440

Appearances
Sub Appearances
Goals

Boam SW	Finch D	Frude RG	Goodfellow J	Hollins DM	Hopkinson ME	Jones DAB	Keeley R	Ledger RH	Melling T	Partridge M	Pate AM	Quigley J	Roberts DE	Sharkey D	Todd RC	Walker M	Waller P	
5			11	1	3		7	9	10		2	4		8			6	1
5			11	1	3		8		10	7		4	2	9			6	2
5		10*	11	1	3	12	7		9			4	2	8			6	3
5			11	1	3	7	12	9	10			4	2	8*			6	4
5			11	1	3	7	8	9	10			4	2				6	5
5			11	1	3	7		9	10			4	2	8			6	6
5			11	1	3		7	9		8		4	2	10			6	7
5		7	10	1	3	11		9		8		4	2				6	8
5				1	3	11	7	8		10*	2	4	9	12			6	9
5				1	3	11	7	9*		12	2	10	4	8			6	10
5				1	3	11	7	9			2	10	4	8			6	11
5			11	1	3*	9	7	12			2	10	4	8			6	12
5			11	1	3	10	7	9			2	4		8			6	13
5			11	1	3	10	7	9			2	4	6	8				14
5			11	1	3	7		9			2	10	4	8			6	15
5				1	3	11	8	9		7	2	10	4				6	16
5				1	3	11	8			9	2	10	4		7		6	17
5			11	1	3*	10		9		12	2	8	4		7		6	18
5			11	1	3		7	9			2	10	4	8			6	19
5			11	1	3		7	9			2	10	4	8*	12		6	20
5			11	1	3	10	7	9			2	4		8			6	21
5			11	1	3		7	9			2	4	10	8			6	22
5			11	1	3		7	9			2	4	10	8			6	23
5			11	1	3		7	9			2	4	10	8			6	24
5			11	1	3		7	9			2	4	10	8			6	25
5			11	1	3		7	9			2	4	10	8			6	26
5			11	1	3	12	7	9			2	4	10*	8			6	27
5			11	1	3		7	9			2	4	10	8			6	28
5			11	1	3	12	7	9			2	4	10*	8			6	29
5			11	1	3	10		9		7	2	4		8			6	30
5	1		11		3		7	9			2	4	10	8			6	31
5	1		10			11	7			8	2	4	3	9			6	32
5				1	3	12	11			8	2	4	10	9*		7	6	33
5				1	3		11			8	2	4	10	9		7	6	34
5			11	1	3		7			8	2	4	10	9			6	35
5			11	1	3	8	7				2	4	10	9			6	36
5		12	11*	1	3	8	7				2	4	10	9			6	37
5			11	1	3		7			9	2	4	10	8			6	38
5			11	1	3		7	9			2	4	10	8			6	39
5			11	1	3		7	9			2	4	10	8			6	40
5			11	1			12	3		9	2	4	10	8*	7		6	41
5			11	1	3			9		7	2	4	10	8			6	42
5			11	1	3		12	9*		7	2	4	10	8			6	43
5			11	1	3		7			9	2	4	10	8			6	44
5			11	1	3		7	9			2	4	10	8			6	45
5			11	1	3		7	9			2	4	10	8			6	46
46	2	2	39	44	44	19	37	34	6	16	39	46	42	40	3	2	45	
		1				4	3	1		2				1	1			
1			6		1	4	4	9	2	3		2	10	13			1	
																		2 own-goals
5			11	1	3		7	9			2	10	4	8			6	1
5			11	1	3		7	9			2	10	4	8			6	2
5			11	1	3		7	9			2	10	4	8			6	R
5			11	1	3		7	9			2	4	10	8			6	3
5			11	1	3	12	7	9*			2	4	10	8			6	4
5			11	1	3		7	9			2	4	10	8			6	5
5			11	1	3		7	9			2	4	10	8			6	6
7			7	7	7		7	7			7	7	7	7			7	
						1												
							3	3					4	4				
5			11	1	3		8		10	7	2*	4	12	9			6	1
1			1	1	1		1		1	1	1	1		1			1	
													1					
							1											

1969-70

Manager: Tom Eggleston

1	Aug	9	(h)	Gillingham	W	1-0	Partridge	6,034
2		16	(a)	Doncaster R	L	0-2		10,960
3		23	(h)	Walsall	D	0-0		6,696
4		26	(a)	Rotherham U	D	2-2	Stenson, Roberts	6,266
5		30	(a)	Orient	L	0-1		6,018
6	Sep	6	(h)	Bradford C	W	2-1	Ledger, Goodfellow	6,895
7		13	(a)	Barrow	W	1-0	Sharkey	4,755
8		15	(h)	Brighton & HA	W	1-0	Ledger	6,804
9		20	(h)	Bristol R	D	1-1	Sharkey	6,742
10		27	(a)	Shrewsbury T	D	0-0		3,801
11		30	(a)	Bury	L	0-1		3,302
12	Oct	4	(h)	Plymouth A	L	1-2	Opp own-goal	6,443
13		6	(h)	Doncaster R	L	1-2	Roberts	9,454
14		11	(a)	Stockport C	W	3-1	Jones 2, Roberts	4,409
15		18	(h)	Reading	W	2-1	Boam, Jones	5,174
16		25	(a)	Halifax T	W	2-1	Keeley, Jones	3,625
17	Nov	1	(h)	Tranmere R	L	1-2	Bates	5,965
18		3	(h)	Rochdale	L	1-2	Bates	4,588
19		8	(a)	Southport	W	1-0	Stenson	2,088
20		22	(a)	Fulham	D	1-1	Stenson	8,088
21		24	(a)	Rochdale	L	1-2	Roberts	6,833
22	Dec	13	(h)	Barrow	W	4-2	Roberts 2, Bates, Goodfellow (pen)	5,068
23		26	(a)	Walsall	L	0-1		7,499
24		27	(h)	Orient	W	4-1	Roberts 2, Stenson, Opp own-goal	7,828
25	Jan	10	(a)	Bristol R	L	1-4	Roberts	5,896
26		17	(h)	Shrewsbury T	W	2-0	Stenson, Jones	6,218
27		31	(a)	Plymouth A	L	0-1		9,181
28	Feb	21	(h)	Halifax T	D	3-3	Partridge 2, Goodfellow	6,152
29		23	(h)	Bury	W	3-1	Partridge, Jones, Goodfellow	7,041
30		28	(a)	Tranmere R	D	1-1	Jones	2,955
31	Mar	4	(a)	Torquay U	W	2-0	Partridge, Walker	4,322
32		9	(h)	Barnsley	W	2-0	Roberts, Opp own-goal	7,936
33		14	(a)	Luton T	D	2-2	Partridge, Roberts	12,690
34		16	(h)	Bournemouth	W	2-0	Partridge, Jones	8,223
35		21	(h)	Torquay U	W	2-0	Partridge, Roberts	6,601
36		23	(h)	Stockport C	W	4-1	Partridge 2, Stenson, Roberts	7,829
37		28	(a)	Barnsley	D	1-1	Stenson	8,760
38		30	(a)	Reading	L	0-1		8,780
39	Apr	1	(h)	Southport	W	5-0	Roberts 3, McKenzie 2	7,008
40		4	(h)	Rotherham U	W	2-0	Partridge, McKenzie	9,166
41		6	(h)	Fulham	L	2-3	Partridge, Jones	10,322
42		10	(a)	Gillingham	D	3-3	Partridge, Jones, Roberts	3,982
43		15	(a)	Brighton & HA	W	2-1	Roberts, Goodfellow	10,274
44		18	(a)	Bournemouth	L	0-1		4,872
45		20	(h)	Luton T	D	0-0		10,301
46		22	(a)	Bradford C	W	1-0	Goodfellow	4,148

FINAL LEAGUE POSITION: 6th in Division Three

Appearances
Sub Appearances
Goals

FA Cup

1	Nov	15	(a)	Bury	D	2-2	Keeley, Stenson	4,336
R		19	(h)	Bury	W	2-0	Partridge, Bates	6,766
2	Dec	6	(a)	Shrewsbury T	W	2-1	Keeley, Roberts	5,661
3	Jan	3	(h)	Barnsley	W	3-2	Waller, Partridge, Goodfellow (pen)	14,387
4		24	(a)	Blackpool	W	2-0	Jones 2	23,715
5	Feb	7	(a)	Leeds U	L	0-2		48,093

Appearances
Sub Appearances
Goals

League Cup

1	Aug		(h)	Notts C	W	3-1	Waller, Bates, Opp own-goal	6,727
2	Sep	3	(h)	Queen's Park R	D	2-2	Ledger, Goodfellow	9,749
R		8	(a)	Queen's Park R	L	0-3		17,135

Appearances
Sub Appearances
Goals

Bates B	Boam SW	Brown GC	Goodfellow J	Hollins DM	Hopkinson ME	Jones DAB	Keeley R	Ledger RH	McKenzie D	Partridge M	Pate AM	Quigley J	Roberts DE	Saunders J	Sharkey D	Stenson J	Walker C	Waller P	
11	5	1				12	7			8	2		10*		9	4	3	6	1
7	5	1	11			12				8	2		10		9*	4	3	6	2
11	5	1	10							7	2	4			9	8	3	6	3
11	5	1				7				10	2	4	9			8	3	6	4
11*	5	1				7		12		10	2	4	9			8	3	6	5
	5		11	1				9		7	2	4			10	8	3	6	6
	5	1	11							7	2	4	10		9	8	3	6	7
7*	5	1	11					12			2	4	10		9	8	3	6	8
7	5	1	11*					12			2	4	10		9	8	3	6	9
11*	5	1					12			7	2	10	9		8	4	3	6	10
11	5	1								7	2	10	9		8	4	3	6	11
11	5	1					7	9		8	2	10		6		4	3		12
11	5	1								7	2	10	9	6	8	4	3		13
11	5			1		7				9	2	6	10		8	4	3		14
11	5			1		7				9	2	6	10		8	4	3		15
11	5			1	7	9	6			8	2		10			4	3		16
11	5			1		9	7			8	2	4	10*			12	3	6	17
11	5			1	3	9	7				2	4	10			8		6	18
11	5			1		9	7				2	4	10			8	3	6	19
11	5			1			7			9	2	4	10			8	3	6	20
11	5			1			7			9	2	4	10		8		3	6	21
11	5		8	1		12	7*			9	2	4	10				3	6	22
	5		7	1		9				11	2	4	10			8	3	6	23
	5	1	11			9				7	2	4	10			8	3	6	24
	5	1	11			9				7	2	4	10			8	3	6	25
	5	1	11			9				7	2	4	10			8	3	6	26
	5	1	11			9				7	2	4	10			8	3	6	27
	5		11	1		9	7*			10	2	4	6		12	8	3		28
	5		11	1		9				7	2	4	10			8	3	6	29
	5	1	11			9				7	2	4	10			8	3	6	30
	5	1	11			9				7	2	4	10			8	3	6	31
	5	1	11			9			12	7	2	4	10			8*	3	6	32
	5	1	11			9			12	7	2*	4	10			8	3	6	33
	5	1	11			9				7	2	4	10			8	3	6	34
	5	1	11			9				7	2	4	10			8	3	6	35
	5	1	11			9				7	2	4	10			8	3	6	36
	5	1	11			9				7	2	4	10			8	3	6	37
	5	1	11			9			12	7	2	4	10			8*	3	6	38
	5	1	11			9			8	7	2	4	10				3	6	39
	5	1	11			9			8	7	2	4	10				3	6	40
	5	1	11			9			8	7	2	4	10				3	6	41
	5	1				9			11	7	2	4	10			8	3	6	42
	5	1	11						8	7	2	4	10			9	3	6	43
	5	1	11			9			7		2	4	10			8	3	6	44
	5	1	11			9			7		2	4	10			8	3	6	45
	5	1	11			9	7				2	4	10		8		3	6	46
20	46	33	30	13	2	31	11	2	7	39	46	43	43	2	14	39	45	40	
						3	1	3	3						1	1			
3	1		6			10	1	2	3	13			18		2	7	1		

3 own-goals

11	5			1		9*	7			12	2	4	10			8	3	6	1
11	5			1			7			9	2	4	10			8	3	6	R
11	5		8	1		12	7			9	2	4	10*				3	6	2
	5		11	1	12	9				7	2	4	10			8*	3	6	3
	5	1	11			9				7	2	4	10			8	3	6	4
	5	1	11			9*	12			7	2	4	10			8	3	6	5
3	6	2	4	4		4	3			5	6	6	6			5	6	6	
					1	1	1			1									
1			1			2	2			2			1			1		1	

11	5			1			7			8	2		10		9	4	3	6	1
	5	1	11		4			9		7	2				10	8	3	6	2
	4	1	11							7	2		10	5	9	8	3	6	R
1	3	2	2	1	1		1	1		3	3		2	1	3	3	3	3	
1			1					1										1	

1 own-goal

1970-71

Manager: W.Basford

1	Aug	15	(a)	Doncaster R	W 2-1	Stenson, D.Roberts	8,147
2		22	(h)	Brighton & HA	W 1-0	Opp own-goal	7,988
3		28	(a)	Shrewsbury T	L 2-5	Partridge 2	5,807
4		31	(a)	Aston Villa	W 1-0	Partridge	30,856
5	Sep	4	(h)	Plymouth A	L 1-5	D.Roberts	12,500
6		12	(a)	Swansea C	W 4-2	Stenson 2, Jones, Opp own-goal	7,408
7		19	(h)	Wrexham	D 1-1	Goodfellow	7,185
8		26	(a)	Gillingham	D 2-2	Goodfellow, Jones	4,706
9		28	(h)	Port Vale	W 2-0	Walker, D.Roberts	8,118
10	Oct	3	(h)	Rochdale	W 3-2	Stenson 2, Jones	7,039
11		10	(a)	Preston NE	L 1-2	Stenson	12,052
12		14	(h)	Walsall	D 2-2	Thompson, Jones	6,911
13		17	(h)	Doncaster R	W 2-1	D.Roberts, Jones	7,601
14		20	(a)	Bristol R	L 0-2		12,230
15		24	(h)	Reading	D 0-0		6,510
16		30	(a)	Tranmere R	L 1-4	Jones	3,194
17	Nov	7	(h)	Halifax T	W 3-2	R.Roberts, Boam, Stenson	5,594
18		9	(h)	Rotherham U	D 1-1	Stenson	7,739
19		14	(a)	Torquay U	D 0-0		5,484
20		28	(a)	Bradford C	D 1-1	R.Roberts	5,709
21	Dec	5	(h)	Fulham	W 1-0	D.Roberts	8,052
22		19	(a)	Brighton & HA	L 0-2		6,583
23		26	(h)	Barnsley	L 1-2	Thompson	5,940
24	Jan	2	(a)	Chesterfield	D 2-2	D.Roberts 2	16,474
25		9	(a)	Port Vale	L 0-2		4,412
26		16	(h)	Bristol R	W 4-1	Thompson 2, D.Roberts, Opp own-goal	6,357
27		28	(a)	Bury	D 0-0		3,585
28		30	(h)	Bradford C	L 3-5	Walker, D.Roberts, Jones	4,360
29	Feb	6	(a)	Fulham	D 0-0		9,374
30		13	(h)	Bury	W 1-0	Stenson (pen)	4,631
31		20	(a)	Rotherham U	L 1-2	D.Roberts	7,361
32		27	(h)	Tranmere R	W 6-2	D.Roberts 4, Stenson, Thompson	4,326
33	Mar	6	(a)	Reading	L 0-1		4,365
34		9	(a)	Walsall	W 1-0	Stenson (pen)	3,364
35		13	(h)	Torquay U	D 0-0		5,710
36		15	(h)	Chesterfield	D 2-2	Jones, Stenson (pen)	13,187
37		20	(a)	Halifax T	W 1-0	D.Roberts	6,667
38		27	(a)	Plymouth A	D 0-0		8,925
39	Apr	3	(h)	Shrewsbury T	D 1-1	Jones	4,289
40		10	(a)	Barnsley	L 0-1		5,061
41		12	(a)	Rochdale	D 1-1	D.Roberts	3,898
42		13	(h)	Swansea C	W 2-0	D.Roberts 2	5,400
43		17	(h)	Preston NE	W 3-1	D.Roberts 2, Thompson	7,185
44		24	(a)	Wrexham	L 0-4		8,024
45		26	(h)	Aston Villa	W 2-0	D.Roberts, Thompson	9,666
46	May	1	(h)	Gillingham	W 2-0	D.Roberts, Thompson	4,252

FINAL LEAGUE POSITION: 7th in Division Three

Appearances
Sub Appearances
Goals

FA Cup

1	Nov	21	(h)	Wrexham	W 2-0	D.Roberts, Stenson	6,285
2	Dec	12	(a)	Scunthorpe U	L 0-3		7,656

Appearances
Sub Appearances
Goals

League Cup

1	Aug	19	(h)	Chesterfield	W 6-2	Partridge 3, Stenson 2, D.Roberts	11,091
2	Sep	8	(h)	Liverpool	D 0-0		12,532
R		22	(a)	Liverpool	L 2-3*	Stenson, Sutton	31,087

*After extra-time

Appearances
Sub Appearances
Goals

Arnold RJ	Bingham J	Boam SW	Brown GC	Derrick J	Finch D	Goodfellow J	Herriot J	Jarvis AL	Jones DAB	Partridge M	Pate AM	Quigley J	Roberts D	Roberts R	Rose MJ	Saunders T	Stenson J	Sutton J	Thompson D	Walker C	Waller P	
		5							11	7	2	4	9		1		8	10		3	6	1
		5							11	7	2	4	9		1		8	10		3	6	2
		5							11	7	2	4	9		1		8	10		3	6	3
		5	1			10			11	7	2	4	9				8			3	6	4
			1			10			11	7	2	4	9			5	8			3	6	5
			1			7			11		2	4	9			5	8	10		3	6	6
			1			7			11		2	4	9			5	8	10		3	6	7
			1			7			11		2	4	9	10		5	8			3	6	8
			1			7			11		2	4	9	10		5	8			3	6	9
			1			7			11		2	4	9	10		5	8			3	6	10
			1			7*			11		2	4	9	10		5	8	12		3	6	11
			1						11		2		9	4		5	8	10	7	3	6	12
		5	1						11		2	10	9*	4			8	12	7	3	6	13
		5	1						11		2	10	9	4			8		7	3	6	14
		5			1	12			11		2	10	9	4			8*		7	3	6	15
		5			1				11		2	10	9	4			8		7	3	6	16
		5				11	1				2	10	9	4			8		7	3	6	17
		5				11	1		12		2		9	4			8*	10	7	3	6	18
		5				11	1				2		9	4			10	8	7	3	6	19
		5				11	1				2		9	4			8	10	7	3	6	20
		5				11	1				2		9	4			8	10	7	3	6	21
		5	1			11			12		2		9	4			8	10*	7	3	6	22
	10	5	1			11					2		9	4			8		7	3	6	23
	11	5	1						8		2		9	4			10		7	3	6	24
	10*	5	1			12			11		2		9	4			8		7	3	6	25
		5	1						11		2		9	4		6	8		7	3	10	26
		5	1						11		2		9	4		6	8		7	3	10	27
		5	1			12			11*		2		9	4		10	8		7	3	6	28
1		5							11		2		9	4		10	8		7	3	6	29
1		5							11		2		9	4		10	8		7	3	6	30
1		5				12			11		2		9	4*		10	8		7	3	6	31
1		5							11		2		9	4		10	8		7	3	6	32
1	12	5							11		2		9	4*		10	8		7	3	6	33
1	11	5							9		2			10		6	4		7	3	8	34
1		5						10	11		2		9	4		6	8		7	3		35
1		5						10	11		2		9	8		6	4		7	3		36
1		5		12				10*	11		2		9	8		6	4		7	3		37
1		5						10	11		2		9	8		6	4		7	3		38
1		5		7				10	11		2		9	8		6*	4			3	12	39
1		5						10	11*		2		9	8		6	4		7	3	12	40
1		5		4				10	11		2		9	8		6			7	3		41
1		5						10	11		2		9	8		6	4		7	3		42
1		5						10	11		2		9	8		6	4		7	3		43
1		5						10	11		2		9	8		6	4		7	3		44
1		5						10	11		2		9	8		6	4		7	3		45
		5	1					10*	11		2		9	8		6	4		7	3	12	46
17	4	38	19	2	2	15	5	12	39	5	46	16	45	39	3	29	45	11	34	46	34	
	1			1		4			2									2			3	
		1				2			9	3			22	2			12		8	2		

3 own-goals

		5			1	11					2		9	4			8	10	7	3	6	1
		5	1			11*			12		2		9	4			8	10	7	3	6	2
		2	1		1	2					2		2	2			2	2	2	2	2	
									1													
													1				1					

		5							11	7	2	4	9		1		8	10		3	6	1
			1						11	7	2	4	9			5	8	10		3	6	2
			1			7			11		2	4	9			5	8	10		3	6	R
		1	2			1			3	2	3	3	3		1	2	3	3		3	3	
										3			1				3	1				

1971-72

Manager: W.Basford to November 1971, then D.Williams.

1	Aug	14	(h)	Halifax T	D 0-0		5,801
2		21	(a)	Rochdale	L 1-2	Opp own-goal	3,458
3		28	(h)	Brighton & HA	L 0-3		4,131
4	Sep	4	(a)	Plymouth A	L 1-3	Stenson (pen)	8,343
5		11	(h)	Swansea C	L 0-2		3,547
6		18	(a)	Chesterfield	L 0-2		9,950
7		22	(a)	Aston Villa	W 1-0	Jones	28,106
8		25	(h)	Rotherham U	L 0-1		4,797
9		27	(a)	Tranmere R	D 2-2	Thompson, Fairbrother	2,455
10	Oct	2	(a)	Bolton W	L 0-2		8,751
11		9	(h)	Bristol R	D 0-0		3,830
12		16	(a)	Halifax T	D 1-1	Fairbrother	3,864
13		18	(h)	Barnsley	D 0-0		3,692
14		23	(a)	Blackburn R	D 1-1	Fairbrother	7,103
15		29	(h)	Bournemouth	L 0-5		6,602
16	Nov	6	(a)	Notts C	L 0-2		16,905
17		13	(h)	Port Vale	L 0-1		5,986
18		27	(a)	York C	W 2-1	Wignall, R.Roberts	3,921
19	Dec	4	(h)	Torquay U	D 0-0		5,138
20		18	(h)	Plymouth A	L 2-3	Thompson, Fairbrother	3,782
21		27	(a)	Walsall	L 1-2	Thompson	7,001
22	Jan	1	(h)	Chesterfield	W 2-1	Wignall, Fairbrother	8,319
23		8	(a)	Brighton & HA	L 0-1		10,616
24		15	(a)	Bradford C	D 2-2	Fairbrother 2	4,098
25		22	(h)	Tranmere R	D 1-1	Fairbrother	4,740
26		29	(a)	Barnsley	D 1-1	Thompson	3,676
27	Feb	5	(h)	Oldham A	W 2-1	Wignall, Fairbrother	4,385
28		12	(h)	Blackburn R	W 1-0	Wignall	5,146
29		19	(a)	Bournemouth	D 1-1	Opp own-goal	13,417
30		26	(h)	Notts C	D 1-1	R.Roberts	16,758
31	Mar	4	(a)	Port Vale	L 0-1		2,809
32		11	(a)	Bristol R	L 1-2	Fairbrother	5,574
33		13	(a)	Wrexham	D 1-1	Saunders	2,358
34		18	(h)	Rochdale	W 3-1	Saunders, Wignall, Fairbrother	5,109
35		20	(h)	Shrewsbury T	D 2-2	D.Roberts, Fairbrother	5,961
36		24	(a)	Swansea C	D 1-1	Wignall	3,494
37		27	(h)	Bolton W	W 1-0	Wignall	5,398
38	Apr	1	(h)	Walsall	D 1-1	Fairbrother	5,770
39		3	(a)	Rotherham U	L 1-3	Fairbrother	5,518
40		8	(a)	Oldham A	L 1-2	Wignall	5,587
41		15	(h)	York C	D 0-0		5,006
42		19	(a)	Shrewsbury T	L 2-4	Fairbrother 2	2,693
43		23	(a)	Torquay U	W 1-0	Longhorn	3,825
44		24	(h)	Aston Villa	D 1-1	Fairbrother	12,454
45		29	(h)	Bradford C	D 1-1	Stenson	4,231
46	May	1	(h)	Wrexham	D 1-1	Fairbrother	6,678

FINAL LEAGUE POSITION: 21st in Division Three (Relegated)

Appearances
Sub Appearances
Goals

FA Cup

1	Nov	20	(a)	Chester	D 1-1	Bingham	3,669
R		22	(h)	Chester	W 4-3	Thompson, Fairbrother, Bingham, R.Roberts (pen)	5,310
2	Dec	11	(h)	Tranmere R	D 2-2	Thompson, Fairbrother	5,634
R		15	(a)	Tranmere R	L 2-4	Fairbrother 2	5,703

Appearances
Sub Appearances
Goals

League Cup

1	Aug	18	(a)	Chesterfield	D 0-0		12,261
R		23	(h)	Chesterfield	L 0-5		9,291

Appearances
Sub Appearances
Goals

Bingham J	Book K	Brown G	Crawford PG	Ellis S	Fairbrother J	Foster B	Foster C	Harford R	Harrington C	Haselden J	Jarvis AL	Jones DAB	Longhorn D	Pate AM	Roberts DE	Roberts R	Saunders J	Stenson JA	Thompson D	Walker C	Waller P	Wignall F	
		1						5	11		10			2	9	4		8	7	3	6		1
		1						5	11*		10	12		2	9	4		8	7	3	6		2
11		1						5			10			2	9	4	6	8	7*	3	12		3
8			1			3	6		11		10*	7		2		12	5	4			9		4
10			1					5	11		7	9		2		12	6	4		3*	8		5
11	1				8	3					10	9*		2		12	5	4	7		6		6
11*	1				7	3		9			10	12		2		8	5	4			6		7
	1				7	3		9*	12		10	11		2		8	5	4			6		8
	1				11	3					10			2	9	8	5	4	7		6		9
		1			11						10*	12		2	9	8	5	4	7	3	6		10
		1			11						10			2	9	8	5	4	7	3	6		11
		1			11						10	12		2	9*	8	5	4	7	3	6		12
		1			11						10			2	9	8	5	4	7	3	6		13
		1			11						10			2	9	8	5	4	7	3	6		14
		1			11						10	12		2	9	8	5	4*	7	3	6		15
12		1			11			5			10	8*		2	9		6		7	3	4		16
12		1			11*						10			2	9		5	4	7	3	6	8	17
11		1			8						10			2		4	5		7	3	6	9	18
11		1			10						8			2		4	5		7	3	6	9	19
11		1			10						8		4	2			5	9*	7	3	6	12	20
		1			9						10*		11	2		4	5	12	7	3	6	8	21
11		1			9						10		7	2		4	5			3	6	8	22
		1		6	9						10*		11	2		4	5		7	3	12	8	23
11		1		5	9								10	2		4	6		7	3		8	24
11		1		5	9								10	2		4	6		7	3		8	25
11		1		5	9						8		10	2		4	6		7	3			26
		1		5	9				11*				10	2		4	6		7	3	12	8	27
		1			9*				11	6	12		10	2		4	5		7	3		8	28
		1			9				12	6	10*		11	2		4	5		7	3		8	29
		1			9					6	10		11	2		4	5		7	3		8	30
		1			9				12	5	10*		11	2		4	6		7	3		8	31
		1		5	9						10		11	2		4	6		7	3		8	32
		1		5	9				12		11*		10	2		4	6	8	7	3			33
		1		5	9				11		12		10	2		4	6		7*	3		8	34
		1		5	9						11		10	2	7*	4	6	12		3		8	35
		1		5	9						11		10	2		4	6		7	3		8	36
		1		5	9						11		10	2		4	6		7	3		8	37
		1		5	9*				12		11		10	2		4	6		7	3		8	38
		1		5	9				12		11*		10	2		4	6		7	3		8	39
		1		5	9						11*		10	2	12	4	6		7	3		8	40
11		1		5	9								10	2		4	6		7	3		8	41
11		1		5	9						8*		10	2		4	6		7	3		12	42
		1		5	9	4					10		11	2	8*		6	12	7	3			43
		1		5	9	3					11		10	4	8		6		7	2			44
		1		5	9	3					11		10*	4		12	6	8	7	2			45
		1		5	9	4					11*		12	2		8	6		7	3		10	46
14	4	40	2	20	41	9	1	7	7	4	40	5	26	46	15	37	44	19	40	41	21	23	
2									6		2	5	1		1	4		3			3	2	
					18							1	1		1	2	2	2	4			8	

2 own-goals

11		1			10						8			2	9	4	5		7	3	6		1
11		1			8						10			2		4	5	9	7	3	6		R
11		1			9						10			2		4*	5	12	7	3	6	8	2
12		1			10				11		8			2			5	9*	7	3	6	4	R
3		4			4				1		4			4	1	3	4	2	4	4	4	2	
1																		1					
2					4											1			2				

		1						5	11		10			2	9	4		8	7	3	6		1
8		1						5	11		10			2	9	4			7	3	6		R
1		2						2	2		2			2	2	2		1	2	2	2		

1972-73

Manager: D.Williams

1	Aug	12	(h)	Northampton T	W	1-0	Wignall	4,301
2		19	(a)	Doncaster R	W	1-0	Fairbrother	3,540
3		26	(h)	Exeter C	W	3-0	Ellis 2 (2 pens), McCaffrey	4,177
4		30	(h)	Cambridge U	W	3-1	Walker, Longhorn, Fairbrother	5,216
5	Sep	2	(a)	Newport C	W	1-0	Fairbrother	4,813
6		9	(h)	Bury	D	1-1	Fairbrother	4,386
7		16	(a)	Aldershot	W	1-0	Thompson	4,779
8		18	(h)	Gillingham	W	2-0	Wignall, Fairbrother	5,389
9		23	(h)	Barnsley	W	3-1	Fairbrother 2, McCaffrey	6,096
10		25	(a)	Stockport C	L	1-2	Thompson	4,605
11		30	(a)	Darlington	W	3-2	Longhorn, Wignall, Fairbrother	1,604
12	Oct	7	(h)	Southport	D	3-3	Wignall, Fairbrother, Bentley	7,312
13		9	(h)	Peterborough U	W	4-2	Walker, Fairbrother 3	5,378
14		14	(a)	Bradford C	D	1-1	Roberts	3,383
15		21	(h)	Chester	W	4-1	Fairbrother 2, Laverick, McCaffrey	5,787
16		25	(a)	Hereford U	L	1-3	Wignall	10,095
17		28	(a)	Colchester U	D	1-1	Ellis (pen)	3,789
18	Nov	4	(h)	Stockport C	W	1-0	Walker	5,114
19		11	(a)	Gillingham	L	1-2	Bird	3,066
20		25	(a)	Lincoln C	D	1-1	Fairbrother	6,675
21	Dec	2	(h)	Reading	D	1-1	Cottam	4,492
22		9	(a)	Workington	L	0-2		1,219
23		16	(a)	Crewe A	W	4-0	Ellis, Thompson, Roberts, Fairbrother	2,439
24		23	(h)	Hartlepool	W	2-0	Fairbrother, McCaffrey	4,208
25		26	(a)	Barnsley	D	1-1	Matthews	5,670
26		30	(h)	Doncaster R	D	0-0		5,188
27	Jan	6	(a)	Exeter C	L	2-4	Thompson, Fairbrother	6,744
28		13	(h)	Hereford U	D	1-1	Ellis	5,530
29		27	(a)	Bury	L	0-1		3,068
30	Feb	3	(a)	Peterborough U	L	0-1		7,224
31		10	(h)	Aldershot	W	2-0	Bird, Wignall	4,289
32		16	(a)	Northampton T	L	0-1		2,288
33		24	(h)	Crewe A	W	5-1	Ellis, McKenzie, Wignall, Fairbrother, Thompson	3,665
34	Mar	2	(a)	Southport	L	1-3	McKenzie	5,656
35		5	(h)	Workington	W	4-0	McKenzie 2, Thompson, Opp own-goal	4,551
36		10	(h)	Bradford C	W	4-1	McKenzie 3, Fairbrother	5,300
37		17	(a)	Chester	D	2-2	Laverick, Opp own-goal	1,964
38		21	(a)	Torquay U	D	1-1	Roberts	2,804
39		24	(h)	Colchester U	D	1-1	Ellis	4,664
40		26	(h)	Newport C	D	0-0		6,402
41		31	(h)	Lincoln C	L	0-2		5,277
42	Apr	7	(a)	Reading	L	0-2		6,935
43		14	(h)	Torquay U	W	2-1	Roberts, McCaffrey	3,451
44		20	(a)	Hartlepool	D	1-1	Thompson	2,863
45		24	(h)	Darlington	W	5-0	Roberts 3, Thompson, McCaffrey	5,130
46		28	(a)	Cambridge U	L	2-3	Roberts, McCaffrey	10,542

FINAL LEAGUE POSITION: 6th in Division Four

Appearances
Sub Appearances
Goals

FA Cup

1	Nov	18	(a)	York C	L	1-2	Fairbrother	4,316

Appearances
Sub Appearances
Goals

League Cup

1	Aug	16	(h)	Lincoln C	W	3-1	Pate, Longhorn, Laverick	4,642
2	Sep	5	(a)	Charlton A	L	3-4	Walker, Wignall, McCaffrey	5,218

Appearances
Sub Appearances
Goals

Arnold R	Bentley D	Bird K	Brown G	Cottam J	Crawford A	Ellis S	Fairbrother J	Foster B	Foster C	Green A	Jarvis A	Laverick M	Longhorn D	Matthews P	McCaffrey J	McKenzie D	Pate A	Roberts D	Sainty J	Saunders J	Thompson D	Walker C	Wignall F	
			1			5	9	12		7*		10	4		11		2			6		3	8	1
			1			5	9				12	10	4		11*		2			6	7	3	8	2
			1			5	9					10	4		11		2			6	7	3	8	3
			1			5	9					10	4		11		2			6	7	3	8	4
			1			5	9				10		4		11		2			6	7	3	8	5
			1			5	9				12	10*	4		11		2			6	7	3	8	6
			1			5	9				10		4		11		2			6	7	3	8	7
			1			5	9				10	12	4		11		2			6	7*	3	8	8
	12		1			5	9				10*		4		11		2			6	7	3	8	9
	10		1			5	8				12		4		11		2			6	7	3*	9	10
	12		1			5	9				10*		4		11		2			6	7	3	8	11
	12		1			5	9				10*		4		11		2			6	7	3	8	12
			1			5	9				10		4		11		2	8		6	7	3		13
			1			5	9				10*		4		11		2	12		6	7	3	8	14
		6	1			5	9	3				7	4		11		2					10	8	15
		6	1			5	9	12				10	4		11		2				7*	3	8	16
		6	1			5	9	3				10	4		11		2					7	8	17
		6	1			5	9	3				10	4		11*		2	8			12	7		18
		6	1			5	9					10	4		11		2				7	3	8	19
			1	5			9		6		12		4		11		2	8*	10		7	3		20
		6	1	5			9						4		11		2		10		7	3	8	21
		6	1			5	9						4	8	11		2		10		7	3		22
			1			5	9*		6		4	12		10	11		2	8			7	3		23
			1			5	9		6		4			10	11		2	8			7	3		24
			1			5	9		6		4		12	10	11		2	8*			7	3		25
		6	1			5	9				10		4		11		2	8			7	3		26
		6	1			5	9						4	10	11		2	8*			7	3	12	27
		6	1			5	9	3				12	4	10	11		2					7*	8	28
		6	1		12	5	9	3			8		4	7*	11		2						10	29
		6	1		11	5	9	3			8		4	10		7	2							30
		6	1			5	12				10		4		11	8*	2				7	3	9	31
			1			5	9		6		4		10		11		2				7	3	8	32
			1*			5	9		6		4		10		11	7	2				12	3	8	33
1		6				5	9				4		10		11	8	2				7	3		34
1		6				5	9				4*		10		11	8	2				7	3	12	35
1		6				5	9				4		10		11	8	2				7	3		36
1		6				5	9					12	10	4	11		2				7*	3	8	37
1		6				5	9	3					10	4	11		2	8			7			38
1		6				5	9*	3				12	10	4	11		2	8			7			39
1		6				5		3				4	10		11		2	8			7		9	40
1		6				5	9	3				4	10		11*		2	8			7		12	41
1		6				5	10	7*					8	4	11		2	12			9	3		42
1		6				5	9				10			4	11		2	8			7	3		43
1		6				5	9				4			10	11		2	8*			7	3	12	44
1		6				5					4			10	11		2	8			7	3	9	45
1		6				5	12				4*			10	11		2	8			7	3	9	46
13	1	26	33	2	1	44	42	11	6	1	24	12	39	16	45	6	46	16	3	14	38	40	27	
	3				1		2	2			4	5	1					2			2		4	
	1	2		1		7	20					2	2	1	7	7		8			8	3	7	

2 own-goals

Arnold R	Bentley D	Bird K	Brown G	Cottam J	Crawford A	Ellis S	Fairbrother J	Foster B	Foster C	Green A	Jarvis A	Laverick M	Longhorn D	Matthews P	McCaffrey J	McKenzie D	Pate A	Roberts D	Sainty J	Saunders J	Thompson D	Walker C	Wignall F	
		6*	1			5	9		12		10	11	4				2			7	3	8		1
		1	1			1	1				1	1	1				1			1	1	1		
									1															
							1																	

Arnold R	Bentley D	Bird K	Brown G	Cottam J	Crawford A	Ellis S	Fairbrother J	Foster B	Foster C	Green A	Jarvis A	Laverick M	Longhorn D	Matthews P	McCaffrey J	McKenzie D	Pate A	Roberts D	Sainty J	Saunders J	Thompson D	Walker C	Wignall F	
			1			5	9					10	4		11		2			6	7	3	8	1
			1			5	9				10		4		11		2			6	7	3	8	2
			2			2	2				1	1	2		2		2			2	2	2	2	
												1	1		1		1					1	1	

1973-74

Manager: D.Williams to March, then D.Smith from April 1974.

1	Aug	25	(a)	Peterborough U	L	1-2	Eccles	7,003
2	Sep	1	(h)	Northampton T	W	2-0	Roberts, Eccles	3,109
3		8	(a)	Barnsley	D	1-1	Thompson	2,302
4		10	(a)	Stockport C	D	1-1	Eccles	3,665
5		15	(h)	Swansea C	W	2-1	Bird, Roberts	3,249
6		17	(h)	Chester	W	3-0	Eccles 3	3,936
7		22	(a)	Crewe A	D	1-1	Roberts	1,776
8		29	(h)	Darlington	W	1-0	Jones	3,154
9	Oct	3	(a)	Chester	D	1-1	Laverick	2,547
10		9	(a)	Newport C	L	0-2		3,044
11		13	(h)	Hartlepool	W	2-0	Roberts, Laverick	3,078
12		20	(a)	Reading	L	0-3		6,376
13		22	(h)	Stockport C	W	5-0	Eccles 3, Roberts, Longhorn	3,443
14		27	(h)	Torquay U	W	2-1	Bird, Eccles (pen)	3,924
15	Nov	3	(a)	Brentford	L	1-4	McCaffrey	4,331
16		10	(h)	Colchester U	D	2-2	Eccles, Longhorn	3,033
17		14	(a)	Bradford C	L	1-3	Bird	3,276
18		17	(h)	Gillingham	D	2-2	Roberts, McCaffrey	3,004
19	Dec	1	(h)	Rotherham U	W	3-0	Eccles, Christopher, Opp own-goal	2,778
20		8	(a)	Scunthorpe U	L	3-5	Eccles, Walker, McCaffrey	2,420
21		22	(a)	Darlington	L	0-1		1,603
22		26	(h)	Lincoln C	W	4-3	Eccles 2, Peplow, Opp own-goal	4,476
23		29	(h)	Barnsley	D	2-2	Peplow, Walker	4,239
24	Jan	1	(a)	Northampton T	L	0-2		6,231
25		12	(a)	Swansea C	L	0-2		4,196
26		20	(h)	Peterborough U	W	2-1	Peplow, Eccles	6,913
27		27	(a)	Bury	L	0-2		6,242
28	Feb	10	(h)	Crewe A	L	1-2	Eccles (pen)	2,668
29		17	(a)	Hartlepool	L	0-4		4,038
30		24	(h)	Newport C	W	2-1	Lathan, Roberts	3,006
31	Mar	3	(a)	Lincoln C	D	1-1	Eccles (pen)	2,615
32		9	(a)	Exeter C	D	1-1	Lathan	3,669
33		10	(a)	Torquay U	L	0-4		2,702
34		16	(h)	Reading	D	1-1	Eccles	2,182
35		18	(h)	Exeter C	D	3-3	Laverick 2, Bird	2,406
36		22	(a)	Colchester U	L	0-1		4,695
37		26	(a)	Doncaster R	D	0-0		1,894
38		30	(h)	Brentford	D	1-1	Lathan	1,909
39	Apr	1	(h)	Bury	L	1-2	Lathan	2,626
40		6	(h)	Bradford C	D	0-0		2,113
41		13	(a)	Gillingham	D	2-2	Bird, Lathan	7,872
42		15	(a)	Workington	D	0-0		1,094
43		17	(h)	Workington	W	2-0	Bird, Eccles	2,329
44		20	(h)	Scunthorpe U	D	2-2	Bird, C.Foster	2,342
45		27	(a)	Rotherham U	L	1-2	Laverick	2,329
46		29	(h)	Doncaster R	W	2-0	Edwards, Bird	2,474

FINAL LEAGUE POSITION: 17th in Division Four

Appearances
Sub Appearances
Goals

FA Cup

1	Nov	24	(a)	York C	D	0-0		4,254
R	Dec	10	(h)	York C	W	5-3	C.Foster, Thompson, Eccles, Walker, McCaffrey	4,733
2		15	(h)	Scunthorpe U	D	1-1	Eccles	4,511
R		18	(a)	Scunthorpe U	L	0-1		2,679

Appearances
Sub Appearances
Goals

League Cup

1	Aug	29	(h)	Chesterfield	D	1-1	Laverick	6,321
R	Sep	3	(a)	Chesterfield	L	0-1		5,711

Appearances
Sub Appearances
Goals

Arnold R	Bird K	Brown G	Burrows F	Christopher P	Cook T	Eccles T	Edwards R	Foster B	Foster C	Grozier W	Jones P	Lathan J	Laverick M	Longhorn D	Lyon D	Matthews P	McCaffrey J	Parry AJ	Pate A	Peplow S	Roberts D	Thompson D	Todd S	Walker C	
	5	1				9			4				8	6			11		2		10	7		3	1
	5	1				9			4				6	10			11		2		8	7		3	2
	4	1				9		3	5		8*		6	12			11		2		10	7			3
1	6					9	5				12		4*	10			11		2		8	7		3	4
1	6					9	5						4	10			11		2		8	7		3	5
1	6					9	5						4	10			11		2		8	7		3	6
1	6					9	5				12		4	8*			11		2		10	7		3	7
1	6					9	5				7		4	10			11		2		8			3	8
1	6					9	5						4	10			11		2		8	7		3	9
1	6					9	5				12		4	10			11*		2		8	7		3	10
1	6					9*	5				12		4	10			11		2		8	7		3	11
1	6					9	5				11*		4	10			12		2		8	7		3	12
1	6					9	5						4	10			11		2		8	7		3	13
1	6					9	5		12		8*		4	10			11		2			7		3	14
1	6					9	5						10	4			11		2		8	7		3	15
1	6					9	5				12		4	10			11		2		8*	7		3	16
1	6			8		9	5		4		11			10					2			7		3	17
1	6			7		9	5		10				12	4			11		2*		8			3	18
1				7		9		3	6					10	5		11		2		8			4	19
1				7*		9		3	5				12	6	4		11		2		8			10	20
	5	1				9		3*	4				12	8			11		2		10	7		6	21
	6	1				9		3	5					4		11			2	7	8			10	22
	6	1				9		3	5				12	4		11*			2	7	8			10	23
	6	1				9	5	3						4		8*	11		2	7	12			10	24
	6	1				9	5	3*	11		8			4			12		2		10			7	25
	6	1				9	12						10	4		8*	11		2	7	5			3	26
	6	1				9	5	12					10*	4		7	11		2		8			3	27
	6	1		7*		9	5	3					12	4			11		2		8			10	28
1	6			7		9		3	5					4		11*		12	2		8			10	29
1	6					9	5				4	7					11		2		8		3	10	30
1	10					9	5	8*			4	7	12				11		2				6	3	31
1	6		5			9			3			8	7				11		2				4	10	32
1	6		5			9	12	3	8*			7	10				11		2				4		33
1	6		5			9		3				7	10				11		8				4	2	34
1	6		5			9	2		12			7	8				11		10				4*	3	35
1	6		5			9	4	3	8			7	11				12		2*					10	36
1	6					9	4	3	8			7	11			5			2					10	37
1	5					9	2	3	4			7	10*			12	11		6					8	38
	6	1		8		9	4		5		3	7					11		2					10	39
	5	1				9		3	4		8	7				6	11		2					10	40
	6	1				9	5	3	12		4	7	10			11*			2					8	41
	6	1				9	3		5		4	7	11				8		2					10	42
	6	1				9	3	12	5		4*	7	11				8		2					10	43
	4	1	5			9*		12	6			7	11			10	8		2					3	44
1	4			12			5	3	7		11	8	10*			6	9		2						45
1	6				9		5		4	3	10	7				11	8		2						46
29	44	17	6	7	1	44	31	19	24	1	15	17	30	28	2	12	37		46	4	27	17	6	42	
				1			2	3	3		5		6	1		1	3	1			1				
	8			1		20	1		1		1	5	5	2			3			3	7	1		2	

2 own-goals

Arnold R	Bird K	Brown G	Burrows F	Christopher P	Cook T	Eccles T	Edwards R	Foster B	Foster C	Grozier W	Jones P	Lathan J	Laverick M	Longhorn D	Lyon D	Matthews P	McCaffrey J	Parry AJ	Pate A	Peplow S	Roberts D	Thompson D	Todd S	Walker C	
1	4					9		3	5				6	10			11		2		8			7	1
		1		8		9		3	6					4			11		2		5	7		10	R
	6	1				9		3	5					4			11		2		8	7		10	2
	6	1		8*		9		3	5				12	4			11		2			7		10	R
1	3	3		2		4		4	4				1	4			4		4		3	3		4	
													1												
						2			1								1					1		1	

Arnold R	Bird K	Brown G	Burrows F	Christopher P	Cook T	Eccles T	Edwards R	Foster B	Foster C	Grozier W	Jones P	Lathan J	Laverick M	Longhorn D	Lyon D	Matthews P	McCaffrey J	Parry AJ	Pate A	Peplow S	Roberts D	Thompson D	Todd S	Walker C	
	6	1				9	5						4	10			11		2		8	7		3	1
	6	1				9		12	5		11		4	10					2*		8	7		3	R
	2	2				2	1		1		1		2	2			1		2		2	2		2	
								1																	
													1												

1974-75

Manager: D.Smith

1	Aug	17	(h)	Southport	W 2-1	C.Foster, O'Connor	3,109
2		24	(a)	Scunthorpe U	W 1-0	Clarke	2,794
3		30	(h)	Rochdale	W 2-0	Clarke, O'Connor	3,769
4	Sep	7	(a)	Exeter C	W 1-0	Eccles	3,276
5		14	(h)	Crewe A	D 0-0		4,340
6		20	(a)	Stockport C	L 2-3	Matthews, Lathan	2,152
7		24	(a)	Cambridge U	D 2-2	Clarke, Hodgson	3,627
8		27	(h)	Chester	D 0-0		3,182
9	Oct	1	(a)	Swansea C	W 2-1	Clarke 2	2,273
10		5	(h)	Darlington	W 4-2	Laverick 2, Kruse, Clarke	3,400
11		7	(h)	Swansea C	W 3-0	Clarke, Laverick, McCaffrey	3,672
12		12	(a)	Workington	W 3-1	McCaffrey 2, Hodgson	1,309
13		15	(a)	Barnsley	W 3-1	Clarke 2, Lathan	4,748
14		19	(h)	Reading	D 1-1	Hodgson	4,982
15		21	(h)	Barnsley	W 2-1	Clarke, Hodgson	5,287
16		26	(a)	Hartlepool	L 1-2	Clarke	2,572
17		28	(h)	Northampton T	W 3-0	Clarke, Eccles, C.Foster	5,305
18	Nov	2	(h)	Bradford C	W 3-0	Clarke 2, Lathan	5,147
19		9	(a)	Brentford	W 3-2	Bird, Clarke, McCaffrey	5,560
20		16	(h)	Doncaster R	W 5-2	Clarke 3, Eccles, Bird	5,634
21		30	(a)	Torquay U	W 2-0	Matthews, Eccles	2,979
22	Dec	7	(h)	Shrewsbury T	W 3-1	Latham 2, Eccles	10,036
23		21	(h)	Rotherham U	D 1-1	Hodgson	8,559
24		26	(a)	Crewe A	W 2-0	Bird, Hodgson	2,571
25		28	(h)	Newport C	W 3-0	Eccles 2, Clarke	7,920
26	Jan	11	(a)	Shrewsbury T	W 1-0	McCaffrey	8,913
27		18	(h)	Torquay U	W 3-0	Eccles 2 (1 pen), Clarke	7,532
28	Feb	1	(h)	Brentford	D 1-1	Eccles	11,334
29		8	(a)	Bradford C	D 1-1	Hodgson	4,970
30		22	(a)	Doncaster R	L 3-4	Eccles 2, C.Foster	7,278
31		25	(a)	Lincoln C	D 0-0		13,408
32	Mar	1	(a)	Rochdale	W 1-0	Clarke	2,317
33		7	(h)	Cambridge U	W 2-1	Clarke, Eccles	9,152
34		15	(a)	Chester	D 0-0		7,518
35		18	(a)	Southport	D 1-1	McCaffrey (pen)	2,004
36		21	(h)	Exeter C	W 3-2	Bird, Lathan, Griffin	8,412
37		25	(a)	Northampton T	W 2-0	Griffin, Hodgson	3,846
38		29	(a)	Rotherham U	L 1-2	Clarke	11,669
39		31	(a)	Newport C	L 1-2	Eccles (pen)	3,662
40	Apr	1	(h)	Stockport C	D 1-1	Eccles (pen)	10,224
41		5	(h)	Hartlepool	W 2-0	Clarke, Hodgson	8,835
42		12	(a)	Darlington	L 1-2	Clarke	2,827
43		14	(h)	Lincoln C	W 3-1	Clarke, Bird, Lathan	14,351
44		19	(h)	Workington	W 1-0	Eccles	9,754
45		21	(h)	Scunthorpe U	W 7-0	Clarke 2, Lathan 2, Bird, Eccles, Hodgson	11,020
46		26	(a)	Reading	D 1-1	Bird	5,378

FINAL LEAGUE POSITION: 1st in Division Four

Appearances
Sub Appearances
Goals

FA Cup

1	Nov	23	(h)	Wrexham	W 3-1	Eccles 2, McCaffrey	7,443
2	Dec	14	(a)	Wigan A	D 1-1	Eccles	15,560
R		16	(h)	Wigan A	W 3-1	O'Connor 2, Hodgson	11,209
3	Jan	3	(h)	Cambridge U	W 1-0	Clarke	10,486
4		24	(a)	Bury	W 2-1	Clarke, McCaffrey	16,623
5	Feb	15	(h)	Carlisle U	L 0-1		18,293

Appearances
Sub Appearances
Goals

League Cup

1	Aug	20	(a)	Doncaster R	L 1-2	O'Connor	3,078

Appearances
Sub Appearances
Goals

Arnold R	Bird K	Clarke R	Eccles T	Foster B	Foster C	Griffin K	Hailwood D	Hodgson G	Kruse P	Lathan J	Laverick M	Llewellyn D	Madden L	Matthews P	McCaffrey J	O'Conner D	Pate A	Shore W	Tones J	Walker C	
1	6	7	9	11	5			10						4		8	2			3	1
1		10	9		5			11		7	6	4				8	2			3	2
1		10	9		5			11		7	4*	6			12	8	2			3	3
1		10	9		5			11		7		6		4		8	2			3	4
1		10	9*		5			11		7		6		4	12	8	2			3	5
1		10	9		5			11		7		6		4		8	2			3	6
1		10	9		5			11	6	7		12		4		8	2			3*	7
1		10	9	3	5			11	6	7		12		4		8*	2				8
1		8	9	3	6			7	5	4				11		10	2				9
1		8		3	5			9	6	7	10			4	11		2				10
1		10		3	5			11	6	7	9			4	8		2				11
1		9		3	5			8	6	7	10*			4	11	12	2				12
1		9		3	5			10		7	8	6		4	11		2				13
1		9		3	5			8		7	10			4*	11	12	2		6		14
1		9		3	5			10		7	8			4	11		2		6		15
1		9		3	5			8		7	10*			4	11	12	2		6		16
1		9	8	3	5			10		7				4	11		2	6			17
1	6	10	9	3	5			8		7				4	11		2				18
1	6	10	9	3	5			8		7				4	11		2				19
1	6	10	9	3	5			8		7*	12			4	11		2				20
1	6	9	8	3	5			10		7				4	11		2				21
1	6	9	8	3	5			10		7				4	11		2				22
1	6	10		3	5			8		7				4	11	9	2				23
1	6	9	8	3	5			10		7				4	11		2*			12	24
1	6	9	8	3	5			10		7				4	11		2				25
1	6	10	9	3	5			8		7				4	11		2				26
1	6	10	9	3	5			8		7				4	11*	12	2				27
1	6	8	9	3	5			10		7				4*	11	12	2				28
1	6	8	9	3	5			10		7				4	11		2				29
1	6	8	9	3	5			10		7				4	11		2				30
1	6	8	9*	3	5			10		7				4	11		2			12	31
1	6	9		3	5		10*	8		7				4	11		2			12	32
1	6	9	8*	3	5					7				4	11	12	2			10	33
1	6	10		3	5					7				4	11	8	2			9	34
1	6	9		3	5	8		10		7				4	11		2				35
1	6	9		3	5	8		10		7				4	11		2				36
1	6	9		3	5	8*		10		7	12			4	11		2				37
1	6	9		3	5	8*		10		7				4	11		2			12	38
1	6	9	8*	3	5			10		7				4	11		2			12	39
1	6*	9	8	3	5			10		7			12	4	11		2				40
1		9	8	3	5			10		7			6	4	11		2				41
1		9	8	3	5			10		7*			6	4	11		2			12	42
1	5	9	8	3				10		7			6	4	11		2				43
1	5	9	8	3				10		7			6	4	11		2				44
1	6	9	8	3				10		7			5	4	11		2				45
1	6	9	8*	3	12			10		7			5	4	11		2				46
46	28	46	32	40	42	4	1	44	6	45	9	6	6	44	37	11	46	1	3	9	
					1						2	2	1		2	6				6	
	7	28	17		3	2		10	1	9	3			2	6	2					

Arnold R	Bird K	Clarke R	Eccles T	Foster B	Foster C	Griffin K	Hailwood D	Hodgson G	Kruse P	Lathan J	Laverick M	Llewellyn D	Madden L	Matthews P	McCaffrey J	O'Conner D	Pate A	Shore W	Tones J	Walker C	
1	6	9*	8	3	5			10		7	12			4	11		2				1
1	4	8	9	3	5			10		7				6	11		2				2
1	6	9		3	5			10		7				4	11	8	2				R
1	6	10	9	3	5			8		7				4	11		2				3
1	5	10	9	3	6			8		7				4	11		2				4
1	6	9	8	3	5			8		7				4	11		2				5
6	6	6	5	6	6			6		6				6	6	1	6				
											1										
		2	3					1							2	2					

Arnold R	Bird K	Clarke R	Eccles T	Foster B	Foster C	Griffin K	Hailwood D	Hodgson G	Kruse P	Lathan J	Laverick M	Llewellyn D	Madden L	Matthews P	McCaffrey J	O'Conner D	Pate A	Shore W	Tones J	Walker C	
1	3*	10	11	5	4			7			6				12	9	2			8	1
1	1	1	1	1	1			1			1					1	1			1	
															1						
																1					

1975-76

Manager: D.Smith to April 1976

1	Aug	16	(h)	Shrewsbury T	L 1-2	McDonald	6,951
2		23	(a)	Colchester U	W 2-0	Bird, Clarke	3,333
3		30	(h)	Chester	D 1-1	McDonald (pen)	6,164
4	Sep	6	(a)	Aldershot	L 1-2	Hodgson	3,289
5		13	(h)	Cardiff C	L 1-4	Eccles (pen)	6,682
6		20	(a)	Gillingham	L 1-3	Eccles (pen)	5,742
7		23	(a)	Bury	L 1-2	McDonald	5,896
8		27	(h)	Walsall	W 4-1	Clarke 3, Hodgson	5,450
9	Oct	4	(a)	Millwall	L 0-1		6,792
10		11	(h)	Peterborough U	D 1-1	Clarke	6,983
11		17	(a)	Southend U	D 2-2	Bird, Clarke	3,248
12		25	(h)	Preston NE	L 0-1		6,677
13	Nov	1	(a)	Wrexham	L 0-1		2,701
14		8	(h)	Halifax T	D 1-1	Bird	5,288
15		15	(a)	Grimsby T	L 1-4	Bird	4,659
16		29	(a)	Crystal P	L 1-4	Hodgson	15,701
17	Dec	6	(h)	Swindon T	W 3-1	Bird, Clarke, Randall	5,487
18		20	(a)	Rotherham U	L 1-2	Hodgson	6,067
19		26	(h)	Chesterfield	L 0-1		8,607
20		27	(a)	Sheffield W	D 0-0		15,430
21	Jan	3	(h)	Port Vale	W 3-1	Clarke 2, Randall	5,417
22		10	(a)	Chester	D 1-1	Randall	4,623
23		17	(h)	Gillingham	D 1-1	Opp own-goal	5,939
24		20	(a)	Cardiff C	L 0-1		10,161
25		31	(a)	Brighton & HA	L 0-1		11,918
26	Feb	7	(h)	Hereford U	D 2-2	Bird, Clarke	5,997
27		11	(a)	Hereford U	L 0-1		8,302
28		14	(a)	Halifax T	W 2-1	Clarke, Saxby	2,378
29		21	(h)	Grimsby T	W 1-0	Clarke	6,094
30		23	(h)	Bury	D 1-1	Clarke	6,610
31		28	(a)	Preston NE	W 2-0	Clarke, Matthews	6,954
32	Mar	1	(h)	Brighton & HA	W 1-0	McDonald	8,321
33		6	(h)	Wrexham	D 0-0		6,473
34		8	(h)	Millwall	D 1-1	McCaffrey	7,435
35		13	(a)	Peterborough U	W 3-0	Clarke 2, McCaffrey	7,497
36		15	(h)	Southend U	W 3-1	Clarke 3	8,043
37		20	(h)	Crystal P	D 1-1	Laverick	12,990
38		27	(a)	Swindon T	W 2-0	Clarke, Laverick	6,789
39		29	(h)	Rotherham U	D 1-1	C.Foster	9,098
40	Apr	2	(a)	Shrewsbury T	W 2-1	Clarke, Hodgson	4,580
41		6	(a)	Walsall	W 1-0	Hodgson	6,481
42		10	(h)	Aldershot	W 1-0	Mackenzie	7,179
43		17	(a)	Chesterfield	W 2-1	Laverick, Eccles (pen)	10,616
44		19	(h)	Sheffield W	W 3-0	Pate, Clarke, Hodgson	13,410
45		20	(a)	Port Vale	D 2-2	Clarke 2	4,239
46		24	(h)	Colchester U	D 0-0		7,407

FINAL LEAGUE POSITION: 11th in Division Three

Appearances
Sub Appearances
Goals

FA Cup

1	Nov	23	(h)	Wrexham	D 1-1	Eccles	6,279
R		24	(a)	Wrexham	D 1-1*	Eccles	4,468
2R	Dec	8	(n†)	Wrexham	W 2-1	Laverick, Opp own-goal	1,470
2		11	(h)	Lincoln C	L 1-2	McDonald	8,466

*After extra-time. †Played at Villa Park, Birmingham.

Appearances
Sub Appearances
Goals

League Cup

1	Aug	20	(h)	Scunthorpe U	W 4-0	McDonald 2, Bird, Laverick	4,810
		26	(a)	Scunthorpe U	W 2-0	Lathan, Laverick	1,412
2	Sep	10	(a)	Wrexham	W 2-1	Bird, Clarke	3,644
3	Oct	8	(h)	Coventry C	W 2-0	Clarke, Eccles	10,027
4	Nov	12	(h)	Wolves	W 1-0	McDonald	12,725
5	Dec	3	(a)	Manchester C	L 2-4	Bird, Clarke	30,022

Appearances
Sub Appearances
Goals

Arnold R	Bird K	Brown R	Clarke R	Eccles T	Evans P	Foster B	Foster C	Hodgson G	Lathan J	Laverick M	Madden L	Matthews P	McCaffrey J	McDonald I	Mackenzie I	O'Brien N	Pate A	Randall K	Saxby M	Uzelac S	Wood I	
1	6		9			3	12	11	10*			8	7	4	5	2						1
1	2		9	12		3	6	10		8			11	7	5*	4						2
1	2		9			3	6	10	12	8			11*	7	5	4						3
1	4*		9	11		3	6	10	12					7	5	8	2					4
1	4			12		3	6	10	7				11*	9	5	8	2					5
1			9	12		3	6	11	7	10*				8	5	4	2					6
1	2		11	9		3	6	10	7*	12				8	5	4						7
1	4		9	7		3	6	10		12		8		11	5*		2					8
1	5		9	8		3	6	10		7		4		11			2					9
1	6		9	8			5	10		7		4	12	11*			2				3	10
1	6		9	8		3	5	10		4		7		11			2					11
1	6		9	8		3*	5	10		12		4	11	7			2					12
	5		9	8	1	3	4	10				7	11*	6	12		2					13
	6		9	8	1	3		10			4	7		11	5		2					14
	6		9		1	3		10			5	8		4	11		2	7				15
	6	1	9	8		3		10			5	7		4			2	11				16
	6		9		1	3	12	8				7	11	4*	5		2	10				17
	2		9		1	3	6	10				8	11	4	5			7				18
	2		9		1	3	6	10				7	11	4	5*		12	8				19
1	4		9			3	5	10	7				11	6			2	8				20
1	6		9			3	5	10	7				11	4			2	8				21
1	5		9			3	6	10	7	11				4			2	8				22
1	5		9			3	6	10	7				11	4			2	8				23
1	6		9			3		10	7				11	4	5		2	8				24
1	6		9			3		10	7			12	11	4*	5		2	8				25
1	6		9	8				10				4	11		5		2	7			3	26
1	6*		9	8		3		10				4	11	12	5		2	7				27
1			9	8		3		10				4	11		5		2	7	6			28
1			9	8		3		10				4	11		5		2	7		6		29
1			9	8		3		10				4	11	12	5		2	7*		6		30
1			9	8		3	6	10				4*	11	7	5		2		12			31
1			9	8		3	6	10		4			11	7	5		2					32
1			9	8		3	6	10		4			11	7	5		2					33
1			9	8		3	6	10		4			11	7	5		2					34
1			9	8		3	6	10		4			11	7	5		2					35
1			9			3	6	10		4			11	7	5		2	8				36
1			9	8		3	6	10		4			11	7	5		2					37
1			9	8		3	6	10		7		4	11		5		2					38
1			9			3	6	10		4		7	11		5		2	8				39
1			9	8		3	6	10		4		7	11		5		2					40
1			9	8		3	6	10		4		7	11		5		2					41
1			9	8		3	6	10		4		7	11		5		2					42
1			9	8		3	6	10		4		7	11		5		2					43
1			9	8		3	6	10		4		7	11		5		2					44
1	12		9	8		3	6	10		4		7*	11		5		2					45
1	12		9	8		3	6	10		4		7	11		5		2*					46
39	26	1	45	29	6	44	34	46	10	22	3	28	35	32	36	7	40	18	1	2	2	
	2			3			2		2	3		1	1	2	1		1		1			
	6		24	3			1	7		3		1	2	4	1		1	3	1			

1 own-goal

Arnold R	Bird K	Brown R	Clarke R	Eccles T	Evans P	Foster B	Foster C	Hodgson G	Lathan J	Laverick M	Madden L	Matthews P	McCaffrey J	McDonald I	Mackenzie I	O'Brien N	Pate A	Randall K	Saxby M	Uzelac S	Wood I	
	6	1	9	8		3	12	10			5	7*		4	11		2					1
	6	1	9	8		3		10			5	7		4	11		2					R
	6		9		1	3		10		8		7	11	4	5		2					2R
	6	1	9			3		10				7	11	4	5		2	8				2
	4	3	4	2	1	4		4		1	2	4	2	4	4		4	1				
							1															
				2						1				1								

1 own-goal

Arnold R	Bird K	Brown R	Clarke R	Eccles T	Evans P	Foster B	Foster C	Hodgson G	Lathan J	Laverick M	Madden L	Matthews P	McCaffrey J	McDonald I	Mackenzie I	O'Brien N	Pate A	Randall K	Saxby M	Uzelac S	Wood I	
1	2		9	12		3	6	11		8			7*	10	5	4						1
1	2		9			3	6	11	5	8			7*	10		4	12					
1	4		9			3	6	10	7				11		5	8	2					2
1	6		9	8		3	12	10		4		7		11	5*		2					3
	6		9	8	1	3		10			5	7		4	11		2					4
	6	1	9	8		3		10			5	7	11*	4	12		2					5
4	6	1	6	3	1	6	3	6	2	3	2	3	4	5	4	3	4					
				1			1								1		1					
	3		3	1					1	2				3								

1976-77

Manager: Peter Morris

1	Aug	21	(h)	Preston NE	W 3-1	Eccles 2, McCaffrey	5,688
2		28	(a)	Rotherham U	L 0-3		5,358
3	Sep	4	(h)	Grimsby T	W 3-0	Eccles 3 (1 pen)	5,220
4		7	(a)	Oxford U	W 3-0	Eccles, Randall, C.Foster	3,822
5		11	(a)	York C	W 1-0	Eccles	2,481
6		18	(h)	Tranmere R	D 1-1	Randall	5,859
7		25	(a)	Crystal P	L 0-2		14,286
8	Oct	2	(h)	Bury	W 5-0	Miller 2, Randall 2, Matthews	6,516
9		9	(a)	Peterborough U	L 1-2	McCaffrey	7,031
10		16	(a)	Chester	L 0-1		4,033
11		23	(h)	Brighton & HA	D 1-1	C.Foster	7,240
12		30	(a)	Sheffield W	W 2-0	Miller, Matthews	15,559
13	Nov	2	(a)	Shrewsbury T	D 0-0		6,161
14		6	(h)	Lincoln C	W 3-1	Hodgson, McCaffrey, Opp own-goal	8,232
15		8	(h)	Reading	W 4-0	Randall 4 (2 pens)	6,793
16		13	(a)	Gillingham	L 1-3	Hodgson	5,457
17		27	(h)	Swindon T	D 1-1	Hodgson	6,663
18	Dec	18	(h)	Wrexham	W 2-0	Miller, Hodgson	5,399
19		27	(a)	Chesterfield	W 1-0	Randall	11,726
20		28	(h)	Port Vale	W 2-1	Moss, Randall	7,979
21	Jan	11	(h)	Sheffield W	W 1-0	Moss	13,714
22		18	(a)	Portsmouth	D 2-2	Moss, Miller	10,720
23		22	(a)	Preston NE	W 2-1	Moss, C.Foster	8,500
24	Feb	5	(h)	Rotherham U	W 3-1	Moss, Morris, Randall (pen)	11,527
25		7	(h)	Oxford U	W 3-0	Moss 2, Bird	8,206
26		12	(a)	Grimsby T	W 1-0	C.Foster	5,322
27		15	(a)	Lincoln C	L 2-3	Bird, McEwan	9,588
28		19	(h)	York C	W 4-1	Randall 2, Bird, Morris	7,576
29		28	(h)	Walsall	W 3-0	Bird, Morris, Opp own-goal	8,029
30	Mar	5	(h)	Crystal P	W 1-0	C.Foster	10,944
31		8	(a)	Northampton T	W 1-0	Randall	7,288
32		12	(a)	Bury	L 0-2		5,321
33		19	(h)	Peterborough U	D 1-1	Cooke	7,728
34		21	(a)	Tranmere R	L 0-4		2,121
35		26	(h)	Chester	D 1-1	Moss	6,967
36	Apr	2	(a)	Brighton & HA	L 1-3	Moss	22,954
37		9	(a)	Port Vale	W 4-1	Bird 2, C.Foster, Randall	4,389
38		11	(h)	Chesterfield	W 2-1	Bird, Moss	11,905
39		12	(h)	Shrewsbury T	W 1-0	McEwan	9,840
40		16	(a)	Reading	L 0-1		4,900
41		19	(a)	Walsall	W 2-1	Moss, Opp own-goal	7,601
42		23	(h)	Gillingham	D 2-2	Randall, C.Foster	8,191
43		30	(a)	Swindon T	W 1-0	C.Foster	5,788
44	May	2	(h)	Portsmouth	W 2-0	Randall, C.Foster	10,774
45		7	(h)	Northampton T	W 3-0	Bird, McEwan, Moss	11,114
46		14	(a)	Wrexham	W 1-0	Moss	20,764

FINAL LEAGUE POSITION: 1st in Division Three

Appearances
Sub Appearances
Goals

FA Cup

1	Nov	20	(a)	Huddersfield T	D 0-0		9,025
R		22	(h)	Huddersfield T	W 2-1	Eccles, Randall	9,036
2	Dec	15	(h)	Matlock T	L 2-5	Matthews, C.Foster	8,181

Appearances
Sub Appearances
Goals

League Cup

1	Aug	14	(h)	Scunthorpe U	W 2-0	Eccles, McCaffrey	5,224
		17	(a)	Scunthorpe U	W 0-2		3,164
R		24	(a)	Scunthorpe U	L 1-2	McCaffrey	4,319

Appearances
Sub Appearances
Goals

Arnold R	Bird K	Cooke R	Eccles T	Foster B	Foster C	Hodgson G	Laverick M	Matthews P	McCaffrey J	McDonald I	McEwan W	Miller J	Mackenzie I	Morris P	Moss E	Pate A	Randall K	Saxby M	Wood I	
1	6		8	3		10			11			7	5	4		2	9			1
1			9	3	6	10			11			7	5	4		2	8			2
1			9	3	6	10			11			7	5	4		2	8			3
1	5		8	3	6	10		4	11			7				2	9			4
1	5		9	3	6	10		4	11	12		7*				2	8			5
1	5		9	3	6	10		4	11			7				2	8			6
1	5		9	3	6	10		4	11*	12		7				2	8			7
1			8	3	6	10		4	11			7	5			2	9			8
1	12		9	3	6	10		4	11			7	5*			2	8			9
1		9*		3	6	10		4	11	12		7	5			2	8			10
1			8	3	6	10		4	11			7	5			2	9			11
1	2				6	10		8		11		7	5	4			9		3	12
1	2				6	10		4		11		7	5	8			9		3	13
1	2*				6	10		8	12	11		7	5	4			9		3	14
1		12			6	10		4*	11	8		7	5	2			9		3	15
1				3	6	10			11	8		7	5	4		2	9			16
1				2	6	10			11	8		7	5	4			9		3	17
1	2			3	6	10		8				7	5	4	9		11			18
1	2			3	6	10		7	12			11	5*	4	8		9			19
1	2			3	6	10		4	11*	12		7			8		9	5		20
1	2	12		3	6	10		4	11			7			8		9*	5		21
1	2	12		3	6	10		4*				11		7	8		9	5		22
1	2			3	6	10					4	7		8	9		11	5		23
1	2	12		3	6	10					4	7		8	9		11*	5		24
1	2			3	6	10					4	11		7	8		9	5		25
1	2			3	6	10				4		11		7	8		9	5		26
1	2			3	6	10					4	11		7	8		9	5		27
1	2			3	6	10					4	11	5	7	8		9			28
1	2			3	6	10					4	11	5	7	8		9			29
1	2			3	6	10					4	11	5	7	8		9			30
1	2	7		3	6	10				11	4		5		8		9			31
1	6	12				10				11*	4	7			8	2	9	5	3	32
1	2	9		3	6	10				12	4	11	5*	7	8					33
1	2			3	6	10					4	11		7	9		8	5		34
1	5	12		3	6	10					4	11*		7	8	2	9			35
1	2			3	5	10				9	4	11		7	8				6	36
1	2			3	5	10				12	4	11		7*	9		8		6	37
1	2			3	5	10					4	11	7		8		9		6	38
1	2			3	5	10					4	11	7		8		9		6	39
1	2			3	6	10					4	11	5	7	8		9			40
1	2			3	6	10				11	4		5*	7	8		9		12	41
1	2			3	5	10				12	4	11*		7	8		9		6	42
1	2			3	6	10				11	4		5	7	9		8			43
1	2			3	6	10				11	4		5	7	8		9			44
1	2				6	10		12		11	4*		5	7	8		9		3	45
1	2				6	10				11	4		5	7	8		9		3	46
46	37	3	10	39	44	46		17	16	15	23	40	28	32	29	14	44	10	13	
	1	6						1	2	7									1	
	8	1	7		9	4		2	3		3	5		3	13		17			

3 own-goals

1		8			6	10			11	4		7	5	2			9		3	1
1			8		6	10			11	4		7	5	2			9		3	R
1			8	3	6	10		4	11			7	5	2			9			2
3		1	2	1	3	3		1	3	2		3	3	3			3		2	
			1		1			1									1			

1	6		9	3		10	8		11			7	5	4		2				1
1	6		9	3		10	8		11			7	5	4		2				
1	6		9	3		10			11			7	5	4		2	8			R
3	3		3	3		3	2		3			3	3	3		3	1			
			1						2											

1977-78

Manager: Peter Morris to 22 February, then Billy Bingham from 24 February 1978.

1	Aug	20	(h)	Stoke C	W	2-1	Syrett, Sharkey (pen)	14,077
2		23	(a)	Crystal P	L	1-3	Syrett	19,001
3		27	(a)	Southampton	L	0-1		15,981
4	Sep	3	(h)	Brighton & HA	L	1-2	Syrett	8,622
5		10	(h)	Millwall	D	0-0		7,655
6		17	(a)	Cardiff C	D	1-1	Moss	6,896
7		24	(h)	Burnley	W	4-1	Syrett, Moss, Hodgson, Sharkey (pen)	8,274
8	Oct	1	(a)	Hull C	W	2-0	Moss 2	6,263
9		4	(a)	Bristol R	L	1-3	Moss	4,980
10		8	(h)	Sheffield U	D	1-1	Aston	14,268
11		15	(a)	Bolton W	L	0-2		18,937
12		22	(h)	Sunderland	L	1-2	Syrett	12,827
13		29	(h)	Notts C	L	1-3	Bird	11,236
14	Nov	5	(a)	Charlton A	D	2-2	Moss, Syrett	9,068
15		12	(h)	Luton T	W	3-1	Sharkey, Syrett, Miller	7,522
16		19	(a)	Blackburn R	L	1-3	Sharkey	8,886
17		26	(h)	Oldham A	L	0-2		7,302
18	Dec	3	(a)	Orient	L	2-4	Bird, Miller	4,426
19		10	(h)	Blackpool	L	1-3	Sharkey (pen)	6,975
20		17	(h)	Luton T	D	1-1	Syrett	6,401
21		26	(h)	Fulham	W	2-1	Bird, C.Foster	8,457
22		27	(a)	Tottenham H	D	1-1	Bird	36,288
23		31	(h)	Crystal P	L	1-3	Aston	9,291
24	Jan	2	(a)	Stoke C	D	1-1	Goodwin	13,834
25		14	(h)	Southampton	L	1-2	Syrett	8,673
26		21	(a)	Brighton & HA	L	1-5	Opp own-goal	22,647
27	Feb	11	(h)	Cardiff C	D	2-2	Wood, Hodgson	6,538
28		25	(h)	Hull C	W	1-0	C.Foster	7,181
29	Mar	4	(a)	Sheffield U	L	0-2		14,916
30		11	(h)	Bolton W	L	0-1		12,329
31		14	(a)	Burnley	L	0-2		9,961
32		18	(a)	Sunderland	L	0-1		14,033
33		21	(a)	Notts C	L	0-1		10,587
34		25	(h)	Tottenham H	D	3-3	Syrett 3	12,106
35		27	(a)	Fulham	W	2-0	Syrett, C.Foster	7,088
36	Apr	1	(h)	Charlton A	L	0-3		6,591
37		8	(a)	Oldham A	W	1-0	Miller	7,224
38		15	(h)	Blackburn R	D	2-2	Syrett 2 (1 pen)	5,848
39		22	(a)	Blackpool	W	2-1	Syrett (pen), Miller	5,376
40		24	(h)	Bristol R	W	3-0	Aston 2, Miller	6,121
41		29	(h)	Orient	D	1-1	Pate	6,336
42	May	2	(a)	Millwall	L	0-1		7,500

FINAL LEAGUE POSITION: 21st in Division Two (Relegated)

Appearances
Sub Appearances
Goals

FA Cup

3	Jan	6	(h)	Plymouth A	W	1-0	Miller	7,402
4	Feb	6	(a)	Bolton W	L	0-1		23,830

Appearances
Sub Appearances
Goals

League Cup

1	Aug	13	(h)	Lincoln C	L	0-1		6,735
		17	(a)	Lincoln C	D	0-0		5,761

Appearances
Sub Appearances
Goals

Arnold R	Aston J	Bird K	Cooke R	Curtis R	Foster B	Foster C	Goodwin D	Hodgson G	Martin D	Matthews P	McDonald I	McEwan W	Miller J	Mackenzie I	Morris P	Moss E	Pate A	Phillips I	Randall K	Saxby M	Sharkey P	Syrett D	Wood I	
1		2				6		10				4	11	5		8					7	9	3	1
1		2				6		10				4	11*	5		8			12		7	9	3	2
1		2				6		10				4	11*	5		8			12		7	9	3	3
1		2				6		10				4	11*	5		8			12		7	9	3	4
1	11	2				5		10				4				8		3	12		7	9*	6	5
1	11	2				5		10		4						8		3			7	9	6	6
1	11	2				5		10		4						8		3			7	9	6	7
1	11	2						10		4						8		3		5	7	9	6	8
1	11	2				5		10		4						8		3			7	9	6	9
1	11	2				5		10				4				8		3			7	9	6	10
1	11	2				5		10				4				8		3			7	9	6	11
1	11	2				5		10				4			7	8		3				9	6	12
1	11	2				5		10				4			7	8		3				9	6	13
1		2						10					11		4	8		3		5	7	9	6	14
1		2						10					11		4	8		3		5	7	9	6	15
1	12	2					8	10					11		4			3*		5	7	9	6	16
1	12	2					8	10					11		4			3*		5	7	9	6	17
1	12	2			3		8*	10					11	5	4						7	9	6	18
1	8	2			3	5		10					11		4						7	9	6	19
1	11	2			3	5	8*	10					7							12	4	9	6	20
1	11	2	8		3	5		10					7								4	9	6	21
1	11	2	8*		3	5		10					7							12	4	9	6	22
1	11	2	8*		3	5	12	10					7								4	9	6	23
1	11	2*	12		3	5	8	10					7								4	9	6	24
1	11*				3	5	8	10					7				2	12			4	9	6	25
1	12	2*	8		3	5		10					7					11			4	9	6	26
1	11			2	3	5		10							7			8			4	9	6	27
1	11*			2	3	5	8	10					7					12			4	9	6	28
1	11			2*	3	5	8	10					7							4	12	9	6	29
1				2	3	5	8	10	11*				7					12		4		9	6	30
1	12			2	3	4	8	10	11				7							5		9*	6	31
1	12				3		8	10	11				7				2			5	4*	9	6	32
1					3	4	12	10	8				11*				2			5	7	9	6	33
1		2			3	4		10	8				11							5	7	9	6	34
1		2			3	4	12	10	8				11*							5	7	9	6	35
1	12	2			3	4		10	11				7							5	8*	9	6	36
1	11	6			3	4		10	8				7				2			5		9		37
1	11*	6	12		3	4		10	8				7				2			5		9		38
1	11	6			3	4		10	8				7				2			5		9		39
1	11	6			3	4		10	8				7				2			5		9		40
1	11	6			3	4		10	8				7				2			5		9		41
1		6			3	4	11	10	8				7				2			5		9		42
42	24	34	4	5	25	35	12	42	13	4		9	32	5	9	15	9	15		19	31	42	36	
	7		2				3											3	4	2	1			
	4	4				3	1	2					5			6	1				5	16	1	

1 own-goal

1	11				3	5	8	10					7*				2	12			4*	9	6	3
1					2	5	8*	10					11		7			3		12	4	9	6	4
2	1				2	2	2	2					2		1		1	1			2	2	2	
																		1		1				
													1											

1		2				6		10		11	12	4	7*	5		8						9	3	1
1		2				6		10		7		4	11	5		8						9	3	
2		2				2		2		2		2	2	2		2						2	2	
											1													

1978-79

Manager: Billy Bingham

1	Aug	19	(a)	Exeter C	D 0-0		3,704
2		21	(h)	Gillingham	D 1-1	Bird	5,745
3		26	(h)	Southend U	D 1-1	Goodwin	5,500
4	Sep	2	(a)	Swindon T	L 0-1		6,195
5		9	(a)	Plymouth A	W 4-1	Syrett, Miller, Martin, M.Saxby	6,052
6		16	(h)	Sheffield W	D 1-1	Goodwin	11,366
7		23	(a)	Rotherham U	L 0-2		5,350
8		27	(a)	Oxford U	L 2-3	Bird, Allen	3,998
9		30	(h)	Carlisle U	W 1-0	Miller	4,716
10	Oct	7	(a)	Shrewsbury T	D 2-2	Bird, Moss	4,338
11		14	(h)	Walsall	L 1-3	Martin	6,066
12		17	(a)	Swansea C	L 2-3	Goodwin, Allen	10,985
13		21	(a)	Blackpool	L 0-2		6,633
14		28	(h)	Colchester U	D 1-1	Moss	4,515
15	Nov	4	(a)	Lincoln C	W 1-0	Martin	3,614
16		11	(h)	Swindon T	L 0-1		4,721
17		13	(h)	Tranmere R	D 0-0		3,929
18		17	(a)	Southend U	D 1-1	Syrett	7,532
19	Dec	2	(a)	Watford	D 1-1	Goodwin	4,157
20		9	(h)	Brentford	W 2-1	McClelland, Curtis (pen)	4,003
21		23	(h)	Peterborough U	D 1-1	Opp own-goal	3,671
22		26	(a)	Hull C	L 0-3		4,700
23		30	(a)	Bury	D 0-0		4,009
24	Feb	10	(a)	Carlisle U	L 0-1		4,934
25		24	(a)	Walsall	D 1-1	Bird	4,157
26	Mar	3	(h)	Blackpool	D 1-1	Curtis (pen)	4,829
27		9	(a)	Colchester U	L 0-1		2,866
28		12	(h)	Plymouth A	W 5-0	Carter 2, Syrett 2, Hamilton	4,325
29		24	(a)	Gillingham	D 0-0		6,935
30		26	(h)	Exeter C	D 1-1	Allen	4,562
31		31	(a)	Chester	D 1-1	Austin	2,205
32	Apr	3	(a)	Sheffield W	W 2-1	Austin, M.Saxby	11,065
33		7	(h)	Watford	L 0-3		7,944
34		14	(h)	Hull C	L 0-2		5,138
35		16	(a)	Chesterfield	L 0-1		4,931
36		17	(a)	Peterborough U	W 2-1	Austin, Miller	4,178
37		21	(h)	Bury	W 3-0	Curtis, Carter, Opp own-goal	3,976
38		23	(h)	Swansea C	D 2-2	Allen, Curtis (pen)	6,420
39		28	(a)	Brentford	L 0-1		6,830
40		30	(a)	Tranmere R	W 2-1	Carter, G.Saxby	1,121
41	May	5	(h)	Chester	W 2-0	Austin, Curtis (pen)	4,173
42		7	(h)	Shrewsbury T	D 2-2	Allen, Curtis (pen)	6,413
43		11	(h)	Lincoln C	W 2-0	Austin, M.Saxby	4,388
44		14	(h)	Oxford U	D 1-1	Miller	4,138
45		19	(h)	Rotherham U	L 0-1		3,913
46		21	(h)	Chesterfield	W 2-1	M.Saxby, Opp own-goal	4,159

FINAL LEAGUE POSITION: 18th in Division Three

Appearances
Sub Appearances
Goals

FA Cup

1	Nov	25	(h)	Shrewsbury T	L 0-2		4,481

Appearances
Sub Appearances
Goals

League Cup

1	Aug	12	(h)	Darlington	L 0-1		4,930
		15	(a)	Darlington	D 2-2	Bird, Miller	5,000

Appearances
Sub Appearances
Goals

Allen R	Arnold R	Austin T	Bird K	Carter M	Coffey M	Curtis R	Dawkins D	Foster B	Foster C	Goodwin D	Gratton J	Hamilton N	Hodgson G	Martin D	McClelland J	Miller J	Moss E	New M	Phillips I	Saxby G	Saxby M	Syrett D	Wood I	
11	1		4			2		3					10	8	6	7					5	9*	12	1
11	1		2		4*			3					10	8	6	7					5	9	12	2
11	1		2					3		4			10	8	6	7					5	9		3
11*	1		2					3		4			10	8	6	7					5	9	12	4
	1		11			2		3*	12	4			10	8	6	7					5	9		5
	1		11			2		3		4			10	8	6*	7	12				5	9		6
11*	1		7		12	2		3		4				10	6		8				5	9		7
11	1		4		10	2		3		9				8*	6	7				12	5			8
11	1		2					3						10*	6	7	8		12	4	5	9		9
11	1		2					3		8				10*	6	7	9		12	4	5			10
12	1		2					3		10				11	6	4*	8		9	7	5			11
11	1		2*			12		3		9					6	7	8		10	4	5			12
11*	1		7			2		3	12	10					6		8			4	5	9		13
12	1		3					3		4				10*	2	7	8		11		6	9		14
	1		6					3	4	10				11	2	7	8				5	9		15
12	1		6			2		3		8				11*	10	7				4	5	9		16
12	1		6*			2		3	8	10					11	7				4	5	9		17
11	1					2		3	4	10	7*				6	8					5	9	12	18
	1		6			2		3*	4	10				7	11		8				5	9	12	19
	1		6			2*	3		10	4				7	11		8				5	9	12	20
	1		4				2	3	10	11				7	6		8				5	9		21
	1		6				2	3	10	4				7*	11		8				5	9	12	22
12	1		4				2		10	11				8	6	7*					5	9	3	23
10	1		11			4	2			12		7		8*	6						5	9	3	24
11	1		10			4	2	3		8*		7			6						5	9	12	25
	1		4	7		6	2	3		11		8*		10							5	9	12	26
12			6	8		4	2	3				7		10	9	11*		1			5			27
12			6	8		4	2	3				7		10		11		1			5	9*		28
12			4	9		5	2	3				11		8	6	7*		1			10			29
11			6	8		4	2	3				7		10	9			1			5			30
9*		8	6	7		4	2	3				10		11				1			5		12	31
		9	6	8		4*	2	3		11		7		10				1			5		12	32
12		9	6	7		4	2	3		10*		8		11				1			5			33
12	1	9	6	8		4	2	3				10*		11		7					5			34
	1	9	6	8		4	2	3				7		10	12	11*					5			35
7		9	10	8		4	2							11	6	12		1			5		3*	36
11		9	10	8		4	2					12			6	7*		1			5		3	37
7*		9	10	8		4	2					12			6	11		1			5		3	38
7		9	2	8		4								10	6	11		1		12	5		3*	39
7		9	6	8		4	2	3						10				1		11	5			40
11		9	6	8		4	2	3		7*						12		1		10	5			41
7		9	6	8		4	2	3	12							10		1		11*	5			42
7		9	6	8		4	2	3				11*				12		1		10	5			43
7		9	6				2	3	4			10			12	11		1		8*	5			44
10		9	6			4	2	3				11			12	7		1		8*	5			45
7		9				4	2	3	12	11		10*			6			1		8	5			46
26	28	16	44	18	2	33	26	39	9	26	1	16	6	33	33	28	12	18	3	14	46	23	6	
10					1	1			4	1		2			3	3	1		2	2			11	
5		5	4	4		6				4		1		3	1	4	2			1	4	4		

3 own-goals

11	1		6			2		3		8					4	7					5	9	10	1
1	1		1			1		1		1					1	1					1	1	1	

12	1		2		11*			3	4				10	8	6	7					5	9		1
11	1		2		12			3	4*				10	8	6	7					5	9		
1	2		2		1			2	2				2	2	2	2					2	2		
1					1																			
			1													1								

1979-80

Manager: Mick Jones

1	Aug	18	(h)	Chesterfield	W 3-2	Curtis, Bird, Allen	5,623
2		21	(a)	Rotherham U	L 1-2	Austin	4,490
3		25	(a)	Exeter C	L 1-2	Austin	3,475
4	Sep	1	(h)	Hull C	D 1-1	Austin	4,320
5		8	(a)	Barnsley	L 0-1		10,588
6		15	(h)	Oxford U	W 1-0	Austin	4,217
7		18	(a)	Colchester U	L 1-2	Bird	2,346
8		22	(h)	Sheffield U	L 3-4	Taylor, Austin, Allen	11,272
9		29	(a)	Reading	L 0-1		5,878
10	Oct	1	(h)	Colchester U	L 0-1		3,500
11		6	(a)	Sheffield W	D 0-0		13,072
12		8	(h)	Rotherham U	W 5-1	Austin 3, Taylor 2	6,308
13		13	(h)	Bury	W 1-0	Hamilton	4,486
14		20	(a)	Millwall	D 2-2	Lathan, Austin	6,049
15		23	(a)	Carlisle U	D 1-1	Austin	4,898
16		27	(h)	Gillingham	W 2-0	Bird, Taylor	4,598
17	Nov	3	(a)	Chesterfield	L 0-2		7,601
18		6	(h)	Carlisle U	W 2-1	Bird, Taylor	3,000
19		10	(h)	Swindon T	D 1-1	Taylor	4,425
20		17	(a)	Chester	L 0-1		2,920
21	Dec	1	(h)	Blackpool	D 1-1	Austin	4,324
22		8	(a)	Grimsby T	L 1-2	Austin	7,663
23		21	(h)	Plymouth A	D 0-0		3,000
24		26	(a)	Blackburn R	D 0-0		8,531
25		29	(h)	Exeter C	L 0-1		3,711
26	Jan	12	(a)	Hull C	L 1-3	Allen	4,243
27		26	(h)	Wimbledon	D 1-1	Bird	3,895
28	Feb	2	(a)	Oxford U	L 1-3	Pollard	2,871
29		9	(a)	Sheffield U	L 0-1		14,921
30		16	(h)	Reading	D 2-2	Pollard, Austin (pen)	3,112
31		23	(a)	Bury	W 2-0	Pollard, Austin	3,606
32	Mar	1	(h)	Millwall	W 1-0	Austin (pen)	4,162
33		8	(a)	Gillingham	L 0-2		4,572
34		10	(h)	Brentford	D 0-0		3,000
35		15	(h)	Sheffield W	D 1-1	Opp own-goal	16,109
36		17	(a)	Southend U	D 1-1	Allen	2,793
37		22	(a)	Swindon T	L 1-2	Opp own-goal	7,990
38		29	(h)	Chester	W 2-1	Austin 2	3,097
39	Apr	1	(a)	Plymouth A	D 0-0		4,669
40		5	(h)	Blackburn R	L 0-1		7,385
41		7	(a)	Brentford	L 0-2		6,060
42		12	(h)	Southend U	W 3-1	Austin 2, McClelland	3,314
43		14	(h)	Barnsley	L 1-4	Bird	6,789
44		19	(a)	Blackpool	D 1-1	Bird	5,677
45		26	(h)	Grimsby T	D 0-0		10,100
46	May	3	(a)	Wimbledon	L 2-3	Taylor, Pollard	2,149

FINAL LEAGUE POSITION: 23rd in Division Three (Relegated)

Appearances
Sub Appearances
Goals

FA Cup

1	Nov	24	(a)	Blyth Spartans	W 2-0	McClelland, Allen	4,433
2	Dec	15	(a)	Doncaster R	W 2-1	Austin, Curtis	7,952
3	Jan	5	(h)	Brighton & HA	L 0-2		8,204

Appearances
Sub Appearances
Goals

League Cup

1	Aug	1	(h)	York C	W 1-0	Taylor	3,117
		14	(a)	York C	L 2-3*	Wood, Hamilton	2,590
2		29	(a)	Reading	L 3-4	Bird, Taylor, Allen	5,779
	Sep	4	(h)	Reading	W 4-2	Austin 2, McClelland, Taylor	4,326
3		25	(h)	Queen's Park R	L 0-3		9,485

*Mansfield won on away-goals rule

Appearances
Sub Appearances
Goals

Allen R	Arnold R	Austin T	Bird K	Burrows A	Caldwell D	Curtis R	Dawkins D	Foster B	Goodwin D	Hamilton N	Lathan J	Mann A	McClelland J	Miller J	McJannet L	New M	Pollard B	Saxby G	Taylor S	Thompson GB	Thompson BL	Wood I	
11		9	6			4	2	3	7	10						1			8			5	1
11		9	6			4	2	3	7*	10						1			8		12	5	2
11	1	9	6			4	2	3		10	8								7			5	3
11	1	10	4			6	2	3		8	7		5						9				4
11	1	10	4			6	2	3		8	7		5						9				5
11	1	10	4			6	2	3		8	7		5						9				6
11	1	9	5			4	2	3		10	7		6						8				7
11	1	10	4			6	2			8	7		5						9			3	8
11*	1	9	5		12	4	2			10	8		6						7			3	9
11	1	9	5		12		2	3*	8	10	7		6									4	10
11	1	9	5				2			10	8	4	6						7			3	11
11	1	9	5				2			4	7	10	6						8			3	12
11	1	9	4				2			6	7	10	5						8			3	13
11*	1	9	4			12	2			10	7	6	5						8			3	14
11	1	9	5				2			4	7	10	6						8			3	15
11	1	9	5*			12	2			4	7	10	6						8			3	16
11	1	9	5				2			4	7	10	6						8			3	17
11*	1	9	5			12	2			4	7	10	6						8			3	18
11	1	9				5				4	7	10*	6						8	2	12	3	19
11	1	9	5			4					7		6						8	2	10	3	20
11	1	9	5							4	7	10	6						8	2		3	21
	1	9	5			4					7	11	6						8	2	10	3	22
12	1	9	5			4					10*	11	6						8	2	7	3	23
11	1	9	5			4					10	3	6						8	2	7		24
12	1	9	5			4		3			8*	11	6						10	2	7		25
11		9	5			4		3	8		7*	10	6			1				2	12		26
11	1	9	5			4				12		10	6				7		8	2*		3	27
8	1	9	5			4	2			11		3	6	12			7					3*	28
8	1	9		5		4	2			10*		3	6	11			7		12				29
11	1	9	6			4	2			10		3	5	7			8						30
11	1	9		5		4	2			10		3	6	7			8						31
11	1	9		6		4	2			10		3	5	7			8						32
11	1	9		6		4	2			10*		3	5	7			8		12				33
11	1	9		6		4*	2			10		3	5	7			8		12				34
10	1	9	4	6			2				8	3	5	7*			11		12				35
11	1	9	7	6		4	2				10	3	5				8						36
11	1	9	7	6		4	2*				10	3	5				8		12				37
10	1	9	8	6		4	2					3	5	7			11						38
11	1	9	10	6		4	2				7	3	5				8						39
11	1	9	10*	6		4	2					3	5	7			8		12				40
11*	1	9		6	7	4	2				10	3	5				8		12				41
12	1	9		6		4	2	3		11*		10	5				8		7				42
	1	9	4	6			2	3		11		10	5				8		7				43
12	1	9	4	6			2*	3		11		10	5				8		7				44
12	1	9	4	6				3		10		11*	5		2		8		7				45
12	1	9	4	6				3		11*		10	5		2		8		7				46
38	43	46	38	17	1	31	35	15	4	32	29	35	43	9	2	3	20		30	9	5	21	
6					2	3				1				1					7		3		
4		19	7			1				1	1		1				4		7				

2 own-goals

11	1	9	5			12	2			4	7	10*	6						8			3	1
	1	9	5			4	2				7	11	6						8		10	3	2
11	1	9	5	12		4	2	3*				10	6						8		7		3
2	3	3	3			2	3	1		1	2	3	3						3		2	2	
				1		1																	
1		1				1							1										

11	1	9	6			4	2	3		10								7	8			5	1
11	1	9	6			4	2	3	12	10								7*	8			5	
11	1	9	6			4	2	3		10	7		12						8			5*	2
11	1	9	5			4	2	3		10	7		6						8				
11	1	9	5			4*	2		12	10	7		6						8			3	3
5	5	5	5			5	5	4		5	3		2					2	5			4	
									2				1										
1		2	1							1			1						3			1	

1980-81

Manager: Mick Jones

1	Aug	16	(a)	Halifax T	W 2-0	Austin 2	1,682
2		18	(h)	York C	L 0-1		4,080
3		23	(h)	Hereford U	W 4-0	Bird, Burrows, Caldwell, Austin	3,103
4		30	(a)	Port Vale	D 0-0		2,558
5	Sep	6	(h)	Darlington	W 1-0	Hamilton	3,001
6		13	(a)	Bury	L 1-4	McClelland	2,668
7		15	(h)	Wimbledon	W 1-0	McClelland	2,903
8		20	(a)	Aldershot	L 0-1		3,607
9		27	(h)	Wigan A	W 3-1	Hamilton, Allen, Pollard	3,402
10		30	(a)	Wimbledon	L 1-2	Austin	2,052
11	Oct	3	(a)	Southend U	L 0-2		4,443
12		6	(h)	Tranmere R	D 1-1	Allen	1,925
13		11	(h)	Bradford C	W 1-0	Bird	3,234
14		18	(a)	Bournemouth	W 1-0	Bird	3,335
15		21	(a)	Hartlepool U	W 1-0	McClelland	3,369
16		25	(h)	Peterborough U	W 2-1	Allen, Parkinson (pen)	4,883
17		27	(h)	Northampton T	W 2-0	Allen, Parkinson (pen)	3,560
18	Nov	1	(a)	Rochdale	W 4-1	Austin 3 (1 pen), Mann	2,636
19		3	(a)	Tranmere R	L 0-1		2,048
20		8	(h)	Torquay U	D 1-1	Bird	3,266
21		11	(a)	York C	L 0-2		2,204
22		15	(h)	Halifax T	L 0-1		2,561
23		29	(a)	Crewe A	W 2-1	Caldwell, Parkinson (pen)	2,482
24	Dec	6	(h)	Stockport C	W 1-0	Allen	2,873
25		19	(a)	Doncaster R	L 1-2	Caldwell	3,620
26		26	(h)	Scunthorpe U	W 1-0	Allen	4,261
27		27	(a)	Lincoln C	D 1-1	Opp own-goal	8,522
28	Jan	10	(a)	Northampton T	W 1-0	McClelland	2,985
29		17	(h)	Crewe A	W 4-1	Wood, Mann, Caldwell, Lumby	3,202
30		24	(h)	Port Vale	W 5-0	Wood 2, McClelland, Caldwell 2	3,864
31		31	(a)	Hereford U	L 1-2	Lumby (pen)	2,672
32	Feb	7	(h)	Bury	W 2-0	Bird, Caldwell	3,514
33		15	(a)	Darlington	D 2-2	McClelland, Allen	5,932
34		21	(a)	Wigan A	L 0-2		4,032
35	Mar	7	(h)	Southend U	L 0-1		4,379
36		14	(a)	Bradford C	W 2-0	Allen, Parkinson (pen)	2,986
37		16	(h)	Hartlepool U	L 0-1		3,737
38		21	(h)	Bournemouth	D 1-1	Opp own-goal	2,606
39		28	(a)	Peterborough U	L 0-1		4,904
40	Apr	4	(h)	Rochdale	D 2-2	Wood, Lumby	2,597
41		6	(h)	Aldershot	L 1-2	Burrows	2,748
42		12	(a)	Torquay U	D 1-1	Burrows	1,699
43		18	(h)	Lincoln C	W 2-0	Caldwell, Thomson	4,771
44		20	(a)	Scunthorpe U	L 0-2		1,850
45	May	1	(a)	Stockport C	L 1-2	Allen	2,236
46		6	(h)	Doncaster R	D 1-1	Lumby (pen)	4,506

FINAL LEAGUE POSITION: 7th in Division Four

Appearances
Sub Appearances
Goals

FA Cup

1	Nov	22	(h)	Rochdale	W 3-1	Caldwell, Parkinson 2 (2 pens)	3,280
2	Dec	13	(a)	Mossley	W 3-1	Caldwell, Thomson, Allen (pen)	3,680
3	Jan	3	(h)	Carlisle U	D 2-2	Bird, Parkinson	5,598
R		6	(a)	Carlisle U	L 1-2	Pollard	6,929

Appearances
Sub Appearances
Goals

League Cup

1	Aug	8	(a)	Doncaster R	D 1-1	Caldwell	4,201
		11	(h)	Doncaster R	W 2-0	Austin, Pollard	3,420
2		26	(h)	Barnsley	D 0-0		6,294
	Sep	2	(a)	Barnsley	L 2-4*	McClelland, Parkinson (pen)	10,566

*After extra-time

Appearances
Sub Appearances
Goals

Allen R	Arnold R	Austin T	Bird K	Burrows A	Caldwell D	Dawkins D	Foster B	Hamilton N	Johnson S	Lumby J	Mann A	McClelland J	McJannet L	Parkinson N	Phillips B	Pollard B	Sutton S	Thomson B	Wood I	Woodhead S	
	1	9	4	6	8	2					3	5		10	7	11					1
	1	9	4	6	8	2					3	5		10	7	11					2
	1	9	4	6	8	2					3	5		10	7	11					3
	1	9	4	6	8	2					3	5		10	7	11					4
12	1	9		6	8*	2		4			3	5		10	7	11					5
	1	9	4	6*	8	2		12			3	5		10	7	11					6
7	1	9	6			2		4			3	5		10	8	11					7
7	1	9	6			2*		4			3	5		10	8	11		12			8
7	1	9	6			2		4			3	5		10	8	11					9
7	1	9	6			2		4			3	5		10	8	11					10
7	1	9	6		12	2		4*			3	5		10	8	11					11
7*	1	9	6		12	2		4			3	5		10	8	11					12
7	1	9	6				3	4			8	5	2	10		11					13
7	1	9	6				3	4			8	5	2*	10		11			12		14
7	1	9	6				3	4			8	5	2	10		11					15
7*	1	9	6		12		3	4			8	5	2	10		11					16
7	1	9	6				3	4			8	5	2	10		11					17
7*	1	9	6				3	4			8	5	2	10		11			12		18
7	1	9	6				3	4				5	2	10		11		12	8*		19
7	1	9	6				3	4			8	5	2	10		11					20
7	1	9	6				3	4			8	5	2	10		11					21
7	1	9*	6		12		3	4			8	5	2	10				11			22
7	1		6		9		3	4			8	5	2	10		12		11			23
7	1		6		9		3	4			8	5	2	10				11			24
7	1		6		9		3*	4			8	5	2		10	12		11			25
7	1		6		9			4	3		8	5	2	10				11			26
7*	1		6		9			4			8	5	2	10		12		11	3		27
	1		6		9			4		7	8	5	2		10			11	3		28
	1		6		9			4		10	8	5	2		7			11	3		29
	1		6		9			4		10	8	5	2		7			11	3		30
	1		6		9			4*		10	8	5	2		7	12		11	3		31
7	1		6*	12	9			4			8	5	2	10				11	3		32
7	1			6	9			4			8	5	2	10				11	3		33
7	1			6	9			4*			8	5	2	10		12		11	3		34
7	1		6					4			8	5	2	10		9		11	3		35
7	1		6	4							8	5	2	10		9		11	3		36
7*	1			4	9					8	6	5	2	10		12		11	3		37
7	1		6	4						9	8	5	2	10				11	3		38
			6	4	7			12		9	8	5	2	10*			1	11	3		39
7			6	4	9					12	8	5	2	10*			1	11	3		40
7			4	5				10		9	8	6	2			11	1		3		41
7			4	5	12			10		9*	8	6	2				1	11	3		42
7			4	5	9			10			8	6	2			12	1	11	3*		43
7			4	5	9			10*			8	6	2			12	1	11	3		44
7			4	5				10		9	8*	6	2			12	1	11	3		45
7			4	5				10		9		6	2			8	1	11*	3	12	46
35	38	22	42	19	23	12	13	36	1	11	44	46	34	35	17	25	8	24	21		
1				1	5			2		1						9		2	2	1	
9		7	5	3	8			2		4	2	6		4		1		1	4		

2 own-goals

Allen R	Arnold R	Austin T	Bird K	Burrows A	Caldwell D	Dawkins D	Foster B	Hamilton N	Johnson S	Lumby J	Mann A	McClelland J	McJannet L	Parkinson N	Phillips B	Pollard B	Sutton S	Thomson B	Wood I	Woodhead S	
7	1		6		9		3	4			8	5	2	10				11			1
7	1		6		9		3	4			8	5	2		10			11			2
	1		6		9			4			8	5	2	10		7		11	3		3
	1		6	12	9			4			8	5	2		10	7*		11	3		R
2	4		4		4		2	4			4	4	4	2	2	2		4	2		
				1																	
1			1		2									3		1		1			

Allen R	Arnold R	Austin T	Bird K	Burrows A	Caldwell D	Dawkins D	Foster B	Hamilton N	Johnson S	Lumby J	Mann A	McClelland J	McJannet L	Parkinson N	Phillips B	Pollard B	Sutton S	Thomson B	Wood I	Woodhead S	
	1	9	4	6	8	2					3	5		10	7	11					1
	1	9	4	6	8	2					3	5		10	7	11					
	1	9	4	6	8	2					3	5		10	7	11					2
	1	9	4	6	8	2*		12			3	5		10	7	11					
	4	4	4	4	4	4					4	4		4	4	4					
								1													
		1			1							1		1		1					

1981-82

Manager: Stuart Boam

1	Aug	29	(a)	Peterborough U	L 0-1		4,310
2	Sep	5	(h)	Bournemouth	L 0-1		2,950
3		12	(a)	Port Vale	D 0-0		3,043
4		19	(h)	Bury	D 1-1	Lumby	2,501
5		21	(h)	Northampton T	W 4-1	Burrows, Mann, Lumby, Nicholson	2,612
6		26	(a)	Aldershot	W 3-2	Burrows, Lumby, Boam	2,486
7		30	(a)	Torquay U	L 0-2		3,100
8	Oct	3	(h)	Blackpool	D 2-2	Bird, Caldwell	3,466
9		10	(h)	Hull C	D 3-3	Lumby 2, Caldwell	3,464
10		17	(a)	Darlington	L 0-1		1,576
11		20	(a)	Sheffield U	L 1-4	Caldwell	12,727
12		24	(h)	Crewe A	L 0-1		2,531
13		30	(a)	Stockport C	L 0-3		2,081
14	Nov	2	(h)	Colchester U	L 1-3	Morgan	2,294
15		7	(a)	Halifax T	L 1-2	Caldwell	1,447
16		14	(h)	Rochdale	W 4-3	Bell 2, Morgan, Parkinson (pen)	2,300
17		28	(h)	Hereford U	W 2-1	Wood, Lumby	1,898
18	Dec	5	(a)	Tranmere R	D 2-2	Morgan 2	1,317
19	Jan	2	(h)	Wigan A	L 1-2	Wood	2,173
20		16	(h)	Hartlepool U	W 3-2	Morgan, Caldwell, Parkinson	2,011
21		20	(a)	Bradford C	W 4-3	Lumby 2, Morgan, Parkinson	3,729
22		23	(h)	Peterborough U	L 1-2	Parkinson (pen)	3,242
23		30	(a)	Bury	L 2-3	Bell, Lumby	2,954
24	Feb	2	(a)	Scunthorpe U	L 0-1		2,099
25		6	(h)	Port Vale	L 1-3	Bell	2,690
26		9	(a)	Northampton T	D 1-1	Lumby	1,945
27		13	(a)	Blackpool	W 3-2	Cannell, Lumby, Parkinson	3,017
28		20	(h)	Aldershot	W 1-0	Parkinson	2,001
29		23	(a)	Bournemouth	L 0-1		5,725
30		27	(a)	Hull C	L 0-2		4,958
31	Mar	6	(h)	Darlington	L 2-3	Lumby, Nicholson	1,538
32		8	(h)	Sheffield U	D 1-1	Wood	8,951
33		13	(a)	Crewe A	W 2-0	Bell, Cannell	1,476
34		16	(a)	Colchester U	W 1-0	Lumby	2,000
35		20	(h)	Stockport C	D 2-2	Lumby, Parkinson (pen)	2,159
36		27	(h)	Halifax T	W 3-2	Caldwell 2, Cannell	2,197
37	Apr	3	(a)	Rochdale	D 1-1	Parkinson	1,276
38		5	(h)	York C	L 0-2		2,388
39		10	(a)	York C	L 1-2	Wood	2,155
40		13	(h)	Scunthorpe U	D 1-1	Caldwell	2,202
41		17	(h)	Tranmere R	W 3-0	Bird, Nicholson, Parkinson (pen)	1,995
42		24	(a)	Hereford U	L 1-3	Cannell	2,852
43	May	1	(h)	Torquay U	W 3-1	Nicholson 2, Caldwell	1,392
44		5	(a)	Hartlepool U	L 0-3		1,202
45		8	(a)	Wigan A	L 1-3	Burrows	8,517
46		15	(h)	Bradford C	L 0-2		3,107

FINAL LEAGUE POSITION: 20th in Division Four

Appearances
Sub Appearances
Goals

FA Cup

1	Nov	21	(h)	Doncaster R	L 0-1		5,456

Appearances
Sub Appearances
Goals

League Cup

1	Sep	1	(a)	Scunthorpe U	D 0-0		2,249
		14	(h)	Scunthorpe U	W 2-0	Lumby 2	2,258
2	Oct	7	(a)	Bradford C	W 4-3	Bird, Lumby, Wood, Smith (og)	4,293
		26	(h)	Bradford C	L 0-2		3,622

Appearances
Sub Appearances
Goals

Arnold R	Bell C	Bird K	Boam S	Brown G	Burrows A	Calderwood C	Caldwell D	Cannell P	Foster B	Lumby J	Mann A	McJannet L	Morgan T	Nicholson G	Parkinson N	Thomson B	Wood I	Woodhead S	
1	4	6	5							9	12	2		11*	8	7	3	10	1
1	4	6	5							9	12	2		11	8*	7	3	10	2
1	4	6	5				10			9	8	3		11		7	2		3
1	4	6	5				10			9	8	2		11		7	3		4
1	4	6			5		10			9	8	2		11		7	3		5
1	4	6	12		5		10			9	8	2		11		7*	3		6
1	4	6	12		5		10			9	8	2		11		7*	3		7
1	4	6	12		5		10		3	9	8	2		11		7*			8
1	4	6			5		10		3	9*	8			11	12	7	2		9
1	4	6			5		10		3		8	2		11	12	7		9*	10
1	4	6			5		10		3	9	8	2		11		7			11
1	4	6	12		5		10		3	9	8	2		11		7*			12
1	4	6			5		10			9	8	2		11	7		3		13
1	4	6			5		10				9	2	8	11	12	7	3*		14
1	4	6			5		10				9	2	8	12	11	7*	3		15
1	4				5		10		3		9	2	8		11	7	6		16
1	4				5		10		3	7	9	2	8		11		6		17
1	4				5		10		3	7	9	2	8		11		6		18
1	4				5		10		3	9	7	2	8		11		6		19
1	4				5		10	9	3		7	2	8		11		6		20
1	4				5		10*	9	3	12	7	2	8		11		6		21
1	4*				5			9	3	10	7	2	8		11	12	6		22
1	4	12			5			9	3	10	7	2	8*		11		6		23
	4			1	5		10		3	9		2	8*	7	11	12	6		24
1	4				5				3	9		2	8	10	11	7	6		25
1	4				5			8	3	9		2		10	11	7	6		26
1	4				5			8	3	9		2		10	11	7	6		27
1	4				5			8	3	9		2		10	11	7	6		28
1	4				5		12	8	3	9		2		10	11	7*	6		29
1	4				5		12	8	3	9*		2		10	11	7	6		30
1	4				5			8	3	9		2		10	11	7	6		31
1	4				5			8	3	9*	7	2		10	11	12	6		32
1	4				5	6		8		9	7	2		10	11		3		33
1	4				5			8	3	9	7	2		10		11	6		34
1	4				5			8	3	9	7	2		10	12	11*	6		35
1	4	2			5		11	8	3	9	7			10			6		36
1	4	2			5		8		3	9	7			10	11		6		37
1	4	2			5		8*		3	9	7			10	11		6	12	38
1	4	2					8	7		9	3			10	11		6	5	39
1	4				5		8	7		9	3			10	11		6	2	40
1	4	6			5		8	7		9	3			10	11			2	41
1	4	6			5		8	7		9*	3			10	11	12		2	42
1	4	6			5		8	7*		9	3	12		10	11			2	43
1	4	6			5		8	7	3	9		2		10				11	44
1	4	6			5		8	9			3	2		10	11			7	45
1		6			5		8	9			3	2		10	11	7		4	46
45	45	25	4	1	41	1	31	23	28	38	35	37	12	37	31	25	36	11	
		1	4				2			1	2	1		1	4	4		1	
	5	2	1		3		9	4		14	1		6	5	9		4		

Arnold R	Bell C	Bird K	Boam S	Brown G	Burrows A	Calderwood C	Caldwell D	Cannell P	Foster B	Lumby J	Mann A	McJannet L	Morgan T	Nicholson G	Parkinson N	Thomson B	Wood I	Woodhead S	
1	4*				5		10		3		9	2	8	12	11	7	6		1
1	1				1		1		1		1	1	1		1	1	1		
														1					

Arnold R	Bell C	Bird K	Boam S	Brown G	Burrows A	Calderwood C	Caldwell D	Cannell P	Foster B	Lumby J	Mann A	McJannet L	Morgan T	Nicholson G	Parkinson N	Thomson B	Wood I	Woodhead S	
1	4	6	5				10*			9	12	2		11	8	7	3		1
1	4	6	5				10*			9	8	2		11		7	3	12	
1	4	6			5		10		3	9	8	2*		11		7	12		2
1	4*	6			5		10			9	8	2		11	12	7	3		
4	4	4	2		2		4		1	4	3	4		4	1	4	3		
											1				1		1	1	
		1								3							1		

1 own-goal

1982-83

Manager: Stuart Boam to February 1983, then Ian Greaves.

1	Aug	28	(h)	Blackpool	W 2-1	Waddle, Dungworth (pen)	2,627
2	Sep	3	(a)	Halifax T	D 0-0		2,225
3		6	(h)	Tranmere R	L 0-3		1,280
4		11	(h)	Port Vale	L 0-2		2,313
5		18	(a)	Hereford U	W 2-0	Nicholson 2	1,960
6		25	(h)	Rochdale	W 2-1	Waddle 2	2,001
7		27	(h)	Peterborough U	D 0-0		2,414
8	Oct	1	(a)	Crewe A	W 2-1	Day, Waddle	1,787
9		9	(h)	Bury	L 1-4	Bell	2,415
10		16	(a)	Chester	W 3-1	Caldwell 2, Woodhead (pen)	1,668
11		18	(h)	Scunthorpe U	L 0-2		2,647
12		23	(a)	Swindon T	L 0-4		3,917
13		30	(h)	Darlington	L 0-2		1,816
14	Nov	3	(a)	Hartlepool U	W 4-0	Ayre, Caldwell, Nicholson, Woodhead (pen)	1,325
15		5	(a)	Colchester U	L 0-2		2,009
16		13	(h)	Bristol C	D 1-1	Opp own-goal	1,979
17		27	(a)	York C	L 1-6	Nicholson	2,119
18	Dec	4	(h)	Stockport C	W 1-0	Bell	1,661
19		17	(h)	Torquay U	W 2-1	Dungworth, Caldwell	1,293
20		27	(a)	Wimbledon	D 1-1	Nicholson	2,517
21		28	(h)	Northampton T	W 2-0	Matthews, Caldwell	2,841
22	Jan	1	(a)	Aldershot	L 1-2	Ayre	2,235
23		3	(h)	Hull C	W 3-1	Dungworth 2 (1 pen), Nicholson	4,560
24		8	(h)	Halifax T	L 1-2	Dungworth (pen)	2,398
25		15	(a)	Blackpool	L 1-2	Nicholson	2,217
26		22	(h)	Hereford U	L 0-1		1,655
27		29	(a)	Port Vale	L 1-4	Hutchinson	4,102
28	Feb	5	(a)	Rochdale	D 2-2	Matthews, Dungworth	1,028
29		19	(a)	Bury	L 0-1		2,304
30		26	(h)	Chester	W 2-1	Matthews, Hutchinson	1,803
31	Mar	1	(a)	Scunthorpe U	D 2-2	Bell, Bird	3,562
32		5	(h)	Swindon T	W 1-0	Dungworth (pen)	2,101
33		12	(a)	Darlington	D 0-0		952
34		14	(h)	Hartlepool U	W 3-0	Dungworth 3 (1 pen)	1,991
35		19	(h)	Colchester U	D 1-1	Nicholson	2,371
36		26	(a)	Bristol C	L 1-3	Caldwell	4,919
37		28	(h)	Crewe A	W 1-0	Caldwell	2,245
38	Apr	2	(a)	Northampton T	W 2-1	Caldwell 2	1,988
39		5	(h)	Wimbledon	D 2-2	Dungworth 2 (1 pen)	3,519
40		8	(a)	Stockport C	D 1-1	Dungworth	2,197
41		16	(h)	Tranmere R	D 1-1	Bell	2,468
42		23	(a)	Torquay U	L 1-3	Ayre	1,546
43		30	(h)	York C	D 2-2	Dungworth, Caldwell	2,288
44	May	2	(a)	Hull C	D 2-2	Bell 2	8,735
45		7	(a)	Peterborough U	L 2-3	Bird, Thorpe	2,200
46		14	(h)	Aldershot	W 4-1	Kearney, Bell, Woodhead, Hutchinson	1,786

FINAL LEAGUE POSITION: 10th in Division Four

Appearances
Sub Appearances
Goals

FA Cup

1	Nov	20	(h)	Stockport C	W 3-2	Dungworth 2, Bell	2,215
2	Dec	11	(h)	Bradford C	D 1-1	Dungworth (pen)	2,962
R		15	(a)	Bradford C	L 2-3	Bell, Dungworth	3,081

Appearances
Sub Appearances
Goals

League Cup

1	Sep	1	(a)	Bradford C	L 0-1		3,265
		13	(h)	Bradford C	L 0-2		2,260

Appearances
Sub Appearances
Goals

Arnold R	Ayre W	Bell C	Bird K	Blackhall R	Boam S	Calderwood C	Caldwell D	Cannell P	Coles D	Day C	Dungworth J	Gallagher B	Hutchinson R	Kearney M	Kennedy K	Laidlaw J	Laws J	Lowery A	Matthews J	Nicholson G	Reynolds M	Rhodes M	Sindall M	Thorpe A	Waddle A	Woodhead S	
1	5	2	6				8*			4	10				3	11			7						9	12	1
1	5	2	6				8*			4	10				3	11			7	12					9		2
1	5	2	6				8			4	10*				3	11			7	12					9		3
1	5		6							4	10				3	11			7	8					9	2	4
1	5	12	6*		11			10		4					3				7	8					9	2	5
1	5		6		11			10		4	12				3				7*	8					9	2	6
1	5	7	6		11			10		4					3					8					9	2	7
1	5	7	6		11			12		4	10*				3					8					9	2	8
1	5	7	6		11*					4	10				3				12	8					9	2	9
1	5	4	6		11		10	9*		12					3				7	8						2	10
1	5	4	6		11		10	9		12					3*				7	8						2	11
1	5	11	6							4	8		10		3				7						9	2	12
1	5	4	6				12				10*				3				7	11			8		9	2	13
1	5		6*	2			10				12								7	11	3		8		9	4	14
1	5			2			10				8								7	11	3		6		9	4	15
1	5			2		6	8				12		10		3				7	11					9	4*	16
1*	5	4				6	8				9		10		3				7	11	2					12	17
1	5	4	2			6	10*				9		8		3				7	11						12	18
1	5	4	2			6	10				9		8		3				7	11*						12	19
1	5	4	2			6	10				9		8		3				7	11							20
1	5	4	2			6	10				9		8		3				7	11							21
1	5	4	2			6	10				9		8		3				7	11*						12	22
1	5	4		2		6	10*				9		8		3				7	11						12	23
1	5	4		2*		6	10				9		8		3				7	11						12	24
1	5	11	6				10					7	8		3				4	9						2	25
1	5	11				6		9				7	8		3				4	10						2	26
1	5	10*	7			6					9	12	8		3				4	11						2	27
1	5	7				6	10				9		8		3				4	11						2	28
1	5			2		6	10				9		8		3				4	11						7	29
1	5	12		2		6	10				9*		8		3				4	11						7	30
1	5	9	12	2		6	10						8*		3				4	11						7	31
1	5	8		2		6	10				9				3				4	11						7	32
1	5	8		2		6	10				9				3				4	11						7	33
1	5	8		2		6	10				9				3				4	11						7	34
1		4	5	2		6	10				9			3						11		8				7	35
1		8	5*	2		6	10				9			3	12						11	4				7	36
1			5	2		6	10				9			3					4	11		8				7	37
1		7	5			6	10				9			3					4	11		8*	12			2	38
1	6	7	5*				10				9		8	3					4	11			12			2	39
	5	7				6	10		1		9		8	3					4	11						2	40
	5	7				6			1		9		8	3					4	11			10			2	41
1	5	7				6					9		8	3	12				4	11*			10			2	42
	5	7*	6				11		1		9		8	3			12		4				10			2	43
1	5	7				6	10				9		8	3					4				11			2	44
1	5	4	3			6	10				9		8					7					11*	12		2	45
1	5	4		2		6	10				9		8	3									11*	12		7	46
43	42	37	28	15	7	28	34	6	3	10	36	2	25	11	32	4		1	39	37	4	4	9		14	35	
		2	1				1	1		2	3	1			2		1		1	2			2	2		7	
	3	7	2				10			1	14		3	1					3	8				1	4	3	

1 own-goal

1	5	4		2*		6	10				9		8		3				7	11						12	1
1	5	4	2			6	10				9		8		3				7	11							2
1	5	4	2			6	10				9		8		3				7	11							R
3	3	3	2	1		3	3				3		3		3				3	3							
																										1	
		2									4																

1	5	2	6				8			4	10				3	11			7						9		1
1	5		6					9		4	10				3	11			7	8						2	
2	2	1	2				1	1		2	2				2	2			2	1					1	1	

1983-84

Manager: Ian Greaves

1	Aug	27	(a)	Bristol C	L 0-4		5,784
2	Sep	3	(h)	Doncaster R	L 1-2	Opp own-goal	2,957
3		6	(h)	Stockport C	L 1-2	Opp own-goal	2,166
4		9	(a)	Halifax T	D 0-0		1,725
5		17	(h)	Tranmere R	W 1-0	Nicholson	2,002
6		24	(a)	Peterborough U	L 0-3		3,490
7		27	(a)	Blackpool	L 0-2		3,461
8	Oct	1	(h)	Aldershot	W 5-2	Caldwell 3, Lowery, Barrowclough	1,836
9		8	(a)	Bury	D 2-2	Caldwell, Barrowclough (pen)	2,468
10		15	(h)	Torquay U	L 1-3	Lowery	1,939
11		19	(a)	Reading	L 0-4		3,551
12		22	(h)	Hartlepool U	W 5-0	Caldwell 4, Lowery	1,906
13		29	(a)	Hereford U	D 0-0		3,110
14	Nov	1	(h)	Rochdale	W 3-0	Caldwell 2, Dungworth	2,535
15		5	(a)	Wrexham	W 3-2	Nicholson 2, Keegan	1,633
16		12	(h)	Colchester U	D 0-0		3,042
17		26	(h)	Swindon T	D 2-2	Dungworth, Nicholson	3,327
18	Dec	3	(a)	Darlington	L 0-3		1,630
19		18	(a)	Northampton T	L 1-2	Lowery	2,628
20		26	(h)	Chesterfield	L 0-1		6,734
21		27	(a)	Chester C	W 4-0	Lowery, Barrowclough, Caldwell, Nicholson	1,432
22		31	(h)	Crewe A	D 3-3	Woodhead, Kearney, Caldwell	2,625
23	Jan	2	(a)	York C	L 1-2	Barrowclough	5,682
24		7	(a)	Doncaster R	L 1-3	Kearney	3,804
25		30	(a)	Tranmere R	L 0-1		1,482
26	Feb	4	(a)	Aldershot	L 1-7	Barrowclough	1,629
27		11	(h)	Peterborough U	D 0-0		2,799
28		14	(a)	Rochdale	D 0-0		1,095
29		18	(h)	Hereford U	D 1-1	Barrowclough	1,868
30		25	(a)	Hartlepool U	L 1-4	Ayre	1,730
31	Mar	3	(h)	Reading	W 2-0	Barrowclough, Nicholson	1,950
32		6	(h)	Wrexham	L 3-4	Ayre 2, Caldwell	1,986
33		10	(a)	Colchester U	L 0-1		2,007
34		17	(h)	Bury	D 1-1	Ayre	1,673
35		24	(a)	Torquay U	L 0-1		1,447
36		27	(h)	Bristol C	L 0-1		1,826
37		31	(h)	Blackpool	D 1-1	Juryeff	2,007
38	Apr	6	(a)	Stockport C	W 4-0	Barrowclough, Matthews, Juryeff, Caldwell	1,933
39		10	(h)	Halifax T	W 7-1	Juryeff 3, Lowery, Barrowclough, Matthews, Caldwell	1,696
40		14	(h)	Darlington	W 1-0	Caldwell	2,084
41		21	(h)	Chesterfield	D 0-0		4,364
42		24	(h)	Chester C	W 3-1	Barrowclough, Matthews, Nicholson	2,346
43		29	(a)	Swindon T	D 1-1	Nicholson	1,941
44	May	5	(h)	York C	L 0-1		3,355
45		7	(a)	Crewe A	W 3-1	Caldwell 3	1,810
46		12	(h)	Northampton T	W 3-1	Caldwell 2, Calderwood	2,141

FINAL LEAGUE POSITION: 19th in Division Four

Appearances
Sub Appearances
Goals

FA Cup

1	Nov	19	(h)	Doncaster R	W 3-0	Calderwood, Caldwell, Barrowclough	5,027
2	Dec	10	(a)	Bolton W	L 0-2		6,934

Appearances
Sub Appearances
Goals

League Cup

1	Aug	30	(h)	Huddersfield T	L 1-2	Barrowclough (pen)	3,734
	Sep	13	(a)	Huddersfield T	L 1-5	Caldwell	5,190

Appearances
Sub Appearances
Goals

Arnold R	Ayre W	Barrowclough S	Calderwood C	Caldwell D	Daines B	Dungworth J	Foster GW	Frain P	Galloway M	Hitchcock K	Hutchinson R	Juryeff I	Kearney M	Kee P	Keegan G	Lowery A	Matthews J	Nicholson G	Partridge J	Sindall M	Storer S	Taylor P	Whitworth S	Woodhead S	
1		7	6	10		9*	5				8		3			11	4						2	12	1
1		7*	6	10		12	5				8		3			11				4			2	9	2
1			6	10		11	5				9		3			4	7	12		8*			2		3
1		12	6	10		9	5				8		3			4	7	11*					2		4
1						9	5		6		8		3			4	7	11		10*			2	12	5
1		7		12		9	5		6		8					4	10*	11	3				2		6
1		12	6	10		9*	5				8					4		11		7			2	3	7
1		9	6	10*			5		12		8					4		11		7			2	3	8
1		9	6	10			5				8					4		11		7			2	3	9
1			6	10		9*	5				8					4	12	11		7			2	3	10
1		9	6	10			5								8	4	7	11					2	3	11
		9	6	10*	1		5								8	4	7	11			12		2	3	12
		9	6		1	10	5								8	4	7	11					2	3	13
		9	6	10*	1	12	5								8	4	7	11					2	3	14
		9*	6		1	10	5								8	4	7	11		12			2	3	15
			6		1	10	5		9						8	4	7	11					2	3	16
	6			10	1	9	5						3		8		7	11					2	4	17
				10	1		5		6				3		8	9	7	11					2	4	18
	6	9		10	1		5								8	4	7	11					2	3	19
	6	9		10	1		5								8	4	7	11					2	3	20
	6	9		10	1		5		7				8			4		11					2	3	21
	6			10	1	9	5		7				4			8		11					2	3	22
	6	9		10	1		5		7				8			4		11					2	3	23
	6	9		10	1	12	5		7				8			4		11*					2	3	24
	6	9			1	10		11	7				8		5*	4		12					2	3	25
	5	8			1	9		12	6				3			4		11		10			2	7*	26
	5	7		10	1		6						9			4	8	11					2	3	27
	5	8		10	1		6						9			4	7	11					2	3	28
	5	7	9	10	1		6									4	8	11					2	3	29
	5	7	9	10	1		6		12							4	8	11					2*	3	30
	5	9		10	1		6								7	4	8	11				3		2	31
	5	9	12	10	1		6								7	4	8	11*				3		2	32
	5	9	6	10						1					7	4	8	11				3		2	33
	5	9	6	10						1			3		7	4	8	11						2	34
	5	11		10			6			1		9	3*		7	4	8	12						2	35
	5	7	12	10			6			1		9				4	8	11*					3	2	36
	5		7	10			6			1		9				4	8	11					3	2	37
		7	5*	10			6		12	1		9			11	4	8						3	2	38
		7	5	10			6			1		9			11	4	8						3	2	39
	5	7	12	10*			6			1		9				4	8			11			3	2	40
	5	11	7				6			1		9				4	8	10					3	2	41
		7	10				5		6	1		9*		12		4	8	11					3	2	42
		7	4	10			5		8	1		9				6		11					3	2	43
	6	7	8	10			5		12	1		9*				4		11					3	2	44
	6	7	2	10			5			1		9				4		11					3	8	45
	6	7	2	10			5		12	1		9*				4		11					3	8	46
11	25	36	27	37	21	14	42	1	12	14	10	12	17		18	45	31	38	1	9		3	41	41	
		2	3	1		3		1	5					1			1	3		1	1			2	
	4	10	1	21		2						5	2		1	6	3	8						1	

2 own-goals

		9	6	10	1		5								8	4	7	11					2	3	1
		9*		10	1		5		6				12		8	4	7	11					2	3	2
		2	1	2	2		2		1						2	2	2	2					2	2	
													1												
		1	1	1																					

1		7	6	10			5				8		3			11				4			2	9	1
1			6	10		9	5				8		3			4	7	11					2		
2		1	2	2		1	2				2		2			2	1	1		1			2	1	
		1		1																					

1984-85

Manager: Ian Greaves

1	Aug	25	(a)	Port Vale	W	1-0	Caldwell	3,552
2	Sep	1	(h)	Rochdale	W	5-1	Caldwell 2, Kearney, Lowery, Vinter	2,627
3		8	(a)	Peterborough U	L	0-1		3,502
4		15	(h)	Crewe A	L	0-1		2,681
5		19	(h)	Colchester U	L	0-1		2,084
6		22	(a)	Stockport C	D	1-1	Caldwell	1,635
7		29	(h)	Swindon T	D	0-0		2,224
8	Oct	3	(a)	Exeter C	D	0-0		2,097
9		6	(a)	Hereford U	L	0-3		3,479
10		13	(h)	Torquay U	W	1-0	Garner	2,000
11		20	(h)	Wrexham	W	1-0	Kearney	1,779
12		23	(a)	Aldershot	D	0-0		1,765
13		27	(a)	Hartlepool U	D	0-0		4,349
14	Nov	3	(h)	Tranmere R	D	0-0		2,001
15		7	(h)	Chester C	W	2-0	Caldwell 2	1,789
16		10	(a)	Halifax T	L	0-1		1,237
17		24	(h)	Bury	L	0-2		2,575
18	Dec	1	(a)	Blackpool	L	0-1		2,796
19		22	(h)	Northampton T	W	2-0	Caldwell 2	1,775
20		26	(a)	Chesterfield	D	0-0		6,960
21		29	(a)	Southend U	W	3-1	Woodhead, Vinter, Galloway	2,334
22	Jan	1	(h)	Darlington	W	2-0	Galloway, Whatmore	8,112
23		26	(a)	Crewe A	D	1-1	Galloway	1,764
24	Feb	2	(a)	Swindon T	L	0-1		2,664
25		22	(a)	Tranmere R	D	0-0		1,273
26		26	(a)	Colchester U	L	1-2	Vinter	2,267
27	Mar	2	(h)	Hartlepool U	W	2-0	Luke 2	1,940
28		6	(h)	Aldershot	L	1-2	Luke	2,086
29		9	(a)	Wrexham	D	2-2	Luke 2	1,426
30		13	(h)	Port Vale	D	1-1	Whatmore	2,159
31		19	(a)	Torquay U	L	0-1		1,114
32		23	(h)	Hereford U	D	1-1	Whitworth (pen)	2,178
33		27	(h)	Peterborough U	D	0-0		1,945
34		30	(a)	Chester C	W	3-0	Woodhead, Whatmore, Lowery	1,535
35	Apr	3	(h)	Exeter C	D	2-2	Kearney, Whitworth (pen)	1,703
36		6	(h)	Chesterfield	D	0-0		6,029
37		8	(a)	Darlington	L	1-3	Whatmore	4,564
38		13	(h)	Halifax T	W	2-1	Whatmore, Luke	1,928
39		17	(h)	Stockport C	W	1-0	Whatmore	1,903
40		20	(a)	Bury	D	0-0		3,218
41		24	(h)	Scunthorpe U	L	0-1		1,963
42		27	(h)	Blackpool	D	1-1	Lowery	3,030
43		30	(a)	Northampton T	L	0-1		2,350
44	May	4	(a)	Scunthorpe U	D	2-2	Garner, Caldwell	1,705
45		6	(h)	Southend U	W	1-0	Kearney (pen)	1,819
46		14	(a)	Rochdale	L	1-2	Whatmore	1,098

FINAL LEAGUE POSITION: 14th in Division Four

Appearances
Sub Appearances
Goals

FA Cup

1	Nov	17	(h)	Rotherham U	W	2-1	Lowery, Caldwell	4,161
2	Dec	8	(a)	Bradford C	L	1-2	Barrowclough	5,729

Appearances
Sub Appearances
Goals

League Cup

1	Aug	29	(a)	Scunthorpe U	W	1-0	Vinter	2,106
	Sep	5	(h)	Scunthorpe U	L	1-2*	Barrowclough	3,107

*After extra-time

Appearances
Sub Appearances
Goals

Allen J	Barrowclough S	Beasley A	Calderwood C	Caldwell D	Cunningham J	Foster GW	Foster N	Galloway M	Garner P	Hitchcock K	Howard L	Jones C	Kearney M	Logan D	Lowery A	Luke N	McKernon C	Pollard G	Robinson L	Vinter M	Whatmore N	Whitworth S	Woodhead S	
	11		4	10		5				1			3		7	8		6		9		2		1
12	11		4	10*		5				1			3		7	8		6		9		2		2
	11		4	10		5		6		1			3		7*	8				9		2	12	3
	11		4	10		5		6*	12	1			3		7	8				9		2		4
9*			4	10		5		12	6	1			3		7	8				11		2		5
	11		4	10		5		12	6	1			3		7	8				9*			2	6
	11		4	10		5			6	1			3		7	8				9		2		7
	11		4	10*		5		12	6	1			3		7	8				9		2		8
	11		4			5		10		1			3		7	8				9		2	6	9
	11		4			5		10	6	1			3		7	8				9		2		10
	11					5		10	6	1			3		7	8		4		9		2		11
	11					5		10	6	1			3		7	8		4		9		2*	12	12
			11			5		10	6	1			3		7	8		4		9			2	13
			11	10		5			6	1			3		7	8		4		9			2	14
	12		11	10		5			6	1			3		7	8		4*		9			2	15
			11	10		5				1			3	6	7	8		4		9			2	16
	11		6	10		5		9		1			3		7	8		4*		12		2		17
	11		6	10*		5				1			3		7	8		4		12	9	2		18
			6	10		5			4	1			3		7					8	9	2	11	19
	11	1	6			5			4				3		7					8	9	2	10	20
		1	6			5		11	4				3		7					8	9	2	10	21
		1	6			5		11*	4				3		7	12				8	9	2	10	22
			6			5		10	4	1			3		7	12				8	9	2*	11	23
			6			5		10	4	1			3		7			2		8	9		11	24
			6			5		10*	4	1			3		7	12				8	9	2	11	25
			6			5		10	4	1		11	3		7					8	9	2		26
			6			5		10	4	1		11	3		7	8						2	9	27
			6			5		10	4	1	12	11	3		7	8						2	9*	28
			6			5		10*	4	1		11	3		7	8					9	2	12	29
						5		12	4	1		11*		3	7	8		6			9	2	10	30
			6			5		12	4	1				3	7	8	11*				9	2	10	31
			6			5		11	4	1				3	7				8		9	2	10	32
			6	9		5		10	4	1			11	3	7		12		8*			2		33
			6			5		12	4	1			3	11	7	9*					8	2	10	34
			6			5		12	4	1			10	3	7	9					8	2	11*	35
			6			5			4	1			10	3	7	9			11		8	2		36
			6			5		12	4	1			10	3	7	9			11*		8	2		37
			6			5	3*	10	4	1					7	9		12			8	2	11	38
			6			5		11	4	1				3	7	9				10	8	2		39
			6					11	4*	1			12	3	7	9		5		10	8	2		40
			6	12				11	4	1				3	7	9*		5		10	8	2		41
	12		6	9		5			4	1			11	3*	7					10	8	2		42
			6	9*	12	5			4	1			11	3	7					10	8	2		43
				9*	11	5			4	1				3	7			6	12	10	8	2		44
			6	9	7	5			4	1			11	3		10		2			8			45
					11	5*			4	1				3	7	9		6	12	10	8	2		46
1	14	3	41	19	3	44	1	23	38	43		5	37	17	45	33	1	17	4	31	26	39	21	
1	2			1	1			8	1		1		1			3	1	1	2	2			3	
				9				3	2				4		3	6				3	7	2	2	

	11		6	10		5		9		1			3		7	8		4				2		1
	11		6	10		5			4	1			3		7	8					9	2		2
	2		2	2		2		1	1	2			2		2	2		1			1	2		
	1			1											1									

	11		4	10		5				1			3		7	8		6		9		2		1
	11		4	10		5		12		1			3			8		6*		9		2	7	
	2		2	2		2				2			2		1	2		2		2		2	1	
								1																
	1																			1				

1985-86

Manager: Ian Greaves

1	Aug	17	(h)	Hereford U	W 4-0	Cassells 3, Chamberlain	2,405
2		24	(a)	Port Vale	D 0-0		2,930
3		27	(h)	Halifax T	W 2-0	Vinter, Chamberlain	3,299
4		31	(a)	Northampton T	L 0-1		2,739
5	Sep	7	(h)	Wrexham	D 1-1	Whatmore	3,026
6		14	(a)	Aldershot	W 2-1	Kearney, Cassells	1,307
7		18	(h)	Orient	D 1-1	Chamberlain	4,128
8		21	(a)	Scunthorpe U	W 3-0	Pollard, Whatmore, Vinter	1,780
9		28	(h)	Southend U	W 3-0	Kearney (pen), Vinter, Westley (og)	3,701
10	Oct	2	(a)	Chester C	L 0-1		2,127
11		5	(a)	Cambridge U	L 2-4	Chamberlain, Kearney (pen)	1,957
12		12	(h)	Colchester U	W 2-1	Luke, Chamberlain	3,364
13		19	(h)	Exeter C	W 2-1	Lowery, Kearney	3,289
14		22	(a)	Tranmere R	W 2-1	Kearney, Chamberlain	1,540
15		26	(h)	Torquay U	W 4-0	Whatmore 2, Lowery, Chamberlain	3,506
16	Nov	2	(a)	Hartlepool U	D 1-1	Chamberlain	4,220
17		5	(a)	Burnley	L 1-2	Kearney	2,200
18		9	(h)	Crewe A	D 2-2	Kent, Chamberlain	3,243
19		23	(a)	Swindon T	L 1-2	Ramsey (og)	4,784
20		30	(h)	Rochdale	W 3-2	Whatmore 2, Luke	2,586
21	Dec	14	(a)	Peterborough U	L 2-4	Garner, Kent	3,128
22		22	(h)	Port Vale	W 2-1	Garner, Kent	3,722
23		26	(h)	Stockport C	W 4-2	Lowery 2, Garner, Chamberlain	4,206
24	Jan	1	(a)	Preston NE	W 2-0	Cassells, Chamberlain	3,702
25		11	(h)	Northampton T	W 1-0	Kearney (pen)	3,829
26		18	(a)	Hereford U	L 2-4	Logan, Kent	2,885
27		25	(h)	Aldershot	W 2-0	Whatmore 2	3,097
28	Feb	1	(a)	Wrexham	W 2-1	Vinter, Cassells	1,363
29		8	(a)	Exeter C	W 1-0	Kent	1,798
30		15	(a)	Orient	W 1-0	Kent	3,713
31	Mar	4	(h)	Chester C	D 0-0		3,957
32		8	(h)	Cambridge U	W 2-0	Cassells, Chamberlain	3,373
33		14	(a)	Colchester U	D 0-0		1,956
34		22	(a)	Torquay U	W 2-1	Luke, Cassells	1,880
35		25	(h)	Scunthorpe U	D 1-1	Garner	3,991
36		29	(h)	Preston NE	L 2-3	Cassells, Chamberlain	3,733
37		31	(a)	Stockport C	W 2-0	Cassells, Chamberlain	4,635
38	Apr	5	(h)	Burnley	D 0-0		3,671
39		11	(a)	Crewe A	L 1-2	Kent	2,099
40		15	(a)	Southend U	L 1-3	Lowery	1,044
41		19	(h)	Swindon T	D 1-1	Chamberlain	8,416
42		22	(h)	Hartlepool U	W 4-0	Cassells 2, Chamberlain, Kelly (og)	5,523
43		26	(a)	Rochdale	D 1-1	Cassells	1,936
44		29	(h)	Tranmere R	D 0-0		3,470
45	May	3	(h)	Peterborough U	L 0-1		3,008
46		5	(a)	Halifax T	W 2-1	Kent, Whatmore	1,414

FINAL LEAGUE POSITION: 3rd in Division Four (Promoted)

Appearances
Sub Appearances
Goals

FA Cup

1	Nov	16	(h)	Port Vale	D 1-1	Chamberlain	5,207
R		18	(a)	Port Vale	L 0-1		6,749

Appearances
Sub Appearances
Goals

League Cup

1	Aug	21	(h)	Middlesbrough	W 2-0	Vinter, Chamberlain	3,179
	Sep	3	(a)	Middlesbrough	D 4-4	Graham, Kearney, Vinter, Chamberlain	4,051
2		25	(h)	Chelsea	D 2-2	Pollard, Cassells	6,018
	Oct	9	(a)	Chelsea	L 0-2		11,664

Appearances
Sub Appearances
Goals

Cassells K	Chamberlain N	Collins R	Foster GW	Galloway M	Garner P	Graham M	Gunn B	Hitchcock K	Kearney M	Kent K	Kenworthy A	Logan D	Lowery A	Luke N	McKernon C	Pollard G	Robinson L	Stringfellow I	Vinter M	Whatmore N	
9	7		5		3	2		1	11				4*	12		6			10	8	1
9	7		5			2		1	11			3	4	12		6			10*	8	2
9	7		5	2*		3		1	11			3	4	12		6			10	8	3
9	7		5			2		1	11			3	4	12		6			10	8*	4
9	7		5			2		1	11			3	4			6			10	8	5
9	7		5			2		1	11			3	4			6			10	8	6
9	7		5			2		1	11	12		3	4			6			10	8*	7
9	7		5	12		2		1	11			3	4			6			10	8*	8
9	7		5			2		1	11			3		4		6			10	8	9
9	7		5	6		2		1	11			3	4						10	8	10
	7		5	6		2		1	11	9		3	4						10	8	11
9*	7		5			2		1		10		3	4	11	12	6				8	12
9	7		5			2		1	11	12		3	4			6			10*	8	13
	7		5			2		1	11	10		3	4	9		6				8	14
	7		5			2		1	11	10		3	4		9	6				8	15
	7		5	12		2		1	11	10		3	4	9*		6				8	16
	7		5	9		2		1	11	10		3	4			6				8	17
9	7		5			2		1	11	10		3	4			6				8	18
9	7		5		11	2		1				3	4			6			10	8	19
9			5*		11	2		1		7				4	3	6	12		10	8	20
9	7		5		11	2		1		10		3	4*	8	12	6					21
9	7		5		8	2		1	11	10		3	4			6					22
9	7		5		8	2		1	11	10		3	4			6					23
9	7		5		8	2		1	11	10		3	4			6					24
9	7	12	5		8	2		1	11	10		3	4			6*					25
9	7		5		8	2		1	6	10		3	4						11		26
9	7		5		3	2		1	11				4			6			10	8	27
9*		12	5		3	2		1	11	7			4			6			10	8	28
9			5		3	2		1	11	7			4			6			10	8	29
	9		5		3	2		1	11	7			4			6	10			8	30
9	12		5		3	2		1	11*	7			4			6			10	8	31
9	11		5		3	2		1		7			4		12	6	10			8*	32
9	11	12	5		3	2		1		7*	8		4		10	6					33
10	11	9	5		3	2		1			8		4	7		6					34
10		9	5		3	2		1		11			4	7		6			8		35
10	7	9	5		3	2	8	1			6		4*		11					12	36
10	7	9	5		3	2	6	1		11	8				4						37
10	7	9*	5		3	2	6	1		11	8		4		12						38
10	7		5		3	2	6	1		11	8		4							9	39
10			5		3	2	6	1		7	11		4						8	9	40
10	11		5		3	2		1		7	8		4			6	9				41
10	11	12	5		3*	2		1		7	8		4		9	6					42
10	9	8	5			2		1	11	7	3					6	4				43
10	8	9*	5		3	2		1	11	7	6						4	12			44
10	7		5		3	2		1	11	9	6		4*					12		8	45
10			5		3	2		1	11	9	6*				7		4	12		8	46
40	39	7	46	4	28	45	5	46	31	31	13	24	40	8	7	35	6		21	30	
	1	4		2						2				4	4		1	3		1	
13	16				4				7	8		1	5	3		1			4	9	

3 own-goals

9	7		5			2		1	11	10		3	4			6			12	8*	1
9	7*		5			2		1	11	8		3	4			6			10	12	R
2	2		2			2		2	2	2		2	2			2			1	1	
																			1	1	
	1																				

9	7		5		3	2		1	11				4			6			10	8	1
9	7		5			2		1	11			3	4			6			10	8	
9	7		5			2		1	11	8		3	4			6			10		2
	7		5			2		1		9		3	4	11		6			10	8	
3	4		4		1	4		4	3	2		3	4	1		4			4	3	
1	2					1			1							1			2		

1986-87

Manager: Ian Greaves

1	Aug	23	(h)	Doncaster R	W 2-1	Lowery, Kearney	3,966
2		30	(a)	Darlington	L 1-2	Cassells	2,043
3	Sep	7	(h)	Chesterfield	D 1-1	Lowery	4,771
4		13	(a)	Bristol R	D 0-0		2,802
5		16	(a)	Bury	D 1-1	Garner	2,023
6		20	(h)	Bournemouth	D 1-1	Chamberlain	2,891
7		27	(a)	Carlisle U	W 2-1	Chamberlain 2	2,817
8		30	(h)	Gillingham	W 1-0	Stringfellow	3,045
9	Oct	4	(a)	York C	W 3-1	Kent, Kearney, Stringfellow	4,163
10		11	(h)	Brentford	W 1-0	Stringfellow	3,453
11		18	(a)	Chester C	D 1-1	Stringfellow	2,377
12	Nov	1	(a)	Rotherham U	D 2-2	Kent, Cassells	3,385
13		4	(a)	Bristol C	D 0-0		6,407
14		8	(h)	Swindon T	D 0-0		3,908
15		22	(h)	Bolton W	D 2-2	Lowery, Garner	3,096
16		25	(h)	Newport C	W 1-0	Whatmore	2,319
17		29	(a)	Walsall	L 0-2		5,702
18	Dec	6	(h)	Blackpool	D 1-1	Cassells (pen)	2,931
19		13	(a)	Fulham	D 1-1	Lowery	3,563
20		21	(h)	Wigan A	L 1-5	Collins	3,035
21		26	(a)	Notts C	D 0-0		8,180
22		27	(h)	Middlesbrough	D 1-1	Kearney	5,035
23	Jan	1	(h)	Port Vale	L 0-1		3,043
24		3	(a)	Bolton W	W 1-0	Cassells	5,048
25		25	(a)	Chesterfield	W 1-0	Cassells	4,080
26		31	(h)	Bristol R	W 5-0	Cassells 4, Whatmore	2,718
27	Feb	7	(h)	Bury	L 1-3	Whatmore	3,051
28		14	(a)	Bournemouth	L 1-4	Whatmore	5,261
29		17	(a)	Doncaster R	L 0-1		1,563
30		21	(h)	Carlisle U	W 2-0	Kent, Kearney	2,082
31		28	(a)	Gillingham	L 0-2		4,564
32	Mar	3	(h)	Rotherham U	D 0-0		2,455
33		7	(a)	Blackpool	W 2-1	Lowery, Kent	3,032
34		14	(h)	Chester C	L 2-3	Kent, Cassells	2,743
35		17	(a)	Newport C	W 3-0	Kent, Kearney, Moore	1,383
36		21	(a)	Brentford	L 1-3	Cassells	3,389
37		28	(h)	York C	D 1-1	Kearney	2,326
38	Apr	3	(a)	Swindon T	L 0-3		8,192
39		11	(h)	Bristol C	W 2-0	Kearney 2 (1 pen)	2,884
40		18	(a)	Port Vale	L 2-3	Cassells 2	2,625
41		21	(h)	Notts C	L 1-2	Kent	6,090
42		25	(a)	Wigan A	L 0-3		3,395
43		28	(h)	Darlington	W 1-0	Cassells	1,938
44	May	2	(h)	Walsall	W 2-0	Cassells, Kearney (pen)	3,389
45		4	(a)	Middlesbrough	L 0-1		13,542
46		9	(h)	Fulham	D 1-1	Kearney	2,759

FINAL LEAGUE POSITION: 10th in Division Three

Appearances
Sub Appearances
Goals

FA Cup

1	Nov	16	(a)	Darlington	L 1-2	Foster	2,118

Appearances
Sub Appearances
Goals

League Cup

1	Aug	26	(a)	Walsall	L 0-1		3,942
	Sep	2	(h)	Walsall	L 2-4	Kent, Cassells (pen)	3,069

Appearances
Sub Appearances
Goals

Andersen N	Cassells K	Chamberlain N	Chambers S	Chandler J	Coleman S	Collins R	Danskin J	Foster GW	Garner P	Graham M	Hitchcock K	Hodges D	Kearney M	Kent K	Kenworthy A	Logan D	Lowery A	McKernon C	Moore J	Pollard G	Robinson L	Stringfellow I	Smith R	Whatmore N	Williams S	
	10	9						5		2	1		8	7	6	3	4	11								1
	10	9						5		2	1		8*	7	6	3	4	11			12					2
	10	9*						5		2	1		8	7	6	3	4	11				12				3
	10	11						5	8	2	1		6	7		3	4	9								4
	10	11						5	8	2	1		6	7		3	4	9*				12				5
	10	11						5		2	1		8	7		3	4	12		6		9*				6
	10	11						5		2	1		8	7		3	4			6		9				7
	10	11						5		2	1		8	7		3	4			6		9				8
	10	11						5		2	1		8	7		3	4			6		9				9
	10	11						5		2	1		8	7	6	3	4					9				10
12	10	11*						5		2	1		8	7	6	3	4					9				11
	10							5		2	1		8	7	6	3	4	11				9				12
	10							5		2	1		8	7	6	3	4	11				9				13
	10							5		2	1		8	7	6	3	4	11				9				14
	10							5	11	2	1		8*	7	6	3	4	12						9		15
	10							5	11	2	1		6	7		3	4				8			9		16
	10			11				5		2	1		8	7	6	3	4							9		17
	10			11				5		2	1		8	7	6	3	4							9		18
	10		2*	11				5	8	12	1			7	6	3	4							9		19
	10		2	11		9		5	8		1		6	7		3	4									20
	10			11		9		5	3	2	1		8	7	6		4									21
	10			11		9*		5	3	2	1		8	7	6		4	12								22
	10	8*				9		5		2	1		11	7	6	3	4					12				23
	10							5		2	1		11	7	6	3	4	9				12		8*		24
	10								12	2	1		11	7	6	3	4	9		5		8*				25
	10							5	8	2	1		11	7	6	3	4							9		26
	10							5	8	2	1	12	11	7	6	3*		4						9		27
	10							5	8	2	1		11	7	6	3	4							9		28
	10*	12						5	3	2	1		11	7	6		4	8						9		29
	10	8						5	3	2	1		11	7	6		4							9		30
8*	10							5	3	2	1			7	6		4	12		11				9		31
	10	11	8*					5	3	2	1			7	6		4					12		9		32
	10	12						5	3*	2	1		11	7	6		4		8					9		33
	10		8*					5	3	2	1		11	7	6		4	12	9							34
	10*	12						5	3	2	1		11	7	6		4		9	8						35
	10							5	3	2	1		11	7	6*		4		9	8		12				36
	10	12					8	5	3	2	1		11	7			4		9*	6						37
	10	11					8	5		2	1		3	7			4	9*		6			12			38
12	10						8*	5		2	1		11	7	3		4			6		9				39
	10	9			3		8	5		2	1		11	7	6		4									40
2	10						8	5			1		3	7	6		4					12	11*		9	41
2	10	9*					8	5			1	12	11	7	6		4			3						42
2	10						8	5			1		11	7	3		4			6		9*			12	43
2	10				6		8	5			1	4	11	7	3							12			9*	44
	10						8	5		2	1		11	7	3		4			6		12			9*	45
	10*						8	5	3	2	1		11	7	6		4					12		9		46
5	46	17	4	6	2	4	10	45	21	40	46	1	43	46	36	26	44	13	5	14	1	12	1	15	3	
2		4							1	1		2						5			1	10	1		1	
	15	3				1			2				10	7			5		1			4		4		

Andersen N	Cassells K	Chamberlain N	Chambers S	Chandler J	Coleman S	Collins R	Danskin J	Foster GW	Garner P	Graham M	Hitchcock K	Hodges D	Kearney M	Kent K	Kenworthy A	Logan D	Lowery A	McKernon C	Moore J	Pollard G	Robinson L	Stringfellow I	Smith R	Whatmore N	Williams S	
	10							5	11†	2	1		8	7	6	3	4	14				9*		12		1
	1							1	1	1	1		1	1	1	1	1					1				
																		1						1		
								1																		

Andersen N	Cassells K	Chamberlain N	Chambers S	Chandler J	Coleman S	Collins R	Danskin J	Foster GW	Garner P	Graham M	Hitchcock K	Hodges D	Kearney M	Kent K	Kenworthy A	Logan D	Lowery A	McKernon C	Moore J	Pollard G	Robinson L	Stringfellow I	Smith R	Whatmore N	Williams S	
	10	9						5		2	1		8	7	6	3	4	11								1
	10	11						5	8	2	1			7	6	3	4					9				
	2	2						2	1	2	2		1	2	2	2	2	1				1				
	1													1												

1987-88

Manager: Ian Greaves

1	Aug	15	(h)	Bristol C	W 2-0	Cassells, Stringfellow	5,441
2		29	(h)	Chesterfield	L 0-1		5,224
3		31	(a)	Sunderland	L 1-4	Stringfellow	13,994
4	Sep	4	(h)	Fulham	L 0-2		3,586
5		12	(a)	Grimsby T	W 3-2	Charles, Cassells, Hodges	3,410
6		15	(h)	Wigan A	L 0-1		3,267
7		19	(h)	Southend U	W 1-0	Stringfellow	2,854
8		26	(a)	Rotherham U	L 1-2	Kent	3,839
9		29	(h)	Doncaster R	W 2-0	Stringfellow 2	3,159
10	Oct	3	(a)	Bristol R	L 1-2	Charles	2,980
11		11	(a)	Notts C	D 1-1	Cassells	8,564
12		17	(h)	Gillingham	D 2-2	Stringfellow, Cassells	2,957
13		20	(h)	Northampton T	W 3-1	Charles, Hodges, Coleman	3,645
14		24	(a)	Chester C	W 2-0	Cassells, Charles	2,456
15		31	(h)	Blackpool	D 0-0		3,221
16	Nov	3	(a)	Bury	L 0-1		2,248
17		7	(h)	Preston NE	D 0-0		3,631
18		21	(h)	Brighton & HA	D 1-1	Kent	3,284
19		28	(a)	Walsall	L 1-2	Charles	4,227
20	Dec	12	(a)	Brentford	D 2-2	Stringfellow, Cassells	3,729
21		20	(h)	Port Vale	W 4-0	Kent 4	3,173
22		26	(h)	Rotherham U	L 0-1		4,763
23		28	(a)	York C	D 2-2	Kent, Charles	2,781
24	Jan	1	(a)	Chesterfield	L 1-3	Cassells	5,070
25		2	(h)	Grimsby T	W 1-0	Ryan	3,315
26		15	(a)	Southend U	L 1-2	Cassells	3,091
27	Feb	6	(a)	Fulham	D 0-0		3,330
28		13	(h)	York C	W 2-1	Charles, Owen	2,749
29		20	(a)	Bristol C	W 2-1	Graham, Kent	9,528
30		27	(h)	Bristol R	W 1-0	Cassells	3,191
31	Mar	1	(a)	Doncaster R	W 2-0	Cassells, Coleman	1,987
32		5	(a)	Gillingham	D 0-0		3,720
33		12	(h)	Notts C	D 1-1	Owen	7,997
34		19	(a)	Blackpool	L 0-2		2,847
35		22	(h)	Aldershot	W 1-0	Charles	2,344
36		26	(h)	Chester C	L 1-2	Charles (pen)	2,918
37		28	(a)	Wigan A	L 1-2	Kent	3,217
38	Apr	2	(a)	Preston NE	L 0-1		6,254
39		5	(h)	Walsall	L 1-3	Charles (pen)	4,900
40		10	(a)	Northampton T	L 0-2		6,917
41		19	(a)	Aldershot	L 0-3		2,339
42		23	(h)	Bury	D 0-0		2,381
43		26	(h)	Sunderland	L 0-4		6,930
44		30	(a)	Brighton & HA	L 1-3	Stringfellow	11,493
45	May	2	(h)	Brentford	W 2-1	Kent, Charles (pen)	2,663
46		7	(a)	Port Vale	D 1-1	Owen	3,167

FINAL LEAGUE POSITION: 19th in Division Three

Appearances
Sub Appearances
Goals

FA Cup

1	Nov	14	(a)	Preston NE	D 1-1	Stringfellow	7,415
R		17	(h)	Preston NE	W 4-2	Cassells 2, Kent, Charles (pen)	4,682
2	Dec	5	(h)	Lincoln C	W 4-3	Lowery, Foster, Kent, Cassells	5,671
3	Jan	9	(h)	Bath C	W 4-0	Charles 2, Ryan, Withey (og)	5,080
4		30	(h)	Wimbledon	L 1-2	Kent	10,642

Appearances
Sub Appearances
Goals

League Cup

1	Aug	18	(h)	Birmingham C	D 2-2	Stringfellow 2	4,425
		25	(a)	Birmingham C	W 1-0	Cassells	6,054
2	Sep	23	(a)	Oxford U	D 1-1	Kent	4,713
	Oct	6	(h)	Oxford U	L 0-2		6,295

Appearances
Sub Appearances
Goals

Andersen N	Beasley A	Cassells K	Chambers S	Charles S	Coleman S	Danskin J	Eves M	Foster GW	Garner P	Graham M	Hitchcock K	Hodges D	Kearney M	Kent K	Kenworthy A	Lowery A	McKernon C	Marks M	Owen G	Ryan J	Steele E	Stringfellow I	Whatmore N	Williams S	
		10	12	11	6			5		2	1	8*	3	7		4						9			1
		10		11	6			5		2	1	8*	3	7		4	12					9			2
		10		11	6			5		2	1	8*	3	7	12	4						9			3
12		10		11				5		2	1	8	3*	7	6	4						9†	14		4
		10		11				5	3	2	1	8		7	6	4						9			5
12		10		11	3			5		2	1	8*		7	6	4						9†	14		6
		10	12	11	3			5		2	1	8*		7	6	4						9			7
		10	12	11	3			5		2	1	8*		7	6	4	14					9†			8
			12	11	3			5		2	1	8		7	6*	4	10					9			9
		10		11	3			5		2	1	8*		7		4	12			6		9			10
		10		11	6			5		2	1	8		7		4	9			3					11
		10	14	11	6			5		2	1	8†		7		4	9*			3		12			12
		10		11	6			5		2	1	8				4	7			3		9*		12	13
		10		11	6			5		2	1	12		7		4	8			3		9*			14
		10	12	11	6		9	5		2	1			7		4	8*			3					15
		10	8*	11	6		9	5		2	1			7		4				3		12			16
		10	12	11	6		9	5		2	1			7		4	8*			3					17
12		10		11	6			5		2	1			7	8	4				3		9*			18
		10		11	6			5		2	1			7	8	4				3		9*	12		19
12		10		11	6			5		2	1			7	8	4				3		9*			20
14		10†		11	6			5	12	2	1	9*		7	8	4				3					21
5†	1	10		11	6				12	2		9*		7	8	4				3			14		22
12	1	10		11	6				3	2		9		7	8*	4				5					23
		10		11	6			5	3	2	1			7		4				8		9*	12		24
		10		11	6			5	3	2	1	9*		7		4	12			8					25
		10		11	6			5	3	2	1			7		4		12	8	9*					26
		10		11	6			5	3	2	1			7		4	8			9					27
		10		11	6			5	3	2	1			8		4*			7	9		12			28
		10		11	6			5	12	2	1			9	8	4*			7	3					29
		10		11	6			5		2	1			9	8	4			7	3					30
		10		11	6			5	3	2	1			9	8	4			7						31
		10		11	6			5	3	2	1			9	8	4			7*			12			32
		10*		11	6			5	3	2	1			9	8	4			7			12			33
		10		11	6			5	12	2	1			9†	8	4			7	3*		14			34
		10		11	6			5	12	2	1			9	8		4		7	3*					35
	1	10		11	6			5	3†	2*				9	8	4			7	12		14			36
	1	10		11	6			5	3	2				9	8	4			7						37
	1	10		11	6			5	3	2				9	8	4†			7*	14		12			38
	1	10*		11	6			5		2				4	8		12		7	3		9			39
12	1			11	6			5		2				9	8	4			7	3		10*			40
	1			11	6			5	3	2		7		9	8	4			12			10*			41
				11	6			5		2		7		10	8	4				3	1	9*	12		42
12				11	6			5		2		7		10	8	4				3*	1	9			43
12				11	6			5		2		7*		9	8	4				3	1	10†		14	44
7*		10		11	6			5		2				9	8	4			12	3	1				45
8		10		11	6			5		2				9		4			7	3	1				46
3	8	40	1	46	44		3	44	14	46	33	21	4	45	29	44	9		15	30	5	22			
9			7						5			1			1		4	1	2	2		8	6	2	
		10		11	2					1		2		10					3	1		8			

		10		11	6			5		2	1			7	8	4				3		9			1
		10		11	6			5		2	1			7	8	4				3		9			R
14		10		11	6			5		2	1	12		7	8	4†				3		9*			2
			9	11	6	12		5	3	2	1			8		4	7			10*					3
		9		11	6			5	3	2	1			10		4	7*			8		12			4
		4	1	5	5			5	2	5	5			5	3	5	2			5		3			
1						1						1										1			
		3		3				1						3		1				1		1			

1 own-goal

		10	8*	11†	6	12		5		2	1		3	7		4	14					9			1
		10		11	6			5		2	1	8	3	7		4						9			
8		10		11				5	3	2	1			7	6	4	12					9*			2
		10	14	11	3			5		2	1	8†		7		4	12			6		9*			
1		4	1	4	3			4	1	4	4	2	2	4	1	4				1		4			
			1			1											3								
		1												1								2			

1988-89

Manager: Ian Greaves to 6 February 1989, then George Foster (player-manager).

1	Aug	27	(h)	Northampton T	D	1-1	Charles	4,042
2	Sep	3	(a)	Wigan A	D	0-0		2,154
3		10	(h)	Fulham	W	3-1	Cassell 2, Hodges	2,734
4		17	(a)	Blackpool	D	1-1	Owen	4,012
5		20	(h)	Gillingham	W	2-1	Cassells, Stringfellow	3,153
6		24	(a)	Bury	W	1-0	Cassells	2,412
7	Oct	1	(h)	Notts C	D	1-1	Hodges	5,907
8		4	(a)	Southend U	D	1-1	Hodges	2,436
9		8	(h)	Bristol R	W	2-1	Charles 2 (1 pen)	3,381
10		15	(a)	Reading	L	0-1		6,604
11		22	(h)	Cardiff C	D	2-2	Cassells 2	3,566
12		26	(a)	Chester C	D	0-0		1,805
13		29	(h)	Bristol C	D	2-2	Kent, Charles	3,800
14	Nov	5	(a)	Preston NE	L	0-2		6,434
15		8	(a)	Swansea C	L	1-3	Hodges	3,526
16		12	(h)	Brentford	W	1-0	Charles	3,181
17		26	(h)	Aldershot	D	1-1	Coleman	2,715
18	Dec	3	(a)	Chesterfield	W	3-1	Coleman 2, Hunter (og)	4,236
19		17	(a)	Wolves	L	2-6	Coleman, Leishman	12,134
20		26	(h)	Port Vale	L	0-1		5,124
21		31	(h)	Huddersfield T	W	1-0	Owen	4,628
22	Jan	2	(a)	Bolton W	D	0-0		4,935
23		14	(h)	Wigan A	L	0-1		2,788
24		21	(a)	Fulham	D	1-1	Cassells	4,148
25		28	(h)	Blackpool	L	0-1		2,735
26	Feb	4	(a)	Notts C	L	1-2	Cassells	5,924
27		11	(h)	Southend U	W	4-0	Cassells 2, Kent, Charles	2,414
28		18	(a)	Bristol R	D	0-0		4,669
29		25	(h)	Reading	W	2-1	Owen 2	3,012
30		28	(h)	Chester C	W	2-0	Kearney, Charles	2,796
31	Mar	4	(a)	Cardiff C	D	0-0		3,217
32		11	(h)	Preston NE	L	0-3		4,706
33		18	(a)	Northampton T	L	1-2	Berry (og)	2,821
34		21	(a)	Bristol C	L	0-2		5,075
35		25	(h)	Bolton W	D	1-1	Christie	3,253
36		27	(a)	Port Vale	W	2-1	Coleman, Owen	8,198
37	Apr	1	(h)	Wolves	W	3-1	Cassells 2, Kent	9,207
38		4	(h)	Sheffield U	L	0-1		8,528
39		8	(a)	Huddersfield T	L	0-2		5,327
40		15	(a)	Gillingham	L	0-3		2,594
41		22	(h)	Bury	D	1-1	Kent	2,826
42		25	(a)	Sheffield U	W	2-1	Kent, Cassells	11,638
43		29	(a)	Brentford	L	0-1		5,231
44	May	2	(h)	Swansea C	D	0-0		2,550
45		6	(h)	Chesterfield	W	3-1	Kearney, Cassells, Hathaway	4,756
46		13	(a)	Aldershot	D	0-0		1,549

FINAL LEAGUE POSITION: 15th in Division Three

Appearances
Sub Appearances
Goals

FA Cup

1	Nov	19	(h)	Sheffield U	D	1-1	Kent	9,101
R	Nov	22	(a)	Sheffield U	L	1-2	Kearney	12,879

Appearances
Sub Appearances
Goals

League Cup

1	Aug	30	(a)	Notts C	L	0-5		4,428
	Sep	6	(h)	Notts C	W	1-0	Hodges	2,695

Appearances
Sub Appearances
Goals

Andersen N	Beasley A	Cassells K	Chambers S	Charles S	Christie T	Coleman S	Cox B	Foster GW	Garner P	Graham M	Gray K	Hathaway I	Hodges D	Kearney M	Kent K	Kenworthy A	Leishman G	Lowery A	McKernon C	Owen G	Pearcey J	Place M	Ryan J	Stringfellow I	Williams S	
		10		11		6	1	5		2				8	9	3		4*		7			12			1
		10		11		6	1	5					9	8		3		4	2	7						2
		10	4	11		6	1	5					9	8		3			2	7						3
		10		11		6	1	5					9	8		3			2	7			4			4
		10		11		6	1	5					9	8		3			2	7			4*	12		5
		10		11		6	1	5					9	8	14	3*		4†	2	7				12		6
		10		11		6	1	5					9	8	12	3*		4	2	7						7
		10		11		6	1	5					9	8	12			4*	2	7		3				8
			4	11		6	1	5					9	8	10				2	7		3				9
			4†	11		6	1	5	14				9	8	10*				2	7		3	12			10
		10		11*		6	1	5	3				9†	8	4				2	7			12	14		11
		10		11		6	1	5					9	8	4				2	7			3			12
		10*		11		6	1	5					9	8	4				2	7			3	12		13
				11		6	1	5					9†	8*	10	12		4	2	7			3	14		14
2*				11		6	1	5					9	8	10†			4		7		14	3	12		15
				11*		6	1	5					9	12	10	8		4	2	7			3			16
				12		6	1	5					9†	11	10	8		4*	2	7			3	14		17
			12	8		6	1	5					9	11	10	3		4	2*	7†				14		18
		10		8		6	1	5	12				7†	11		3	14	4	2				9*			19
		10		11		6	1	5					4	8	7	3	9*		2			12				20
		10		11		6	1	5					4	8	7	3	9*		2	12						21
		10		11		6	1	5					4	8	9	3		12	2	7*						22
		10		11		6	1	5					4	8	9*	3			2	7			12			23
		10		11		6	1	5					4	8	9	3			2	7						24
		10		11		6	1	5					4	8	9		3		2	7*			12			25
		10		11		6	1	5					4	3	9		8*		2	7			12			26
		10		8		6	1	5					4	3	9		12		2	7*			11			27
		10		8		6	1	5					4	3	9		12		2	7*			11			28
		10		8		6	1	5					4	3	9					7		2	11			29
		10		8		6	1						4	3	9	5	12			7*		2	11			30
		10		8		6	1						4	3	9*	5	7		2			12	11			31
		10		8		6†	1					14	4	3		5	12		2	7*		9	11			32
		10		8		6	1	5				12	4	3			9*		2	7			11			33
		10		8		6	1	5				7	4*	3	9				2	12			11			34
		10*		8	9	6	1	5					12	3	4				2	7			11			35
		10		8	9	6	1	5						3	4				2	7			11			36
		10		8	9	6	1	5				12		3	4				2	7*			11			37
		10*		8	9	6	1	5					12	3	4				2	7			11			38
		10		8	9	6	1	5				11*	3†		4		12		2	7					14	39
	1	10		8	9			5				12	4*	3	4				2	7		6				40
	1	10		8	9	6		5				12		3	4*				2	7		11				41
	1	10*		11	9	6		5				14		3	8				2	7		4†	12			42
	1			8	9	6						12	10	3	4				2	7		5	11*			43
	1			11	9	6		5				12		3	4				2	7		8*	10			44
	1*	10		8	9	6		5			7	11		3	4				2						12	45
		12	14	8	9*	6		5				11†	10	3	4				2		1				7	46
1	6	36	3	45	12	45	39	42	1	1	1	4	37	44	36	19	6	11	42	39	1	11	23		1	
		1	2	1					2			8	2	1	3	1	6	1		2		3	7	8	2	
		14		7	1	5						1	4	2	5		1			5				1		

2 own-goals

				11*		6	1	5					9	12	10	3		4	2	7			8			1
				11		6	1	5					9†	12	10	3		4	2	7			8*	14		R
				2		2	2	2					2		2	2		2	2	2			2			
														2										1		
														1	1											

		10		11		6	1	5		2				8*		3		4		7			12	9		1
		9		11		6	1	5					10	8		3		4	2					7		
		2		2		2	2	2		1			1	2		2		2	1	1				2		
																							1			
													1													

1989-90

Manager: George Foster

1	Aug	19	(a)	Chester C	W 2-0	Christie, Charles	2,293
2		26	(h)	Bristol R	L 0-1		3,050
3	Sep	2	(a)	Fulham	L 0-1		4,551
4		9	(h)	Cardiff C	W 1-0	Charles	2,766
5		16	(a)	Bury	L 0-3		2,821
6		23	(h)	Blackpool	L 0-3		2,629
7		30	(a)	Bolton W	D 1-1	Charles	5,797
8	Oct	7	(a)	Shrewsbury T	W 1-0	Gorman (og)	3,148
9		14	(h)	Walsall	L 0-2		3,229
10		17	(a)	Tranmere R	D 1-1	Charles (pen)	6,938
11		21	(h)	Bristol C	W 1-0	Christie	2,937
12		24	(h)	Swansea C	W 4-0	Stringfellow 2, Christie, Kent	2,643
13		28	(a)	Reading	L 0-1		3,242
14		31	(h)	Preston NE	D 2-2	Wilkinson 2	3,129
15	Nov	4	(h)	Notts C	L 1-3	Wilkinson	6,016
16		10	(a)	Crewe A	L 1-2	Christie	3,333
17		25	(a)	Leyton O	L 1-3	Wilkinson	3,317
18	Dec	2	(h)	Huddersfield T	L 1-2	Kearney	2,966
19		17	(a)	Brentford	L 1-2	Wilkinson	5,022
20		26	(h)	Rotherham U	W 3-1	Smalley, Stringfellow, Christie	6,304
21		30	(h)	Northampton T	L 1-2	Christie	3,200
22	Jan	1	(a)	Wigan A	L 0-4		2,477
23		13	(a)	Bristol R	D 1-1	Leishman	5,339
24		20	(h)	Chester C	W 1-0	Wilkinson	2,257
25	Feb	3	(a)	Blackpool	L 1-3	Wilkinson	4,402
26		10	(h)	Bury	W 1-0	Wilkinson	2,424
27		13	(h)	Fulham	W 3-0	Charles, Christie, Hathaway	2,255
28		17	(a)	Huddersfield T	L 0-1		5,441
29		24	(h)	Leyton O	W 1-0	Wilkinson	2,542
30	Mar	3	(a)	Birmingham C	L 1-4	Christie	5,139
31		6	(h)	Bolton W	L 0-1		3,334
32		10	(a)	Swansea C	L 0-1		3,304
33		17	(h)	Shrewsbury T	W 2-1	Charles, Christie	2,230
34		20	(a)	Walsall	L 0-1		3,017
35		24	(h)	Tranmere R	W 1-0	Wilkinson	3,362
36		27	(a)	Cardiff C	L 0-1		2,280
37		31	(a)	Bristol C	D 1-1	Kearney	11,773
38	Apr	3	(h)	Birmingham C	W 5-2	Wilkinson 5	4,163
39		7	(h)	Reading	D 1-1	Christie (pen)	2,563
40		10	(a)	Preston NE	L 0-4		5,035
41		14	(h)	Wigan A	W 1-0	Charles	2,421
42		16	(a)	Rotherham U	D 0-0		5,096
43		21	(h)	Brentford	L 2-3	Clark, Christie	2,346
44		24	(a)	Northampton T	W 2-1	Kearney, Christie	2,119
45		28	(h)	Crewe A	W 2-1	Swain (og), Hodges	3,071
46	May	5	(a)	Notts C	L 2-4	Kent, Christie (pen)	6,943

FINAL LEAGUE POSITION: 15th in Division Three

Appearances
Sub Appearances
Goals

FA Cup

1	Nov	19	(a)	Wigan A	L 0-2		3,057

Appearances
Sub Appearances
Goals

League Cup

1	Aug	22	(h)	Northampton T	D 1-1	Stringfellow	3,095
	Sep	5	(a)	Northampton T	W 2-0	Stringfellow, Christie	3,936
2		19	(h)	Luton T	L 3-4	Stringfellow, Christie 2	5,361
	Oct	3	(a)	Luton T	L 2-7	Wilkinson, Kearney	6,519

Appearances
Sub Appearances
Goals

Beasley A	Charles S	Chambers S	Christie T	Clark M	Coleman S	Cox B	Fairclough W	Foster G	Gray K	Hathaway I	Hodges D	Hunt D	Kearney M	Kent K	Kenworthy D	Leishman G	Lowery T	McDonald G	McKernon C	Murray M	O'Riordan D	Pearcey J	Place M	Prindiville S	Smalley M	Stringfellow I	Wilkinson S	
1	10		9		6			5				4	11				7		2					3		8		1
		12			6	1		5		10		4	11			9	7		2					3*		8		2
	10		9		6	1		5				4	11				7		2					3		8		3
	10		9		6	1		5		7		4	11						2					3		8		4
	10		9		6	1		5				4	11				7	12	2					3*		8		5
	10		9			1				2	12	4	11		5	14	7*						6†	3		8		6
1	10		9					5*		12	2	4	11				7				6			3		8		7
1	10		12					5		14		2†	11	7			4				6*			3		8	9	8
1	10		12					5		3		2	11	7			4*				6					8	9	9
	10		4			1		5	3		12	2	11	7							6					8*	9	10
	10		4			1		5	3			2	11	7							6					8	9	11
	10		4			1		5	3			2	11	7							6					8	9	12
	10		4			1		5	6			2	11	7										3		8	9	13
	10		4			1		5	6	12		2	11	7										3*		8	9	14
	10		4			1		5	6	11		2	3	7			8*									12	9	15
	10		4			1		5	6			2	3	7			11									8	9	16
	12		4			1		5	6*	14		10	3	7†			8		2					11			9	17
	10		4			1		5		11			6				7		2					3	8	12	9*	18
	10		4			1		5				3	8	7						2					6	11	9	19
1	10		4					5				3	11	7						2					6	8	9	20
1	10		4					5				3	11	7				8		2					6		9	21
1	10	11	4					5	6*		14	12	3	7						2					8		9†	22
1	10*	12	4					5				8	11	7		14				2				3	6†		9	23
1		10	4					5			12		11	7		14	8*			2				3†	6		9	24
1	10	11*	4					5		12	8			7						2				3	6		9	25
1	10		4					5	8	11				7						2				3	6		9	26
1	10		4					5		11			8	7						2				3	6		9	27
1	10		4					5	11				8	7						2				3	6		9	28
1	10		4					5		11			8	7						2				3	6		9	29
1	10		4						5	11			8	7						2				3	6		9	30
1	10†		4*				11		5	14	12		8	7						2				3	6		9	31
1			4				10		5	11	3		8	7						2					6		9	32
1	11		4	8			10	5					3	7						2					6		9	33
1	11*		4	8			10	5		12			3	7						2					6		9	34
1	11		4	8			10	5					3	7						2					6		9	35
1	11		4	8			10	5					3	7						2					6		9	36
1	11	12	4	8*			10	5			14		3	7†						2					6		9	37
	11		4	8*			10	5			12		3	7						2		1			6		9	38
	11		4	8				5			10			7						2		1		3	6		9	39
	11	3†	4	8				5	10*	14	12			7						2		1			6		9	40
	11		4	8				5	6		10		3	7						2		1					9	41
	11		4	8			10	5					3	7						2		1			6		9	42
1	11		4	8			10	5			12		3	7						2					6		9*	43
1	11		4	8			10	5			9		3	7						2					6			44
1	11		4	8			10*	5			9		3	7						2					6		12	45
1	11*		4	8			10	5		12	9		3	7						2					6			46
26	42	4	43	14	5	15	13	42	16	11	8	21	42	38	1	1	13	1	7	28	6	5	1	22	28	17	36	
	1	3	2							9	9	1				3		1								2	1	
	7		13	1						1	1		3	2		1									1	3	15	

2 own-goals

	10		4			1		5	12		11*	2	6	7			8							3		14	9†	1
	1		1			1		1			1	1	1	1			1							1			1	
									1																	1		

1	10*	12	9†		6			5				4	11			14	7		2					3		8		1
	10		9		6	1		5				4	11				7		2					3		8		
	10		9		6	1		6		3		4	11				7*		2					12		8		2
1	10		9						5	12	2	4	11				7							3		8	6	
2	4		4		3	2		3	1	1	1	4	4				4		3					3		4	1	
		1								1						1								1				
			3										1													3	1	

Mansfield In Other Competitions

Watney Cup

1973-74
Round 1
Aug 11 v Hull City (h) 0-3
Arnold; Pate, Walker, Jones, Edwards, Bird, Thompson, D.Roberts, Eccles, Matthews(McCaffrey), Longhorn.
Att: 6,137

Anglo/Scottish Cup

1975-76
Preliminary Round
Aug 2 v West Bromwich Albion (a) 1-1
Bird
Arnold; Pate, B.Foster, McDonald, Mackenzie (C.Foster), Bird, McCaffrey, Matthews, Clarke, Eccles, Hodgson.
Att: 5,713
Qualifying Round
Aug 6 v Leicester City (h) 2-0
Whitworth (og), Matthews
Arnold; Pate, B.Foster, McDonald, Mackenzie, Bird, McCaffrey, Matthews, Clarke, O'Brien, Hodgson.
Att: 6,496
Qualifying Round
Aug 9 v Hull City (h) 2-1
McDonald, Clarke
Arnold; Pate, B.Foster, McDonald, Mackenzie, Bird, McCaffrey, Matthews, Clarke, O'Brien(C.Foster), Hodgson.
Att: 5,757
Quarter-final (1st leg)
Sep 15 v Ayr United (a) 1-0
McDonald
Arnold; Pate, B.Foster, Lathan, Mackenzie, C.Foster, O'Brien, McDonald, Eccles, Hodgson, McCaffrey (Laverick).
Att: 3,817
Quarter-final (2nd leg)
Sep 29 v Ayr United (h) 2-0 (agg 3-0)
McDonald, Clarke
Arnold; Pate, B.Foster, Bird, Laverick, C.Foster, Matthews, Eccles(McCaffrey), Clarke, Hodgson, McDonald.
Att: 7,149
Semi-final (1st leg)
Oct 21 v Middlesbrough (a) 0-3
Arnold; Pate, B.Foster, Laverick, C.Foster, Bird, Matthews, Eccles(McCaffrey), Clarke, Hodgson, McDonald.
Att: 14,929
Semi-final (2nd leg)
Nov 3 v Middlesbrough (h) 0-2 (agg 0-5)
Evans; Pate, B.Foster, McDonald, Madden, Mackenzie, Matthews, Eccles(Laverick), Clarke, Hodgson, Bird.
Att: 7,115

1978-79
Preliminary Round
Jul 31 v Notts County (h) 1-0
Syrett
Arnold; Bird, B.Foster, C.Foster, Saxby, McClelland, Miller, Martin, Syrett, Hodgson, Goodwin(Coffey).
Att: 5,345
Preliminary Round
Aug 5 v Orient (a) 1-0
Syrett
Arnold; Bird, B.Foster, C.Foster, Saxby, McClelland, Miller, Martin, Syrett, Hodgson, Allen(Coffey).
Att: 3,385
Preliminary Round
Aug 9 v Norwich City (a) 1-1
Syrett
Arnold; Bird, B.Foster, C.Foster, Saxby, McClelland, Miller, Martin, Syrett, Hodgson, Allen(Coffey).
Att: unknown
Quarter-final (1st leg)
Sep 13 v Partick Thistle (a) 0-1
Arnold; Bird, Wood, Curtis, Saxby, McClelland, Miller, Martin, Syrett, Hodgson, Goodwin(C.Foster).
Att: 6,000
Quarter-final (2nd leg)
Oct 3 v Partick Thistle (h) 3-2 (agg 3-3 a.e.t.)
Goodwin 2, G.Saxby (penalties: Bird, B.Foster, G.Saxby)
Arnold(New); Bird, B.Foster, Miller, M.Saxby, McClelland, G.Saxby, Moss, Syrett, Goodwin (Phillips), Martin.
Att: 5,287
Mansfield won 3-1 on penalties.
Semi-final (1st leg)
Oct 31 v Burnley (h) 1-2
Goodwin
Arnold; McClelland, B.Foster, Goodwin, M.Saxby, Bird, Miller(Allen), Moss, Syrett, Phillips, Martin.
Att: 5,515
Semi-final (2nd leg)
Nov 7 v Burnley (a) 1-0 (agg 2-2 a.e.t.)
Syrett (penalties: Bird, Curtis, Goodwin, B.Foster, Syrett, M.Saxby, McClelland.
Arnold; Curtis, B.Foster, G.Saxby, M.Saxby, McClelland, Miller, Bird, Syrett, Goodwin, Martin.
Att: 6,871
Burnley won 8-7 on penalties.

1979-80
Preliminary Round
Jul 31 v Sheffield United (a) 0-1
Arnold; Dawkins, B.Foster, Curtis, Wood, Bird (Goodwin), G.Saxby, Taylor, Austin, Hamilton, Allen.
Att: 4,875
Preliminary Round
Aug 4 v Notts County (h) 0-1
Arnold; Dawkins, B.Foster, Curtis, Wood, Bird, G.Saxby, Taylor(Goodwin), Austin, Hamilton, Allen.
Att: 3,527
Preliminary Round
Aug 8 v Cambridge United (a) 1-1
Curtis
Arnold; Dawkins, B.Foster, Curtis, Wood, Bird, G.Saxby, Taylor, Austin, Hamilton, Allen.
Att: 4,260

Football League Trophy

1982-83
Preliminary Round
Aug 14 v Peterborough United (a) 1-4
Bird
Arnold; Bird, Kennedy, Bell, Boam, Calderwood, Matthews, Cannell(Waddle), Dungworth, Laidlaw, Nicholson(Caldwell).
Att: 1,873
Preliminary Round
Aug 16 v Northampton Town (h) 1-2
Ayre
Arnold; Bird, Kennedy, Bell, Boam, Ayre, Matthews, Caldwell, Waddell, Dungworth, Laidlaw.
Att: 1,485
Preliminary Round
21 Aug v Norwich City (h) 1-4
Dungworth
Arnold; Bell, Kennedy, Woodhead, Bird, Ayre, Matthews, Caldwell, Waddle, Dungworth, Laidlaw.
Att: 1,985

Associate Members Cup

1983-84
Round 1
Feb 21 v Darlington (h) 1-3
Barrowclough
Daines; Whitworth, Galloway(Caldwell), Lowery, Ayre, Calderwood, Barrowclough, Matthews, Foster, Woodhead, Nicholson.
Att: 1,086

Freight/Rover Trophy

1984-85
Round 1 (1st leg)
Jan 22 v Hull City (a) 2-2
Lowery, Whatmore
Hitchcock; Whitworth, Kearney, Garner, Foster, Calderwood, Lowery, Luke, Whatmore, Woodhead, Galloway.
Att: 2,310

Round 1 (2nd leg)
Feb 6 v Hull City (h) 2-1 (agg 4-3)
Lowery, Luke
Hitchcock; Pollard, Kearney, Garner, Foster, Calderwood, Lowery, Vinter, Whatmore(Luke), Galloway, Woodhead.
Att: 2,116

Round 2
Feb 20 v Bradford City (a) 2-1
Galloway, Whatmore
Hitchcock; Whitworth, Kearney, Garner(Luke), Foster, Calderwood, Lowery, Vinter, Whatmore, Galloway, Woodhead.
Att: 2,160

Round 3
Apr 10 v Burnley (h) 1-1 a.e.t.
Whatmore (penalties: Whitworth, Woodhead, Galloway, Whatmore, Foster)
Hitchcock; Whitworth, Logan(Pollard), Garner, Foster, Calderwood, Lowery, Whatmore, Luke, Kearney(Galloway), Woodhead.
Att: 22,540
Mansfield won 5-4 on penalties.
Semi-final
May 9 v Bolton Wanderers (a) 2-1
Kearney, Caldwell
Hitchcock; Whitworth, Logan(Luke), Garner, Foster, Calderwood, Lowery(Pollard), Vinter, Whatmore, Caldwell, Kearney.
Att: 6,706
Area Final
May 20 v Wigan Athletic (h) 1-1 a.e.t.
G.Foster (penalty: Pollard)
Hitchcock; Whitworth, Logan(Pollard), Garner, Foster, Calderwood, Lowery, Whatmore, Caldwell, Vinter, Kearney(Luke).
Att: 9,214
Wigan won 3-1 on penalties.

1985-86
Preliminary Round
Jan 21 v Doncaster Rovers (a) 0-1
Hitchcock; Graham, Logan, Lowery, Foster, Kearney, Chamberlain, Garner(Kent), Cassells, Collins (Whatmore), Vinter.
Att: 1,584
Preliminary Round
Mar 11 v Notts County (h) 1-0
Lowery
Hitchcock; Graham, Garner, Lowery, Foster, Kenworthy, Kent, Vinter, Collins(Luke), Robinson, Chamberlain.
Att: 3,447
Preliminary Round Replay
Mar 17 v Doncaster Rovers (h) 4-2
Collins 2, Cassells, Chamberlain
Beasley; Graham, Garner, McKernon, Foster, Kenworthy, Luke, Vinter, Collins, Cassells(Lowery), Chamberlain.
Att: 2,895
All three clubs in group finished with identical records.
Preliminary Round Replay
Mar 20 v Notts County (a) 1-0
Luke
Beasley; Graham, Garner, Lowery, Foster, Kenworthy, Luke, Vinter, Whatmore, McKernon(Andersen), Chamberlain.
Att: 2,409
Quarter-final
Mar 27 v Darlington (a) 0-3
Hitchcock; Graham, Garner(Andersen), McKernon, Foster, Pollard, Luke, Coleman(Cunningham), Vinter, Collins, Whatmore.
Att: 1,457

1986-87
Preliminary Round
Dec 2 v Halifax Town (h) 2-2
Kent, Chandler
Hitchcock; Graham, Logan, Lowery, Foster, Kenworthy(Garner), Kent, Kearney, Whatmore, Cassells, Chamberlain.
Att: 1,944
Preliminary Round
Dec 9 v Rotherham United (a) 1-1
Chandler
Hitchcock; Chambers, Logan, Lowery, Foster, Kenworthy, Kent, Garner, Whatmore(Stringfellow), Cassells, Chandler(Kearney).
Att: 1,317
Round 1
Jan 27 v York City (a) 1-0
Whatmore
Hitchcock; Graham, Logan, Lowery(Blair), Pollard, Kenworthy, Kent, Whatmore, Garner, Cassells, Kearney.
Att: 2,061
Quarter-final
Feb 26 v Bury (a) 2-1
Lowery, Kent
Hitchcock; Graham, Pollard, Lowery, Foster, Kenworthy, Kent, Garner, Whatmore, Cassells, Kearney.
Att: 2,455
Semi-final
Mar 10 v Middlesbrough (a) 1-0
Kearney (pen)
Hitchcock; Graham, Garner, Lowery, Foster, Kenworthy, Kent, Chamberlain, Whatmore, Cassells, Kearney.
Att: 11,754
Area Final (1st leg)
Apr 8 v Chester City (h) 2-0
Stringfellow, Cassells
Hitchcock; Graham, Garner, Lowery, Foster, Pollard, Kent, Danskin, Stringfellow, Cassells, Kearney.
Att: 7,767
Area Final (2nd leg)
Apr 15 v Chester City (a) 0-1 (agg 2-1)
Hitchcock; Graham, Garner(Kenworthy), Lowery, Foster, Pollard, Kent, Danskin, Stringfellow (Chamberlain), Cassells, Kearney.
Att: 8,787
Final
May 24 v Bristol City (Wembley) 1-1 a.e.t.
Kent (penalties: Kent, Kearney, Pollard, Stringfellow, Kenworthy)
Hitchcock; Graham, Garner, Lowery, Foster, Kenworthy, Kent, Danskin(Pollard), Whatmore (Stringfellow), Cassells, Kearney.
Att: 58,586 *Receipts: £324,592*
Mansfield won 5-4 on penalties.

1987-88
Preliminary Round
Oct 13 v Doncaster Rovers (a) 1-0
Lowery
Hitchcock; Graham, Ryan, Lowery(Chambers), Foster, Coleman, Kent, Hodges, McKernon, Cassells, Charles.
Att: 1,280
Preliminary Round
Oct 27 v Hartlepool United (h) 3-2
Cassells, Eves, Smith (og)
Beasley; Graham, Ryan, Lowery, Foster, Coleman, Kent, McKernon(Hodges), Eves, Cassells, Charles.
Att: 2,710
Round 1
Jan 19 v Scunthorpe United (h) 1-0
Kent
Hitchcock; Graham, Garner, Lowery, Foster, Coleman, Kent, Marks(Stubbins), Ryan, Cassells, Charles
Att: 3,637
Round 2
Feb 16 v Preston North End (a) 1-2
Kent
Hitchcock; Graham, Garner(Stringfellow), Lowery, Foster, Coleman, Kent, Kenworthy, Ryan, Cassells, Charles.
Att: 5,332

Sherpa Van Trophy

1988-89
Preliminary Round
Nov 29 v Notts County (h) 1-1
Kearney
Cox; McKernon, Kenworthy, Lowery, Foster, Coleman, Owen(Charles), Ryan(Hodges), Stringfellow, Kent, Kearney.
Att: 2,477

Preliminary Round
Dec 10 v Chesterfield (a) 1-2
Coleman
Cox; Andersen, Kenworthy, Lowery, Foster, Coleman, Kent(Ryan), Charles, Hodges, Stringfellow (Leishman), Kearney.
Att: 2,640

Leyland/DAF Trophy

1989-90
Preliminary Round
Nov 28 v Leyton Orient (a) 0-2
Cox; McKernon, Kearney, Christie, Foster, Prindiville, Hunt, Lowery, Wilkinson(Stringfellow), Charles (Kent), Hathaway.
Att: 1,133

Preliminary Round
Dec 9 v Brentford (h) 2-1
Charles 2
Cox; Hunt(Gray), Prindiville, Christie, Foster, Stringfellow, Kent, Kearney, Wilkinson, Charles, Hathaway.
Att: 1,455

Preliminary Round Replay
Jan 9 v Leyton Orient (h) 2-1
Gray, Kearney
Beasley; Murray, Prindiville, Christie, Foster, Gray, Kent, Hunt, Wilkinson, Chambers, Kearney.
Att: 1,938
Both teams finished group matches with identical records.

Round 1
Jan 17 v Maidstone United (a) 1-2
Christie
Beasley; Murray, Prindiville(Chambers), Christie, Foster, Gray, Kent, Hunt, Wilkinson, Leishman (McDonald), Kearney.
Att: 1,020

Ray Clarke shoots against Middlesbrough in the Anglo-Scottish Cup. The Stags lost 5-0 on aggregate.

Nottinghamshire FA County Cup

1936-37
Semi-final
Oct 14 v Notts County (h) 1-5
Rattray
Jones; Perfect, Moran, Brown, Hart, Speed, Rattray, Atkinson, Harston, Anderson, Roy.
Att: unknown

1937-38
Semi-final
Oct 21 v Newark Town (h) 3-0
Crawshaw 2, Fielding
Peebles; Smith, Bungay, O'Connor, Paterson, Barke, Fielding, Shaw, Crawshaw, Sams, Johnston.
Att: 501
Final
Nov 3 v Nottingham Forest (a) 2-1
Sams, Johnston
Hughes; Stimpson, Speed, O'Connor, Paterson, Barke, Horne, Stamps, Crawshaw, Sams, Johnston.
Att: 3,304

1938-39
Oct 19 v Notts County (a) 3-2
Somerfield 3
Hughes; Stimpson, Bungay, O'Neil, Barke, Collier, Turner, Bell, Carter, Somerfield, Wilson.
Att: unknown
Final
Nov 2 v Nottingham Forest (a) 2-2 a.e.t.
Dutton, Wilson
Hughes; Stimpson, Bungay, Collier, Barke, Speed, Turner, Bell, Somerfield, Dutton, Wilson.
Att: 1,500

1960-61
Final
May 5 v Nottingham Forest (a) 0-1 a.e.t.
Wyllie; Toon, Humble, Williams, Phillips, Coates, Wragg, Delapenha, Hollett, Jones, Stringfellow.
Att: 5,516

1961-62
Final
May 11 v Nottingham Forest (a) 2-3 a.e.t.
Hollett, R.Chapman
Treharne; Toon, Humble, Williams, Phillips, Morris, Wagstaff, Straw, R.Chapman, Hollett, Hall.
Att: 6,214

1962-63
Semi-final
May 23 v Notts County (a) 2-4
S.Chapman, Morris (pen)
Treharne; Toon, Jones, S.Chapman, Gill, Morris, B.Hall, Coates, Wagstaff, Hollett, Scanlon.
Att: 7,432

1963-64
Semi-final
Jan 25 v Nottingham Forest (a) 1-3
Wagstaff
Treharne; Jones, Humble, S.Chapman, Gill, Morris, B.Hall, Govan, R.Chapman, Wagstaff, Scanlon.
Att: 13,419

1964-65
Semi-final
May 3 v Notts County (h) 1-0
Curry
Humphreys; Nelson, Toon, I.Hall, Gill, Morris, Gregson, Macready, Curry, Middleton, Scanlon.
Att: 5,775
Final
May 8 v Nottingham Forest (a) 0-5
Humphreys; Nelson, Toon, Poynton, Gill, Morris, Gregson, Macready, Curry, Middleton, Scanlon.
Att: 9,074

1965-66
No Competition

1966-67
Semi-final
Oct 25 v Notts County (a) 0-4
Wilson; Mallinson, Richardson, Morris, Williams, Ferns, Brace, Rowland, Curry, McGeorge, Gregson.
Att: 3,424

1967-68
Semi-final
Mar 25 v Notts County (h) 0-1
Hollins; Pate, Stanton, Waller, Boam, Roberts, Melling, Sharkey, Ledger, Goodfellow, Rowland.
Att: 5,378

1968-69
Semi-final
May 3 v Notts County (h) 1-3
Needham (og)
Ogden; Pate, Hopkinson, Walker, Saunders, Waller, Todd(Partridge 80 mins), Keeley, Ledger, Frude, Jones.
Att: 3,958

1969-70
Semi-final
Oct 22 v Notts County (a) 0-2
Hollins; Pate, Walker, Stenson, Boam, Quigley, Jones, Partridge, Ledger, Roberts, Bates.
Att: unknown

1970-71
Semi-final
Mar 30 v Notts County (a) 1-0
D.Roberts
Arnold; Pate, Walker, Stenson, Boam, Saunders, Derrick, R.Roberts, D.Roberts, Jarvis, Jones.
Att: 11,147
Final
May 4 v Nottingham Forest (a) 1-0
D.Roberts
Brown; Pate, Walker, Stenson, Boam, Saunders, Thompson, R.Roberts, D.Roberts, Jarvis, Jones.
Att: 9,022

Mark Kearney (right) receives the Notts FA County Cup in 1989 from Notts FA chairman, John Crampton.

1971-72
Final
May 15 v Notts County (h) 3-1
Thompson, Wignall, Longhorn
Brown; Walker, B.Foster, Pate, Ellis, Saunders, Thompson, Wignall, Fairbrother, Longhorn, Laverick.
Att: 7,496

1972-73
Final
May 7 v Nottingham Forest (h) 0-1
Arnold; Pate, Walker, Matthews, Bird, C.Foster, Thompson, Laverick, D.Roberts, Longhorn, McCaffrey.
Att: 8,409

1973-74
Semi-final
May 1 v Notts County (a) 2-4
Edwards, Bolton (og)
Arnold; Pate, Walker, C.Foster, Edwards, Bird, Lathan, McCaffrey(Jones 45 mins), Cook, Donovan, Matthews
Att: 3, 327

1974-75
Semi-final
May 1 v Notts County (h) 0-0
Arnold; Pate, B.Foster, Matthews, Madden, Bird, Lathan, Eccles, Clarke, Hodgson, McCaffrey.
Att: 7,728
Notts County won 5-4 on penalties.

1975-76
Semi-final
Jan 23 v Nottingham Forest (a) 0-1
Arnold; Pate, B.Foster, McDonald, Mackenzie, Bird, Lathan, Eccles(Laverick 77 mins), Clarke, Matthews, McCaffrey.
Att: 4,885

1976-77
Semi-final
May 10 v Nottingham Forest (h) 1-2
Moss
Arnold; Bird, Wood, McEwan, Mackenzie, C.Foster, Matthews, Moss, Randall, Hodgson, McDonald.
Att: 9,679

1977-78
Semi-final
May 8 v Notts County (h) 2-0
Bird, Martin
Arnold(Phillips 49 mins); G.Saxby, B.Foster, C.Foster, M.Saxby, Bird, Miller, Martin, Syrett, Johnson, Goodwin.
Att: 4,105

1978-79
Final (from previous season)
Sep 19 v Nottingham Forest (a) 0-4
Arnold; Bird, B.Foster, Curtis, M.Saxby, McClelland, Goodwin, Moss, Syrett, Hodgson, Martin.
Att: 5,399
Semi-final
Mar 5 v Notts County (h) 3-0
Curtis 2 (1 pen), Carter
New; Dawkins, B.Foster, Curtis, M.Saxby, Bird(Allen 45 mins), Hamilton, Carter, McClelland, Goodwin, Miller.
Att: 2,763
Final
May 23 v Nottingham Forest (a) 1-3
Allen
New; Dawkins, B.Foster, Curtis, M.Saxby, Bird, Allen, G.Saxby, Austin, Hamilton, Goodwin.
Att: 9,165

1979-80
Semi-final
Nov 12 v Notts County (h) 2-2
Taylor, Thomson
New; Dawkins, Johnson, Hamilton, Curtis, McClelland, Thomson(Caldwell 69 mins), Taylor, Austin, Lathan, Allen.
Att: 2,590
Notts County won 9-8 on penalties.

1980-81
Semi-final
Apr 13 v Notts County (a) 2-1
Pollard, Thomson
Sutton; McJannet, Wood, Hamilton, Burrows, McClelland, Allen, Mann, Caldwell, Pollard, Thomson (Woodhead 80 mins).
Att: 1,979
Final
May 4 v Nottingham Forest (a) 1-2
Thomson
Sutton; McJannet, Wood, Pollard, Burrows, McClelland, Allen, Parkinson(Woodhead 83 mins), Lumby, Hamilton, Thomson.
Att: 3,405

1981-82
Semi-final
Apr 19 v Notts County (h) 1-1
Lumby
Arnold; McJannet, Mann, Woodhead, Burrows, Bird, Cannell, Caldwell, Lumby, Nicholson, Parkinson.
Att: 1,985
Notts County won 5-4 on penalties.

1982-83
Semi-final
Apr 27 v Notts County (a) 1-2
Caldwell
Coles; Woodhead, Kearney, Matthews, Ayre, Bird, Bell (Sindall 60 mins), Hutchinson, Dungworth, Caldwell, Lowery
Att: 1,225

1983-84
Semi-final
Feb 28 v Notts County (h) 4-0
Caldwell 2, Lowery, Barrowclough
Daines; Woodhead, Taylor(Calderwood 86 mins), Lowery, Ayre, Foster, Keegan(Sindall 85 mins), Matthews, Barrowclough, Caldwell, Nicholson.
Att: 1,303
Final
May 18 v Nottingham Forest (a) 0-3
Hitchcock; Calderwood, Logan, Lowery, Ayre, Foster, Barrowclough, Woodhead, Juryeff(Galloway 64 mins), Caldwell, Nicholson.
Att: 2,480

1984-85
Competition held over to following season.

1985-86
Semi-final (1984-85)
Aug 10 v Notts County (a) 2-2
Kearney, Vinter
Hitchcock; Graham, Logan, Lowery, Foster, Pollard, Luke, Whatmore, Kent, Vinter, Kearney.
Att: 1,490
Notts won 3-2 on penalties.
Semi-final
May 7 v Nottingham Forest (h) 0-1
Hitchcock; Graham, Logan, Robinson, Foster, Pollard, Kent, McKernon, Whatmore, Chamberlain (Stringfellow 82 mins), Kearney(Lowery 82 mins).
Att: 3,165

1986-87
Semi-final
Aug 12 v Notts County (h) 3-0
Lowery 2, Cassells
Hitchcock; Graham, Logan, Lowery, Foster, Kenworthy, Kent, Kearney, Chamberlain, Cassells, Brazil(Robinson 58 mins).
Att: 1,954
Final
Aug 17 v Nottingham Forest (a) 1-1
Cassells (1 pen)
Hitchcock; Graham, Logan, Lowery(Robinson 45 mins), Foster, Kenworthy, Kent, Kearney, Chamberlain, Cassells, McKernon.
Att: 3,718
Mansfield won 4-3 on penalties.

1987-88
Final
Aug 11 v Notts County (h) 2-2
Stringfellow, Kearney (1 pen)
Hitchcock; Graham, Kearney, Hodges, Coleman, Kenworthy, Kent, Chambers(Danskin 63 mins), Stringfellow, Cassells, Charles.
Att: 3,876
Mansfield won 5-4 on penalties.

1988-89
Final
23 Aug v Notts County (h) 3-2
Cassells 2, Laws (og)
Cox; Graham, Garner(Kenworthy 6 mins), Lowery(Ryan 45 mins), Foster, Coleman, Owen, Kearney, Kent, Cassells, Charles.
Att: 3,933

1989-90
Final
May 8 v Nottingham Forest (h) 0-4
Beasley; Chambers, Kearney, Christie, Foster, Smalley, Kent, Clark, Hodges(Stringfellow), Fairclough, Charles.
Att: 6,119

1990-91
Semi-final
Aug 22 v Notts County (h) 3-3
Wilkinson 2, Stringfellow.
Beasley; Murray, Kearney, Fairclough, Foster, Smalley, Kent, Chambers, Wilkinson, Stringfellow, Charles.
Att: 2,271
Mansfield won 4-1 on penalties.
Final
Aug 25 v Nottingham Forest (a) 0-5
Beasley; Murray, Kearney, Clark, Foster, Smalley, Kent, Chambers, Wilkinson, Stringfellow, Charles.
Att: 6,254

Stuart Boam (with cup) and the Stags celebrate the 1-0 win over Forest in 1970-71.

Mansfield Town Against Foreign Opposition

Although Mansfield Town have never enjoyed the heady heights of European competition, they have, over the years, played occasional friendly games against foreign opposition, most recently in 1986 when they met the Canadian national team. Below are listed details of these games

1931
Sep 23 v Netherlands FA (a) 2-1
Jepson 2
Wilson; Clifford, England, Wake, Chambers, Blackburn, Gilhespy, Readman, Jepson, Broome, Baxter.
Played under floodlights.

1932
Feb 20 v Red Star Club Français (a) 3-4
Bowater 2, Broome
Staples; Clifford, England, Wake, Robinson, Weightman, Storer, Broome, Fisher, Featherby, Bowater.
Att: 3,000

The Mansfield party that travelled to The Hague in September 1931. The Stags won the match 2-1, thanks to two goals from Jepson.

Feb 21 v Rennes University (a) 3-3
Fisher, Broome, Prazek (og)
Staples; Clifford, England, Wake, Robinson, Weightman, Storer, Broome, Fisher, Featherby, Bowater.

1956
Apr 23 v Rampla (Uruguay) (h) 2-3
Murray, Jepson
Wright; McGregor, Bradley, Fox, Warner, Watson, Murray, Darwin, Jepson, Smith, Mitten.

1957
May 1 v Blauw Witt (Holland) (h) 3-1
Morris 2, Uphill
Elliott; Chamberlain, Swinscoe, Jayes, Anderson, Uphill, Morris, Darwin, Mitten, Watson, Dickinson.

1965
Oct 19 v St Gallen (Switzerland) 2-0
Anderson, Poynton
Treharne; Nelson, Humble, Hall, Gill, Lee, Anderson, Middleton, Curry, Poynton, Scanlon
Att: 5,342

1986
Aug 8 v Canadian National Team (h) 3-0
Kearney 2, Chamberlain
Hitchcock; Graham, Logan, Lowery(Robinson 64) Foster(Coleman 80), Kenworthy, Kent(McKernon 56), Kearney, Chamberlain(Andersen 74), Cassells (Stringfellow 45), Brazil.
Att: 2,466

Before World War Two, the famous amateur side, Corinthians, often played prestigious friendly games against Football League sides. Although by the 1930s the Corinthians were not the power they were in Victorian and Edwardian days, they still enjoyed the occasional decent FA Cup run and were an attraction to Field Mill when they met the Stags on 11 February 1932. Mansfield won 2-1 with goals from Prior, Hoyland. The Stags team was: Clough; Anthoney, England, Davies, S.Robinson, Slack, Prior, Readman, Brailsford, Hoyland, Bowater.

The Reserves pictured in action in their first-ever season, against Lincoln Reserves at Field Mill.

Mansfield Town Reserves

AFTER their election to the Football League in 1931, Mansfield Town retained their reserve team in the Midland Counties League until 1933-4, when they once more entered the Central Combination. Club officials were adamant that their supporters were 'fed up' with the Midland League and this had been shown by the poor attendances at Field Mill.

They admitted, however, that from a footballing point of view, there would be little difference between the Midland Counties League and the Combination. But they believed that because there were more local clubs in the competition, better attendances would be the result.

The Stags finished sixth in their initial season of their new venture and raised this to third the following season. However, in 1935-6, a great number of clubs resigned to join other competitions and left only nine clubs in the Combination.

It was decided to divide the season into two competitions, the first half for the championship and the second half for the Byron Cup, which was to be played on a League basis.

Mansfield Town Reserves finished fourth in the league and joint third with Ilkeston Town in the cup competition, with Ollerton Colliery achieving the league and cup double, after a cup play-off with Newark Town which was won 2-0 by the colliery side.

Despite the difficulties, the Central Combination decided to carry on the following season, but the Stags, Forest and Newark Town resigned and were successful in their bids to rejoin the Midland Counties League, for the 1936-7 season.

The Stags remained loyal to the competition until the end of the 1957-8 season, when along with Nottingham Forest Reserves and Notts County Reserves, they were admitted to the Football Combination.

In 1939, at the outbreak of war, after the original ban on matches had been lifted, only eight of the 22 clubs in membership indicated that they were prepared to carry on for the rest of the season.

Consequently, the main competition was abandoned and a wartime competition was initiated, although three of the eight clubs, Burton Town, Scarborough and Shrewsbury Town were excluded because of the problems of travel.

The second competition, started on 10 February, also proved to be unsatisfactory because of several adverse circumstances. Here is Mansfield Town's Midland Counties League record:

First Team

	P	W	D	L	F	A	Pts	Pos
1921-22	42	20	7	15	68	57	47	8
1922-23	42	17	6	19	79	64	40	13
1923-24	42	31	6	5	98	31	68	1
1924-25	28	20	4	4	82	27	44	1
1925-26	40	23	7	10	120	54	53	2
1927-28	44	19	11	14	118	97	49	10
1928-29	50	31	10	9	133	72	72	1
1929-30	50	25	4	21	126	98	54	10
1930-31	46	19	11	16	103	95	49	10

Reserves

1931-32	46	16	12	18	86	86	44	10
1932-33*	44	16	9	19	108	97	41	13
1936-37	42	11	9	22	57	100	31	19
1937-38	42	18	3	21	69	67	39	15
1938-39	42	11	7	24	80	111	29	19
1945-46	36	7	8	21	66	104	22	19
1946-47	42	7	6	29	84	126	20	20
1947-48	42	12	9	21	63	82	33	18
1948-49	22	9	8	25	49	81	26	21
1949-50	46	17	6	23	65	93	40	17
1950-51	42	17	13	12	69	50	47	8
1951-52	42	12	13	17	63	65	37	15
1952-53	46	16	10	20	86	95	42	14
1953-54	46	17	3	26	80	120	37	20
1954-55	46	12	11	23	79	104	35	19
1955-56	46	10	7	29	85	141	27	22
1956-57	46	4	6	36	55	173	14	24
1957-58**	46	18	8	20	108	105	44	14

* Left to join the Central Combination
** Left to join the Football Combination

Central Combination

1933-34	32	14	11	7	106	75	35	6
1934-35	28	16	5	7	80	56	37	3

1935-36 League position 4th:
Byron Cup competition joint third

Football Combination

Second Division

1959-60	38	10	13	15	68	86	33	14
1960-61	38	10	8	20	67	93	28	18

Saturday Section

1961-62	34	4	4	26	34	107	12	18
1962-63	34	12	6	16	59	88	30	13

Second Division

1963-64	34	12	6	16	59	88	30	13
1964-65	34	9	7	18	84	89	25	17
1965-66	38	8	7	23	54	12	23	30
1966-67	24	5	3	16	38	71	13	12
1967-68	24	5	3	16	13	44	12	9

Cup Competition

16	5	5	6	20	23	15	5

Subsequently, Mansfield Town withdrew their reserve side from the Football Combination to join the newly-formed North Midlands League in the 1969-70 season, which was also a competition strictly for the reserve teams of Football League clubs. After only one season, however, the team was withdrawn on the advice of manager Tom Eggleston, although they were reinstated for the 1971-2 campaign.

The Stags competed in the North Midlands League for ten years until the end of the 1981-2 season, relying for several seasons after this on the Midland Intermediate League to serve both the Reserves and 'A' team, not a completely satisfactory state of affairs.

Then in season 1987-8, the Central League extended their competition to a Second Division and Mansfield's application to join was successful. A spate of injuries, however, meant that the Stags had to rely mainly on their 16-year-old players during the initial season and they finished next to bottom and had to apply for re-election.

This was successful and the following season, although once again too many of the club's 'A' team players also had to take an early baptism into more senior soccer, because injuries had once again taken their toll of the senior players, the final position had improved, albeit only slightly, to fourth from bottom, well clear of the need to seek re-election.

By now, the Central League had secured sponsorship from the holiday firm Pontins and in 1989-90, with the Stags coming to terms with the requirements of the competition, their final placing was sixth from bottom, to maintain the steady improvement, 15 points clear of the re-election zone.

Stags Internationals

OF all the players to have worn Mansfield Town's colours, only **John McClelland** was actively involved on the international scene whilst on the Stags' playing staff. During his international career, McClelland twice took part in the final stages of the World Cup for Northern Ireland, under the managership of former Stags boss Billy Bingham.

All told, McClelland gained 52 full caps, six of them as a Mansfield player. His full list is as follows:

Mansfield Town: 1980 v Scotland (sub), Australia (3 times); 1981 v Sweden, Scotland.
Glasgow Rangers: 1981 v Scotland, Sweden, 1982 v Scotland, Wales, Yugoslavia, Honduras, Spain, Austria, France; 1983 v Austria, West Germany, Albania (twice), Turkey, Scotland, England, Wales; 1984 v Austria, Turkey, West Germany, Scotland, England, Wales, Finland; 1985 v Romania.
Watford: 1985 v Finland, Iceland, England, Spain, Turkey; 1986 v Turkey, France (sub); 1987 v England (twice), Turkey, Israel, Yugoslavia; 1989 v Republic of Ireland, Hungary, Spain (twice), Malta.

Other full internationals to have played for Mansfield Town include **Dave Hollins**, who was capped for Wales on 11 occasions whilst with Newcastle United as follows: 1962 v Brazil (sub), Mexico; 1963 v Northern Ireland, Hungary; 1964 v England; 1965 v Northern Ireland, Greece, Italy; 1966 v Scotland, Denmark, Brazil.

Freddie Steele collected six England caps whilst with Stoke City, all in 1937, against Scotland, Wales, Northern Ireland, Norway, Finland and Sweden.

Full-back **Steve Whitworth** played for England in seven internationals whilst with Leicester City. In 1975 he was capped against West Germany, Cyprus, Northern Ireland, Wales and Scotland, and in 1976 against Sweden and Portugal.

Another former Leicester City full-back, who moved to Mansfield Town in 1947, **David O.Jones,** was capped by Wales on seven occasions as follows: 1934 v England, Northern Ireland; 1935 v England, Scotland; 1936 v England, Northern Ireland; 1937 v Northern Ireland.

One of Mansfield Town's most popular pre-war goalkeepers was **Jack Hughes,** who gained one Welsh cap whilst with Blackburn Rovers, against Northern Ireland in 1935.

Centre-half **Ernie Hart** cost Mansfield £350 when he joined the Stags from Leeds United in time for the start of the 1936-7 season. And considering Hart had been capped for England on eight occasions whilst with United, his fee was considered something of a bargain. Hart was first capped in 1929, against Wales. His other international appearances were: 1930 v Wales, Northern Ireland; 1933 v Scotland, Austria; 1934 v Scotland, Hungary, Czechoslovakia.

Alan Jarvis, whose career at Mansfield was cut short when he was struck in the eye by a ball when playing squash during the 1973 close season, gained three Welsh caps in 1967, when he was with Hull City. These were against England, Wales and Scotland.

Striker **Frank Wignall** was capped twice by England in 1964-5 whilst with Nottingham Forest, against Wales and Holland.

Top Appearances

Figures are for Football League appearances only. Number in brackets is the number of substitute appearances made which are included in larger figure.

400+

ARNOLD R 440

PATE A ....413(1)

300+

BRADLEY D 384

WRIGHT D..........379
MORRIS PJ ....328(1)
BIRD K................377(5)
FOSTER G...........305

200+

WATSON S..........292

FOSTER B...........287(5)
FOX O................248
BARKS E 213
KENT K ....204(8)
CHESSELL S........256
KEARNEY M ....230(2)
TOON C..............213
GROGAN J 201
LOWERY A ....244(1)
WALKER C ....229(6)
FOSTER C...........205(10)
ROBERTS D ....200(6)

100+

HUMBLE W.........198

TREHARNE C 191
BOAM SW...........190(4)
HODGSON G 184
COOLE W............182
HITCHCOCK K.....182
WAGSTAFF K 181
McCAFFREY J .....178(8)
PLUMMER N 166
LEWIS J..............163
JOHNSON H 163
CASSELLS K........163(1)
COATES D 159
WALLER P..........159(6)
CALDWELL D......157(12)
CHAPMAN S 155
WILLIAMS G 154
WOOD I..............149(14)
HALL I...............145
BROWN G 143
MURRAY K.........140
REEVE K 139
GILL J................139(1)
CHAPMAN R 136
CHARLES S.........134(1)
GRAHAM M ....133(1)
THOMPSON D .....131(2)
ENGLAND E 130
JONES D.............130(14)
DARWIN G..........126
McCLELLAND .....125(3)
MATTHEWS P......124(3)
WOODHEAD S.....122(14)
SLACK W............120
ATKINSON G.......119
McGREGOR W 119
ECCLES T ....118(3)
MANN A.............116(2)
NICHOLSON G.....116(4)
ALLEN RP...........116(17)
DELAPENHA L 115
JAYES B 115
BARKE JL 114
OSCROFT H 113
MILLER J ....113(4)
HOLLINS D 111
GARNER P..........110(8)
SCANLON A 108
STENSON J..........107(4)
QUIGLEY J..........105
LATHAN J...........103(2)
PHILLIPS B 102
CURRY W 102
SPEED F.............100
MITTEN C...........100
KENWORTHY A ...100(2)
CALDERWOOD C 100(3)
GOODFELLOW J 100(4)

Top Goalscorers

Figures are for Football League appearances only.

1931-32	Johnson....32	Bowater....10	Broome....8
1932-33	Johnson....30	Bowater....18	Hoyland....9
1933-34	Johnson....18	Kilcar....12	Methven....9
1934-35	Johnson....17	Hunt....14	Bytheway....12
1935-36	Harston....26	Atkinson....10	Anderson....8
1936-37	Harston....55	Atkinson....10	Anderson....8
1937-38	Crawshaw....25	Read....9	Horne....6
1938-39	Dutton....12	Carter....7	Somerfield....6
1946-47	Bryant....15	Copestake....7	Hogg....6
1947-48	Banks....14	Oscroft....11	Cooling....7
1948-49	Oscroft....14	Banks....7	Cooling....7
1949-50	Steele....18	Oscroft....12	Reeve....8
1950-51	Coole....16	Ottewell....15	Steele....14
1951-52	Reeve....21	Fox....10	Donaldson....9
1952-53	Marron....16	Reeve....10	Fox....5
1953-54	Murray....21	Darwin....17	Daley....12
1954-55	Adam....13	Daley....12	Murray....12
1955-56	Jepson....22	Darwin....19	Murray....17
1956-57	Darwin....19	Jepson....13	Mitten....11
1957-58	Thomas....23	Morris....15	Chapman S....15
1958-59	Thomas....21	Uphill....19	Delapenha....9
1959-60	Hollett....15	Fitzsimmons....15	Jones....13
1960-61	Wragg....11	Hollett....10	Wagstaff....9
1961-62	Chapman R....20	Wagstaff....12	Straw....11
1962-63	Wagstaff....34	Chapman R....30	Hollett....9
1963-64	Wagstaff....29	Chapman R....19	Hall B....6
1964-65	Middleton....16	Curry....15	Wagstaff, Chapman R....9
1965-66	Curry....14	Anderson....9	Middleton....8
1966-67	Curry....22	Brace....21	Morris....13
1967-68	Jones....8	Morris....7	Rowland....7
1968-69	Sharkey....13	Roberts....10	Ledger....9
1969-70	Roberts....18	Partridge....13	Jones....10
1970-71	Roberts....22	Stenson....12	Jones....9
1971-72	Fairbrother....18	Wignall....8	Thompson....4
1972-73	Fairbrother....20	Roberts....8	Thompson....8
1973-74	Eccles....20	Bird....8	Roberts....7
1974-75	Clarke....28	Eccles....17	Hodgson....10
1975-76	Clarke....24	Hodgson....7	Bird....6
1976-77	Randall....17	Moss....13	Foster....9
1977-78	Syrett....16	Moss....6	Miller....5
1978-79	Curtis....6	Allen....5	Austin....5
1979-80	Austin....19	Taylor....7	Bird....7
1980-81	Allen....9	Caldwell....8	Austin....7
1981-82	Lumby....14	Parkinson....9	Caldwell....9
1982-83	Dungworth....14	Caldwell....10	Nicholson....8
1983-84	Caldwell....21	Barrowclough....10	Nicholson....8
1984-85	Caldwell....9	Whatmore....7	Luke....6
1985-86	Chamberlain....16	Cassells....13	Whatmore....9
1986-87	Cassells....16	Kearney....10	Kent....6
1987-88	Charles....12	Kent....10	Cassells....9
1988-89	Cassells....14	Charles....7	Coleman, Kent, Owen...5
1989-90	Wilkinson....15	Christie....13	Charles....7

Above: Terry Eccles scoring one of his two goals against Newport when the Stags won 3-0 in December 1974. Eccles finished that season with 17 goals.

Left: Much travelled Dave Caldwell (second left) beats Blackpool's goalkeeper to earn a 2-2 draw during 1981-2 as he grabbed nine goals to finish third in the top goalscorers that term.

Dudley Roberts (right) scores a 50th minute goal to give Mansfield a 2-0 victory over Wrexham in the FA Cup tie at Field Mill in October 1970. Roberts topped Stags' goalscorers that season with 18 and followed it the next year with 22.

Stags Hat-tricks

(Football League unless otherwise stated)

1931-32	Johnson	28 Mar v Luton T	(h)	5-2	
1932-33	Johnson	5 Sep v New Brighton	(h)	5-0	
	Johnson	5 Nov v Darlington	(h)	3-3	
	Readman	27 Dec v Rotherham U	(h)	9-2	
	Hoyland	27 Dec v Rotherham U	(h)	9-2	
	Bowater	27 Dec v Rotherham U	(h)	9-2	
1933-34	Methven	31 Mar v Carlisle U	(h)	6-0	
1935-36	Allen	14 Sep v Darlington	(h)	4-2	
	Harston	19 Oct v Southport	(a)	3-3	(Debut)
	Harston	22 Feb v Southport	(h)	5-1	
	Harston	14 Apr v Gateshead	(h)	3-1	
1936-37	Harston	1 Sep v Rochdale	(a)	3-1	
	Harston	9 Sep v Rochdale	(h)	6-2	(Scored 5)
	Harston	10 Oct v Halifax T	(h)	3-0	
	Harston	17 Oct v Hull C	(h)	5-2	(Scored 4)
	Harston	25 Nov v Barrow	(a)	4-0	(FA Cup)
	Harston	23 Jan v Hartlepools U	(h)	8-2	(Scored 7)
	Harston	27 Mar v Port Vale	(h)	7-1	(Scored 5)
	Harston	30 Mar v Wrexham	(h)	3-0	(1 penalty)
1937-38	Crawshaw	28 Aug v Northampton T	(h)	4-1	(Debut)
	Crawshaw	26 Mar v Reading	(h)	5-1	(Scored 4)
1938-39	Somerfield	19 Nov v Northampton T	(a)	4-3	
1947-48	Banks	28 Feb v Halifax T	(h)	3-1	
1948-49	Mercer	30 Oct v Stockport Co	(h)	4-0	
	Mercer	27 Nov v Gloucester C	(h)	4-0	(FA Cup)
1949-50	Steele	29 Oct v Hartlepools U	(h)	7-1	
	Oscroft	29 Oct v Hartlepools U	(h)	7-1	(2 penalties)
1951-52	Evans	8 Mar v Chester	(a)	5-1	
	Reeve	15 Apr v Halifax T	(h)	4-2	
1952-53	Fox	22 Nov v Scarborough	(a)	8-0	(FA Cup)
1953-54	Murray	6 Feb v Grimsby T	(h)	5-1	
1955-56	Darwin	31 Dec v Hartlepools U	(h)	5-1	
	Darwin	4 Feb v Wrexham	(h)	6-1	
	Murray	24 Mar v Rochdale	(h)	6-0	
	Jepson	9 Apr v Bradford	(h)	5-0	
1956-57	Chapman S	3 Nov v Darlington	(h)	7-3	
	Darwin	6 Apr v Wrexham	(h)	3-1	
1957-58	Thomas	19 Apr v Bury	(h)	6-4	
1959-60	Fitzsimmons	7 Nov v Bournemouth & BA	(h)	3-4	
	Hollett	2 Apr v Accrington S	(h)	4-1	
1960-61	Hollett	19 Nov v Barrow	(h)	5-1	
1962-63	Wagstaff	22 Aug v Exeter C	(a)	3-0	
	Chapman R	1 Oct v Tranmere R	(h)	6-1	
	Hollet	5 Nov v Hounslow T	(h)	9-2	(FA Cup)
	Chapman R	5 Nov v Hounslow T	(h)	9-2	(FA Cup)
	Wagstaff	26 Nov v Crystal Palace	(h)	7-2	(FA Cup)
	Wagstaff	9 Mar v Oldham A	(h)	4-2	
	Wagstaff	6 Apr v Southport	(h)	6-1	(Scored 4)
1963-64	Chapman R	16 Sep v Notts Co	(h)	4-0	

Above: Clarke's second of three against Southend in the 3-1 victory in March 1970.

Right: Eccles on his way to a hat-trick during the 5-0 win over Stockport in October 1973.

Below: Kevin Randall's diving header gives Mansfield a 2-0 lead over Reading in November 1976 and went on to score two more as the Stags won 4-0.

	Chapman R	9 Nov v Southend U ....(h)	4-1	
	Coates	30 Mar v Bristol C............(h)	4-0	
1964-65	Curry	26 Feb v Workington ....(a)	5-1	
	Curry	15 Mar v Queen's Park R .....(h)	8-1	
	Middleton	15 Mar v Queen's Park R .....(h)	8-1	
	Curry	5 Apr v Southend U ....(h)	6-1	(Scored 4)
1969-70	Roberts	1 Apr v Southport ....(h)	5-0	
1970-71	Partridge	19 Aug v Chesterfield ....(h)	6-2	(League Cup)
	Roberts	27 Feb v Tranmere R ....(h)	6-2	(Scored 4)
1972-73	Fairbrother	9 Oct v Peterborough U.......(h)	4-2	
	McKenzie	10 Mar v Bradford C ....(h)	4-1	(On loan)
	Roberts	24 Apr v Darlington ....(h)	5-0	
1973-74	Eccles	17 Sep v Chester..............(h)	3-0	
	Eccles	22 Oct v Stockport Co ....(h)	5-0	
1974-75	Clarke	16 Nov v Doncaster R ....(h)	5-2	
1975-76	Clarke	27 Sep v Walsall..............(h)	4-1	
	Clarke	15 Mar v Southend U.........(h)	3-1	
1976-77	Eccles	4 Sep v Grimsby T............(h)	3-1	(1 penalty)
	Randall	8 Nov v Reading..............(h)	4-0	(Scored 4, 2 pens)
1977-78	Syrett	25 Mar v Tottenham H ....(h)	3-3	
1979-80	Austin	8 Oct v Rotherham U.........(h)	5-1	
1980-81	Austin	1 Nov v Rochdale.............(a)	4-1	(1 penalty)
1982-83	Dungworth	14 Mar v Hartlepool U ....(h)	3-0	(1 penalty)
1983-84	Caldwell	1 Oct v Aldershot.............(h)	5-2	
	Caldwell	22 Oct v Hartlepool U ....(h)	5-0	(Scored 4)
	Juryeff	10 Apr v Halifax T ....(h)	7-1	(On loan)
	Caldwell	7 May v Crewe Alex ....(a)	3-1	
1985-86	Cassells	17 Aug v Hereford U ....(h)	4-0	(Debut)
1986-87	Cassells	31 Jan v Bristol R ....(h)	5-0	(Scored 4)
1987-88	Kent	20 Dec v Port Vale ....(h)	4-0	(Scored 4)
1989-90	Wilkinson	3 April v Birmingham C ......(h)	5-2	(Scored 5)

Ever-Presents

England 1931-32
Slack 1933-34
Dransfield 1935-36
Barke 1937-38
Stimpson 1938-39
Grogan 1948-49, 1950-51
Chessell 1950-51
Lewis 1950-51, 1951-52
Bradley.........................1951-52
Wright 1951-52, 1953-54, 1955-56
Morris F 1957-58
Wyllie 1960-61
Toon 1961-62
Treharne.............1962-63, 1963-64
Humble 1963-64
Wagstaff 1963-64
Gill 1964-65
Morris P 1964-65
Mitchinson 1966-67
Boam.................1968-69, 1969-70
Quigley.........................1968-69
Pate 1969-70, 1970-71, 1971-72,
..............1972-73, 1973-74, 1974-75
Walker 1970-71
Arnold 1974-75, 1976-77, 1977-78
Clarke..........................1974-75
Hodgson 1975-76, 1976-77, 1977-78
Syrett 1977-78
Saxby M 1978-79
Austin..........................1979-80
McClelland 1980-81
Foster G........................1985-86
Hitchcock.............1985-86, 1986-87
Cassells........................1986-87
Kent 1986-87
Charles.........................1987-88
Graham 1987-88

Field Mill Scandals

FOR ardent Mansfield Town supporters — and at that time attendances of between 7,000 and 8,000 were by no means unusual — 1953 must have been a traumatic year.

At the club's annual meeting in January, shareholders were told that a financial report was not available because the accounts were in the hands of the police, who were investigating alleged discrepancies in the club's books.

The meeting was adjourned after a committee had been formed to look into Mansfield Town's affairs, which it was admitted were in a parlous state. Near to bankruptcy, the club were in danger of having to fold.

Indeed, when the annual meeting was reconvened on Monday, 23 March, the packed audience of shareholders were told that the Stags were hopelessly insolvent and had only £44 to meet the following week's wage bill of £360. They needed to seek time from their creditors if the club was to be saved from extinction.

In the local Press, manager George Jobey suggested that Field Mill should be sold in an effort to solve the problems, but such action was discounted. There was a further adjournment of the annual meeting to give the appointed committee further time to investigate the club's affairs.

When the AGM was resumed for a second time, on Monday, 20 April 1953, Councillor J.B.Jenkins, who was director-secretary of Mansfield Brewery, revealed that the club had liabilities of £14,000.

He reported that a new board of directors had been elected, with the immediate task of ensuring that Mansfield Town would be able to operate the following season.

Councillor Jenkins emphasized that land and freehold buildings at Field Mill must not be touched. It was the club's only free asset and would be pounced upon by preferential creditors.

The shareholders appointed Councillor Jenkins as the club's new chairman and approved the efforts being made to save Mansfield Town.

There was, however, to be a sad and startling turn of events. At the end of February, William James Warner (29), a former secretary of the club, was sent for trial on charges of £2,344 theft and fraud.

The charges related mainly to the falsifying of PAYE returns to the Inland Revenue, the misappropriation of season-ticket income and proceeds from benefit matches for players.

It was revealed that the deficiency in the club's affairs totalled £3,060, but Warner was only responsible for £2,344 of that money.

Warner, who was assistant secretary to honorary secretary Bert Mee before taking over his post when Mee resigned on 21 November 1951, was subsequently cleared of 15 charges of theft, falsification of accounts and omissions from the books, but fined £75 for making false income tax returns.

Warner had claimed that he was covering up for monies taken from the club safe by the former player-manager Freddie Steele, and for illegal payments to players.

After a joint FA and Football League inquiry later in the year, the club was fined £500 and Steele £200. Several former players were cautioned and former officials and directors banned from participating in football affairs.

Mansfield Town received another body blow in 1964, when a national Sunday newspaper, *The People*, which had exposed details of bribery and betting in football a year earlier involving international players in December 1962, turned their attention to Mansfield Town.

When the paper reported the previous scandal, they named the former Everton and Charlton Athletic star Jimmy Gauld, who was a Mansfield Town player towards the end of the 1960-61 season, although he played only four matches before breaking a leg. Gauld was identified as the instigator of a scheme which involved bribing players to lose a match with the intention of bringing off a betting coup. He was later to serve a term of imprisonment.

In their edition of 26 April 1964, when Mansfield were coming to the end of their first season back in the Third Division, *The People* accused five Stags players of putting up money to bribe their opponents to lose a match which thus ensured Mansfield promotion.

The paper also alleged that in season 1959-60, several Mansfield players 'sold' two points to Tranmere Rovers, who required them to steer clear of relegation, whilst Mansfield were already down.

Mansfield's captain, Brian Phillips, and the late Roy Chapman were named as being involved in the scheme and Phillips was later banned from soccer for life. But in 1971 he appealed against the suspension, which was lifted, and redeemed himself by managing local club, Rainworth Miners' Welfare, to the FA Vase Final at Wembley. He also acted as coach to the Notts FA's representative teams.

MANSF...

FINED £500

Mansfield Town Football Club has been fined £500 by the Football Association. And former player-manager Freddie Steele, now manager of Northern Section leaders Port Vale, will have to pay £250.

These are the two main penalties imposed after last Thursday's joint F.A. and Football League inquiry in Nottingham.

and Mr. W. M. Hornby, the former chairman, is suspended permanently from all football and football management.

Past and present officials and players are concerned,

The full report of last Thursday's joint commission reads as follow:

"The directors, ex-officials and ex-players of the Mansfield Town Club were asked to answer charges of alleged breaches of the Football Association and Football League rules and regulations made by the former secretary of the club, Mr. W. J. Warner. Among the charges were allegations that illegal payments had been made to player-manager F. C. Steele, and players, D. O. Jones, G. R. Antonio, and J. Grogan.

a. *Steele admitted that he had received the alleged payments from Mr. W. M. Hornby (former chairman of Mansfield).*

b. *D. O. Jones admitted in a letter to the commission that he had received the alleged sums of money from the club.*

c. *Antonio admitted receiving the alleged amounts from Mr. Hornby, but explained that they were in the na...*

payments of £150, £87 5s. and £57 10s respectively, to player D. O. Jones.

c. *that on or about February 25th, 1950, and May 2nd, 1950, Mr. W. M. Hornby made irregular payments of £75 and £175 respectively to player G. R. Antonio.*

d. *that on or about November 20th, 1947, Mr. E. M. Smith made an irregular payment of £50 to player J. Grogan.*

e. *that Mr. J. A. Taylor made a loan of £400 to Antonio, contrary to the regulations of the Football League.*

DECISIONS

"The commission decided:

a. *That Mr. W. M. Hornby, former chairman of the club, be suspended permanently from all football and football management.*

b. *That Mr. E. M. Smith, former vice-chairman of the club, be suspended sine die from all football and football management.*

c. *That Mr. J. A. Taylor, a director of the club, be suspended from football and foot-... the end*

"The commission met at Nottingham on Thursday, December 10th, and the following attended:

"Mansfield directors, Messrs. A. C. Shillington, W. R. Ward, J. A. Taylor and W. H. Mein; former directors, Messrs. E. M. Smith and C. A. Ripley; hon. secretary and director, Mr. H. N. Mee; former secretary/assistant manager, Mr. S. Mercer; former player-manager, Mr. F. C. Steele; former players, Messrs. J. Grogan and G. R. Antonio (now Rowlands); former secretary Mr. W. J. Warner.

"Mr. J. B. Jenkins, present chairman, also attended. Mr. W. M. Hornby, former chairman, and D. O. Jones, former player were given an opportunity to appear before the commission but failed to do so."

After the findings of the commission had been announced Coun. J. B. Jenkins said: "So far as the club is concerned, it is now under new control, and though the fine imposed will strain our resources we are going to start afresh and fight on to restore the reputation of Mansfield Town."

The former chairman, Mr. Hornby, who is a wine and spirit merchant at Mansfield and has a farm at Arnold, refused to comment. George Antonio, now player-ma...

MANSFIELD AND NORTH NOTTINGHAMSHIRE

CHRONICLE ADVERTISER

Published in the Centre of Sherwood Forest

THURSDAY 16th JULY 1953

NEW PIANOS

KENT & COOPER LTD.

Leeming St. Mansfield

MORE EX-PLAYERS IN WITNESS BOX AT WARNER TRIAL

Freddie Steele, former Mansfield Town player-manager, denied suggestions that he had paid for a television set from Club funds, when yesterday he gave evidence on the third day of the trial of the Club's former secretary, 29-years-old William James Warner, of Nottingham Road, Mansfield.

Warner faces 16 charges of theft and falsification of accounts, and the case is being heard by Mr. Justice Gorman at a special sitting of Notts. Assizes, which is expected to last until next week.

Wearing a brown suit, the accused sat in the dock beside a warder. Among the few people in the public galleries were his mother, father and sister.

YOUNG DANES MEET THEIR HOSTS

CHRONICLE ADVERTISER

Published in the Centre of Sherwood Forest

THURSDAY, 23rd JULY 1953

WARNER VERDICT MAY BE REACHED TO-DAY

Summing up at Notts. Assizes on Tuesday, the seventh day of the trial of 29-year-old William James Warner on 15 charges of theft or fraud involving £247 while secretary of Mansfield Town Football Club, Mr. Justice Gorman said: "If you come to the conclusion that a witness is lying — that is, deliberately concocting a story either to save his own skin or to throw blame on someone else — then you know how to treat his evidence."

After speaking for over two hours, the Judge adjourned the hearing until today, when he will continue his summing-up. A verdict may be reached tonight.

HOSPITAL'S REPLY TO TRADES COUNCIL'S STATEMENT

ANCIENT DOCUMENTS OPENED AT WOODHOUSE CHURCH

This team 'won' by bribery

THE SOCCER SCANDAL OF THE CENTURY

● This is the most sensational report of all in "The People's" investigation of the great Soccer Bribes scandal.

● Here are the facts about a group of players who bought promotion-winning points for their team by bribing members of the opposing side.

By MICHAEL GABBERT, PETER CAMPLING and a team of 'People' investigators

MANSFIELD TOWN are well up the Third Division table. But Mansfield Town have no right to be in the Division at all. They should immediately be sent back to the Fourth Division, from which they were promoted at the end of last season.

FIVE MANSFIELD MEN PUT MONEY INTO THE KITTY ◄AND HE HANDED IT OVER TO A HARTLEPOOLS PLAYER

Sunday, April 12, 1964

PEOPLE

FRANK FEARLESS FREE

THE PAPER THAT LOOKS AHEAD

TODAY a shattering exposure

TOP SOCCER STARS BRIBED

These are the guilty men

They agreed to 'fix' a First Division match

LAYNE SWAN KAY

THE PEOPLE

THE PAPER THAT LOOKS AHEAD

GAULD CONFESSES

SOCCER BRIBES

'Players offered to throw matches to get in on wins of £1,000 a week'

By Michael Gabbert and Peter Campling

MANSFIELD TOWN CAREER RECORDS

Below are the career records of all players who have made a first-team appearance for Mansfield Town. They do not include appearances during the war seasons 1939-46, the three League matches played prior to the start of the war in season 1939-40, the match against Accrington Stanley in the 1961-2 season when the club resigned from the League and its record was expunged and any County Cup matches. The years refer to the first and last seasons played. Included in the 'Others' column are appearances in the Watney Cup, Associate Members Cup, Anglo-Scottish Cup and Freight/Rover Trophy competitions. These players had more than one spell at Mansfield: S.W.Boam (player, player-manager); G.Brown; S.Chapman; R.Edwards; J.Lathan; D.McKenzie (on loan); P.J.Morris (player, player-manager). R.Brown was a non-contract player, T.Cummings played a few matches in his first two seasons as player-manager, but then concentrated on managing the side only.

		League		FA Cup		FL Cup		Others		TOTAL	
	Played	App	Gls	App	Gls	App	Gls	App	Gls	App	Gls
ADAM C	1952-55	93	6	5	3	0	0	0	0	98	9
ADAM J	1954-55	39	10	1	1	0	0	0	0	40	11
AKERS W	1945-46	0	0	2	0	0	0	0	0	2	0
ALDREAD P	1965-67	11/1	3	0	0	0	0	0	0	11/1	3
ALLCOCK K	1947-48	1	0	0	0	0	0	0	0	1	0
ALLEN F	1953-55	6	0	0	0	0	0	0	0	6	0
ALLEN J	1935-36	8	5	0	0	0	0	0	0	8	5
ALLEN John	1984-85	1/1	0	0	0	0	0	0	0	1/1	0
ALLEN RP	1978-81	99/17	18	5	2	6/1	1	0	0	110/18	21
ANDERSON GR	1935-37	37	16	2	1	0	0	0	0	39	17
ANDERSON N	1985-89	9/11	0	0/1	0	1	0	1/2	0	11/14	0
ANDERSON RJ	1956-60	41	4	3	0	0	0	0	0	44	4
ANTHONEY C	1932-33	39	1	1	0	0	0	0	0	40	1
ANTONIO G	1949-51	67	8	2	1	0	0	0	0	69	9
ARNOLD R	1970-84	440	0	26	0	29	0	20	0	515	0
ASHALL T	1934-35	2	0	0	0	0	0	0	0	2	0
ASHLEY J	1933-36	69	0	5	0	4	0	0	0	78	0

Rod Arnold

Mansfield Town pictured in 1950. Back row (left to right): Antonio, Grogan, Wright, Bradley, Fox, Lewis. Front: Coole, Godwin, Steele, Reeve, McCarter.

		League		FA Cup		FL Cup		Others		TOTAL	
	Played	App	Gls	App	Gls	App	Gls	App	Gls	App	Gls
ASKEY C	1962-64	30	2	5	3	2	0	0	0	37	5
ASTON J	1977-78	24/7	4	1	0	0	0	0	0	25/7	4
ATKINSON G	1934-37	119	31	6	2	4	0	0	0	129	33
AUSTIN T	1978-81	84	31	3	1	9	3	0	0	96	35
AYRE W	1982-84	67	7	3	0	2	0	1	0	73	7
BAIRD J	1946-48	9	0	0	0	0	0	0	0	9	0
BANKS G	1947-49	63	21	6	0	0	0	0	0	69	21
BARKE JL	1937-47	114	0	16	0	3	0	0	0	133	0
BARKS E	1948-55	213	6	12	1	0	0	0	0	225	7
BARKS W	1934-35	4	0	0	0	1	0	0	0	5	0
BARLOW G	1934-36	11	0	0	0	0	0	0	0	11	0
BARROWCLOUGH S	1983-84	40/4	10	4	2	3	2	1	1	48/4	15
BARTLEY P	1935-36	2	0	0	0	0	0	0	0	2	0
BATES B	1969-70	20	3	3	1	1	1	0	0	24	5
BAXTER TW	1931-32	14	1	0	0	0	0	0	0	14	1
BEASLEY A	1984-	45	0	0	0	2	0	6	0	53	0
BELL C	1981-83	82/2	12	4	2	5	0	0	0	91/2	14
BELL E	1938-39	28	1	6	1	2	1	0	0	36	4
BENTLEY D *	1972-73	1/3	1	0	0	0	0	0	0	1/3	1
BERRY W	1956-57	10	1	0	0	0	0	0	0	10	1
BETTS E	1946-47	19	5	0	0	0	0	0	0	19	5
BILLINGTON C	1958-59	1	0	0	0	0	0	0	0	1	0
BINGHAM J	1970-72	18/3	0	3/1	2	1	0	0	0	22/4	2
BINNIE L	1946-47	20	0	1	0	0	0	0	0	21	0
BIRD K	1972-83	372/5	55	24	1	31	6	18	1	445/5	63
BISBY C	1935-36	9	0	0	0	0	0	0	0	9	0
BLACK D	1935-39	46	0	6	0	2	0	0	0	54	0
BLACKBURN GF	1931-32	14	0	0	0	0	0	0	0	14	0

Sid Carter

Dave Caldwell

Charlie Bell

Keith Cassells

Ernest Bramley

Derek Dawkins

Billy Ayre

		League		FA Cup		FL Cup		Others		TOTAL	
	Played	App	Gls	App	Gls	App	Gls	App	Gls	App	Gls
BLACKHALL R	1982-83	15	0	1	0	0	0	0	0	16	0
BLAIR J	1986-87	0	0	0	0	0	0	0/1	0	0/1	0
BOAM SW	1966-83	186/4	4	16	0	7	0	0	0	209/4	4
BONER D	1963-64	12	1	0	0	2	2	0	0	14	3
BOOK K *	1971-72	4	0	0	0	0	0	0	0	4	0
BOWATER G	1931-33	60	28	1	0	0	0	0	0	61	28
BRACE S	1966-68	55/2	25	8	3	4	2	0	0	67/2	30
BRADLEY D	1949-62	384	6	25	0	4	0	0	0	413	6
BRAMLEY A	1949-53	19	0	2	0	0	0	0	0	21	0
BRAMLEY E	1938-47	45	1	3	0	0	0	0	0	48	1
BRIGGS R	1936-37	2	0	0	0	0	0	0	0	2	0
BROOME WH	1931-33	48	9	1	0	0	0	0	0	49	9
BROWN A	1935-37	46	0	2	0	1	0	0	0	49	0
BROWN Albert	1947-48	17	2	1	0	0	0	0	0	18	2
BROWN Alex	1946-47	5	0	1	0	0	0	0	0	6	0
BROWN G	1969-81	143	0	10	0	10	0	0	0	163	0
BROWN REE	1975-76	1	0	3	0	1	0	0	0	5	0
BRYANT E	1946-47	35	17	0	0	0	0	0	0	35	17
BURNS N	1965-67	7/3	0	0	0	1	1	0	0	8/3	1
BURROWS A	1979-82	77/1	6	1/2	0	6	0	0	0	84/3	6
BURROWS F *	1973-74	6	0	0	0	0	0	0	0	6	0
BUNGAY R	1936-39	87	5	9	0	0	0	0	0	96	5
BUTLER E	1932-34	46	5	0	0	1	0	0	0	47	5
BUTT L	1947-48	15	4	2	1	0	0	0	0	17	5
BYTHEWAY G	1933-36	87	23	3	0	4	0	0	0	94	23
CALDERWOOD C	1981-85	97/3	1	6	1	4	0	7	1	114/3	3
CALDWELL D	1979-85	145/12	57	12	4	13	2	4/2	1	174/14	64
CALVERLEY A	1946-47	30	1	0	0	0	0	0	0	30	0

Stuart Boam

Stewart Brace

Graham Brown

		League		FA Cup		FL Cup		Others		TOTAL	
	Played	App	Gls	App	Gls	App	Gls	App	Gls	App	Gls
CANN R	1957-58	1	0	0	0	0	0	0	0	1	0
CANNELL P	1981-83	29/1	4	0	0	1	0	0	0	30/1	4
CARR A	1934-35	12	0	1	0	1	0	0	0	14	0
CARTER M *	1978-79	18	4	0	0	0	0	0	0	18	4
CARTER S	1938-47	39	11	0	0	1	0	0	0	40	11
CARTWRIGHT H	1936-37	5	1	0	0	1	0	0	0	6	1
CASSELLS K	1985-89	162/1	52	7	3	11	3	14	3	194/1	61
CHADBOURNE W	1946-48	9	3	0	0	0	0	0	0	9	3
CHAMBERLAIN D	1956-58	43	0	3	0	0	0	0	0	46	0
CHAMBERLAIN N	1985-87	56/5	19	2	1	6	2	5/1	1	69/6	23
CHAMBERS B	1931-33	10	0	0	0	0	0	0	0	10	0
CHAMBERS S	1986	12/8	0	1	0	1	0	2/1	0	16/9	0
CHANDLER J *	1986-87	6	0	0	0	0	0	2	2	8	2
CHAPMAN R	1961-65	136	78	8	6	6	4	0	0	150	88
CHAPMAN S	1956-64	155	40	11	2	3	0	0	0	169	42
CHARLES S	1987	133/1	26	8	3	10	0	7/1	3	158/2	32
CHEESEBOROUGH A	1965-57	24	0	2	0	3	0	0	0	29	0
CHESSELL S	1945-54	256	7	19	0	0	0	0	0	275	7
CHRISTIE T	1988	55/2	14	1	0	4	3	4	1	64/2	18
CHRISTOPHER P	1973-64	7/1	1	2	0	0	0	0	0	9/1	1
CLARK M	1989-90	14	1	0	0	0	0	0	0	14	1
CLARK P	1960-61	2	0	1	0	1	0	0	0	4	0
CLARKE R	1974-76	91	52	10	2	7	3	0	0	108	57
CLAYTON J	1933-34	15	1	2	0	2	0	0	0	19	1
CLENSHAW L	1935-36	27	6	1	0	2	0	0	0	30	6
CLIFFORD G	1932-32	39	0	1	0	0	0	0	0	40	0
CLOUGH J	1932-33	30	0	0	0	0	0	0	0	30	0
COATES D	1959-64	159	17	6	1	8	1	0	0	173	19

Paul Cannell signs for the Stags watched by manager Stuart Boam (right) and coach Geoff Allen.

		League		FA Cup		FL Cup		Others		TOTAL	
	Played	App	Gls	App	Gls	App	Gls	App	Gls	App	Gls
COCHRANE C	1947-48	1	0	0	0	0	0	0	0	1	0
COFFEY M	1978-79	2/1	0	0	0	1/1	0	0	0	3/2	0
COLEMAN J	1966-68	43	1	5	0	1/2	0	0	0	49/2	1
COLEMAN S	1985-90	96	7	7	0	9	0	7	1	119	8
COLES D	1982-83	3	0	0	0	0	0	0	0	3	0
COLLIER A	1938-39	21	0	4	0	1	0	0	0	26	0
COLLINS R	1985-87	11/6	1	0	0	0	0	4	2	15/5	3
COOK T	1973-74	1	0	0	0	0	0	0	0	1	0
COOKE R	1976-78	7/8	1	1	0	0	0	0	0	9/8	1
COOKE T	1934-37	15	1	0	0	0	0	0	0	15	1
COOLE W	1947-54	182	35	11	3	0	0	0	0	193	38
COOLING R	1947-50	65	14	3	2	0	0	0	0	68	16
COOPER J	1964-65	7	4	1	0	1	0	0	0	9	4
COPESTAKE O	1946-47	31	7	1	0	0	0	0	0	32	7
COTTAM J *	1972-73	2	1	0	0	0	0	0	0	2	1
COX B	1988-90	54	0	3	0	4	0	4	0	65	0
CRAWFORD A *	1972-73	1/1	0	0	0	0	0	0	0	1/1	0
CRAWFORD G *	1971-72	2	0	0	0	0	0	0	0	2	0
CRAWSHAW H	1937-38	41	25	3	1	1	0	0	0	45	26
CROFT C	1947-50	85	5	6	0	0	0	0	0	91	5
CROMACK V	1945-47	10	0	2	0	0	0	0	0	12	0
CROPPER R	1932-33	6	1	1	0	0	0	0	0	7	1
CROWE C	1956-58	37	0	4	0	0	0	0	0	41	0
CUMMINGS T	1962-64	10	0	0	0	1	0	0	0	11	0
CUNNINGHAM J	1984-86	3/1	0	0	0	0	0	0/1	0	3/2	0
CUPIT W	1932-33	2	0	0	0	0	0	0	0	2	0
CURRY W	1964-68	102	53	6	3	5	1	0	0	113	57
CURTIN D	1965-66	3	0	0	0	0	0	0	0	3	0

Gordon Chadbourne

Len Butt

John Dungworth

Bill Dallman

Ken Allcock

Ray Blackhall

Dick Edwards

		League		FA Cup		FL Cup		Others		TOTAL	
	Played	App	Gls	App	Gls	App	Gls	App	Gls	App	Gls
CURTIS R	1977-80	69/4	7	3/1	1	5	0	0	0	77/5	8
CUTHBERTSON J	1953-54	3	0	0	0	0	0	0	0	3	0
DAINES B	1983-84	21	0	2	0	0	0	1	0	24	0
DALEY A	1953-56	97	25	3	0	0	0	0	0	100	25
DALLMAN W	1946-48	5	0	0	0	0	0	0	0	5	0
DANSKIN J	1986-88	10	0	0/1	0	0/1	0	3	0	13/2	0
DARVILLE H	1935-36	13	0	1	0	2	0	0	0	15	0
DARWIN G	1953-57	126	63	6	1	0	0	0	0	132	64
DAVIES R	1932-33	18	0	0	0	0	0	0	0	18	0
DAVIS C	1932-32	5	1	0	0	0	0	0	0	5	1
DAWKINS D	1978-81	73	0	3	0	9	0	0	0	85	0
DAY C	1982-83	10/2	1	0	0	2	0	0	0	12/2	1
DEATH W	1931-32	14	2	1	1	0	0	0	0	15	3
DELAPENHA L	1958-61	115	27	5	0	0	0	0	0	120	27
DELLOW R	1934-35	24	10	3	2	0	0	0	0	27	12
DERCO F	1966-67	1	0	0	0	0	0	0	0	1	0
DERRICK J *	1970-71	2/1	0	0	0	0	0	0	0	2/1	0
DEVEY R	1947-50	76	4	6	0	0	0	0	0	82	4
DICKSON W	1956-57	19	0	0	0	0	0	0	0	19	0
DONALDSON W	1950-52	52	10	5	2	0	0	0	0	57	12
DOWNIE J	1958-59	18	4	0	0	0	0	0	0	18	0
DRANSFIELD E	1934-37	78	1	4	0	3	0	0	0	85	1
DUNGWORTH J	1982-84	50/6	16	3	4	3	0	0	0	56/6	20
DUTTON T	1938-39	39	12	6	2	2	0	0	0	47	14
EATON J	1952-54	4	1	0	0	0	0	0	0	4	1
ECCLES T	1973-77	115/3	47	13	8	9/1	2	0	0	137/4	57
EDMONDS A	1934-35	33	4	3	0	1	0	0	0	37	4
EDWARDS J	1933-34	20	0	0	0	2	0	0	0	22	0

Charlie Croft

Walter Edwards

Harry Hill

Roddie Collins

George Banks

Ray Cooling

Billy Coole

Neil Burns

Colin Calderwood

		League		FA Cup		FL Cup		Others		TOTAL	
	Played	App	Gls	App	Gls	App	Gls	App	Gls	App	Gls
EDWARDS R	1966-74	76/2	2	1	0	2	0	0	0	79/2	2
EDWARDS W	1947-49	25	5	1	0	0	0	0	0	26	5
ELLIOT F	1956-58	63	0	6	0	0	0	0	0	69	0
ELLIS S	1971-73	64	7	1	0	2	0	0	0	67	7
EMERY A	1959-61	26	0	1	0	1	0	0	0	28	0
ENGLAND E	1931-35	130	3	6	0	1	1	0	0	137	4
EVANS P	1975-76	6	0	1	0	1	0	0	0	8	0
EVANS R	1949-53	39	12	0	0	0	0	0	0	39	12
EVERETT Harold	1946-47	15	0	0	0	0	0	0	0	15	0
EVERETT Harry	1945-47	3	0	6	0	0	0	0	0	9	0
EVES M *	1987-88	3	0	0	0	0	0	1	1	4	1
FAIRBROTHER J	1971-73	83/2	38	5	5	2	0	0	0	90/2	43
FAIRCLOUGH W	1989-	13	0	0	0	0	0	0	0	13	0
FAWCETT D	1934-36	72	0	3	0	3	0	0	0	78	0
FEATHERBY LW	1931-32	22	5	0	0	0	0	0	0	22	0
FERNS P	1966-68	55/1	1	4	0	3	0	0	0	62/1	1
FIELD E	1935-36	2	0	0	0	0	0	0	0	2	0
FIELDING H	1937-38	4	0	0	0	0	0	0	0	4	0
FIELDS N	1951-53	20	0	2	0	0	0	0	0	22	0
FINCH D	1968-71	4	0	0	0	0	0	0	0	4	0
FISHER F	1931-33	10	6	0	0	0	0	0	0	10	6
FITZSIMMONS A	1959-61	62	23	5	2	1	0	0	0	68	25
FLOWERS I	1938-39	7	2	0	0	0	0	0	0	7	2
FLOWERS M	1956-57	3	0	0	0	0	0	0	0	3	0
FOSTER B	1971-82	282/5	0	22	0	17/1	0	17	0	338/6	0
FOSTER C	1971-79	195/10	17	15/2	2	9/1	0	7	0	226/13	19
FOSTER G	1983-	305	0	15	2	19	0	29	1	368	3
FOSTER N	1984-85	1	0	0	0	0	0	0	0	1	0

Barry Foster

George Foster

Alex Livingstone

Paul Evans

Gordon Hodgson

Keith Kennedy

Phil Ferns

		League		FA Cup		FL Cup		Others		TOTAL	
	Played	App	Gls	App	Gls	App	Gls	App	Gls	App	Gls
FOSTER W	1932-34	10	2	2	0	1	1	0	0	13	3
FOX O	1950-57	248	30	10	4	0	0	0	0	258	34
FOX W	1946-50	62	0	2	0	0	0	0	0	64	0
FRAIN P *	1983-84	1/1	0	0	0	0	0	0	0	1/1	0
FRASER D	1958-59	6	1	0	0	0	0	0	0	6	1
FRUDE R	1967-69	14/1	0	1	0	0	0	0	0	15/1	0
GABBITAS H	1935-36	1	0	0	0	0	0	0	0	1	0
GALLAGHER B *	1982-83	2/1	0	0	0	0	0	0	0	2/1	0
GALLOWAY M	1983-86	39/15	3	2	0	0/1	0	4/1	1	45/17	4
GARDINER A	1938-39	27	4	2	0	1	1	0	0	30	5
GARNER P	1984-89	102/8	8	4	0	2	0	20/1	0	128/9	8
GASKELL A	1954-56	42	17	1	0	0	0	0	0	43	17
GAULD J	1960-61	4	3	0	0	0	0	0	0	4	3
GEDDES A	1951-52	11	2	0	0	0	0	0	0	11	2
GILHESPY C	1931-32	19	4	1	0	0	0	0	0	20	4
GILL J	1961-66	138/1	0	6	0	8	0	0	0	152/1	0
GILMORE H	1935-36	20	0	1	0	2	0	0	0	23	0
GLAZZARD J	1956-58	21	10	1	0	0	0	0	0	22	10
GLOVER G	1967-68	18/1	0	0	0	0	0	0	0	18/1	0
GODWIN V	1949-51	31	9	0	0	0	0	0	0	31	9
GOODACRE R	1933-34	18	1	0	0	2	0	0	0	20	1
GOODFELLOW J	1967-71	96/4	14	13	1	4	1	0	0	113/4	16
GOODWIN D	1977-80	42/4	5	3	0	0/2	0	0	0	45/6	5
GOODWIN E	1953-55	9	0	0	0	0	0	0	0	9	0
GOVAN C	1963-64	10	0	0	0	0	0	0	0	10	0
GRAHAM G	1964-65	18	3	2	0	1	0	0	0	21	3
GRAHAM M	1985-89	132/1	1	8	0	11	1	16	0	167/1	2
GRATTAN J *	1978-79	1	0	0	0	0	0	0	0	1	0

Stan Keery

Paul Kee

Colin Harrington

Mike Graham

		League		FA Cup		FL Cup		Others		TOTAL	
	Played	App	Gls	App	Gls	App	Gls	App	Gls	App	Gls
GRAY K	1988-	17	0	0/1	0	1	0	2/1	1	20/2	1
GREEN A	1972-73	1	0	0	0	0	0	0	0	1	0
GREGSON J	1964-67	75/1	5	1	0	5	0	0	0	81/1	5
GRIFFIN K	1974-75	4	2	0	0	0	0	0	0	4	2
GRIFFITHS K	1957-59	42	7	2	0	0	0	0	0	44	7
GROGAN J	1947-52	201	0	16	0	0	0	0	0	217	0
GROZIER W	1972-73	1	0	0	0	0	0	0	0	1	0
GRUNDY W	1935-36	5	0	0	0	0	0	0	0	5	0
GUNN G *	1985-86	5	0	0	0	0	0	0	0	5	0
HAILWOOD D	1974-75	1	0	0	0	0	0	0	0	1	0
HALL B	1958-65	72	19	4	3	5	2	0	0	81	24
HALL I	1962-68	145	10	10	3	4	0	0	0	159	13
HAMILTON N	1978-81	84/5	4	5	0	5/1	1	0	0	94/6	5
HARFORD R	1971-72	7	0	0	0	2	0	0	0	9	0
HARKIN J	1938-47	23	5	2	1	1	0	0	0	26	6
HARPER D	1946-47	21	1	1	0	0	0	0	0	22	1
HARRINGTON C	1971-72	7/6	0	1	0	2	0	0	0	10/6	0
HARSTON E	1935-37	70	81	3	4	2	0	0	0	75	85
HART E	1936-37	28	0	2	0	0	0	0	0	30	0
HASELDEN J *	1971-72	4	0	0	0	0	0	0	0	4	0
HATHAWAY I	1988	15/17	2	0	0	1/1	0	2	0	14/10	2
HAWKSFORD E	1952-53	1	0	0	0	0	0	0	0	1	0
HAWLEY S	1934-35	4	1	0	0	1	0	0	0	5	1
HEATHER J	1953-54	1	0	0	0	0	0	0	0	1	0
HERRING C	1932-33	2	0	0	0	0	0	0	0	2	0
HERRIOT J *	1970-71	5	0	0	0	0	0	0	0	5	0
HEWITT H	1945-47	1	0	4	0	0	0	0	0	5	0
HILL A	1936-37	2	0	0	0	0	0	0	0	2	0

Billy Grozier

Mansfield Town pictured in 1969-70. Back row (left to right): C.Walker, P.Waller, S.Boam, D.Finch, D.Roberts, D.Hollins, J.Saunders, B.Ledger, M.Hopkinson. Front: J.Stenson, D.Jones, J.Goodfellow, D.Sharkey, J.Quigley, B.Bates, M.Partridge, R.Keeley, A.Pate.

		League		FA Cup		FL Cup		Others		TOTAL	
	Played	App	Gls	App	Gls	App	Gls	App	Gls	App	Gls
HILL H	1933-34	22	5	2	0	1	0	0	0	25	5
HILL WH	1947-48	2	0	0	0	0	0	0	0	2	0
HITCHCOCK K	1983-88	182	0	10	0	12	0	20	0	224	0
HODGES D	1986-	67/14	7	3/1	0	4	1	2/2	0	76/17	8
HODGETTS J	1938-39	1	0	0	0	0	0	0	0	1	0
HODGSON G	1974-79	184	23	15	1	14	0	0	0	213	24
HODGSON S	1948-49	2	0	0	0	0	0	0	0	2	0
HOGG AR	1958-60	11	0	0	0	0	0	0	0	11	0
HOGG F	1946-48	35	8	5	1	0	0	0	0	40	9
HOLLETT I	1958-65	98	40	3	5	6	2	0	0	107	47
HOLLINS D	1966-70	111	0	12	0	3	0	0	0	126	0
HOLMES M	1937-38	17	4	2	1	0	0	0	0	19	5
HOPKINSON M	1968-70	46	1	7/1	0	2	0	0	0	55/1	1
HORNE A	1936-38	44	9	3	0	1	0	0	0	48	9
HOWARD L	1984-85	0/1	0	0	0	0	0	0	0	0/1	0
HOYLAND W	1932-33	25	9	1	0	0	0	0	0	26	9
HUDSON W	1954-55	8	1	0	0	0	0	0	0	8	1
HUFTON C	1934-36	4	0	0	0	0	0	0	0	4	0
HUGHES J	1937-39	76	0	3	0	2	0	0	0	81	0
HUMBLE W	1959-66	198	1	10	1	5	0	0	0	213	2
HUMPHREYS A	1964-68	58	0	3	0	3	0	0	0	64	0
HUNT D	1989-	21/1	0	1	0	4	0	4	0	30/1	0
HUNT S	1934-35	29	14	3	4	0	0	0	0	32	18
HUNTER J	1934-36	26	5	0	0	1	1	0	0	27	6
HUTCHINSON R	1982-84	35	3	3	0	2	0	0	0	40	3
IBBOTTSON W	1948-49	2	2	0	0	0	0	0	0	2	2
JARVIS A	1970-73	76/6	0	5	0	3	0	0	0	84/6	0
JAYES B	1956-60	115	1	10	0	0	0	0	0	125	1

Jimmy Goodfellow

Ray Keeley

Trevor Morgan

Mick Laverick

Laurie Madden

Duncan McKenzie

		League		FA Cup		FL Cup		Others		TOTAL	
	Played	App	Gls	App	Gls	App	Gls	App	Gls	App	Gls
JEFFRIES W	1946-47	2	0	0	0	0	0	0	0	2	0
JEPSON A	1934-35	2	0	1	0	0	0	0	0	3	0
JEPSON B	1953-57	55	36	3	2	0	0	0	0	58	38
JEPSON J	1931-32	1	0	0	0	0	0	0	0	1	0
JOHNSON H	1931-36	163	104	7	8	2	2	0	0	172	114
JOHNSON S	1980-81	1	0	0	0	0	0	0	0	1	0
JOHNSTON C	1937-38	36	4	3	1	1	0	0	0	40	5
JONES C	1984-85	5	0	0	0	0	0	0	0	5	0
JONES DO	1947-49	74	0	6	0	0	0	0	0	80	0
JONES DAB	1967-72	116/14	32	4/3	2	3	0	0	0	123/17	34
JONES G	1959-61	45	18	5	1	1	0	0	0	51	19
JONES M	1962-66	91	0	3	0	4	0	0	0	98	0
JONES O	1936-37	14	0	2	0	0	0	0	0	16	0
JONES P	1973-74	15/5	1	0	0	1	0	0	0	16/5	1
JURYEFF IM *	1983-84	12	5	0	0	0	0	0	0	12	5
KAY K	1947-48	1	0	0	0	0	0	0	0	1	0
KEARNEY M	1982-	228/2	29	6/3	1	16	2	20	3	270/5	35
KEE P	1983-84	0/1	0	0	0	0	0	0	0	0/1	0
KEEGAN G	1983-84	8	1	2	0	0	0	0	0	20	1
KEELEY R	1968-70	48/4	5	10/1	5	2	1	0	0	60/5	11
KEELING H	1933-34	8	0	0	0	0	0	0	0	8	0
KEERY S	1957-59	53	17	4	0	0	0	0	0	57	17
KEMP S	1958-59	3	1	0	0	0	0	0	0	3	1
KENT K	1985-	196/5	32	11	4	8	2	18/2	5	233/7	43
KENNEDY K	1982-83	32/2	0	3	0	2	0	0	0	37/2	0
KENWORTHY A	1985-90	98/2	0	6	0	5	0	12/1	0	121/3	0
KILCAR S	1933-35	31	14	0	0	3	0	0	0	34	14
KIRK W	1933-34	7	1	0	0	1	0	0	0	8	1

Ernie Moss

Peter Morris

Jim McCaffrey

Jim Lumby

Billy McEwan

John Haselden

Michael Galloway

Ian McDonald

Dennis Longhorn

John Lathan

		League		FA Cup		FL Cup		Others		TOTAL	
	Played	App	Gls	App	Gls	App	Gls	App	Gls	App	Gls
KIRKHAM R	1957-60	42	0	0	0	0	0	0	0	42	0
KNOX T	1966-68	34	5	1	0	1	1	0	0	36	6
KRUSE P *	1974-75	6	1	0	0	0	0	0	0	6	1
LAIDLAW J	1982-83	4	0	0	0	2	0	0	0	6	0
LAMBERT B	1954-60	24	0	4	0	0	0	0	0	28	0
LATHAN J	1973-80	101/2	15	8	0	5	1	0	0	114/2	16
LAVERICK M	1972-75	73/16	13	3/2	1	9	4	0	0	85/18	17
LAWS J	1982-83	0/1	0	0	0	0	0	0	0	0/1	0
LEDGER R	1967-70	51/6	14	7	3	1	1	0	0	59/6	18
LEE H	1955-56	3	2	0	0	0	0	0	0	3	2
LEISHMAN G	1988-	7/9	2	0	0	0	0	1/1	0	8/10	2
LENNON A	1948-49	3	0	0	0	0	0	0	0	3	0
LEWIS J	1948-53	163	11	13	1	0	0	0	0	176	12
LIDDLE D	1946-47	1	0	0	0	0	0	0	0	1	0
LILL J	1953-56	3	0	0	0	0	0	0	0	3	0
LINACRE W	1955-56	13	0	2	0	0	0	0	0	15	0
LITTLEDYKE R	1936-37	9	1	0	0	0	0	0	0	9	1
LIVIE G	1952-54	21	0	0	0	0	0	0	0	21	0
LIVINGSTONE A	1933-35	43	1	0	0	1	0	0	0	44	1
LLEWLLYN D	1974-75	6/2	0	0	0	0	0	0	0	6/2	0
LLOYD C	1931-33	5	0	0	0	0	0	0	0	5	0
LOCKIE T	1935-36	14	1	1	0	2	0	0	0	17	1
LOGAN D	1984-87	67/1	1	3	0	5	0	7	0	82/1	1
LONGHORN D	1971-74	93/3	5	5	0	3	1	0	0	101/3	6
LOWERY A	1982-	243/1	19	15	2	19	0	25/1	5	302/2	26
LUKE N	1984-86	41/9	9	2	0	3/1	0	5/4	2	51/10	11
LUMBY J	1981-82	49/2	18	0	0	4	3	0	0	53/2	21
LYON D *	1973-74	2	0	0	0	0	0	0	0	2	0

John Quigley

Ian Phillips

Ian Mackenzie

Arthur Mann

Les McJannet

		League		FA Cup		FL Cup		Others		TOTAL	
	Played	App	Gls	App	Gls	App	Gls	App	Gls	App	Gls
McBRIDE V	1958-59	10	0	1	0	0	0	0	0	11	0
McCAFFREY J	1972-77	170/8	21	15	3	10/1	3	0	0	195/9	27
McCARTER J	1948-50	67	10	5	1	0	0	0	0	72	11
McCLELLAND J	1978-81	122/3	8	8	1	8/1	2	0	0	138/4	11
McDONALD G	1989-90	1/1	0	0	0	0	0	0/1	0	1/2	0
McDONALD I	1975-78	47/9	4	6	1	5/1	3	0	0	58/10	8
McDONALD R	1954-56	13	0	0	0	0	0	0	0	13	0
McEWANS W	1976-77	32	3	0	0	2	0	0	0	34	3
McGEORGE J	1966-67	5/4	0	0	0	0	0	0	0	5/4	0
McGOWAN J	1961-62	3	0	0	0	0	0	0	0	3	0
McGREGOR W	1953-56	119	0	5	0	0	0	0	0	124	0
McJANNET L	1979-82	73/1	0	5	0	4	0	0	0	82/1	0
McKENZIE D *	1969-73	13/3	10	0	0	0	0	0	0	13/3	10
MACKENZIE I	1975-78	69/1	0	3	0	5	0	0	0	77/1	0
McKERNON C	1984-90	79/15	0	4/1	0	5/3	0	7/1	0	95/20	0
McKINNEY W	1966-68	51/1	2	4	0	3	0	0	0	58/1	2
McREADY B	1964-66	49/1	11	1	1	2	1	0	0	52/1	12
MADDEN L	1974-76	9	0	2	0	2	0	0	0	13	0
MADDISON A	1933-34	0	0	1	0	1	0	0	0	2	0
MALLINSON D	1965-66	10/1	1	0	0	0	0	0	0	10/1	1
MANN A	1979-82	114/2	3	8	0	7/1	0	0	0	129/3	3
MARKS M *	1987-88	0/1	0	0	0	0	0	1	0	1/1	0
MARRON C	1952-54	53	25	3	2	0	0	0	0	56	27
MARSH W	1945-46	0	0	4	0	0	0	0	0	4	0
MARTIN D	1977-79	46	3	0	0	2	0	0	0	48	3
MATTHEWS J	1982-84	70/2	6	5	0	3	0	1	0	79/2	6
MATTHEWS P	1972-78	121/3	6	11	1	5	0	0	0	137/3	7
MAYFIELD L	1949-53	34	0	0	0	0	0	0	0	34	0

Sandy Pate

Noel Parkinson

Les Smith

Harry Oscroft

Dudley Roberts

Gary Nicholson

		League		FA Cup		FL Cup		Others		TOTAL	
	Played	App	Gls	App	Gls	App	Gls	App	Gls	App	Gls
MEE G	1933-34	11	0	0	0	0	0	0	0	11	0
MEE NB	1938-39	13	1	0	0	1	0	0	0	14	1
MELLING T	1967-69	33	7	1	1	1	0	0	0	35	8
MELLOR K	1957-59	66	0	5	0	0	0	0	0	71	0
MERCER S	1948-49	12	3	6	4	0	0	0	0	18	7
METHVEN H	1933-34	10	9	0	0	2	0	0	0	12	9
MIDDLETON H	1964-66	45/1	24	2	0	2	1	0	0	49/1	25
MILLER J	1976-80	109/4	14	6	1	7	1	0	0	122/4	16
MITCHINSON T	1965-68	76	15	4	2	4	1	0	0	84	18
MITTEN C	1955-58	100	25	6	2	0	0	0	0	106	27
MITTEN J	1957-58	3	0	0	0	0	0	0	0	3	0
MOORE B	1960-61	4	0	1	0	1	0	0	0	6	0
MOORE J *	1986-87	5	1	0	0	0	0	0	0	5	1
MORAN J	1935-37	30	0	2	0	0	0	0	0	33	0
MORGAN T	1981-82	12	6	1	0	0	0	0	0	13	6
MORRIS A	1937-38	1	0	0	0	0	0	0	0	1	0
MORRIS F	1956-58	56	17	4	2	0	0	0	0	60	19
MORRIS PJ	1960-78	327/1	53	19	0	18	0	0	0	364/1	53
MOSS E	1976-79	56/1	21	0	0	2	0	0	0	58/1	21
MUNNINGS E	1933-34	29	7	2	0	1	0	0	0	32	7
MURRAY K	1953-57	140	60	5	1	0	0	0	0	145	61
MURRAY M	1989-	28	0	0	0	0	0	2	0	30	0
NELSON C	1964-66	38	0	1	0	2	0	0	0	41	0
NETTLESHIP R	1946-47	1	0	0	0	0	0	0	0	1	0
NEW M	1978-80	21	0	0	0	0	0	0	0	21	0
NICHOLSON G	1881-84	112/4	21	5/1	0	7	0	1	0	125/5	21
NUGENT C	1958-60	52	7	2	1	0	0	0	0	54	8
OAKLEY J	1945-46	0	0	4	0	0	0	0	0	4	0

F.T.Perfect

Mansfield Town in 1950-51. Back row (left to right): S.Carter (trainer), G.Antonio, J.Grogan, S.Chessell, D.Wright, L.Mayfield, J.Lewis. Front: W.Coole, O.Fox, K.Reeve, W.Donaldson, E.Barks.

		League		FA Cup		FL Cup		Others		TOTAL	
	Played	App	Gls	App	Gls	App	Gls	App	Gls	App	Gls
O'BRIEN N	1975-76	7	0	0	0	3	0	0	0	10	0
O'CONNOR D	1974-75	11/6	2	1	2	1	1	0	0	13/6	5
O'CONNOR F	1937-39	18	0	2	1	1	0	0	0	21	1
OGILVIE J	1959-61	24	1	0	0	0	0	0	0	24	1
O'HARA D	1961-62	3	1	0	0	1	0	0	0	4	1
OLDHAM J	1966-67	0/1	0	0	0	0	0	0	0	0/1	0
O'RIORDAN D	1989-90	5	0	0	0	0	0	0	0	5	0
OSCROFT H	1946-50	113	40	8	3	0	0	0	0	121	43
OTTEWELL S	1949-52	67	21	7	1	0	0	0	0	74	22
OWEN G	1987-89	54/4	8	2	0	1	0	1	0	58/4	8
PAGE S	1934-35	0	0	0	0	1	0	0	0	1	0
PARKER E	1934-36	15	4	1	0	0	0	0	0	16	4
PARKINSON N	1980-82	66/4	13	3	3	5/1	1	0	0	74/5	17
PARRY A	1973-74	0/1	0	0	0	0	0	0	0	0/1	0
PARSONS J	1932-33	2	0	0	0	0	0	0	0	2	0
PARTRIDGE J	1983-84	1	0	0	0	0	0	0	0	1	0
PARTRIDGE M	1967-71	65/2	20	5/1	2	6	2	0	0	76/3	25
PATE A	1967-68	412/1	2	36	0	21/1	1	0	0	469/2	3
PATERSON W	1937-39	61	0	5	0	1	0	0	0	66	0
PEARCEY J	1988-	6	0	0	0	0	0	0	0	6	0
PEPLOW S *	1973-74	4	3	0	0	0	0	0	0	4	3
PERFECT F	1936-37	13	0	2	0	1	0	0	0	16	0
PETERS T	1948-49	6	2	0	0	0	0	0	0	6	2
PHILLIPS B	1960-63	102	3	8	0	5	0	0	0	115	3
PHILLIPS B	1980-81	17	0	2	0	4	0	0	0	23	0
PHILLIPS I	1977-79	18/5	0	1/1	0	0	0	0	0	19/6	0
PHOENIX A	1931-32	2	0	0	0	0	0	0	0	3	0
PLACE M	1988-90	12/3	0	0	0	0	0	0	0	12/3	0

Andy Shore

Mark Reynolds

Pat Sharkey

John Stenson

		League		FA Cup		FL Cup		Others		TOTAL	
	Played	App	Gls	App	Gls	App	Gls	App	Gls	App	Gls
PLUMMER N	1952-56	166	5	8	0	0	0	0	0	174	5
POLLARD B	1979-82	45/9	5	2	1	4	1	0	0	51/9	7
POLLARD G	1984-87	66/1	1	3	0	6	1	6/2	0	81/3	2
POOLE CJ	1945-51	16	1	6	1	0	0	0	0	22	2
POOLE G	1936-37	1	0	0	0	0	0	0	0	1	0
POYNTON W	1964-66	20	0	1	0	2	0	0	0	23	0
PRENTICE D	1933-34	19	1	0	0	2	2	0	0	21	3
PRESGRAVE G	1936-37	5	1	0	0	0	0	0	0	5	1
PRICE J	1932-33	32	7	0	0	0	0	0	0	32	7
PRINDIVILLE S	1989	22	0	1	0	3/1	0	4	0	30/1	0
PRIOR J	1932-33	32	7	0	0	0	0	0	0	32	7
PRITCHARD T	1935-36	1	0	0	0	0	0	0	0	1	0
QUIGLEY J	1968-71	105	2	13	0	4	0	0	0	122	2
RANDALL K	1975-77	62/4	20	4	1	1	0	0	0	67/4	21
RATTRAY C	1936-37	336	5	2	0	1	0	0	0	39	5
RAYNOR F	1933-34	17	8	2	1	1	0	0	0	20	9
RAYNOR G	1932-33	9	1	1	0	0	0	0	0	10	1
READ C	1937-38	22	9	0	0	0	0	0	0	22	9
READMAN J	1932-33	73	12	2	0	0	0	0	0	75	12
REEVE K	1949-54	139	62	6	0	0	0	0	0	145	62
REVEL G	1952-53	1	0	0	0	0	0	0	0	1	0
REYNOLDS M	1982-83	4	0	0	0	0	0	0	0	4	0
RHODES M *	1982-83	4	0	0	0	0	0	0	0	4	0
RICHARDS A	1961-62	3	0	0	0	0	0	0	0	3	0
RICHARDSON W	1965-68	61/2	0	3	0	4	0	0	0	68/2	0
RINGSTEAD A	1959-60	27	3	3	0	0	0	0	0	30	3
RIPLEY K	1958-60	31	5	0	0	0	0	0	0	31	5
ROBERTS D	1967-74	194/6	66	19	6	9/1	1	0	0	222/7	73

Mansfield in 1924. Back row (left to right): H.Bostock, J.Simpson, H.W.Beaumont, B.Platter. Third row: R.Gunton, F.Warmby, S.Musgrave, W.Taylor, G.H.Whitsed, R.Belcher, W.Fenton, W.Harrison. Second row: W.Mason, E.Horsley, S.Hunt, G.Annable, J.H.Baynes, S.Patrick, J.J.Coleman. Front row: J.Baxter, R.Slack.

		League		FA Cup		FL Cup		Others		TOTAL	
	Played	App	Gls	App	Gls	App	Gls	App	Gls	App	Gls
ROBERTS R	1970-72	76/4	4	5	1	2	0	0	0	83/4	5
ROBINSON A	1931-32	12	0	0	0	0	0	0	0	12	0
ROBINSON L	1984-87	11/4	0	0	0	0	0	1	0	12/4	0
ROBINSON S	1931-34	61	1	3	0	0	0	0	0	64	1
ROSE M *	1970-71	3	0	0	0	0	0	0	0	3	0
ROY J	1936-37	25	2	2	0	1	0	0	0	28	2
ROWLAND J	1966-68	49	16	3	0	1	0	0	0	53	16
ROWLANDS J	1967-68	12/1	3	0	0	0	0	0	0	12/1	3
RUDKIN G	1937-38	1	0	0	0	0	0	0	0	1	0
RUSHBY A	1956-58	20	0	0	0	0	0	0	0	20	0
RYAN E	1954-57	20	0	1	0	0	0	0	0	21	0
RYAN J	1987-89	53/9	1	7	1	1/1	0	5/1	0	66/11	2
SAINTY J *	1972-73	3	0	0	0	0	0	0	0	3	0
SAMS A	1937-38	11	2	1	0	1	0	0	0	13	2
SAUNDERS J	1969-73	89	2	4	0	5	0	0	0	98	2
SAVIN K	1957-59	68	0	4	0	0	0	0	0	72	0
SAXBY G	1978-80	14/2	1	0	0	2	0	0	0	16/2	1
SAXBY M	1975-79	76/3	5	1/1	0	2	0	0	0	79/4	5
SCANLON A	1962-66	108	21	3	0	5	3	0	0	116	24
SCOTT K	1952-53	5	2	2	0	0	0	0	0	7	2
SEARSON H	1947-49	42	0	3	0	0	0	0	0	45	0
SHARKEY D	1967-70	67/2	17	7	4	4	0	0	0	78/2	21
SHARKEY P	1977-78	31/1	5	2	0	0	0	0	0	33/1	5
SHAW F	1937-38	22	1	0	0	1	0	0	0	23	1
SHELL F	197-48	22	1	2	0	0	0	0	0	24	1
SHORE A	1974-75	1	0	0	0	0	0	0	0	1	0
SIMPSON G	1953-54	8	0	0	0	0	0	0	0	8	0
SINCLAIR D	1953-54	1	0	0	0	0	0	0	0	1	0

E.Vaux

Mansfield Town in the 1963-4 season. Back row (left to right): S.Carter (trainer), S.Chapman, C.Toon, P.Morris, C.Treharne, J.Gill, M.Jones, W.Humble, T.Cummings (manager). Front: B.Hall, C.Askey, D.Coates, K.Wagstaff, I.Hollett, A.Scanlon, R.Chapman.

		League		FA Cup		FL Cup		Others		TOTAL	
	Played	App	Gls	App	Gls	App	Gls	App	Gls	App	Gls
SINDALL M	1982-84	18/3	0	0	0	1	0	0	0	19/3	0
SIVITER E	1932-34	2	0	0	0	0	0	0	0	2	0
SLACK W	1932-36	120	0	6	0	5	0	0	0	131	0
SMALL T	1931-32	2	0	0	0	0	0	0	0	2	0
SMALLEY M	1989-	28	1	0	0	0	0	0	0	28	1
SMITH F	1955-57	31	4	0	0	0	0	0	0	31	4
SMITH L	1946-48	38	0	6	0	0	0	0	0	44	0
SMITH R	1986-87	1/1	0	0	0	0	0	0	0	1/1	0
SMITH T	1960-61	8	0	0	0	0	0	0	0	8	0
SOMERFIELD A	1938-39	15	6	6	4	0	0	0	0	21	10
SPEED F	1936-39	100	5	10	0	4	0	0	0	114	5
STAINTON	1955-57	9	0	2	0	0	0	0	0	11	0
STAMPS JD	1937-38	1	0	0	0	0	0	0	0	1	0
STANIFORTH C	1931-32	8	2	0	0	0	0	0	0	8	2
STANTON T	1967-68	37	1	1	1	0	0	0	0	38	2
STAPLES A	1931-32	13	0	0	0	0	0	0	0	13	0
STATHAM A	1938-39	2	0	0	0	0	0	0	0	2	0
STATHAM T	1956-60	26	0	0	0	0	0	0	0	26	0
STEELE E *	1987-88	5	0	0	0	0	0	0	0	5	0
STEELE F	1949-52	53	39	9	5	0	0	0	0	62	44
STENSON J	1969-72	103/4	21	9/1	2	7	3	0	0	119/5	25
STIMPSON G	1937-39	82	0	9	0	3	0	0	0	94	0
STORER J	1931-32	13	1	0	0	0	0	0	0	13	1
STORER S	1983-84	0/1	0	0	0	0	0	0	0	0/1	0
STRAW R	1961-63	44	12	2	1	3	1	0	0	49	14
STRINGFELLOW I	1985-	51/31	16	4/3	1	11	5	4/4	1	70/38	23
STRINGFELLOW M	1960-62	57	10	4	1	4	1	0	0	65	12
STUBBINS P	1987-88	0	0	0	0	0	0	0/1	0	0/1	0

Steve Sutton

Brian Pollard

Ian Wood

Alan Waddle signs for the Stags watched by manager Stuart Boam.

Phil Waller

Simon Woodhead

John Tones

		League		FA Cup		FL Cup		Others		TOTAL	
	Played	App	Gls	App	Gls	App	Gls	App	Gls	App	Gls
SUTTON J	1970-71	11/2	0	2	0	3	1	0	0	16/2	1
SUTTON S *	1980-81	8	0	0	0	0	0	0	0	8	0
SWINSCOE T	1956-59	14	0	1	0	0	0	0	0	15	0
SYRETT D	1977-79	65	20	3	0	4	0	0	0	72	20
TARRAT B	1960-61	3	0	0	0	0	0	0	0	3	0
TAYLOR J	1959-60	5	2	0	0	0	0	0	0	5	2
TAYLOR P	1983-84	3	0	0	0	0	0	0	0	3	0
TAYLOR S	1979-80	30/7	7	3	0	5	3	0	0	38/7	10
THOMAS B	1957-60	72	48	1	1	0	0	0	0	73	49
THOMAS J	1957-59	41	0	1	0	0	0	0	0	42	0
THOMPSON D	1970-74	129/2	21	10	3	6	0	0	0	145/2	24
THOMPSON GB	1979-80	9	0	0	0	0	0	0	0	9	0
THOMSON B	1979-82	54/9	1	5	1	4	0	0	0	63/9	2
THORPE A	1982-83	0/2	1	0	0	0	0	0	0	0/2	1
THORPE L	1945-47	5	0	6	1	0	0	0	0	11	1
TODD R	1968-69	3/1	0	0	0	0	0	0	0	3/1	0
TODD S *	1973-74	6	0	0	0	0	0	0	0	6	0
TONES J	1974-75	3	0	0	0	0	0	0	0	3	0
TOON C	1957-66	213	1	12	0	6	0	0	0	231	1
TREHARNE C	1961-66	191	0	11	0	10	0	0	0	212	0
TURNER J	1937-39	58	9	5	0	2	0	0	0	65	9
TYRER A	1963-65	41	5	1	0	3	1	0	0	45	6
UPHILL D	1956-59	83	38	1	2	0	0	0	0	84	40
UZELAC S *	1975-76	2	0	0	0	0	0	0	0	2	0
VAUGHAN T	1958-59	6	2	0	0	0	0	0	0	6	0
VAUX E	1936-38	29	0	0	0	1	0	0	0	30	0
VINTER M	1984-86	52/2	7	1/1	0	6	3	9	0	68/3	10
WADDLE A	1982-83	14	4	0	0	1	0	0	0	15	4

Bill Williams

Mansfield Town line-up for 1956-7. Back row (left to right): K.Murray, T.Stanton, B.Jayes, D.Wright, D.Bradley, B.Jepson, R. Warner, B.Berry. Front: B.Lambert, D.Ryan, O.Fox, G.Darwin, S.Watson, B.Bishop, D.Smith.

		League		FA Cup		FL Cup		Others		TOTAL	
	Played	App	Gls	App	Gls	App	Gls	App	Gls	App	Gls
WAGSTAFF K	1960-65	181	93	8	7	7	5	0	0	196	105
WAINWRIGHT W	1936-37	3	0	0	0	0	0	0	0	3	0
WAKE H	1931-32	20	1	0	0	0	0	0	0	20	1
WALKER C	1969-75	223/6	8	17	1	13	1	0	0	253/6	10
WALKER M	1968-69	2	0	0	0	0	0	0	0	2	0
WALLER P	1967-72	153/6	1	19	1	9	1	0	0	181/6	3
WANNACOTT C	1932-33	15	2	0	0	0	0	0	0	15	2
WARNER R	1954-55	33	0	0	0	0	0	0	0	33	0
WATKIN W	1955-56	25	4	2	1	0	0	0	0	27	5
WATSON S	1951-61	292	9	14	2	1	0	0	0	307	11
WATSON V	1952-54	14	9	2	0	0	0	0	0	16	9
WEIGHTMAN A	1931-33	45	1	2	0	0	0	0	0	47	12
WEIR J	1962-63	18	3	4	1	1	0	0	0	23	4
WESTLAND J	1946-47	10	0	1	0	0	0	0	0	11	0
WHATMORE N	1984-88	71/5	20	2/2	0	4	0	14/1	1	91/8	21
WHEATLEY W	1948-50	38	3	3	0	0	0	0	0	41	3
WHITE C	1931-32	1	0	0	0	0	0	0	0	1	0
WHITE W	1954-55	3	0	0	0	0	0	0	0	3	0
WHITTAM E	1935-36	20	4	1	0	2	1	0	0	23	5
WHITWORTH S	1983-85	80	2	4	0	4	0	6	0	94	2
WIGNALL F	1971-73	50/6	15	3	0	2	1	0	0	55/6	16
WILKINSON S	1989-	36/1	15	1	0	1	1	4	0	42/1	16
WILLIAMS C	1933-34	22	0	2	0	1	0	0	0	25	0
WILLIAMS G	1957-62	154	5	6	0	3	0	0	0	163	5
WILLIAMS S	1986-90	4/7	0	0	0	0	0	0	0	4/7	0
WILLIAMS W	1965-68	47/2	2	3	0	4	1	0	0	54/2	3
WILSON A	1938-39	20/2	6	1	1	1	1	0	0	27	4
WILSON J	1931-33	41	0	2	0	0	0	0	0	43	0

		League		FA Cup		FL Cup		Others		TOTAL	
	Played	App	Gls	App	Gls	App	Gls	App	Gls	App	Gls
WILSON James	1954-56	19	1	1	0	0	0	0	0	20	1
WOMWELL D	1945-46	0	0	6	5	0	0	0	0	6	5
WONNACOTT C	1932-33	15	0	2	0	0	0	0	0	17	0
WOOD I	1975-82	135/14	9	10	0	9/1	2	0	0	154/15	11
WOOD L	1935-38	46	3	1	0	0	0	0	0	47	3
WOOD W	1933-34	5	0	0	0	1	0	0	0	6	0
WOODHEAD S	1980-85	108/14	6	2/1	0	3/1	0	5	0	118/16	6
WRAGG D	1959-61	46	13	1	1	0	0	0	0	47	14
WRIGHT D	1946-47	379	0	20	0	0	0	0	0	399	0
WRIGHT E	1934-37	47	0	0	0	2	0	0	0	49	0
WRIGHT V	1952-53	2	0	0	0	0	0	0	0	2	0
WYLLIE R	1959-62	92	0	5	0	3	0	0	0	100	0

SUBSCRIBERS

Presentation Copies
1 Mansfield Town Football Club
2 The Football League • 3 The Football Association

4 Stan Searl
5 Ian Greaves
6 Joe Eaton
7 Paul Richardson
8 J A Harris
9 Raymond Shaw
10 A N Other
11 K P Wood
12 John Lathan
13 Derek Hyde
14 Harry Kay
15 William James Grier
16 Dave Parine
17 Roberto J Gamble
18 David Earnshaw
19 Errick Peterson
20 Peter Lunn
21 R K Shoesmith
22 Douglas Lamming
23 Harald Löhr
24 B H Standish
25 Moira & Frederick Furness
26 John Motson
27 Duncan Watt
28 P H Whitehead
29 Maurice Golesworthy
30 D T Bryant
31 Anton H Knaflic
32 Sports Marketing (Australia)
33 Brian H Hobbs
34 Ian Willott
35 Chris Minchin
36 Gordon Small
37 David Downs
38 Angus W Rodger
39 Colin Cameron
40 Paul Golabowski
41 Paul H Bannister
42 J Ringrose
43 Douglas Bidgood
44 David J Godfrey
45 Lars-Olof Wendler
46 John Treleven
47 J Mulrennan
48 P Marks
49 David Keats
50 J D M Whitaker
51 Stuart W Holland
52 Kevin C Wyatt
53 Paul Vibert
54 Christer Svensson
55 Richard D N Wells
56 Keith Coburn
57 Roger Hudson
58 W D Phillips
59 Roger Wash
60 Gilbert Monnereau
61 Diamant Yosef
62 Geir Juva
63 Harry Thompson
64 Fred Lee
65 Keith B Ducker
66 Philip Scoble
67 J Gardiner
68 Trond Isaksen
69 Raymond A Kelly
70 I Watts
71 T D Culshaw
72 Alan Davies
73 John van den Elsen
74 J S Pyke
75 C J Morton
76 Terry Frost
77 Gary James — 'The Blue'
78 David Gregg
79 Peter Baxter
80 Dave Harrison
81 L A Zammit
82 Brian Tabner
83 David Coulson
84 Denis Sturman
85 P Ploughman
86 Robert Hollingworth
87 Mark Smith
88 Kevin Charles
89 Colin Belcher
90 Richard Nigel Jordan
91 Andrew Ernest Tooth
92 Michael R Burden
93 Brian Easom
94 A R Speed
95 Patrick Sleigh
96 David Mark Blinkhorn
97 M Walker
98 Stephen M Burdon
99 Stephen M Burdon
100 Paul Taylor
101 Jack Ford
102 P E Gajda
103 Mark Wallis
104 D J Parkin
105 A Clarke
106 C P Barnard
107 S J Abbott
108 M Horton
109 Trevor Phillips
110 Alan Clarke
111 Martin Neale
112 Chris Bradshaw
113 R Paling
114 Neal Matthews
115 Martin Matthews
116 F Beale
117 Peter Chester
118 John W Bellamy
119 Andy Shore
120 Neil G Walker
121 David Samuel Hill
122 A E Warsop
123 Ian Cosford
124 John Slade
125 Roy Needham
126 P D Harrison
127 Andrew Smith
128 W Williams
129 A W Miles
130 Stephen Robert Parish
131 Peter Williams
132 S R Simpson
133 Ronald Neil Buttery

134 Michael Postles
135 Ashley Blick
136 Richard Allen
137 J R Purseglove
138 Martin Cook
139 Ian McCraighy
140 Antony Cope
141 Simon Coope
142 L Keeling
143 J A Retter
144 Paul Jerome
145 Dave Hillam
146 Dennis Dodd
147 John Partlow
148 David James Green
149 Peter Kowalenko
150 S Higginson
151 Stephen Arnold
152 C J Beckerton
153 Paul Stevens
154 Paul Cassidy
155 Richard Peter Smith
156 M Kowalenko
157 John Marshall Fell
158 Anthony Hall
159 M N Fell
160 James Slack
161 John Gray
162 Ted Wilson
163 Anthony Gdula
164 Alan Wheatley
165 B R Butler
166 Eric Heesom
167 Michael Joyce
168 Jon Robinson
169 Mike Purkiss
170 Eric Wint
171 Robert Johnson
172 Fraser David Shooter
173 R L Hudson
174 Mick Gardner
175 Carol Gardner
176 Keith L & Anthony M Beaumont
177 Philip J Sims
178 J R Revill
179 J R Revill
180 J R Revill
181 Christopher Eaton
182 David Richardson
183 Mark Gallagher
184 John Selby
185 Arthur Timmons
186 Tim Booler
187 Andrew Anderson
188 Stanley A Robinson
189 Alan Hindley
190 A Naylor
191 J T Parr
192 Trevor Harrison
193 Cameron Ellis
194 A T Jones
195 Jim Walker
196 M R Pearce
197 Geoffrey Wright
198 Tony Bluff
199 Filippo Rossi
200 J T Wass
201 Cyril Parkes
202 Douglas Allen Tattersall
203 Edwin Arthur Tattersall
204 Vaughan P Skirrey
205 Dave Green
206 Mervyn Powell
207 John Penrose
208 P R Davidson
209 Trevor Breedon
210 Derek Truswell
211 Melvin David Piasecki
212 C Holmes
213 Andrew Steven Oliver
214 Richard Stocken
215 Norman Green
216 A N Davis
217 David Pease
218 Peter Pickup
219 James Fuller
220 Roger J Turner
221 Michael Brown
222 D Burrows
223 Stephen Burns
224 Alan J Belcher
225 Richard Lee North
226 P H Mercer
227 Dennis Hursthouse
228 W H Taylor
229 Kevin Seaman
230 Ian Gill
231 Craig Kirk
232 Andrew Whittle
233 J Buitenga
234 C Egan
235 Jeremy Wain
236 Michael Anthony Priest
237 Ian Halfpenny
238 P D Middleton
239 Martin Cunningham
240 J Campbell
241 W O Woodin
242 Robert Harpham
243 Ian Baguley
244 Paul Gillett
245 John Rowley
246 Andy Bunting
247 Adrian Johnson
248 Paul Phelan
249 Kostas Fotopoulos
250 Tasos Botsis
251 Ian Griffiths
252 Gerald Hill
253 J W Milner
254 Derrick Hassall
255 Roy Robertson
256 Deborah Robertson
257 Tracy Robertson
258 S Patrick
259 J R Wright
260 Surapot Saengchote
261 John Slater
262 Thomas Frank Lamb
263 M J W Holden
264 Michael Briggs

265 Darren Shaw
266 Field Mill Fred
267 W H Cutts
268 John Bodicoat
269 Peter Overton
270 John Richard Evans
271 Kenneth Hardstaff
272 David Hardstaff
273 Paul Dean
274 David Bamford
275 Chris Roper
276 David Cantrell
277 P K Dowsing
278 J D Clothier
279 P J Wood
280 A R Dawes
281 Geoffrey Hall
282 David Herbert
283 Railway Stag (Gary)
284 Richard Parkes
285 Geoff Allman
286 Mark Willows
287 Colin Dobell
288 K N Underhill
289 Benjamin Smith
290 N Drabble
291 S P Tomlin
292 A H Atkins
293 A Young
294 M Swart
295 P W Stevenson
296 Paul Stevenson
297 Stefan Guy
298 Anders Johansson
299 Q C M Olsthoorn
300 G D Painter
301 Tonny Otten
302 R G Woolman
303 R W Lane
304 Simons Martin
305 David Lumb
306 David Helliwell
307 C L Place
308 A N Place
309 Michael J Innes
310 Ray Hodkin
311 Daniel Reece
312 Duncan Reece
313 Martin Reece
314 I W Hall
315 John Vardy
316 Brian Evans
317 Mick Roffe
318 David Roffe
319 J Marriott
320 J Marriott
321 A Mellors
322 Graham P Oglesby
323 Barry Salmon
324 Roy Harrison
325 Roger Grayson
326 David Jelley
327 Ian Marsh
328 W A Spencer
329 G D Hyde
330 Adrian Fenwick
331 Stuart A Rowlands
332 Linda M Rowlands
333 John Clive Painter
334 R & J E May
335 David Crawford
336 Neil Goddard
337 Mark Saxton
338 R V Calmels
339 P Gallagher
340 Esa Kautonen
341 K Quibell
342 C J G Shaw
343 Ian Richard Smith
344 Keith Parnill
345 Donald H J Betcher
346 Nial & Kris Walden
347 Bernard Savage
348 Keith Lamb
349 David Parkes
350 Bill & Gareth Moody
351 Carl Southwell
352 Dean Owen
353 P H Moult
354 P C Lee
355 A C K Lawrence
356 M C Lawrence
357 D R Priest